The Language of Journalism

The Language of Journalism

Volume One: Newspaper Culture

Melvin J. Lasky

BEING A FIRST VOLUME,
wherein
THE LANGUAGE OF JOURNALISM IS EXAMINED,
ITS SPLENDORS AND MISERIES –
including
CLICHÉS & TRIVIA,
SENSATIONALISM & PRURIENCE,
WIT & WITLESSNESS,
FICTION & FACTION,
PSEUDERY & JABBERWOCKY,
SCOOPS & HOAXES,
RACISM & SEXISM,
PROFANITY & OBSCENITY,
VIRTUE & REALITY,
CULTURE & ANARCHY –
AND THE ABUSE OF SLANG, STYLE,
&
THE HABITS OF WRITING GOOD PROSE

Transaction Publishers
New Brunswick (U.S.A.) and London (U.K.)

Copyright © 2000 by Transaction Publishers, New Brunswick, New Jersey.

This book is printed on acid-free paper that meets the American National Standard for Permanence of Paper for Printed Library Materials.

Library of Congress Catalog Number: 00-034408
ISBN: 0-7658-0001-2
Printed in the United States of America

Library of Congress Cataloging-in-Publication Data

Lasky, Melvin J.
  The language of journalism / Melvin J. Lasky
    p. cm.
  Includes bibliographical references and index.
  Contents: v. 1. Newspaper culture.
  ISBN 0-7658-0001-2 (v. 1 : alk. paper)
  1. Newspapers—Language. 2. Journalism—Language. I. Title.

PN4783 .L37 2000
070.4' 01'4—dc21   00-034408

Confucius, it is told, was once asked what he would do first if it were left to him to govern a nation.

He replied:

"To correct language...

If language is not correct, then what is said is not what is meant;
If what is said is not what is meant, then what ought to be done remains undone;
If this remains undone, morals and art will deteriorate;
If morals and art deteriorate, justice will go astray;
If justice does go astray, the people will stand about in helpless confusion.

Hence there must be no arbitrariness in what is said.
This matters above everything."

* * *

And as in uffish thought he stood,
The Jabberwock, with eyes of flame,
Came whiffling through the tulgey wood,
and burbled as it came!

One, two! One, two! And through and through
The vorpal blade went snicker-snack!
He left it dead, and with its head
He went galumphing back.

"And hast thou slain the Jabberwock?"
"Come to my arms, my beamish boy!
O frabjous day! Callooh! Callay!"
He chortled in his joy.

—Lewis Carroll,
"The Jabberwocky"

Contents

Part 3: The Quest for Meaning

Preface

These pages are, I readily admit, the result of a life-long addiction: a compulsive, if also pleasurable, devotion to the reading of newspapers. One of my earliest memories of my father is of him sitting in his chair in our living room, reading the *New York Times*, pursing his lips to overcome a slight stammer and calling my attention (I was an obedient, if uncomprehending toddler) to some story or other that had pleased him or puzzled him in that morning's paper. One of my last memories of my aged mother was her reminding me to take away from her night-table, next to the bed in which she spent her last days, a crumpled bunch of clippings which she had been collecting for me, as she always had over long and opinionated decades (they were mostly polemical columns from her favorite New York columnists).

When I reflect for a moment on how I came to write this volume (and those to come) on "newspaper culture" or what the papers say, I find myself nostalgically aware of how the elements of nature and nurture played their role. Like most New York schoolboys I learned at an early age how to fold one's newspaper and discreetly turn the pages on crowded, strap-hanging interborough subway rides. In those years, consistent with one's revolt against the father, the morning paper was not his *Times* but my *Herald-Tribune*, not his *World-Telegram* but my *New York Post*.

As time went by, the side-effects of the addiction became part of the intellectual kicks of a more academic environment. We had a small circle of students in City College, dominated by our awesome mentor in all things historical or topical, Dr. B.N. Nelson.[1] We met once or twice a week, after classes, in some uptown or downtown cafeteria where we chatted earnestly about what happened to be new, by which we meant the news that we had happened to find strange or illuminating in the day's papers. Nelson dignified the gossip by calling it the study of "the visible surface of things," and he would regale us (he was a medieval historian) with tales of famous palimpsests and their secret sub-texts.

We were learning to be *penetrating*, to discern *"hidden meanings"*; and we devoured even the sleazy tabloids and stuffed, like bookmarks, our academic textbooks with apposite cuttings. I recall my adolescent pride when I earned the circle's (and the master's) praise: I had "solved" a famous prewar murder case. In a lost corner of a jump-story in the *Daily Mirror* or the *Journal-American* (both of which were still being published then) I had found a revealing item reporting the names of the books and authors which the brutal young killer (named Lonergan, I recall) had been reading before the commission of his crime, thus establishing a "deeper" motive or, at least, a literary *motif.* (What had Caesar's murderers been reading before the Ides of March? What titles were at hand in Canterbury when Thomas à Becket was laid low in the cathedral?)

I think of it now as constituting a special kind of what scholars call empirical research. In the hazy perspective of memory our "investigative reporting" was roughly equivalent to Michael Ventris' breaking the Greek code of Linear B (and opening up the true history of classical Cretan culture) or Theodor Mommsen's poking around with ancient coins and epigraphs (in order to re-tell the story of the Roman Empire like-it-was). But, truth to tell, the pastime was for over half-a-lifetime sheer fun and games, and no such newspaper addicts were ever alone. The Nelson circle over five-cent cups of coffee—in one of the Bickford's cafeterias near Washington Square or Morningside Heights—became, in time, a cosmopolitan international. There were many in far-away exotic places who, above and beyond their intellectual duty to the printed word, pored over the quotidian press, underlining quotations, scribbling in the margin, tearing out as neatly as one could the precious finds which could one day provide exquisite footnotes to history. I exchanged cuttings with François Bondy in Zurich, Edward Shils in Chicago, Dr. Hellmut Jaesrich in Berlin, George Urban in Munich, Leo Labedz in London, Friedrich Torberg in Vienna; and when we chanced to meet, armed with *faits divers*, the occasion soon became a small press festival. We recited our special scoops and eagerly bartered Xerox copies. Torberg was especially good on suggestive misprints, Bondy on embarrassing double negatives, Shils on clichés and buzz-words, Labedz on what in the East European press the GPU/KGB had failed to notice. Some of us were building up a formidable library of clues to the larger meaning of things which had been preserved, according to our hypothesis, in the visible and readable surfaces of the day. The old credo still obtained, as in the early days when we were (as Eliot says) dropping questions on our plates and measuring out our lives in coffee-spoons.

And so the addiction was both nature and nurture. Still, who knows newspapers who only newspapers know? This is often one of the shortcomings of our schools of journalism. What the papers say is dissected in a near-sighted "content-analysis"; journalist pronounces upon journalist (for good stories, or engaged campaigning, or defective ethics). But a far-sighted critique would be to focus on that larger set of values, ideas, and attitudes which the democratic press is deemed to be fulfilling in our media-dependent society...or failing miserably. For my own part, flaunting no comprehensive philosophy of communication or totally committed politics, I confine my analysis of the language of journalism, the uncertainties of its faltering style, its hectic quest for incisive meanings (and the other media matters with which I will be dealing in this book) more to an *implicit* critique—naturally involving elements of my personal attitude, my own sense of logic and reason (and, I hope, of humor)—and rather less to an *explicit* message and all-encompassing media manifesto. I have been influenced by H.L. Mencken's[2] devotion to the drama of the word, not by his half-intellectual tendentiousness. I have been attracted by Marshall McLuhan's thematic adventurousness, not by his overheated or undercooled categories.

While I am about it, I might as well confess to a number of other sources which might help the reader to explain what I have been, consciously or unintentionally, doing in these thousand pages. To some, I fear, the enterprise might appear a gigantic emptying of file-boxes (a conventional reproach for work studded with detail): outing huge collections of newspaper cuttings, and second-guessing them with glosses and annotations about style, meaning, vocabulary, and the like. There was once a book by B.H. Haggin, a distinguished New York critic, entitled *Music for the Man Who Enjoys Hamlet*; and this is a sort of a companion effort for readers who take thought, take the trouble to work at—and work through—their newspapers; for the media we may have may be our best, if not only, source of knowledge of the external world, offering us a singular chance to grasp what is happening in our times. Assembling many and diverse things, it will, I trust, be taken to be the work of a man who was, as befits his calling as an editor and publisher, subject to many and multifarious influences. Some were intellectual onslaughts: difficult to accept, painful to resist. Others were eccentric, if lasting, impressions on a New York schoolboy whose mind was first exposed to logic and the scientific method by Morris Raphael Cohen and Ernest Nagel[3]...and also to their very opposite: the romantic fallacies of Marx and Trotsky, illogical and unscientific, but which may still have left traces in the pages to follow. Still others taught me to be concerned with "the color of things" and not only with their meaning, with the shape and sound of words and not merely with their artless message. Among them were two old-timers at the *New Yorker*: Frank Sullivan who instructed a generation of literary aspirants – standing at the crossroads, looking through the window of opportunity – how to sneer (with a smile) at a cliché; and A.J. Liebling on how to laugh at "the wayward press." Without further explication my ideal reader will be detecting further traces of influence from that elegant master of language, Jacques Barzun; from the late Sidney Hook, an indefatigable polemicist who nevertheless preached "the culture of controversy"; from S.M. Levitas, publisher and fatherly censor at the *New Leader*, a social-democratic paper in Manhattan, with whom I learned how it is that some difficult truths sometimes, somehow, get lost in the printing shop, on galley, on page-proofs just before press-time... and from his young managing editor of the time, Daniel Bell, who wrote an enviable weekly column entitled "Clippings without Comment" (I often provided the comment by sub-editing into the text pointed captions). The earliest professional advice came at a green teenager from his curmudgeonly "faculty advisor" at the *Clinton News*, Raphael Philipson...and equipped with the elementary journalistic rules of how to write a lead (who-what-how-when *etc.*), and where to cut a story (from the bottom), together with a dozen proof-reading marks (to *stet* what had been cut), I went on to become a sports writer, a film and theater critic, a book reviewer, and a special foreign correspondent for the *New York Sunday Times* – what a distinction in its day!—associating with the likes of Lester Markel, James ("Scotty") Reston, A.M. Rosenthal, Sydney Gruson, C.L. ("Cy") Sulzberger, et al.

One last prewar recollection and acknowledgement: of my gratitude to Dwight Macdonald,[4] unforgettable editor of *Partisan Review* (and, later, *Politics*) who became before his death in 1982 (and especially after) a so-called "American cult figure" (largely because of his intensely eccentric criticism of the movies). He published in *Partisan Review* my very first serious article and invited me to my first Greenwich Village cocktail party (1941) at which I, to my eternal embarrassment, asked only for a glass of milk; but as a result of which my very sober conversations with Mary McCarthy, Philip Rahv, and Clement Greenberg left me with a new sense of intellectual acuity. Macdonald was a Yankee cracker-barrel ideologue with whom, after inviting him to London to help edit *Encounter*, I fell out uproariously. But for me, and for many young writers whom he favored, he was present at the creation of a special New York intellectual culture: in part political commitment, in part high journalism, bound together by an admirably cranky devotion to language and personal style. I thought of him often in the writing of the book.

I shall leave to the unswayed opinion of the reader what I owe to the lesson of the subsequent forty years during which, in Berlin and in London, I edited two international intellectual journals, *Der Monat*[5] (1948-1962) and *Encounter* (1958-1990), both devoted to literature and politics and enjoying some recognizable relationship to the newspaper culture of our time.

Last and least—but still pertinent to the wild profusion of echo and allusion in the pages to come—I must mention that grand and infuriating work by that seventeenth-century master of flamboyant allusiveness, Robert Burton. I was introduced to his classic but little-read book, *The Anatomy of Melancholy* (1621), by a once famous London man-of-letters, Daniel George, who was preparing a small paperback edition of what he judged to be "a storehouse of learning, wisdom, and entertainment."* I have been reading in it ever since. I still have not determined what all the three beguiling volumes amount to in terms of theology and/or intellectual discipline, but it profited me even where it corrupted. (Samuel Johnson thought he overloaded the books with quotation; Burton was a "chain-quoter.") I have not been the same since. Whatever it may have been that Burton was after, possibly to win indisputably a long-forgotten argument and save a precious truth, he drew upon everything that came his way, from "the whole world's literature, sacred and profane, for precept and example, for legend and history and fiction, for every possible illustration or embellishment of his theme...." Who can fail to envy his magisterial performance?

---

* Robert Burton, *The Anatomy of Love* (ed. Daniel George, paperback in the New English Library, 1962). The full scholarly text—"it can be eloquent, vigorous, coarse, poetic, concise, prolix"—has been published in three annotated volumes by the Oxford University Press: *The Anatomy of Melancholy* (eds. Faulkner, Kiessling, Blair, 1989/1994).

     The original book, published in 1621, went through five editions in Burton's lifetime (he died at the age of 63 in the year 1639).

If, in the beginning, there was the word or, as the biologist Richard Dawkins might say, the literary gene, compelling and word-devouring; and then there came to it an intellectual and academic element which the German philosopher Hegel, also a newspaper addict, considered a stimulant to insight and even truth...there is a third influence which derives from the transatlantic factor. It is the fact that I have lived most of my professional life as an editor and journalist as an American in Europe. This has proved to be "a defining moment" in several senses.

Most Europeans have had two souls in their breast, cultivating (on the one hand) their Eurocentrism with a pride in the Old World as the still living source of civilization and alternating (on the other) with a secret Goethean surmise that *"Amerika, du hast es besser,"* a notion of America having it better—doing it better, making it better—as befits the last best hope of mankind.

Most Americans had their roots in the Old World and uprooted them, exhibited pride in having established a New World, but periodically showed pious signs (as in the troubled credos of Jefferson, of Hawthorne, of Henry Adams and Henry James) of admiration and envy of lost motherlands.

Journalists are no exceptions to the rule of ambivalence. There have been recently two notable judgements[6] on the state of Anglo-American deference, one from an editor of the *New Republic*, the brilliant American weekly, who happened to be a Briton, the other from the American editor whom he replaced. The former (Andrew Sullivan) comes down on the Goethean side: American journalism, he finds, is indeed "better." It doesn't have the flash and the wit and elegance of English writing but, then again, it doesn't have its superficiality, irresponsibility and, in the end, its unseriousness. His reply to the query, "Why do the British chatter so wittily but say nothing of any substance?" is, substantially, a contrast with

> the admirable earnestness of *The New York Times* and the *Washington Post*, with their po-faced foreign reporting and deadpan political analysis....The subjects of race, ethnicity, pluralism, feminism, sexuality have all seen their most vivid exploration in the US. When the Brits discuss race or the underclass they import American writers.....The London *Zeitgeist* tends towards entertaining dilettantism, rather than addressing serious public concerns....[What is] readable, witty and sprightly, reeks of lassitude and decadence....The country positively sighs with cultural exhaustion.

Be that as it may (and it is true), the opposite—as in the famous paradox of Karl Kraus—is also true. The Oxford man's "Yankee-philia" is matched by the Washington man's "Anglophilia." As Michael Kinsley admitted, in the mirror-imagery of recurrent transatlantic illusionism, his own deference ran the other way—in admiration of the nimble quickness, the fluent finish and, to be sure, the good grammar (most of the time) that is expended on a London newspaper's daily output: "Perhaps it's just my Anglophilia, but I still think that English journalism is remarkably lucid and intelligent, on average, compared with that in America." We will leave it at that: a tie, a draw, a Mexican stand-off , and yet another example of the Anglo-American difference which is that of a shared culture separated by a common language.*

The standards and innovations, virtues and vices, differ in transatlantic perspective, but I treat them together in an interchangeable and, at times, a unified perspective, just as a literary critic, inquiring into the state of the contemporary novel or poetry or modern English-language literature in general, must perforce deal with writers from both sides of the Atlantic: James Joyce and T.S. Eliot, George Orwell and Ernest Hemingway, Evelyn Waugh and Saul Bellow, Kingsley Amis and John Updike. Paying attention in this way can illuminate the inter-related manner the Americans as well as the British report on the world around them.

The reader will also note my effort to introduce a third "newspaper culture," in order to have a sort of control-test in matters of national parallelism (sophistication, populism, taboos) and international diffusion (slang, profanity, buzz-words). And so I have used in many chapters the serious German press, above all that distinguished West-German daily, the *Frankfurter Allgemeine Zeitung*, which matches up with the *New York Times*, the *Washington Post*, and the *International Herald-Tribune* (published in Paris but owned jointly by the *Times* and the *Post*). In England the sources for most of my references are to the *Times* (now owned by the *ur*-Australian, Rupert Murdoch), the *Daily Telegraph* (now owned by the Canadian, Conrad Black), and the *Guardian* (formerly of Manchester distinction). Occasionally I have added some

---

* I have delimited this Anglo-American comparative strategy to modest proportions: for I intend to be mainly concerned with English-language journalism, and within that vast enterprise the mainstream publications of New York, Washington, and London.

It would be fascinating and instructive to examine how the controlled Chinese press and the free Japanese newspapers have coped with the difficulties of modernism: slang, profanity, new coinages, buzz-words, etc. I have taken only an occasional side-glance at what the Germans have been doing as they wrestle with such problems of newspaper culture.

weekly and monthly magazines in accumulating examples to attest to the splendors and miseries of our Anglo-American journalism. Two London dailies, both of which in their way aspire to be taken "seriously," also figure in the handbookish case-study materials assembled (*viz.* the *Daily Mail* and the *Evening Standard*). I have written as if the *New Yorker*'s famous "old lady in Dubuque" (immortalized in Harold Ross' phrase for the great non-reading reader in tennis shoes)—even if she doesn't subscribe to any of the publications herein examined for what they tell us about the state of life and letters today—will be influenced or even, sooner or later, be caught up by the "cultural mechanisms" I have been considering. For better or worse, I see the "filtering through" or trickle-down effect everywhere in our copy-cat cultures.

I used to try and follow more newspapers than I do now, picking up at the nearest international kiosks *Le Monde* fairly regularly, along with the *Corriere della Sera* (not to miss a reportage by Luigi Barzini) and, later, Indro Montanelli's *Il Giornale*. Rather more frequently I took the *Neue Zürcher Zeitung*, leafing through them all diligently, clipping them assiduously. The cannibalized remnants were, mostly, stuffed away in small used envelopes, but every now and then an odd batch of miscellaneous cuttings were air-mailed to a friendly editor abroad or to a foreign correspondent who might be stimulated to do a bright, thoughtful piece.

But I never lived long enough in France or Italy or Switzerland to feel any special empathy with their journals, to peer over the top of my newspaper and make out the three-dimensional realities in strange local colors which the reporters were supposed to be recording. With some effort I discouraged myself from trying to match what these papers were saying with the kind of life-and-letters I had come to experience in lands where I had lived long chunks of my own life. So I decided more modestly to confine the research for this book to the United States, where I was born and educated (and in whose armed services I did wartime duty); to postwar Germany where I edited and published a German-language monthly magazine (and it achieved a certain cultural influence and notoriety); and to Britain where my Anglo-American intellectual journal, *Encounter*, rarely gave me (and, I dare say, my readers) a dull moment.

And now that my life is approaching a ninth decade, and I still manage to devour my bundle of the daily and periodical press, I realize poignantly, almost with a sense of distress and displacement, that my autobiography is a pieced-together patchwork, a tale of three cities.

Without renewing daily contact with the latest messages coming from New York, Berlin, and London I can no longer be sure—as the philosopher said (to refer to Hegel once again), explaining his own nervous devotion to the morning press—that the realities are out there. To be sure, I pay attention less to the "new appointments" than to yesterday's obituaries but, for all that, I continue to be curious, as an old and obsessive devotee should, as to whether my former schoolmates are still around and what my old clan of writers and poets, those ever-warring intellectuals, have now been up to. Over and above that, the unfolding account of yesterday's events, of what by tomorrow will already be history—the continuing story, the headlines for what happens next—still keeps me on tenterhooks. We all live our lives with print and paper, and sooner or later we too become a news-item or, with luck, a jump-story to be continued next day.

In all of this I have tried wherever possible—and it has not been uniformly possible—to repress my own subjective value-judgments as to the merits and demerits of the American, the British, and the Continental European traditions of journalism. I have spent most of my life reading what these papers have to say, and I have, as an American publisher, tried to pick and choose among attractive foreign models for printing a page, telling a story, for supporting a cause or winning an argument. As an inveterate magpie—my first published pieces were published in a schoolboy journal of that name in the Bronx—I have always succumbed (alas) to the sentimentalism that, wherever I was, the grass was always greener on the other side. This is the nervous tic of bi-national, and indeed, cosmopolitan experience. The past induces nostalgia—my father reading his copy of the *New York Times* for fifty years of his life, and trusting every word the paper thought fit to print. The future is another country: now England (where every writer knows his Shakespeare and the King James Bible, and his prose echoes accordingly), now Germany (where they compose stories and dispatches, editorials and *feuilletons*, as if the high-brow readership included Goethe, Heine and Nietzsche). As for my first loves—the New York press which included such defunct unforgettable rags as the *Daily Mirror*, the *Sun*, Roy Howard's *World-Telegram*, Hearst's *Journal-American*, and the superb *New York Herald-Tribune**—one's provisional prejudices and tentative judgements vary, as I say, with the

---

* See Richard Kluger's loyal tribute to past glories in his history of *"The Trib," The Paper: The Life and Death of the New York Herald Tribune* (1986).

distance or the *locus in quo* of the reader, and also what I, a transplanted American in Europe, have been forced to recognize as the recurrent "transatlantic illusion." The great ocean divides; sail across it, fly over it, turn our backs on it, the great tides still unite and separate New and Old Worlds.

I have chosen some thousand "practical examples" and have made an effort to relate them to some general attitude toward life and letters. I do not pretend, as I say, to have a general theory either of literature or language; and I like to think of Rousseau—discoursing in his essay on the *Origin of Language*[7] (written in the early 1750s but published only after its author's death in 1781)—rather modestly closing with an apology for his "superficial reflections, but which others more profound may arise." What might arise

> would be the subject of a very philosophical examination to show by examples how much the character, the morals and the interests of a people influence their language.

I can only hope that my collection of examples, my *chrestomathy* (the tag is Mencken's), can lead the reader in the right direction to a greater critical reflectiveness.

Finally, three lines of heartfelt acknowledgement. To my patient wife, Helga Hegewisch, who was busy writing her own books and generously refrained (most of the time) from taking umbrage at the litter in the house, and from criticizing my "messing about" with "mere" newspapers. To my beloved sister Floria Lasky Altman, keeper of the family tradition, who kept the clippings coming. And to my friend and self-styled amanuensis Marc Svetov who (like most admirable and indispensable assistants, with an eye for bibliography and an ear for punctuation) earned the classic encomium: without whom this work would have been finished so much earlier.

M. J. L.
February 1999

Part 1

A Question of Style

"For words of a feather tend to stick together, and if one strays behind, it is likely to incur danger in life."

—Edward Sapir, Language: An Introduction to the Study of Speech (1921)

"It is not the word that I fear, but the emotion which produces the word...."

—Epictetus (50-138 AD), "Discourses"[1]

"But words are things, and a small drop of ink falling like dew, upon a thought, produces that which makes thousands, perhaps millions, think..."

—Lord Byron, "Don Juan" (1818)[2]

Part I

A Question of Self

1

Words Win, Language Loses

The Infinity of a Split

The appalling casualness of the current use of language, remarked upon by so many literary critics today—deficiencies in grammar and vocabulary, ignorance of shades of meaning, indifference to traditional and/or reasonable rules of proper usage—could be a subject for a thousand-page lexicographical study. For the purposes of this work—which only occasionally, in a very few places also aspires to be a contribution to the "semantic sensitivity awareness" of aspiring journalists on some utopian ideal paper—I will confine this opening section to a few representative notes illustrating the cultural zero-sum game in which the new words win and the old language loses.

First, a word of defeatism. Let me begin with the fiasco which amounts to the least of our troubles—the vain struggle to maintain that splendid old grammarian's precept not to split infinitives. The last-ditch sticklers for that tiny rule of literary rectitude have been repulsed, rebuffed, routed. Here are the casualties strewn across the battlefield of just yesterday's newspapers. My "body count" is taken from a week's perusal of the Anglo-American press:

> He emphasized the government's failure *to effectively enforce* the immigration laws.... He decided *to personally attack* Columbia after six years of service there.... An industrial tribunal also criticized the TSB for failing *to fully investigate* the allegations.... Damon Hill even went so far as *to playfully advise* photographers to position themselves on the outside.... The protocol always called for him *to confidently greet* visitors.... She had problems when she began *to voraciously eat* everything in sight.... Hartford, Connecticut, is the first community *to completely privatize* its public school system.... Salem, the sheikh's bodyguard, used a tape-recorder of his own *to covertly monitor* his conversations with FBI controllers...

3

How old this bad habit is can be surmised by a paragraph reprinted recently in the *International Herald Tribune* under its rubric "75 Years Ago." It was a report of a London riot in Trafalgar Square (1919) against an American prohibitionist who vainly tried to convert an apparently pro-alcoholic "crowd of frenzied collegians":

> The students intended *to publicly duck* Mr. Johnson into a barrel of beer.[3]

Even Africans, who obviously learned proper English in the West, are doing it. A spokesman in Mobutu's Zaire was quoted as saying in Kinshasa about the chances of gaining political power for a new reformer on the scene, named Kengo wa Dondo:

> The trick for us is to incrementally extend legitimation to Kengo without letting Mobutu hijack it for himself.[4]

He must have felt free to split and splatter in this way because he was talking to the State Department's deputy secretary of state, who is a former editor of *Time* magazine (now no longer a bastion of old fashioned values as in Henry Luce's day).

The prize for the longest rupture of the year (at least among the splits that have come my way) was captured by the *Daily Telegraph* when it reported on a TV broadcaster's exposé of P.R. shenanigans:

> During the programme, he used the names of 14 MPs to, according to another motion, "establish Ian Greer Associates' credentials with its prospective clients."

The most unkindest cut of all is when the split is elevated (from the unobtrusive 8-point text) to the blatant headline, and the 24-point Bodoni type screams out at you—

D.A. THREATENS TO PUBLICLY EXPOSE SECRET FILE

Sometimes it is a cozy matter of bunching up the phrase to keep you warm.

> Unfazed in the chilly air, Marla Maples in a slinky dress marched to the ladies room and buddied-up to the hot-air dryers *to better heat up* her ample torso.[5]

With so many colleagues who share my mild horror and chronic dismay at this kind of thing—indifference to grammar is, I suspect, linked ultimately to indifference to meaning and truth—I have long since admitted defeat. But I still, like the hapless Charlie away from his assembly line, twist and twinge, and go on to register irritation at each day's specimen (naturally excepting those dozen classic cases where there's no sensible alternative to splitting). Still, there is mounting evidence that reporters or their sub-editors go out of their way to show how liberated they are: to really and truly write well is to consistently and blatantly split infinitives. The mood on the other side is, alas, triumphalist. The poet (T.S. Eliot, somewhere) had it right: words split, language breaks up, the wasteland cometh...

We didn't think we have the creativity to dramatically distinguish our products on our own.

Mr. Barry announced sweeping changes in the Defense Department to better cope with the danger.

Indeed General Mladic traveled from one execution site to another to personally oversee the extermination.[6]

The usual sub-standard delinquencies have almost made a normal rhythm of the bifurcated infinitive, for this is the way that ill-clad sentences can appear in public these days. The gait is pedestrian but no longer seems conspicuous.

The new European Commission will find it difficult to quickly resuscitate a piece of [TV-Quota] legislation.

A computer hack who blocked radio-station phone-lines so that he could be the winning contest-caller admitted using his computer to fraudulently win two Porsches and at least two trips to Hawaii.

NATO commanders can deter attacks to an extent, but it's very difficult to actually prevent the place being occupied.[7]

See a verb coming and you reach out to fill the open space. I sense a note of aggressiveness in the practice, and also a bit of an effort to be somewhat unusual and even original. The *Herald-Tribune* headline writer contrived this head across three front-page columns for a *Washington Post* story about how to (almost) get away with political corruption:

HOW TO (LEGALLY) GET FOREIGN GIFTS

Foreign languages have their own native problems with verbs, not necessarily akin to the splitting of the Anglo-Saxon infinitives, but in English everybody is doing it, if one believes Alessandra Stanley (reporting from Russia for the *New York Times*) who is quoting one of her Moscow sources, a Mr. Umar Dzhabraiov, about his quarrel with a high ex-Soviet bureaucrat: "He has the ability to initially convince people he is right." Does Russian have splittable verbs? or was he prompted or interpreted, and otherwise helped along by the up-to-the-minute Ms. Stanley?[8]

Chaucer, as academics have reported, split a handful of infinitives, but the modern practice may have begun by giving wide latitude to the raw, untutored talents who were permitted to write as they pleased. Now it is on the verge of becoming a grammatical imperative. Sub-editors, and indeed headline writers, move the adverb crisply into the once-forbidden space, splitting the infinitive with the pioneer spirit of an Abe Lincoln splitting rails. No, our district attorneys will not be exposing the secret files publicly; nor will our ministers be confessing their failures publicly (or even publicly confessing those self-same failures). The four-column headline in the *International Herald Tribune* presumably following the style books of its sponsors, the *New York Times* and the *Washington Post* (with an assist from the *Los Angeles Times*), read:

E.U. MINISTERS TO PUBLICLY CONFESS FAILURES.[9]

I am afraid it's time for the rest of us to publicly confess: We just can't stop them. The split is infinite, and permanent.

One would have to risk being totally humorless to go on about it (as I am, half-heartedly, trying to do), when the whole matter of grammatical proprieties has become a subject for jokes and a peg for fun columnists. One wag (Dave Barry of the *Miami Herald*) has been posing as a "Language Person" who was named "the Official Grammarian for the 1996 Summer Olympic." In that capacity he would be "testing the athletes' urine at random for split infinitives and traces of illegal gerunds." As for the "diphthong," there was nothing suspicious about that and, in fact, he was persuaded by one dictionary or another that it was "a word that is used to form a good name for a rock band (e.g., Earl Piedmont & the Diphthongs)."[10] This may well be, as I say, the least of our troubles in a raging sea of adversities. We probably won't be, as a direct consequence of barbarian practices in our language, approaching the End of Civilization as we have known it. Yet the admirable Karl Kraus spent a lifetime in tragic Vienna arguing just this—if a shade too melodramatically, but then the apocalyptic wasteland did come in the form of two great world wars.

As Kraus insisted in his philology of nit-picking, they who violate the essence of language will in turn be violated. They are the condemned victims of a society plagued by dark and pernicious ambiguities, and increasingly alienated from proper standards of order, truth and meaning. And for Kraus—as for H.L. Mencken, our greatest philological critic—grammar and rhetoric were the clues to catastrophes. Kraus seized upon every little item in the press or erratic phrase in parliament as pieces of evidence for the dire future, what he called in his formidable play of that name, *Die Letzten Tage der Menschheit* (*The Last Days of Mankind*).*

---

*   See, in English, Harry Zohn's book *Karl Kraus* (1971); the Zohn anthology of translations, *In these Great Times: a Karl Kraus Reader* (1976); and Erich Heller's brilliant essay in *The Disinherited Mind* (1952). In German there is Hans Weigel's biography (1986); a valuable Kraus volume in the *Text + Kritik* series (ed. Arnold, 1975); and of course Karl Kraus' oeuvre, the most pertinent volume being *Aphorismen* (1986), a convenient anthology published in Frankfurt as a Suhrkamp paperback.

I will not withhold my sneaking admiration for an old-fashioned and recalcitrant school of thought which is attempting, against all odds, to hold fast to traditional rules of grammar and syntax. In his weekly department on "*Usage and Abusage*," one newspaper columnist has been arguing for years against splitting the infinitive and was especially upset when the Chambers Dictionary people, in the summer of 1996, finally gave up the ghost and conceded that the once-taboo practice was now "perfectly in order." The *Daily Telegraph's* authority on the subject (whose brief, alas, does not extend to any other column or page in his own paper) was "insulted." As he wrote,

> Free speech includes the freedom to mangle it, as we all do at one time or another, in informal circumstances. But, as I wrote here only a year ago when Oxford kindly sanctioned the dreaded split, anyone with an ounce of feeling for speech rhythm knows that it is ugly and angular, and will avoid it.

Some of the thousand bits of favorable evidence, beginning with the Bard, were again trotted out in support of the case for the prosecution. How odd and indeed absurd it would have been had Shakespeare written "*To be or to not be*" or "*A consummation to devoutly be wished*"! The split puts a limp into the natural flow of words, although no one will deny that Shakespeare ignored grammar when it suited him; but not *euphony* (and he knew enough Greek to know it meant "good sound").

Insulted traditionalists keep on cringing and groaning. A BBC reporter said the other day, "They are intending to now study it closely." And what is wrong, pray, with "now to study it closely" or "to study it closely now"? Yet how long will we want to expend our ingenuity by rephrasing all the split infinitives that come our way in the course of a day? If we maintain our beleaguered and almost lost positions, then it must surely be not a mere matter of literary style but more than that, one of essential life-style. As one English lexicographer (Fritz Spiegl) writes, pulling himself up to his full cultural height—

> Our freedom also allows us to decide whether we wash, shave, or scrub our fingernails. When out camping or mountaineering we let niceties go by the board and offend no one. Equally it is good manners in the drawing room to observe conventions when not to do so might make others uncomfortable, or think less of one. Nobody complains about good manners—or good grammar.
>
> That is why I faintly resent being told by Chambers that a four-day stubble and dirty nails are now acceptable.

Acceptable to whom? Or should we write, "Who to?"[11]

I share little or none of the emotional involvement of my grammarian friends who in their pedantic loyalties cheer on all who dare to employ the traditional rules and chastise or otherwise condemn to obloquy those who carelessly or deliberately herd themselves among the splitters. But I do aver that when I unexpectedly find, rare as this is becoming, an unsplit infinitive a special rhythm and even an extra shot of persuasive power seems to hover over the construction. Here is an English columnist discussing pregnancy and the state of the abortion debate; and she is arguing for more candor about the little-mentioned after-effects of terminal foetal surgery, suggesting only that "Violently to interrupt this delicate and powerful process is likely to cause trouble." This sentence as constructed is, I submit, a touch stronger, or more expressive and elegant, than if violence had also been done to the infinitives.[12]

Railing in their very own self-interest against the imaginary rules that petty linguistic tyrants have sought to lay upon the English language, novelists, poets, and other serious craftsmen in modern literature have often insisted that there is simply no grammatical reason whatsoever against splitting an infinitive. Often the avoidance of one lands the writer in trouble; Fowler and other texts are full of examples, and the general liberal conclusion is that "We will split infinitives rather than be barbarous or artificial." Among the literary men who lined themselves up in opposition to the "anti-split infinitive fanatics" was Kingsley Amis, but despairing that the old "rule" would ever yield to reason, he made in the end his own reasonable, if gloomy, compromise in his guide to modern usage, *The King's English* (1997):

> whatever anybody may say, split infinitives are still to be avoided in most circumstances.... I personally think that to split an infinitive is perfectly legitimate, but I do my best never to split one in public and I would certainly not advise anybody else to do so, even today.

He was not quite aware that it was no longer a matter of ungainly departures from natural word orders by a careful writer eager to get on with his felicitous phrasing. Good prose in our time is being overwhelmed by forces much larger than quibbles about solecisms. Fowler's successor, Robert Burchfield, is still trying to keep his finger in the hole of the dam:

> Avoid splitting infinitives whenever possible, but do not suffer undue remorse if a split infinitive is unavoidable for the natural and unambiguous completion of a sentence already begun.[13]

This guidance makes a sensible arrangement with the *faits accomplis* in serious prose wherein a Philip Roth shows "*a willingness to not always, in every circumstance think the very best*" of being natural—when a John Updike "*shares a curious dry ability to without actually saying anything make*" him feel unambiguous—and even Kingsley Amis "*managed to quite like*" the rule-of-thumb.

In daily journalism it is another matter. The avalanche which has been triggered by the enthused faction of our newspaper splitters—as in our many examples—comes from (to paraphrase one of the splitters) "*seeming to just deliberately and maliciously draw attention*" to the fact that anything goes, no rules obtain, everything is as good as anything else. We are all post-modernists now.

The *Times* of London was judicious, if a tad light-hearted, in its summing-up (1992) of the grand debate over adverbial deployment: "The most diligent search can find no modern grammarian to pedantically, to dogmatically, to invariably condemn a split infinitive." Well, this may be as good a place as any at which to formally conclude our discussion, before running the risk of trying flatly to forbid enlisting a reader in a lost cause.[14] Is this last clause ambiguous? Is it a flat prohibition? A flat try? So be it.

In the Passing Parade of Words

When wars over words break out—and verbal animals, or bipeds with a gift for speech, have never been able to keep the peace for very long—there are usually two opposing camps confronting each other in the hostilities. The one has styled itself for as long as literacy has been known as classically tone-giving heroes. Their message—from Jahweh's monolinguists in Babel (Genesis 11) to the Hebrew formalists (in Judges 12.6), from Homer's Greek to Napoleon's French—rings down in history, loud and clear and unmistakable. The others, upstart strangers from beyond one's own frontiers, speaking an alien tongue, or some shibboleth of a language, sometimes armed only with an obscure argot or a broad dialect, have always been dismissed as barbarians. Since human language grows and changes, and even victorious vocabularies get transformed over the centuries, some speech forms become richer, some increasingly obsolete. Barbaric usages continue generally to circulate until the appointed guardians of the language, hidebound or permissive as they may be, sit and pronounce judgment. Classical grammarians defend the old locutions; liberal etymologists are prepared to concede yet another prescriptive stronghold to the offenders. We are continually making war, trying to make peace. In our days, new up-to-date standard editions of great classic dictionaries are a sort of armistice, a kind of solution.

As I write, the Oxford University Press has just published the *New Oxford Dictionary of English* (1998), and it flaunts an impressive association with the immense authority of its august grandmother, the *O.E.D.* Language is now described with a fresh eye (and newcomers include *bimbo, phone sex, dumb down...*). Odd words are authenticated for proper and approved use (like *lunch box* for an athlete's bulging male genitals, or *to bobbitt*, named after the jealous woman who vindictively cut off her husband's penis, an act, so etymologists assure us, quite different from castration). Controversial twists and turns in grammatical usage get to be finally resolved: *viz.*, since *he* or *she* is tiresomely long-winded one is permitted to say, "Every child needs to know that they are loved." These changes usually cause some mild relief in pedagogical circles, weary of dithering, and arouse a modest stir of criticism, as in the traditional objection that what is legitimate is determined by the people's habits and are no longer decreed by their betters. On all such issues the people vote comfortably for what comes naturally. Small wonder that some skeptics, including humorists who habitually depend on nuances of meaning, accent, and inflection, despair in a semantic world where words have lost their bearings and are given no new guidelines, except that anything goes if enough of you out there go along with it. Controversy raged, for the English still feel that after all it is *their* language and, accordingly, its legitimate defenders; but it was hard to distinguish in all the brouhaha the high indignation from the hijinks. The first letter the *Times* printed in the putatively furious discussion that was to follow was one sentence long, under the head "*To boldly go*":

> Sir, May I be the first to roundly condemn *The Oxford Dictionary of English* for allowing the use of split infinitives?...Yours, etc.[15]

In 1906, in his "The Enlarged Devil's Dictionary," Ambrose Bierce defined "Dictionary" as

> A malevolent literary device for cramping the growth of the language and making it hard and inelastic. The present dictionary [namely, his own] is, however, one of the most useful ever produced. It is a compendium of everything that is known up to date of its completion, and will drive a screw, repair a red wagon or apply for a divorce. It is a good substitute for measles, and will make rats come out of their holes to die. It is a dead shot for worms, and children cry for it.[16]

There is a reasonable element of absurdity in many of the rules of a mature and sophisticated language, and even excitable literary polemicists persist with a Biercean sense of irony. The playwright Keith Waterhouse thought that the Oxford green light for the split infinitive was "a slippery slope" and predicted the coming of the Association for the Annihilation of the Aberrant Apostrophes (AAAA). He reported that the Confederation of Trader's in Bananas have already petitioned dictionary's editors for a *carte blanche* "to scatter their produce with random apostrophes like glitter on a Christmas tree." Kindergarten teachers, concerned for the well-being of their pre-literate charges, have asked for the apostrophe to be abolished entirely, as have lobbyists for the replacement of gas meters. The dictionary makers are impressed with the phenomenon of casual, if momentarily incorrect, punctuation and give signs that if this is the calm before the storm, they may well be ready to give up the ghost, or throw in the towel. Thousands of aberrant apostrophes have been collected, as Waterhouse reports in the *Daily Mail*, and

> they include ladie's wigs, a visitor's car park, and rule's for member's of a dog owner's club to the effect that puppie's injection's must be entered into their vacci-

nation book's, and that flat shoe's must be worn for training session's. There are references without number to toilet's, surgerie's, college's, security camera's, to childrens portion's always being available, and—a rare find—a Royal Society of Medicine scale of fee's.

The AAAA has also spotted the recent strain of apostrophic deviation: the slipped apostrophe (reported by readers to be more painful than a slipped disc), as in "Antiques,...Saturdays,...Hairdresser's."[17]

Be that as it may, in the case of the split infinitive there are still two formidable camps, although mugwumpery in the middle has for almost the whole of the century reinforced the school of compromise. We are reminded that as long ago as 1926 the mighty traditionalist H.W. Fowler in his *Dictionary of Modern English Usage* said there is nothing wrong with splitting infinitives, and he mocked "those who do not know but do care, who would as soon be caught putting their knives in their mouths as splitting an infinitive but have only hazy notions of what constitutes that deplorable breach of etiquette." Fowler thought that such people were guilty of "tame acceptance of the misinterpreted opinions of others, for they will subject their sentences to the queerest distortions, all to escape imaginary split infinitives."

"That's me," confessed a distinguished British journalist, now editing the *Spectator*. All his life, as his friends and readers know, he has suffered under the fear of being thought the sort of person who splits his infinitives.[18]

The anxiety over correctness or rectitude has only grown—paradoxically enough, for a permissive age—but, then, so have dissidence, contrariness, and eccentricity. One writer notes with distaste that "aboriginally" has been dropped because it is no longer used, not because it might offend native Australians; consequently, he is tempted to join in a crusade to restore *aboriginally* to its former adverbial glory. Others object to the dismaying nod to topicality (*viz.*, the inclusion of the word *Eurosceptic*); the saddening loss of the old-time religion (e.g., the dropping of "Christian name"); the awful anticipation that the next edition will feature a "Monica" as a term for the sexual act popularized by *that woman*...a Miss Lewinsky.

If this latter is one of those earthier terms ingested with glee into the language, would they not have appealed more to Boswell than to Samuel Johnson? Would the classic English lexicographer have balked at the Oxford pronouncement that infinitives may now be split at will? The consensus appeared to be that grammatical rules are all a matter of taste and snobbery; and, in a free country "with no language gestapo," who prefers to be slightly sniffy about the current exercises in "plastic language" may continue to go his or her—*their*—way. Still: language is, among other human fundamentals, part of the ground we stand on, and when words slip and stumble the earth seems to move and quake. Two-letter prepositions and even tiny misplaced apostrophes—although the Germans do their quotation marks, and the Spanish their question marks, upside down—appear to matter. One historian (Andrew Roberts in the *Sunday Times*) reconciled himself to the idea that, after all, history is only one damned battle after another: "The citadel of the split infinitive having been stormed, it is now time to man the barricades in defence of the beleaguered apostrophe."[19] One last word about lost causes which, apparently, will always be with us. But then no cause is ever finally lost until the last straggler surrenders the flag. I detect no sign of defeatism from Simon Jenkins in the *Times*:

> Grammar is serious. The capacity to use it is what separates us from the apes. It defines our species and enables us to do more than grunt, warn and mate.... We recognise, judge and react to each other through the subtleties of grammar. Its rules hold the key to human diplomacy and should never be changed without the utmost care.

Given this high seriousness, it is no easy question whether to split or not to split. Words are free, argues Jenkins, but grammar is too important to be left to grammarians who don't see why infinitives matter. The *Times* columnist waxes lyrical:

> Whole departments are devoted to the infinitive as verbal and as substantive. Others study the many grammatical cases in which this noble mood so glories. It appears as a nominative in, *To know is to love*; accusative in, *God gave us to see*; and dative or purposive in, *He has gone to visit his mother*.

Here the battle is to defend that "paragon of grammatical subtlety," namely the English infinitive, that "grammatical titan." Some are already plotting to get rid of the preposition, and by eliminating the *to* from the infinitive render the split obsolete. Are we in the English-speaking world ready for *Know is Love* or *God gave us see*? These notions and sentiments can be said (and have been) in other languages (French, German, *inter alia*); but Jenkins sees here the threatening shadow of pidgin and Creole. Lose the battle of Oxford, and night has fallen:

> These fine scholars are the space scientists of the language. They are lost in its black holes and quasars. When they tell us to shift course, we can shift. Until then, the Earth is still round, time does not bend and splitting infinitives is not normal or useful. It is ugly and sloppy, to be done only in emergencies.

This is not to be confounded with old-fashioned absolutism; it accommodates the concessions which grammarians from Fowler to Burchfield have made. The emergency also includes, be it noted, the urgencies of poetry. One of the most famous splits is Byron's *"To slowly trace the forest's shady scene."* Jenkins' defense is an admirable example of what I have called rules of reasonable absurdity, here moderated by poetic needs. Byron overcomes ugliness only by the purity of his meter and the balancing strength of *slowly* and *trace*. Had he written "to slowly go" he would have (so Jenkins) killed the line.

> The split infinitive debate is always welcome. It emphasizes what is vital to language, the rhythm and power that grammar bestows on the passing parade of words. [20]

Or so, as I hope, say all of us. This firm, apodictic tone is an echo of a self-confident century which produced that classic work of 1879, the first, formidable edition of the *Oxford English Dictionary*. I have frequently in these pages dwelt on the many virtues and a few of the vices of this many-volumed achievement; but one historical incident in the scholarly story of its compilation throws a provocative shadow, and it should not go unmentioned. It is told in a recent biography by Simon Winchester of Dr. William Minor of the United States, who contributed to the *O.E.D*. It is a weird story—even in "A Tale of Murder, Madness and Love of Words"—for Dr. Minor was an American surgeon and a homicidal lunatic.* It was only when James Murray, the editor of the first edition of the dictionary, went to visit his collaborator that he realized that the doctor was a resident in an asylum for the clinically insane.

Perhaps the anecdote should be left there. But the whole history of language—from its highest flights into philosophy, theology, and poetry to its low tabloid usefulness—has been connected with a measure of manic obsessiveness. It suggests that the ideal love of words can be darkly associated with other, even fatal attractions, and that way lies madness.[21]

The Uses of Illiteracy

But back to the split infinitive and related crack-ups. In a Dublin story which first explained why an IRA bomb "failed to fully explode" the writer went on to offer this maxim of wisdom, for whatever good it does for the Irish peace process: "In a zero-sum society, perception is all." Where no grammar is (i.e., no sense in sentences), gibberish can't be far behind.

This leads us to another related misdemeanour which is surely more troubling: blindness to the color of words and their shades of implicit meaning. On the same day, in the same paper, in a story from Cairo about the first successes in the world conference about "female fertility rights" (which had been criticized by Islamic governments and welcomed by militant Western campaigners), a leading New York spokesperson named Ellen

---

* From the Simon Winchester book, originally entitled *The Surgeon of Crowthorne* (1997), the *Sunday Times*' resident etymologist picked up the tidbit (16 August 1998), p. 5): "...Dr. Minor eventually cut off his own penis with the penknife he used for cutting book pages, an action dignified in the latest edition of the *OED* with its own verb 'to Bobbitt'...."

Chesler was quoted as saying with some pride: "Women will really be *collaborators*...." And this in the same week when the French wartime sins of *collaboration* with the Nazis received world-wide attention with President François Mitterand's confession that he had been a Pétainist in Vichy France. Certain tainted words can't be washed clean; nor should they be spoken mindlessly. Language is a beautiful thing: what a shame to waste it on political illiterates.

And on cultural illiterates too. For years the word "culture" has been bandied about and so systematically abused that its meaning has been contorted to extend to a thousand omni-cultural situations, all thought to be included in the so-called scientific meaning of the term as used by the classical anthropologists (Franz Boas, Ruth Benedict, Claude Lévi-Strauss, et al.). We are told of the *"culture of poverty"* in urban slums (so poor there's no room for culture at all); the *"culture of murder"* in civil war-wracked Yugoslavia; the *"culture of dependency"* in crisis-ridden welfare states; the *"culture of corruption"* in the *Tangentopoli* of contemporary Italy; the *"culture of evidence"* when lawyers and judges get together to sing the praises of justice and fair trial; the *"culture of deviance"* in the gay bathhouses of New York and San Francisco; the *"culture of the black-market"* in post-Communist Russian society.

In recent years, as black intellectual discourse has moved into a place at American centers of discussion, culture as an argumentative concept has served as a weapon on both sides of a racial debate. One black writer in the *New Yorker* tries to explain sympathetically why the black community was almost unanimous in its approval of the trial decision of not guilty in the O.J. Simpson murder case. The white community was practically unanimous in its opinion (nay, certainty) that he was the murderer, and that it was a sign of madness to ignore the mountain of persuasive evidence. Professor Henry Louis Gates, Jr., is saddened at the cultural divide. He writes,

> How can conversation begin when we disagree about reality?...For many whites a sincere belief in Simpson's innocence looks less like the culture of protest than the culture of psychosis. [22]

Gates goes on to mention Simpson's "ironic status in a *culture of celebrity"*; the possibility that other villains were involved in our *"drug culture of violence"*; the influence of "the white gatekeepers of a *media culture"* (convinced that black folk are "not merely counter-normative but crazy"); and he winds up with something called *"outlaw culture"* (by which he says that he means, in case we are still with him, "the tendency—which unites our lumpenproles with our post-modern ironists—to celebrate transgression for its own sake"). Culture seems to have its finger in every pie.

Nor is this all. I will be, subsequently, devoting a long chapter in explication of the 57 varieties of cultural experience. In this place, before one gets swamped and drowned in despair, I want only to ask, hopefully: What will happen when we will be needing the word in its luminous earlier meaning? It used to be conjugated: high culture, middlebrow culture, low or popular or mass culture; and then, no-culture-at-all, what the Russians disdainfully call *nyetkulturny*. Who will grasp that something ideal-aesthetical was originally implied and not some verbal shards of an anthropologist researching in the field?

Culture Lives!

The day may have already come. I note that when the pundits have exhausted the nostrums which have failed to be pertinent to the on-going carnage in the Balkans (U.N. Peace-keeping...Redrawing the Maps-and-Frontiers...Blockade...Air-Strikes...Humanitarian Aid...Embargo...Safe Havens...etc., etc.), they are turning to... culture. The *New York Times* (14 September 1994) came up with the surprising headline:

BOSNIA: CULTURE OFFERS THE SEEDS OF SURVIVAL

In view of the prevailing hunger and starvation in Sarajevo, it might have been supposed that seeds were offering the culture of survival, or, alternatively, survival was offering the seeds of culture. In any event the culture being referred in this case was not the old prevailing humbug (the "culture of despair ... of fratricide ... of ethnic cleansing") but, quite simply, music and art and theatre, and even fashion shows. These were beginning to flower in Bosnia, and (opined the hopeful *Times* analysts), "these moments of culture" could "save the nation."

In a not unrelated development (as the sub-editors like to say, "combining dispatches"), another pundit desperately invoked the old culture of lost meaning, in order to make vivid the warning against the latest European strategy to move along "two tracks" in the process of unification. This would be, as Brian Beedham argued (in the *Herald Tribune*, 14 September 1994), "the folly of uniting Europe while slicing it into two." Journalism when it gets aggressive is like the intelligentsia going to war: culture is conscripted, and history is recruited off the streets.

The glory that was Greece in the 4th and 5th centuries B.C., required no All-Greek Parliament sitting in Thebes, no commission with an office in Corinth, no pan-Hellenic army commanded (one fears) from Sparta. The great new philosophy and culture and politics that burst upon the world in those centuries was at least a product of Greece's very diversity and variety. When Greece was eventually made into a single state by that cold outsider, Philip of Macedon—the light never shone so brightly again.

One can almost hear the futile argument going on, with the Continental pundit manipulating quotations from Herodotus and Aeschylus—and did not Philip's son, Alexander, uniting the whole known world of his day, an empire from the Mediterranean to the Ganges, have as his cultural adviser none other than Aristotle?

In order to fully and vividly comprehend the dangers of all this, and to possibly effectively avoid them, I suggest the following two rules-of-thumb in the context of "the culture of grammar" and "of intellectual discourse."

Cease-and-desist from the linguistic mayhem of the day, its splits, cracks, and fashionable seizures. Avoid splitting infinitives unless under grievous duress: expatriation, repatriation, or other forms of cruel and unusual punishment. More than that, refrain modestly from the sexual harassment of the muse of history, Clio. And indeed when you hear the historic word *Kulchur* (Ezra Pound's spelling, not mine), reach for your blue pencil or punch sharply on your *delete* key.

Full Confrontal

On a memorable Tuesday in December—it was the day before the Pearl Harbor anniversary—hopes ran high for peace between the hostile grammarian camps. The *Washington Post* published a book review (*IHT*, 6 December 1994) about that "gentleman spy," Allen Dulles; and although the author of the biography, Peter Grose, was a former member of a friendly and allied institution, the *New York Times*, he came under obligatory fire from the sharpshooting critic: "A bit frustrating is the reluctance of Grose...to confront fully the sense of elitism and self-righteousness that imbued Dulles and his comrades." It might well have been easier, in these times, *to fully confront* such delicate problems. But if a man is reluctant to split an infinitive, how sharp can the cutting edge of his pen be?

Was, then, the *Post* and the *IHT* relenting on its ongoing grammatical assault? No, it was a false lull. The guns kept firing. On the same day, in the same edition of the *Herald Tribune* and on the weightier editorial page, a dispatch from Washington pointed up the new challenges which the incoming president of Mexico would face. One half hoped he would be able to confront them fully all on his own. No such luck. U.S. policy was "pushing Mexico to fully embrace dramatic democratic reforms in the short run." And if that were not enough for the day, the writer went on to advise, "He needs to radically restructure a corrupt judicial and legal system." As for us, forlorn souls, if we can push ourselves to fully confront our increasingly corrupted language, then we will need to radically restructure the acceptable rules of language.

2

The Equality of Sentences

Chomsky, Pinker, and Cognitive Science

I am skeptical as to whether the scientists, studying what they hold to be instinctive cultural behavior or accounting for the distinctive linguistic achievements of the superior human animal, can be of very much help to us. In our own time we have moved from revolution to counter-revolution in one Harvard generation. In the 1950s, with scholars like J.B. Watson and B.F. Skinner, we breathed in an atmosphere which relativized human achievement in terms of rats scurrying in mazes and dogs salivating to bells. Now, quite the contrary, having moved from a behaviorist biology, dour and cynical, to a new scientific romanticism, the semantic and "cognitive" scholars are entranced by the splendid universalism of human capacities.

Once again, the rights and wrongs—or evaluating what is better and what is worse, the ethical imperative of challenging and choosing—is lost in the mechanics of rigorous theory. One "cognitive scientist" sees not only the "Universal Grammar" of Chomsky but goes on to pay lyrical tribute to every ingenious form of human babble and burble, from the garbled patter of baby talk to the fractured chatter of half-illiterates. It is all part of a seamless web, the cognitive triumph, and (to quote a follower of Chomsky, Professor Steven Pinker)* "a system of great richness and beauty."

In this scientific (or rather: academic) atmosphere it becomes incorrect to attempt to devise or maintain rules and standards for the use of speech and prose. This is peremptorily put down as "just guides to etiquette." Small wonder that in this kind of cognitive euphoria with its suspension of judgmental disapproval, one finds every kind of jabber to be a species of loquacity. Pinker

---

* Steven Pinker, *The Language Instinct* (1994), ch. 1, p. 21.

17

quotes Chomsky's semantic truth as "Virtually every sentence that a person utters or understands is a brand-new combination of words, appearing for the first time in the history of the universe." So it is that all sentences become equal in space. This applies (in Pinker's judgment) to

> even the notorious syntax-fracturing professional athlete and the, you know, like, inarticulate teenage skateboarder.
>
> In nature's talent show we are simply a species of primate with our own act, a knack for communicating information about who did what to whom by modulating the sounds we make when we exhale.

This is the ultimate semantic democracy—each and every sound is free and equal, and has one cosmic vote. Language has achieved the grand utopia in which the exhalations of a Shakespeare and a Goethe are matched and the equally free vaporings of "seemingly homely abilities ... an immigrant struggling with a second language, a stroke patient with a first one." Everything has a galactic originality; in addition to which it is all rich and beautiful.

In this kind of astral soup of the constellations, what we will be trying to do in these pages is not even worth a pinch of salt. And yet, by not losing oneself in the stars and safely taking up a rather more this-worldly position where wonder gets tempered by humane critical reason, we can rediscover the immemorial legitimacy of taking a stand. "Rich" chatter can be puerile patter, "beautiful" babble may mask immoderate modulation, even foul-breath'd exhalation. An immigrant's language struggles can produce the memorable greenhorn inspirations of Leo Rosten's *The Education of Hyman Kaplan* (I omit the author's asterisks lest they confuse and mislead); or, mainly, they can issue in endless and forgettable fractures of the intractable new mother tongue.

Why (one must ask the defenders of cognition), if language is so infallibly original, are the dreary words and sentences in our—the adjective is William James'—"debauched" culture seeming more and more to sound the same?

The Bible of Prescriptivists

The views of "modern English usage" of Henry Fowler, Ernest Gower, and Robert Burchfield are formidable landmarks in our language, but, as my reader will be painfully aware, most of the prose which I cite in this book from various English-language newspapers on both sides of the Atlantic has been composed in a state of blithe neglect of the formal rules and traditional regulations devised, and defended to the last breath, by grammarians. It takes a temperament of a true believer to accept Fowler's classic work (revised by Gower, and now both rewritten by Burchfield) as having the status of holy writ. That extraordinary historical writer, A.J.P. Taylor, thought it was "perhaps the greatest book ever published by the Oxford University Press." And a recent reviewer in a lively, well-written and widely read Sunday newspaper confessed that he also considered it "the Bible of prescriptivists":

> prescriptivists being those people—well, most of us really—who insist that there is a right way and a wrong way to write and speak, with an emphasis on the wrong.

Some of the most persistent critics of contemporary journalism belong to this band of instinctive grammatical moralizers. Is there, for example, anything grammatically "wrong" in saying "*due to low customer levels*"? Why is it "better and more perspicuous" to say (as one editor instucts us) "because there are not many customers"? Whereupon the question pops up: Why, then, is it better to say "*perspicuous*" rather than "more understandable"? There is much bluff and not a little arrogance in the polemical world of the philologists. As Fowler himself put it, at the outset of his exercise in authoritive *esprit*: "We should assume a cheerful attitude of infallibility." American authorities have tended to reverse the credo to the grim and inflexible assumption of an attitude of tolerance and permissiveness. A viable mid-Atlantic compromise might be a modulation of both extremes to an acceptance of this rule-of-thumb: *As much of tradition as possible, as much of change as necessary.* Read your favorite morning paper assiduously for a fortnight, and see whether it can work. Meanwhile,

> the language moves on. Vogue words come and go, clichés wax and wane. Inflections are increasingly ignored. I bet your grandson will never use a *whom*. Ten years ago Burchfield said that the *whom* in "Whom is she looking for?" should be "maintained where possible." No longer. In a long entry in the *New Fowler's Modern English Usage*, you will find that *who* (for *whom*) has graduated from "informal" to "acceptable."

Who then will be left to resist when all are finding progress and change to be irresistible?[1]

Fowler, as rewritten by Burchfield, has been accused in (of all places) the *New York Times* of having been transformed

> from an upholder of standards into a passive observer of trends....The more you sample, the more you are troubled by the degree to which tolerance lapses into passive acceptance in the face of regrettable change.

The dissenting suspicions here are those of Christopher Lehmann-Haupt, one of the few writers on the *Times* who take some trouble with the sentences he writes (and hence, by implication at least, a mourner for lost standards of journalistic prose in what his own paper has been publishing). The criticism is deepened by the new and lackadaisical attitudes to a current cliché (to which we will return) "life-style." This buzzword has, as Burchfield records, been assailed as "obnoxious" and as "an unnecessary and clumsy excrescence on the language." Yet the new Fowler cannot rouse itself to more than a weary conclusion that it "looks like surviving...[in] its extended sense" and that "it will pass into uncontested standard use as time goes on." Only a small, almost inaudible caution is offered.

Of course, if the simplex *life*, or the traditional phrase *way of life*, would in context adequately convey the required meaning, one of these should be used instead.[2]

But in the vast extension of required meanings for the old Adlerian concept—and also in the handful of examples I have presented here—a recourse to a "simplex" in the old traditionally standard way will not "adequately convey" what the new coinage aspires to communicate. The intended meanings are different, special, and often incommunicable. The trouble with *life-style* is not that it is obnoxious or unnecessary, but that it now is intended to mean so many ineffable multifarious things, from the wholeness of a biographical experience to any one of its momentary highlights—from (in Blake's words) worlds and eternities to grains of sand—that there seems to be no viable way to get around its universal conscription.[3]

3

The Slang of an In-Lingo

Semantics of Silence

"In-language" can be the technical vocabulary of the specialist—from the astronomer, predicting the new galactic movement of Shoemaker-Levy, to the biologist, tracing the mad-cow obscurities of Creuzfeldt-Jacob, and to the zoologist, classifying all other species-specific properties. Here, very often, only a dictionary can be of help, but one can do without such assistance rather happily, if you accept, inconsolably, that there are some things on heaven and earth which, at least for you, remain inexplicable. Indeed, speaking personally, I find it good to be reminded on occasion of my own dark areas of ignorance, and moreover, that some matters are difficult and recondite, and some contemporaries do have brainier capacities.... These may well include, regularly featured on the financial pages of your favorite journal, the authoritative analyses of the relationship between inflation and the *M-3* when it is disturbed by the eccentricities of derivatives. Or, at the very least, those tantalizing, evasive dispatches, intended mostly for the young, of the latest news in computer technology:

> [T]he lab's two full-time designers plunder the trendiest fields in mathematics, whether chaos theory or fractal geometry, and fashion it into futuristic images using high-powered computer hardware and graphics techniques such as ray tracing—which simulates how light beams bounce off virtual objects.[1]

And yet the due respect for authoritative mumbo-jumbo may be kow-towing to false gods. Where language is academic and abstract, and its precise meaning just beyond the reader's grasp, there is room for hoax and pastiche, and who knows exactly what the score is? I am not convinced that the professor of genetics at the University of London is playing it straight when he reports on some latest research in his column "View from the Lab" in a British newspaper (*Daily Telegraph*). Dr. Steve Jones writes,

21

Physicists at UCLA are working in the new field of sonoluminescence. Pass a loud noise through a liquid, and bubbles form. As they collapse, they give off bright and astonishingly regular flashes of light. The information in the sound has been translated into a different medium.

Surely, here's the chance for the ultimate in subliminal study. Encode the data into some suitably loathsome rap music, play it very loud and—in principle at least—the sonoluminescence agitation in the retina should pass the knowledge straight in with no effort at all.[2]

Can this be a scientist's squelch at his lazy lab students who now have some hope of avoiding conscious learning altogether? It could be, I suspect, a joke; but jokes with feints and fancy footwork—with no punch-line—are no laughing matter. Sonoluminescence leaves me in the dark.

Everyday slang is also, at least at the outset, a variety of in-language; but most of it tends to turn obsolete when it becomes rudely "outed." "With-it" characters have to get along without it when the general public catches on. One London wordsmith, aware of the evanescence of the short-lived vocabulary he diligently studies, has referred to the brief shelf-life of his subject as "Frantic Semantics." As an example he offers "*cred*," as in: "His cred hit rock-bottom when he married a Nicaraguan socialite." or "He's well cred: used to be a burglar":

> *Cred* abbreviates and incorporates credibility, credentials, credence. The term 'street-cred' surfaced in 1977 in the music business. Those with 'real cred' were *on* stage but *of* the street. Now widely used on the street and across young consumer industries, 'real cred' can be applied to your reputation or roots, accent or attitude, hemline or hairstyle.

How long will cred's cred last? Possibly as long as "super" did before it dropped to "cool," or "Right on" until it crossed over from black jive to pop white salutation. In the world of frantic semantics very little remains on the stage and of the street for more than a season. Our lexicographer of cred knows the end is nigh:

> To confuse matters, '*Show your cred*' may be a request to *(a)* display a credit card, *(b)* deport oneself in an erotic manner, or *(c)* fax over a note on letter-headed paper. [3]

Thus, in-language lasts a spell longer when it is protected by an armor of obscurity, reinforced by secrecy, and underpinned by a dire necessity to keep the password from getting into the hands of the enemy on the other side of the street. Chicago gangland slang was for many years almost impenetrable to outsiders but declined when the "gangsters" managed effectively to "rub" themselves out, by taking each other "for a ride." It lived on only in the Hollywood dialogue of Jimmy Cagney and Edward G. Robinson.

Sociologists of the East or West Side of innumerable urban centres have explored the phenomenon of Underworld or *underclass* language; and the sweet sing-song lyrics in *West Side Story* are not "typical" or "characteristic" only because Messrs. Bernstein and Sondheim wanted the gang rivalries to be understood by everybody on Broadway.

And, of course, the Broadway vocabulary, second-hand and necessarily bowdlerized, changes with the repertory. A recent stage revival of *Pal Joey*, set in Chicago at the end of the Depression, tries to up-date the lingo of that day but only succeeds in evoking in one London critic an affecting nostalgia for the way they, presumably, used to talk.

> John O'Hara's book is full of wonderful wise-guy slang: women are 'mice', singing is 'making with the throat' and when you want someone to push off you tell him to 'take a powder the hell out of here.' [4]

Can one still get inside this kind of talk?

Penetrating the impenetrable is no paradox, for even the most secretive of gangs thirst for the notorious publicity which in the end dries them out, or at least parches their penchant for phrase-making. A BBC reporter, investigating gun-toting juvenile violence in Phoenix, Arizona (where one teenager was killed by the gang-leader for not properly murdering a designated victim), learned a bit of "gang argot":

> To be *'strapped'* is to be armed, and by extension a *'strap'* is a gun; to *'flex'*, *'talk mesh'* or *'woof'* is to boast about being tough, and to *'show'* is to prove that you can live up to your boast; a friend is *'a homeboy'* and girls are *'bitches'*; to be *'smoked'* is to be shot dead. And, in a curious reversal of the orthodoxy of the 30 years since the civil rights movement, black gang members call other blacks *'niggers.'* [5]

The style will surely change and the words will drop out, even if the killings go on. The homicidal teenage delinquents, flourishing their "straps," may resort more and more to what the BBC man in Phoenix calls "an extremely sophisticated vocabulary of hand signs." We must leave it at that, for they are in the nature of things unprintable.

In the end, *"smoking"* or the deadly homicidal act, reduces itself, as in the Roman Coliseum of the old Flavian Empire, to wordless signals like "Thumbs Down" (and then the Christian gets fed to the lions). Historians of homicide underscore the sinister quietness of great assassins, killers without even a war-cry. The vocal support of language—a slogan, or a vindictive imprecation, or a whole manifesto of hate—is so essential to rationalize or symbolize the foul deed, but it is quite unnecessary for "motiveless malignity." Murder, like the best of handguns, carries a silencer.

In the Land of Jargontua

What the press is itself guilty of, it hastens to expose in others. Prolixity is the name of the sin, and each newspaper style book recites the virtues of simplicity, clarity, instant comprehension. Several recall, instructively, the mockery of Sir Ernest Bowers when confronted with the lax standards of official English and the British bureaucracy's propensity to invent words, to use a long one when a short one would do, and to use ten words when three would be enough.

What barnacular song do the puddering sirens sing, to lure the writer into the land of jargontua?

This surely would not have been chastening for some Treasury official who was only proceeding with his job of making obscure of what the Queen's subjects have no business knowing. To follow slavishly Bowers' counsel would have been positively deleterious in the prose of our newspaper culture, for its very lyricism suggests what a loss it would have been to the daily reader never to have run into a long word again, never to puzzle over a bright new coinage, never to get a breather from staccato sentences that seem to cut out when stories begin to get really interesting.

But we know what is being gotten at—verbiage, prolixity, flab—"the lobotomized quality" (in Peter Drucker's phrase) of much academic prose, the impenetrable density of almost all business and bureaucratic prose. One journalist recalled what H.G. Wells's Mr. Polly termed *"sequippledanian verboojuice."* Another concluded that such prose is not really written but "boiler-plated together in committee-speak." But, then, who is there still around who remembers what boiler-plate represented in the life of newspaper editors? I can faintly recall as a young "subber" on a local newspaper in the Bronx filling some empty column by taking over something syndicated from a ready supply of routine articles, all stereotyped for instant publication. What we find nowadays making its way into print is giving boiler-plate a bad name. A few excerpts:

Core competencies are not just another way of describing vertical integration.

Differences in value creation insights and parenting characteristics are reflected in different criteria for heartland businesses.

Leaders need to take their businesses ahead of proconsumerism and the process-cost curve.

Our idea is that, eventually, within any holon in the holonic network, all support and management processes will be outsourced.

One correspondent, overwhelmed by such random polysyllables and "making no concession to style and little to syntax," gave vent to his contempt for holons and proconsumers and even, in desperation, longed for the humanizing touch of a split infinitive. He was being, as he readily confessed, positively holonic.[6]

In the hands of first-class journalists, phrases, sentences, whole paragraphs stand out and gleam, making even the technical obscurities generally "comprehensible."

Mike Zwerin, who stars in the *International Herald Tribune* regularly, writes of some hitherto unknown (to me) jazz musician named Clark Terry: "The operative blurb for jazz is 'expect the unexpected'. It's all about risk. Risk implies the possibility of failure. You tell your story in real time." [7]

One fears that these highfalutin' maxims can be applied meaningfully to diplomats and footballers and grand-chefs. But this could only apply to trumpeter Miles Davis, if only I could translate it; still, the imagery is vivid:

> As always he played principally off silence. Shortly before he died, I watched him shuffle painfully from stage-right to stage-left, his horn tucked under an arm. It took eight bars of a slow blues to get there. Along about bar six, thousands of lit cigarettes were held high in tribute.

These kinds of things will never happen again once the tobacco ban becomes total. But other bits of pictorial journalism will emerge, and will be welcomed.

In isolation, of course, the slangy elements remain puzzling, and too many of them will weary the reader. You can't get through a paper easily when you have to stop for a new buzzword, and even mother-language Anglo-Americans get so stopped, by phrases which they have to decipher. It may take only a couple of seconds extra but it sure slows you down: "Four years ago Clark Terry, at the age of 69, thought he needed more slack." I had to explain to a European reader that this meant not "slack" as in a loose rope but as in "less work" and "more vacation time." Okay, the couple of seconds are up and we move on to other slow-down reading-time bumps in the road.

I do not even pretend to understand the cryptic mysteries of English journalism when it comes to reporting on cricket games. I read them often in the London papers with a mix of fascination and sheer uncomprehending ignorance. But no matter, the dark impenetrable areas of in-language spill over into other equally indecipherable sports lingo, native perhaps to the British Islanders (but I doubt even indigenous readers get it all).

During the World Cup in the U.S.A. of summer of 1994, the *Sunday Times* had splendid soccer coverage, and spiced it with feigned astonishment of how awry the sport had become since they, the English, first invented it. The paper ran a putatively funny series of items called "Culture Clash," the fifth of which was (in its entirety, bewildered readers getting no extra clue):

No. 5. 'Nutmegging' called 'tunneling' by an American TV station. [8] What *can* this mean? Neither one nor the other catch-phrase will be understood by outsiders to the in-vocabulary. And since these, presumably, will constitute a vast majority of a paper's readers, who will be bright and knowing but not necessarily cognoscenti of recondite semantics, one can assume they have known neither to nutmeg nor to tunnel, whatever that may entail.

In-language is often unavoidable, especially in stories involving "expertise." Still, the woolly words and phrases can, like mittens, be turned inside out, even if they wear a little roughly. But one should beware of "inside dealing"—it's a punishable misdemeanor on the stock exchange and well-nigh criminal in the marketplace of inflated meanings and over-usage.

The mechanisms for such verbal productivity may be too intricate for brief analysis. The whys and wherefores of "grunge"—and even "jazz"—may be lost in time; but, possibly, if one pays close attention to the phrasemaking in the next short cycle or tide of the coming years, we can spot the trick. In some easy cases it appears elementary and obvious, and indeed so self-evident that it is hardly capable of taking wing. One of the latest usages in the black community is the new enthusiastic buzz for approval and admiration—*"Man, your car* [presumably a Porsche or a Ferrari] *is—ba-a-d!" Bad* here means good, indeed even great! It is a kind of negative metaphorics, and the catching popularity of such opposites is subjected to mysterious fevers of infectiousness. Simple systems of transpositions as in pig Latin and in Cockney back-rhyme rise and fall in curves which cover long periods of time; but they remain specialized and practically private methods of coded conversation which are occasional and thus still viable. What of single, individual words which have to make it on their own? Does simplicity guarantee longevity, or does simple-mindedness wear thin and always give way to something fresher as, perhaps, "Right on!" gave way to "cool, man..." and "swell" to "super" to "brilliant"*?*

For my own part, I have little confidence in Cool remaining with us for very long. In my morning newspaper I find a three-column headline over a *Washington Post* story:

AMERICANS ARE COOLING TO CLINTON

No problem there; the public opinion polls serve to register the political temperature for us. But on the same front-page there is an obligatory pop-culture story:

"COOL" RECORD LABELS REGAIN THE BEAT

Which leads us into temptation: the word, predictably, will soon disappear in a mire of confusions and contradictions. "Bad" will surely never displace "good," and what is called *cool* as a synonym for what is still being called *hot* can only be slang of limited duration. The *Herald Tribune*'s story from London was an account of "cutting-edge musical talents" who run new and prospering record companies, and their commercial smallness is conveniently based on the latest disc-technology which enables them to compete effectively with the giants in the industry (Sony, EMI, Polygram). What is the secret of their success?

> "It is because we are cool," the spokesman for Creation Records said. "It is the one undefinable thing that Sony and the other majors cannot have—being cool and having everyone know that you are cool."

But what is this *coolness* which is making cultural history by "swinging the balance back towards the little guys...the indies [i.e. the industry independents]"? Here the cutting-edge is not proving to be so sharp. A bit of obligatory alliteration gets in our way: this battle for survival "in the global marketplace from Boston and Barcelona to Brasilia and Bangkok." Still, a touch of the old lingo reinforces my surmise:

> Not even the majors...have the wherewithal to cater to all tastes in all parts of the world, or even necessarily to be aware of the hottest musical trends at any given time.

The *hottest* is the *coolest!* And a spokesman for one of the "hot indies" named Go! Discs expresses gratitude to "the digital revolution" which has made possible commercial-quality recordings on personal computers in their bedrooms and basements. Evidently some like it hot and cool at once, and they conclude: "Advances in technology have given the independents a new edge, making it far easier and cheaper to turn a hot musical idea into a compact disk." In other, Orwellian, words: hot means cool (or vice versa). That being so, the latest news in the papers is that the Majors are now "taking equity stakes" in the Indies...until the market overheats and sales freeze over. [9]

The uses of another kind of lower literacy are limited by factors of age and social class. Street gangs in urban ghettoes can spend a scrappy lifetime perfecting their handful of signals and war-cries. Young children in the middle-income American families—"our kids," as we usually call them—specialize in their pop-fed "in-lingo" only for the half-dozen seasons or so when their pubertarian energies and sensitivities first get involved with the "teenage culture." One New York critic (David Denby), writing in the *New Yorker* more as "a concerned parent" than as a sociologist, has observed,

> my sons talk in the private language they've worked up from exposure to the shows, movies, computer games, rap music, and basketball players that matter to them. Children have always spoken in tongues, living inside their jokes and insults—as

my friends and I did it forty years ago—but in recent years the talk has grown quicker, more jangled and allusive, shifting at near-electronic speeds.... The children channel-surf their own minds.

As for the "bad language," used on all improper occasions, this helpless parent consoles himself with a compromise of an attitude: "The kids know that the profane rap lyrics are a violation; they speak the words with an almost ecstatic sense of release." But still, neither the ecstasy nor the adolescent liberation communicate across generations:

> I don't like the way my boys talk—I don't like the way they think. The crude, bottom-line attitudes they've picked up, the nutty obsessive profanity, the echo chamber of voices and attitudes, set my teeth on edge....What American parent hasn't felt that spasm? Your kid is rude and surly.[10]

He who writes in terms of *bottom-lines* and *nutty* and *teeth on edge* would, as the cliché expert, deserve the next spasm.

The Cult of Chic Obscurity

Half of any current in-lingo will fall by the wayside in a season but, as in the old dilemma, one doesn't know in advance which half. One is always surprised that useful and indeed ingenious coinages catch on and take their place in the language.

Evanescence is the rule; but nobody can be sure about what will survive. I, for one, am attracted currently to the sinister phenomenon of *white-anting*. It may well become popular and even get to be a ubiquitous buzzword. It emerged in an explanation of what "*Shoddipush*" meant, to wit: "the deadly syndrome that white-ants most businesses." It is nothing less than a short-hand tag for describing the economic force that drives excellence out and shoddiness in. The original phrasemaker came from Australia where it was "like termites eating your house, but over there it's white ants." One can always use in the context the word "undermine" with instant comprehensibility, but the colloquialism is more colorful and eye-stopping. Of course, this excuse can constitute the defense of all jargon, even the most impenetrable, on the misguided basis that (as one grammarian notes) "its usefulness is to quickly and effectively communicate an idea or a concept"—and if it is done with such dispatch of infinitive-splitting, then all's well. But this is a pious hope of the true believers of Jargontua, a land in which no birds sing or ideas flourish.

There is no implication here that this phenomenon in our newspaper culture is only "contemporary" or peculiar to the modern world. This is, I suspect, not only a semantic feature of the fast-paced industrial civilization, uncontrollable in its impulse for the new and different and in its changeable forms of communication (journalism, radio, television, advertising slogans, pop songs, etc.). Whole industries prosper on the fetish of innovation, but immemorial is the human delight in the new.

History and literature offer the longer perspective. Recall those ancient passages in Horace (65-8 B.C.) expressing his Roman hope that "new words and words of yesterday's framing will find acceptance" and his Latin insistence on "the right of adding, if I can, something to the store in giving to the world new names for things." He was convinced that "Each generation has been allowed, and will be allowed still to issue words that bear the mint-mark of the day." But, resourceful poet and critic that he was, even he did not (and could not) know which of the new words, "like a young generation, would bloom and thrive."[11]

Consider the following table which the *Financial Times* offered its readers in its firm editorial conviction that the "distortions and indignities" that are being daily inflicted on the English language in business or economic news are "inspired." Even three words will do.

Column 1	*Column 2*	*Column 3*
0. Integrated	0. Management	0. Options
1. Total	1. Organizational	1. Flexibility
2. Systematized	2. Monitored	2. Capability
3. Parallel	3. Reciprocal	3. Mobility
4. Functional	4. Digital	4. Progamming
5. Responsive	5. Logistical	5. Concept
6. Optional	6. Transitional	6. Time-phase
7. Synchronised	7. Incremental	7. Projection
8. Compatible	8. Third-generation	8. Hardware
9. Balanced	9. Policy	9. Contingency

Thus, to come up with instant gibberish one can use this simple device by choosing any three-digit number and then selecting the corresponding buzzword from each column. Accordingly, 2-5-9 produces "systematized logistical contingency." The *FT* warns us that no one will know what you are talking about but you are unlikely to be challenged. It would be an obvious exaggeration to moan that the possibilities are infinite; they are not. The box offers a lot of scope—8-8-6 gives us a "compatible third-generation time-phase." But, in fact, the total number of hard-chic phrases possible with the handy phrase generator is $10 \times 10 \times 10 = 1,000$ "totally incomprehensible, meaningless obfuscations."

I wonder whether there is real hope here, despite the efforts of civilized newspapers like the *Financial Times* and the *Wall Street Journal* to use gentle satiric thrusts against the enemy. Irony tends to get ironed out in the marketplace. One New York-based consultant defended jargon as "an extension to the language," claiming that "it creates a sub-culture":

> So it's very important, not only from a writing perspective but just purely from a management perspective, that the use of jargon and terminology is aligned with the culture that one is looking to instil or maintain within a business. [12]

I am afraid that if one has culture as an ally we need to have no enemies. For, as we shall see in subsequent chapters, *culture*—and all of its parts and particles from *cult* to *cultural*—has itself become contaminated, and is one of the more toxifying sources of gibberish and obscurity. If we "align with culture" we have met the enemy and they is us.

Current hi-tech culture leads directly to "technobabble," the sort of language which "empowers knowledge workers with multidimensional analysis of transactional data." There is an additional argot here to be flourished by "boffins, nerds, bean-counters or legal eagles"; for these *geeks* can live and work in language of "breathtaking tortuousness and opacity." The psycho-culture gives us insight into the mental sub-structures which have to cope with "Organizational dress as a symbol of multilayered identities."

The culture of sociological inquiry gives us the likes of U.N.-officialese about a "new system for the promulgation of administrative issuances," which leads on *via* "self-similar rulesets" to "that system wherein the prospective connections are observed as syntax."

All this in the serious, quality press has become scheduled as a round of daily fun-and-games, on the editorial suspicion that people like to read about other people's "plain bad English." In point of fact, one editor (of the *Financial Times*) has instituted a "Business Jargon Competition," and skirting ever so slightly the legal limits of libel and slander recruited a panel of judges, who are charged with openly ridiculing syntax, bringing lofty rhetoric down-to-earth, unmixing metaphors, etc., crowning the winners for their impenetrable texts. The rules are simple, and prize-winning gobbledygook has had to meet three principal criteria.

> First, it took an astonishingly long time to say astonishingly little.
> Second, it used big words and grand phrases—preferably infused with mala-propisms, mixed metaphors and muddled grammar or syntax—to conceal banal, platitudinous thoughts.
> Third, and most important, it has to be utterly incomprehensible—to a point where its obscurity deepened with each reading. [13]

As I have suggested, the dastardly phrase is more than the sum of its parts which are often "big words"—prize-winners in recent years have been "holistic...paradigm...interface." Dictionary-makers of the seventeenth century used to refer to the like as "hard words," and Shakespeare was among the first to try and popularize them (amongst which one could find, for example, the Italianate "revolution"). Special and extenuating circumstances are well-known where a truth has to be, at first, stated obscurely before it can be put clearly. Nevertheless, our contemporary problem is not *hard* but *easy* words, over-simplifying discourse and blocking intellectual effort.

The computer world, *aka,* "cyberspace," has provided in its rapid expansion most of the reader's difficulties with so-called "hard words" still to be found in our newspapers. Apart from the daily crossword feature, it is the source of more puzzlement for the general reader than any other type of technical story. There, to decipher meaningfully, even more than the names of new scientific discoveries or the devious stratagems in shady high finance, we need the passing help of specialist dictionaries.

What, for example, is *"dirty data"?* It is apparently when, in the effort to transform computer-stored data into "knowledge," the new technologies do not (as they, properly programmed, should) let businesses transform "info overload" into "a rich vein of usable knowledge." The opposite is, presumably, *clean data*—which is the hallmark of entrepreneurial success, and hence of substantial profits and dividends. Thus, what is also referred to as *"discovery-driven inquiry"*—which one would have thought to be tantamount to normal commercial curiosity—can achieve a decisive refinement of customer relationships. It is also called by some geeks *"data mining,"* which leads one inevitably to the proverbial theorem that every gold-rush produces fool's gold; and the gold found in data mining is no exception. One newspaper reports a grave warning by no less an authority than the man from IBM's "Business Intelligence Solutions Unit": "You can wind up with some totally useless information, like the possibility that people whose names have an '*e*' as the third letter are the least profitable." Or that 82 percent of motorcycle owners buy frozen fish. One company, mining its complete sales data, discovered that "black lingerie sells better in the north, other colors in the south, and that white is the top choice of brides." Here the computer seems to be playing dirty tricks or practical jokes.

Still, the database has been known to come up with ingenious correlations. One giant U.S. retailer wanted to find out what were its most frequently linked purchases—and it found the unlikely combination of...beer and diapers. How could this be, and why? One distinguished professor of marketing and retailing at an international business school was interviewed and he confirmed the following: "When these two items were placed next to each other in the stores, sales of both soared." Everybody in the grocery business soon went and did likewise—even to Safeway's data mining about the usefulness of carrying twenty-eight different brands of orange juice. Cleanly programmed research came up on the screen with the names of eight best-selling brands (although one would have thought that a stubby pencil in any old Mom-and-Pop shop could make the simple calculation, and proceed to stock up the identified winners). Less obvious and positively deceptive is the managerial dilemma involving the keeping of some 200 cheese brands in stock. "With data mining they discovered that some of the lowest-selling cheeses were purchased by their top-spending customers. " What a dilemma!

Data cleansing is essential, we are told, for the raw data can amount to *gigabytes* and even *terabytes* (i.e., thousands of gigabytes). The large Sears company has four terabytes in its warehouse. IBM is currently developing seventy-five terabytes in the database for the U.S. Department of Energy. This would dwarf all other technologies, especially in its built-in knack of raising quasi-philosophical, near-metaphysical questions that need to be answered by all "end-users" who would otherwise be faced with the catastrophe of "bad information." "It means defining, for example, 'what's a customer?' or 'what is a profitable account?'... These are not technical issues and can take a long time to resolve."[14] One needs the patience of a *geek*,* his eyes and ears fine-tuned to the gold in a gigabyte. Diaper-buying beer-drinkers, good; fish-eating motorcyclists, bad. Between the risk of "information fragmentation" and the ultimate reassurance for corporate confidence that "human insight remains paramount," the geek has his career cut out for him, and giving straight-talking interviews to the newspapers is part of it. In the end some plain language emerges if one can hold out during the passing obscurities.

Sort of/Kind of

In Washington—and no other political capital is essentially different—language needs to reserve a special area where ambiguity, or hesitancy, or uncertainty can blur precise meanings; for in many critical situations politicians dare not commit themselves too soon or too clearly (and hence definitively). Would Senator Robert Dole, whose new Republican majority had the Democratic administration on the run, stoop to make compromises, and thus avoid the obstacle of a presidential veto, in connection with new legislation? President Clinton hinted his readiness. Could Dole, the leading opposition candidate for the presidency, at the time, afford to be seen joining forces? Or, indeed, could President Clinton? It was an "iffy" question. And the answer, as reported in the *New York Times*, illustrated the characteristic—and indispensable—uses of the "sort of/kind of" syndrome we will be documenting.

> "If this [the change in the Social Security system] is going to work, we've got to be in it together," said Mr. Dole, who hopes to take Mr. Clinton's job in the 1996 presidential election. "It will happen only if everybody sort of joins hands." [15]

---

*   For the *"geek"* and his *"geek culture,"* see "The Culture of Disney Land & Geek Culture," volume three.

Well, is there going to be a laying on of hands or isn't there?

But, perhaps, in the case of Senator Dole, a proper reading of this particular usage has, conceivably, more to do with disability than with lexicography. One editor whom I asked about this quickly rejected the semantic aspect and pointed out, *sotto voce,* with suitable delicacy, that the good senator, whose arm had been wounded in World War II, had a manual problem and was therefore predisposed to such evasive phrases. I found this an outlandish, even outrageous, resort to a kind of biological determinism of vocabulary. (As if all men with muscular impairment were secretly reluctant to utter such embarrassing phrases as: "strong-arm tactics...a firm grip on the problem...handshakes of good will.")

No, I remain with my uncertainty principle in political jargon. The alternative explanation is not only politically incorrect ("handicappism") but actually wrong. Would President Franklin D. Roosevelt, tragically crippled and confined to his wheelchair, have been tempted in his famous arguments with Congress and the Supreme Court to enjoin his opponents to "sort of take a walk" or his supporters to "kind of" wrench themselves away from the "paralyzing" effect of fearing "fear itself"? Precision and a manly simplicity are all. FDR may not have been able to stand on his legs, but his language was sturdy. And, incidentally, President Harry S. Truman did not famously rally his forces to achieve a historic victory by admonishing them to fight on and "sort of give 'em hell!"—nor did he take full and personal responsibility with the White House adage "the buck kind of stops here."

I jest, but only to argue that language (not lameness) rules.

When the gentle and soft-spoken Senator Dole had won his decisive victory in the primaries over his Republican Party rivals, he decided (if that is not too strong a word) to take a short break; and short it was indeed, as the AP reported what appeared to be a decision to go back to politics: "Bob Dole, saying he was 'sort of glad' to be wrapping up a weekend vacation in Florida: 'I'm sunned out, I think.'" [16]

The Paris editors of the *Herald-Tribune*, with their wonted verbal sensitivity as Americans living abroad, sensed that there was something unusual about this sentence and featured it in their "Quote/Unquote" column of the day— which, of course, guarantees that they will be getting more of the same, proliferating to fill the bright space, even perhaps from one of their Cartesian French readers an updating of a classic maxim suggesting that "I (kind of) think, therefore I (sort of) am." All old philosophies need a touch of skeptical uncertainty about them.

The very next day the editors of the same paper could not resist yet another quotation which kept their stylistic reputation sort of clean. It was an off-hand remark by the actor Christopher Reeve whose public appearance at the Academy Awards ceremonies astonished (and delighted) Hollywood; for he had been totally paralyzed after a horseback accident and was reluctant to show himself for fear of embarrassing moments of spasm. "Superman" mustered enough strength and self-control to propel himself on to the stage and later explained his composure: "I sort of willed myself to not have anything go wrong."[17] Not even the strength of Superman was enough to break the addiction of the press to language as she is spoke, especially with a grammatical tremor.

When the endemic vagueness of the phrase reaches up and into the White House it must be considered as a sign of the generally diffuse presidential political style rather than a slip in some speechwriter's prose. On the occasion of the tragic death of his valued cabinet member, Ron Brown, a flamboyant black lawyer who was serving as secretary of commerce and whose plane crashed on a trade mission in Bosnia, Bill Clinton was moved to praise him as "one of the best advisors and ablest people" he had ever known. Brown had been the chairman of the Democratic Party; and he had rallied it so valiantly as to elect a little-known Arkansas governor against President Bush, running for reelection in 1992. For services rendered he had wanted to become the first "Negro" secretary of state in American history but in the shuffle had to be content with the lesser post. The president was evidently still making it up to him in his funeral tribute: "[T]he Commerce post was sort of ready made for him at this moment in history, and he loved it very much." [18] At any moment in time the phrase is sort-of-ready-made for the fuzz and haze which can carry extra suggestibility. For politicians who are "making it" it is kind of useful to know that history was sort of waiting for them.

Whatever the larger causes or psychic factors involved in the spread of this kind of vocabulary, building into all manner of statements, attitudes and claims an element of hesitation or uncertainty or confusion, it contaminates more and more professional diction. We have seen bankers and economists stuttering their way into a sort of/kind of incoherence, and it could be that such verbal waywardness does not seriously affect in the end the bottom line—although it is hard to see imprecision in such matters not exacting its price. As for the dilution of the language of diplomacy, the managers of foreign policy and international relations have since the days of Metternich and Talleyrand had their coded way of subtly sending signals that affect war and peace, *entente* and *détente*. One surmises that nowadays a little sloppy speech and a few bits of ungainly grammar may only serve the purposes of good will between peoples and order among the nations.

Or so it seemed in a recent Cambodian crisis. The late Pol Pot had just been captured; the Khmer Rouge was wracked with violent internal dissension; the old militant Hun Sen was locked in struggle with his co-Prime Minister Norodom Ranariddh—and mayhem was breaking out in Phnom Penh. Bodyguards were killing each other, and a rocket had landed in the garden of the U.S. ambassador. Accordingly the official two-day visit of the U.S. Secretary of State Madeleine

Albright, was cancelled for security reasons. But wasn't the airport safe? Then she might (and, later, did) make a quick landing to confer with the two prime ministers there.

It was disclosed gravely that Prince Ranariddh, accustomed to the formalities of royal arrangements, considered the whole affair "a major breach of protocol" and "an insult." Was it truly as bad as all that? The *Washington Post* correspondent reported only that the aborted visit had turned into "something of a diplomatic fiasco." This was something of a nice step back; and the retreat from the brink was furthered by a reformulation that it was only "kind of insulting to Cambodia." This was sort of watering the problem down; and the happy final dilution came from the foreign diplomats in the capital who sided with the Cambodians but only agreed that "this sort of thing just is not done."

If events do not take a turn for the worse, don't count on gunboat diplomacy. Words have saved the day—"kind of/sort of" has struck a blow for peace. Or, seen another way, sloppy grammar can cushion rough diplomacy.[19]

The Quest for Uncertainty

This proliferating tone of uncertainty, or of defensive hesitation, is evidently appearing in other languages, and is of increasing concern to those newspaper editors who have to serve as confident guardians of proper or conventional style. A critic in the leading German daily, the *Frankfurter Allgemeine Zeitung*, is disturbed by the ubiquitous usage of the uncertainty adverb, *eher*. This is functioning in the same complex self-effacing way to put a cautious touch of conditional doubt to whatever is being put forward as being (sort of, kind of) true. He notes that even in his own paper, fastidious in such things almost to stuffiness, the Bonn correspondent did not just downright repeat that Herr Scharping is not "*zornig* [angry]" but "*eher zornig*"; and Chancellor Kohl was not "*unzufrieden* [unhappy]" but "*eher unzufrieden.*" *Eher* serves in the same manner as *rather* did (in yesterday's English), and sort of / *kind of* (in today's idiom). The *FAZ*'s sharp-eyed grammarian, Dr. Kurt Reumann, observes,

> Strange world, in which nobody is any longer something precisely, but always "kind of/sort of [*eher*]"...Pavarotti is kind of fat. The Eiffel Tower is sort of high....Our popular, alcoholic actor Harald Juhnke is like on the wagon, and "sort of confident [*eher zuversichtlich*]" of staying there....
>
> Why should this be? Probably because nobody wants to stand by exactly what he has been saying. [20]

To stand fast—in clipped literality, *ipsissima verba*—is to take a risk. There is always a chance of being caught out, a danger of inaccuracy or impropriety or incorrectness, or even libel. A qualifying adverb provides a guarantee, an insurance policy against possible self-incrimination (as in Richard Gott's "sort-of-guilty" evasiveness, see below) and other hazards of verbal malpractice. The angry reaction of an overweight Pavarotti (and his lawyers) may thereby be disarmed. Like calculated ambiguity or deliberate vagueness, this equivocal form of sloppiness has a hidden safety net.

Needless to say, there are cases when the locution serves no tactical purpose whatsoever and is written with the kind of mindlessness which always characterizes careless writing (or, perhaps, the affectation of same). Here is a senior sportswriter on the *New York Times* reporting the conversation between two highly paid basketball stars (Messrs. Patrick Ewing and Charley Barkley):

> "Hey, I read you're making $18 million this season," Barkley shouted at Ewing from a distance of a foot. "I never met anybody who was making $18 million a year."
>
> "Aw, get lost," Ewing sort of said, laughing at his colleague...[21]

Whether this immortal exchange, sort of recorded forever in newsprint, was worth chopping down a single pulp tree in the Canadian forest, I seriously doubt, for this is, I feel, more of an ecologist's problem than a grammarian's.

As we have seen, the mixed motives can vary for helpless semantics. The latter, by which I mean a whole vocabulary gone astray, is the element which concerns us most in these pages. For the devious words and errant phrases that are increasingly in circulation receive grammatical authentication nowadays by semanticists and other wordsmiths (*viz.*, newspaper editors and their headline writers) who are keen to accommodate, at any price, the language to popular tastes and to this morning's latest trends and new coinages.

I do not know exactly how lexicographers weigh the various usages of new words and phrases—or popular demotic errors—before the makers of dictionaries can include them in their newest editions. It could be that a sighting in a recondite book or journal counts for less than one in a national mass-circulation magazine, or for vastly more when it is heard in a coast-to-coast TV-broadcast. In any case the deviant and dismal examples I have been documenting reach a crowning achievement of recognition when they finally make it into front-page newspaper headlines. This may count for double.

Thus, from Tokyo the dispatch from the *New York Times* correspondent, reporting the compromise resolution passed by Japan's parliament to the effect that it expressed "remorse" but not "contrition" for World War II crimes, was headlined on page one by the *International Herald Tribune*:

JAPAN SAYS

IT IS SORRY

— SORT OF –

FOR THE WAR [22]

If this sort of thing—we see the sort of/kind of syndrome involved in the cases of Dole (above) and of Simpson and of Gott (below)—persists in politics and history, one can expect soon to be reading how President Lyndon B. Johnson, taking advantage of the ambiguous Tonkin Gulf Resolution, "declared—sort of—war on North Vietnam." And indeed how, in the collapse of the Soviet Union somewhere between Comrades Gorbachev and Yeltsin, "the Russians turned their backs on Communism—sort of..." It is an incoherence handcuffed to a wisecrack.

These kind of things happen when in the course of human events it sort of becomes necessary to sound illiterate rather than grammatically fussy. It is to be down-to-earth, colloquial and simplicity itself—rather than risk putting a clear thought in a crisp sentence. The habitual use of whimsical one-syllable locutions like "sort of" introduces a persistent jocular note, as if every fact or attitude becomes more accessible, and even more meaningful, if it is couched in the form of an easy-going gag. In the end it turns out only to be a weak-witted verbal gesture. A rough meaning, arguably, is communicated; but so did the primitive efforts of Neanderthal Man before grunt-speak evolved into human language.

Like in the O.J. Simpson Trial

The "sort of/kind of/like" principle of uncertainty has also been detected by William Safire in a column of 1995, commenting on the language used in the O.J. Simpson trial, then in its opening disputatious stages. He noted that "there seems to be a widespread use of the fuzzy *kinda sorta*." [23] Witnesses rambled on sloppily, almost into incoherence; but the legal professionals in the courtroom also reflected the current standards of speech and discourse, which have long since been quite indifferent to the older, ambitious verbal habits of self-discipline and pride in the use of words. Judge Lance Ito explained to the jury, "These opening statements are normally given by attorneys *to sort of* give you an overall view of the evidence." The prosecutor, Ms. Marcia Clark, was also quoted as describing some guest-housing units that were figuring in the testimony as—"It's *kind of* one long building..." Small wonder that in the vapid spirit of the courtroom the witnesses were not prompted to state clearly, simply, precisely what they had seen or heard. A former police officer, Ronald Shipp, who was a friend and companion of O.J. Simpson, testified that the U.S. football star on trial for murder of his wife "*kind of* jokingly said, 'I've had some dreams of killing her...'"

Lexicographers have been quick to pinpoint the abuse of "kind of" and "sort of" as adverbials. I quote Safire here, for he tends to take the turn from the texts towards grammatical analysis and to the place where lexicographers spin their rules (whereas our special interest lies in the other direction, at the place where ideas lurk and cultural fashions shape changing usage—

The British grammarian Sir Randolph Quirk has identified these terms, in informal speech, as "downtoners for adjectives and adverbs," ways to tone down the force of the words that follow. "The informality of expressions used on both sides of the bar," the lexicographer Anne Soukhanov adds, "not to mention pervasive use of the non-standard adverb *like*, simply points up the stress factors inherent in a trial."

But the stress factors have become the unavoidable ingredients of the way we speak (and, increasingly, write) nowadays. Carelessness gives way to indifference and the standardization of bad habits. To open one's mouth to say something, to communicate with a measure of clarity and accuracy (and good grammar usually helps), becomes a trial in itself. One hesitates to say something for fear that what would come out is not exactly what one intended.

We are living in a time where the stress factor is becoming inherent in the very act of the spoken and written word. Everybody seems to be worrying: the slightest slip—on the part of politicians and editors, doctors and lawyers, admen and comedians, et al.—can get one hauled up on charges of verbal malpractice. Or even worse, as in the case of President Clinton's famous evasiveness ("It all depends on what you mean by 'is'...."), linguistic inexactitude is an impeachable offense.

On Not Speaking English So Good

The trouble with American journalism, if I may dare a seditious thought, is that it's always quoting Americans, and they don't speak English so good: like, I mean, you know, being sort of ungrammatical and kind of splitting infinitives—and kind of getting sentences half-wrong, sort of, hopefully. Now that the media are getting more and more international, talking to and publishing in every story a few fast quotes from foreign-speaking experts, U.S. newspapers are getting into even deeper trouble. The correspondents, like little jitney Hemingways, still want to get the conversation absolutely right, with the authentic phrase visible and the natural tone audible. (Magic Johnson: "Wow, did I blow it! Man, I need a cool shot of sumpin'...")

The other day there was a spectacular German bankruptcy which was given world-wide news coverage, and Stephen Kinzer of the *New York Times*, reporting from Frankfurt, needed one of those fast good quotes from a local German banking expert. He talked to a certain Eberhard Weiershäuser who said at the drop of a hat, "The affair will negatively impact Germany as a financial center...."

Well, this kind of language is certainly not calculated to positively impact English as a model of clear and simple communication. Perhaps Mr. Kinzer should have touched it up a bit, or Herr Weiershäuser could have retranslated it and tried again. But then he might only have come up with an old *Stasi* secret-police standby about the impact of *"feindlich-negative Kräfte"* in the hoary DDR, a cliché of subversive-negativism, and that might have been even more sinister.

For now, such ungainly circumlocutions, aspiring to be portentous, are tiresome but otherwise harmless. Journalists who should (and do) know better go in for a little coquetry with these downmarket demotic devices and coyly come up with something like these kind of, or sort of, things: "Well, Murdoch sort of owns these media, doesn't he?"

Well, he does or he doesn't. Part ownership (a matter of 24 percent of the stock of a European TV-station) would not prove the point the story was supposed to be making, namely that one Murdoch-owned newspaper was following a different political line from another of his media outlets. This is sort of misleading, isn't it?

But sort of meaningful is the ironic usage, as in the following example. Enid Nemy is reporting for the *New York Times* on the grand reopening of the refurbished Plaza Hotel by Manhattan's Central Park, and she shines up her prose for the occasion. "The rejuvenated 87-year-old glitters almost as blindingly as it did originally, when some of the gold leaf had to be toned down with bronze varnish." She notes that there are still nips and tucks to be made, but no matter: "Donald J. Trump modestly calls it 'the finest hotel in the country,' but then Trump sort of owns it, with a few banks." [24] The non-grammatical slip is used to suggest the financial illegitimacy of the millionaire real-estate high-flyer (at that moment near bankruptcy). It can also be taken as a sign of the changing conception of property rights in America (sort-of-ownership); or, alternatively, the stranglehold of what Lenin used to call finance-capitalism on individual entrepreneurs, with banks running the whole show. Useful sort of a word, no?

The more I ponder my collection of "sort-of/kind-of" usages, the more I sink in unwilling admiration of its adverbial-cum-prepositional ingenuity. It can also serve as a bureaucratic camouflage, or as an organizational cover-up wherein this six-letter toss-off used in all its impropriety does an effective public-relations job. In an interview with Alan Friedman of the *International Herald Tribune* (26 September 1994, p. 2), Mr. Lewis Preston, the J.P. Morgan financier who became the president of the World Bank in 1991, conceded that "until a year ago the Bank did not even have a cost accounting system," that there were too many "boon-doggle projects," that loans amounting to billions had been disbursed without meeting what they call "the requirement of conditionality," etc. And this is the way he then summed up the bottom line: "So the bank got stuck with a budget that kind of distorted things." It could have been the unkindest cut of all: the most powerful banking institution in the world was hovering for years on the frontiers of fraud and waste and know-nothingism. Mr. Preston's snappy and very streetwise "kind-of-distorted-things" almost brought the bank back into intellectual solvency. As he says, "the bank is trying to be more transparent," to see things more clearly. *More light!* (which was the phrase, *Mehr Licht!*, on Goethe's lips when he died).

There was, alas, not time enough at the World Bank to institute a new calculus before yet another president, Mr. James Wolfensohn succeeding Lewis Preston, had an innovative financial approach of his very own. It reminded some Londoners of a Kingsley Amis anecdote in which Philip Toynbee was inspired to write an epic in blank verse and then was further inspired to go through the verse making it blanker. This classic work of supererogation has now, as a reporter notes, been matched by James Wolfensohn at the World Bank: "He has gone through the costs and come up with proposals for making them costlier." [25]

But bad habits are ultimately a self-defeating trap, and a bit of charm or irony will not neutralize what I will be calling (see below) the pseudo-Wordsworthian error of journalism's absolute commitment to the old Romantic credo of reproducing "the natural speech of the common people." In the *New York Times'* famous (i.e., "exclusive" and, in sports circles, "sensational") interviews with the teen-age champion, aka known as "the tennis phenom," Jennifer Capriati, the then eighteen-year-old is pictured as on the verge of an inspiring comeback. She had been on "self-destruct" after "a year of entropy" but now had turned the corner. As Ms. Robin Finn quotes her as explaining, "You're considered a celebrity, you kind of have no rights to privacy.... I felt like people were watching me. ... After that I kind of forgot about everything." [26]

And after that came an arrest by police on drug charges, and related troubles, so that grammar should be the least of her worries. She is kind of eager to "tell it like it is" and so is the *New York Times*, sort of, hopefully. So are we all.

A last word about telling-like-it-is, for it can always be told more accurately. Good writers can phonetically reproduce speech down to every inflection which Professor Higgins would be proud to have detected. The novelist Thomas Wolfe had this ingenious talent, and also his namesake, the "father of New Journalism" Tom Wolfe; humorists from Mark Twain to Clive James have sparkled thereat.

But I note a measure of "racism" in the press when it tries its more mediocre hand at phonetics. Folksy white characters, like Western ballad singers, are allowed their "Ah'm gonna sing now" or "Musta bin outa mah mind"; and cool black jazz musicians are always given their "kinda played it like Django." It's a populistic nostalgia for true old-timer sounds, mixed with a new "wannabe" grammar and orthography where anything goes. There is about it, I detect, also a sad salute to the abortive campaign for something called "Black English" whereby every race, ethnic minority, and "aspiring culture" enjoys its linguistic self-determination. In this spirit every expression "wuz" considered to have its inalienable right to grammatical incorrectness, and no P.C.

(political correctness) or G.C. (grammatical correctness) bullying was constitutional.

One doesn't know whether to cry or to laugh—we have just moved from Uncle Tom to Ish Kabbible to Peter Sellers in all his comic Bombay glory. All accents are equal; to err is only human, and slips-of-the-tongue (when not Freudian signals) are taken to be mere signs of the fallibility of all our speech cultures.

The pace of change in slang, or the swiftness of the current of what Saussure called "diachronic" drift in fashionable phraseology, can leave one embarrassingly stranded. In-lingo which becomes out is either ignored as if listeners suddenly became hard-of-hearing, or a handy interpreter saves the situation by translating simultaneously from the new *in* to the old *out*, or the other way round. Here is a *Times* reviewer doing us a good turn in reporting about "a sincere, plain, friendless girl." It doesn't sound promising but the real trouble is linguistic, for she is "apt to say such old-fashioned things as 'I'm not all that on walking,' meaning she's not keen on it." [27] Not keen on it? Not *into* it, I would have thought. But even that, by now, may have to retranslated. This kind of in-and-out lingo is on a fast track, and any slow drawl is likely to be overtaken, even overlapped.

4

Sort of Suspicious, Kind of Guilty

Artful Dodging and the Gott Case

These circumlocutions—sterner critics would call them lapses in style—have in their very grammatical imprecision and slangy equivocation a built-in uncertainty. This can be, mostly, attributed to the vagaries of colloquial conversation where little or no mental exertion accompanies whatever is being talked about. In a more serious vein, the issues involved in the exchange of sentiments or opinions require rather more mental activity than the speakers (or writers) care to make, or are capable of exercising. If there is some doubt about the complicity of a suspicious character, then he becomes "sort of guilty." If there is an emotional complexity to a marriage or an affair, the couple can be said to be "kind of happy." Sort-of/kind-of is here a lazily scrawled short-hand for sharper analyses of situations which cannot be accurately described in words of one syllable.

I have already referred to a critical playfulness in which, more than that, a sly put-down is intended—"Trump sort of owns the hotel," which implies that whether he does, or doesn't, there is something odd or fishy about his property rights (probably wildly overdrawn on his bank loans). There is also a usage by artful dodgers who are neither accidently nor playfully imprecise but find it necessary to conscript loose grammatical formulations in a somewhat more sinister semantic cover-up.

Thus, there were the recent disclosures about a senior *Guardian* editor, Richard Gott. He was a stalwart for decades in the radical left's sympathetic commentaries about Castro, Afro-Asian insurrections, third world liberation movements, progress in Communist China, Pol Pot's (and Erich Honecker's) socialist idealism, and paused only for bouts of acrimonious polemics against reactionary American Cold War policies. He was for over twenty-five years the *Guardian*'s flamboyant features editor, literary editor, and roving foreign correspondent—and he (under some staff pressure) promptly resigned. It was true that he was "associated" with the Soviet KGB over many decades and admitted taking "red gold." But he denied all guilt that he was a "paid agent," that is, took money for anything but expenses to meet his Secret Service friends from Moscow in Vienna or Athens or wherever. The *Guardian* accepted his resignation with embarrassment. The editor, Peter Preston, conceded that he had been "betrayed," and the "confidence" of his trusting liberal-left readership had been duplicitously misused.

The London newspaper competition, the *Sunday Times* and the *Sunday Telegraph* in the forefront of the pack, spared no effort or expense to rub it in. The former station-chief of the KGB in London, Oleg Gordievsky, was interviewed to telling and damaging effect (he had indeed approved goodly sums to be paid to the agent in question, etc., etc.).

How, then, did Richard Gott react? He had been an ideologue of the Left *par excellence*, always on the front line where rebels fought and ideas clashed, but now his usefulness was over. For he'd also been a bit of a Scarlet Pimpernel, here and there and everywhere, an eccentric and cultivated gent who knew his spy literature from E. Philips Oppenheim and Somerset Maugham to Len Deighton and John Le Carré, all of whom must have supplied him with enough role models (i.e., mole models) to fantasize his sense of reality.

In a long interview with a *Guardian* writer which filled a full page of the *Guardian* (13 December 1994), Gott went on and on about how it was just one of those things, harmless fun-and-games, exciting in its way, but only a small adventure on the frontiers of the Cold War. One phrase stands out: "I suppose I just sort of thought it was quite fun..."

Here are all the evasive signals of prevarication, tell-tale imprecision to cover up dissimulation—suppose ... just ... quite ... and last, but not least, "sort of."

And what kind of questions did all those KGB officers (including Col. Titov) put to him? "Sort of political questions." Anyway, "this fellow called Titov was a bit of a thug, and I didn't terribly care for him..." *Bit* of? *Terribly* care? ... He was a thug, or he wasn't. He cared for him, or he didn't. But no such self-confident precision can go with dissembling.

And what of his thousands of *Guardian* pieces of political reportage and ideological manifestoes, defending peace, progress, and the revolutionary struggle? "[A]nyway those sort of pieces were written as sort of *jeu d'esprit,* pieces written against the tide." And what of his own motivations in dealing with the KGB?

> I'm a benign and friendly person...and I think that the KGB didn't have that many friendly people to talk to...in distant parts they are lonely and depressed.... Neal Ascherson had a thing saying it was vanity. I think it was sort of arrogance... these sort of things can't touch me because I am the sort of person I am and I am not likely to be suborned.

An unlikely story. Sort of arrogant. Sort of vain. Sort of suspicious. Kind of guilty.

Karl Kraus would have been inspired by the Richard Gott case, indeed could have read profound meanings in it: You begin with bits of sloppy speech and playful prose, covering up for diffuse sentiments—and then, in "the last days," the whole world begins to fall in on you.

Signals of Prevarication

The buzzwords echo like an incessant refrain in all newspaper prose, aspiring to recapture the natural speech of the eventful characters who crop up in its columns. Sort of/kind of often gives semiotic signals on occasions rather more important than even the confessions of international espionage (although not, perhaps, in the evidence for the Heisenbergian principle of human uncertainty). Cinema-going book-readers will recall the high-climactic dialogue in Tarantino's *Natural Born Killers* (the film directed by Oliver Stone, 1992-94) when Mickey Knox, the serial killer, finally decides to dispose of the TV-star Wayne Gale—whose hand-held camera had brought the whole bloody prison riot, break-out and incredible escape to the live-action screens of a hundred million Americans. Wayne tries to protest: "Just wait....Wait! I kinda felt that during this whole escape thing that a kind of bond developed between the three of us. We're kinda in this together, right?" The appeal to the so-called Patty Hearst syndrome (i.e., overwhelming fear driving captives into sympathy with their captors) was to no avail. Mickey promises that the removal of Wayne would be the one, *last* killing. The drama had to end, the story had to be finished—on, finally, a tender touch. As Mickey tries to explain to Wayne Gale, who was assured television immortality for his unprecedented on-the-spot documentary of a massacre,"It's not about you...I sort of like you. It's just that killing you, and what you represent is a sort of... statement."* The serial killer—the number of his massacred victims runs into the hundreds—wants, at the end, to register a general, radical protest; but apparently not everybody agrees that any statement at all, even a small reference to what can be construed as an *apologia pro vita sua*, is pertinent, plausible, or advisable.

Some critics in the Western press have taken the whole enterprise (story, script, screenplay, feature film, video cassette; all seen or read by millions) to be an unconscionable "exercise in evil." The whole infernal work was itself exactly representative of "the culture of horror" it purports to indict.

---

* The scene occurs in Chapter 19, p. 223, of the Penguin edition of the novel (based on a story by Quentin Tarantino). In Faber & Faber's text of the original Tarantino screen-play the dialogue only includes "a kind of bond developed" (p. 118). The "*statement*"— which, in any case, is not in Tarantino's unpedantic style but rather in Oliver Stone's ideology—is...sort of superfluous.

Oliver Stone prefers to argue that "the Greeks got there first [i.e., Homer, Aeschylus, et al.]—and with buckets of blood and gouged-out eyeballs." He likes to believe that, in the words of one of his characters, "love beats the demon." It's a sort of a simple faith, a kind of a pulp-fiction philosophy, which can sustain a film career in contemporary Hollywood.[1]

48   The Lan...

paign of '96.
just learn
A sen
with a
"He
le

5

Of Plastic Prose, in Bits and Pieces

In a Sporting Manner

The trouble with the metaphorical imperative that has increasingly taken over U.S. political reporting is that one can hardly tell when figures of speech end and hard electoral figures begin. The press program is half scorecard, half joke book. And one *Times* columnist, Russell Baker, who alternates fun-poking with viewing-with-alarm, offers a remark on the "tragic" state of our American political language with a comical anecdote about "old-fashioned political reporting"; and his point is either cynical or ironical (or both). The good old days being indelibly burned into journalistic memory, Baker recalls Eddie Folliard of the *Washington Post*—

> "It's time to take off the gloves," Eddie would say one day before October 10 [i.e. less than a month before Election Day] before tapping out a story that began: President Whoever "took off the gloves today." [1]

Taking off one's gloves in October is equivalent to putting them on aggressively in any other part of the year. It means the punch is being telegraphed; the knock-out blow, either in leather or bare-knuckled, is on its way.

Nor, as I regret to say, do the more solemn items of the day's news, the largest questions of national politics and foreign policy, get treated in a dissimilar manner. More often than not we get plastic prose, in little bits and broken pieces. It may be thought of as "news analysis" or an important column of weighty comment but it emerges as thin and as emaciated as the local fashion models on the current catwalks. The endemic "trouble with words" is lacquered over by the fast colorful quotations that give such vividness to the popular reporting on the sports pages. One pollster is explaining the complex course of statistically measuring the ups-and-downs of the Clinton-Dole cam-

"It's like the other team had an uncontested layup drill, and we
at those baskets count," he said. [2]

or political correspondent of the *Times*, R.W. Apple, Jr., follows on
small variation in the athletic metaphor, pinning down Dole's tactics:
was thus in the awkward position of needing to land a knock-out, or at
st a knockdown, punch, while keeping a smile on his face."

As for the president, after a month or two of the campaign, he "was never
seriously bloodied." So, at the end of the first TV debate, "Mr. Dole badly
needed to make it to the end of the fight on his feet, and he did so." [3]

The politics of pugilism is proceeding apace as all the sparring partners
keep punching away at the bag. "We're hardly in the final round," said Dole's
chief spokesman, "and Bill Clinton still has a glass jaw. All we need to do is
land the right punch." [4] After the second and final TV match the *Post*'s editorial writer was also watching the bout closely for a *k.o.* blow and was quick
with a ringside perception to the effect (as he knowingly put it), "You could
say the President slipped the punch, but in fact the punch was never thrown." [5]

Be that as it may in the punch-drunk world of blows "slipped" and/or
unthrown, a *Times* pundit pondered in another editorial whether Dole could
"juice up his floundering campaign," after doing "a good job sketching his
road map for the weeks ahead," by "delivering some sort of oratorical body
blow to Bill Clinton...." Or could he "loop back...to take a half-hearted stab at
the question of Whitewater pardons"? [6] What he did do was to try and bring
Ross Perot, the third Presidential candidate, into the game (and then out) by
proposing his withdrawal, his "pulling out of the race." This tricky "gambit"
was justified by the dubious notion that "if he half hits it, it's a home run." [7]
The mixed metaphors scurried across the pages, hopping haphazardly from
column to column. Yet another commentator turned (if I am not getting the
conceit wrong) to Indy or formula-one racing when he opined that some unexpected change in the league tables "would take a real blowout by the Democrats... No blowout was apparent."

At the end, the hapless Republican candidate lost: Dole was defeated,
downed, routed, knocked out, presumably because he failed to mount an aggressive campaign, make a battle of it, take the offensive, score against the
enemy, outpoint or outpitch or outslug his opponent. He himself was directly
confronted with his campaign shortcomings; and why, pray, didn't he hit out,
bloody the Arkansas Kid's vulnerable nose, crack his glass jaw, buckle his
knees, counterattack in the clinches where he knew his man to be so weak?
Dole replied to a correspondent of the *Washington Post* who pressed him about
his failure to "attack Mr. Clinton's character...to criticize Mr. Clinton's personal life"—indeed in the vogue word of yesteryear "to sock it to him"—"you
can't pull a punch you never intended to throw."[8] To climb into the ring and
hold back on throwing punches is the definition of a loser, for (in our classic

American phrase for political challenge) "throwing one's hat in the ring" is not quite enough. He should have stayed back in the gym, trying out his fists on the punching bag.

Boxing wisdom, you see, explains all. And when the mode finally changes and we are out of the ring, away from the stadium, off the roaring runway, far from home-plate, we get only school-girls' tricks in snappy writing—as in these remarks by Ms. Maureen Dowd (who is becoming notorious for eponymous dowdy prose)*: *"Washington.-* Bill Clinton has given us the Limbo Presidency. (Bill be limbo, Bill be quick, Bill go under the limbo stick.)" This is only for starters; she ends with this about the dour Dole who was not nearly as effective as his opponent in flashing a keep-smiling Americanism: "And maybe what he's selling is just as much America. But we don't elect the twilight of our souls." [9]

She is always exhibiting her schoolgirl certainties, and she uses her column to reprimand all and sundry who do not live up to the clique's credo. When the president crosses the line, she primly registers that "Mr. Clinton acts like a big baby...." And if a White House advisor is at fault, then "the baby's baby is Mr. Morris...." Nobody is so confident about life's wisdom as an adolescent who thinks that she has put away childish things: "So we have the spectacle of one childish man coaching another childish man on how to act more mature." [10] And we have also the ongoing spectacle of a jejune commentator, confined to immature language and a teen-age superciliousness, trying to cope mewlishly with some of the most complex and melancholy affairs of state. It seems to be all a gag, calling only for those new-age qualities of intellect and personality prized as "funky...feisty...flaky...." Or something like that.

Again, in another tedious screed about how wearisome she finds life all around her: *"Washington.*—I never thought I'd say this, but I'm tired of sex. I have eros fatigue." How tiresome of her! (And this in the morning paper, so early in the day, with only a cup of coffee behind most readers.) [11] A note of literary desperation has always been known to creep into the prose of the columnists sooner or later, as any anthology of American punditry will reveal. (A convenient collection is the excellent anthology assembled by Karl E. Meyer, an editor on the *New York Times,* whose own father was a prolific regular for the *New York Post* and a stylist whose daily stint enchanted me as a teen-ager.) Doing five or four or even three pieces a week, year after year, becomes a burdensome chore and drives one to tricks and wayward devices. I think now of the most talented of the newspapermen—among them I rank Heywood Broun, H.L.

---

*   I apologize for the low blow; one should avoid, I know, nomenclatural epithets. Also I intend here no gender discrimination; "school-boy" tricks are no better. In fact in all of this dowdy prose there is a kind of reversion to teen-age lingo which, a generation or two ago, would not have been accepted by the precocious adolescent editors of a self-respecting high-school newspaper (say, the [DeWitt] *Clinton News* in the Bronx).

Mencken, Walter Lippmann, Joseph Alsop, Max Lerner (and indeed Ernest L. Meyer), not to mention those sports writers Red Smith and Jimmy Cannon, and on a slightly more idiosyncratic or eccentric level: Dorothy Thompson, Franklin P. Adams (F.P.A.), Ben Hecht, Westbrook Pegler, Ring Lardner. They managed with a certain finesse to maintain their literary equanimity over long periods of journalistic productivity.

In recent times, when populistic pressures have added to the strain, there has been, as we have amply seen, a frenetic note in the regular efforts to inform and entertain, to be original and quotable and get to be the-talk-of-the-town, at least for a day. Maureen Dowd is probably less to blame for her contributions to the grotesque current image of the serious American columnist than the recent editors of the *New York Times* who encouraged the kind of show-biz writing which they would deplore in their teen-age children, getting a good education in private Manhattan academies. Here is Ms. Dowd commenting in the *Times* on the rush to write memoirs and viewing with alarm our "exhibitionist era" when New York book publishers are frantically signing up all-and-sundry to reveal the inside stories of their lives and times:

> We have revenge memoirs. Good mommy memoirs. Bad mommy memoirs. Bad daddy memoirs. Very bad surrogate daddy memoirs. Celebrity memoirs. Nonentity memoirs. Pubescent memoirs. Senescent memoirs. Anyone remotely associated with a celebrity memoirs. I-could-have-run-I-did-run-I-might-still-run-for-president memoirs.

This doesn't have enough wit to carry on in such staccato fashion as if it were a comical singing telegram. But it is another way of easily filling the space without taking the old-fashioned trouble of composing straightforward sentences amounting to a forceful and, possibly, elegant paragraph.[12]

Ms. Dowd's suspicion of a kind of spiritual *Götterdämmerung*—or an equally Wagnerian "twilight of our souls"—was actually at issue in the 1996 campaign is a moot question; but getting it right or wrong in one's sporting metaphor indubitably was. Even the smallest errors of a campaigning politician are deemed to be outlandish, especially when they are spotted to be in conflict with the few well-known facts about foreign far-away countries. One remembers President Ford slipping up on whether Poland, in the Cold War days, was or was not a Communist country; also countless would-be American ambassadors who didn't quite know the location (out there in Asia? in deepest Africa?) of the land to which they aspired accreditation. Egregious mistakes involving athletic lore are even more memorable, and in fact are taken at once in a spirit of comedy and with a seriousness that implies important political ineptitude. Thus, the *New York Times* had fun with the "Brooklyn" affair ("ERROR: WILD PITCH TO DODGERS") and scored another costly point against the presidential candidate it had other good reasons to disapprove of:

West Hills, California.—Bob Dole was in the right place at the right time and trying to hitch his fortunes to the right baseball team. The only thing he got wrong was the city—by 39 years and nearly 3,000 miles (4,800 kilometers).

A miss being as good as a kilometer, the Dole camp could only explain it as "mixing seriousness with a bit of mirth," and the *Times'* reporter skeptically recorded that the man who placed the Dodgers in Brooklyn, New York, rather than Los Angeles, California, had been "only joking."

I will, in a subsequent chapter, be sketching "the literary origins" of this kind of writing, pinpointing among others Ernest Hemingway. But since Ms. Dowd is so special—capable of packing almost twice as many sentences into an 800-word space on the op-ed page of the *New York Times* as all of the paper's other columnists—Hemingway should be mentioned twice, for his influence has thrown a hard, mean punch. Maureen Dowd once poked fun at the commercial cult of the novelist and smiled at the peddling for $600 of "a Hemingway Mont Blanc pen" which *"refuses to write long sentences."* But was she welcoming or regretting the fact that nowadays "along with other macho writers such as Jack London, Irwin Shaw and Norman Mailer, his work has gone out of fashion..."? She did recommend *A Farewell to Arms* as "superior," yet still noted that "Hemingway was already a parody of himself when he died." Did he, then, deserve to be "booted off college curriculums filled with more multiculturally correct, if not always as talented, women, minority and gay writers"? In her evident ambivalence her own prose blurs into a parody within a parody:

> *Fort Lauderdale*—For years people have come to Key West to celebrate Papa. The town was small. And it grew large with tourists.
> The sun was warm and it was good. You could drink a Corsican wine that had a great authority and a low price. It was a very Corsican wine...

Would the lady consider abandoning writing her columns with that Mont Blanc fountain pen? [13]

But the difficulty may lie deeper than the writing instrument; when she goes abroad and composes her column, say, from England she may be tempted even to use a quill. In any event the result is not less unimpressive:

> *Coventry, England*—John Major peered at leather swatches in teal, oatmeal, cream, coffee and warm charcoal.
> 'Fascinating', he murmured... [14]

Finding stories as newsworthy and significant as this to call the attention of her New York readers, too busy to fascinate easily, she didn't even have to leave Times Square. After all, it's becoming a fun place, and the old paper is as lively as a teen-ager. Each section of the paper has to be ectoplasmic in its energy, jumping with human interest, loud or rude or insistent, or all at once in some meaningful cacophany. Here is a story in "The Arts" section, between two serious reports on a dramatization of T.S. Eliot's *The Waste Land* and the latest activities of the New York Philharmonic. To compensate for so much aesthetic earnestness so early on a Saturday morning there is also a story with the following headlines:

OH, ALL THOSE WACKY CELEBRITIES!

Such Fun They Have!

They Joke! They Josh!

They Take Cheap Shots!

The gossipy account of an entertainment-industry dinner at Manhattan's Roseland was in a similar vein of heavy irony and deep inside knowledge— "Yes, this is the same event at which Ted Danson caused a furor by appearing in blackface three years ago, when Whoopi Goldberg was the one being roasted...." It was like a swell time was had by all.[15]

The Folksy Affectation of Simplicity

I have been alluding in these pages to "plastic prose," with its artificial collage of little bits and broken pieces of semi-intellectual references and half-grammatical presentation. As this school of journalistic style would have it, it goes on. And on. Unavoidably so. (Why stop now?)... Here is a columnist writing in the *International Herald Tribune* (6 November 1996), although it may be one of Joe Murray's pieces reprinted from his Texas paper, the *Lufkin Daily News*, or from the Cox Newspapers for whom he is a senior writer. The column begins with a short punchy opening paragraph, intended instantly to grab reader attention:

"*Angelina County, Texas.*—Elections come and go. America goes on."

It concludes some two dozen truncated sentences later:

"Elections come and go. America goes on, for better or worse."[16]

On some more challenging occasion, the *IHT*'s mentor paper, the *New York Times*, will rise to the moment of opportunity and attempt a somewhat longer sentence, adumbrating a rather more complex political observation. After all, foreign affairs have their outlandish complications and even so apodictical an analyst as Thomas Friedman will want to hesitate sometimes, draw a long breath, and exhale dependent clauses, or parenthetical remarks, or a dangling participle or two. On the subject of Middle East terrorism and some "strange moves" on the part of Saudi Arabia, Friedman is busy puzzling out the tantalizing clues:

Maybe things are just as they appear—maybe Iran and its agents really did blow up the Dharan barracks and maybe Jaafar Chueikhat got a pistachio stuck in his throat and did choke to death in a Syrian prison before he could tell his story. Maybe. And maybe not.[17]

After this dramatic effect of staccato uncertainty, others can go on (and on) with their simple certainties, in a few three-word sentences or less. On rare literary days, in the course of editorial events, the presentable prose on the op-ed page manages to slip away on to greener fields, as in the *Times'* half-page of elegant excerpts from the classic nineteenth-century French historical work about *Russia in 1839* by the brilliant Marquis de Custine. (Custine, as attested to by George Kennan, was uncannily prophetic.) Then it is up to the Times Square headline writers to save the day, and keep the tone elementary for Dick and Jane—

A LONG-AGO LOOK AT RUSSIA
(SO WHAT ELSE IS NEW?)[18]

Here is Frank Rich, coming in fast (on 7 November 1996) with his post-election commentary ("FOUR MORE YEARS, BUT WHO'S COUNTING?"), and keeping it to the familiar stand-up comic tradition of replying to one's own rhetorical questions: *"New York.*—Don't you feel better already?" Perish the thought. Or maybe not. Frank Rich, wide-awake master of exemplary coherence, concludes by offering a rhetorical stratagem for countering American political insomnia. He recommends something better than counting sheep. It is in fact a bit of fun-and-games by the bed-time recitation of the soporific language of campaign oratory, especially its bromidic phrases, "squeezing as many of them into a single sentence as possible" (and even then he doesn't quite manage it, by strict count, before nodding off):

> Bridge. The most optimistic bridge in America. It takes a village to build the most optimistic bridge in America. It takes a village of peasants with pitchforks to build the most optimistic bridge in America. It takes a village of peasants with pitchforks dancing the Macarena to build the most optimistic bridge in America. It takes a...zzzzzzz.[19]

If even the *Times'* own man nods off in the midst of his own prose, can a reader be blamed for asking wearily, so what else is really new?

The old legendary figure of the newspaper world, the "copy editor"— hunched over stories for the morning edition, pencil in hand, dedicated to the maintenance of high journalistic standards—seems no longer to exist. There are still discernible efforts to be quick with the news, to be accurate rather than erratic; but there appears to be nobody around who is concerned with grievous lapses of language and style, someone who can stop the self-indulgent excesses of careless writers who allow themselves to get away with anything. Here is Frank Rich once more, showing his sympathy for the critique of the "frivolous" Hollywood Manifesto which protested the treatment of the sect of Scientologists in Germany ("like the Holocaust of the Jews"). He associates himself in his *New York Times* column with the critical commentators—at home and abroad—who have called the comparison "grotesque... tasteless...outrageous...absurd." He adds his two cents as crisply or eloquently as he can: "In a word—Oy!"[20] Tastelessness is a bottomless pit; you can always sink a little lower.

I am afraid we will get no respite from the onslaught of low-pop phraseology, lightly disguised as smart-aleck writing. Thomas Friedman is telling us in the *New York Times* all about how he would summarily handle the foreign policy trouble with Iraq (by taking a hint from the influential Iraqi newspaper, *Babel*) and putting a financial squeeze on Damascus :"Guess who owns *Babel*? Saddam Hussein's evil son, Uday. Think about that..." After taking thought—and after noting "When Saddam got mad at Uday last year and decided to punish him, he did so by personally dousing Uday's collection of antique sports cars with gasoline and torching it...."—we are regaled by a pseudo-eloquent conclusion to this effect: "Saddam really knows how to hurt a guy. So should we. Follow the money." [21] The final three-word phrase has his concise advice on the best way to counter the Iraqi dictator: to "attack his ample cash flow." As the foreign-policy commentator for the *New York Times*, Friedman was obviously making a valiant effort to keep the complex—and hence shunned—issues of world politics at the center of national attention; and he tried to do the best he knew how, arguing now in urgent telegrammese and then with twee baby-talk—

Mr. Clinton doesn't know it, but his last four years were a foreign-policy honeymoon. The honeymoon is over....

Bill Clinton has it oh so lucky these past four years.... He was blessed with local leaders who were huge bulldozers ready to effectively tackle the really hard issues and do it in a way that defused them as political problems....

Mr. Netanyahu can have real negotiations between leaders or a real war between peoples. Those are his choices. There is nothing in between. There never was.[22]

There is a homely, home-spun element in this affected simplicity, and it apes the artificial way that experts and other authorities feel is their best informal and ingratiating manner. Here is the senior Presidential advisor opining about the '96 campaign at its mid-way point: "It sure doesn't feel like five weeks out—it feels like another day at the office...." With two *like's* in a folksy sentence, can *sort of/kind of* (one each) be far behind? The rhythm of the phrase demands it, and George Stephanopoulos goes on to oblige: "If you just sort of read the local newspapers and watch television, it's just kind of not happening...." Is the not-happening only the pause of half-time, or the lull in the action at a time-out, or is somebody not playing the game for real? "The challenger has to take the ball to the hoop, and Dole is just not doing that."[23]

One never suspected how much the New York reader has suffered from the plague of functional illiteracy, afflicting whole generations of metropolitan school-children, until one becomes aware of how systematically all newspapers (including the most serious paper in town) go in for "dumbing down." Only a non-reader with serious handicaps could take this opening of a Friedman column, and then try and go on from there: "Sometimes you can tell a lot about a country by what is on the front pages of its newspapers. Sometimes you can tell even more by what is on the back...."[24] Sometimes you can "tell a lot"—and even more—by not trying to sound like a dumb-bell, writing for the left-back class.

It is as if the man can't read without moving his lips, can't count without using his fingers. To any and all complex problems of international affairs he tots up the elementary factors involved, gives them a brief paragraph each, and comes swiftly to the bottom line. Here he is writing from Zurich (2 February 1998) about the three (3) options which confront U.S. foreign policy in the Middle East with a "Hamlet-esque choice." (The young Danish Prince had it, at least in Shakespeare's version, somewhat easier, for he could rather early on walk away from options like Rosencrantz, Laertes, and Hecuba.) The President can finish the 1991 Gulf War (option 1); or he can opt for (3) a certain disinterested aloofness (which, alas, Laertes neglected, thus coming to a tragic end). This diplomatic problem is, in Friedman's bitter aphorism, also known (although only a soft-drink expert might know what it means), "When you've got lemons, make lemonade." So we are left with option 2—bombing Iraq and destroying Saddam's weapon-making capability. Does this choice also have its problems? Friedman comes up with a variant option, called *2-b* which might re-insure the success of *2-a*. Here's where Shakespeare comes in, at the point at which all of Iraq has been made a no-fly zone. If you've followed the argument in the *Times'* op-ed column up till now—it isn't easy, but then Adolph Ochs didn't found a great newspaper for simpletons—then you're ready for the dramatic *denouément*, namely, he doesn't really believe there is an option *2-b*! It is probably such stuff as dreams are made of. "There is only option 2—bombing Iraq, over and over and over again...." With a final flourish as if Fortinbras, armed to the teeth, was at long last coming on to the final scene, Friedman rings down the curtain: "So, 2-b or not 2-b? There is no question. There is no 2-b. There is only option 2, over and over and over again..."[25] Small wonder that foreign policy advice from Times Square is going down like a bomb in the counsels of state.

Once upon a time the *New York Times* had a number of fairly strict editorial taskmasters, and one of them—Theodore M. Bernstein, in his published style-book*—confessed, "This scrivener never matriculated in the Write-Like-Talk School, and does not believe in it." His successors evidently do not share his conviction that "writing is and must be a more precise form of expression than extemporaneous speaking." Nowadays even the headlines on the *Times*' editorial page, and its page opposite, are written as if they were sound effects accompanying the music up-and-under or the canned audience-response in a studio sit-com.... Indefatigably on the road, our foreign-affairs commentator tells us from Istanbul and from Moscow—

TURKEY WINGS IT
Islamists vs. The Paradigm

GET REAL ON RUSSIA
Yeltsin vs. Zyuganov—a no-brainer [26]

From Istanbul Thomas Friedman explains to us what "the Paradigm" is (and the vogue-word was so stretched that its meaning escaped me**). He goes on

---

*   Theodore M. Bernstein, *Watch Your Language: A lively, informal guide to better writing, emanating from the News Room of The New York Times* (1958), pp. 4, 6. The elegant preface by Jacques Barzun reads today as if he, at least, knew that the good old cause of "language watchers" was a forlorn one.

**   After several readings I feel compelled in this place to record that "The Paradigm" is for Friedman those "very powerful set of rules and standards for how countries have to behave if they are going to attract investment capital to grow..." —"You can call these rules 'The Paradigm'." He can, if he will. I lost him when those who accept The Paradigm are "the winners," all the others become "losers or left-behinds."
      This is playing a school-yard game, with school-boy language, touched up by a bit of Greek which, in my *Longman's Dictionary of Contemporary English* (1978, p. 786), is defined mainly as "an example or pattern of a word, showing all its forms in grammar...." Exemplary patterns of words are, come to think of it, what good writing is all about.
      I have heard it claimed that "paradigm" could be literally ascribed to Copernicus; but this is a misunderstanding. Professor Thomas Kuhn's influential book on *The Copernican Revolution* (1957) popularized the word by arguing that the Copernican theory represented not a mere new discovery about the solar system but a genuine "scientific revolution" which, in his definition, was when the presuppositions of new knowledge shifted paradigms. Real revolutions shift the basic and conventional models of life and thought. In this case the hitherto exemplary premises of both cosmology and science were transformed.
      Its recent buzzword snobbishness has not only made it a disagreeable cliché of pretentious conversation but a figure of fun. In Tom Wolfe's best-selling novel, *A Man in Full* (1998), the leading character objects to the bromidic use of the word—
      "...But this word *paradigm* absolutely drove him up the wall....The damned word meant nothing at all, near as he could make out, and yet it was always 'shifting', whatever it was. In fact that was the only thing that the 'paradigm' ever seemed to do. It only shifted...." (p. 66).

to admonish us: "So what's happening in Turkey is much more complicated....
So watch Turkey, but don't panic." As for Russia, he offers his own "brainy"
opinions and has no patience with any other views: "Enough of this nonsense."
He handles his readers as if they were growing up to be street-smart kids but
are still having difficulties doing the assigned home-work. His school-mas-
terly manner is ingratiating: "While traveling you are often asked what you do
for a living. Lately I answer that I'm a foreign affairs columnist and that means
I cover wars...." One war which the *Times* has evidently lost was the one in
which Ted Bernstein was a combattant—taking arms against "*a black rot*"
which was demoralizing language, sounding off against "the battle cry" of
popular or fashionable conventions which hold: "Whatever the people say is
okay by me; the people speak real good."

Friedman, like so many top-flight newspapermen, has an irrepressible talent for writing speeches; and many colleagues have, in fact, served as presidential ghost-writers (Max Freedman for L.B.J., Bill Safire for Nixon, Pat
Buchanan for Reagan). Here is Tom Friedman, flexing his literary muscles as
a would-be strong man for Bill Clinton, beefing up his policy on China in
recommended remarks to a group of business leaders at the White House:

> Wake up, you morons! You are so greedy and short-sighted. You profit from your
> dealings with China. But you refuse to acknowledge that those dealings take place
> in an overall framework of U.S.-China relations, and that framework is now erod-
> ing. Yet you won't lift a finger to help shore it up. You ostriches make me sick!

The only open question remaining is who the ostrich is and who the moron,
whose head is in the sand and whose is in those arid areas where only a dry,
brainless sub-literacy flowers.[27]

The *Times* style, then, has been subjected to severe changes since the old
and classical days of Anne O'Hare McCormick and Simeon Strunsky, of Brooks
Atkinson and Bosley Crowther—indeed of Theodore Bernstein's rigorous
house-book of guidelines to good writing and accurate reporting. The winds
of change have left everywhere a certain breeziness which flies over lightly the
traditional markers. In a sentence which is supposed to be easily readable if not
strictly true, the *Times* dramatizes the historic post-Cold War situation: "Every
Cold War President with a serious problem in a faraway place could call on the
CIA, pay off a foreign potentate, rent a guerrilla group, or send in the Marines."[28]
This is foreign policy for the man who reads Frederick Forsyth or Tom Clancy—
the famed and feared Lester Markel (1894-1977), who presided over the *Times'*
international coverage for many decades, would have demanded facts not fiction.

Friedman often makes the effort in his various dispatches to characterize
the differing styles of contemporary diplomacy and only winds up in the end
defining his very own style of diplomatic writing. Thus, he recommends to the
Israelis and to the Egyptians, at the moment in an aggressive stalemate of the

Middle East peace process, to try "more of the Jim-Baker in-your-face diplomacy style"; and in the event that they would not readily grasp what that might be, he explains that he means "a Bakeresque taste for knuckle-breaking, strategic leaking and other diplomatic contact sports." What is unsportingly going on, as he writes from Cairo, is intolerable; and he presumably said as much to Prime Minister Mubarak, at the moment doing his bit of "Netanyahu bashing," when he met him for one of his in-your-face-to-face interviews—

> This has got to stop. It's cheap. It's counter-productive and it's throwing out the bathwater with the Bibi [as the Israeli Prime Minister is nicknamed by his friends].[29]

With slang on the Hudson and puns on the Nile, the flow of the *Times'* editorial argument is strong and swift. Also timely. More than that: instantly readable. In a word or two: informed, authoritative.

Our columnist is attracted to the clichés of the day as to a magnet; he collects them, sticks them together, puts them on exhibit three-a-week on the op-ed page. Here he is going on about "culture" in Hong Kong where he is taken by yet another vapid variation of the ubiquitous buzzword—

> Hong Kong is a bridge culture. China is a fortress culture.... Bridge cultures live off tolls—they make a little bit of money on each transaction.... China's image is the Great Wall...[30]

Does this, slightly polished up by platitude, tell us more than we already know? It is surely well-known that the small insular British Crown Colony (as it then was) had become very rich and that the old Chinese land mass has huddled for centuries, for millennia, behind its traditional entrenchments. Add a few "cultures," and you have an up-to-the-minute cultural conflict.

He is didactic all the way from Cairo to Casablanca whence he writes, "Pay attention to Morocco. Pay close attention." As soon as we are sitting still and upright in our seats, all ears and hands clasped, he proceeds to tell us "what's' going on here...."[31]

And in putting his finger on the official ignorance of foreign affairs among Washington politicians—as contrasted, presumably, to the sophisticated knowledgeability and pregnant incisiveness of the Washington press corps—he offers this conclusion to yet another hectoring column: "Lawmakers, fearful of being accused of junketing, don't travel anymore. Those who don't travel don't know. Those who don't know don't care."[32]

In all of this one can detect that *déformation professionelle* of self-indulgent journalism, the sign of omniscience, worn on the jacket like a colored ribbon, daintily and demurely peeking out of the lapel: "China is going to have a free press. Oh, its leaders don't know that yet, but they are being pushed straight in that direction..."[33] What took philosophers of history life-times to discern patterns in the *Zeitgeist* we can now—oh, it's a breeze—get served up two or three times a week by the pundits in their columns. That cutesy "*oh*" rescues modesty from the jaws of arrogance. The tones have, of course, something of the artificial thinness of a ventriloquist's dummy; yet there is a method in the unabashed pretense. One can, as a pundit, assume the mantle of authority without sounding insolent or supercilious. The repetition of the simple stylistic twist, turning on the falsetto, suggests that the writer is toying with the language and he doesn't really mean it literally. As in Friedman's column on "a fateful moment in Arab-Israeli diplomacy" (6 January 1997) when his analysis and recommendations were prefaced by, "President Clinton, pay attention."[34] The tiny full-stop indicates a gentlemanly relationship; a rude exclamation point would have been too loud, too boisterous, and self-defeating! Surely a modicum of deference must be shown to the actual bearers of authority and power, even by headstrong newspaper columnists.

He is nothing if not peremptory. How does he estimate the hopes for ethnic harmony in Bosnia after the Dayton accords? "*Fat chance.*" What is his attitude to the talk in the *NATO* capitals of mounting a military peace-keeping operation? "*Enough Eurobabble.*" His sententious knowledgeability is like chewing gum, with a small wad going a long way. From Cairo he gives us the news about the dramatic change in Egypt's world role:

> we are moving from a world in which the big eat the small to a world in which the fast eat the slow. Egypt has led the Arab world because it was big. It can lead in the 21st century only if it is fast.

Blow hard enough into this kind of pipe and you can get bubbles.[35]

Friedman is so taken with this last turn of phrase about bigness and fastness that he is soon, a dozen columns later, to be found re-cycling it, as if it were a familiar maxim which had become proverbial: "in this era of globalization when, as they say, it's no longer the big who eat the small, but the fast who eat the slow."[36] At this rate he will in good time be proclaiming that the thin outrun the fat, and even (as they say) scrawny birds can outfly pretty butterflies. It makes little difference whether any single remark is true or clear or incisive, it is apparently the rhythm which is meaningful. "Culture," he writes in February 1997, "matters a lot in this new world"; but "the trick is getting the right balance": "For instance, Germany is too much Alan Greenspan and not enough Benetton. Italy is too much Benetton and not enough Greenspan." And what of France, he hears a *Times* reader asking? Well, as the Friedman refrain goes, "France is not enough of either." The trick indeed is in the balance—a name here, another country there, and three full-stops in quick order.

There was an extended period during the winter of 1998-99 when there was no word from Friedman who, presumably, had taken leave to tend to another assignment. Readers who welcomed the pause found his return to politics, and its deeper meanings, just more business as usual. His first column in mid-January '99 picked up where he had left off—"*Washington*—Say, I've been away for the past four months writing a book. Has anything happened while I was gone?"[37] Not that we could bring him up-to-date, especially with what he referred to as the president's "reckless affair with an underwear-flashing intern"; and failing that he warned us that he would be "diving right into things," and, as is his wont, flashing his stabbing insights. On the Washington impeachment process which he almost missed but returned in time to explain, in his elegant manner, the complex causes and consequences:

> Mr. Clinton made the Republicans crazy, and it is easy to see why: He took all their good stuff—welfare reform, balanced budget, and defense spending. I'd be crazy too.

This was reassuring; for a moment we might have thought that his book-writing stint had exhausted all his reserves of purple prose.

If the prose-style leader in American journalism, the most serious *Times* of New York, feels the need for snap-shot prose, for short sentences with a few words of one syllable, little wonder that the tabloids, in turn, strip communication even further and have to make do with elongated over-exposed photographs to seduce a mass circulation. Evidently Friedman is meeting even this challenge with an innovative attention-grabbing "*intro*" which will ensure entrapping the reader for the distance. Here are two examples of new-style crackling leads which lead on snappily from the pop of old-style leads:

> *Washington.*—So it's all O.K. now? That's the word from the Clinton folks....

> *New York.*—I can't believe I'm writing this sentence, but it's true....[38]

As I say, when the broad-sheets reduce prose to these bare-bones there is no way left for the tabloids to go and still use newsprint and the standard alphabet (although the *Daily News* calls the President "*Prez*" and the *New York Post* calls the Mayor "*hizzoner*").

As Marshall McLuhan might have been tempted to say, the mixed metaphor has become the media message. A careless mélange of analogies and similes offers a semblance of analysis and insight. None of these conceits function to extend meanings or illustrate insight; not extension but implosion is the end effect, and it leaves only a dismal mess. This slovenliness in what the papers say, and how they are saying it, is bringing the whole of democratic discourse close to the rubbish bin. A useful critique has less to do with philology than with garbage disposal.

Anglo-American Differences

In rare moments of self-conscious introspection, there is a flash of concern whether this kind of mumbo-jumbo is actually grasped in some meaningful or reflective way by the great American public and especially by listeners and readers abroad. Will this crackling mix of sporting color and staccato three-word sentences, compressed into one-sentence paragraphs, really *communicate?* reach out? get through? Jim Hoagland, the *Washington Post*'s columnist, appears to be concerned :

> Part of the problem lies in translation. No, not from English to French or Swahili, but from baseball to soccer, the global pastime. How to explain America's intense passion and its king-sized character flaws to nations that revere a game that allows a 0-0 tie to stand as a final result?[39]

Perhaps an element of self-critical awareness in the American sporting ideology—that, for example, the so-called *"World Series"* is merely a national championship, running only from coast-to-coast in one country*—would signal a more effective, more persuasive role in the international policies on behalf of, say, a new world order. But within the "baseball world" (viz., the U.S., Cuba, and Japan) there has been no sign of improved king-size understandings; nor has the spreading global popularity of basketball, tennis, and even American football indicated any universal progress in shared semantics. Could it be that the style that has afflicted our political language like hollow-cheeked malnutrition actually has other sources of infection?

A suspiciously similar phenomenon can be detected in Britain where the so-called political culture has fed itself for centuries on diverging Anglo-American linguistic traditions. Same language, different metaphors. Cricket and rugby are also national games which are revered with a passion: but the day is long since gone when a Fleet Street daily newspaper would cheer the Prime Minister for "hitting 'em for six" or holding the loyal Opposition in contempt for never "getting the ball out of the scrum." The conceits of sports as a reservoir for the language of victory, rivalry and defeat in democratic political competition will be giving way, one surmises, to yet another analogizing vocabulary. The sporting metaphor in British politics, unlike its centrality in the U.S., is on the decorative periphery, and is mostly employed to suggest, casually, a charming many-sidedness. Thus, the chancellor of the exchequer (then Kenneth Clark), in his Budget Day speech before the House of Commons (26 November 1996) which fulfilled his promise to "lower taxes" (a bit), said that the basic rate of income tax, reduced by a penny, was now at its lowest "since Baldwin was Prime Minister, Edward VIII abdicated and Wally Hammond scored a double century at the Oval...." Who could ever forget Wally?[40]

---

* The point is a staple of old-world criticism of new-world provincial naiveté, often made superciliously. A New York correspondent for *The Independent* (London, 22 October 1996, p. 24), reporting from Yankee Stadium, writes: "Never has a sporting event attracted such hyperbole. They call it the World Series when it is nothing of the sort. What could be more domestic to the United States than baseball?..." One simple answer: baseball in Japan.

The parliamentary sketch writer for the *Times*, Matthew Parris, a former M.P. himself, has come up with a theory. He observed in the autumn of the 1996 Tory Party conference at Bournemouth that one of the major speeches

> contained little more than a hundred words, arranged in paragraphs, none of which contained more than one sentence. Only two paragraphs contained more than a dozen words....[41]

The décor of political rhetoric has, of course, gone over to the imagistic style of ad-agency staging, and Parris suspects that "as in the visual, so with the spoken word." He argues (and here the transatlantic implications are clear),

> The modern conference speech unconsciously echoes the advertising copywriter's style of the 1980's. Advertising has moved on since then, the industry accepting that consumers can tackle sentences with quite complex sentence structures; but to the politicians of the Nineties, the Eighties are still the latest thing....

The headline over the piece is notable:

POLITICAL SPEECHES NOW ECHO 1980s ADVERTISING

Short Paragraphs. Verbless Sentences. Like This.

Nor is the new stylistic rhythm confined to the right-wing of the political spectrum, as if conservatives were naturally closer to the dynamic world of business enterprise and to its noisy bands of sloganeering ad-men and copy-writing publicity agents. A correspondent covering the British Labour Party conference for a Tory paper has discovered the underlying principle of "per-petual emotion"; and with Tony Blair's impassioned speech envisioning his post-Socialist utopia he detected both contemporary as well as traditional sources for the fragmentation of political grammar.

For this was what always happens (so the account goes) to the way people speak when they are under intense pressure. The feelings become so strong that the bonds of language disintegrate. One can go so far as to say that "both Othello and Lear" lose the ability to articulate whole sentences as their mo-ments of crisis approach, and they too "descend to a sort of broken, magnifi-cent ferocity." Whether the feelings are really strong (or only perfunctory)—and the break is critical (or only simulated)—is, I feel, arguable. Yet to parody it, is to expose its rhetorical tricks:

> No verbs. But lots of feelings. The modern political speech. A speech for us. For all time. Where argument has gone. Forgotten. Part of the baggage of the old way. In our speeches now, today, in all of our hearts: something else. Something richer, purer, simpler. Something easier on the mind. Feelings. What matters to us. As human beings. As people. Together. Now. And for all time. For a thousand years. Or maybe two. Or ten.

On these margins of the articulate there were in the Tony Blair speech, by count, 115 verbless sentences in all. This stripped-down expressiveness offers a good replica of intensity for the politician in the phonetic mode:

> He will feel he must dance along the cliff edge of being unable to express himself at all to show how deeply he means it, how deeply he feels it, and then amaze us by his ability to remain coherent even under these pressures.[42]

Needless to say, such performances on the great stage of popular politics in a mass-media democracy require a not inconsiderable personal endowment of verbal ingenuity and rhetorical talent. We are talking about the supreme leaders, not their deputies or running mates or vice-presidents. Here a *Post* snap-shot of Veepee Al Gore trying to communicate in "the debased era of modern political discourse":

> Throughout the debate Mr. Gore spoke so robotically and with such painstaking enunciation that he appeared to be targeting such potential swing voters as lip readers, closed-captioning stenographers, 6-year-olds, brain-surgery patients, people for whom English is a fourth language, and the scientists at MIT attempting to prove that it is possible for a computer to think and communicate like a human being.[43]

The Coming of the "Soccer Moms"

Meanwhile, back in the White House the president was reported to be enjoying substantially more success with a constituency target group called, for some obscure electoral reason, "soccer moms." *Soccer?* There goes a whole theory of transatlantic differences on "how to explain America"!

Jim Hoagland of the *Washington Post* had over-simplified that oceanic difference in the national sporting cultures; and just as on the other side Ian Thomsen of the *International Herald Tribune* abandoned European hopes for a successful transplantation of the game of soccer at the very moment when events were wrong-footing all theories. In the one case, the very phrase "*soccer moms*" should have suggested, with a fanfare of trumpets, that there was a growing familiarity, even cosiness with the idea of a once-strange and foreign game; and in a matter of weeks, during the autumn presidential campaign, the unused tag had become an English buzzword, repeated incessantly in the London press. The foreign correspondents were evidently puzzled by the phrase but, having little or no time for etymological research, simply bluffed their way to knowing usage. The technical American explanation, coming from the new U.S. soccer associations, is replete with odd details. Apparently "kids' soccer teams" consist of fourteen players, thus yielding "six moms per team." Given the figure of 5 million American kids (under nineteen) who are turning up for soccer games, or practice, the official estimate is that "there are at least a million *soccer moms*...." Which offered an occasion for the wit of William Safire to pen a useful psychological profile:

think of this mom as being in her 30s, harried, family-oriented, carpool-pallored, ethnically diverse, with her vote up for grabs. And as the *soccer mom* goes, so goes the election, if she's not too tired to get to the polls.[44]

The word was also cautiously defined by Mark Steyn for the *Sunday Telegraph*'s readers as "suburban mothers who drive their children to sports practice"; and by the *Times*' man as "white suburban mothers who daily juggle the conflicting demands of work and family." They both assumed the good women were all soccer devotees, for Jack Kemp was lashed out at for being "incapable of any non-footballing analogy. Most of his offerings are impenetrable to the soccer mom."[45] What a fall was there! Foreign soccer may decide American elections; native football puzzles patriots.

Ian Thomsen had added a cunning account to the speculation as to why the game that the British had invented and had spread irresistably throughout the world would never, regrettably, catch on in the States. The conventional explanation ranged from its low-scoring slowness (Americans like points and goals galore, with a couple of home runs thrown in) to its interdiction on the use of hands (and all popular U.S. sports are "hand-driven, manual-powered"). More than that, argued Thomsen (19 October 1996),—

It's because American sports are like the movies, while soccer is more like real life....

All of the popular American sports—football, basketball, baseball and hockey—are built on the excitement of the last minute....[It must] result in a huge come-from-behind victory or upset of some other kind....The game builds and builds to a wriggling climax in the final seconds (not to be overtly sexual about it)....

Great games are decided on the last play. Movies and sports create mirror images of each other. They both want realistic conflict, suspense, and the big ending.... Soccer is more like real life because real life usually doesn't come down to the final seconds...[46]

On the very weekend of publication of this quasi-metaphysical theory of comparative gamesmanship, worthy of the school of a Thorstein Veblen or T.W. Adorno, came the proof of the pudding. In a stadium in Foxboro, Massachusetts, as the *New York Times* reported, "Major League Soccer ended its inaugural season in grand style...." One team, *D.C. United*, had trailed two goals behind when a "heroic" comeback tied the score. The teams continued to play in extra time until a United player named Eddie Pope scored with a powerful header after 3 minutes 25 seconds into the "sudden-death overtime." A last minute thriller! With a climax! Like real life....

The *Times* in New York reported that "soccer fever is alive in the United States and it's going to stay...." The *Independent* in London confirmed that a nation was "enthralled by a cup final that promises to lift the game into a new dimension." It ventured to predict "the years to come when the best of millions of American children for whom soccer has become the predominant sport take on and—as they surely will— beat the world."

Journalists ought by now to know better. In the big game as in real life—and in high politics—things turn out unexpectedly. One pundit who was prudently wise before-the-event polished up a plastic proverb to the effect that *"You never can tell...."* You never can.[47]

A sneaking hope was that those "soccer moms" would also be providing some last-minute real-life surprises. Not a chance. They should have watched the "football moms"—or even the "baseball pops"—if they wanted wriggling climaxes.

It is in the nature of fashion to change and to be re-designed, and it indulges itself irrepressibly in novelty and variety. Looking back over a century of up-to-date avant-gardism, there would seem to be no limits to its inventiveness, at once playful and ingenious. But there are (to use the current fashionable word) discernible parameters*—even familiar perimeters—beyond which even the most imaginative modishness cannot go. It is obvious that in the world of *haute couture* there are not infinite possibilities—the latest hem-lines can go either up or down, skirts can become either tighter or looser, the silk can be plain or iridescent. In the world of industrial models, the Detroit designers can go on stretching their limousines or persist in compacting their smaller passenger cars. As for stylish journalism as it currently sashays down the columns of our newspapers, the reporter's sentence can get either longer...or shorter.

Can they shrink or be shrivelled even smaller than what I have identified as the one- or two-word sentences in a two- or three-sentence paragraph? Only the slightest little bit. Does it, then, have only one way to go? But the re-birth of an old standard-length sentence with a clause or two (and a parenthetical thought) appears to be no option; it would take a major counter-cultural turn to break with the punchy vernacular which, after all, reflects the populism of accessible democratic simplicity. In our examples we have not only the sports writers but the political pundits in our newspapers going in for the truncated telegrammese. The latter are represented by the staccato tones of Friedman of the *Times*. Here is a sports story, also in the *Times* (which cannot get enough of the abbreviated demotic), registering several upsets in thrilling end-of-season football games involving the Dallas Cowboys and their closest rivals (the Jack-

---

* As Kingsley Amis has noted in his *The King's English* (1997, p. 151) parameter is a mathematical expression which is "far too technical and difficult for verbal novelty-hunters and seekers after poshness...." (It denotes "a quantity constant in case considered, but varying in different cases.") Its "newish meaning," *limits* as in "the *parameters* of discussion" has saddled us, so long as the vogue is in fashion, with yet another "repulsive word."

I note that the buzzword has reached the barracks. The professional journal of the U.S. Army War Office is called *Parameters*. Once, in more old-fashioned military times, it might have been called *Perimeters*.

sonville Jaguars, the Carolina Panthers, and the Denver Broncos): "Football fans everywhere are rubbing their eyes.... This is shocking. This is numbing. This is fun."[48] If these kind of three-word sentences in one- or two-sentence paragraphs get increasingly popular, it may well put a heavy and even unbearable strain on the literary ingenuity of journalists as well as the editorial patience of their copy editors. Even such witless one-liners take thought to devise, and the daily deadline waits for no frill or flourish. We may have no choice but to write at greater length; it takes too much time to concentrate on being brief. To come up on a regular basis with so much thin dyslexic brevity can be too much for all but the most facile masters of mini-prose.

The Wrong Profession?

The attrition of vocabulary and the anaemia of sentence-structure—and even the shrunken shape of paragraphs—is rooted in a kind of populism, a wise-guy pretense at being low-brow which is intended to be charming, comical, and above all easily readable and understandable by the maximum number of readers in a hopefully growing circulation. It amounts to a self-imposed intellectual down-sizing, or dumbing-down. Even the most distinguished of newspapers, once famed for their sturdy straightforward no-nonsense prose, are now composed in a slangy style which approaches the dim-witted demotic. Here is the *New York Times* reporter being coy about his difficulties with language and how, in writing an investigative story about a Manhattan course in successful business management techniques, he had performed miserably in the vocabulary test. After all, as he recognized, "Vocabulary is not an aptitude —and thus can be improved with study." He could understand why it was stressed as crucial for managerial success:

> Now you'd think that a reporter for The New York Times would have no trouble with words like *rancor, obtuse, acrid* and *indigent*. And you'd be right—for the most part. But when I encountered gems like *tyro, salubrious,* and *effrontery* I waffled.
> This was not going to turn out as I expected...[49]

He could not, nor did he want to, avoid "exposing a weak vocabulary," and there was a certain modest pride in an inferior performance. "Lackluster" he confessed that it was, and he was happy to remain one of the backward boys. At the conclusion of the course, the Manhattan school director discouraged the *Times'* man from taking up any career which required language skills:

> Journalism was definitely out, as was a career in law. (Sorry, Mom.) ...But to be an effective manager, he said, I would need a larger vocabulary. He suggested I buy a primer.

Given this penchant for low-stylized know-nothingism, it should come as no surprise that even the gravest of public issues tend to get described in words of one syllable and in sentences that end as quickly as they begin. (Sorry, you guys.)

To be sure, this atomized literary presentation, made up of ragged fragments stuck together with quick daubs of attitude, is an all-purpose style to deal with any bit of news of the day. What they all have in common is the put-on camouflage, a half-baked attempt at sub-literacy. So when one New York museum director announced that some of his contemporary exhibits made of plastic had been disintegrating (Yeats's "Things fall apart" is the unavoidable, inevitable quote), the *Times'* op-ed page editor published a comment from a local "novelist and essayist" which began "*New York*—Yikes! Plastic is mortal?..."

There was more of the same over twenty brief paragraphs, and she concluded, "I used to think my pink cup was still out there somewhere. Nothing lasts forever. Not even Dynel."[50] The title of the piece was embarrassingly candid: "Plastic is Us." Were the *Times* editors, in a rare self-deprecating moment, speaking for themselves, or only for the rest of us?

One last thing. Like some other observers, I see the confluence of yet another current of linguistic change in the end-of-the-century transformation of our political rhetoric—the tide of profanity. We see the onset of bawdy words and sassy tones, easily and casually spoken, and recorded in full and correct realism—or, when absolutely necessary and under editorial duress, marked revealingly as deleted or amended expletives. Two-sentence paragraphs with three-word phrases may, in future perorations, be giving way to four-letter words. P— or f*** off are already synonyms of sorts for *ave atque vale*. But the alien invasion of asterisks, dots, and hyphens—and other underground techniques of participatory obscenity—I leave to a later place in this book.

6

Life-Style Crosses the Ocean and Returns

Translating Alfred Adler

Our times have witnessed a democratization of cultural life, ranging from the mass extension of education for the millions to the paperback publishing revolution. As a consequence there has been a certain expansion of the vocabulary available to both the writers and the readers of newspapers which are classified as being written in something approaching standard prose. Whether or not real educational standards have risen (as a few claim) or genuine literacy has declined (as others bitterly argue), there has emerged a "new world of wordes."* We can read in the morning edition of our favorite paper a whole host of hitherto recondite references—to "Kafkaesque" doings at the U.N. and other political bureaucracies; to a Washington administration's "paradigms" of political power; to the "charisma" of outstanding public figures; to "Proustian" elements in the remembrance of recent tragic European events; to "existentialist" or, latterly, "post-modernist" or "structuralist" trends in New York café society controversies.

As for "paradigm," such high-falutin' words do not soar for very long. They are overweight, and are taken lightly, for all their pretentiousness, only by the jokesters who write newspaper headlines who swiftly get to work in order to puncture them. Over an important *Wall Street Journal* story of the collapse of U.N. policy in Cambodia as factional civil war broke out (in July 1997), the front-page headline read,

---

*   This is one of history's "eternal recurrences." My reference in quotation marks is to John Florio's *A World of Wordes* (1598) and his revised edition, *New World of Words* (1611). There is also, before the century is out, a new *New World of Words* (1696). And so on through the centuries as the dictionaries grow ever thicker, more substantial.

PARADIGM LOST[1]

I have also heard a jingle which runs to the refrain, "*O brother, can you spare a paradigm?...*" Between such desperate puns, the normal shelf-life of a vogue word is reduced to a mere long weekend.

Some current coinages come and go; popularized by book titles or chic phrase-makers on stage or screen with a snippet from a song or an ad jingle, they are *en vogue* for a season and get quickly displaced. Highbrow literature constantly rallies to replenish lowbrow demotic. Marx's "dialectic" and "ideology" give way to Dr. Marcuse's "repressive tolerance" and Dr. Fromm's "alienation" which, in turn, become old-fashioned and fall into obsolescence.

Yet some concepts, borrowed for populistic purposes from our intellectual life, have more than passing significance and serve in our newspaper culture— more than that, in society at large—in fundamental and revealing ways. Can it be an accident that they emerge in the way they did? One surely wouldn't wager that abstruse, if relatively well-known, phrases like "negative capability" (Keats, as used by T.S. Eliot)—or any one of a half-dozen philosophical phrases (as used by Heidegger or Popper, Sartre or Wittgenstein)—would ever catch on. Still, two technical terms in academic disciplines of several generations ago have indeed proved contagious—*culture* from the professors of anthropology, and *life-style* from the doctors of psychology; and I will be paying special attention to their phenomenal linguistic career to the extent that they have shaped, colored, or otherwise transformed the language of journalism.

I am not necessarily implying in all or any of the above (or below) that a casual tone in journalese is impermissible, nor that, in the attempt to be more mature (or at least sound half-way cultivated or educated), the journalistic expropriation of an academic intellectual concept can only be inexcusably superficial. "Culture" (to which I will address myself subsequently) is a prime example. All characteristics of behavior, no matter how scantily registered in newspaper reportage, can be useful—"in the last analysis"—to the most profound case study. Moreover, thoughtful journalists often use vogue words with a self-conscious touch of irony, a sense of stylistic distance of their own, which contributes to cracking or breaking up the stereotypes just a little.

Thus, in the usual course of contemplating the fatuity of the court claim of poor Maya Flick (the former wife of the immensely rich Mick Flick, who says she cannot live on her divorce settlement of £9 million), Ms. Minette Marrin, a bright Sunday columnist in London, is careful not to be so unfeeling as to call her greedy, or a typical product of our acquisitive society, a.k.a. our culture of avarice. She avows that we are dealing here with identity, with self-esteem, and with something called the "social role of valorisation." In fact the former Mrs. Flick argues herself that it is not just the loss of income but of a "life-style" that has driven her to sue: "The children are used to life-styles. I am used to a life-style." These include, we learn, elegant weekly dinners for twelve, maintaining a Labrador at a cost of £4,000, a smart nanny at £25,000 a year, and other such stylish expenditures, which all go to support the claim for a revised divorce settlement of the inadequate previous sum. I imagine Alfred Adler (and indeed his sometime translator, Nigel Dennis) would have responded to all these clinical details with a smile of *Schadenfreude*, and surely would have agreed with Ms. Marrin's shrewd one-liner of a conclusion: "And the loss of a life-style, for the very rich, is the loss of a self-style, and in the end perhaps of a self."[2]

Nigel Dennis used to be one of Alfred Adler's translators; when he co-edited *Encounter* with me in the1970s he once told me that his book, *Cards of Identity* (1955)—a brilliant, if neglected novel—was written completely "in the spirit of Adler." His cards of identity could have been cards of life-styles: for the idea was that every personality is a self-constructed fiction and "what marvelous ingenuity went into the fabrication of selves." Thus, this Adlerian masterpiece is "a novel of characters who are their own novels." (This is what sometimes happens when we live in a culture of subtlety.)*

In its subsequent adjustment to the American way of life, "life-style" had among its other verbal virtues proved capable of trans-continental accommodation, fitting itself with panache into the world of chic (with its fashions in furniture, food, and fun) and into even more permanent things. It struck me as a kind of ultimate achievement when it went on to impinge on the writing of obituaries, in a sort of triumph of death-style. When the *Los Angeles Times* reported the passing at fifty-three of one of its ablest correspondents—he had last specialized in reporting "the demise of communism in Eastern Europe"—it noted that this assignment had capped his career as an observer with a sharp eye for the styles of life and death. The *L.A. Times* paid tribute to their man who "during more than two decades with the *Los Angeles Times*...wrote about a variety of changing lifestyles in Southern California, in New York, as Nairobi bureau chief and finally from Warsaw."[3]

It could be that life-style at its pulsating best has intimations of mortality.

"*Lebenstil*" was an attractive phrase coined by the psychologist Alfred Adler (1870-1937) who lived and worked in the USA in his years of exile from Hitler's Europe. The term was translated usefully, in the days of the wartime anti-Nazi emigration, as "the style of life" and then "life-style." It made its debut in the New York press, and subsequently became jargonized as in one "whimsical" newspaper headline—"The *Life-style* of Some Favorite Inhabitants of the Zoo" (*New York Times*, 5 April 1967, p. 41, my italics). In the postwar days of the so-called Americanization of Germany, it returned across

---

* See Nigel Dennis' article, "Alfred Adler and the Style of Life," in *Encounter*, August 1970, and Heinz L. Ansbacher, editor of Adler's writings in German: "Life Style: A Historical and Systematic Review," in *Journal for Individual Psychology* 23 (1967), pp. 191-212.

the ocean to become a West German buzzword in a thousand contexts. The re-export was not in its Adlerian original form—which was in German—but as "lifestyle"..in English! Life-style had crossed the ocean, toured the States, and came back as an alien with a foreign passport. These are the perils of catch-phrases when they travel.

It would not be amiss to add here a remark about the nature of the differ-ence when words emigrate and acculturate, or otherwise betray the tell-tale symptoms and side-effects of *Wanderlust*.

In Adler's work the term *Lebensstil* first appeared in 1926, but he adapted it for his own psychological theories from earlier usages, most likely from the sociological writings of his great contemporary, Max Weber. (Weber used it to characterize social-collectivities, whereas with Adler it referred to an indi-vidual psychology.) One Adlerian explained the change with the analogy that "culture is to the larger group what life style is to the individual."

Adler's original phrase, *der Lebensstil*, was an ambitious concept and in-deed a profound theory—after all, he was competing with Freud and Jung—attempting to deal with the complexities of human personality. It encapsulated a psychological view of existence in which each individual is seen striving for a viable "style of life," inventing or re-creating him- or herself into a more or less viable *Lebensstil*, although often failing distressingly. The buzzword in our own time, whether used in English or in up-to-the-minute German or vice versa, was a rather more humdrum tag as in: "remembering the *Lebensstil* of the hippies" or: "*das life-style im amerikanischen Suburbia*." It was middle-brow slang, and referred to what Adler (and all the other doctors of the uncon-scious soul) would take to be the most outward attributes, inessential and doubt-less superficial—the cut of one's clothes or one's hair, the tunes one hummed and the catch-words that caught one's fancy, the problems of suburban com-muting.

Dr. Ansbacher, the editor of Alfred Adler's writings, registers the curious fact that probably the very first usage was in 1811, and it occurs in an English translation of a book by an obscure nineteenth-century German author named Adlerjung (sic)—thus linking, by an outlandish coincidence, not only the two languages but two of the Founding Fathers in our story of a phrase which has become a buzzword in at least two "newspaper cultures." But these serious distinctions pertain to days gone by. When both terms become vulgarized and trivialized as catch-words, the phrase-mongering grows wild and irrepress-ible.

After Adler, its circulation was stimulated by the writings of Talcott Par-sons, Erik Erikson, among many others. In some of their theories "life-style" became pigeon-holed in various clinical categories before moving out into the big time: "obsessive-compulsive life-style, paranoid hysterical life-style, im-pulsive life-style," and so on. In all of these, the linkage is, mostly, to sexual behavior. Whole books went on to link in similar fashion other forms of life-style behavior to masochism, fanaticism, and greed, to crime and to everyday patterns of buying and selling in a consumer society.

The end is nigh: as one psychology professor has written, quite humorlessly, "Finally, people will grow old and face death in accordance with their life styles." But others saw the joke in life-styles shaping death-styles; and burial rites became—with Evelyn Waugh, with Jessica Mitford—a subject for irony, sarcasm, and even lively social protest.

In good times it became yet another phraseological pigeonhole in which to cram higgledy-piggledy any newsworthy items in the way of obituary drama, funereal surprises, and post-mortem angles. "Life-style" which began in the *Times* in a story about monkeys in the Bronx Zoo (1967) now winds up, also in the *Times*, in a banner headline (1997) about—

THE DEATHSTYLES OF THE RICH AND FAMOUS[4]

The real estate magnate, Harry Helmsley, had just died at the age of eighty-seven, and had just been buried in a gigantic and very expensive mausoleum in the Bronx's Woodlawn cemetery. The *Times'* obit prompted one intellectually curious New York reporter to ponder burial rites over the centuries from the Egyptian Pharaohs to Frank Woolworth (who had two sphinxes imported to guard his grave) and the Vanderbilts (who made an exact copy of "a twelfth-century chapel in Arles, France"). What ever could be "the basic allure of a luxurious grave"? Why this "scramble for eternal status"? Is it merely, in the *Times'* own phrase, "to leave an impressive impression"? With this bit of word-play we leave the *New York Times*, and its mortal readership (not all necessarily rich and famous) touchingly puzzled by one of the profoundest issues in the morning's news: "But why do people pay lip-service to spiritual fulfillment and then pay through the nose to save their material remains?" Newspapers are there to print the news, but they try hard on occasion to answer all the stylish questions of the moment about life and death.

"Deathstyle" as an expression is basically a pun; "Lifestyle" as a theoretical construct is also very weak and wobbly, and could hardly convince anybody whose life-style included having occasional second thoughts. For Alfred Adler it was (1) "consistent," (2) "constant," (3) "causal." But what of lives which are demonstrably contradictory (and conspicuously unstable)? Could, then, the consistency consist of being contradictory...and the constancy in being inconstant? As for causality, a famous American economist who used the term as an analytical tool for his manpower studies remarked that "even sexual behavior depends on the values men live by" (i.e., their way of life, their life-style). But, then, on what does the choice of values depend? Especially in the case of cynics, skeptics, nihilists and others who do not value values![5]

Adler and his followers were lucky in their *Leitbild*—the predecessor of *Lebensstil* in their technical vocabulary—which achieved semantic immortality; for it is rare that felicitous words emerge from the thickets of academic jargon into the light of day. The notable exceptions are, of course, Freud and Jung, for they were good writers and skillful phrase-makers. Max Weber's followers gave us "role-model"; Keynesian economists "multiplier effect"; and C. Wright Mills' sociology "the power structure." But think of the Mode-of-Being School which comes up with "Existence differentiates itself in various modes-of-existence....Each mode-of-existence integrates various modalities-of-existence such as perceiving, feeling, touching, and thinking."[6] A half-dozen words, all straining for modishness, but clogged down by frail hyphens too anaemic to hold catch-phrases together.

No, the newspaper culture has reasons to be grateful: some academics perceived, felt, touched and thought a little better than the others.

Transatlantic Variations

Fast ocean liners, to the deep regret of transatlantic travellers, no longer cross the ocean in both directions; but linguistic crossovers help to turn the great old barrier between America and Europe into a little lake, even a pond. There is in some semantic sector—usually the vocabulary of pop (and the "youth culture" generally)—instant transportation. What Manhattan coins as new buzzwords lands safely before the season is out in the old-world boroughs of Paris and Berlin and is daily passed on in the French and German newspapers as legitimate currency. Even as legal tender it takes some time for the transported words to get their land-legs, and they are often observed to have a sea-sick wobble.

But, as we have seen in the prime and pioneering examples of *Kultur* and *avant-garde* and *Lebensstil*, the ocean-crossings seem to be compulsive, if not compulsory. There is always the continental option for the Anglo-American words to go native, to get a proper translated equivalent. (The French-Canadians in Quebec even make it a legal requirement.) The sinister experiences, however, of the German as well as the Italian language under totalitarian control have tilted the linguistic game away from nationalism to a free and easy acceptance of foreign formulas. Mussolini's hidebound attempt to get the Italians (and all the tourists) to refer to a hotel as an *Albergo* and Hitler's effort to replace telephone with *Fernsprecher*—among other futile chauvinistic measures to resist linguistic incursions from abroad—have left postwar semantics open and receptive.

In German, for example, the jazz world has taken its revenge (the *Führer* had forbidden "nasty nigger music") by dancing and singing almost exclusively in Anglo-American in-lingo. The disc jockeys are known as that; and if not, in the abbreviation DJ (pronounced by some *deejay*, by others in the local German phonetics, day-yutt). Their latest influence over what hits make the uppermost best-sellers "on the charts" is necessarily explained in English by the *Frankfurter Allgemeine Zeitung*—which, when it has a choice, prefers to translate and use a traditional German style (except in the case of profanities and obscenities which sound better in a second language). It is called "*scratching*," a technique which amounts to re-composing rock numbers by needle-damaging them. It has so fascinated pop devotees on the German scene that a full-length book has recently been published in Hamburg on "DJ-Culture." The *FAZ* review of it put it into context of "*Popkultur,*" domesticating that ancient Teutonic verbal icon, *Kultur;* it made indigenous adaptations from the wilder American usages, but respectfully left the latest culture of the disc-jockeys in its original English phrase. The K-word has been having to share power with its foreign allies.[7]

The newspaper reader's simple litmus-paper test of the efficacy of a buzzword is the naive question: How did we ever get along without it? What did we ever say before we had the bright phonetic idea of combining those two desirable goods in our modern consumer culture (both available in large economy sizes): "life" and "style"? The combination, at first hyphenated and then re-packaged for and by itself, is irresistible. What could rival its user-seductiveness? And it comes in various shapes and colors—even, when the metaphorical imperative runs a little wild, emerges in "clusters," as in this *New York Times* dispatch:

WASHINGTON.—Dick Morris once said that every time Bill Clinton had a problem, he got a poll in his head.

In 1995, worried that the Clintons last vacation sailing with Jackie O. at Martha's Vineyard had not been suitably populist, Mr. Morris recommended that the president go on a mountain vacation with high-tech gear. A White House poll on "lifestyle clusters" had shown that swing voters liked camping, hiking, and technology.

Needless to say, the president dutifully obeyed the laws of "lifestyle clusters" and went camping and hiking in a national park. In vain. He was reported to be "grumpy afterward," for it was "the first vacation I've taken that didn't help me in the polls."[8] It could be that the choice of the Far Western national park was not quite politically correct, or even indeed that lifestyles do not in fact "cluster" or, at least, are not known to get together to form representative samples.

Whatever the explanation, we are left with the question: What has the expressive phrase within itself that gives it energy, resonance, and general congeniality? Life is not necessarily good, and styles can be egregiously bad. Nevertheless, it has (as one popular grammarian put it) "a certain oomph" (which only served him to open up yet another etymological problem).* Fowler/ Burchfield mildly disapproves of lifestyle but gives the word credit for its speedy success, its adaptable generality, and (in contrast to other phrases currently *en vogue*) its likely survivability in high or standard usage. For now it is clearly having a very good run of things, equipped as it is with that element of universally recognized "plastic" which enables it, on presentation, to be ticketed and fly anywhere.

Great words, like good wines, lose very much in long journeys. "*Angst*," for another example, lost its tang on the way to other shores. It too has been assimilated and given transatlantic citizenship. As a buzzword in English— pronounced with a broad and lower-case *ae*—it is a gelatin-like thing that makes vaguely sad reference to worrisome concerns and fears. The original is closer to deep-seated terror, to dread and anxiety (and W.H. Auden tried to suggest this in his poem of 1948, entitled "The Age of Anxiety").

It is a long way from the Vienna of Freud's *Angst* and Adler's *Lebensstil* to America's eastern élite coastline, to the newspeak of the *Washington Post* which had the snappy idea of naming what was to become its most popular newspaper supplement "Style." The pleonastic "Life-" has been usefully omitted. (Who could be interested in Death-Style except some morbid furr'iners like Evelyn Waugh and Jessica Mitford and, lately, Manhattan obit writers?) The *Washington Post* supplement, catering to affluent élites who live stylish lives, has dealt engagingly for thirty years now with the very latest, from trendy fashions in local boutiques to tasty innovations in ethnic cuisine. The *Sunday Times* publishes in London a similar separate section entitled "The Culture" (subsequently adding to it a supplement called "Style"). Trying to keep up with the competition, the *Observer* calls one of its color-magazine supplements: *Life* (presumably violating the Henry Luce copyright), and its special feature therein is captioned: "Lifestyle." The combinations are exhausted. The circle is closed.

And yet, and yet.... The buzzword has had the good fortune to have yet another lease of life, and its current career as a "life-style culture" I will be treating in a subsequent chapter.**

Insuring for All Risks

Some characters who have emerged famously in the newspapers as celebrities appear to be all style and no content. The public relations men of the pop-cultural world are among the great persuaders of our time, and our press obliges us with an endless gallery of portraits of pop stars who, had not certain ani-

---

*   "Oomph," *Oxford Modern Slang* (1992), p. 156: "sex appeal, attractiveness, energy." Jonothan Green, *The Slang Thesaurus* (1986), p. 9, 69, 80: "bang, bounce, flash, pep, piss, pizzazz, punch, snap, socko, steam, wollop, zap, zing, zowie...."
* *   See "The Culture of Life-Style" in volume three.

mating phrases been invented, wouldn't even exist. Here is a certain Bob Brozman: "a singer and a guitarist who incorporates a master's degree in ethnomusicology into his act and lifestyle."[9] His act is, evidently, a result of "how technology affects the transmission of musical culture." But he is not an uncritical acquiescent product of that transmission belt since he is convinced that "our culture gets more and more superficial." Fortunately there are still some escape hatches through which he has squeezed his own life-style: a reclusive farm-house in California, with wife and daughter, remembering "the vintage guitar world" (i.e., a time for gigs before the coming of loud and noisy electric resonators). There are also "cultural traps," and he has constantly to be concerned about Hawaiian music, his specialty; for, after all, the Hawaiians had learned about the guitar from the Mexicans who were imported to work the ranches. His studies in "ethno-musicology" led him to the conclusion that "Hawaiians were, basically, playing the blues of the Pacific." Of which anomaly he is perceptive enough to remark, "This is the sort of thing that can happen when two cultures collide." If that's the only sort of thing that can happen in such a cosmic collision, all our life-styles are pretty much safe for a while yet.

But for how long? Only the insurance companies can know, calculating as carefully as they can with the probabilities of personal accident and medical attention. They have been studying life and death for a long time now, but never so resourcefully as under the aspect (by now it has become almost the totality) of the life-style, which category takes pride of place in their actuarial tables. They have, for example, factored into insurance policy applications not merely the relevant information about cigarette smoking, alcoholism, good and bad cholesterol, etc., but whether sporting activities are, or are not, a feature of the applicant's style of life. An enterprising American insurer, Indianapolis Life, has offered heavily discounted policies to "anyone who can prove they have completed a full or half-marathon within the past six months." The Sun Alliance offers a 12.5 percent discount for people who fall within its "healthy living criteria." A set or two of tennis, a dozen strokes in the neighborhood swimming-pool, or a bit of an early morning jog, will *not* do! You've got to be into the *whole* life-style, a factor half-magical half-mathematical, which can indeed convert the debilitating rat-race into a classical marathon:

> Their actuaries reckon that if people are fit enough to compete in such events, they must also have lifestyles healthy enough to reduce the risk of death—and they want to extend the cheap premiums on offer to competitors in other sports.[10]

Life-style will keep you *in* and protected; a death-style will keep you *out*, or have you paying as much as your life is worth. It's rapidly becoming a buyer's market if you can offer "a sporting life-style."

To be sure, the evidence correlating sports and other forms of strenuous exercise to life-span is a moot question among longevity experts. But the insurance companies are ready to take a risk, and already a good many American golf clubhouses display advertising about what discounts can be had for a "healthy life-style." I am told that they even cover against the cost of a round of drinks that follow a hole-in-one.

There is something poetical, even mystical, to all this; but then Franz Kafka and Wallace Stevens didn't work in insurance companies for nothing. Novelists and poets can claim to have their own life-styles, but they are not likely to be eligible for discounts. Still, the insurance culture might be persuaded to accept D.H. Lawrence's maxim that "one sheds one's sicknesses in books." If true, then the life-style of the literati can have an effect, if not on immortality, but on shelling out a little less for living a little bit longer. Invest in life-styles, it will pay off.

If "life-style" has to do with low-strumming guitars, and their cultural and technological implication, it has also to do with telephone calls—with making many (hundreds, maybe), or making just a few (nothing obsessive, really) as in the case of Princess Diana who had been reported to have been ringing one lover or another in desperate efforts to get in touch. Her Royal Highness (as she then was) denied this. As she said in her famous BBC interview (in November 1995), "No, I didn't, I didn't. But that again was a huge move to discredit me, and very nearly did me in, the injustice of it...." About those so-called "nuisance phone calls" (letting the number ring and ring, and then hanging up), she explained,

> I was reputed to have made 300 telephone calls in a very short space of time which, bearing in mind my lifestyle* at that time, made me a very busy lady.... I used to, yes, I had rung up, yes... a few times, but certainly not in an obsessive manner.[11]

Certain life-styles can insure one—yes, protect one—against nuisances and their obsessions.

Making a Meal of It.

Is there anybody now alive who doesn't have a life-style? The rich certainly have it, with their notorious exhibition of conspicuous consumption. Their lives have "texture, light, scale and color." Or so we are instructed by

---

*   The easy-going English charm of the old stolid Adlerian phrase didn't here make it quite back to Germany. In the German text as printed in the *Bild Zeitung* (22 Nov. 1995, p. 6), the translator avoids the re-translatese of "Lebensstil" and misses out on the bearable lightness of the Princess' less than candid reply. The *Bild*'s rendering makes it into a rather more pompous excuse of having to look after all her duties ("*Ich musste doch auch meine Pflichten als Prinzessin von Wales noch erfuellen*").

In English, the quote is snippety, hence charming; in German, it suggests the earnestness of a dutiful daughter, hence perhaps also winning, in its way, but only for an earnest heavier readership. Still, Diana was exceedingly popular in Germany.

Ms. Cheryl MacLachlan, who is introduced to us as "an American who spent a lot of time in Europe"—as the American editor of *Esquire* magazine in Paris, she has made "many side-trips to Milan" and even to London. According to an admiring reporter (Ms. Laura Colby, in the *International Herald-Tribune*), she has published a number of knowledgeable books which "aspired to re-create the charming home life she experienced there [in the Old World] back in the States."

The first and most successful was entitled *Bringing France Home* (1995), and the home-making reader is assured that "you learn quite a bit about French culture—the closeness of the chairs, for instance, shows the importance conversation has in the country's family and social life."[12] You also learn, we might conclude, quite a bit about America, at least Ms. MacLachlan's America; for she is one of those eternal Jamesian transatlantic heroines who, for more than a century now, have always to learn for the first time "what Maisie knew" and what disoriented Isabel Archer. She confesses, with the freshness of a bottom carbon-copy:

I fell in love with Europe. Every time I returned to New York, I would be depressed for a couple of days. There is a certain texture to life in Europe that's missing in the United States.

Thanks to her efforts America will be having it better, for her second volume brings Italy home ("Italians don't cover everything with fabrics, the floors are often left bare"), and her third book deals with Sweden ("Ikea with a touch of 18th-century elegance inspired under King Gustav III").

Here the transatlantic quest—which began with a longing for a new world with its hope for utopia and a prospect of gold—is confined to a glimpse of "a gracious life-style." One is looking for "right angles, clean lines, and always the feeling for space..." Especially the latter, since it produces "very distinct silhouettes." As Peter Schlemihl came to realize, shadow is all.

Which raises the awkward question whether there can be any "life-style" among the poor. The down-trodden and oppressed—presumably among the Gatzes until Jay, the Great Gatsby, created a Long Island life-style with "texture" and "over-scale objects"—have no life (as we all know, deep down in our troubled social consciences), and, accordingly, can have no style. This, semantically, is the goal-difference in the current league tables between those migrant Teutonisms, *Kultur* and *Lebensstil*. Among the poor there can be a "culture of poverty...of despair...of crowded angles," far from the graciousness and spaciousness of the rich who are so different. The culture concept is more flexible, less confining than life-style which still has—as culture used to have—a built-in class prejudice. In a new world order, embracing the developing third world, the poor will be getting themselves a life, and the life, in turn, will get itself a style, and—who knows?—perhaps we will get to be "bringing home" the new texture of light, scale, and color in what was deepest Asia and darkest Africa.

As little as she may realize it, Cheryl MacLachlan has helped to bring home to us the tragedy of *Lebensstil*, of a life-style divided against itself. Humankind is separated by "diaphanous curtains." But: comes the chic revolution we will all be free and equal and affirmative under the elegant laws of life-style, guaranteeing above all each person's right to space and grace. More than even that (as Ms. MacLachlan puts it cryptically), "Nothing should ever be left white by default." In the end, since one buzzword deserves another, we will be destined to enjoy a multi-colored life-style culture.

What used to be conveniently departmentalized in newspaper supplements and magazines which were conventionally devoted to Homes and Gardens and suchlike, is now embraced in an integrated, organic, interpenetrated creation of modern design. It not only includes the old central pieces—a flowering indoor plant, a Chinese wall scroll, a pre-Columbian mask, etc.—but puts at the very heart of the new chic that which used to be the household routine of rather peripheral items.

Such as paint. Only yesterday a prospering U.S. company like Sherwin-Williams could supply a whole nation of do-it-yourself house-painters with Deluxe-glo colors that would keep suburban life up-with-the-Joneses. Today there is new luster and luminescence available, and at the moment there is cutthroat competition between somebody called Martha Stewart (who invented a distinctive national post-Freudian emotion called "paint envy") and the Ralph Lauren groups (who simply refer to the products, now selling in the millions, as "designer paints"). In any case the *Newsweek* headline in its section on "Society & the Arts" (6 January 1996, p. 50) read,

> *"Martha and Ralph Don't Just Paint—*
> *It's a Major Lifestyle Fetish!"*

Evidently, so far as I have learned, the colors are redolent—truly resplendent walls even have a visceral impact, sometimes "feeling softer than any baby's skin you've ever felt, enjoyable," certainly "more beautiful than stone." At the moment there is still a "Yuppie porn" quality to the naming of the fancy finishes; and surely Alfred Adler (and even Nigel Dennis) would have been mildly bewildered by "Crested Butte... Porch Awning... Dressage Red...Spinaker Blue...." But since, as the designers insist, "the new paint fetishism, after all, is about lifestyle and philosophy" there have been serious intellectual efforts to give a certain dignity and coherence to Lauren's "400 snootily named colors." *Newsweek* tells us "Lauren's 400 colors are grouped by lifestyle (Thoroughbred, Country, Santa Fe and Sport)...." One or two more, it is hinted, may be added by next spring. A lifestyle, like life itself, can always be made more beautiful.[13]

Still, for now, all that is life-style glistens like gold, for the pursuit of such happiness is at the moment confined to the rich; and only in America are the rich so free as to enjoy such a wide choice, as if they were the sole heirs and heiresses to all that was brilliant in millennia of life-style cultures.

The *Washington Post* makes the effort to keep the capital city at the center of what it calls "couture-level interior design." The paper even has a special "home & design editor," a Ms. Linda Hales (at the time of writing), and we will be returning to her in a moment. The journalistic specialty has a special difficulty; and it lies, obviously, in the devious differences between haute couture (covered by fashion-watchers in Paris) and the complications (from real estate to fixtures in the kitchen) of doing up an English manor house in Virginia or a French chateau in Maryland. The latest fashions in dresses that one is supposed to wear can be short and frilly or long and plain (or vice versa). As I have lamented before, the limitation of hemlines going up or down (except for the promise of Hong Kong split-skirts) accentuates the fact that the scope of the vertical arts is still very restricted as compared to the extensiveness of a horizontal culture where the inspiration can be global, ranging as far East or West as the traffic will bear. Old China and all the Oriental points en route are often favored. Northern and Southern Europe, as we have just seen, can be held up for imitation, occasionally alternating with the bamboo cultures of the South Pacific or the wagon-train America of the Wild West.

Family houses are serious affairs; they are lived in, almost every day and night. (Even if one French stylist has complained of doing up grand kitchens with every conceivable gadget...and nothing ever gets cooked.) Haute couture gowns are different. Who was ever seen wearing a "Versace" before Gianni Versace was brutally murdered in Florida? Who was ever caught out flouncing a Vivienne Westwood at even the fanciest of fancy balls? Couture-level interior designers, not unlike great chefs who do haute cuisine, have it better. They have the whole world as their oyster, and the pearls therein last longer than a season.

So, then, what does Ms. Linda Hales tell us in the *Post* about what is inspiring awe and admiration in style-conscious Americans? So many are eager (and cash-capable) of building their dream house, doing up their castle in the sky. (The reader, as I warned, must be prepared for "the sociology" of furniture-fittings, and even for "the aesthetic" of keeping-pets-in-the-house, among other complexities.)

Washington.—Back in the '80s, when Wall Street hit its stride, Americans of means dressed their houses to look like an English aristocrat's crumbling country estate. They overcame a lack of centuries-old architecture by glazing walls, lavishing faded chintz on down-stuffed sofas, lining up instant collections of Chinese Export porcelain and allowing dogs everywhere (real ones on the floor, imitations on needlepoint pillows, china for the mantel and oil paintings on the walls).

We have already been alerted for a surprise, a change of vast cultural proportions, by the four-column headline,

FORGET CHINTZ, THIS YEAR IT'S PROVENCE

The news from the *Washington Post* is, you see, that style-conscious Americans have transferred their gaze to sunnier climes; and it is the French country house, not the drafty English one, that inspires the theory of our leisure class:

> Colorful Provençal cottons brighten suburban breakfast bars. Tract mansion bedrooms are plumped up with pillows of toile de Jouy. Televisions peek from 19th-century armoires converted to entertainment centers. Prized French limestone, ironwork and baskets are transforming the all-important family room into a cocoon of casual elegance.

If the historic importance of this phenomenon might be escaping some readers, stumped on many an appellation of French fineries, there is reinforcement by a good local quote, an observation from Sally McCormick McConnell (a founder of *French Country Living*, a furnishing store in the affluent suburb of Great Falls, Virginia): "It reflects a shift we see in our lifestyles."

We had better believe it. For the overall U.S. market for home furnishings has been estimated at $64 billion in a prospering economy, and Sally McC. McC. suspects that "the hunger for things of a French country nature could reach $3 billion." Indeed the swing of the style pendulum could make a few storekeepers rich enough to own a Provençal farmhouse of their own.

It all depends now on who—"in the face-off between fans of George III and updated Louis XIV"—is likely to win the cultural war. One report from the front, as the *Post* correspondent records, was "headline grabbing"; for a Parisian big-gun named Jacques Grange was being so effective that he had "made the salon of French manor house or a Parisian apartment seem like the place to be." If this discovery—the place to be—gave a new meaning to the positions of Sartrean existentialism, history provided an even more important lesson for the style of being: "Mix periods as if you'd had the good fortune to inherit it all." Could it be that "this kind of intellectualizing" might well endanger the whole movement? French designers sense the closeness of nothingness and being. They concede that their life-style "can lead to a wonderfully personal space or be a license for chaos...." Hostile agents whisper about "the influence of Rimbaud"—on, for example, a notorious design of a space, dark and brown, featuring a few eccentric furnishings (including a gigantic winged bathtub)—with the purple explanation, in verse, "It is as if the wind of poetry had shattered a room."[14]

And, naturally, life-style must also extend to real estate:

> He's building what he calls "boutique hotels" in Miami Beach and Jamaica. He [Chris Blackwell] travels to West Africa to buy materials to cover the floors and walls and such. He wants to create a "lifestyle collection of tiny hotels"—small properties with appropriate technology like central accounting, marketing, reservations and management; but "each with its own personality."[15]

It was a strange wind that blew Adler's *Lebensstil* from the counsels on the meaning of life to a dark, brown room with hardly anything in it. Freud and Jung who had both kept a watchful eye on Alfred Adler and on French affairs might have made something of it.

I am afraid that newspaper stylists are not the only culpable sector of the literati responsible for the inflation of the current usage of life-style and, ultimately, the deflation of the meaningful original usefulness. Even the scholars among the classical linguists—lexicographers who should know better (but, perhaps, because of that)—stoop to flirting demurely with the tired demotic. I note that the distinguished Cambridge University Press's so-called "Encyclopedist," while professing his devotion to "the power, range and beauty of the [English] language to express new orders of meaning," recommends a journal called *English Today* (*ET*) in the following way:

> For anyone who wishes to maintain a healthy English language lifestyle, I prescribe the reading of *ET* three times a day after meals."*

In some dismay, I am tempted likewise to prescribe that, preferably before meals, one should try to restrain the appetite for vapid and insipid chic buzzwords. The health of the language can only suffer from the widespread gluttony for sweet and fatty phrases.

---

*   David Crystal, *The Cambridge Encyclopedia of the English Language* (1995), pp. vi–vii.

7

Teutonics, or Refighting World War II

Accent of the Positive

I would have thought it by now to be a non-story: the lingering Franconian inflection of Dr. Henry Kissinger's vaguely guttural accent in English. But no; his recent publication of a new book, a huge tome on *"Diplomacy,"* elicited old-time anti-Teutonic cracks in the Washington press corps, as if it heralded some new crisis in German-American relations. The former Fürth-born U.S. secretary of state left Hitler's Germany in 1938 as a teenage refugee; but never, for all his years in Harvard, managed to lose his tell-tale trace of an accent. It continues to be "heavy," reported the *Washington Post* recently, and quoted him as philosophizing about *"de end of de Secund Wuhld Wuhr."*

But still it was all in the spirit of good fun. In the history of the German accent in America we have long since entered the peaceful postwar era, at least if you can take a little friendly joke. A great turning-point in the armistice process was that very popular California *"Laugh-In"* TV-show wherein every week (in the 1970s) a tiny fellow wearing a large *Wehrmacht* helmet peeked out of his look-out bush and intoned this cryptic comment: *"Vehrry Inntahrestingh."* Even the stereotyped SS-character in Gestapo-style leather jacket became a Monty Python comic character, always threatening *"Vee haff vayz uff mehking yoo tukk!"*

But the recent reports of Brecht by the (East) Berliner Ensemble seems to be threatening a new *"Ossie"* phase of hostilities. Bert Brecht always flaunted his theory of *"Verfremdung,"* and, sure enough, a bit of alienation is setting in. The London reception of Vanessa Redgrave's recent attempt to put on a show called "Brecht in Hollywood" was cool, critical, caustic, positively *"Wessie"* in its hostility. Brechtian veteran Ekkehard Schall (who was the Master's son-in-law) was cruelly dismissed as speaking "incomprehensible English," and the *Frankfurter Allgemeine Zeitung*'s own London critic, Gina Thomas, recorded that he had absolutely ruined the drama of *Galileo* with "a caricature of a German accent." Even the gifted Vanessa Redgrave, trying out her schoolgirl German in renditions of the Brecht-Weill songs (presumably the notes came out even worse than the words), got some of the worst notices of her life.

Now for the good news. Not since the word *Blitzkrieg* bombed itself into the English vocabulary has there been such a linguistic victory. The U.S. Vice President Al Gore has been preaching the future of something he called, a bit ponderously, "Information Superhighways" and not even the abbreviated catchphrase "info-way" could catch on. Then we were instructed on the authority of the *Herald Tribune*'s William Safire, that seismically subtle semanticist, that it was a Teutonized version of the word which was currently being used: "*Infobahn*"! Should it catch on, it will be joining the handful of "Anglicized" words like *Zeitgeist* and *Schadenfreude* and *Kindergarten*, as semantic success stories. Maybe they do have ways of making us talk.

World War II against the despised German enemy is being fought, and won, every weekend on British television as fifty-year-old films get repeated on the various channels and their late-night movie shows. Occasionally a news item makes the morning newspaper which suggests that the battle is still raging, if with cooler emotions. Thus, a startling report had it that

> The ME-109, scourge of RAF crews throughout the Second World War, has just claimed its latest victim—more than 50 years after the Battle of Britain. A ground crewman at Duxford Airfield in Cambridgeshire has achieved the dubious distinction of being the first Briton to be injured by a Messerschmitt in half a century.

If the curious and unfortunate incident put one in mind of those Pacific island tales where dazed Japanese soldiers, decades after General Douglas MacArthur's famous island-hopping victories, stumbled out of their hiding-places, armed to the teeth and ready to resist, then perish the thought. It was sheer accident as an English crewman, misjudging the aero-dynamics of the Imperial War Museum's specimen being given a routine display flight, was blown away by the roaring Daimler-Benz engines. A newsworthy mishap?—only if the reporter wrote his story as if it were a continuing drama of wartime tragedies, thus,

LUFTWAFFE CLAIMS FIRST BRITISH VICTIM IN 50 YEARS

The casualty amounted to "proof that old German fighter planes never really change...." This could not have been intended seriously, for there were at present a thousand German fighter-planes flying in NATO formations alongside their British RAF allies. Yet even a journalistic playfulness takes on the colors of the familiar deep-seated prejudice, and it gets marked down on the scorecard

of sensitive German observers as yet another cross-channel obstacle, even if
they should've taken it as a journalistic joke:

> Those who believe machinery can have a soul might reflect on the humiliations
> suffered by the 53-year-old plane. Captured by the British when its airfield was
> over-run in the Western Desert, it was shipped back to Britain, painted in RAF
> colours and flown against Spitfires and Hurricanes in vital evaluations exercises.
> Who can blame the Messerschmitt for wanting just once in its life to bite back?[1]

If the stereotypes are sticky enough, even whimsy comes to reinforce the
nasty old antipathies. American attitudes have a shorter shelf-life, and the canned
goods are usually staler: schoolboy resentments about learning a very foreign-
sounding language, old jokes ridiculing (à la Mark Twain) ponderous sentence-
structures. Such flights of anti-Germanism that can be registered in the U.S. press
are just that flighty, and only have local and passing political significance.

The ideological opposition to Pat Buchanan's candidacy for president in
the Republican primaries (in the spring of '96) mixed with, and contributed
to, preexisting ethnic hostilities: to the Irish, to the German. The former is
obvious: the man is of Irish ancestry, and there are Protestant and English
prejudices abroad in the land. But what has he to do with Germany? Nothing.
Still, when in his clever journalistic way Buchanan formulated something that
could be taken to be abstract, lofty, complex, or otherwise slightly puzzling,
he was said to be "speaking German." Germany was the land of metaphysics
and meaninglessness—everybody knew that, didn't they? There were some—
not many, but a few—voters who supported Buchanan, were attracted by his
style. One group was quoted as saying: "They like him—'but his speeches are
better in the original German'"[2] "Kidding the Kraut" was a shared transatlantic joke, a lingering irrepressible antipathy.

I keep a file of English clippings called "*Teutonics*" and, for a year or two,
surprisingly enough, it was beginning to bulge with Anglo-German good news.
The new atmosphere made even Goethe quotable in the popular British press.
One of those sophisticated lady columnists was going on (as is their wont)
about feminist matters, and then out of the blue came this warning signal (yet
again) of an historic cultural armistice: "Lady Thatcher was, and is 'all woman'.
I would go further. Lady Thatcher is what Goethe once called *Das Ewig
Weibliche*— roughly, the eternal woman."[3] I would also go further. Roughly, a
kind of Anglo-German peace appeared to have broken out. If Goethe, then can
Nietzsche or even Bismarck or *Der Alte Fritz* be far behind? If a spiteful hate-
the-Hun ex-prime minister, now Baroness in the House of Lords, can be drawn
into a Teutonic coupling, what fine hopes for a grand Europa-wide reconcili-
ation do loom! For a year or so we even enjoyed an Indian summer with a
young athlete named Jürgen Klinsmann. Could it be that only athletics, in
their best Olympic idealism, have ways of making us talk together?

Sport is the joy of the gods, as Homer knew; and perhaps a footballer from Stuttgart, playing in London for Tottenham Hotspurs, could add his divine touch to the struggle for a measure of fairness and tribal tolerance. He became in a year the most celebrated foreign star in the land; he scored goals and won games; he spoke fluent English and made jokes; he was liked, almost loved by the fans.

On Hating the Huns

The Klinsmann story of the summer of 1994, will, I surmise, take its place in the history of postwar Anglo-German relations. There have been other high-points before which were promptly, too hurriedly, taken to be turning points, only to be followed by yet another cycle of low-points.

I remember the euphoria in the young West German *Bundesrepublik* when the first president in Bonn was invited to travel to England to meet everybody in and around Buckingham Palace, and then the coldness when the old-fashioned scholarly gentleman named Theodor Heuss scolded the Oxford students for always keeping their hands ("how impolite can you get?") in their trouser pockets. Then the surprising successes of Wagnerian operas in Covent Garden re-extended friendly hands across the North Sea. Only to be followed by a series of scare stories about a revival of Nazism involving a whole host of characters from old General Remer to the young Franz-Joseph Strauss. This was in the 1950s.

The essential trouble in the ensuing decades was that both the BBC-TV and the ITV Channels kept broadcasting (and then replaying them on the late-night shows) the never-ending series of films about "England's finest hour" and Churchill's famous victory in World War II—with the Brits winning the war over the beastly Krauts every Wednesday and twice on weekends. To be sure, there were some small ameliorations in tone and temper in the popular series of English heroic escapes from German prisoner-of-war camps. Those miraculous scooped-out tunnels, even in Colditz! Those cunning breakouts during friendly soccer matches on the playing fields of the Stalag!

Slowly but surely the Wehrmacht commandants became sympathetic characters whose tragedy was that the Gestapo villains had more power. And then even the Gestapo developed human streaks—only to be outmaneuvered by the hateful SS who really ran the Stalag and had the criminal responsibility for doing our lads in. There were one or two other variations on the standard plot.

And then came a magnificent German piece of cinema, a filming of Lothar Buchheim's novel *Das Boot* (1978) which had the power and warm humanity of an earlier postwar film of Erich Maria Remarque's *All Quiet on the Western Front* (1931). One London film critic was moved to write that he had never realized that even those sinister automatons who ran that insidious U-Boat campaign against Allied ships were capable of fear, emotion, hysteria, cowardice, simple humanity.

And even this glowing moral high point did not survive the showings of Claude Lanzmann's overwhelming eight-hour documentary *Shoah* about Auschwitz—Chancellor Kohl's unfortunate visit (with the then-President Ronald Reagan) to the SS-graves at Bitburg—Steven Spielberg's heartrending *Schindler's List*—and other poignant reminders of an ineradicable evil that passeth all understanding.

Prejudices have long memories, and what appears to be dormant often awakens to wonted vigor and virulence. We can do little more than tally some of the ups and downs; but the scorecard is never finished until the last inning, the last whistle. The happy Klinsmann story in English football can only be a passing incident in a continuing free-for-all contest.

The game goes on, and the current state of play involves a souvenir, misplaced but unforgotten, from the World Championship Soccer victory in 1966 with the English national team defeating the Germans. There was a disputed last-second goal; it finalized the victory, but the coveted, historic orange football disappeared. On the occasion of the thirtieth anniversary, an aging German defender (Jürgen Haller) confessed that he had walked off with the "trophy"; and he was now returning it to its proper "owner," the English forward (Geoff Hurst) who had scored the third controversial goal that had beaten Germany. The London tabloid press had been searching for the kidnapped souvenir, demanding its return forthwith, offering generous rewards for finders or tipsters. Fleet Street columnists accused an insidious "enemy" of grave misdemeanors running all the way from unfair-play and bad sportsmanship to something close to a Neo-Nazi "postwar crime." The serious broadsheet press reported to its readers the progress of the quest, the heat of one tabloid's campaign and the coolness of another's counter-attack. As a matter of fact no less than eight bright orange footballs were offered, from all corners of the German *Bundesrepublik*, with claims to be the genuine article, the real cow-hide thing from the playing field of Wembley. Obviously concerned about authenticity, almost as if it were a saintly relic, the *Times* reassured its readers that "dye and leather now face tests as stringent as those used on the Turin shroud." After all it had been "a 30-years War for football's Holy Grail."[4]

In the last round it was the *Daily Mirror* reporter who turned up in London with the bright orange leather ball for which Rupert Murdoch's *Sun* had offered a £80,000 reward. And, in the *Daily Telegraph*'s story, there were combat scenes worthy of an aftermath to World War II:

> What should have been the return of a valued memento to a national sporting hero degenerated into Fleet Street farce yesterday. The competition between rival tabloids to bring back to England the ball with which Geoff Hurst scored a World Cup final hat-trick 30 years ago led to scuffles between journalists at Stansted airport, in Essex. Police had to intervene....

The losing tabloid labeled the Haller family the *'Greediest Krauts on Earth'* while its rivals trumpeted its triumph in getting its *'Hans on Hurst's ball'*....

The "Krauts" considered themselves lucky that this time only puns were being dropped on them; and Hellmut or Hans (or whoever) proved themselves quite gallant in the final surrender scene of yet another unconditional capitulation.[5]

Ugly Germans and Aryan Heroes

But here, as I have been trying to suggest, there are no final happy ends, no fortunate fade-outs of a problem which has been a plague for centuries in foreign relations and the newspaper culture. When foreigners want to "speak together" they always get fitfully separated by their foreign languages: by their peculiar accents, ambiguous pronunciations, and, more than that, by the elusive suggestiveness of words and phrases that are burdened with the self-same alienation which wants to be overcome.

For example, one enthusiastic British newspaper referred to Jürgen Klinsmann as "the blonde *Aryan* hero," quite innocent of the fact that this for the Germans was no compliment—indeed an embarrassing reminder of the dark past, so much so that it is practically a taboo word in the Germany of today. In addition to which English sports writing (unlike German) is playful, ironic, comic, flamboyant, irresponsible to the point of manic puns and parody—and this certainly does not go down well in translation. The usual linguistic practices reasserted themselves. The euphoria about an "Aryan hero" cheered on by a million English enthusiasts was, as should have been expected, short-lived.

Paradoxically enough, good news does not go down well at all, for postwar Germany has grown to live with the foreign image of "the Ugly German." News to the contrary is not exactly welcome for it reminds them of the infamous lines of one of their famous poets who was arrogant enough to predict, in the style of *"Deutschland über alles,"* that *"Am deutschen Wesen soll die Welt genesen...."* (Roughly: the German spirit will be the elixir of the world.) Possibly alone among the great peoples of the world, they have given up on being liked, loved, thought of with affection. In the four-column headline in the *Frankfurter Allgemeine Zeitung* (14 October 1994) which reports lengthily on the Klinsmann story in England there is an alarmed note. Is this, again, the all-conquering *"deutsche Wesen"*? But it tries valiantly to play it down by reckoning the success story as a *commercial* win, a *good-business* victory, in fact "the most important export since Gottlieb Daimler's automobile a hundred years ago"—not at all a testimonial to their character and its winning ways.

The account in the *FAZ* was printed on the sports pages but it was actually written by its experienced political correspondent Bernard Heimrich, who evidently seemed to be at a loss as to what his readers, long accustomed to earnest analyses of the achievements of Boris Becker and Franz Beckenbauer, could be expected to understand of what Klinsmann, the kinsman, was all about. Herr Heimrich tried to explain. He took pains to make everything clear. As a good foreign correspondent he assumed nothing, expatiated on everything. Every madcap metaphor or puerile pun was footnoted. And so he ran the risk of all explicators of jokes, to wit, nobody in the end being at all sure how seriously to take anything. I imagine slight shivers ran down the back of the *FAZ* readership when they read, in conclusion, what the *Daily Star* was quoted as saying, namely, *"He's Done What Hitler Failed to Do—He's Conquered England!"* A cynical wag whom I know added: *"Jawohl, Vee haff vaze of vinning losst Vars...,"* with which we are back where we started.

One paragraph in the Frankfurt report is worth preserving, for it illustrates the trials and tribulations of conscientious journalism. It quotes a bilingual *News of the World* headline about an angry moment (and every moment of a star's life has to be recorded by the tabloids): "MEIN FURY!" (The parenthetical explanation: "as in 'MEIN KAMPF' by Adolf Hitler.")

There was more where that came from, and thoughtful English editors always obliged readers by putting the single explanations of their frenetic word-play into parentheses, viz.:

A *sub-headline:* "We catch Klinsmann with his Panzers down!" ("Rommel, Guderian.")

A *comment:* "German soccer ace Jürgen Klinsmann launched a fuhr-ious blitz ..." (*"Fuhr-ious* is again the *Führer,* and *blitz* was his *Blitzkrieg."*)

Another *crack:* "Klinsmann stormed off to his room and trooped inside." ("The *SS* is referred to in this country as the 'Stormtroopers'.")

A *passing remark:* "Unless you catch him hun-prepared." ("Hunned.")

The final *FAZ* illustration of sardonic English humor is a bit bowdlerized and actually belongs to another chapter where scatological neuroses in our newspaper culture have their proper place.

The climax: "Then the Messerschmitt really hits the fan." (And now the prudish explanation reads, "it's a complex play of words which is better not gone into.")

Why a newspaper, which, as I have documented in another place, publishes without hesitation f-words, s-words, a-words, and all the others (some of the capital letters in German are, needless to say, different) should suddenly be overcome by modesty when confronted by the punning anagram hidden in the wings of their most famous airplane-maker, is also, I suspect, very complex. Mark it down to recurring turbulence in the stormy atmosphere of Anglo-German relations. One good year almost came to an end peacefully but for another outbreak.

The British Foreign Office finally released released the hitherto-secret papers of a "dangerous Tscherrmann spy" who was executed during World War I. He was Roger Casement, a so-called martyr to the cause of the "Easter uprising" and of Irish anti-British nationalism. He was hanged for treason in 1916. Among the "confidential" items made public was an enemy pamphlet (in German) and hence incriminating enough to be pictured in facsimile photos accompanying the London news-stories. Its irritating title, opening up old and long-invisible WW I wounds, was: *GOTT STRAFE ENGLAND* (1915). The German word, *strafe* (to punish) has, of course, gone into our language as a sinister verb: "to attack with heavy gunfire from low-flying aircraft."* Possibly the Messerschmitts of the day were involved. It was an altogether nasty bit of business. Just to mention it was not necessarily being especially beastly to the Germans.[6]

The spiral loops back again. When in the Cabinet re-shuffle of 1995 Prime Minister Major conceded the post of deputy prime minister to one of his loyal supporters (and possible rivals the day after tomorrow), newspapers reverted to their usual fun-and-games in which their Germanophobia is usually couched in these days, some fifty years after the end of World War II. One reported, "Cabinet Obergruppenführer Michael Heseltine has wasted no time establishing his authority in his new post as Deputy Prime Minister."[7] The headline, which ostensibly was based on an uninformed exaggeration of the powerful role in the Nazi-SS hierarchy which an Obergruppenführer was thought to have held, read darkly: "HE WHO MUST BE OBEYED." Obviously because any kind of Führer would have ways of making you fall in line....

It is as if the final military command was still looking for the vaunted "last redoubt" of 1945. Each day might offer the last target for a "search and destroy" action. Hostilities could flare up anywhere at any time. A British art critic travels to Venice to write a newspaper report on the Biennale (of 1997) and still finds the English and the Germans locked in combat. The German pavilion ("full blown Nazi architecture") he found "gloomy and haughty" and it was filled, as he reported, with "staring giant skulls...that reminded one that you will soon die." The U.K.'s pavilion ("a former tearoom") offered him, mercy be, "immediate respite" although it was also devoted to the late war:

> Elsewhere in the world, it is officially over. In that corner of the Biennale garden in which the British pavilion stares across at the German, the struggle continues.[8]

Apart from that, all was quiet on the Venetian front where everybody was conforming to the stereotypes of national character:

> So, the British are cool. The Germans are haughty. The Japanese are inscrutable. The French are a mess. The Israelis are dangerously provocative....Even the Italians had their historic inability [to complete their exhibition on time].

A remark by Thomas Mann (from *Death in Venice*) seemed to be an apt quotation at this point. "Some of necessity go astray, because for them there is no such thing as the right path." But, come to think of it, wasn't this an alien, enemy thought? Mann was, of course, German, so he would think that.

---

*   *Longman Dictionary of Contemporary English* (London, 1978), p. 100. The *Shorter OED* (Oxford, 1980), vol. II, p. 2141.

Part 2

The Art of Quotation

*"Newspapers always excite curiosity. No one ever lays one
down without a feeling of disappointment...."*

Charles Lamb, "Last Essays of Elia" (1823/1833)

*"Language exists to communicate whatever it can communi-
cate. Some things it communicates so badly that we never
attempt to communicate them by words if any other
medium is available."*

C.S. Lewis, "Studies in Words" (1960)

*"He that is once admitted to the right of reason is made a
freeman of the whole estate. What Plato has thought, he may
think; what a saint has felt, he may feel; what at any time has
befallen any man, he can understand....*
*"There is a relation between the hours of our life and the
centuries of time....We, as we read, must become Greeks,
Romans, Turks, priest and king, martyr and executioner; must
fasten these images to some reality in our secret experience....*
*"I have no expectation that any man will read history aright
who thinks that what was done in a remote age, by men whose
names have resounded far, has any deeper sense than what he
is doing today....He will see how deep is the chain of affinity."*

Ralph Waldo Emerson (1841)[1]

"Only superficial things can manage not to be insignificant."

Paul Valéry (1922)

8

The Little Goose Feet

Starting and Finishing

Up until very recently there were distinguished newspapers of record that had a thing about quotations. There was simply much too much room for error in direct ascription; and almost everything, except for published documents and set speeches and the like, was given in indirect paraphrase. Many leading reporters were not able to make stenographic notes at press conferences; and even if they could, they might not be able to read them accurately or transcribe them faithfully. In the event, opinions and personal remarks as well as expostulations and indiscretions were "cleaned up" and all came out in good, grey, somewhat boring prose without quotation marks.

I myself was almost caught out, when editing *Encounter* in London, with a quotation in an article by a scholar who had taken it from a report in the *Frankfurter Allgemeine Zeitung*. Ostensibly, it made the point, but it seemed to be just not quite right: the words fitted awkwardly in the mouth of Ulrike Meinhof, then the spokeswoman for the RAF terrorist group in West Germany. On checking it I found that it was not a direct quotation at all but a rewritten editorial summary of some rather outlandish statement she had made. The *FAZ* was not trying to mislead; it was playing it safe with an explosive off-the-cuff remark which would serve to alienate such liberal sympathies that the '68ers notion of "defensive violence" could still command.

But now that journalistic safety lies securely in tape recordings and film sound-tracks, there is no reason to evade the responsibilities of what the Germans call *"Gänsefüßchen"* (little goose-feet), the English "inverted commas," and the Americans simply "quote-unquote". In the last analysis, they preserve the evidence, and protect the truth (so long, as we shall see, the fraudsters have not yet perfected the art of digital faking, on tape, on film, and ultimately on anything).

For a while there were transitional problems. Courts would not admit tape-recordings as incontrovertible proof for what somebody had actually said. I recall a famous incident in the 1950s when a renowned statesman was re-corded praising his mortal enemies; the words sounded real, the accent and inflection impeccable. But the tape was a political hoax, put together on the studio tape-cutting table from bits-and-pieces of old speeches and interviews. This may still play a role in some countries where the courts, trying libel cases against newspapers, take a very strict interpretation (about "hearsay"); but, in general, the profession of journalism has been liberated into that brave free world of "telling it like it is."

Difficulties remain when a writer doesn't have a scrap of hard evidence but publishes the disputed remark the way she affirms she heard it—as in the notorious *New Yorker* case when Janet Malcolm "ruined" the reputation of Jeffrey Masson in psychoanalytical circles by citing an outrageous remark about Freud, and she couldn't find it on tape, or even on a handwritten note, to show the judge.

For the rest there are no technical reasons for the press not to get it abso-lutely right, and to be seen to have gotten it literally correct. Beyond that literal verisimilitude, there are philosophical problems, ethical issues, aesthetic considerations—and I will be considering these in this section—but, apart from slanderous motivations or a magnetic tangle in the Sony 90-minute high-energy tape, there are no obvious grounds for not believing that what the pa-per said the man said he did in fact say.

Presidents of the United States—and they are in this not alone in the corri-dors of power—are often manglers of their own language. Should the raw protocol be touched up? Hansard allows English parliamentarians to revise their texts before the House of Commons transcripts go to press.

Once the *New York Times*—it was during the Administration of General Eisenhower—published the White House transcripts of Ike's press conferences as they were actually given, stutterings and all. I found the full-page "docu-mentary record" mean-spirited, and, even worse, unreadable. I argued at the time with Lester Markel, a senior *Times* editor of the day, that this is *not* what I, for one, had heard the day before from the incumbent in the White House. The ear skips "er's" and "ah's" which stud the President's speech and concen-trates on grasping the meaning, if any; but the eye gets increasingly annoyed and gives up on the "illiteracy" of it all. In the end the *New York Times* aban-doned the practice, and obviously concluded that minor speech defects were not truly "news fit to print." But the bigger issue—philosophical, if you will—

has not definitively gone away. When is a quote not a quote? What do we over-hear when we hear? How do we, in point of fact, get a wrong picture of things when the snapshot is graphic and genuine to its last black-and-white (or lurid red-and-blue) detail?

I once published a transcript of a fascinating argument about race and rac-ism (it involved the American black novelist James Baldwin, the English jour-nalist Peregrine Worsthorne, and Colin MacInnes, the Australian author) which had been originally a television broadcast. The moderator of the heated debate (the philosopher Bryan Magee) insisted on having the stenographic text "ed-ited for publication" with the usual semantic cleansing. I declined, trying to make the point that what we *heard* as an important and revealing discussion (and it *was* that, to watch and to listen to) must be reproduced on the printed page in its stenographic totality—including brilliant interruptions, tempera-mental interjections, furious expostulations, and above all, up and under, a constant plaintive cry from every side to *"let me finish, let me finish!"* The first stenographic account was pretty close to incomprehensible gibberish. Where the ear searches for order, the eye spots chaos.

Philosophers, as I say, have long since puzzled over the "epistemological paradox" which relativizes the correspondences of eye and ear as objective recorders of the sights and sounds we happen to register.

In the ensuing post-Eisenhower decades, as I have been delighted to ob-serve, this small, but reverberating problem in journalistic practice has been taken with deadly seriousness in the world of academe. Specialist professors have devel-oped this attentiveness to the transcription of what is called "non-verbal speech particles" into a fairly recondite branch of "communciations science."

The journal *Language* (50: pp. 696-735) published a widely used notation system oddly entitled "A Simplest Systematics for the Organization of Turn-Taking in Conversation." It serves as theory and practice for "conversation analysis" with a research methodology which includes symbols to show timing, emphasis, vocal dynamics, nonverbal utterances and other features of speech – among them *"uh huh"* and *"hah hah,"* frequently employing misspellings in an attempt to indicate precise pronunciation. The *arrow* symbol (-) in quotations shows a marked rise in intonation. But a *comma* (,) denotes continuing intonation that is "too subtle to be indicated with a question mark or period." *Chevron brackets* (» «) indicate "talk that is spo-ken faster than the surrounding talk." One or two or three *h*'s represent "au-dible outbreaths, sighing, or nonverbal laughter" (but with a "superscripted period" [·*h*] audible inbreaths); whereas the *pt* symbol indicates an audible lip smack. [:] indicates a stretching or an extension of "the sound that it follows." As for single parenthesis enclosing numbers (.4), they represent seconds and tenths of seconds of pauses in talk, whereas a pause too brief to be timed is simply (.).

Taken together the system seemed to provide enough evidence, or "evidentiary perspective," for a dozen U.S. professors in the field—most holding chairs in the subject which has come to be called "Interpersonal Communication Studies"—to re-analyze every word and phrase in the famous Anita Hill-Clarence Thomas hearings in Washington (October 1991) and come to a decisive and triumphal vindication of one side in this much-disputed affair.

Let me quote from the academic volume entitled *Lynching the Language* (1996, published by the University of Illinois Press). One of the dramatic passages, an exchange between Senator Arlen Specter (Republican from Pennsylvania) and Anita Hill, valiantly trying to cope with cross-examination, came in transcription to read like this:

Specter: did yo:u (.2) ca:ll (.) the: (.) »telephone log« i:ssue (.) garbage (.1) unquote=
Hill: =I believe »that the« issue *i:z* garbage (.1) when you look *a:t* (.) hhh (.)what (.) you:re (.) u:h (.) what se:ems »to be« im*pli:ed* by (.) *fro:m* (.) »the telephone« (.) log (.) yes (.) that i:z garbage (.5)
Specter: »have you« *se:en* (.) the (.) records (.2) »ov the« telephone lo:gs (.) »Pro[fessor Hill«"]
Hill: [»yes I«   ] have (.7)
Specter: »do you« den:y the a.ccuracy (.) »ov these« telephone lo:gs=
Hill: =*n:o* (.) »I do« no:t (.)
Specter: »then you« (.) no:w conce:de (.) »that you« had ca:lled (.2) »Judge Thomas« (.1) eleven ti:mes (.1)
Hill: I »do not« den:y the a:ccuracy »ov these« lo:gs (.1) hhh I (.) cannot den:y »that theyre« accurate (.) hhh um (.) »and I« will conce:de that (.) those »phone calls« were made (.) yes (.)
Specter: so (.) »theyre not« garbage (.) ....

This, in some bizarre and *quasi*-occult way, especially when rigorously applied to Judge Thomas' testimony, maximized the collection of "cues of nonverbal deception" which included—

underlying anxiety or nervousness (perspiration, shaking, blinking, frequent shaking of the body, self-adapters [drumming fingers on a desk], object adapters [clicking a pen], increased non-fluencies [ah—uh—uh], facial play).

Particularly innovative was the use of one "determinant of witness credibility," namely,

underlying reticence of withdrawal (fewer illustrative gestures, less forward body lean, reduced eye contact, longer delay in verbal responses, shorter words/sentences).

All these (and more) were associated with the following excerpt from Judge Thomas' testimony before the same Senate Judiciary Committee. The final decision ultimately confirmed his appointment to the Supreme Court, and

Senators were pleased to learn that, at the end, the results of public opinion surveys indicated some 46-60 percent of Americans believed Thomas' side of the story, only 20-37 percent Anita Hill's. Our academics dissented. They had, after all, quoted Judge Thomas to this devastating effect:

Thomas: I think that (.1) this (.) to*da:y* (.1) »iz a« travesty (.2) I think that »it iz« (.) disgu:sting (.2) I (.) think (.) *thi:s* (.1) hearing (.4) should never (.1) occu:r (.1) »in America« (.2) this »iz uh« *ca:se* (.) »in which« thi *slea:ze* (.2) this *di:rt* (.2) waz *sea:rch*ed fo:r (.) by (.) *sta:ffers* .... dredged up (.1) »and this« *go:ss*ip (.1) hhh »and these« *li:es* (.) displa:yed (.) »in this« manner (.1) »how would« *an:y* person (.) like it (.2) the Su*pre:me* Court (.) »iz not« (.) »worth it« (.2) no *jo:b* (.) iz »worth it« (.1) »I'm not« he:re »for that« (.1) I'm here (.) for *m:y* name (.1) my *fa:m*ily (.1) my *li:fe* (.1) »and my« integrity (.2) I think something iz *dread*fully *wro:ng* (.) »with this« country (.) when *a:ny* person (.1) *a:ny* person (.1) »in this« free coun-try (.1) »could be« subjected »to this« (.1) this »iz not« (.) »uh closed« *ro:om* (.2) .... matters (.) privately (.1) or »in uh« closed environment (.) this »iz uh« *circus* (.) this »iz uh« *na:t*ional dis*grace* (.2) »and from« *m:y* standpoint (.2) »az uh« *Black* American (.1) az »far az« *I m* conce:rned (.1) it »iz uh *hi:gh tech ly:nch*ing (.1) for uppity *bla:cks* (.1) who in *a:ny* wa:y (.) *deign* »to think« (.) for themselves (.1) to *do:* (.) »for themselves« (.1) »to have« *diff*erent ideas (.) and »it iz uh« *me:ss*age (.1) that »ubless you« co:w *to:w* (.) »to an« old order (.1) *thi:s* (.) »iz what« will ha:ppen »to you« (.2) you »will be« *ly:nch*ed .

All told, the practitioners of this new art of quotation claimed that this kind of analysis added up to "a compelling argument that Professor Hill was telling the truth" (i.e., about "the pain" of her sexual harassment by Judge Clarence Thomas, now serving honorably on the highest court of the land). The devices for such studying of "intercultural communication" with a sharp eye (and an ear), out to detect "verbal deception" techniques and "impression manage-ment" rhetoric, were ingenious as applied to this special case. It is a moot question whether it can be extended to the whole range of human utterance. Up to date there are precious few signs in the newspaper world that these kinds of "systematics" are being employed by editors and journalists to clarify what the papers have to say and what its quoted protagonists have been talking about. It is also an open question of who in fact was "lynching language."[2]

Behind the Confession

Honorable journalists are they all, and neither their honor nor their accu-racy can be impugned. Still, in the use and abuse of the art of quotation there is a determination to be made—for most quotations in our newspapers of record are "straight," that is, meant to be accurate, and are indeed authen-tic; but a certain slyness which makes for mischief is not to be overlooked. As we have seen, a quotation can be a form of devastating put-down. The reporter knows it, the reader gets it. The ethics of arranging an unrelenting self-exposure may be dubious, but the practice is widespread and is also, I suppose, inexpungeable. Sometimes the satirical element slips in almost undetectably; often the political passion or irony is irrepressible, and the „hidden agenda" may well show.

Not so long ago the *New York Times* (and the *International Herald Tribune* did the same) devoted much space to the story of one David B. Philipson who left a busy life in the Bronx to enrol himself in a Carthusian monastery "for a life of silence and solitude." He appeared to be a serious and admirable fellow, and there was no evidence that the reporter (Francis X. Clines) thought him to be in any way a figure of fun. But it could be a funny story, and in the very first paragraph he began to tap what he felt to be a rich vein of humor. For this is what Mr. Philipson would be now missing out on the in-world from coast to coast—

> What? Never to hear a Letterman Top-10 list again? Never to learn the O.J. verdict? Or see if the Carville-Matalin nuptials go pffft but produce another "gosh weren't they a wacky twosome" bestseller? Never to master E-mail or track the lost Harriman fortune? Never to accept fresh-ground pepper at the latest hyped bistro? Or savor that better world we all hope for when Forrest Gump recedes mercifully to video replay?[3]

These are, roughly, seven portentous questions, meaningful perhaps to a rather small proportion of the non-American *IHT* readership; but we all want to be taken up (and in) by in-language and we know what Francis X. Clines is driving at: The thirty-six-year-old Mr. Philipson may well have a hard time of it by making this withdrawal to a severe life of godly contemplation in the Vermont woods.

The list of life's losses—which also included Polish *borscht*, *merlot* red wine, *cappuccino*, stereo music—was intended to be touching, even moving.

But what were these sacrifices all in aid of? What philosophy moved his act of monkish renunciation? What theology informed his new faith? The only clue we are given is a single paragraph of direct quotation from the Fordham University lay minister, as he still then was, who had spent ten years "setting up social outreach programmes for students and scouting the poorest parts of the world from India to Appalachia." (Two questions of my own: what were the students outreaching for? and for what were the scouts scouting?) The man's credo was simple:

> "The people of the Third World have a special quality and I found myself wanting to become like them," Mr. Philipson said. "To be on an equal footing with them because I saw value in how they embraced their own life situation."

This must be one of the most depressing passages I have run across in a month's melancholy reading of the daily press, replete with the clichés, platitudes, and bromides of a newspaper culture that has lost its way. I am not sure whether Mr. Clines knew what a jewel of a quote he had when he noted and taped this credo; the late Lionel Trilling might have despaired over it, as yet another example of "inauthenticity" in modern feeling. Rough questions abound. What Third World—Rwanda and Angola in genocide? Somalia and Mozambique in fratricide? Liberia and Zaire in homicide? What was their special quality apart from dying ignominiously and in vain? How will he be becoming "like them" in Vermont? When does he step forward (or down) onto "equal footing"? Merely "seeing value" is not enough, only an airy and value-less concession which avoids the question of how *much* value: a little? a lot? *sufficient* for a mind-bending life-changing break in all of our "life situations"? Nor would it be less diffuse if he saw "some merit" or even "much virtue" in the life of the poor, sick, and maltreated. For they do not "embrace their life situations," they are smothered and crushed by them: the special quality of their lives being mute inglorious extinction in death situations.

But it could be that the quotation that has given me so much trouble was not meant dead-seriously. Without resorting to the rumblings of heavy outrage that I have given way to, the story might well be taken to be a putdown of poor David B. Philipson, the moral of the story being that he should have stayed on with his borscht and cappuccino and the "Grateful Dead" (presumably a hot rock group of the moment) before venturing into the unscouted higher out-reaches of spirituality. Perhaps, if journalism goes on seeing value in accounts of converts in ongoing change-of-life situations, it may do well to supply us with a useful scorecard of true saints and wayward sinners.

Expensive Words

I was only being half playful in my previous suggestions that from little acorns huge oaks grow—that, namely, from the permissive muddle of indif-ference and ignorance in which splitting infinitives can flourish comes a larger confusion in which it seems too late to be finding a clear way out. For my own part, if I spot a story with my favorite little misdemeanor, pernickety tiny thing that it is, I am oddly certain that the fault lines will begin to quake disastrously before the end.

Consider this text about the billion-dollar crisis in the U.S. Navy's budget in one forthcoming year. Here is the minor tremor (and I admit I am among the last semanticists registering such shakes on my own personal Richter scale): "We can no longer afford to physically deploy forces in every region of con-cern."[4] This is the U.S. Air Force chief-of-staff speaking, and what the general truly can't afford is to use a word which is ambivalent and to squeeze it in where it doesn't belong. What the Air Force general wants are the billions in the Pentagon budget which are being reserved for the U.S. Navy "to physi-cally deploy" in every conceivable region of global concern. The Navy is going full-steam ahead building aircraft carriers ("flattops") which are, it admits in a surprising concession, not needed for fighting at all. The strategic conception is to maintain a deterrent U.S. military peacetime presence in the Persian Gulf, the Mediterranean, off Korea, etc. etc. The estimate, as reported, is that it costs nearly $1 million a day to operate a carrier.

But does such deterrence actually need a "physical" presence? The Air Force theoreticians countered the Navy's position by making a valuable distinction between "real" and "virtual" presence. What was being offered was a billion-dollar gloss on the concept of "virtual reality." Words were being split, phrases divided. The argumentative generals and admirals may be able to make war, but they could not make meanings clear. How could you be *present* without being *physically* there? Couldn't the shade of difference between "virtual" and "real" involve, possibly, victory or defeat in a war?

The Air Force general, a clever wordsmith named Ronald Fogleman, was quick to provide an example of how with several billion dollars more he and his fliers could provide *both* real and virtual presence. It appears that releasing, say, the Air Force's satellite photographs of Iraqi troop movements might affect Saddam Hussein's behavior more than flying Navy aircraft over Iraqi territory.

For his own (and the Navy's) part, the admiral took this as a cheap shot against his aircraft carriers. The Air Force was only trying to provide a "cheaper alternative service." He was appropriately upset and dismissive, for a ship was costly and press releases were inexpensive. How to be virtually present on all the seven seas? "I don't know what that means....I guess we're never going to have a 'virtual navy.'" Well, if he doesn't stop splitting infinitives and neglecting to spit-and-polish up his meanings, one guesses he will be short of a fortune when the next budget comes up for Congressional approval. Semantics can cost you dearly; clear and positive thinking doesn't come cheap.

One should not overlook here, as in all social problems, what used to be called "the economic interpretation of history." There is sometimes a "materialist" factor involved, for such bridging or filling phrases are assets that occupy space and take time, and so are worth money and can be as good as gold.

In the nineteenth century, popular French novelists who had their tales serialized in the Paris newspapers were paid by the line. As a result, Alexandre Dumas' musketeers had snappy one-line-one-paragraph conversations elongated by characteristic interjections such as *"Morbleu!"* or *"Sans blague!"* When the frugal French newspaper owner changed the mode of literary payment, Dumas' D'Artagnan now made all his points convincingly and there was no word from Athos, Porthos, or Aramis indicating their (unpaid) responses.

Fillers can be very expensive, and some television critics have detected a related cost-cutting scheme. Thomas Sutcliffe, writing in the *Independent* (4 January 1995) notes in a new series of detective thrillers, the odd languor that steals over programmes that want to make the money stretch; they've paid a lot for this so there's no question of rushing it. In this respect court-room drama is useful as it provided the perfect excuse to use lines twice.

"We had a row of sorts," says the witness.

"A...row...of...sorts," says John Thaw [famed on British TV for his policeman's cunning], in tones of menacing rumination—and a little more of that expensive time is nibbled away....

It takes all sorts of writers to fill the space and the time which the print and the electronic media have at their disposal, and some of them are ingenious enough to contrive instructive little scams. As we have seen, the mixed motives can vary: tricky politics, greedy economics, helpless semantics.

The impact of certain World War II troubles had different consequences during the long postwar period in Anglo-American newspaper writing, on both sides of the Atlantic. The shortages of rationed newsprint shrunk the British newspapers for a decade and more; and the mini-stories and compact dispatches made for lean and austere reporting with quotations especially at a premium. On the contrary, the *New York Times* and other American dailies suffered under few restrictions and could go on and on, self-indulgently, in their old expansive selves. If Americans seem to be long-winded, the English appear short of breath. Consequently, most pieces in the British press are still dispatched with an unusual concision; U.S. reviewers writing about, say, the new films or a Broadway première ramble on and take easily double the space to come to an evaluation or a recommendation. Melodramatic news events (a fire, a crash, a murder) which call for the on-the-scene incorporation of the *vox populi* are often interminably padded by instant interviews, off-the-cuff remarks, snippets of response from next-door neighbors, snappy anecdotes, colorful utterances from innocent bystanders in various states of shock and suspicion, very little of which is essential or even relevant. At best, as in long chunks of American reportage, the reporter's transcriptions of talk at the scene of the happening is professionally ambitious and in the best quotes aspire to, well, quotability. I stayed the course in the *New York Times'* extensive account from Bergen County, New Jersey, of "Teen-Age Sweethearts Charged With Murdering Their Baby" (18 November 1996); and I was rewarded in the very last paragraph by the final explications of the "Romeo-and-Juliet tragedy" which had distressed an affluent suburban community. The owner of the local Ramapo delicatessen expressed himself tentatively, skeptically, almost philosophically when he told the *Times* reporter, "I believe there is something that will come out that will explain how they got from who they were to where they are." All the news that's fit to print is there in that one-liner; and it was a pithy ending to a sad story. The man from the *New York Post* also wanted to be in tune with the metaphysics of what had happened to the "two nice young American kids" in Ramapo:

They were two typical teens whose love story began in the plush surroundings of exclusive suburbs. It ended in a dumpster behind a cheap motel where, cops say, they snuffed out the life of their newborn son.

In the *Post* which had a half-dozen reporters talking to everybody in the county and assembling innumerable human-interest details, the best quote came from a man who repined against cruel fate: "Who can re-invent the world? They're children." Hemingway, among others, thought there was literature in such lines, and he, along with Theodore Dreiser, John Steinbeck, Arthur Miller, Saul Bellow, et al., tried to prove it.[5]

9

Television and Press "War"

Pictures and Print

What I have generally referred to as the war between the picture and the word, the electronic image and the printed message, is usually conducted between the newspapers and the television's small screen (although the battle between Books and Films is part of it). Still, it can have skirmishes quite distant from the hostile clarity of the front lines.

The conflict ranges from the large confrontation between vested financial interests to the personal vendettas among the talking heads in front of the TV camera and the unseen writing fingers at newspaper consoles. But the message is still: word good, picture bad.

What happens to the reputation of a fine writer and excellent literary critic like Clive James when he becomes a TV star, doing funny programs to canned laughter and wise-cracking with the best of the stand-up comics? TV audience-ratings register that he is "better than ever." But TV critics in the press are merciless in their reviews. Here is the *Daily Telegraph* commenting on James's BBC program entitled "Letter from Bombay" (22 February 1995):

> Like so many telly personalities [writes Hugh Massingberd], James has long since succumbed to self-parody; one dreads the constant thud of leaden puns and laboured quips with hammy pauses, 'funny' inflections and an overweening air of satisfaction at his own cleverness.

More than that. For not only the intellectuality but also the physiology is going down the tubes. The newspaperman, aloof behind the clean cool computer, says that watching Clive James in India, he

> became concerned about the alarming amount of sweat he was exuding. Each time the hatless figure lumbered into shot, a fount of perspiration would announce itself in an unexpected valley of his shirting....Even Nixon wasn't as bad as this.

Don't rub it in. We get the point: by-line man, good—small-screen star, all wet. Keep dry by reading your morning (or even the afternoon) newspaper. No sweat.

Wittingly or no, every effort is made by the press to put down television's excursions into sexuality and the soft-porn language which may pertain thereto. The pictures are mocked, the dialogue ridiculed. The London *Times'* TV critic, a Matthew Bond, is almost alarmed when a certain character in a BBC border-line show suddenly hunts for unread newspaper articles as he asks his secretary what she knows about nymphomania. "Well," she paused, sending a million newspapers nervously aflutter. "I think it's a bit like me and a box of chocolates."[1] "Phew," expostulated a relieved Mr. Bond, "perhaps that article wasn't quite so interesting."

Our newspapers have their good days when they can pretend to be virtuous and quite above such lascivious things like nymphs eating aphrodisiac candies. Mr. Bond rises to full contempt for the film-scene in which "three American marines arrive wearing silver lamé jockstraps"—what could be more "silly"? One feeble joke was singled out for praise, possibly calculated to discourage any newspaper-reader from turning on his TV set for a tickle. "One nice line about a couple who last had sex in 1959 (Macmillan told them they'd never had it so good, so they didn't try it again)." Conventional, traditional verbal foreplay—in this case a relatively innocent pun on Prime Minister Harold Macmillan's famous boast of unprecedented prosperity in Great Britain—is something that a sexually harassed print media world thinks it can live with.

And yet the guardians of the Word against the Picture must be ever vigilant: the word being the true image of art and life, the picture merely a flimsy snapshot of perspectives in depth. Literary critics were alarmed recently at the newspaper reports that *Lolita*, that "perverse masterpiece" by Vladimir Nabokov, was to be filmed again. The first attempt in the 1950s to translate the novel into cinema had been distressing enough; and now a film director named Andrew Lyne was to try again. The press, it will come as no surprise to my readers who have been following the vendetta so far, rushed to help him off to a bad start. As the estimable Bryan Appleyard wrote in the *Independent* (4 January 1995):

> Lyne made his name with those glossy, abysmal porno-shockers *9½ Weeks* and *Fatal Attraction*. Both were crude exploitations of fashionable sexual anxieties, scarcely a promising apprenticeship for taking on Nabokov....Lyne decided to reject the script he had commissioned from Harold Pinter. Presumably by now he has in some slavering Hollywood hack with a back-to-front baseball cap.

We already know that the film will be "a glossy travesty." But the novel, that distinguished thing, is "a profound meditation," and (in Lionel Trilling's words) "one of the few examples of rapture in modern writing."

Another good blow has been struck for Gutenberg!

In other words, when all is said and done, if one still wants what D.H. Lawrence called sex-in-the-head, abandon naughty picture postcards and blue films and return to our favorite form of reading matter, good books, wherein a story of love and even lust can attain high art and may be enjoyed in the quiet privacy of your favorite easy-chair. Away with potato couches!

On battlefield terrain when there are no clear demarcations between the rival armies there is a deceptive truce. Newspaper owners, especially in the U.S., very often control television stations and film studios; TV directors and correspondents are sometimes literate cultivated men who write articles and indeed books. They have a stake in both camps, and refrain from the internecine media warfare.

On the border lines between Press and Picture there are occasional moments of goodwill and even fraternization. I myself appeared regularly for almost thirty years on a prime-time German-language television program in which journalists had pride-of-place and appeared to be given much credence because they were writers, wordsmiths, literate students of some subject, rather than mere chat-show chatterers or "talking heads." The fact that most of the panel who appeared in Cologne on Werner Höfer's historic "*Frühschoppen*" series were foreign correspondents gave them a bit of advantageous glamour for the million viewers. (But then, as outsiders, they were a bit disadvantaged, because they were not native speakers but had to be serious and eloquent in a language not their own.) A popular American series, also on Sundays, invites the viewers to *Meet the Press* in a fair and hospitable way, and no foul blows have been recorded.

Quite another thing was the British effort to review the Press in a regular TV program over many decades. It was called *What the Papers Say* (I am obviously indebted to it), and it was lively, funny, satirical, condescending, and in the end contemptuous.

When print journalists were conducting it—the best of them was the late Brian Inglis, author and former editor of the *Spectator*—the tenor was critical but just and informative. When TV-personalities took over, veterans of chat and canned laughter, the jokes became feeble and vapid. The message imparted was that, their hated rivals in so-called news-gathering, the Press, tabloids and broadsheets alike, were worth looking at only for their inanities; and trust your tuned-in television team to set them right.

Finally, I note a new TV program on the German network, *Sat-1*, entitled *Die Menschen hinter den Schlagzeilen* (the people behind the headlines). One despairing reviewer noted that television had stolen almost every line from the newspapers except...the headline. And now *this!*—and it *was* a steal. An enterprising chap named Ulrich Meyer quickly recruited front-page names on to his show—a deserted wife of a film star, a local mum who took on "whole Sicily" in order to get her kidnapped child back, etc. His interviews, live on camera with the hot-off-the-press protagonists of sensation, were supposed to tell the real story which the papers had over-looked, or exaggerated, or simply made up. He won some, he lost some. He was nonplussed when one headliner confessed that the story, as it actu-ally transpired, was identical with the account published in the newspa-pers:

> "Really and truly?" he asked with obvious discomfort. "Really and truly!" came the reply.

The *Frankfurter Allgemeine Zeitung* gloated. Its own headline (5 January 1995) was triumphalist in its print-media pride: "*Ehrlich? Ehrlich!*" Journalism had won a rare honest-to-goodness victory over showmanship.

Of Trash and Rubbish

In the conflict between the Press and the TV—variously presented here as the Word against the Picture, active literacy *vs.* passive viewability (or the print addict as against the couch potato)—there are, as so often in combat and hostilities, curious interludes. A strange truce may break out—particularly when, as in the most prominent case of Rupert Murdoch, the same group owns newspapers, publishing houses, television stations, and film studios. There may even be a startling *renversement des alliances*—in which the most critical sec-tor of the serious press will come to the defense of the most putrid perfor-mances on the TV screen, presumably (as in the Hitler-Stalin Pact) because the preservation of the bad is, I suspect, somehow seen to be more advanta-geous to its long-term interests than the onset of the worse. What is the fuzzy logic behind this strange choice of "the lesser evil" whereby the shoddier gets the nod?

Obviously, the worst prospect for the quality in our daily newspaper culture is the increasing and unstoppable mass popularity of the fare that television offers every day and night. Dramatic moving-pictures of news (wars, fires, accidents, political crises), often in real time—soap-op-era stories of love and hate and human trouble (and all of life can be cap-tured in a police precinct, hospital ward, and sit-com living-room)—mass-produced B-films which are so skillfully paced that even with the endlessly exciting car-chase, wildly hurtling through the traffic of rainy metropoli-tan streets, they only manage in the end to induce a sleepy relaxation in the millions.

Many newspaper columnists have already written obituaries on the end of the Printed Word as we know it; yet, over the last forty years at least, they have proved to be premature. Television has gone from strength to strength in the audience ratings throughout the world. But the Press has conspicuously survived; and not least among its saving graces has been, as I have tried to document, a torrent of relentless criticism against Television where it has shown itself to be most vulnerable—its irresponsibility, superficiality, mindlessness, sheer insipidity.

But what price success? How will the competitive scores stand if newspaper criticism actually serves to improve the quality of television performance? Would it be better for the cultivated reading world, or worse? It would be naive to think that the major American networks do not prefer a high-quality *PBS* (Public Broadcast Service) which caters to the small (and ever dwindling?) minority tastes that are happy with BBC imports, with Alistair Cooke forever introducing handsome and civilized English costume dramas of Jane Austen and Thomas Hardy. As for the BBC itself, it is forever struggling with its conscience about going "down-market" in order to overtake the gross popularity of the prospering private and commercial opposition.

In Germany the same agonizing qualms are afflicting the two traditional public—and highbrow—TV networks (ARD and ZDF). They think they have to "vulgarize" (i.e., even more) in order to maintain their audiences who are flocking to the proliferating competition whose profitable advertising revenues have enabled them to improve their news, up-grade their talk-shows, and outbid all others for Hollywood's hit films. Indeed they are even better off in every way since the public and press outcry against their original attempt to seduce viewers by late-night soft-porn blue movies forced them to think up more intelligent (less sleazy, more "decent") programming.

And it is in such distressed circumstances that we find the high-brow critics of the serious British press coming to the perverse defense of a grotesque phenomenon on the television screen which specializes in the bad, the bawdy, and the beastly (their alliteration). A writer in the *Independent* makes his plea under the headline,

THE CASE FOR UNDERRATED "TRASH TV"[2]

At the outset the critical evaluation is conventional and only apparently negative, in its familiar "egg-head's lament" over the coarse and the tawdry: "*Trash TV* is essentially ephemeral, valueless TV without any redeeming features and with only one intention: entertainment." So far, so bad. The demerits among other execrable items include "wacky breakfast TV shows...third-rate game-shows...lousy emcees spouting banalities...filthy back-of-the-classroom guffaws...entirely pointless sporting contests...mindlessly entertaining underclass wit...the glorious absurdity of it all...."

Where there is glory there is always power to be envied, and a sneaking dash of admiration does intrude itself (and in the columns of an excellent if circulation-anaemic newspaper which has been having painful troubles maintaining its own hold on its public) when it registers the fact that the programs of *Trash TV* have been so popular that they have been credited with causing a serious decline in cinema attendances:

> That a show that features fourth-rate celebs, members of the public who have had middling wins on the lottery and the presenter can hold the same ear-to-ear smile for 15 minutes should be held responsible for the fall of the British film industry is surely testament to the power of *Trash*.

What can the secret be, the clue to this power and glory? Certain rivals thought they had come upon it, concocted their copy-cat versions, and failed ignominiously. Why? Because they did not truly "fit into the genre": "They aren't trash, they're rubbish." Evidently it is a question of mindlessness over matter; for, as the argument runs, "*Trash TV* is good because it does not know that it is bad." Calculated—and hence less innocent—exercises in something called "ironic postmodernism" are futile and will be quite incapable of attracting huge audiences. Only the shared appetite for authentic kitsch will make the connection. Samuel Johnson had hit upon the fatal attraction in his bitter explanation of a rival's success with the public, namely: "His folly appealed to their folly." Still, the distinction between trash and rubbish, a piece of medieval scholasticism which would count the number of garbage men dancing on the point of a rusty needle, may have its tactical uses. It also has, come to think of it, a dash of Bourbon insouciance about it, rejecting a diet of garbage...but "Let them have trash."

In any case our newspaper culture will be needing all the defense stratagems it can muster. Journals like the worthy *Independent* have accepted, for a momentary skirmish, an ally with a non-culture of its own. Its value is minus; it is operating well below a three-figure IQ line; it is mentally deficient. But it has, in these hard times, something called "negative equity" (where, in the real-estate business, the mortgage-debt exceeds the depressed property re-sale price). Any kind of equity is held to be better than none.

In the end it would appear that in the skirmishes of the TV/Press wars the meretricious is better than the meritorious, for it obviates having to praise the enemy and it does provide bigger and better targets. In the end the trash will be relentlessly rubbished.

We are not dealing here with occasional bursts of spite, malice or bad temper on the part of newspaper reviewers, who find themselves on the edge of exhaustion after ceaseless exposure to mediocre (and worse) television fare. The streak of negativism can reflect, on occasion, the larger and long-term interests of a newspaper industry which may be doomed to extinction by its pictorial media rivals. But this is not necessarily the case, for the critics involved often are in the employment of owners who themselves have substantial interests in TV empires.

Consider a case of a notable polemical salvo by a *Sunday Times* writer who works, ultimately, for press baron Rupert Murdoch, who is also a mogul in the realm of film and television. The critic in question is A.A. Gill, a journalist of the younger generation and an aspiring novelist, who does a weekly review in the "Culture" section of the paper, replete with fairly good jokes and unexpectedly percipient remarks. Every once in a while he omits reviewing some big and ambitious TV program, and takes the trouble to say why. On one day in March (1997) he explained why he refused to see and write about an ITV program called *No Child of Mine*, a so-called docu-drama on the subject of "Child Abuse" which had been dominating the headlines from Brussels to Djakarta and back. What were his reasons for not switching on (in ostensible neglect of his journalistic duties)? It is, after all, what he's paid to do. What he came up with was a principled objection to this TV genre which combines facts and fiction and is known as "faction"—which, he contended, is "deeply immoral, prurient, and fraudulent."

Why, then, are the exposés of "child abuse"—from beastliness in the family to prostitution and pornography—legitimate in published journalistic accounts and not in the dramatic reconstruction which all television producers, sooner or later, get around to making? As A.A. Gill writes,

> Film-makers who make faction hold up the as-told-to truth as an unarguable shield against artistic or moral criticism. "This really happened, so we have to show you. Your criticism isn't with my program, it's with life and society."

This is held to be "wholly bogus," although he concedes that everything you see on the screen is fake in one way or another, for "the very act of you sitting in one place looking at another place is artifice." Drama documentary "relies on the audience's trust—and then manipulates it." Should we, then, not listen to victims (or their impersonators) telling us the "truth"?

> Television as victim confessional and cathartic therapy is repellent. If the victims are willing, even eager, to relive their tragedy by proxy, this mustn't be a carte blanche. The damaged should be protected from themselves and their understandable desire to make their damage public. Every week editors stop lots and lots of people [from] appearing on television; whether or not they'll make a good dramatic film shouldn't be the only criterion.

This is the crux of the matter: criteria, and the ethics thereof. "Docudramas" have over the years become ever more shocking, and true stories have had to justify themselves, not on merit or public worth, but against last week's anguished offering. This can only result in the dulling of the viewer's sense of outrage. When will we be getting the "Multiple Baby Sex Murder of the Week"? Moving, as is the journalist's wont in the intra-media wars, towards the high moral ground, Gill writes in the *Sunday Times* (which, be it recorded, has on good week-ends its own low lurid moments),

> The bottom line with all drama documentaries is abuse....The victim's distress is abused, and real characters who aren't consulted or are portrayed as villains are abused. The process of law is abused, and playwriting as a vehicle for telling greater truth is abused by being hanged on the scaffold of "fact". But, most important, *you* are abused by being made complicit in the act.

How such consequences differ from the effects of, say, complicitous prose is a question for another time. For now the anguished cry of the writer is heard in the land: "if you really love television, the best thing you can do for the good of the medium is switch it off."[3] As I say, this protest against pictures that deceive, and facts that fail in their duty to the truth, is not to be taken as petty or idiosyncratic. It is an echoing battle cry in the war between the forces of pen-and-paper and the camp of film-and-sprockets. Imperial interests are involved, but also the touching defense of a traditional cultural faith in literature and the printed word.

In America where this kind of reader's pride came relatively late, there is a particular sensitivity in the community of the scribes. I can remember with what youthful pangs of upset we received the news that one of our favorite by-lines, that of the *New York Times'* brilliant film critic of the 1930s and '40s, Frank S. Nugent, was leaving the newspaper world for a job in Hollywood. We felt somehow betrayed. And in that spirit there was also an element of *Schadenfreude* when writers of the stature of William Faulkner and F. Scott Fitzgerald had their scenarios re-written beyond recognition and failed utterly to make a mark in the film world of the California studios. Decades later it is still turning out to be, in the current stereotype, a war of two cultures—East is the word, and West is the picture, and never the twain should meet.

The Shrinking Attention-Span

The major conflict does not, of course, preclude minor internecine warfare between rival camps in the picture world. Word-determined newspaper habits get increasingly subverted by the TV experience; and journalists get drawn into the field of criss-cross fire, for the front lines of the opposing camps are not hard-and-fast. Movie critics see a lot of television and bring into the cinema TV-determined habits and tastes.

Thus, a literate and cultivated maker of feature films like Robert Altman is incensed at many of the published reviews of his work (the latest, for the moment, being *Prêt-à-Porter*). He feels that for shrunken minds everything is becoming too complicated. His plots develop subplots; characters in his story change their characters. Are the TV-addicted cinema critics too dull-witted? In one outburst against the press Altman said: "You're a child of television. You have no attention span."[4] In the quarrels of a previous generation, the Fourth Estate's charge against Hollywood fans ran: You are all children of the movies, living your lives on the aluminum screen—you'll all grow up to be illiterates. It is not unknown that in some bouts of mutual recrimination both accusations can come true.

As a correlate to this medially induced reduced force of concentration, let us examine what the papers say and how they say it. How do, for example, the new non-journalistic leads in news stories solve the tricky problem in their initial human interest paragraphs? The new "leads" have been devised, of course, as a technique for awakening the reader's appetite, to arouse his curiosity, and lengthen his attention span. Presumably it does so serve. But some readers are allergic to teasing, and get no further than the first sentence: "Cole Grady was earning $52,000 a year as a technician at a herbicide plant in Muscatine, Iowa...." If news from Iowa bores and turns the reader away, he would be missing an informative report on how technological factors are affecting the U.S. work-force and, especially, families in the Middle West. Similarly, I almost missed an interesting dispatch from Grozny by the *New York Times* correspondent on the Chechnya war front, evaluating the chances of a final Russian defeat and a victory for the guerrilla rebellion. It began, "*Grozny, Russia*—The word was on the streets by the beginning of the month...." Street-wise readers usually ignore month-old street words.[5]

In some of these ways, mostly puerile and picayune, print journalism tries to vie with the enviable techniques of pictorial reportage—by imitating, in some manner, the film story's capacity for quick cutting and fade-outs, for montage and close-ups, and all the rest. Even the structure of a news dispatch is shaped, bent, and twisted so as to capture attention and stimulate instant interest. The traditional "lead" paragraph of a reportorial account these days has given way to something that teases rather than sums up in the old classical manner of who-what-why-how, and so on. Thus, in a front-page story from the *Washington Post* correspondent in Tokyo, we are lured into a puzzling melodrama which only further reading (and it jumps in a continuation some eight pages further on) can solve. "*Tokyo.*—Hirofumi Kiuchi's heart was failing him and so, he felt, was his country." Our curiosities seduced, the tale went on to tell a significant case of how "tradition, culture and religious concerns" have blocked recent medical advances from taking hold in Japanese hospital practices. Our protagonist, Kiuchi-*san*, could not get a heart transplant in his own country but had to travel abroad where his "soul" was not considered endangered by the surgical invasion.

Again, on the same day, the Antwerp correspondent entices us with

On the E-19 Outside Antwerp, Belgium—Robin Earith pauses for a morning coffee to the din of traffic plying one of Europe's busier highways.

Between that pause that refreshes and the column-long details of snarled traffic on all the European highways we are regaled by the argument about changes in automobile-and-truck taxation and, especially, in electronic road pricing which would enable governments to split all kinds of alternatives (and infinitives) when they are finally "allowed to automatically levy fees on vehicles at peak hours in urban ring roads and in city centers."[6]

This prose technique of indirection will, as in the old saw, get you everywhere so long as you start from anywhere. But the prose has to be in good shape (a trim one-sentence opening paragraph) and be able to deliver a quick first-round punch; little else matters. No editor can really care about what beverages are being drunk (a double-whiskey would have served as well) or whether transplantees lose their patriotic roots (Kiuchi-*san* might have gotten a new cornea or kidney without causing damage to his "soul"). A casual culture of carelessness is taking over in our newspaper offices. Sentences dangle precariously like participles, and all metaphors can be mixed when infinitives are split. A *New York Times* story, reporting on a decision by Bill Gates' Microsoft Inc. to release new software in order to accommodate the growing use of the Internet, wrote that it is being designed "to seamlessly blend the multimedia technology of the Internet's World Wide Web with the Microsoft Windows 95 operating system." The multi-blender goes on to multi-stitch the various conceits that hold the story together on a reader-accessible level. The decades-old metaphor of creating and storing information as "files" in "folders" gives way, in a sea change, to "a new paradigm for personal computing" (also known as "moving into a new world"), etc.[7]

Take another example of journalistic soap-opera which would appear to be so thin and threadbare as to be on the verge of imminent unravelment but is, alas, likely to go on for some time yet. My collection of cuttings about this (a few examples open this chapter) is still expanding. The *New York Times* correspondent in Yugoslavia was on to an important political development: the increasing bitterness in Kosovo which was about to erupt in an anti-Serb revolt. This, in the context of the successful demonstrations in Belgrade and the visible weaknesses of the Milosevic régime, is what the professionals call a big story. How should it be written? Well, Chris Hedges writes it in the way he thinks (and, presumably, his editors back in Times Square) is stylish and captivating and full of the human interest and personal tension that makes readers read on:

Orllan, Yugoslavia.—Bajram Pajaziti walked solemnly down the hillside from his brother's grave, past a line of silent, motionless mourners, and stopped at the door of his father's small, white-washed home to pull off his shoes.

This is the first paragraph, the "lead." And why is Bajram taking off his shoes? Because, as the second paragraph will tell us, "it is a ritual he had repeated several times in this remote mountain village" since his brother Zahir, thirty-four, had been killed with two other ethnic Albanians in Kosovo. And why had they been killed? Because they were members of the Kosovo Liberation Army and had been in a gun-battle with the pro-Serbian local police.

Well, Mr. Hedges almost lost me there. But after only an additional paragraph of sugar-coating the human-interest details, he went on soberly to report the hard news that the Albanian disaffection in Kosovo had been intensifying to the point of sporadic violent clashes. More than that, the guerrilla movement, while still embryonic, might be capable of de-stabilizing the Yugoslav province which was governed by Belgrade in the interests of the Serbian minority. In an additional thousand words the dispatch provided facts, analysis, revealing quotations by the insurgents, their persecutors, and by a number of foreign diplomatic observers.

In case you were wondering what had happened to Bajram Pajaziti, left shoeless on the first page, twenty paragraphs ago, he turns up again in the last lines, visiting his brother's hilltop grave, mourning for a martyr who "died, as he lived, for his people." This is the way foreign news has to be presented these days: if you're fishing for readers, bait the hook first, pull in the catch later.[8]

Yet another reporter, Ms. Christine Spolar, writing for the *Washington Post* from Warsaw, teases the reader in a front-page story which will take up, sooner or later, a serious matter first raised by the revelations about the first woman secretary of state, Madeleine Albright and her Jewish parents' Nazi-time conversion from Judaism to Roman Catholicism. Like some aging coquette, trying hard to mime her old come-hither look, the *Post* reporter flirts with us and dallies with our attention-span:

Warsaw.—The phone in the one-room office in a building in central Warsaw begins to ring every Thursday just as the sun dips into the soft gray horizon. The anonymous callers have one secret to tell....

The secret is soon told, and so is the news of the sole surviving Warsaw synagogue having recently been set ablaze; and the additional news of the anguish and bewilderment of hundreds of Poles, in a current state of shock about their "secret adoptions" and their "tactical baptisms." Were they really Jews? or "of Jewish descent"? Then the Thursday call will just make the connection, for the telephone should never ring as the dipping Friday sun makes for the Sabbath eve. Identity crises need to be handled sensitively, and are in any case a long, roundabout, and continuing story.[9]

If this is interesting (and it is), then we know when Mark Twain's classical remark is recalled—to the effect that journalism is the art of getting readers to read a story in which they are not really interested—that it is a witticism but is not strictly true. The functions of journalism are already a hopeless task when artfulness becomes a mere primping trick to avoid boring the newspaper's customers. The information is tarted up, and the flirtatious contact is fleeting and unsatisfying. Something less cosmetic is more suitable for the serious relationship between reporter and reader.

As in the relationship of "limited war" to "total war," the restrained aggression and delimited use of vulgarisms in a major newspaper of quality and seriousness, in Britain as well as the United States, represents a working compromise between the older conventions and the new possibilities of verbal innovation. Compared to the frenzied violence of hard-porn it is a low-intensity experience. This middling position swings, as we have seen, from an occasional venture into the total frontal across a whole variety of foreplays, slow and steady but only for starters. At times, the attentive reader will note, there is a curious lull, or what appears to be one. It is what Byron once called (in his *Don Juan*) "a short armistice with truth...." Or, rather, with truth-telling in the hasty, passing sense of journalistic documentation: *Tell it like it is*...because it actually happened yesterday and that is demonstrably (for a transcription or a short-hand note is usually available) the way the who-and-what-and-how-and-why expressed itself, quote unquote. This quasi-Jeffersonian commitment to the high idealism of a free press is regularly coupled with the need to appeal to the lowest common denominator of a mixed readership which will be held loyally fast with a dash of "dirty realism."

We can see this rather clearly in the style of our newspaper culture, in the way our newspapers cover this mixed motivation in our television fare. Thus, one TV critic reiterates his cynical attitude to the renewed promise of one major network "to clean up its act":

> I doubt if it will because whatever its executives may say in public, they know that filth and violence make for great ratings, and that nothing gains an audience's attention faster than a solemn announcement that "Some viewers may find the following programme offensive".[10]

The standard punning summing-up runs: *peak-time* for them, *pique-time* for us. But us are not really piqued at all, for they do roughly the same thing all the time, except in those especially sensitive periods when one or another "public outcry" goes up, and everybody is on his best behavior for the duration of a short armistice. Thereafter comes another pictorial season of blood-and-guts, and ordinary black-and-white print can never hope to compete in the contest of commandeering attention-spans.

A last word on the ultimate residue of the dualism between word and picture in our media culture. As in all fundamental clashes, from the class struggle upwards, there emerges a double standard of moral judgment, far removed from the pretence of a universal standard of objectivity. As a result much of what our newspaper culture argues in severe judgementalism is tinged with conspicuous hypocrisy. This is particularly obvious in all matters that touch on sexual themes.

We have had in recent years films about women strippers and now male strippers (viz., *The Full Monty,* 1997), all of which have been subjected to the harshest press criticism. Especially on the count of what is called cultural courage. Daring movie producers, fearful of losing some of their audience by going "too far," make their little compromises. They are innovative enough to break new ground, to do for the human body on film what was never done by Hollywood and therefore restricted to the soft- (or hard-) porn circuit of blue cinemas. The film reporters were promised, in the case of *The Full Monty,* what the script specified was a "full frontal naked star jump." As a producer explained his professional problem:

> We wanted to create something magical with the final shot. I felt six naked bums were quite sweet and fun—let the imagination do the work—whereas six sets of genitals might have seemed a bit, er, medical....

This was not good enough, not brave enough for the critics on the *Sunday Times*. One felt decidedly cheated by not having "all revealed," and one penned the harsh judgment that the climax was "in the final analysis, six sausages short of the full Monty."[11] No excuses would be acceptable. There had been, as was conceded, many complex considerations to the filming of new cultural phenomena of public nudity, all revolving about male insecurities about self-esteem ("worries about penis size, involuntary erections, pendulous beer guts, and impotence," etc.). Still, the troupe had promised to "go all the way" (and thus, according to the film's devious plot, recover their civic dignity)—and it had failed.

The formidable film critic, Tom Shone, was especially severe. He ruled that furtive bump-and-grind routines "wouldn't hold f*** all," and certainly would not compensate for the loss of full-frontal nudity.

> Far from seeing the full Monty, all we get is a bit of bare butts....[I]n place of real nudity, what we get is a whole lot of soul- and chest-baring....[B]asically this is a movie about bare bottoms....

Readers (and film-goers) may not quite credit the chagrin. This is the bitterness of "disappointment at this failure of nerve" on the part of writers who regularly choose not to go "the full Gutenberg" and accept to spell the *f-word* with three asterisks. As in all writing about the sexual mores which still have an aura of taboo about them, conspicuous hypocrisy rules; double standards are inevitable. As one of our press punsters ventured to say, always straining after pertinence (and even insight): what's sauce for the goose is not sauce for the gender.[12]

When the Kissing Had to Stop

In the running polemic between the two classic media, newspapers and television, the most characteristic ploy in the argument is the familiar and immemorial *tu quoque.*

In the televised critiques of "what the papers say" the impression is usually left on the viewer of how superficial, contradictory, and absurd daily journalism always is—given, especially, the sensationalism of cynical tabloid editors. For its part, its recurrent sanctimonious reportage of the depths to which electronic media have been sinking to cater to the lowest mass-cultural taste (with nudity, profanity, not to mention bloody violence), the press regularly insinuates the charge that the men and women who work in the upstart medium are somehow a breed apart. Journalists who write, alone at their desk, are nice and normal people; writers who play with pictures, hand-holding cameras and toying with actresses in studios or on location, are a scandalously dissolute lot. Thus, one newspaper headline reads,

ARE TV PEOPLE OVERSEXED?
The Sex Lives of People Who Work
in Television Dictate How Much Sex
We See on Screen

Much is made in this exposé of the coincidence that the great era of television expansion in the West occurred in the 1960s, a swinging era of sexual revolution. Even more is made of the bromidic life-style wisdom that when raunchy young men and nubile young women grow older, they may grow weary, slow down, change their minds, feel differently. Here is a retired old-time TV producer (and new-time novelist) joining the fray and confessing her sins:

As one of the sexual revolutionaries and campaigners against censorship, I ought to feel elated by how much sex there is on television. Back in the Sixties, when I started my television career...isn't that what we wanted? We yearned for freely-expressed, all-holds-allowed glorious sex for everyone to see and four-letter words bouncing into broadcast vocabulary....

She has had it all, Elisabeth Leigh has; she had it her way, and now she looks back:

Thankfully gone are the days when the head of an ITV company came unexpectedly in person to the cutting room to confiscate a pantomime scene of simulated sex between King Kong and a nun which I'd shot on a respectable New York stage. ("I can't allow that. People might think it's real.") I was outraged when I heard later he'd added it to his private collection of out-takes, presumably for exclusive showings in the boardroom....

The revolutionary experience was, as so many others have been, dramatically chastening:

> Sex seems to have been relegated to something you have to learn to do, like making profiteroles or growing camelias. Did we fight for sexual freedom to end up with a close-up of a condom?

What of the notion that television is populated by "depraved actors and crews in a permanent state of sexual frenzy"? She says that this was "more or less true—once." Evidently a new generation learns to make the beds differently (and when made, not even to lie in them). Miss Leigh, now far from the cutting room, observes with a novelist's touch: "But the more sexual activity there has been on the screen, it seems, the less has gone on behind it." As in the enriched memories of war veterans and the anecdotes of deep-sea fishermen things were so different in the old heroic days. "A well-known film and TV actress (you've seen her on your screen; we mustn't reveal her name) told me: 'If you weren't f***ing, you weren't on location.'" Obviously the chastened Elisabeth Leigh fought for the revolution of sexual freedom in order to wind up in the London *Evening Standard* with close-ups of bawdy colleagues:

> I once heard the late Donald Baverstock, the inspiring head of Yorkshire Television, bellow across an open-plan office to his minions: 'There's not enough f***ing going on around here.' For him, lively sex meant lively programs....

As in all revolutionary situations when the kissing has to stop, the desperate heavy-breathers turn to artificial respiration. The Jacobins, catching their second breath in the Terror of '93, bellowed in the Paris prisons that there was not enough guillotining going on around there (and added a few more names for the chop). The Bolsheviks, going on to a second and third round of Stalinist show trials in the 1930s, bellowed through the Lubianka there weren't enough confessions being confessed around there (and they tightened a few more screws). For all of them, lively purges meant lively progress.

But the "terror" in Miss Leigh's press war against the diehard TV extremists who distorted (even "betrayed") the sexual revolution is only mild and cultural, the harmless excess of a naive erotic utopianism. It was the ideology of a Tynan, following *Lady Chatterley's Lover*, in the belief that the more *f-words* going around the greater the liberation. It was the promise of *Hair*, singing of the dawn of the age of Aquarius, prophesying an idyll of sexual bliss. It was the credo of a whole army of free spirits from de Sade to Felix Salten and Henry Miller, for all of whom there was never enough of a good thing; and, as we will be hearing, it was a war cry that was echoed by the noisy combatants in the rear-guard (Messrs. Osborne, Amis, Selby, et al.).

What was currently agitating the observers of the scabrous scene was the instruction left by the late Dennis Potter (*Pennies from Heaven*; *The Singing Detective*) that not a line, not a word, could be changed or omitted from his last two new plays scheduled (in April 1996) for major production on both the BBC and the ITV in Britain. One play had the *f-word* forty times in its hour-long text; the other, a faltering forty-one times in almost two hours. (Potter did not prescribe how loud the volume had to be on for one to be properly invigorated by the artistic resonance of his inviolable dialogue.) Our old disenchanted veterans may feel "bemused and a little sad" about so much loyalty to old-fashioned orthdoxies; but they remain sentimental enough to be still fired by the old ideal that naked sexological truth will make ye free:

> Our heroes were outrageous creative talents like Potter and Ken Russell. We were also fired by another ideal. We believed that the physical closeness and affection peculiar to a film crew or a group of actors, although lasting only for a matter of weeks, would transfer to the screen. If it worked for Bogey and Bacall, if it worked for Truffaut...it would work for us.

After the revolution comes the winter of discontent. If in the sixties there may have been more sex behind the cameras than in front of them, a cool reversal appears to have taken place. Now, as Ms. Leigh authoritatively reports to the *Standard* (whose editors keep close tabs on what the TV crowd is really up to), "more simulated sex scenes are shot for the small screen than ever before. But behind the scenes, real sex is happening less and less." A Thermidorean reaction has set in. Budgets are tight; schedules are restricting; rehearsals oppress; accountants rule; time is rationed. And fear has come again:

> the dread that carefree affectionate sex might end in Aids prevails, especially in a profession (acting) where so many of the males are gay or bisexual. All this has terrorised the television industry.

But down in the Fourth Estate things are fairly straight and normal in the *status quo ante bellum*. The media enemy may enjoy the popularity of million-fold ratings among the youth but is in the process of castrating himself. There is life and hope in the old printed word yet. If you keep those asterisks flying, if you take care not to spell out everything in full, and risk post-coital sadness, even impotence, then you can keep going on for a long time to come.[13]

Oohs, Ahs, and a Wee Bit of Bother

The competitive struggle, at least in the times where the warring rivalries are not intense, has developed some polite collegial rules of engagement. There are certain Geneva conventions among professional journalists, and little victories can be scored in the skirmishes which respect the gallantry of the enemy. Thus, the broadcasters—necessarily scoring first with news beats of who won and who lost and its on-the-spot drama—are gently treated even when being sternly put down.

It was a relatively happy atmosphere at Royal Troon where a young Texan won the Open Golf Championship (in July 1997) and Tiger Woods made his European debut. The newspaper world's Monday morning quarterbacks (or, rather, caddies) underlined their linguistic indispensability by recording what kind of sports reporting one would have been getting if one had not bought the paper in one's hand—and was restricted to the wireless and the electronic media to keep up with events. Could they even cope? Here is a reporter writing—affectionately, as it happens—about a popular sports commentator named Peter Alliss, and his every slip of the tongue is carefully monitored: "There was a stiff breeze here on Thursday. But today it's...*ooh.*" What's with this expostulation? Is it in the *Oxford Dictionary*? "Oh, Fred [Couples]...*ooh,* he got away with it." And when Ernie Els bunkered at the fifth hole, "*Ooh,* Ernie." Finally, when another ball was seen rolling into the rough, "And that could be...well, I don't know." He still knew no more when, in a rather unfortunate moment, the TV camera's telescopic lens caught Tiger Woods inspecting his right arm-pit through the neck of his shirt. Alliss said: "*Oops!* Well, I..." and left it at that.

The point of the whole exercise in traditional British one-upsmanship was to demonstrate, yet again, the superiority of the written over the spoken word. Complete sentences are capable of telling a better story, and accurate prose is actually more graphic than even a picture. It accounts for the schoolmasterly tone, and the sniffy sense of pedantry: "His specialty is the sentence which lacks many of the grammatical parts for which sentences are famous." The reporter goes so far as to recommend to the broadcaster the lyrics of an old pop-combo song entitled "*Ooh to be Ah.*"

All this might be more amusing and indeed convincing if the standards for composing the written word in just these newspapers hadn't been in such a decline that their own misdemeanors included more grievous lapses than mere *oohs* and *ahs.* Their hanging, dangling clauses are also drawn and quartered.[14]

To be sure, the players themselves have linguistic problems; and once again, conventionally distant microphones and camera lenses have a distinct disadvantage over notebooks in which reporters can record questions and answers of nearby spectators. Tiger Woods was here, and in much else, at the center of attention. In a press conference the well-spoken and eloquent new American star of the golf links surprised many corresponents by confessing that he hadn't been in very good form: "I didn't drive the ball particularly well." One English columnist remarked, with more satisfaction than snootiness, that never in a donkey's years had he heard an American athlete "talking so good."

Still, Tiger would have his problems about the way English-as-she-is-spoken in this windy, remote coastline of Scotland. He was not offering any excuses about the mediocre performances on the old links that he had been turning in to finish so far down in the results. Still ,"People said things they shouldn't have out there...."[15] The microphones had caught nothing, and no TV lip-reader was at hand. What had been said? It would not have amounted to a serious transatlantic incident, but didn't we have a right to know?

> He refused to reveal exactly what spectators had shouted but was clearly upset after finishing 24th on level par. 'The kids came out and supported me, but what was said soured it for me a bit', Woods added....

What might have been lost to posterity—and certainly to my own researches into the expletives that don't ever get quoted (and, on occasions, never even get said)—found its way into the aforementioned notebook of an inquiring reporter who took the trouble to look into the affair. Apparently the incident occurred at the infernal tenth hole at Royal Troon when

> Approaching that tee, which adjoins a caravan park, Woods was hailed by a raucous, beer-bellied group of men and women who were in their element—if not all their clothes.
> 'Awright, how's it going wee man?' he was greeted with. It is to be hoped that someone confirmed to him later that this was the cheeriest of local salutations.
> But, after a slight acknowledgement of the guttural Scottish yell which, to him, must have sounded like dogs barking at each other, Woods decided he needed to answer the first call of nature....

The next natural question to ask was whether the "guttural yell" happened a wee bit before or a wee bit after the golfer had moved towards the handily placed Portaloo some ten yards away. A misunderstood salutation, more patronizing than ethnically cheerful, might well have added to the golfer's discomfort: "poor old Woods was then assailed with the same Scottish voice splitting he morning with 'Oh, I see, you're going for a wee, man.'" The caravan audience "thought it was a hoot," but Tiger Woods "lost his cool" which didn't help his putting problems. At least the newspaper culture, involved in the fine, punning distinctions between urinary slang and affectionate diminutives, did creditably in its search for the facts and the old quest for a wee bit of meaning. A London headline writer added yet another pun to round off the course:

TEED-OFF TIGER

IN WEE SPOT OF BOTHER[16]

10

Mailer's Tales of Oswald

Novelists love to make things up. It is the strength of their storytelling and the source of their imaginative vitality. For these very virtues they are not to be trusted when they turn to recording nonfictional realities. What emerges, more often than not, is a species of historical romance—a documentary novel which is, of course, a contradiction in terms—for it is only a pleasurable and/or instructive departure from the hard slog through confusing facts and the way things actually happened.

In this kind of surrogate history or biography, a likely theory and practice of quotation is the keystone which holds the structure feasibly together. Did the great man truly say what the writer says he said? Does a document really exist which incriminates or exonerates a protagonist in the way the story develops? Can we believe in—in addition to being charmed by—the elements of love or intrigue or dramatic motivation in the historical narrative being unfolded? The canons of scholarship, preserved by the academy, are strict and unswerving. Truth in history must be... true. It can be put more mellifluously than in professorial prose, and without the encumbrances of footnotes and appendices; but the historian must get it right: and be seen to be getting it right.

Norman Mailer's excursion into the riddles of the Kennedy assassination is a case in point. He is not trying his hand once again in colorful journalism, evincing what he once called his need "to speak to one's time," as in his bestselling accounts of the politics of the 1960s, catching tumultuous events on the wing. Here, in one of his new books entitled *Oswald's Tale: an American Mystery* (1995), he busies himself diligently with unpublished KGB transcripts and recollections of Oswald's friends in Soviet Russia before he returned to the U.S.—and to the Texas Schoolbook Depository building in Dallas. For his task he has devised a notable new approach. Even the *New Yorker*, which is never so finicky about such matters includes a footnote to explain it when it published (10 April 1995) a long narrative adapted from the book. It reads, in its full waywardness:

Even as one stains a slide in order to separate the features of its contents more clearly, so Oswald's letters and writings have been corrected here for spelling, clarity, and syntax. Oswald was dyslexic, and his orthography and syntax are so bad at times that the man is not revealed but concealed—in the worst of his letters he seems stupid and illiterate. Therefore, it seems worth giving him some benefit in this direction in order better to perceive the workings of his mind.

For a tiny (if well put) footnote, this is, as I suggest, a venture into extraordinary extremism, even for Norman Mailer. He would disdain the more workaday technique of citing the opaque originals and then to proceed with his interpretive transliterations. Audacious, as always, he goes in for a radical departure in the practices of historical veracity—and his rationalization is as ingenious and pretentious as it is specious and invalid. Consider the entry for 16 October 1959:

> I explain to her [Rimma, his official guide] I wish to apply for Russian citizenship. She is flabbergasted, but agrees to help. She checks with her boss, main office Intourist, then helps me address a letter to Supreme Soviet asking for citizenship.

One wonders what Oswald wrote originally—"flummoxed," perhaps, or "flubbergusted"? Kept in the dark as we are about the dyslexic originals, the primary evidence, we are subjected to a constant temptation to play scrabble with what we are being given in order, precisely, to get the actual words to reveal the real "workings of his mind." (Imagine taking the wild jottings of Nietzsche's last, mad year and correcting them... for any editorial reason whatsoever!)

A few days later Oswald expresses his dejection (21 October):

> Receive word ... I must leave country tonight at 8:00 p.m. as visa expires. I am shocked! My dreams! I retire to my room. I have $100 left. I have waited for two years to be accepted. My fondest dreams are shattered because of a petty official, because of bad planning. I planned too much!

Sounds a shade like a disappointed student, headed for a fail-pass, in one of John Kenneth Galbraith's Harvard seminars where planning (bad? too much?) was the credo.

Echoes alternate with questions. Other questions I am considering, apart from the stylistic one—the art of quotationmanship—can be left aside for now, although other critics have already taken them up in a similarly sceptical spirit.... the politics of the book, for one thing—and, for another, the originality and general plausibility of the theses it offers in the wake of some 2,000 other books on the subject of the Kennedy assassination.

One reviewer (in the *New York Times*) found the 828 pages of the leviathan volume "cumbersome" and rudely dismissed Mailer as "boring and presumptuous, derivative and solipsistic." Mailer scarcely deviates from the conventional conclusions—Oswald as a lone, non-conspiratorial killer—reached by the official Warren Commission almost four decades ago. But loners can be tragic ("rather than absurd"), and Napoleonic in their failure and defeat. Mailer has always been drawn to figures of outsize proportions, and they command his sneaking sympathies. One critic conceded that she didn't have enough "reserves of human sympathy" to respond to Mailer's invitation "to place a sympathetic arm around the killer's shoulders...."* In effect it is "an effort to dress a man—who by most other accounts was a small-time, troubled loser—in the garments of heroism...."** A good reason to be cleaning up his prose.

But, back at the factory in Minsk, Lee Harvey Oswald struggles vainly with his Russian studies and his copy of Dostoevsky's *Idiot*, and a young man's fancy in June turns to love. (Oswald had renounced his U.S. citizenship and was given official Soviet permission to stay and work in the USSR)

> Ella Germann—a silky black-haired Jewish beauty, with fine dark eyes, skin as white as snow, a beautiful smile and good but unpredictable nature. Her only fault was that at 24 she was still a virgin due entirely to her own desire. I met her when she came to work at my factory. I noticed her and perhaps fell in love with her the first moment I saw her.

Lee Harvey? or more like Norman? some little vignette of his that could be out of *The Deer Park* (1955)? or *An American Dream* (1964)? A fellow of infinite jest, he may just be toying with us.

What could the uncorrected versions—the originals—have been like? Not a trace of stupidity or illiteracy up till now. Nor here:

> As my Russian improves, I become increasingly conscious of just what sort of society I live in.... They don't seem to be especially enthusiastic about any of the "collective" duties, a natural feeling.... May be I will move to another socialist country. For example, Czechoslovakia....

> [Ella says] "You understand the world situation, there is too much against you and you don't even know it." I am stunned.... It is the state of fear which is always in the Soviet Union....

> *May 1, 1961:*

> Found us thinking about our future. Despite the fact I married Marina to hurt Ella, I found myself in love with Marina.

Little Maileresque twists of the story in Minsk—erotic complications, ideological disenchantment—before the onset of the big plot in Dallas.

---

*   Michiko Kakutani, in the *N.Y. Times/IHT*, 7 May 1995
**   Thomas Powers, in the *N.Y. Times Book Review*, 30 April 1995.

"They wanted to be pregnant right away," Mailer writes of Lee Oswald and his new, pretty Russian wife, and reveals that Lee wanted to have a boy and was going to call him David. One wonders: *David?* for the deadly power of the sling-shot that would bring down his giant of an enemy? One is, again, driven to playing games, to trivial pursuits: "Their boy, he assured Marina, would some-day be President of the United States." In the light of the fact that Oswald was to kill one White House incumbent to make room, it might have appeared important to transcribe that paraphrased forecast a little more precisely.

But historical precision is not necessarily the qualities of literature. Mailer's most respectful and enthusiastic reviewer, Thomas Powers, thought he de-tected in the Mailer texts "a brilliant linguistic invention"—namely, "a kind of Mailer-patent English that captures Russian rhythms not only of language but of thinking and feeling...." These are the kind of remarks that are best made without benefit of a mastery in the Russian language and its untranslated litera-ture. In any case, the brilliance would be relevant only to the way that Oswald's Russian friends talk and write. But what of "stupid, illiterate, dyslexic" Oswald himself? Isn't he also re-invented in another kind of "Mailer-patent English"? It is more accurate as well as more concise when Powers describes the style as "like a novel," and Mailer, among his twenty-seven previous books, has written some good ones, some bad ones, none of them the true stories we call history.

And so, in the very literary crescendo towards which we have been hurtling in long columns of some forty pages of the *New Yorker*, little remains but the well-constructed play of sentences. (Fade-out, with Marina, as Mailer's music comes up and under.)

> What is left of what once was her beauty are her extraordinary eyes, blue as dia-monds, and they blaze with light as if, in divine compensation for the dead weight of all that will not cease to haunt her, she has been granted a spark from the hour of an apocalypse others have not seen. Perhaps it is the light offered to victims who have suffered like the gods.

For that diamond-blue hour of apocalypse we would gladly take in ex-change some sixty little moments of truth, "sparks" embedded in facts and unadorned testimony. As for that divine suffering like the gods, we should have liked to have had it a few sizes smaller, bits of anguish and distress ex-pressed in their very own broken or unpatented words. All in all, perhaps it is this whole blazing conclusion that should have been "corrected"—"even as one stains a slide," etc.—"in order better to perceive the workings of" Norman Mailer's mind.

On page 60 of the text of *Oswald in the U.S.S.R.* the editors of the *New Yorker* inserted in their random way of publishing poetry a new poem by the Nobel Prize winner Czeslaw Milosz, and we find the poet asking what re-mains "*when words abandon us.*" This is the ultimate question: for now we only ask what remains when words are washed, pressed and folded, and each process shrinks truths, dyes insights, launders meanings?

11

Citations Sown

Sketch-Writers and Tinted Spectacles

The trouble with political quotations—snappy remarks by candidates on the road, empty rhetoric by stand-up parliamentarians, calculated evasions by devious cabinet ministers—is that not only can they be deceitful, dreadful in language and worthless as testimony (except for their own indictment). They are also contagious, and the style of double-talk and vapid banter begins over the years to rub off on readers. Can democracy survive on this self-indulgent fare?

Only rarely in the world's quality press is there a rubric in which the political events of the day are subjected to critical distance in which irony, satire and even a tinge of cynicism shade the tinted spectacles. The British press with its tradition of "parliamentary sketches" is exemplary. By contrast, in Europe the genre is almost unknown in the generally humorless continental press.

During the last twenty or thirty years there have been extraordinary observers sitting in the House of Commons gallery, and their dispatches delivered to the *Times* and the *Daily Telegraph* (here a trio of young men made their journalistic names: Frank Johnson, John O'Sullivan, Edward Pearce), and later to the *Independent*, were memorable. Colin Welch shone in the *Daily Mail*; and incomparable was Bernard Levin writing as "Tadpole" in the *Spectator* (and even President John F. Kennedy was a fan).

To be sure, there was no far-ranging political philosophy involved, and no consistent intellectual statement attempted. They were journalists, writing to a deadline and to a brief: they had to be accurate, to be witty, to be iconoclastic, and to be concise. This was not a branch of punditry, and no permanent contributions were required to be made—in competition, say, with the grave and

127

profound disquisitions of a Walter Bagehot or a Charles Beard or a Tocqueville—to the theory and practice of democracy. In one corner of the daily newspaper, nobly dedicated to all the fine journalistic ideals of truth and the public happiness, a wicked pen could be witty, flippant, salty—and the salt was wherewith the mush and the pap which was served up to us each day by our masters was made tolerable.

I use two current illustrations from the morning newspaper (*Daily Telegraph*, 16 February 1995) which arrived as I write.

The sketch writer is Max Davidson; and the scene, as usual, is the House of Commons in which, the day before, there had been a debate of no real consequence but, from the sound and fury, could have been taken for stormy:

> Mr Gummer had got out of bed the wrong side. The Environment Secretary's mood can be deduced from his wardrobe and, from his selection of a yellow tie with angry red blobs on, the cognoscenti knew to fasten their seat belts. It wasn't a question of whether he would lose his temper, but when and with whom.

Thackeray or Trollope could not have set the scene better. The argument was on the subject of out-of-town shopping malls, and their desirability in the face of the dying small-town family shops. One Labour spokesman defended the people and their human rights to get a bargain-on-the-cheap anywhere. Mr. Gummer was sitting on the fence. As he said, to general confusion, "I am not going to be drawn on Streatham High Street." Whereupon the sketch writer pounced:

> Did the pavement artists of Streatham *want* to draw Mr Gummer? Hadn't they got more suitable subjects for their talents? For a brief, zany moment, one imagined shoppers coming out of Tesco and having to step over a life-size sketch of the minister, yellow tie and all.
>
> At which point, enter Mr Keith Vaz (Lab., Leicester East) with an attack on out-of-town shopping centres. It wasn't a particularly aggressive question, but it sparked a positively ferociously response from the minister.
>
> "The Labour Party," he thundered, "has done more to destroy inner cities than anything else since the War." The Opposition growled its protest. Mr Vaz opened his mouth to say something. But it was too late. Mr Gummer was apoplectic. He had lost it.
>
> "The honourable gentleman ought to retain himself," he shouted, a classic malapropism made funnier by the incandescent anger with which it was delivered. "This party...and this Government...do *not* go back on their promises." It was practically a scream and brought pandemonium....
>
> The tetchiness spread....[There was] a bizarre reference to "a dog-eat-dog situation in which there are more winners than losers". (Surely only the smaller dogs, the ones who got eaten, would qualify as losers?)....

Etc., etc.; and all this, of course in a Tory newspaper which usually can be counted on to be sympathetic with the Conservative Government spokesmen.

In the U.S., this kind of thing is only done occasionally—but with no less wholesome effect—when somebody like Art Buchwald turned his syndicated column to kidding a senator, a congressman, or even the president himself. The jokes were more muted in the elegant pieces by Russell Baker on current gobbledygook, and more frenetic when Dave Barry lets himself loose on political absurdities.

The electoral fever in the U.S. can unleash some quips like the following by Clinton's strategist, James Carville: "You get so nervous you don't know whether to scratch your watch or wind your feet" (*New York Times*). A waste of space? News fit to print? Mildly entertaining? For those of us readers who didn't pore over with a magnifying glass the latest ups-and-downs of the Wall Street stock-exchanges, these homely saws are harmless little turns of phrase which bring a weak, wan smile to our lips.

Still, a handful of journalists will be remembered as flowers in our newspaper culture. All have distinguished themselves, to shift metaphors, as Socratic "gadflies of the State"; and they can be read with pleasure and instruction. Or perhaps I have been spoiled to addiction by the experience, in "olden times," by my father reading out to me the regular exercise in irony, then published by the *New York Times* in a tidy little one-column box, by the famous wit of the day, Will Rogers (1879-1935). My schoolboy impression was that the daily joke, a tidbit of an *aperçu*, was all that stood between political jabberwocky and public sanity.

The dictionaries of quotations preserve for us today some characteristic Will Rogers quips and their relevance suggests that democracy and its discontents cannot long be borne without a sense of humor:

My forefathers didn't come over on the *Mayflower*, but they met the boat.

More men have been elected between sun-down and sun-up than between sun-up and sun-down.

Politics has got so expensive that it takes a lot of money to even get beat with.

Everything is funny as long as it is happening to somebody else. *

And his most pertinent crack (at least for us working our way through a thousand cuttings) remains the coy and forlorn catchphrase:

All I know is just what I read in the papers.

"Sez You? Sez Me!"

For all its occasional abuse in mean-spirited racialist mockery, phonetic transcription is usually a gentle parodic instrument, poking fun with open af-

---

* *Bartlett's Dictionary of Quotations* (16th ed., 1992), pp. 637-8.

fection. A novelist's ear gives us a sentimental reminder in a Sunday newspaper of how Maurice Chevalier sang a famous song: "sank evan for leedle girls...."[1] There are even occasions when the phonetic technique is pertinent and essential to an illuminating discussion of what the news story is all about. It still retains its elements of parody and humour but it has a kernel of truth. How else, for example, can you comprehend that great tragedy in the successful career of Johnny Hallyday, France's *grand rockeur* with a hundred hit-songs behind him but never a one in the Anglo-American big-time? At the ripe age of fifty-one he was still attempting to break the „cultural barrier," and the obstacle appears mainly to be his French accent. The Paris correspondent of the *Times* hastens to inform, for whatever concern it is to the English, that Monsieur Hallyday is putting aside "the language of Descartes to release an album in American (sic), *Rough Town...*." The ambition is get „the requisite gutsy blues sound..." But does he have enough charm and decipherable enunciation to make it where only Maurice Chevalier succeeded before? The *Times* is sceptical.

> Somehow, a Paris accent gets in the way of the image conjured by *"Rough Town, Gotta find a Way Outta Here"*. Perhaps they should have written words without an *'r'* in them so he could have avoided singing lines such as *"You nevairr look back on the rrruins that rrremain like a'urricane..."*[2]

Barring the unlikely event of "Franglais" being approved by the Académie Française as an export incentive for the nation's pop culture, the Paris star has only an outside chance "to convince the US that French rock is not an oxymoron." The hip writer in *InfoMatin* is only whistling in the dark when he rationalizes: "But as the English would say, *'Ze Frenche accent is veri sexy.'*" Is this sort of thing endangering the *Entente* and the peace of Europe? My personal rule of thumb and advice is to suspend all sensitivities about ethnic slights, and related injunctions of political correctness—but to be forewarned that the French will be rather easier to take on than the Irish, the Jews, the Italians, and the Japanese. When the heart of the matter is an accent—the odd lilt of a phrase, a fatal twist in a tricky word—then the comic turn of funny phonetics is surely excusable.

Only a few will resent its being *legit, hokay, baynay, tray byen*, even *velly light* and deserving a *banzai*.

To get a point home, *nuffink* is taboo.

Inverted Commas in Sports

Given the notorious illiteracy of many of our most splendid athletic stars—strong men in a ring, fleet figures on a track, skillful teenagers on a court, admirable champions all!—it condemns the sports reporters to be constantly scraping the barrel in order to get a quotable quote in a fast interview after a triumphal record-breaking event. A bit of slang, an odd phrase, a grammatical error or two, a wild expostulation which can be colorfully transliterated—any and all will do. "Anything goes"—even intimations of profanity—when it can be put between inverted commas.

The practice is all the more compelling for print journalism since it has become hard-pressed to rival the verbal power conveyed on TV-film by a loquacious Cassius Clay after a predicted first-round K.O. of his challenger, or an angry John McEnroe enraged at losing a Grand Slam match after a series of outrageous out-calls by an obviously blind linesman.

In the end, as I suggest, we will be winding up being fed bare scraps, hardly printable. Few boxers have had Mohammed Ali's wit or Gene Tunney's literary education, and the teen-agers who have made it to the top in track or tennis have had their entire adolescence spent in physical training, not in the classroom. Their vocabularies are understandably and excusably limited. They pick up buzzwords from their coaches—and, if they are quick-witted, from the press interviewers themselves—and proceed to talk earnestly about their problems in "mental preparation" or getting "really focused." But usually, their insipid opinions and what passes for critical analyses of a victory or a perceptive explanation of defeat are helpless and inadequate. In the old days the Sports Expert would not deign to quote them.

I used to follow the daily pieces from Forest Hills in the *New York Times*, and Allison Danzig never failed to enchant with his eloquence and acumen. Three or four decades later the tennis story of how the Wimbledon champion was upset by her Spanish rival featured the immortal explanation of Senorita Arantxa Sanchez Vicario of her victory over the world No. 1 player, Steffi Graf—"She's a very gutsy player, but I outgutsied her!" For Allison Danzig the whole match was a prose poem of skill and risk, courage and agility, and a strategic context whose tactical details only he could put in proper words. Guts here, intestinal fortitude there; both were to be avoided like an awful double-fault on match-point.

The same would obtain, *mutatis mutandis*, for masters of sports journalism like John Kieran (also of the *New York Times*), Al Laney (Danzig's tennis rival on the *Herald-Tribune*), Jimmy Cannon of the *N.Y. Post*, Grantland Rice of the *World-Telegram*, and a whole host of others, who would never use a quote when a colorful and incisive phrase of their very own would do. This was equally true of sports writing in British journalism. Even as late as the post-World War II decades. I followed with a loyalist admiration stylists like Geoffrey Green of the *Times* who made literary drama of football and golf, and any other game he was assigned to report—and (blessed be his memory) Neville Cardus of the *Manchester Guardian* where he played a double role: as the finest music critic in England since George Bernard Shaw, and a writer on cricket who made the game into a philosophical ballet even for those readers who couldn't tell a *l.b.w.* (shame on you!) from a *googly* (are they still allowed?).

This is a far cry from the story in the morning's paper about a recent crisis of American baseball. The long strike was over; the new season was in full swing; but the big league fans were still embittered, and were not in full attendance—which was prompting the baseball moguls to try and make the game more attractive, by introducing long-promised reforms (to speed up the slow-moving nine innings, and the like). Here is the report in the *New York Times* (*IHT*, 13 July 1995), giving us the latest controversy about anchoring the hitters in the batter's box, changing the size of the pitcher's strike zone (and also the height of the mound from which he hurls the ball), and various other worrisome innovations. The important interview was with an apparently expert figure named Phil Garner, who is evidently so famous in the sport that he does not need to be precisely identified (so I can't tell you who he is and why his views matter so much); but he is, as far as one can judge from what the *Times* reported of his conversation, a man of very limited vocabulary. The paper, one suspects at this distance, would have been far better off publishing a succinct informative paragraph rather than some nine-hundred-word feature which included this (among more of the same).

> "Four home runs [which had been hit in the All-Star Game between the victorious National League and the American League] is a lot of power," Phil Garner noted, "but it's not a lot of offense".... "They want to change the strike zone and raise the mound (Garner said after the game at the Ball Park in Arlington). That might enable them to play faster, but it will reduce offense. You poll the fans out there tonight and they want to see offense".... "We shouldn't do anything that takes away offense....If you raise the mound and pitchers get more outs, it will reduce the offense....We're messing with things that will decrease the offense," etc. etc.

I take it that Mr. Garner was a reactionary who was against the reforms in question, and that he had been taking offense against changes in the rules and regulations of the American national sport, baseball. Not a few readers who do happen to be inveterate fans might have thought that a journalist could have had the editorial skill to tell us just a bit more over the three columns of type. Regrettably, a newspaper's habit in the era of quotable-quotes of making the interviewee's word-poverty and other linguistic deficiencies their very own is, well,...offensive. I recognize they only want to share the slang, to rap with one of the boys, to tell it like it is, to record the speech natural to common men. But I am afraid—to vary the journalistic vice I have previously registered—it is a case of participatory illiteracy.

The "genius" of great sporting performers lies in their athleticism, not in their literacy. But there was a time in the history of journalism when the sports writers were entranced by champions who spoke prose. World Champion heavyweight boxer, Gene Tunney (who outpointed Jack Dempsey in 1926-27), could quote from Shakespeare by heart, and was, in turn, quoted gratefully by the press. But in recent decades the sports page story did not lie in the good poetry but in the bad prose, enfeebled vocabulary and wild grammar, of young men and women who had no time, beyond their indefatigable devotion to the cutting edge of competition , to sharpen their way of talking. (When it came to writing the obligatory book of their careers, publishers always provided the good ghost.)

On the assumption that readers—as well as the TV-viewers— were eagerly waiting to hear the weary footballer, basketballer, or tennis ace put together a few personalized remarks about victory or defeat, we are overwhelmed by primitive phrases and vapid sentences somehow culled from somebody else's conversation that happened to stick in the mind. "I was mentally strong today...I just lost my competitive edge...I can't say what caused me to play *so bad,* or *so good,* or *so focused* (or *unfocused*)." In today's paper, reporting on the June 1996 French Open, I find the usual space-filling insipidities, here Michael Stich being quoted on his surprising victory: "This is something I never would have believed could or would happen," Stich said. "I don't know why it happened or how it happened, but it happened." The real mystery is why such mindless twaddle, extorted by the publicity machinery of million-dollar sports industry from weary stars who have to make the evening news, ever gets printed.[3] On the other hand, when on some rare occasion an athlete turns up with an unusual facility for perfuming a phrase —e.g. the French football star, Eric Cantona, who led Manchester United to numerous titles and prizes—he is quoted and ridiculed especially for the extravagant metaphor in the verse he himself writes. In the end, he confined himself to scoring incredible last-minute goals, and maintaining a discreet Gallic silence rather than become a figure of fun for journalists who have been accustomed to ungrammatical grunts with the bits of fine language being left to the press professionals of the English word.

Perhaps this is becoming a division of labor that suits both parties; both can profit from what they do best. When sports writers are good, they are very good indeed (and honors have been heaped upon them, from Grantland Rice to Red Smith). Small wonder many have graduated into other sections of the paper. Sports journalists excel in a kind of fast-moving metaphor, possibly because they are always involved in events of pace and speed, and not (as are their newspaper colleagues) in the slow and long drawn-out trends in politics and finance. Writing of the new captain of the England football squad, Michael Parkinson, for example, notes that even in an interview "the body fairly hurls with energy—you feel that if you put a bulb in his mouth it would light up."[4]

A few loquacious athletes can compete with their own one-liners, but what happens to the greenhorn speech difficulties of the immigrant stars? Foreigners, although they are rare birds in high-flying big-league sports, become suitable targets for a few comic turns with mispronunciation and fractured grammar. The Lithuanian accent is not known to have a flourish of its own, so the interviews with the 7-foot-3, three-hundred-pound basketball star (for the Portland Trail Blazers) come up with rather paltry pickings.

> His teammates do not speak a word of Lithuanian but Sabonis' secret is that during his decade as a Blazer recruit he learned quite a bit of English.
> "So, you like beer?' he was asked the other day.
> "Who don't?" Sabonis said.[5]

This poor excuse of a quotable anecdote is far from being a put-down. The powerful Arvydas Sabonis (once again: 2.2 meters, 135 kilos) would not be tempted to lean on the writer who was only making a good-natured, if jejune, effort to bring a sympathetic smile to the reader's lips.

I am not certain whether it is intentional or accidental, but the constant attention paid to every twist and turn of an interviewee's language does one cultural service, after lending some color and human interest to the story. It preserves old slang from becoming quickly obsolete and giving way to new colloquialisms and buzzwords which could have even a shorter shelf-life: "Did we do these things?...You're doggone right we did!"

You may not, as I have not, met a person in the last fifty years who ever said "doggone," a hill-billy dog-patch cracker of an expression if there ever was one. But it is evocative of yesterday's speech, redolent of the old reluctance to use real "cuss-words" which take the name of the Lord in vain; and one is grateful to the reporter who catches it and doesn't "correct" it or "edit it out." He preserves a bit of old slangy phraseology that still has a faded touch of color, a slightly tangy flavor.

While I am in a mood of gratitude, I appreciate also the short-hand descriptions of the various attempts to "clean up the game," whether football, basketball, and even boxing; I like especially the kind of drastic warning to the delinquent athletes that they will be "sent off" or condemned "to the bench" or "to the penalty box" or otherwise "taken out"—"If they go on doing what they're doing they'll be in foul trouble." It is a *terminus technicus*—"committing a professional foul," in soccer—but it sounds almost Shakespearean with its accidental echo of "murder most foul." But then we must not let our athletes get away with murder, must we? In the ethics of sport *should* there be any such contradictory thing as a "professional foul"?

For addicts of some branch of athletics the *New York Times* is indispensable, for they can get detailed dispatches from almost everywhere by their far-flung correspondents. I follow, among other sports, the tennis results, and with gratitude one learned from Robin Finn in Melbourne how the Australian weather was playing havoc with the seeded favorites, who were losing in upsets, one by one. Writing about Boris Becker, we gather that "he blamed the searing summer sun for scrambling his brains like eggs in a frying pan...." Other players "wilted" and "disintegrated"; a few revived with "ice-packs." Although it was winter in our time zones, we got the point. Still, there is white space to fill and post-match interviews to be quoted. How hot was it out there really? And what could anybody drink (a soda water? a cola?) to offset the dehydration? The stories soaked up detail after detail like the wet head-bands on dripping foreheads. Was the reportage all worth it? Then Michael Chang came to the rescue of one of his ball-girls who fainted. The *Times* reporter rushed intrepidly to the interview after close of play in the day's Australian Open. What had he done, and why had he done it?

> Chang provided first aid to a ball-girl who fainted in the third set....Chang furnished a chilled towel to help revive the girl.
> "I think she had a bit too much heat," Chang said.[6]

Was it understatement that made the remark so eminently quotable? Good stories, confided a friendly Sulzberger of the *Times* to me years ago, "just gotta have quotes, otherwise they're not believable." I would have thought that a single sentence, with a few well-chosen words, would have sufficed for the metereological side of the news from Down Under. I still remain conscience-stricken about all those Canadian forests being cut down to make the newsprint to inform us that the heat comes from the blazing sun, that the sweat comes from the perspiration, that indeed you can get too much of all of them. You better believe it, and that's a quote....

In sports the equivalent of the gossip columnist's saw about being famous-for-being-famous is brilliant-for-being-erratic-and-unintentionally-funny. The most celebrated figure in British broadcasting, the "dominant figure in BBC sport" and a "national institution" used to be David Coleman, now over seventy and on the verge of retiring (which event will bring tears to the cheeks of millions of faithful listeners and viewers). Still, quite beyond his achievements—including an eight-hour broadcast from Munich, dramatically following the Black September (1972) assault on the Israeli Olympic athletes—is his vaunted "mastery of the malapropism at a magic moment" (the *Independent*, 26 April 1996). His erratic facility inspired a column in *Private Eye* which first drew attention to the manic propensity for TV sports commentators, unscripted and under pressure, to make gaffes. The press, which has time to choose its words (and even to have them checked and sub-edited), is relentless and indefatigable in quoting "the distinctive voice" as it blunders into what has become immortalized as "*Colemanballs.*" Here is a sampling, prepared by a newspaper which slyly suggests how much the television spectator is missing when *our* sportswriters don't have the last word. They are more finicky, but surely less funny and fulsome:

Here are some names to look forward to—perhaps in the future.

He's 31 this year. Last year he was 30.

And with an alphabetical irony Nigeria follows New Zealand.

I don't think he's ever lost a race at 200 meters, except at 400...

There's a mistake on the scoreboard: they're only showing his Christian names, Ismail Ibrahim.

At the Schools Athletics Championships, you can see the youngsters of the future.

I was keeping my legs and fingers crossed for him.

It's a race that the Kenyans have dominated—but, looking at the records, it's the first time they've won it.[7]

In fact Coleman always disclaimed that the knack for verbal indiscretion that launched the debunking and, possibly, embarrasing *Private Eye* column. (Still, isn't being a notorious figure-of-fun a form of inimitable success in our newspaper culture?) But the man who became famous for "and Juantorena opens his legs and shows his class"; "They're still faster, although their times are still the same"; and "Absolutely right, and just a fraction wrong"; and the surreal "She's really tough, she's remorseful"—will always be re-enjoying his fifteen-minutes of fame in times to come.

There are times in the great sporting occasions when the souls of even the most hardened of professional reporters get sorely tried. Some get their assignments changed, move on to other pages, go in for politics or travel writing. Others hold out and are permitted to lose their patience and deliver themselves of judgments above their usual station. Among the strictest of the occasional moralists is an English writer named *(nomen est omen)* Calvin. Here is Michael Calvin reporting from Suzuka, Japan, on the last days of the 1997 motor racing competition. Two would-be champions are scheduled to give a press conference to "hot up" the Grand Prix atmosphere of Formula One's "phony war" between Jacques Villeneuve and Michael Schumacher. What they said—presumably in anger, resentment, rivalry and envy—went largely unreported. There must have been the usual "juicy bits" and familiar clichés. But this time we were given another story. As Calvin sniffily reported,

As the drivers sat next to each other, delivering a succession of inanities that purported to be a reasoned commentary on their duel for the world championship, they were notably ill at ease....Schumacher smirked, evidently heartened by his rival's discomfort....[8]

As some other rival or even reader must have observed, this was a "kind of gutsy" reaction for a sports writer on the job to reveal; if things go on this way (but they won't) we will be collecting inanities and vapidities and miss out altogether on the virtually real life-and-death melodramas on all the world's playing fields. As it happened Schumacher crashed himself out of the final race by a disgraceful attempt to block Villeneuve's speeding by.

On the other hand, some chaps have all the luck. On the same day, in the same paper, the *Times'* man in Rome, Oliver Holt, was able to fill his assigned space on the sports pages with revealing and intelligent quotations from a football star in the England team, cogitating on the prospects of an all-important international game between England and Italy. The man had been surprisingly appointed as his team captain after he had won a long, successful bout against alcoholism which seemed, in the sober judgement of coach and trainer, "to enhance his qualities as a leader of men...." Tony Adams evidently no longer drinks-and-drives or prattles-babbles. The journalist was almost taken aback by a "thoughtful, searingly introspective conversation":

> Adams not only talks about serenity, but he exudes it, too. He talks slowly now, in such a studied quiet way that it is almost soporific. There is something almost monastic about the tone of his words. Where he might once have yelled and screamed a call to arms, he said, he would try to use his influence to steady young nerves as tomorrow's kick-off approached.

One illustrative quote, and we are done: a common man's speech is uncommonly readable—

> Banging the toilet door has never won football matches. Maybe that was the kind of approach I used to adopt. This time, there might be a process of calming some of the younger boys down.

> You can go over the top with enthusiasm. Calming down and using your brains should be what it is about....It is hard to be serene during a football match but beforehand we can be, can't we? I don't have to go running round the hotel like a nutcase any more....

> I have always been able to motivate people throughout the years and that is maybe why people have put me as captain. I have been able to focus in on certain individuals. I preferred that to looking at myself. Maybe there was too much going on inside me to have a look at me....I can now handle defeat and success and take all that into my private life....I have to pinch myself at times but I do not fear anything any more.

It is the least of my intentions to be poking indiscriminate fun at the sports sub-section of our newspaper culture. There is somewhere a mechanism of a self-parody built into those pages whose origins I cannot quite determine. It certainly was not functioning in the great, classic period of modern journalism when writing about athletics produced exemplary prose (and indeed, as I have mentioned, those masterly journalists who went on to make other literary careers). The great tradition, not to put too fine a point on it, goes back to classical days, and one can read Virgil's pages on ancient games in the *Aeneid* today with much pleasure and excitement.

In our own day there was along the way a professional turning point when our American sports became such a prosperous mass-cultural branch of the entertainment industry that no sports writer could resist the temptation of making his name as an entertainer himself. Show business demands gags; and all of our stadia are a stage. Whether on the playing field or in the press box, histrionics became the order of the day. Language no longer needed to be put on its best behavior; fanatics became *fans*, and the theatrical enthusiasm of the broadcasters (first in radio, and then on television) captured the tumult and the shouting at its most infectious roar. ·

When sportswriters like James Reston (among many others) became distinguished political commentators, they brought to the reporting and analysis of the grave affairs of state an original vivacity which added to prose style in our newspaper culture. Later generations of reporters turned away from the old literary standards which good writing was supposed to entail and which, one thought, was shared in all journalistic departments. I used to read "the Shipping News" in the old *New York Sun* and clipped for my schoolboy scrapbook many admirable pieces of crisp, unaffected prose, quite free of, say, the slang of the water-front. Even the intellectual standards of a paper's cross-word puzzle symbolized a faithful devotion to a stylish and knowledgeable way with words and meanings.

The canned laughter of show business disrupted all that. Every sports story had to perform, for it aspired to be as exciting and rewarding as the cliff-hanging game itself. Why else read all about it? Sports writing became an extension of a called time-out or an over-time, full of murmurs and whisperings but always preserving the *fanzine* tension which filled the stadium on the day and attracted readers even the morning after. I am pleased to offer a last example in this section which constitutes not only evidence for these suggestions but offers proof that these remarks are not being hurled from the outside, in an interpretation which could only reflect the cool distance of a non-playing "foreign" observer. The state of self-criticism in the newspaper world has its healthy, vigorous, and incisive phases—if only what is wrong and indeed ridiculous is put in a way which is fun to read. (Even the *Washington Post*'s "ombudsman" has to turn in lively copy.) Accordingly I turn again for words of wisdom from Dave Barry, the humorous columnist of the *Miami Herald*.

He was (over the Fourth of July 1997) celebrating "The Joys of Being a Sportswriter." He found himself, as he writes, "trying to do what sportswriters really do," namely, "to try and get intelligible statements from large mumbling naked men in the locker room." He was only doing it for his sportswriting wife who was hard-pressed to obtain a few "quotable quotes." The passage is worth reproducing not least because it indicates that even a Miami entertainer knows what's wrong with the show.

> So player quotes are critical; the problem is that the players almost never have anything to say. This is not their fault. They shoot the ball; it goes into the basket, or it doesn't. What is there to say about it?
>
> But reporters are constantly badgering the players for quotes. In response, the players have developed Sports Blather. This is a special language consisting of meaningless words and phrases—such as "execute," "focus," "step up," "find a rhythm," "game plan," "mental errors," and the "next level"—that professional athletes can string together in any random order to form quotes.

A prime example is easily at hand, for our man is sure playing good and is right on for gutsy valor (even to the splitting of an infinitive)—

> "We made some mental mistakes, but...we gamely planned to erroneously focus on stepping up our level of mental rhythm."
>
> Professional athletes regularly make statements just as incoherent as these while hordes of reporters religiously record every word.

On the same day and in the same paper a reporter on the *Washington Post* was recording religiously every word of one Randy Myers, a baseball All-Star relief pitcher in the American League: "Image? I don't have an image," he said, knowing he's got a beaut. This last is only an abbreviated part of a word, but they do get fuller as Thomas Boswell *(nomen est omen)* proceeds with his Boswellian recording of the Interview about the Image. But first it was important for the reader to know, as Dave Barry may not have made absolutely clear, how difficult the task is without falling into "caricature."

> Myers is usually no help on the subject of Myers. You can interview him in four different uniforms over a 10-year period and you still get argumentative answers to simple questions. In his first Orioles game in 1996 he got a save. Twenty reporters gathered beside his locker, but none knew him on sight. So Myers sat directly behind them, nibbling cold cuts, enjoying their ignorance for 15 minutes. When one reporter finally sat beside him and said, "Nice way to start," Myers snapped, "I'm eatin'."

After that prolegomena to the complex subject, the interview can move now into its high mode of quotability:

> "How come you never give interviews?"
>
> "I never give interviews," said Myers.

"How are people going to know how good you are?"
"I'm the best," said Myers.[9]

This, I am afraid, moved me to shedding another tear for that wastefully felled forest tree in far-off Canada, given the chop to make newsprint for such stop-press news.

Unquoting the Quote

In a dispatch from Jerusalem in the aftermath of the bomb violence and the killing of a young Arab presumed to be a terrorist, Clyde Haberman of the *New York Times* quotes an editorial in the newspaper *Ha'aretz* to the effect that if the Arab was in fact involved in murder and terrorism, then "he got the punishment coming to him." Then came a Biblical quote, "for they have sown the wind, and they shall reap the whirlwind." Either the correspondent (less likely) or the sub-editor at the New York foreign-news desk thought it the better part of pedantry to make the attribution specific to every reader, as if the Old Testament epigram could cherish an ethnic argument: "The quotation was from Hosea 8:7."[10]

We of the Pedants Patrol immediately reached for our Bible; and it was indeed accurate, just so. But why, when they were about it, didn't they mention that it was the King James translation, and presumably *Ha'aretz* quoted it in the rather more authentic Hebrew of the prophet in ancient Israel? As for myself I rather like the more compact version of the N.I.V. (p. 842): "They sow the wind and reap the whirlwind." The effort to get things right is laudable and noble, but it sure slows down reading your morning newspaper. At the moment I am trying to decide whether Martin Luther didn't put it even better in his sixteenth-century German version: *"Denn sie säen Wind und werden Sturm ernten."* Isn't the proverb more direct without definite articles? Could it be that the non-repetitive *Wind/Sturm* contrast is a shade more vivid and sinister? Where pedants sow, pedantry reaps to excess.

And, indeed, the pedantic ploy which has plentiful variations can be put into reverse, leaving the reader not with more but with less than he needs to know. William Safire can always be counted upon to give the ongoing thing an extra twist, and as a self-styled *maven* about the art of quotation he has risked—in the *New York Times* yet!—this item of what Stephen Potter coined as one-upmanship. Safire gives the precise ascription but omits the quote, as if we knew the sacred texts by heart.

The '94 election swept Newt Gingrich into the powerful post of Speaker of the U.S. House of Representatives, and his prudent opening statement elicited from Safire the comment that "a partisan tiger was changing his stripes." Gingrich had been notorious for his youthfully impulsive remarks and behaviour, and now he had been "seized with a sudden maturity celebrated in

1 Corintheans 13:11." Safire left it at that, with the Biblical wisdom hanging in the air before us. Our Pedants Patrols everywhere were seen to beat a hasty retreat to their book-lined shelves. The passage in *Corinthians* should have been memorized, by rote, and known outright since—well, childhood: "When I was a child, I spake as a child, I understood as a child, I thought as a child: but when I became a man, I put away childish things."

This King James (1611) version has been altered in characteristic ways by the committee of scholars who put out the translation which is known as the New International Version (1979). The committee prefers "*talked*" to "*spake*" and likes to think that Paul didn't simply "put away childish things," but put these "*ways*" "*behind*" him. Altogether, the N.I.V. likes *like* as against *as,* offering "I reasoned like a child" etc. I suspect that William Safire refrained from giving the passage its full explicit power in the Gingrich affair because it might have landed him into an "*As* vs. *Like*" adverbial quarrel—like, you know, pedantic grammarians are prone to do, as we childishly admit.

We are on tricky and even dangerous ground here. What was the threat of the poet (Burdett) who wrote "The Purple Cow"?—"I'll kill you if you quote it!" But then, as Peacock is always quoted as saying, "A book that furnishes no quotations is no book, it is a plaything."

So, earnestly, my suggested rule-of-thumb would be to quote the Quotation (in full splendour or in rich paraphrase, yet not arousing the wrath of the author)—or to give the Source—but never both together.

For one thing, one runs in newspapers the risk of being embarrassed by a slight typographical error. For example, Hosea slightly misnumbered to 7:8 (which speaks of Ephraim as "a cake not turned" and may turn out, for a family paper, to be obscene). Or: 1 Corinthians erratically printed 11:13 (which only speaks of "uncovered women" and they may not be exactly pertinent).

For another, footnotes—and this may be an excusably pedantic point—do not belong in the body of the text. This is confirmed by any style-book ever written—that is, ever since Pierre Bayle wrote his famous encyclopaedia featuring hundreds of full-page footnotes covered only by a single, lonely line of type at the top of the page.

As for journalists who write for a newspaper like *Le Monde* in Paris—which finds it intellectually chic to publish minute six-point annotations at the foot of their elegant columns—they can do as they please.

12

Words, Words, Words...

The Old Maid of Times Square

I do not mean to give the impression that the Old Maid of Times Square is consistently prudish, wrapping her skirts tightly against the grubby realities that each of its editors had to pass daily on tawdry 42nd Street. She, too, tries hard to keep up and go along—as far as her *amour propre* allows—with the erotomania of the culture of Pop Kulchur. Now and then the *New York Times* finds an opportunity to point a finger at the penchant for explicitness without, of course, ever stepping over the line and being overly explicit itself. These are valiant attempts for the *Times* to "get with it," and within its own lights it is, sort of.

This is the way one of its cultural correspondents, Jon Pareles, deals with the various careers of a pop star known mainly as "Prince" but who has, frankly, "acted oddly through the years...." Alert and informed reporters know that he has sometimes tried "a subject other than sex"—a protest song against housing discrimination, a plea for a pop star's creative freedom (against his record companies). But "soon enough he gets back to his true vocation" which is "creating music that pulses and moans and shimmies with the rhythms of lubricity."[1] Since *lubricity* is defined as "having or showing too great an interest in sex, esp. in a way that is unpleasant or socially unacceptable," there is a semantic minefield here; and the *Times*, as is its wont in these delicate matters, treads warily.[2] It tells us "while Prince didn't invent heavy breathing songs, he did give them a certain slow-rolling groove and a willingness to be explicit"— and it stops just there, just short of being explicitly lubricious itself. It does go on to tell us (perhaps overworking its own odd vocabulary of recondite euphemisms) that he had "publicly toyed with androgyny"; but then, to be fair, adds that "he was, and is, a prodigiously gifted musician." There is a certain melo-

143

drama in the balancing act, a tension between off-beat sex and oddball genius, being in-it and with-it; and it makes for a good story about a star who "dropped his name for an unpronounceable glyph."*

> Trying to adapt to the hip-hop juggernaut, he added rappers to his group and brandished a gun-shaped microphone, but he ended up sounding provincial and awkward.

At least to his metropolitan fans in Times Square. But then they go out of their way to give both the musical prodigy and the aging "Casanova" his due. His new albums have "ingenious musical detail...horn sections syncopations...rippling guitars..." His new contract with the Warner Brothers label guaranteed him "creative freedom" and some $100 million, enough to pay for the best horns and guitars money can buy. And to go on, the *Times* assures us,

> with his crowning obsession: sexuality. In a slow grind, "Shhh," he promises a private seduction. He wants to join a woman in an orgasm-inducing "Endomorphmachine," rapping over a Stones-like guitar riff; "319," another rocker, fantasizing about photography as foreplay.

Surely, this is as far as a report on the *Times*' cultural pages can go; perhaps, in its "Science and Technology" section we will be getting a tad more on that lubricating new machine.

Jefferson Under a Shadow

There are those who see a psycho-intellectual link between the sex and the politics, between the reticence about rude words and a certain shy indecisiveness in the confrontation of rough realities—our whole liberal reluctance to call a spade a spade.

Consider, the editorial views of Brent Staples of the *New York Times* in a recent argument where sexual attitudes ran into basic political principles. How must we think about the possible scandal of Thomas Jefferson over his illegitimate paternity? Did our revered hero of enlightenment and democracy secretly father one or more dusky daughters in an illicit affair with Sally Hemings, a beautiful Negress (as she was then known) who was a slave on his estate in Virginia and his secret companion when he was a diplomat in Paris?

---

*   "Glyph" is, I am informed, short for hieroglyphic in pop-lingo. It was made famous by Prince's legal predicament in which he was forbidden to record under his own (very pronounceable) name. Thus, his choice of an anonymous icon – it identified his albums only with a stylized image which looked like an androgynous combination of male and female medical symbols. The *Shorter Oxford* (vol. I, p. 862) gives *glyph* as "a sculptured mark or symbol."

Evidently, the *Times'* editor advises, we should not lose very much time in thinking about it. A "debunking" biography by an historian named Fawn Brodie, a few years ago, first launched the thesis on an unsuspecting patriotic America; and the thesis for which there was only a slender thread of disputable evidence was subsequently dramatized by Ruth Prawer Jhabvhala in a Hollywood film (1995) called *Jefferson in Paris*. Was she, or was she not? did he, or did he not? Obviously Mr. Staples of the *Times* is less interested in the facts than in the truth: for the truth is apparently a moral and emotional question. As Staples writes,

> The more interesting question is: Why did a man who inherited slaves and a fortune dependent on them, and who lived in a society that was inured to slavery, decide at an early age that slavery was morally wrong and forcefully declare that it ought to be abolished?[3]

No doubt about it, President Jefferson was a hero of Negro emancipation, and no academic rumors of a slave mistress (and up to five children from the alleged liaison) could subvert that reputation for enlightenment. Still, the possible factor of sexual peccadilloes—"a serious passion," according to Ms. Brodie, that lasted thirty-eight years—raises the dark issue in race relations of "miscegenation and mulattoes," and the ensuing identity crises of a sorely tried people. Some scholars have been aghast. Professor Douglas Wilson reasons that an illicit affair with "Dashing Sally" would have violated Jefferson's own standards of "honor and decency." Professor C. Vann Woodward confesses his sadness at the debunking spectacle of the Hemings story being "hung" around Jefferson's neck. As for Brent Staples of the *Times*, himself an American black of African ancestry, he is pleased at the recognition that "Jefferson would remain a towering figure regardless of what happened in the bedroom."

This is a resounding answer to the "more important question." But what of the "less important question"? History, to which good journalism is related, is a seamless web of a great many strands of greater or lesser importance. Yet all the facts matter; and indeed, under some other circumstances, one would have imagined *Times* research of the old investigative persistence digging deeply for the last scrap of evidence. But here journalism is instructed to refrain from key-hole peeping, to call a halt "before the closed door," to manifest a discreet indifference to, or a benign neglect of, "what happened in the bedroom":

> Perhaps they did, but for crying out loud, what's the big deal? Jefferson would still be who he is, the country he fathered still history's envy. The world as we know it would go right on turning.

But could this mind-set be any kind of historian's envy?

The "big deal" which Brent Staples ignores is that no aspect of an historical truth can or should, for hidden or undisclosed reasons, be re-classified as unimportant. Jefferson's own times have been continuously subjected to new research and substantial reinterpretation. We know more about (and understand more sensitively) the heartwrench of the colonial loyalists when Jefferson wrote the Declaration of Independence; about the economic interests as well as the vaunted idealism of all "the Founding Fathers" when they drew up the Constitution; about the illiberal temptations of every young post-Revolutionary régime when it passes repressive Alien and Sedition laws. How would we have known which questions are "interesting" unless we posed them and followed eagerly on from there?

Wherever they landed us in the end, the world-as-we-know-it went right on turning. The editors of the *Times* should be reassured: it always does.

The Infobahn

In the end, when the first heats were over, the German locution came away not with a gold medal but with an honorable silver. The Brussels summit on the "global information world"—English was the only communicable language around the table, in February 1995—settled on the ungainly "Super-highway." the *Wall Street Journal*, however, put "*Infobahn*" into its front-page headline (27 February 1995), possibly only because it is shorter and fits into the 13 ems width. The popular German tabloids (*Bild, BZ*, etc.) did their duty by literal translation and called the electronic wave-of-the-future "*die Super-Autobahn.*" Since Germany is so far behind at the moment in so-called (electronic) information technology the local readership could be forgiven for thinking it to be good news about new road-building to break up the old traffic jams.

Incidentally, the dramatic "technology gap" (or, perhaps, culture-lag) between the United States and its electronic competitors in Europe gave rise to much exceptional writing. Nothing spurs the American journalist on to flights of prose more than a colorful transatlantic contest (with the Yanks in the lead).

To be sure, he has to know how to get into the proper mode, and he does his obligatory bit of splitting at least one infinitive on the way (something about how the engineers, even with "the hottest new kind of digital switching called asynchronic transfer mode," had "to manually program each exchange"). That done, he can transfer into the color purple; and here is one passage from the *Journal*'s story, sub-headlined "The Devil Is in the Details":

> Perched on a packing crate, the young Deutsche Telekom AG engineer is eye-balling a big computer screen and conferring, a phone to each ear, with fellow-technicians back home in Germany. A tangle of orange-sheathed optical fibers, pumping mega-torrents of bits and bytes to and from the show's displays, cascades from a hole in the ceiling and fans out to the banks of the communications gear. From the heat of so much electronics, the room is sweltering despite three fans and a portable air conditioner.

"All this is supposed to be plug-and-play—but it isn't," says his boss, Jürgen Kanzow.

The good news for Wall Street seems to be that the Germans are on their way to losing yet another war.

Boots, Boogaloos, and Giant Raves

Straight and straightlaced conservative journalism of the day was fitfully attracted by the strange exoticism of the youth pop culture of the 'sixties and 'seventies, but only decades later would the *New York Times* get around to take it with what appeared to be intellectual seriousness—it would refer to Patti Smith and the "visionary, shamanistic role" she played in the "incantatory" ideology of punk rock:

> Outside of society
> That's where I wanna be...

This was the hand-on-heart refrain of one of her songs, howled in improvisation at the time, and it became "an anthem," but no one, I am afraid, stands at attention and salutes anymore. We are all insiders now, aliens no longer.

Still, it was for a decade as good a formulation as philosopher Herbert Marcuse devised for the youth movement of would-be outsiders; only a small sector of the academic rebels took to the doctrine of "alienation" and Dr. Marcuse's explication of what the young Karl Marx had written on the subject. A few had looked to Friedrich Engels for light on "the condition of the working-class"; a great many more were moved by what the *Times* calls Patti Smith's "ferocious poem about working on an assembly line, called 'Piss Factory.'"[4]

It is not so much that the oldsters get out of touch, and take sentimental refuge in their "golden oldies." The youngsters come up so fast that there is a new generational gap every fiscal year or two as the pop industry caters to yet another pubertarian brood desperate to find their own note, intoning their own songs and slogans. In a bad season something long since "out" can be recycled to be "in" again. That must be the explanation for the recurring comebacks of has-beens, of forgotten stars of yesteryear—Tony Bennett, Nancy Sinatra, and the like—who suddenly draw millions again into concerts and climb to the top of best-selling charts. As a dispatch from Los Angeles reports (April 1995):

Nancy Sinatra seems intent on resurrection, hoping the second-career lightning that struck Tony Bennett will strike her next. She doesn't want to be an answer to a trivia question, a one-time wonder, the rebel chick with the go-go boots, mini-skirts and hit tune that foot fetishists everywhere hum in their sleep.[5]

For the time being the only hummable daytime tune that is available on re-release is a number called "Somethin's Stupid" which is referred to blithely by the *New York Times* as "that swoony yet suggestively incestuous duet with her father" (i.e., the late Frank Sinatra). A columnist in *Vanity Fair* magazine who has a reputation for being something called "a style-arbiter" has pronounced his judgment: "'Boots' was the rebel yell for a generation, and it worked." But will it work again? Nostalgia for "that mini-skirted bombshell who had 13-year-olds doing the boogaloo" may not be enough, even if one could remember what the boogaloo looked like and how big those go-go boots were....

If amnesia in America can lose you a whole yelling generation, in England the damage can be more modest, amounting possibly only to a stately home. The Earl of Farmouth thought it a splendid idea at first—to hold "house con-certs" at Ragley Hall—in order to keep the ancestral seat, a large country pile in Warwickshire, from crumbling around him. But he had simply forgotten, if he ever knew, that "dance music" nowadays is not exactly a stately step or two and a swirling flourish. It is the noisy part of something which was advertised as a "giant rave." As the *Sunday Telegraph* reported (30 April 1995), warning all the lords and ladies, including the Duke of Marlborough who also had a concert scheduled in his Blenheim Palace,

> Organisers of 'raves', distinguished by the playing of repetitive high-speed elec-tronic music, have in the past trespassed on land and held all-night parties before departing the next morning, leaving scenes of devastation....

The Earl of Yarmouth had been thinking of a black-tie ball for a thousand people, paying-guests all participating in "a quiet civilised function." The agents for the "special event" charged that stately home owners have "an irrational prejudice against dance music," and threatened legal action for breach of con-tract. They patiently explained the varieties of "rave," and insisted that for their part they were only into "'house' and 'garage' music which tends to be slower and more lyrical."

It is reassuring that our newspaper culture has been increasingly more at-tentive to the "style arbitration" which necessarily follows on the circulation drive to win over more young readers. You can learn all about the varieties of "dance music"—and thus save your castle from devastation—even from the *Times*. Its pop critic writes about the problems of

> accommodating all musical tastes, everything from garage to house to techno to hard-house to wild pitch.
> "What about Euro-hand-bag' I hear you cry...."[6]

No such cry could ever pass our lips, not having a clue as to whether so-called "Euro-hand-bag" is for real or for laughs.

Moving about in the in-lingo is like muddling through a maze. It seems that some of the numbers of the aforementioned music are mixed "live" for the new albums which present them ("I Luv You Baby," "Fell It," "Kut It") as "a seamless web of specialist club hits." But there is a snag. Apparently they have been "spliced together over the relentlessly pneumatic beat that used to be known as disco." *Used to be known?* What ever happened to disco? What is its *nom de bruit* these days, or has it gone the way of all boogaloos and rebel yells?

For all that, there are still redeeming features for newspaper readers who can't tell grunge from garage. Even in the narrow intellectual parameters of Pop-Kulchur-criticism one can find many thoughtful and telling remarks which add some lustre to the enterprise of giving Kurt Cobain's *Nirvana* as much space as Sir George Solti's *Cosi fan tutti*. Here is a pop critic named David Cheal, wrestling with an evening of music from a four-piece band called *Hole* which features as the lead singer, Courtney Love (the widow of the twenty-four-year-old Kurt Cobain who killed himself with a shotgun).

> The trouble with *Hole* is that while their music possesses many of the qualities of classic grunge—energy, raucousness, dynamism, volume—they seem to have neglected one important ingredient: tunes.
>
> It's not enough just to think of a riff, then double it, and play it as loudly as you can while your lead singer screams on about sex and violence and all kinds of ugly stuff. It's got to stick in the mind, and there was little here...that was remotely memorable.[7]

One almost feels that one is being present at some grand prehistoric occasion...like a "giant rave" in a Jurassic park, like *pithecanthropus erectus* first inventing the wheel or Neanderthal Man hitting upon a melody he can whistle. Those turning points really do stick in the mind.

13

The Strategy of Misquotation

B.B. and K.K.'s Memorably Misquoted Tag-Lines

Fine writers have a penchant for fine phrases. Occasionally when the inspired formula turns out to be at once thoughtful and memorable it runs into one peculiarly troublesome fate—the felicitous lines tend, more often than not, to be misquoted. Inaccurate and wrenched badly out of the full context, they may finish up implying (and even directly stating) the very opposite of the original literary intention.

I want to take up two flagrant cases of tag-lines which have been cited innumerable times in the world press, famous lines from Bert Brecht and Karl Kraus, illustrating the "art of misquotation." No two better phrasemakers can be found in modern German and Austrian letters: B.B. with his unforgettably Berlin-cynical Marxian twists; K.K. with his large ironies, broad enough to shock old Vienna and the Habsburg empire.

One Brecht quote came to dominate for decades the postwar German debate in Bonn over unilateral disarmament, and it is not often that high politics concerns itself with etymology, theology, and literary citations. But the intellectuals of the German Peace Movement had been going in for a lot of effective quotation, from the Bible to B.B., and had in the 1980s been making much mileage out of a witty line they said they had found in a Brecht text. In the feuilleton pages of the German newspapers it had been quoted a thousand times, and it was also bill-posted as a nationwide placard:

Stell dir vor, es kommt Krieg, und keiner geht hin...

(Just think of it, war breaks out and nobody turns up....)

Nobody less than Chancellor Kohl's right-hand man, the then general-secretary of the CDU (Herr Heiner Geissler), ordered his research staff to look it up

151

and double-check. When they did, Geissler was able to let loose a literary salvo against the *Friedenskämpfer* which may have caused some casualties. For apparently the pertinent "pacifist" sentiment of the poet and playwright had been torn out of the proper context which, not surprisingly, was not peace-loving at all but militant, if not militarist. The very next line in context revealed how far Brecht, as a Marxist and Communist, was from sentimental peace-mongering. It read:

> It would amount to fighting for the cause of the enemy, if one did not fight for one's own cause.

In other words, as the familiar Marxist dialectic had it, pacifism and defeatism meant "objectively" working for the victory of the other side. Not exactly, I would think, the Brechtian message the Peace Movement wanted to convey.

But there is yet another complication. Was it, in point of fact, a quotation from Brecht himself? B.B. was well-known to plagiarize others (on notorious occasion: Villon, Byron, et al.)—had he, somewhere, picked up the line from somebody else? His followers, and there are still a host of Brechtians who revere the Master, were long content to allow the *Zitat* to pass for *echt* without looking for it in the vast body of his work. One skeptical scholar followed the literary trail and came to the conclusion: it neither reflected his politics—he was all for the good comrades "turning up" for war or violent revolutions that he deemed just and necessary—nor could it be found in the printed work or any of his notes and jottings. The archivist in East Berlin who guards the Brecht oeuvre in B.B.'s old apartment, now a museum, kindly called my attention to the definitive research done by one indefatigable *Germanist* for the Academy of the German Language a few years ago. Strange to tell, although it had become a European maxim, the phrase had American origins.

The pseudo-Brechtian phrase had gone through all the newspapers, had been quoted in innumerable speeches and sprayed as graffiti on thousands of walls (especially in the anti-NATO protest-demonstrations of the 1980s). It had also inspired many other turns of phrases which benefited from its catchy twist—"Just think of it, it's Tuesday and nobody's watching *Dallas*.... It's Election Day, and nobody shows up to vote.... It's Sunday and nobody buys the Sunday paper..." etc., etc. But there it was, almost pristine in its original purity, on a page in a book by the American poet Carl Sandburg (1878-1967). In his compilation of *Graffiti* (1971), Robert Reisner associated the tag with the anti-Vietnam demonstrations, "Supposing they had a war and nobody came." Still, Sandburg tells the anecdote some thirty-five years earlier in *The People, Yes* (1936, p. 43) of a little American girl who saw for the first time in her life a military parade and asked about it naively:

The little girl saw her first troop parade and asked, "What are those?"
"Soldiers."
"What are soldiers?"
"They are for war. They fight and each tries to kill as many of the other side as he can."
The girl held still and studied.
"Do you know... I know something?"   ·
"Yes, what is it you know?"
"Sometime they'll give a war and nobody will come."[1]

Some Brechtians have gracefully given pride of place and originality to the American writer who was, like Brecht, "the best poet of his day." Others claim, wittily, that "Marxism" (sic) still had something to do with it. For our indefatigable researcher found a passage in Harpo Marx's autobiography, *Harpo Speaks!*, of which both B.B. and brother Groucho Marx would have been proud. Harpo Marx writes:

My favorite Thornton Wilder story was the one about the time a little girl asked him what war was. Wilder replied, "A million men with guns go out and meet another million men with guns, and they all shoot and try to kill each other." She thought that over, then said, "But suppose nobody shows up?"[2]

It is recorded that both Thornton Wilder and Carl Sandburg lived and worked on their books in the Chicago of the 1930s. Who told the anecdote first, and who repeated it from whom? Or must the sweet cause of universal peace and good-will satisfy itself with the support of yet another good story from Anon.?

In the case of Karl Kraus one certainly knew that he was militant enough to fight for his own cause, but his artful phrase-making has curiously served to befog it.

In 1933, an embittered and outraged Karl Kraus let loose his full contempt for the Nazis who had come to power in the neighboring German Reich; and it ultimately became an Austrian book of some 280 pages entitled *Die dritte Walpurgisnacht*. Unfortunately it began with a line so memorable that nothing else seems to be remembered. One Kraus biographer has collected dozens of recent references to Kraus and the famous opening line: *"Mir fällt zu Hitler nichts ein"* (On the subject of Hitler, nothing occurs to me).

Astonishingly, it is taken to be the full and complete expression of Kraus's political response to the Führer. What an abdication of literary and political responsibility! Could *nothing more* occur to him than that one noncommittal sentence? One literary editor (Fritz J. Raddatz of *Die Zeit*) sat in severe judgment: "This was no *bon mot*, but a declaration of bankruptcy." A writer in *Stern* (which evidently gets nothing right when it comes to Hitleriana) scolded Kraus for not having more "occur" to him. Anti-Nazi writers bemoan his resignation, his withdrawal, indeed his "self-indulgent abandonment of reason."

How could the impeccable Kraus, who would go on and on about a misplaced comma or a dangling participle, remain *silent?*

But, of course, he hadn't—the entire volume is an indictment of Nazi *Unkultur.* This surely is one of the rarest cases in modern writing: a book which began so well that nobody went on to read it.[3]

When Scotspeak Goes Scot-Free

What happened yesterday? what happened anywhere? According to your morning newspaper, aspiring to be a record of contemporary day-to-day history, a wide variety of important events: a few are from abroad involving foreigners, most are of local significance engaging the interests and curiosity of the reader's neighbors and compatriots. What commands banner headlines in our Washington and New York dailies gets only six lines of an agency report, if on the first page, in *Le Monde* or the *Corriere della Sera* or *Die Welt.*

What happened yesterday in London at the House of Commons (I am referring to Thursday, 16 November 1995)? The *New York Times*, which carried no story at all, deemed the Westminster speeches of the day, although concerned with foreign policy, to be of little or no international resonance; and its judgment was probably correct. You can't have space to cover all the fiery political rhetoric which happens to get delivered on any one single day in Parliament, in the Duma, in the Bundestag, in the Dail and the Knesset, by professional politicians whose news-value is in inverse proportion to the length of their texts. Outside these chambers what happened yesterday, which may also produce wide local coverage and even provoke sensational human interest—murders, crimes, airplane crashes, and the like—gets similarly evaluated, selected or omitted, "edited out." Unless it is a war or an alarming dip on the stock market, there is time to catch up in the days and weeks to come, even for a serious paper that prides itself on its up-to-the-minute knowledgeability.

I remember once being asked by a senior editor of the *New York Times*, the legendary Lester Markel of the Sunday edition, to write a long article on the Baader-Meinhof Gang whose campaign of political terrorism in Western Germany had been reaching its peak in the early 1970s. Uncertain as to what "level" I should pitch the piece, I requested the clippings of all that the *Times* had previously published on the subject. They sent me a couple of brief stories of a paragraph each; and so I proceeded to tell the whole history of the Gang from the very beginning, and in some ten thousand words (half of which they generously published).

So what happened yesterday in London in the House of Commons? There's nothing in the American press. But in the (London) *Times* the political sketchwriter was inspired to a massive outburst of nostalgia under a six-column headline:

FOREIGN AFFAIRS EVOKE GLORIES OF A DISTANT AGE

Two of the finest Parliamentary speakers were matching wits, and although the new Tory Foreign Secretary in John Major's cabinet seemed to be getting the nod there were only words of praise (even for his "sub-Churchillian style," a local accolade) for the then Shadow Foreign Secretary in Tony Blair's shadow cabinet. If Mr. Robin Cook was "most masterful," then the Rt. Hon. Malcolm Rifkind was "sharp-toothed and donnishly pugilistic...a high-octane performer...on pep-pills."[4] Watching "the tall, thin, bespectacled and scholarly Mr. Rifkind prosecuting his case in that educated Edinburgh accent of his," the *Times'* man could only conclude: "This was a debate whose style and tone would not have been out of place a century ago...."

Since a newspaper, at least in America, usually pays more attention to content than to style and tone, small wonder that the evocation of the glories of a distant age did not make the front pages in New York and Washington. (Nor even in Paris, where the *Herald-Tribune* minds the overseas store faithfully.) Yet even on the glory road the journalist rises to the evocative occasion in ways that reflect his present-day political commitments. The *Times'* old-fashioned man, still tilting conservative, has a Tory nose for the "antique" atmosphere of "old-fashioned, traditional performers of the highest caliber." What he sniffed, you got.

On the other hand, the *Guardian*, still radical and apoplectic at the sound of Old Empire tones, gave its Parliamentary sketch-writer full rein to vent his fury at what he had been forced to sit and listen to. What he heard, you got. It was an uncontrollable exercise in aural mania, tracking with the savage persistence of an *Inspecteur* Javert the detectable traces of an incorrect accent or a suspicious phonetic peculiarity. It can stand as a brilliant example of what we have been referring to as polemic by transcription, the Quote as Put-down. Simon Hoggart records in the *Guardian*:

> Yesterday the Foreign Secretary attacked a body called the *'Lebber Pardy'* (Her Majesty's Opposition), and spoke sarcastically of his *'iggerness'* (enthusiasm) to hear what they had to say, *'the semm deh'* (within a concurrent 24-hour period)....[5]

There is much more of this sort of comic turn in idiom's delight, amounting almost to a "Berlitz *listen 'n' learn* tape cassette course in Rifkind." In each case you get the handy and useful instructions on how to master the key phrases:

> seven days past: (*'a wick eggo'*)...a binding agreement between nation states, or *'tritty'*....the voters (*'the elick-tritt'*)...You'll be relaxed and convincing when you

talk about *'fullishness'* (stupidity) and describe auhoritatively how *'wi hev sinn they eonly kinclushion'* (we have observed the sole result)....

Making fun of the Scots is, for the English, a national pastime, often ending (as in the historic past) to the detriment of Tudor life and Stuart fortune. But these tribes will play games, often viciously, cultivating in all camps the "inner bully" in themselves. Sometimes it is all good clean fun, mostly, with only an occasional dark suspicion that such polemic by pseudo-phonetic transcription can do very well in doing down blacks from Asia and Africa, orientals from China and Japan, Irish and Mexicans and (in the case of Rifkind, when some *Guardian* readers sniffed anti-Semitism) Jews.* Yet, in the end, historians conclude that discrimination begins at home, with bullying in one's own school-yard. As Sir Denis Brogan used to say (with his unmistakeable Celtic burr), Scots tend to dislike the English on principle, but each other in practice. And the *Guardian* used to be edited by sturdy Scots.

But since that day, the *Guardian* has developed other journalistic qualities that have been shining through these pages. Even the Parliamentary sketchwriter (successively on the *Times, Daily Telegraph,* and *Independent,* as well as "Tadpole" for the *Spectator,* see above) has to contribute his *pensum* to the daily quota of off-color remarks. Impudent to the very end, Hoggart manages to insert this in his homily about Scotspeak: "*'sex'* is what coal comes in, and *'feckless'* refers to a virgin."

Thus the neighborhood news, which attracts and excites a vast local readership close to home, becomes a non-story over the border, almost incomprehensible abroad, certainly non-exportable. For those who breathe their atmospherics in other, far-away places, London remains lost "in a Distant Age," disconnected, as out of touch as Timbuctoo. As for Edinburgh, the stately center of the Scots, it all goes to prove how different they are and, accordingly, worthy of national independence with a seat of their own in the U.N. (Even that wouldn't, I suspect, be quite newswor-

---

* The "Quote as Put-down" has, as we have seen on occasion, a secret agenda; the coded quotes in sports-writing can suggest the contempt of literate professionals for highly-paid low-IQ athletes; the phonetic transcriptions in political reportage a hidden partisan racism. Some alert readers do protest. But indignant letters-to-the-editor are, mostly, dismissed as signs of a persecution-complex; some are indeed persecuted, if only verbally so or by editorial accident.

I note in the current *Spectator* (16 September 1995) a letter by its own Publisher, Mr. Conrad Black, apologizing for a recent *Spectator* piece by an ex-Tory Minister, Alan Clark, in which he ranted against the paper's former Editor, Dominic Lawson. Lawson had "slitty eyes" and "loathesome sneering features, pastily glistening." A newspaper reported that it was "a vicious – some would say anti-Semitic – tirade...."

thy enough to command a front-page story these days unless there was a massacre somewhere in it, with hidden mass graves and other violations of human rights.)

Foreign correspondents in the U.S. refrain for the most part from the effort to impart to their readers abroad a sense of the sound of American accents (a Yankee Bostonian twang in the speech of John and Bobby Kennedy, a Bronx-Brooklyn cockney in the speech of New York mayors from Jimmy Walker to Fiorello LaGuardia to Ed Koch). Apart from the British, few foreign readerships would find it useful or entertaining to be instructed in the flavorsome differences between the Texas drawl of LBJ and the broad Harvard flatness of JFK, the patrician golden tones of FDR and the peremptory Midwest ordinariness of Harry S (for nothing) Truman. I do recall Luigi Barzini risking a remark in the *Corriere della Sera* to the effect that President Lyndon B. Johnson's "Great Society" address was the greatest civil-liberties speech he had ever heard "in a Southern accent." (Would his Italian readers have made the apt association and contrast with the illiberal Confederacy of slave-holding states in the South, etc.?) English journalists, finding all Yankee pronunciations to be comically deviant, are tempted to use bits of phonetic transcription to make a light, quick point; and the London reader, even if he has to move his lips, more often than not does "get it." Here is a fairly hostile English report about President Clinton's conspicuous lack of political consistency, moral courage, and (in general) "bravery":

> The Cowardly Lion in *The Wizard of Oz* was also looking for courage, though, when he sang, 'If I Only Had Da Noive'. Whatever his 'courage' or lack of it, Bill Clinton certainly has da noive.

One can wonder, in this particular case, whether the New York man of the *Sunday Telegraph* didn't overdo it just a little by counting on his London readers to get the double-entendre of *"noive."* (That is to say: the weak, hesitant, vacillating President having the nerve to have no nerve...and revealing it in an accent more like Brooklyn than Little Rock).[6]

Most of the attempts, as in the examples above, to transcribe quoted remarks phonetically, making them read as if you were hearing them, are done light-heartedly, to bring a dash of color into a story and also a bit of humor (if, that is, it is done well enough and manages to come up with a laugh). One some rare and grave occasions, not necessarily involving Dr. Henry Kissinger, conversations in high places are being quoted and even the quirks of such recorded talk are intended to influence the serious affairs of state.

In a long interview and profile of one of President Clinton's advisors, Strobe Talbott, the *Washington Post* and its staff writer Michael Dobbs seemed to be doubting Talbott's effectiveness as the White House's counselor on relations with present-day Russia (and some other republics in the former USSR). They played up his "élitist" background (Nelson Stowbridge Talbott III had been educated at Hotchkiss private school and at Yale). They underlined his youthful attitudes during the 1968 student revolt (he was, like his fellow-Rhodes-scholar and Oxford roommate, Bill Clinton, a long-distance Vietnam War protester), and worried about his vulnerability to patriotic critics. They accented his closeness to the erratic views of Khrushchev (he had translated Nikita's *Memoirs*) and, later, of Gorbachov and emphasized his related antipathies to the dissident voices against Soviet totalitarianism. The *Post* and its reporter mustered all the hard evidence they could find and which might answer their banner headline question—*"Is He the Right Architect for Our Russian Policy?"*—in the negative. In addition to which the man was a sentimentalist and a romantic, among other semi-professional deformations of a journalist-turned-diplomat. There were even grumbles at his manicured *Time* magazine prose when it came to writing State Department memoranda.

There was one column-long section in the warts-and-all portrait which is apposite to my concern here with the art of quotation in our newspaper culture. It gave us details of a conversation in Moscow between the young Rhodes scholar from Oxford and Yale and a new-found Russian friend, one Sergei Milyutin. They were both drinking in a café; and the Muscovite, seated at the next table, was eager to strike up a conversation with somebody who looked like a real American. As the *Post* tells it—and its impeccable source must have been one of the two gentlemen in question, or both—Milyutin tried to strike up a bit of small talk: "'D'ya like georrn wain?' Milyutin repeated insistently." Talbott looked puzzled, and then with the query's repetition it dawned upon him that his nice neighbor—again, with a *"D'ya laike geoorn wain?"*—was asking for his opinion on John Wayne. Now Wayne represented the "Green Beret" ideology, a hawk among doves, a Hollywood symbol of patriotic America at war. Talbott put it to Milyutin straight: No, he didn't care for the man. He considered John Wayne to be "an extremist."

"It was now Milyutin's turn to be puzzled. 'Do you like Georgian wine?'..."

Ah, the reader now sighs with relief. Here is, finally, the real question with the sort of spelling that he is used to. Strobe Talbott's friend was not asking possibly embarrassing questions about war and peace but was only offering, friendly-like, to fill the American's empty glass. They had been talking past each other.

The poor prolonged effort at phonetic transcription did not quite ruin the point that the anecdote in the *Washington Post* seemed to want desperately to make. I think I got it. *Time*'s gift to American diplomacy—"the first journalist to rise to such a high position in the State Department"—just didn't know his backwards from his forwards, his Wayne from his wine, confounding "the Duke" in the cowboy movies and the *vino* with a modest little bouquet from Georgia.

It wasn't a very telling story, I admit, not as funny as it would have been in Evelyn Waugh's hands or even when it occurs (and it does) in the East-West satires of Malcolm Bradbury's novels. But I take it as a prime example of the literary efforts in our newspaper culture to "tell it like it is" or, rather, "telling it like it sounds." Someone catches it wrong and mishears it along the way; and since all foreigners talk funny, the burden of the joke is on him. Quotations can be poison, can cut one up or put one down.[7]

There is a last and ironic twist. Burlesquing quotations can come to a sticky end, for the parodic spirit is infectious and even hack journalists can take their mocking revenge on professionals of satiric dialogue should they reveal themselves to be vulnerable by getting an accent wrong or slipping up on the lilt of a drawl.

Martin Amis, the novelist and literary critic, was savaged by a paragrapher in the *Times*' "Diary" after an attempt to be funny (for, at least, the hundredth time, not including the dreary efforts in his father's vast oeuvre*) about the way Americans speak when the ungainly colonial sounds reach sensitive English ears. Amis *fils* was a star at the annual Hay-on-Wye literary festival (1997) and he was reading a new short story. To convey its full ironic impact, he explained, he was going to read it in an American accent. It was an unmitigated disaster, according to the *Times*' diarist, rallying to the cause of anti-Anti-Americanism. Its report claimed that the story wasn't a story at all and Martin Amis' pastiche of an American accent was "hilariously bad and strange":

> He replaced every "c" with a "g" as in "gable television"; "s" became "z" as in "ztreetz"; "p" turned into "b" which gave us "barked the gar"; and he had a weird, elongated way of pronouncing vowels.

To mitigate the bash in the spirit of English fair play the gossip columnist offered this small qualification: "It was quite awful other than those few references to Isobel Fonseca, the lovely mother of his child, who was sitting in the audience with their baby...." But would a pink-cheeked love-child make up for the transatlantic cultural *faux-pas?* This had been a "real jaw-dropper" of a performance from (as the *Times*' caption had it) a "Crazy Limey." Something had gone amiss...which was a poor pun, but probably no better than he deserved.[8]

---

*   My own personal relations with Kingsley Amis, after decades of friendship and editorial collaboration, fell under a shadow. It was not, I am sure, for his frequent comic turns about my own "Noo Yawk" accent (apparently I always pronounced the name of my *Encounter* co-editor, Stephen Spender, as if it were...Steven).

The falling-out was occasioned by his disagreeable remarks about the late Leo Rosten, of whom he said, "Imagine, getting a reputation as a stylish English-language writer for transliterating the ghetto gibberish known as 'Yinglish'...." "Hyman Kaplan" would have known how to defend his mentor "Leonard Q. Ross"; but Rosten was deeply wounded, especially by the nasty chapter about him in Amis' *Memoirs* (1991), pp. 321-323.

Killing with a Quote

Interviews conducted by highly personable journalists, celebrated in newspaper circles in their own right, often have a hidden agenda, a small message between the lines. If the portrait is an encomium, the writer often gives the impression that his or her trained eye has yet again spotted a worthy talent, a candidate waiting to be made king. If the portrait is critical, the by-line suggests with a flourish that the reporter is sophisticated, intelligent, or otherwise superior; the interviewee is pretty much of a fool. The choice of what the interviewee said for quotation, taken in shorthand, or on tape, or in scribbles on the back of an envelope, is necessarily selective; and between the conversation and the day of publication falls a shadow of distortion.

It is easy to be both accurate and accusatory. Contexts do not have to be wrenched to quote a remark and round off an effective put-down. I will be giving a few examples of this, but I do not mean to color the point with conspiratorial overtones. Sometimes an attentive reader takes hastily-typed stories too seriously; very often an element of incompetence or carelessness appears to be suspect, with no dark justification.

I suppose that Ms. Judi Bevan, who contributes a weekly portrait of an important businessman to the economics section of the *Sunday Telegraph*, meant well by doing a long and praiseworthy profile of Professor Wiseman Nkulu who had become the first black chartered accountant in South Africa. She told moving stories of his years in prison and his hopes for "black empowerment." His virtues—professional ability; business acumen; Christian piety; love of family, etc.—were given their due.

On the other hand, his life-style was depicted with a touch of irony—his comfortable house in a "swish" suburb of Johannesburg (where most blacks are maids or gardeners); his driving a BMW-5-series car; his regular workouts in an "exclusive" health and racquet club. All fair enough. A pleasant revealing profile, with a dash of color, and a few warts and all.

But at one point there was, for the western reader of economics news, an embarrassing passage. Professor Nkulu was quoted to this effect on the shortcomings of an American-style capitalism ("too stark") and his preference for a German model: "I feel there is more humanity in the German system. I call it the social market economy." What kind of intellectual pretense was this? ("I call it....") Was the rather shameful note of pomp intentional? If Ms. Bevan was under the impression that Prof. Nkulu actually coined the phrase about a "social market economy," then she is naive and ignorant. If, alternatively, she knows that it is for decades now standard usage among economists—after the ideas of Hayek and Roepke jelled into what Dr. Ludwig Erhard, the father of the "German miracle" in the 1950s, called the *"Sozial-Markt-Wirtschaft"*— then she is making the good man from Johannesburg look naive and ignorant.

This is what I call killing with a quote. Or was the putdown gratuitous? In any case, the whole thing turned out to show a profit; for the Tory paper ran it all under the self-serving (and very misleading) headline: *"South Africa's Black Disciple of Thatcherism."* Our man in Johannesburg was enlisted among the loyalists of Lady Thatcher (and her very un-social market economy), and dragooned away from a hated German rival.

The Wide Open Range of Malpractice

The range of the malpractice here is very wide...at least as wide as the spectrum from slipshod carelessness—which comprises faults of technical transcription as well as lapses of attention-span on the part of reporters. It also embraces the to the lofty and principled indifference which we find in highminded transcribers of reality who are convinced (like Mailer, and Truman Capote, and Lawrence Durrell, and even Rebecca West) that fiction is at least a depth or two more truthful than mere factual accuracy. The former thrives on sloppiness, the latter on a relativism which conveniently proclaims that "anything goes" as well as an old élitist precept that the truth is in the poetry.

An example.

The interviewer in the *New York Times* describes Julian Schnabel as a "43-year-old high-living art-world superstar of the 1980s (his trade-mark was paintings that incorporated broken plates)," and the news is that he has become "a singer and songwriter in the punctured art environment of the 1990s...." The chap seems to be bright but not especially inventive or original. His first hit-song is a country-rock number entitled "Every Silver Lining Has a Cloud." And the reporter goes out of his way to quote the following quotation from Schnabel via Bob Dylan: "What's that Bob Dylan song—'There's a time for everything and every purpose under heaven'?..." As if neither of them—the high-brow *Times* man may well be putting us on—knew anything of the passage in Ecclesiastes (many thousands of years old but it got around in its time) which, at 3:1, observes that "To every thing there is a season, and a time to every purpose under heaven." But, perhaps, after such a long time, there may be more power to an authentication from Dylan than the Divinity.*

As in some dyslexic disability, one little mistake follows erratically a whole fault line. Schnabel describes how he has been working in his summer home at Montauk, Long Island, writing and then taping the songs, and then having someone transcribe them. He confesses that during the transcription "certain mistakes" were made: "One line came out, 'It's like picking stars out of a coffin'...I don't know what I said, but I didn't say that. It sounded so weird that I kept it."[9] Those "weird sounds" cover a multitude of accidental obscuri-

---

*   Actually the song-phrase was from Pete Seeger, not Bob Dylan.

ties. With the surrealists there was a method in the madness, and sometimes aural messages just had to be divorced from literal meanings. With the aleatoric modernists there was system in the casual dice-throwing, and casual and wayward notes truly "belonged" on the theory that what played together stayed together. Nowadays there is also an off-season to every purposelessness under heaven. It only has to sound "weird" enough to earn the ultimate accolade of "*Wow!*"

14

The Interviewer and the Interviewee

We have explored so many aspects of our newspaper culture as exemplified in the regular features of journalistic interviews—from the art of manipulative quotation to the vice of making up the juicier bits in outright fabrication—that it prompts one to think a little about the origins and the history of the form (and to interview a singular practitioner of the art at its best).

We know it today mostly in the bastardized version of a dialogue or a conversation which appears in our newspapers and on our television screens. A lowly reporter asks simple (and often simple-minded) questions of a great statesman. An arrogant TV personality tries to embarrass a man of affairs and make him look silly, helpless, or guilty. A gossip columnist probes hopefully for some scandal or, at least, an indiscretion.

But then one could, of course, also go back over the centuries and the millennia to work out how difficult and complex it has been historically to ask proper questions and elicit worthwhile answers. Certainly, Socrates did not find it easy, for all his philosophical mastery, to put useful questions to all those curious, but often illogical and sometimes lazy, young Athenians in the *agora*. A thousand years later we would find Giordano Bruno bypassing all the difficulties of a genuine dialogue, by writing all the dramatic exchanges himself, as if the Renaissance mind needed no old-fashioned question marks but only the final, authentic full-stop itself. All this, however, would take us too far afield.

The modern usage of the word "interview"—and it has been taken over as a *Fremdwort* in German, French and most other European languages—derives from the English or, rather, an original American coinage. As such, it is just a little more than a century old. In its original meaning or earliest usage it had, of course, nothing to do with journalism, and referred to a formal or ceremonial meeting *(entrevue)* of great persons, as when Henry VIII met François I at the Field of the Cloth of Gold. Montaigne refers to ceremonies in the "interview of Kings."

As late as 1875, an American translator of *Faust* tried to explain certain Goethean phrases by annotating "the interview of Satan with the Lord in the first and second chapters of Job...." By that time, however, some of his readers may have been forgiven for wondering whether the exclusive interview would have been published in heaven or in hell.

Hell, most probably. For the breakthrough of the interview form in modern journalism was widely considered an infernal new device. In 1869 the New York *Nation* observed,

> The "interview," as at present managed, is generally the joint production of some humbug of a hack politician and another humbug of a newspaper reporter.

And in the same year the New York *Daily News* complained,

> A portion of the daily newspapers of New York are bringing the profession of journalism into contempt, so far as they can, by a kind of toadyism or flunkeyism, which they call "interviewing."

In London the *Pall Mall Gazette* (1886) went even further:

> The interview is the worst feature of the new system: it is degrading to the interviewer, disgusting to the interviewee, and tiresome to the public.

Still the new practice—of journalists conversing directly with important persons with the object of obtaining matter for publication—could as well produce a brilliant and accurate document as an irresponsible piece of scandalous gossip. The editors of the *Pall Mall Gazette* had to concede that "Among the permanent gains of the year [1884] the acclimatization of the 'interview' in English journalism certainly should be reckoned...."[1]

For all its "low" origins, the art of interviewing in the context of the so-called New Journalism of the late nineteenth century reached its high point in the "exclusive scoops" which Monsieur de Blowitz, the celebrated Paris correspondent of the *Times* of London, managed to obtain with kings, popes, and chancellors.

The most memorable was in the year 1878 with Prince Bismarck who, during the Berlin Congress of that summer, invited "the prince of journalists" to a private dinner at his apartment in the Wilhelmstrasse. The conversation was evidently frank and free, and M. de Blowitz—whose absolutist credo was that everything that was said to him anywhere belonged to his newspaper and the public—subsequently published a long *Times* interview quoting huge chunks of Bismarck's table-talk, verbatim. Having already published the text of the Berlin Treaty before the signatures were dry on the confidential document (somehow, mysteriously "leaked" to him), M. de Blowitz incurred the wrath of the German chancellor who openly attacked him in the *Reichstag*.

M. de Blowitz found Bismarck an almost overpowering personality, but in his effort to "correct my first impressions and judge the Chancellor with perfect impartiality" he proceeded to quote a German liberal critic who described Bismarck, the "Iron Chancellor," as treating the Germans "as if he had conquered us...." This could not fail to displease. As Blowitz remarked, Bismarck "has such an opinion of his own infallibility that he deems eulogy an impertinence and censure a blasphemy...."

One final, personal impression after some five hours of conversation in the Wilhelmstrasse is worth quoting as the kind of pontifical wisdom which nineteenth-century interviewers went in for at their interpretative best:

> Whatever the greatness or genius of a man, he fails in his mission as leader of a nation when he seeks to substitute his single will for the collective will of the people, and when, instead of training them in the wise exercise of liberty, he tries to make them share the melancholy lot of nations which abdicate in favor of one man, even though a man of genius.[2]

The sterling merit of "the art of interviewing" could be best exemplified in the writing of the late George Urban. I single out here my one personal favorite in the world of professional interviewers, although others have their special virtues: Rudolf Augstein, Barbara Walters, David Frost, Jeremy Paxman, Sir Robin Day, Günter Gaus, Oriana Fallaci, et al. But the depth, finesse and solidity of Urban's work was almost unprecedented in modern journalism. In the first place, it avoided all the traditional pitfalls of ephemeral newspaper efforts: superficiality, sensationalism, sauciness. One can appreciate the iconoclastic interviews of Oriana Fallaci, but at the same time wonder whether it was necessary for her to undress before the Ayatollah Khomeini in Qu'om, or to provoke Lech Walesa to angry impatience in Warsaw. One can value the recorded conversations of Emil Ludwig with Stalin and Mussolini, and of Edgar Snow with Mao Tse-Tung, and still regret their inability to formulate a challenging, not to say disagreeable, question. American television interviews with the visiting Mikhail Gorbachov a few years ago were polite to the point of obsequiousness. The grave consequences were that it ill-prepared a misled public opinion for the rapid changes which swept Gorbachov away and ushered in a post-Soviet era.

Unlike most of his fellow-practitioners, Urban (who died in 1997) was a journalist and historian with wide-ranging scholarly interests. From his early Budapest days as a student in Georg Lukács' philosophy seminar, and his work on the Stefan George *Kreis,* to his later global assignments as an "intellectual consultant" for Radio Free Europe, he had been both a specialist and a generalist in the fields of social science and literature. He had read the books....Perhaps one should take this kind of intellectual preparation for granted, but it is, nevertheless, quite rare.

I won't even bother to make the contrast with interviews whose immortal achievement (as in the notorious *Playboy* session with Jimmy Carter) is the revelation that a puritanical U.S. president was capable of "lusting after women" in his heart. Nor with the interviewers who have become famous on our television screens, for obviously their concern is more with images than ideas, less with elucidation than with embarrassing slips-of-the-tongue.

All of the interviews of George Urban had the great good fortune not to have been prepared under the pressure of urgent deadlines. He had the time—hours, days, weeks—to put his questions, double-check his recorded transcripts, return for clarifications and additions, and even then to revise, at the last minute, for maximum precision. But that is why, in thinking of the work of George Urban, I have been reminded often of Max Weber's remark that there is a kind of *haut journalisme* which is indeed a form of scholarship and akin to the highest intellectual activities.

I suspect that I will not be alone among the readers of these marvelously inquiring "conversations" who will remain tantalized by the temptation to put a few questions of their own to the long-distance questioner; indeed to interview the interviewer. And so I have done below.[3]

"Although the reporter should be fair and objective, one should not be upset by the suspicion that a great many of the dialogues or conversations that were transcribed were not exactly conducted in the spirit of disinterested inquiry, for the interrogative method itself is a rather subtle way of loading any discussion. Certain assumptions are built into the questioning, and they inevitably set the framework in which the answers are elicited. Even when the questioner's frame of reference is rejected (and it often is), the discussion tends to move in step— negative step—with it."

"The interrogative method, while unfavorable to the display of background and contextual information, is a truth-detector of particular sensitivity. It picks up the false, the mendacious and the phoney, but will also register misjudgement, incompetence, and plain folly. It is crude to the extent that the knowledge it conveys is limited by the constraints of question and answer, the yes/no type of communication. But this crudeness imposes a wholesome rigor which the more leisurely historical narrative cannot match."

"But the interrogative mode has its pitfalls too. One must know how dangerous and narrow the line is between the interrogative and the inquisitorial."

"Yes, the interviewee is—voluntarily, but vulnerably—in the hands of the questioner. The interviewer has a responsibility to the man who has agreed to expose himself to his curiosity."

"Is disinterested curiosity enough?"

"No, it may not be firm enough. The political or intellectual commitment of the interlocutor may be so strong that it calls for a balancing commitment of one's own. It may warrant some deviation from the rule that an interview is an exchange of ideas between two informed parties, and not a trial or a cross-examination."

"What about historical eyewitnesses or 'great names'?"

"What one often finds, though not really very unexpectedly, is the narrow perspective and partiality of the men 'who were there'. To have been there is no guarantee of having understood."

"What about 'on-the-scene' reporting?"

"I believe in the interview form, yet one should not overvalue the importance and self-importance of eyewitnesses. One would hesitate to rehearse so trite a conclusion were it not for the current fetishism of 'on-the-scene' reporting, together with Radio- and Television-induced cult of interviewing politicians with an eye and ear on 'Instant History.'"

"Isn't the 'news,' though, in a way a history of our own times?"

"No, I'm afraid not. One feels saddened by the sullen disinclination of human affairs to yield an intelligible story. The 'question and answer' method underlines a truth well-known to students of human affairs: 'history in the raw' is stubborn and chaotic. It carries no 'natural theme,' no 'obvious pattern.' It imparts no 'message.' The themes of history are laboriously hewn out by the historian; and they are contained in, if often anticipated by, his questioning. He alone can impose an articulate form on what is essentially ambivalent, haphazard, grotesque, and accidental."[4]

Part 3

The Quest for Meaning

"Black is a shade of brown. So is white, if you look."
—John Updike (1994)

"If there were a grain of truth
hidden beneath the floor boards he would be prepared
to dig it up with his bare hands."
—Rabbi Israel of Rizin,
speaking of Rabbi Aharon of Karlin (1825)

"If we find words like these...if we find ourselves applying them to
more and more different kinds of things, there is grave reason
to suspect that—whether we know it or not—we are really using them
not to diagnose but to hurt. If so, we are assisting in verbicide.
For this is the downward path which leads to the graveyard
of murdered words. First they are purely descriptive....Then they are
specifically pejorative....Then they become mere pejoratives....Finally
they become terms of abuse and cease to be language in the
full sense at all."
—C.S. Lewis, "Studies in Words" (1960)

"Why are there no simple languages? All human languages, from the
ancient Akkadian language to Zulu in South Africa today, are equally
complex. Such complexity exists for humans alone....
Why are there no simple languages today?...Because there never were
any simple languages. Not ever. Certainly, as far back as we know of
writing, languages were just as complex as today, say, 6000 years or
roughly 240 generations, and only eight times more takes us back to
Cro-Magnon days."
—Professor Robert C. Berwick (M.I.T., 1997)[1]

15

Race and the Color of Things

Black, White, and Other Spurious Shades

How to deal with words and phrases that are loaded with "racial prejudice" and are often omitted or self-censored in the interests of what might be called cultural correctness"?

In New York City in the 1960s and '70s, when Harlem was always about to explode in a "Hot Summer," the *New York Times* tried for a while systematically to omit earlier ethnic designations which would identify "Thomas E. Washington, 19" who had been arrested on criminal charges as "Negro." It was a well-intentioned do-gooder's idea, but it soon backfired. If an "Abraham Levy" was charged by the police, or a "Vito Gianelli," or an "Aloysius Kelly," then clearly it was white folks who were involved. But then the readers quickly took to identifying *all others* with obvious Anglo-Saxon names—the William Hamiltons and the George Clays—as dark culprits who had come up from the South and were doing mischief in Manhattan.

So: by trying to hide the racial identity as a routine bit of factual reporting they swelled the racial suspicions of a mass crime-wave mostly involving "blacks."

In one case—which I took up personally with my friend A.M. Rosenthal, then managing editor of the *New York Times*—one could not know by reading the morning's *Times* that the young Brooklyn student who was killed by the police while trying to escape a drug-dealing arrest was...black. One could not understand the uproar on the college campus; one could not fathom the daily growth of "community tension." Finally, when there were riots involving angry crowds of blacks and the mainly white police, one could deduce that the student who had been shot was in point of fact a negro, or black, or Afro-American. Instead of shedding light, the *Times* left readers in the dark; for the identification of race (it argued) could have been inflammatory and therefore was not "fit to print." The inflammation set in anyway.

The British press, in occasional bouts of similar highmindedness, tries its best to "play down" racial background. But in the quality dailies it emerges, wittingly or unwittingly, in the detailed context of the story; and in the sensational tabloids it becomes obvious when they get hold of a photograph of the culprit in question. The American press did not identify in any way Mr. Jeff Hurt when he was charged for defrauding his Wall Street firm of millions of dollars. The *Sunday Times* of London did a half-page photograph of the dashing well-dressed Harvard-graduate embezzler: he was black and as handsome as Harry Belafonte or Sidney Poitier. His predecessor in the high-finance fraud-league was Michael Milken who had stolen even more millions. The "truth" about their "ancestry" emerged in both cases; and observers of race relations bitterly concluded that "all blacks" and "all Jews" were falling under a shadow of suspicion and mistrust.

In recent times, after the life-and-death of Martin Luther King, much has changed in both the relationships between blacks (or Negroes, or African-Americans) and the white communities of North and South, and especially in the way the press reports on ethnic events and personalities. But whenever a serious altercation comes up—I exclude mass riots, for the TV pictures in "living color" on the evening news immediately identify the cast of characters—there recurs the old dilemma of thoughtful, responsible editors as to specifying exactly who it is that is in the midst of front-page trouble.

What was happening in Lawrence, Massachusetts, was rather less clear, if possible; and in a related confusion I leafed through all the papers I could find in Logan Airport which could clarify the rumors of nearby violence about which I had heard. The banner headlines indicated that the local police were still desperately trying to control the rioting. Troopers were trying to stop angry crowds and gangs on the rampage; firemen were busy putting out fires and disposing of garbage cans burning in the middle of Lawrence streets. Who was fighting whom? and why? For a moment I had a little nostalgia for the hard ideological lines of the Old World, where a class struggle is a class struggle, pitting local workers against greedy capitalists, the old familiar battle between the rich and the poor.

Only a limited amount of light was shed on the subject by the *Boston Globe*, the famous New England newspaper. Its accounts showed the politicians blustering and filibustering in their usual way, and the Lawrence alderman in charge of public safety was quoted as saying, "It was an isolated incident over nothing important. It was not racial. It was simply a warm night, tempers were high....Things just got away with themselves." Accordingly one's immediate suspicion was that it was, once again, "whites" *v.* "blacks." But the press also reported that Puerto Rican women had been complaining that they had been subjected to racial taunts from "Americans." Who they? White Americans? Brown ones, black ones, yellow ones? (On another page, covering another story, the paper used the odd, if now standard, phrase "Native Americans"...referring to some Indian tribes on an Arizona reservation.) That evening in Providence—and perhaps Rhode Island was far enough away to have more perspective—the local evening newspaper revealed that when the police moved in to declare an absolute curfew in Lawrence they had made megaphone announcements in English, Spanish, *and French!* Well, the first is obvious; Spanish, understandably, because this is an area of so-called "Hispanic" settlements and Puerto Ricans, among others, emigrated there because of its attractive ethnicity. But the *French?* It turned out, after much finger-flicking research at the hotel's newspaper stand, that there was a substantial French-Canadian community in Lawrence. Were these the "Americans" who were doing the taunting?

At any rate somebody, in the phrase of the *Journal-Bulletin*, was "raising a ruckus"; and I couldn't quite figure out *who* was "ruckusing," and *why* (it wasn't the hate, it was the humidity). I was pleased to note that after forty-eight hours or so, in which your friendly neighborhood police were described as moving in with "snarling attack dogs on leashes," Lawrence was brought back to law-and-order, and Mayor John J. Buckley could remind one and all that their town had "a long and proud history of being a city of immigrants." The *Boston Globe* reported,

> In an effort to defuse the tense situation last night, area clergymen organized an ecumenical service in front of an abandoned fire house at the corner of Oxford and Lowell Streets. With an electric piano and bongo drums playing in front of a wooden cross, a group from St. Augustine's Roman Catholic Church sang "the Lord's Prayer."

Our press was running true to form, telling us more about everything we didn't have to know, and sedulously omitting the essentials.

I had good reason, even at that time, to suspect that this was not a mere accident of careless reporting under the pressure of a fast-breaking story, but rather a reflection of our new cultural predicament where the precarious balance of disruptive forces dictates that no potentially explosive truths be told. The motives are doubtless well-meaning. Yet how an informed public opinion can ever develop under such self-censored circumstances—much less come to wise and prudent conclusions about properly ordering a multiracial and ethnically plural society—remains unfathomable.

Let's return to the details of how the *New York Times* reported the Brooklyn incident which I have just mentioned. For, in my view, those happened to be more optimistic and hopeful years, and I had been trying to discuss, and to argue, the problem with the distinguished managing editor, Mr. A.M. Rosenthal and his associates. I had been more bewildered every day by the full-page coverage which his paper was energetically devoting to a situation of racial tension in Brooklyn that alarmed the entire nation. Thousands of agitated citizens were milling about the streets; the atmosphere was explosive; police were alerted for riot and violence; the fire brigades were in readiness for arson; shopkeepers were boarding up their shops in fear of looting. What had happened?

Well, apparently, as the fuller story was later to emerge, the academic officials of Brooklyn College had asked the FBI to help with the proliferating hard-drugs problem on the campus. The city had approved, for the metropolitan hospitals were overcrowded with appalling cases; and this was when the pushing had to stop. One suspect was trapped on a street-corner: a young student, of hitherto good record and repute. The FBI moved to the arrest; the young man broke away and fled. At one point in the chase, according to the *New York Times*, he seemed to turn and reach into his jacket. The FBI fired; the student fell dead. In the next twenty-four to forty-eight hours the neighborhood seethed with anger and agitation. A riot of major proportions seemed imminent.

Coming from abroad, one followed the drama with a certain Henry Jamesian innocence: I simply could not quite comprehend what was transpiring. The *Times*, loyal to its famous motto, was only publishing "all the news fit to print." From a Washington newspaper I ultimately, and unfittingly, learned that the shot student was a black, and it was the black or Negro community, amounting to a million in Brooklyn, which seethed with a sense of outrage. How could we know any of this? Or shouldn't we?

The blacks in an all-Negro neighborhood felt "victimized"; one of their own had been "martyred." From a subsequent *Times* report one could learn, in the jump-story paragraph on page 43, that when the young student had turned and reached into his jacket, he was taken to be reaching for a gun; and that when he was searched he had on his person a loaded pistol and a substantial quantity of heroin.

Neither of these facts makes an ugly situation any prettier. But the duty of all the press was to report them, to "tell the truth"—and here the placement of facts, and how the truth is paragraphed, is of decisive importance. It could make the difference, in an agitated community, between riot and remorse, mindless anger and tragic understanding.

Some thirty years later our newspaper culture, at least that high-minded sector of it that is embodied in the style patterns of the *New York Times*, finds itself impaled on the horns of the very same dilemma.

It was Christmas day 1997. A young man named William J. Whitfield—the *Times* has him aged twenty-three, the *News* and the *Post* as twenty-two—was shot dead by the New York police. Whitfield came from the Bedford-Stuyvesant area, but the fatal incident occurred in Canarsie. The *Times'* headline ran:

AFTER CHASE,
POLICE KILL
BROOKLYN MAN

No further identification was to be found in the story. Since the man was un-armed and there seemed to be no established reason for the shooting, the deputy chief of police, Dewey Fong, refused to release the name of the officer who fired the gun. Why had he shot to kill at the man who fled into Milky Way grocery store on Ralph Avenue? The police were still investigating "the exact specifics," and Friday's newspaper-readers would have to be patient for now—and make do by rounding up all the usual suspicions. Had Whitfield been a black man? Were the police officers on the chase all white? Had the victim really been unarmed? ("No weapon was recovered," the police spokesman had said, loftily.) Could this be yet another incident in the sinister chain of so-called "trigger-happy killings" where poor ghetto kids are "taken out" at the slightest excuse of a suspected misdemeanor?

The *Times* remained mum. It was the season of good will, and the only large photograph on page B3 showed a young disabled white boy, Yossi Frank, nine, being cheered up at a Hanukkah party by Jean Collins, a smiling black childcare-counselor at a Brooklyn home for the mentally retarded. A heart-warming moment of civic harmony in the big town! No dark troubling racism disturbed the reader of the special "Metro" section of the *New York Times* that day when Christians and Jews, black and white, were celebrating and making joyful noises unto the Lord.[2]

Not so in New York's two tabloids. The *Post* added extra drama to the story by headlining "MYSTERY SHROUDS SLAYING BY POLICE." It went to considerable investigative trouble to supply sociological detail, colorful stuff that made the victim's last day, only yesterday, especially vivid—"He was in the neighborhood [a neighbor said] to visit his girlfriend, their child and two of her other kids"—"He was coming here for dinner [Whitfield's grandmother said], we made banana pudding for him"—"They blew his heart clean out [the vicim's furious uncle, Xavier Whitfield, said], his heart came out his back." Here were some specifics which could convince a reader that there was somewhere a racial or "multicultural" element involved. The *News* even reported Whitfield on the telephone, just before the fatal incident, ask-ing "What's up, yo'?"

Why spend valuable reading time puzzling out ethnic clues? An exotic dish, a turn of phrase, a salutation were only suggestive, possibly misleading. One isolated fact or another about a victim's color or his race may not (according to an editor's style-code) be considered "relevant"—a head-and-shoulders snapshot, never. In point of fact both the *Post* and the *News* stories featured a prominent column-wide photograph of William J. Whitfield with baseball cap and slight smile. What the *Times*, presumably in its civic concern and cultural caution, deemed not fit to print—which made its standard of relevance an instrument of self-censorship—stared several million New Yorkers in the face that same Friday morning.[3]

Were our worst fears thereby confirmed? It is early days yet. The senior police chiefs and the angry black civil-rights groups will soon be exchanging words. There may be regrettable clashes. Will a free press continue to be helpful, harmful?

A few last, exemplary (if still problematic) items.

I reprint—"in its entirety" (as Harold Ross used to reassure his skeptical *New Yorker* readers, suspecting a tilted context) – a *New York Times* paragraph which was recently included in the daily "Quote/Unquote" feature on the political page of the *Herald-Tribune*. Usually the cited passages are witty or outrageous, extreme or anecdotal or otherwise memorable. Here, with an unusual racial attribution, is Wade Henry, "a black real estate agent from Phoenix, speaking to President Bill Clinton's advisory board on race relations": "I pay taxes. I want value for my dollar. I appreciate you being here, but want something done. If not, then stop wasting my money."[4] The point of the insipid story making it into the morning newspaper may well escape the reader. If it were a brilliant *aperçu* or a notable piece of civic decisiveness, it might well be taken as a small and welcome contribution to better U.S. race relations (viz., mutual respect among all citizens, etc.). As it stands, flat and conventional, it only illustrates the haphazard pointlessness and essential irrelevance of much racial attribution, color identification, or ethnic reference. Where it might be deemed essential to a story, it is often omitted; where it could, correctly or not, be considered inflammatory, it tends to be underplayed or indeed censored; where (in certain sectors of the tabloid press) it is calculated to amuse or titillate, alarm or anger, publishing all the facts is considered basic, unavoidable, and desirable.

Do British editors—after many years of cogitation in their Press Council which periodically produces codes and guide-lines (and grave warnings that failing to observe "the decencies" would prompt government interference)—manage to handle these issues with more conspicuous intelligence or morality? The careful reader of the serious press may well want to suspend judgement, for the revised, improved coverage up till now seems to be still part of the problem, not the solution.

Almost at the same time as our killing in Canarsie with the behavior of the local police and the New York press leaving something to be desired, the *Times* in London covered two criminal incidents which suffice to underline the Anglo-American dilemma as I have been presenting it.

Once again it was "an unarmed suspect" who had been shot and killed in a police raid. He was a thirty-nine-year-old, named James Ashley, and the fatality took place in the southeastern English coastal town of Hastings. The police declined to say whether a warning shot had or had not been fired, but we are

given to understand that "a single bullet from a Heckler & Koch MP 5 semiau-
tomatic carbine" had killed Ashley about whom we learned only that he had a
previous conviction (for manslaughter, following a barroom brawl). Should
we know more? If Ashley had been a Caribbean emigrant, should he have
been identified as "a black" who may have had something to do with "the drug
problem" in his neighborhood? Some say he should be identified as "*a white*"
(if that's what he was) to obviate misunderstanding (or, perhaps, to score tit-
for-tat). Tempers were already rising. Friends of the victim accused the Sussex police of "murder"; and, as the *Times* reported, one friend's statement
read: "I absolutely refuse to let the police murder a friend of mine and then try
to dirty his name in their own pathetic attempt to justify a ruthless killing."
The chief constable of Sussex was quoted as justifying the use of guns ("when
we believe that the target may be violent"). A chief constable in Kent has announced a "complaints inquiry." All in all, a routine if tragic incident, with no
"racial complications" so far as what the papers said is concerned. Should the
follow-up story—of the funeral, of the investigation—suggest otherwise (possibly with a photo of the late James Ashley), then we will know a bit more; but
for now we can only bring to the matter, for better or worse, the suspicions
and/or prejudices which afflict all multiethnic societies.

The same obtains for the second incident (of 16 January 1998) which the
Times put across its front page with the banner headline:

OLD BAILEY BECOMES CLASSROOM FOR RAPE TRIAL OF 10-YEAR-OLDS

There was color enough in the abominable story without overloading it with
racial or ethnic considerations, if any. There was also a complicating inhibit-
ing factor of the age of "the rapists" (children: hence no names, no pictures).
Accordingly, Court 12 of London's Old Bailey had been transformed, like a
stage set, into a modern primary school classroom. The two accused boys would
have been too small to be seen had they had to stand in the dock—so they sat at
low desks and tables, "just as at school." The forbidding figures of the Judge and
the *QC* Barristers played their courtroom roles without—just this one time— their
traditional wigs, "as unintimidating and as relaxed as possible." The nine-year-
old girl who had been stripped and raped by the boys in the school lavatory
was only to be seen, when she was giving evidence, on a video link screen.

The *Times* gave us all, and even more, than we needed to know about this
unprecedented, distressing affair. It sent an artist into the court-room to give
us "an impression of the scene" wherein all chairs were green, all tables properly mahogany, all haircuts straight, all faces a light sepia tint. One felt a twinge
of sadness, a touch of alarm. Was this how life had become in England today?
Am I the only one in a million readers who, with perhaps an editor's *déformation
professionelle*, scanned prose and picture with a sigh of relief that no bigot

could come away with some nasty propaganda fodder (foreign barbarization of English customs-and-mores, etc.)?

Some details were, in point of fact, troubling. One of the girl's cousins had been involved in the rape, and he had been "jumping and laughing and saying I was going to have different kinds of babies." Did this difference mean anything? Were the perpetrators a mixed gang? And what was one detail about the raped girl's background supposed to signify? "She lives with her mother, five brothers and three sisters, but she was born in Jamaica and lived there until a few years ago." What can, and will, English readers make of this? What other colorful details in courtroom 12 of the Old Bailey will be fit to print as the unfortunate story unfolds? I am afraid that no press code will be helpful, with its ambiguous doctrine of "relevance." Alas, we will, in all the days to come, be overwhelmed by an embarrassment of abominations.[5]

Suspicion by Omission

All these, as I say, were no isolated incidents, and they did not come from nowhere. The whole corps of editors and political journalists have nowadays arrogated to themselves a power to disclose and to withhold as they please. The government's secrets are open to prey by investigative journalists; their own media secrets are classified and to be protected by the force of law. They are the arbiters over which facts it is socially constructive and ethically progressive to reveal—and which are to be held back lest regrettable reactionary consequences ensue. This is not only an indefensible, unjustifiable entitlement, but also an outlandishly mistaken strategy.

If memory serves, I think I can remember when the kindly, charitable self-censorship began. It must have been some time after the horrific riots in Harlem in the wartime 1940s (about which Ralph Ellison wrote his impressive novel, *The Invisible Man*) when in New York, and elsewhere, news-stories no longer referred to the race, color, or ethnic origins of persons arrested, criminals sentenced, gang-leaders apprehended. The tactics of benevolence, later "PC," suggested that the tactful omission of the designation of "Negro"—later, black, or whatever—would help assuage troubled race relations. But, as the ironies and paradoxes of good will would have it, the very opposite was soon seen to be the case. Of course, as I have argued, there could be no mistaken identities when "Lepke" Buchalter was indicted and convicted as an accomplice of Murder Incorporated, or when Tammany's notorious Frank Costello came to trial. But what—and I think the challenge worth repeating—of the news items naming a George Jackson, or a Henry Whitehouse, or a William Henry Jones? Good Anglo-Saxon names, all; and when the newspaper reader read of their felonies, was he in point of fact relieved of his "racial suspicions"? Quite the contrary. It was suspicion by omission. Even if Mr. Jackson and Mr. Jones were "Caucasians," and they might well be, the general tendency was, alas, to conclude that all crimes and criminals—if there was no obvious nomenclatural evidence to the contrary ("Bugsy" Siegel, Vito Genovese, et al.)—were to be attributed to you-know-who....

Words and names on the police blotter are too important to be left to the precinct's reporters. Their (or their editors') thoughtless and arbitrary manipulations of journalistic practice in the cause of ethnic benevolence have proved, in this case and in innumerable others, to be part not of the healing process but of the exacerbation of harm and hate. When quacks prescribe, wounds continue to fester.

Nor is the imperative all one-sided, an embarrassing matter of negative image-making. Since none of us is without a certain enlightened sympathy with minorities who have suffered grievous harm due to race, religion, or previous condition of servitude, it is obvious that we would also want to participate in positive image-making, to register the good as well as the bad news. Surely we would want to know whether the George Washington Carver who was elected the other day to edit the *Harvard Law Review* was (as he would be, at long last) the first American Negro (or black, or African-American) to be so honored?

I am not sure that it is altogether satisfactory for human beings to be so "racially tagged," to find themselves in a kind of permanent identity parade. But the "Ethnic Revolution" (as Professor Nathan Glazer was the first to call it some twenty years ago) through which we have been living makes knowing who-is-who inevitable, for purposes of pride as well as shame, for better or worse. Neither educators nor immigration officials, nor housing officers nor hospital doctors, can afford not to pay attention, not to take note. An English community wants to know how its new Asian or West Indian immigrant community is faring—how big it is; what its birth-rate comes to; whether all the children, girls included, attend school regularly; how high the unemployment percentage is. An American "affirmative action" reformer demands to know the color and ethnic origins of applicants for government jobs and medical-school places. A slum doctor in Harlem or Watts is scientifically handicapped without careful correlations between, say, sickle-cell anemia (which evidently afflicts mainly persons of Black African origin) and whatever categories of racial classification we may devise or revise.[6]

But we have in recent years, as I have been suggesting, substituted for the old Victorian taboo of sex the new taboo of so-called "racism." In the course of this transvaluation of values we have become frightened out of our wits by the semantic spooks of a changing vocabulary: by obscenities which have now become standard, by old colorful words which have suddenly been interdicted. "Golliwogs," one notes, are now to be forbidden in England, the little dolls (or the black figurines on your jam jar) constituting nothing less than a "racial slur." An English police inspector was forced to retire the other day because he used the word "nig-nogs"—which, presumably, was taken to suggest *nig* for "niggers" and *nogs* for "wogs," although the etymology was spurious and the term was rather one of some affection and often used by Northumberland grandmothers about their own unruly grandchildren.

Whether or not the semantic clean-up involved in the doctrine of "political correctness" is deemed excessive and even morally untenable, tomorrow's newspapers and next week's television series will betray marks of the new standards and sensitivities. And, one should add, of Adam's old deviousness which will always find ways of getting away with illicit titillation or untoward breaking of taboos. For example, the name of the late Benny Hill stood for several decades in Britain and then in the U.S.A. as a symbol of entertainment which made capital of whatever was comic in the subjects we now have to identify as sexism, racism, and the like. Changing tastes as well as stricter monitoring would—one would have suspected—have made re-runs, repeats, revivals, and altogether the prospects of a comeback highly improbable. Not so. One can always announce that one is eager to illustrate the misdemeanors of yesteryear in order to highlight the virtues of enlightened progress already made.

"BENNY HILL RETURNS" reported the *Times* of London (and will the *Times* of New York be far behind?). And not only "Bawdy Benny"—also *The Black and White Minstrel Show* (which featured black-faced entertainment in the grease-paint manner Al "Mammy" Jolson made famous), not to mention *Miss World* (the bathing-beauty contest which drew the fiery protests of feminist movements all over). Such "vintage delights" were long languishing in the dusty BBC archives; but not for much longer. They are all to be resurrected in an anthology of politically incorrect programing. As the *Times* reports (in March 1998) richly illustrated documentary films, devoted to *One Million Years PC*, will be putting on the once-popular shows "in context for a new generation of viewers." This is an ingeniously indelicate idea whose time has come.

Time magazine, on the occasion of its seventy-fifth anniversary number, is equally inspired to collect the so-called errors or sins of yesteryear, and how they can be digitally re-mastered for up-to-the-minute amusement. In a rare confessional mode it devotes a column—entitled, in the inversion it has always made its own—"Regrets, We Have a Few," famously parodied by Wolcott Gibbs in a *"Timese"* crack: "Backwards ran sentences until reeled the mind." The editors collectively admitted that *"Time's* approach to questions of ethnicity and gender wasn't always what it should have been." Among the editorial regrets was a reference (1929) to Albert Einstein as a "Jew"; and, typically, he didn't take, as all good Americans should, any physical exercise. A description (1935) of Ethiopia's Emperor Haile Selassie as "cocoa-butter-colored." A Pacific War-time counsel (1941) as to how to tell Japanese and Chinese people apart by offering indelicate rules-of-thumb.

Should *Time* have known better even at the time? Stricken staggers the conscience until up-flows the guilt.[7]

An irritability on the subject has been taking on the proportions of a plague-like eczema.* Part of the disease, I have been trying to suggest, is the reprehensible self-censorship in the public prints, a combination of timidity (in the face of small, militant cliques who have appointed themselves to be the keepers of the word) and ideological arrogance. For the manipulators in authority are quite ready to force one and all to become as enlightened, altruistic, and forward-looking as they take themselves to be.

On all these issues I myself am not sure what the ideal or even the advisable provisional solution should be. But surely one can call out to the journalists, in the spirit of Orwellian skepticism, to consider whether they could conceivably be mistaken. The truth may wound, but possibly (as André Gide suggested) only to cure. In any case: Orwell, thou should'st be living at this hour! we have need of thee....

The Risks of Shedding Light

I am struck by one more recent case, thirty years on from the incident in Brooklyn and a decade after the events in Lawrence, Massachusetts, that I have described. Three U.S. Marines were involved in the rape of a twelve-year-old Japanese schoolgirl in the woods near a U.S. military base on the island of Okinawa. Of what interest could it possibly be for a newpaper to record their color, race, religion, or hair-style? Presumably none. They were servicemen, two Marines and a Navy seaman, three young Americans, and wayward enough to get caught up in an ugly mess. They were duly indicted and tried, found guilty and sentenced to 6 ½ to 7 years by an Okinawan court to whom the U.S. Army had been pressured to delegate jurisdiction. Their names were non-committal: Rodrico Harp, 21; Kendrick Ledet, 20; Marcus Gill, 22. A newspaper reader who had not deeply studied and sedulously compared various accounts in the international media would have had no idea that a special "racial" factor was involved in this perhaps most troublesome matter in a half-century of Japanese-U.S. military relationship.

The turning-point in the coverage of the story came when the families of the three guilty servicemen, resident in Georgia and in Texas, suggested in an Atlanta press conference that "the men were being unfairly treated because they were black...." This was a startling way to break the news on an unsuspecting

---

* It is, of course, not a new phenomenon in England. As Cromwell memorably put it – in 1655, thinking of his own Puritan movement's radical-left (Charles Firth, *Oliver Cromwell*, 1900, p. 368):

   "Is there not a strange itch upon the spirit of men? Nothing will satisfy them unless they can press their finger upon their brethren's conscience to pinch him there...."

readership. And when the families embarked on a journey to Okinawa to witness the legal proceedings for themselves, news-agency photographs of the mothers and wives that accompanied the story—as in the *Herald-Tribune* for 5 December 1995 (with an Agence France-Presse picture)—told the rest of the tell-tale story.

Originally, the press had refrained from mentioning the "color question" for the usual enlightened reasons. Surely it is PC and also ethically correct to be reluctant to add to the congeries of bad images which have accompanied racial prejudice against the Negroes ever since they were enslaved and transported over the Atlantic to be the "mud-sill" of American society. Who needs additional stories about inborn laziness, backward intelligence quotas, and sexual violence? The Okinawa affair would be re-casting "the blacks as rapists," and summoning up old and bad memories—even to the appalling message of that almost forgotten Black Power militant, Eldridge Cleaver, who advocated in his best-selling book *Soul On Ice* (1968) the rape of white women as a political weapon of racial compensation.

No, the conscientious editor of a serious newspaper would not pander to the temptations, succumb to the stereotypes, allow his readers to jump to suspect conclusions and think the worst. An important innuendo gap ensued. As I say, no reader could quite comprehend the passions and the embarrassments that were boiling over Okinawa. Doubtless the sorely-pressed Pentagon would have been a mite more willing to turn over white Marines than blacks. And the Japanese islanders who had put up "with a half-century of foreign occupation" were giving vent not only to the normal resentments of such uneasy situations, but also to a traditional sense of tribal solidarity which still expresses itself in a superiority complex against all races whose complexions happen to be a shade darker, or lighter, than themselves. All empires know the panicky colonial message: *Natives Furious—Base Under Siege*. Republics have the sober advantage of a free press which sustains a critical reflectiveness that can save the day. Rough and uncouth news editors of the old school say: Let it all hang out....

Thus, classic defenders of "the whole truth, and nothing but—" position point to the Okinawa incident as yet further proof that the ideals of "political correctness" always yield to journalistic wrongdoing. In the absence of all the facts, of all the devious factors making for tragic conflict, more bad news is bound to come. The best guideline for our troubled newspaper culture could still be the old motto which one famous New York daily (now defunct)—Roy Howard's *World-Telegram*—printed on its editorial page: "*Shed Light, and the People Will Find Their Own Way.*" But the fearful risk of a free and uncensored press is, then again, that the People might not.

Wog, Golliwog, and Likely Stories

No frankness is full, no candor complete; and even when breaking the rules of political correctness there are evasions and circumlocutions. Andrew Alexander of the *Daily Mail* is not known in London for mincing words, and he often takes on the clichés of the day which mask political reality. He was, a short while ago, incensed at the social surveys with their "humbug phrases" about people in a particular group being "more likely" to suffer some disadvantages. Thus, if you are black, the sociologists will say that you are "more likely" to be sent to prison than if you are white; and if you are from an ethnic minority you are "more likely" to be unemployed than if you are white. He makes a valid point, I believe, when he writes,

> The phrase is regularly used to imply either that there *must* be discrimination where differences in achievement are detected or that we are all in the grip of impersonal forces which decide our destiny according to some group membership.

He is led on to ask,

> Why is it, by the way, that these surveys never seem to talk about one group, the Jews? Why are they, as an ethnic minority, not 'more likely to be unemployed'? Why are they not mentioned when claims are made that ethnic minorities are 'more likely' to fail to become Q.C.'s or judges or Cabinet ministers?

What is he trying to imply?—that one minority, evidently more successful, is obviously superior? He would beware of saying so. There are evasions in incorrectitude. And, if on the subject of unemployment likelihoods, he writes about "the idle" and "the work-shy," he bewares of implying that one or two ethnic minorities who make up the bulk of the jobless, are—in the old painful platitude of prejudice—deemed "lazy."

But so many stories of "racial news"—and this is a specialty of Alexander's paper, the *Daily Mail*—are in the grey area of implications and imprecations, all vaguely suspect. One headline read,

SCHOOL MUST TAKE BACK TEACHER
IN "GOLLIWOG JIBE" ROW

The "jibe" (a four-letter word that fits narrow headline space, and thus much loved by newspapers) is an especially interesting one, for it suggests surprisingly that expletives of harmless origin take on more vicious import than normally foul insults.

"Golliwog" (according to my Partridge) was a rather hairy Australian caterpillar and the name came to be applied to a "golliwog doll" which was also hairy and black. It served for a long time as the charming trade-mark on the label of a very popular English jam, jelly, and marmalade brand—until the P.C. pressure on the company as "racist" consigned the smiling little caricature to oblivion.

Now Mr. James Evans, the schoolteacher in question, had difficulties in pronouncing the name of one of his Liverpool students in his roll-call, and then he said allegedly, "Then we'll just have to call her golliwog...." Had he said it? Or had he said (as others testified) "wog"—which could be considered a shade worse? The teacher was one for nicknames, having previously been warned by the school for calling a boy in the playground "Big Nose."

What's in a name? a memory of an Australian caterpillar? an echo of Cyrano de Bergerac? a sticky phrase mis-heard? The teacher says he merely said, "I jolly well can't pronounce that name"; and he was reinstated in the school.

Race in the Shadow of Enlightened Counsel

Since the "happy breed of men" on "this scepter'd isle" has become, with Afro-Asian and Caribbean emigrants and refugees in the millions, a multiracial society, this England has been sorely confronted with most of the American problems which I have been considering. Its press has been wracked with roughly the same dilemmas which trouble the ethics of journalism on either side of the Atlantic. In creating an institution like the voluntary, non-governmental British Press Council, the Britons have often been praised, admired, and envied for the civilized attempt at self-regulation which would be free of the heavy hand of governmental interference. In some lands a Press Council to adjudicate complaints and make recommendations (and sometimes reluctantly calling upon law enforcement) has been transplanted or otherwise imitated. How relevant, then, are the "Anglo-American differences" in this context of comparative multiculturism? Reconsider the question that has dominated the foregoing pages: Should the color or "racial origin" of persons in the news be mentioned, or not?

A complaint had been made to the Press Council against four London newspapers for the "journalistic misdemeanor" of having identified a youth of sixteen who had raped five women and hacked another to death with a broken milk bottle. He had been described (in the *Daily Mail*, the *London Standard*, the *Daily Telegraph*, and the *Daily Express*) as "black" (and also as "slightly built"). This was held to be culpably irrelevant. And the judgment is interesting enough to be quoted—especially so, since it rather sharply contrasts with my original argument about the arrogance of well-meaning journalists (my emphasis was on liberal-enlightened U.S. newspapers) indulging in self-censorship. According to the British Press Council's adjudication,

The Press Council has consistently held that people's race or color should only be introduced into newspaper reports where it is relevant to the story being told.

By this the council means where, for example, in a court report the color or race of a defendent or victim has a direct bearing on the crime alleged. Another obvious example is where publishing a description may assist in the apprehension of a criminal.

The fact that a crime is serious or abhorrent does not itself create such relevance. Indeed, because of the likelihood of serious crime engendering strong emotions in readers, it is more important than usual when reporting them for newspapers to beware of irrelevant references to race or color which may encourage or pander to racial prejudice.

In this case the crimes were appalling, but the fact that the youth convicted was black was irrelevant to them and should not have been introduced into the reports.

The complaints are upheld.

Now this, clearly, puts the shoe on the other foot. I have been very skeptical about such self-censorship in New York or Washington, convinced that one man's "relevance" was another man's "essentials." But now, in London, the censor's pencil was being brandished not by the prudent reporter, or his *bien-pensant* editor, but by the Wise Men of Fleet Street, appointed to be watchdogs of liberty and integrity!

I still feel that, in general, the roots of the problem lie in "our new cultural predicament" where the precarious balance of disruptive forces dictates that no potentially explosive truths be told. Discretion is in the saddle, and the idealism of care and concern leads to "tactful omissions" which in turn lead only to what I called "Suspicion by Omission": namely, that all the heinous crimes of the day are being committed by "you-know-who"....Nevertheless, it is the case that in Britain the press—for a variety of its own reasons (some probably less than honorable, especially in tabloid quarters where sensationalism is the daily style)—takes a rather more straightforward attitude to "reporting the facts" than the ideologues of the struggle against racial prejudice. The *Daily Mail* printed the Press Council's ruling, but replied that it had

no intention of having its editorial judgement usurped or censored by a body whose credentials are becoming increasingly devalued. This paper will continue to make its own judgements on reporting the news and let its readers decide whether they are relevant or not.

The *London Standard* went further and, in its way, rather underlined my paradox about uninformed-readers-jumping-to-undesirable-conclusions:

To be selective about these details, on the principle that a mention of a person's color fosters racial divisiveness, would lead newspaper readers to make prejudiced and inaccurate assumptions about the scale of black crime: the opposite effect to what the Press Council intends.

The *Daily Telegraph* also echoed this viewpoint, for what the Press Council is saying, in effect, is that

> there are certain facts which it is too dangerous for the people to know lest they draw false and divisive inferences from them. Apply this to race and you have opened the door to applying it to everything. What is worse, this principle is particularly perilous when used as a means of promoting racial equality. If the color of defendents in criminal cases cannot be reported what proof can there be that justice is being impartially administered to blacks and whites? The public often makes wild and prejudiced assumptions about the relationship between race and crime; the remedy is not to suppress facts but to reveal them all and discuss them thoroughly.

This may seem to some who know and follow the British press, what used to be called "Fleet Street," to be going at it with a bit too much high-mindedness. Are there no cases where the omission of a "relevant" or "interesting" detail would be morally mandatory?

Suppose for a moment that, on that fateful day in New Delhi, the first announcements of the late Indira Gandhi's assassination could have been (which they probably couldn't) "controlled" or "managed" or "censored" or "cleaned up." There would have been the grave announcement, the news of an assassin's successful murder—but no mention of the dastardly role played therein by the prime minister's Sikh bodyguards. This could have been released some time later, at a cooler calmer date when the emergency shock and uncontrollable hysteria had subsided. Surely the hideous lynching parties might have been circumvented, and possibly tens of thousands of Sikh lives, all violently destroyed during that first night, spared.

This would not, I suspect, quite fit in with the prevailing journalistic philosophy, as witness Alexander Chancellor, former editor in chief of the *Spectator* (London) and a senior editor of the *New Yorker*. Chancellor insists that for a newspaper the main test of "relevance" is whether a piece of information will interest its readers:

> If a person is convicted of an horrendous crime, it is quite natural for the newspaper reader to want to know as much about him as possible—his age, height, background, and so on. Journalists are taught to deliver such facts.
>
> If the facts as revealed happen to be taken by a particular reader as confirmation of his own prejudices, that is not the newspaper's fault. An editor is not a psychiatrist.

Nor, to be sure, is he a Bowdler. Israeli editions of Shakespeare cannot omit that Shylock was a Jew (a fact that is understood in Arabic editions). Nor can Mr. Julius Nyerere, the famous Shakespeare translator into Swahili, "edit out" Othello's blackness for Tanzanian readers. Yet the dilemma remains; for, under certain extreme circumstances, the reporter and editor and cameraman can inadvertently find themselves leading a hue-and-cry, unintentionally inciting to anger and mayhem.*

In the end I suppose I concur with the latitudinarians—despite the fact that in New Delhi, were it my fate to be the all-powerful censor-for-a-day, I would have surely used my blue pencil to save innocent lives, to blue-pencil a provocation, to jam a signal which would lead to massacres. When all is said and done, John Stuart Mill provides better guidelines than does Mrs. Grundy or Mrs. Whitehouse. Fleet Street is right to resist outside meddling. Americans revere the First Amendment. There is much that is wrong and insensitive in our writing about race and crime these days, but nothing that the amateurs of the race-relations industry can set right. I remain convinced that when quacks prescribe, wounds continue to fester.

Still, a decade or two is a long time in race relations, and the last two of the twentieth century may well go down as the bitter stretch during which the stratagem of ethnic benevolence at the expense of disagreeable truth telling was rudely undermined. Harsh communal tensions and indeed murderous political developments—for example, a London bobby hacked to death in a Tottenham riot; Zulu (or Hondo) blacks putting Indian browns to the flames in South African anti-*apartheid* marches—have radically retouched the whole picture. Tender-minded guidelines for discretionary omissions and self-censorship disappeared almost overnight as press reporters had to identify what appeared, in deadly color, on the TV screen. Were the latest victims in the news out of Africa (north and south of the Sahara) white, brown, black? No one could get a firm grasp of the nature of the Balkan violence without *all* the facts, ruthlessly recorded. Taking advantage of a media which was transmitting only *some* of the facts, partisans of Croatia and sympathizers with Islam helped to shape a world public opinion which pointed the "war crimes" finger solely at the Serbs. The "others" were barely mentioned for the ostensible fear of inflaming even more old-time Balkan animosities.

---

*   There always seems to be an ingenious way out, an escape route for rude stereotypes which become impermissible in the present but can, perhaps, be preserved in the past tense. It is a ploy which is generally referred to as "moving the goal-posts." What mustn't be said *now* can be offered as items in the historical present. This goes not only for racial stereotypes but as well for (as we shall see) sexually obscene clichés.

Thus, when H. Rider Haggard's *King Solomon's Mines* (1886) was made into a new film by the director J. Lee Thompson, not a little of the putative "old flavor" is pungently conveyed. As David Castell, the film critic for the *Sunday Telegraph*, (22 December 1985) pointed out:

"...setting the story back in hazily-defined time allows the makers to revert to national stereotypes without offending too violently modern sensibilities. Thus the Germans are bald and guttural and stupid, the Turks are fat and greasy and stupid, and the Africans are noble and savage and very stupid indeed. ('He doesn't trust anything that moves without eating grass,' Quartermain quips of the faithful Umbopo when he won't ride in a motor car.)"

Meanwhile, back on the local London scene, an English school principal was up on charges for identifying the rising crime rate in his school as one of West Indian delinquency. Fleet Street reporters gave a minute-by-minute account of the Middlesex police siege at the end of which a stabbed baby was rescued from her captor—and the photographers with their telescopic lenses made it clear that both the child and her attacker were "Caribbean." At the end of a long story in the *Daily Mail*, it was simply recorded, almost with relief, that it was not a "mixed affair": "All those involved in the siege were black."[8]

Elsewhere in the paper, sports columnists had to discuss the incidents of "Fascist racial abuse" in English football stadia, directed by fans and hooligans against certain players. Armchair followers of the sport wanted to know *which* players, and *what* the vicious epithets were.

A London judge at an industrial tribunal had to decide whether to award damages for a "racial insult" to a secretary in a city office named Maria de Souza; and he held that the remark—"Go and get the typing done by the wog!"—was "not enough to suffer a detriment under the Race Relations Act" and, therefore, the regrettable incident of prejudice could not be pronounced unlawful.

The Catholic headmaster of the English Martyrs School in Leicester, testifying in a case of "racial discrimination" against a dismissed teacher (Mrs. Rasamah Sivasothy), said that she had humiliated and terrified her pupils, and added that "if she had been white she would have been gone long ago."

In each case there were urgencies of establishing the real and unvarnished details of a case, whether out of civic curiosity or legal procedure. And they shattered most previous preconceptions of what is seemly and proper, progressive or civilized, in the public presentation of ethnic nastiness in a "multicultural society" (which evidently did not know how to "live together," and perhaps did not even want to). Nobody knew how to find the right words, ideas, or sentiments, as vagueness gave way to misunderstanding, and small differences became aggravated by agit-prop. One Police Federation chairman in Northamptonshire expressed the pious hope that England's ethnic minorities would become "more English." He was quoted as saying,

> I believe that, when in Rome, you should do as the Romans do. Guests who live here must try to become English. If we are to have a multiracial society, then we must learn to live together.

To which Mr. Michael Prescod, chairman of the Afro-Caribbean Association, angrily replied, "I find what he said repulsive. He has done a disservice and should not be allowed to hold public office."[9]

In these altercations, race and color, ethnicity and indigenous culture, national habits and religious creeds were all confused and confounded, and unceremoniously tossed into what Israel Zangwill once called "the melting pot," which surely has nowhere melted.

Even in the U.S., where the American press is particularly careful on denominational issues—Roman Catholics these days react as sensitively as do pro-Israel Jews, and both are thinner-skinned than the much-belabored Protestant "Wasps"—the self-denying ordinances of journalism and public discourse have been under trial. At the time I found it extremely difficult to follow (especially in the European press, including the *International Herald Tribune*, owned by the *New York Times* and the *Washington Post*) the full ramifications of the case of the young American, named Jonathan Jay Pollard, who was arrested by the FBI for "spying for Israel." The stories on "J.J. Pollard" (no further identification) seemed to confine the issue to one of foreign-policy ethics among friendly military allies. But the full range of the alarm, scandal, consternation which ensued pointed to the fact that Mr. Pollard, being an American Jew, had opened up the old can-of-worms about "dual nationality" and/or "double loyalties." These were old issues which so-called Zionists (and Papists too, after the Kennedy presidency) had hoped to have put behind them, generations ago.

Illusions in New York and London

I trust that I have made it sufficiently clear that stratagems based on obvious and fragile ambivalences cannot hold their vitality for long; and, even more, that a practice of self-censorship founded in goodwill and shoddy language has a built-in self-destruct. "Blacks" (as a whole variety of coloreds well know) were not all black; the whole "black movement" was based on a chromatic deceit; and what some observers have called the lie in the soul has proved corrosive.* "Anti-Discrimination" was not against *all* forms of discrimination; it was tactically preferential. And "equal opportunity" (or, in the USA "affirmative action") meant that some were more equal than others; and for many that signified very negative action.

A few final examples of how threadbare the semantic stratagems— and the flawed ethic of progressivism behind them—have become.

In the left-dominated Haringey Council in North London, then led by a flamboyant West Indian militant named Bernie Grant, the campaign against

---

*   No less so, I should add, than the complex of "whiteness" which led during the centuries of Western Empires in Afro-Asia to a disastrous racial complex. See the astute analysis of colors by Philip Mason in his *Encounter* (April 1968) essay: ..."'but O! My Soul is White'." We need to take such studies to heart, for therein lies the tragedy of: what Dr. Mason called "the Confusion of Biological Accident & Symbolic Metaphor." See also: Philip Mason, *Prospero's Magic: Some Thoughts on Class and Race* (1975). Mason called "the Confusion of Biological Accident & Symbolic Metaphor." See also: Philip Mason, *Prospero's Magic: Some Thoughts on Class and Race* (1975).

racial and sexual discrimination had been running in high gear, fuelled over the recent years with a militant idealism on behalf of the unfortunate "victims of middle-class society." Yet how does it work in practice when jobs come to be filled, Civil Service examinations taken, and equal opportunities at long last installed? As one Haringey councillor put it the other day: "What it amounts to is that if you are white, British and male and applying for a job in Haringey, you may as well forget it."[10]

Some fifty persons applied for an £11,000-a-year appointment. The final twelve who were to be considered were on a special panel's short list. Given its ideological complexion, it proceeded to alter the number of points that had been previously given. Under the heading of "Ability to understand the needs of black and ethnic minorities," the scores of two were doubled, thus advantaging the "black and Asian" candidates. (Evidently the "whites" scored nothing, and Irish candidates only one.) Under the heading of "Ability to communicate the needs of women," the women candidates' scores were doubled; the men scored nothing. Under the heading of "Ability to work on one's own," (oh, that hated middle-class individuality!), well, the whole category was simply scrapped. At the end of the day, the official explanation (from Mr. Nakendra Makanzi) was that it was all "a way of countering discrimination"!

In a sense, what we are going through is yet another tortuous exercise in the arbitrary imposition of Rousseau's "general will" (or what the generals of the Enlightenment's army hold it to be). If necessary, as the fateful phrase in the *Contrat social* (1762) has it, everyone will be "forced to be free": to have the right sentiments, to be above and beyond prejudice, to be enlightened. J.L. Talmon called it, in his intellectual history of the period, the origins of "totalitarian democracy."[11]

For his recent television documentary a BBC producer put cameras into an old Victorian house in Devon where he had assembled a white manager (he had lost his post when Rhodesia became Zimbabwe); a white pensioner from Peckham (where he had been twice mugged by black youths); and a white lawyer (fearful of her property values as the neighborhood became more ethnically mixed). To this group he added a number of sensitive blacks, including a nurse, a welfare councillor, and an academic researcher. The producer, a Rousseauian *bien-pensant* if there ever was one, was convinced that "after a week together, the racists' position would collapse..."

Alas, nothing went right. The bizarre and misguided experiment failed dismally, as most of the group ended with their views as rigid as at the outset, possibly even more so after tears, hateful arguments, and daily bitterness. They had all been foolishly encouraged to act out their prejudices, and the ensuing theater was not therapy but tragedy. The participants, racists and victims alike, had found the manipulated experience "appalling...shocking...depressing." The BBC producer almost seemed to be apologizing when he confessed: "I was just trying to make a good film. I knew that very likely someone would get hurt. It was not meant to be therapeutic for either the whites or the blacks...." As one outraged television critic (Mary Kenny) wrote, in reviewing the screening of the BBC production, *Are you a Racist?*,

> This was a wicked program to have made: its consequences will have been almost wholly detrimental....Written and produced by Edward Goldwyn, it ended with a little sermon to all the poor bloody infantry out there: ..."We must find a way to change the racist views." I say we must also find a way to stop this mischief of stirring up hatred in a society which has been historically characterized by its tolerance.[12]

Finally, an incident in New York which also suggests why the shaky foundation of the "race relations industry" may well be collapsing. In the ruins something new and strange is emerging, with perhaps an even more dispiriting mix of what a harassed and manipulated citizenry may find fair and proper in a darkening struggle for rights, privileges, and self-identities.

No doubt about it, the New York City police force—predominantly white in its leadership—has also been predominantly white in recruitment; and there were inevitable handicaps in its maintaining law-and-order in a metropolitan community of such mixed racial and ethnic character. Time was when police candidates made sure that their application forms were "unexceptionable." Times have changed. What is now happening is that white policemen—who were passed over for promotion to sergeant or lieutenant, under the city's racial-quota plan— are suddenly asking to be reclassified as "blacks" or "Hispanics." The police officers chose to call themselves *white* when they joined the force; but they are now insisting that they are really members of "minority groups," and thus eligible for promotion ahead of whites with higher scores on the test.

Well, they would say that now, wouldn't they?

Can they prove it? Once quotas—ever since the time of Ellis Island and Anglo-Saxon immigration laws, a hated, evil, "un-American" thing—became acceptable, it was only a short step to finding Nazi-like methods of "determining" ancestry, Nuremberg-style, the "full" identity of one's grandfather.[13] Indeed one police commissioner (in charge of "equal opportunity"), Mr. George Sanchez, agreed that "the cops can qualify by proving that either one parent, two grandparents or four great-grandparents were black or born in a Spanish-speaking country." As Sanchez added, "One guy just put down that he *didn't want to be white any more.*" Surely anyone can say that?

The Hispanic Society quickly protested, for this could be the long-awaited backlash even if whites were not exactly standing up, in a last-ditch struggle, for whitehood. Could it be that, since nobody is truly "white" (Aldous Huxley suggested "pinko-gray"), you can call yourself anything you want and take the glittering prizes and annual raises, shiny badges, better pensions, and extra holidays?

There may be a moral here, for in what Goethe called *Farbenlehre*, chromatic lies have caught on, and old deceptions are now newly deceived. The lesson may not have been lost on the Hispanic Society's leader, Mr. Luis Salgado, who in touching tones of wailing mournfulness saw that the affirmations of yesteryear were becoming the negations of tomorrow. Where the community consents to trickery, tricksters grow and flourish. Or, as Salgado put it, "The moment we win something, they find some way of taking it away from us." Defeat has been snatched from the jaws of victory. As he recognized, "There's really nothing we can do, if they can prove what they are."

Well, you can bet on it that some 20 percent are likely to decide that they *"don't like being white any more."* They will be discovering a shadowy grandfather in Haiti or documenting a long-lost grandmother in Brazil (unless Portuguese doesn't technically qualify as "Spanish-speaking"); and a whole host of converts will proceed efficaciously to fill the 20 percent of officer posts reserved under the quota plan and its corrupting temptations.

More illusions shattered![14]

Journalists do not serve the truth when they think it might be a shade more morally expedient to prevaricate. Reformers do not help minorities when they treat majorities with the same subterfuges which have always marked the meanness of discrimination. *Affirmative* cannot mean negative; *equal* dare not signify more-equal or less-equal.

For there appears to be, or so I prefer to believe, some inner logic in the clash of social forces whereby that which is unnaturally promulgated or arbitrarily administered tends, in the short or long run, to destabilize itself and to self-destruct. On all these matters we will still have to be picking ourselves up out of the chaos and the rubble.

Brazil is, to be sure, a source of much multicultural confusion for the more simple-minded black-and-white media world of the Northern Hemisphere. For alone of the mixed societies, with heavy ex-slave populations and/or a colored immigration, it developed a utopian dream of racial harmony and tried to superimpose it on ex-Portuguese colonial realities. A *mestizo* could consider himself white, and it was well known (if, for outsiders, surprising) that mulattoes, *morenos, pardos*, and others with some amount of black ancestry didn't consider themselves black in Brazil. Confusion—which here amounts to a benevolent state of non-prejudice—was worse confounded when official census-takers persisted in classifying the population according to primary colors (in 1990: 42 percent brown, 5 percent black, 52 percent white, and "yellow" almost 1 percent). Small wonder that Brazilians approached the chromatic scale rather differently than a John Updike. A Rio carnival star remarked to a foreign correspondent, "Everybody in Brazil is black, whether they know it or not..." and he, in turn, noted that she was called *"Neguinho do Samba"* (or "Little Black of the Samba"), an affectionate nickname which elsewhere would be derogatory.

In contrast to the former African-slave population in the U.S. which found over the years a viable road to social progress but not a clear, stable, lasting sense of identity, the Brazilian blacks remained poor but relatively free from bouts of rootlessness and regular identity crises. When the word had been dogmatically proscribed in the American press from Harlem to Watts, I happened to see a happy-go-lucky group of Rio de Janeiro athletes in T-shirts which they had labeled "*100 percent Negro.*" I am sure that they didn't subscribe to the old Brazilian fetish of miscegenation, whereby Brazil's future was considered to lay in "whitening" its blacks through the power of "greater white genes," or at least through an injection of European stock. Now blacks are calling themselves "*Afro-Brazilians*" and surmise that more social progress might be achievable in the North American way: pressure politics, sharp profile, militancy, playing the race card. *Newsweek* recently reported a new problem in Brazil: What to do with people who are now "white" but declare themselves "brown" (or even "black") for affirmative-action purposes.

For the time being, a peculiar indigenous fluidity obtains. Foreign observers no longer believe as firmly as they used to that, so far as race was concerned, the Brazilians had a dream of their own and its colorful spirit of open ethnicity was helping it to dance and sing to fulfilment. One can again read familiar stories in our papers and periodicals of popular Brazilians who, despite being black, have a white soul; and of high achievers who began by being born black, turned brown when they received a good education, and were perceived as white when money and honors came their way. Now one can hear more and more of campaigners in the Afro-Brazilian advocacy movement who say, not without a smile, that they are the only blacks in their family..."the black sheep," so to speak. Some observers do foresee a new, effective black power movement. Others watch bemused, as if it were an unpredictable kaleidoscopic scramble:

> For the irony of the Brazilian conundrum [writes Ellis Close in *Newsweek*] is that the conflict that seems necessary for racial progress may mean sacrificing the Brazilian racial cordiality that, for so many people, made the dream of racial paradise seem real.[15]

Chromatic Deceptions

Let me be unequivocally clear about one thing: If an irresponsible editor deliberately panders to the worst prejudices, then it is a reprehensible misdemeanour in journalism. Sometimes the deed is disguised under the cover of factual reporting—"giving all the news"—especially when, as above, the short-sighted convention of a sector of the mainstream liberal press is to omit or to play down. Sometimes this reluctance is based on a semantic confusion not of one's own making.

At the present moment the leading black organization in the U.S. is the NAACP, with the "C" standing for Colored, a term which has long since (except in South Africa, where it referred to nonblack Indians, like Mahatma Gandhi in Capetown) fallen into disusage. This old organization is now (in the late 1990s), according to one black columnist (Michael Meyers in the *New York Post*), trying to regain its place "in the forefront of social change without hating their fellow humans or denigrating America...." It is a rare black leader (or journalist) who still advocates the concept of nonviolent civil rights for which they walked on marches with Martin Luther King. Julian Bond is one, and as the new head of the NAACP he insisted that he would be rejecting racist separatism; the "C" in NAACP "summoned all people because all people have color...."[16]

In the last half-century, the slangy insult "nigger" fell more and more into disrepute, and "Negro" was politely spelled with a capital N. Then it was decided that "Black was Beautiful" (though it was in point of plain fact no more beautiful than white or yellow or purple)—and all journalists were persuaded or pressured to write about "blacks." The latter catch-all category included West Indians who were conspicuously brown and even embraced, for a time, Koreans, Vietnamese, and other Asians, who were "yellow" in the old color scale. "Black" as a blanket description for peoples who were not "white" (read, according to Aldous Huxley, "*pinko-grey*") was a chromatic deception—and it soon broke down. The blacks then now became, in the official description of the movement, "African-Americans." This has not proved very popular with the peoples previously known as "colored" or "Negro," or with the U.S. press (whose editors demurred at being pushed back to referring to citizens as "Italo- or Greco- or Sino-Americans").

With some differences these deceptions and dilemmas also plague the British press. Thus, in the always newsworthy conflicts that have marked the London borough of Brent, ever since the 1970s a centre of "Black Power" politics, the rainbow coalition of "oppressed races" became divided against themselves. The British press reported (on 12 July 1994) on the illegality of a black counsellor's move to oust all Asians from the borough posts and substitute "black officers of African origin." The left-wing Brent Council had a "Race Equality Unit" of twenty-four good jobs. Miss Poline Nyaga, thirty-four, "born in Kenya," was outraged that the local political scene was "dominated" by Afro-Caribbeans; she defected from her Labour group, and went over to the Tories. The headline in the *Daily Mail* had a touch of malice: "*The Black Race Offender.*"

Again: What's in a name? The *Observer* remarked that "Afro-" as an ethnic denomination would be short-lived since Africa, proud and confident in the heady days of Nkrumah and Nyerere, has descended into abject poverty, continuous civil war and worse, even in its most hopeful areas. Who will be ever again searching for "roots" in Rwanda and Somalia? Much blood blurs the way; and much ink will be spilled before any kind of clarity (or journalistic unanimity) emerges.

The controversy which was caused by Keith Richburg, a black *Washington Post* correspondent who wrote a book (*Out of America*, 1997) about his experiences in fratricidal black Africa, was summed up thus by one London paper: "An American has triggered rage and consternation among his fellow black intellectuals by repudiating his African roots and thanking God he was enslaved." Afro-centric idealism is, for the moment, an article of faith in black America; and is politically correct in the white newspaper culture's house-style. Richburg is almost alone in rejecting it as "ignorance and hypocrisy." He recognizes his slave forebears, transferred in chains to the Caribbean and thence to South Carolina, but does not lament his deracination. He writes, rather, "Thank God my ancestor got out because now I am not one of them." This isolated viewpoint among black American writers is an unusual mixture of intellectual dissent and patriotic sentiment; it is oddly Jeffersonian.[17]

"Black" may do for now, for it fits more easily into the headline space. But "Blacks" are not black nor do West-Indians come from West India. Nor are Indians (U.S., red) literally "native Americans." They were there before the eponymous Amerigo Vespucci dreamed of discovering what Christopher Columbus failed to discover (having made it only to the Caribbean); and thus they qualify to be registered as, perhaps, native *pre*-Americans. Come to think of it, "native" is itself problematical, for it has an echo of the old imperial attitude to the indigenous folk, there to be conquered and exploited.

Readers and writers will have to tread warily in these treacherous waters for a long time to come. If one doesn't go in, over one's head, then one can live with the waves and tides. After all, in the Middle East the enemies of Israel, or of the Zionist state, are called "anti-Semites"; whereas they are themselves Semites of Arab provenance. Words have clear and fixed meanings only in dictionaries (and not always there).

Even reading the papers assiduously it is difficult to find out what our friendly neighborhood police have been up to. Evidently the detectives of Greater Manchester have been overdoing it, for at a charity dinner (a jolly, off-color affair filmed by ITV, which bleeped out some of the after-dinner talk) they were seen and heard laughing at the cabaret act of a comedian named Bernard Manning, a shy man in private but a rude and rough customer in public: "I need a *macho* audience to find myself." His patter, which had the officers standing on chairs applauding, was what one paper called discreetly an "appalling tirade." What did he say? At first few quotes emerged. If they were offensive to black people, it would be doubly offensive to repeat them. The papers were properly outraged: "These, of course, are the people responsible for patrolling and policing the streets where young black people try to walk about." Shouldn't we, then, know what is going on in the constables' minds, echoing the stand-up comics whom they just love? Or is general public and politically correct indignation enough? The critic and novelist A.N. Wilson was curious enough to find out and tell us, although he quoted only "the least offensive" of Bernard Manning's remarks, "most of which were scabrous as well as Nazi in flavor": "They think they're English because they're born here. That means because a dog's born in a stable it's a f—ing horse."

In the end the man who came to the charity dinner to delight the police on the beat only illustrated an old Mancunian proverb: some become street-wise, some are born street-stupid.

The Stained Cloak of Ethnicity

For now, we can only wearily concede that every variety of ambiguity, or tricky double-talk, even the most inevitable double-entendre, will have on occasion, sooner or later, a field-day. In the British controversy over the peripatetic Gypsy population, each locality tries to vie with each other in *not* providing sites for the wandering caravans. A *Daily Mail* headline refers to the "GIPSY CURSE" but in the sub-head refers more daintily to "SITES FOR TRAVELLERS." "Travelers" are a traditional term for gypsies, a shade more polite than the generic term which gave the English vocabulary the pejorative verb "*to gyp,*" i.e. to steal, rob, pinch, cheat. It is almost as obsolete as "*to jew down*" (to bargain, haggle, or otherwise buy cheaply) which had been subject to protests against standard dictionary editors for having included it in their pages. (One particular dictionary was adamant; others revised.)

How can one cleanse the stained cloak of ethnicity? A murder is a murder. There's the killer, and here's the corpse. But when it is called, as in the *Daily Telegraph* headline, a "REGGAE ROW," then you begin to sense a different tune.

One Michel Gilfilin, thirty-five, was charged with the murder of John Purbrick, thirty-one. The court heard evidence in Cardiff that "Gilfilin would play his West Indian music loudly at all hours." So it is a Caribbean affair, but with inter- (or intra-?) racial implications. Who can know? Poor Purbrick was obviously not Indian or Chinese. Was he white? And was his killer a Caribbean black? Gilfilin testified: "He knocked at my door, called me a nigger and fell down the stairs." Purbrick's head was smashed and his chest crushed. Gilfilin, a giant of a man, averred he was only defending his music and his honor. A little "Reggae Row" turned out badly for all the races (whatever they were) in the fatal affair. The white (presumably) reporter was being very discreet. He called no names. The nastiness of the story was in the quotes smuggled in between the inverted commas.[18]

In the end the question always comes down to this: Will the paper have the spirit, the courage, the "guts" enough to withstand all the demands of political, cultural, and semantic correctness? The editorial imperative is to report it straight: fully, accurately, avoiding insinuations between-the-lines. The world will not come to an end, nor will there be riots in the streets, if we call a spade a spade (even if some "spades" in that ethnic minority might consider it discriminatory, racial, or whatever).

A reader can't understand the mounting anti-Semitism of "black ideologists" in the U.S.—viz., Louis Farrakhan of the Nation of Islam – if the reporter doesn't ever report the language used, including the "Hymietown" epithets, harmful and wounding though they may be. You can't grasp the *Asylanten* issue in Germany or the Algerian tensions in France if you hold that all foreigners, legally or illegally in the land, are your brethren with whom you are bonded in the deepest fraternal feelings, with the result that you can't ever speak freely about facts, figures and fracas in an open and honest way. The candid proverbial German carpenter used to say: "*Wo gehobelt wird, fallen Späne,*" which my Cassell's German/English Dictionary translates (freely) as "You can't make an omelette without breaking eggs." The realism of the workshop accepts that chips fall where they may; and fall they will.

It is the realistic essence of a self-confident democracy to believe, as we have heard a famous editor say, that by shedding light the readers can find their own way. Amen.

16

The N-Word and the J-Word

From Blacks to Kikes

A curious thing happened to the n-word as it came up from the former slaveholding South, wending its way to Yankee ghettos and echoing darkly in Harlem and other Northern neighborhoods. It shed the softly drawled suffix, as in "nigra," which had served to "put the Negro in his place" in the old antebellum days; and it took on the harsh, peremptory snap of "nigger," the hated expletive of our day.

Nor was this all. Among the colored population itself, variously known as black or African-American, it retained strangely a legitimate demotic usage, in part affectionate, in part self-critical. Among themselves, apparently, the term nigger—nowadays, so reviled and rejected in enlightened white American circles—is all right, okay, even right on.

I can remember the deep disquiet in our liberal world when the black writer and entertainer, Dick Gregory, deigned to entitle his autobiography *Nigger* (1964). In the complex self-awareness which was resulting from a sudden and intense bout of "black consciousness"—running from Martin Luther King to Malcolm X, from Richard Wright to James Baldwin—the public face in a hostile white world called for a new and positive identity. The brothers were no longer, as in Ralph Ellison's novel, "invisible." *Black-was-beautiful, man!* Yet the private face, conspicuously un-black, troubled and uncertain about its real identity (and "roots"), could look into the mirror and, with an agreeable shock of familiar recognition, whisper—or even shout—the n-word. In other circumstances it might have provided the signal for a race riot.

Other minorities have also exhibited this paradoxical pride of self-deprecation. Words which are hateful in the out-group may take on a reassuring affectionate quality in the in-group. Jews, for example, with their well-known penchant for telling anti-Semitic jokes amongst each other (but only there!), can refer to themselves as "Yids" (or "Yeeds," depending on the regional accents). The Yeed, as at my grandfather's table and in Isaac Bashevis Singer's Yiddish tales of the East European *shtetl*, becomes the comical *schlemiel*, always the victim of a *schlemozzle*. But among the Others, the *goyim*, it is the most common appellation for the Jews in the vilest of century-old hate campaigns. Something similar is true of the Irish, or "micks"; of the Italians, or "wops"; of the Poles, or "polacks"; and of many other peoples who, as disparaged ethnic minorities, seek a measure of safety and protection by disconnecting the enemy's vocabulary. Liberal white journalists, reacting too quickly and too simply to any charge by black activists about their "racism," often miss this deviant dimension. One American columnist, Richard Cohen, reports that he found the evidence in the PC case against an old Broadway favorite, "convincing." *Show Boat*, the famous Jerome Kern musical (in which Paul Robeson made the song "Ol' Man River" an international hit), had good intentions but was, in the end, "racist": the lyrics, the music, the whole Southern drama on the Mississippi: "The show is racist. Its blacks are a servile lot, talking stagy 'black-talk' that is downright repellent to contemporary ears." As he argues, especially odious is the melodious line in the original text (it has since been cleaned up) about "Niggers all work on the Mississippi": "If whites sang that line it would be jarring enough. But blacks sing it, which is like Italians singing about wops or Jews about kikes."[1] But they do, Mr. Cohen, they do: on occasion, amongst themselves.

The complaints that *Show Boat* denigrates black Americans increased over the years and plagued its revivals as a popular musical. Paul Robeson himself, forever associated (even in his Moscow exile) with the show-stopping number *Ol' Man River*, and an outspoken campaigner for racial equality in the decades before it became a political force which could command "correctness," gradually amended what he saw as racist overtones in the song's lyrics. Historians record that by the time of the second film version in 1935 he was singing *"There's an ol' man called the Mississippi,/that's the ol' man I don't like to be,"* and changed (in accordance with his ideological militance) *"I'm tired of livin' and scared of dyin'"* to *"I must keep fightin' until I'm dyin'."*

Well, even in the first filming of *Show Boat* in the 1930s the term *"Darkies"* was considered a more acceptable substitute. Understudies usually have a brief moment. *"You get a little drunk"* was held to be a slur on one's drinking habits and so, and not because of its new militant touch (as some suspected), Robeson sang *"You show a little spunk."* This was, again, changed in the London run. The substitution was short-lived since to the English (at the time) "spunk" meant semen. Black-white relations were sexually over-charged enough as it was without any help from unintentional double-entendres. Edna Ferber who wrote the best-selling novel (a story of the white Southern family who ran the river show boat *Cotton Blossom)* reconciled herself to the up-to-date recasting

ing of the daughter Magnolia as a dark-skinned soprano; but Oscar Hammerstein of Broadway fame was stubborn against the *Zeitgeist*—"As the author of these words I have no intention of changing them or permitting any-one else to change them. I further suggest Paul write his own songs and leave mine alone." But Paul and Oscar are long since dead; and into the latest revival of *Show Boat* (1998) the director Hal Prince inserted versions of his own.[2]

The seven decades since *Show Boat* (1927) was surely not an era of racial correctness but certain critics keep a careful scorecard; and one American jour-nalist (Mark Steyn), listening to the songs which Paul Simon (of Simon & Garfunkel fame) wrote for his new musical, *The Capeman*, duly notes in a London newspaper which is, comparatively, free-and-easy about recording such discomfiting realities,

> it's worth nothing that *The Capeman* is the first musical since *Show Boat* in 1927 to use the word 'niggers' in its opening number:
>
>> Afraid to leave the project to cross into another neighborhood
>> The blancos and the nigger gangs, well, they'd kill you if they could....[3]

Transatlantic distance—and a lack of propinquity which shields against a neighborly bad conscience towards former African slaves—gives European journalists, and even British editors (although they have a large colored popu-lation living amongst them), a certain latitude. What cannot (or, perhaps, should not) be uttered on an American stage in musical lyrics or dramatic dialogue— the *Washington Post* can always be relied on to showboat its protest—is put on, with only a slight twinge of embarrassment, in London. At the moment, as I write, *The Front Page*: the old Hecht/MacArthur play about newspapers and their addiction to "scoops" is being performed in a British theater. The story is, as one English reviewer noted, "fueled by cigarettes, drink, and lack of sleep," all the things that were "dying out" (so it is claimed) when contempo-rary journalistic virtues took over. But not as far as the n-word is concerned, and its still virulent derogations: "It was vaguely shocking to walk into the Donmar Warehouse in Covent Garden last week and hear outspoken comments about 'niggers' and 'coons' received with such laughter by a liberal London audience."[4] Ethnic correctness is still not strong enough abroad to induce self-censorship. But some words in the racialist vocabulary do die out or go out of fashion, and our vaguely embarrassed English newspaperman expresses outspoken satisfaction that he and his editor would no longer be capable of recalling the reporter from a kidnap story (he had difficulty getting in to interview the family): "'Don't worry', he was told by the news desk. 'It's not a story. We've just heard the baby's colored.'" Does the movement, in fact, from *colored* to *Negro* to *black* to *African-American* to *nigga* (and in the plural *niggaz)* represent progress? Is it a measure of increasing "multicultural" respect?

Authentic enlightenment is still to be tested when "colored" makes, one day soon, its predictable semantic comeback. The c-word may do more justice to so many different shades of non-white complexion. For one thing, the writers of advertising copy in our newspapers and magazines have already moved a step in that direction. The U.S. cosmetics industry is now paying major attention to a non-white market (from cologne to bath foam) and addresses its potential customers as *"people of color."* Since we are all of some pigment or other, this could make the whole properly toilet-trained population a kind of universal brotherhood (and sisterhood).

Happy is the people who can live with the insults that, inevitably, come their way.

Consider *wop.* One of Luigi Barzini's most famous articles in the *Corriere della Sera* (Milan) was entitled *"Wop come me"* (A Wop Like Me). Italian readers liked it, and made it one of their favorites; it was often reprinted. More than that, "Wop" was derived from the Spanish *guapo,* the term derisively applied by Spanish ruling-class snobs to proud local Neapolitans in occupied and exploited Napoli, but who sometimes tried to dress up in their Sunday best. Consequently, they were marked out as dandies; and surely, in the beginning, it was only a term of mild contempt before it became in time "racially" abusive. A not dissimilar complication can be discerned in other colorful representations of the dandy. His double profile is by turns pejorative (in its dismissiveness of foppery) and positive, even patriotic (as in "Yankee-doodle-dandy" which is taken to be fine and...dandy).[5]

As for the Jews, Leo Rosten has pointed out in his celebrated work *The Joys of Yiddish* (1968) that "kike" was derived from the Hebrew word for what Plato considered the most beautiful ideal form, the circle. This was the sign with which the Jews authenticated their immigration papers on Ellis Island a century ago. It amounted to their "greenhorn's" signature when instructed to *"Make your mark here";* for their literacy was confined to writing in an unacceptable, indecipherable right-to-left Hebrew script. They disdained to make the sign of the cross. They were subsequently called "kikes" after *keichel,* the proud circular mark of their new-world identity, before it became a badge of abuse. In the beginning the Ellis Island immigration officer had called out, rather innocently,

"Here comes another *'Keik'l'!'"*

---

*   *"Kike"* in the *Webster's New World Collegiate Dicitonary* (3rd ed., 1997) is categorized simply as "a vulgar term of hostility and contempt" (p. 742), which phrase is the current standard term for racial expletives. See also *Dago* (p. 347) and *Wop* (p. 1538).

On the subject of *"nigger,"* it explains that it was "originally a dialectal variant of *Negro,"* and that "the term *nigger* is today acceptable only in black English." This is wayward. Can a non-Negro speak "acceptable" black English.

These are all, in William Safire's useful phrase, *Rashomon* words, "gleaming with different facets of meaning..."[6]

The Breaking of Taboos

Like some Wild West bounty hunters, the cultural desperadoes track down taboos wherever they can find them, and they are relentless in their disrespectful pursuit. One London TV producer dismissed all local protests against his showing in one of his prime-time dramas an explicit scene detailing an incestuous affair; his defense was simply that "Taboos are there to be broken," and he vowed "As soon as we find another one, rely on us to try and break that one too." The bounty in the taboo-breaker's ambition amounts to one part scandal and notoriety; one part commercial success and reward; and one part an elated sense of liberation when all taboos have been dispatched and we are all left utterly free and uninhibited.[7]

For the moment, however, there are still a number of taboos around to inhibit us, and thus our press is not quite free—certainly not as carefree as the practitioners of "dirty realism" are in the worlds of the novel, the periodical press, the television, and the cinema—to broach all themes in explicit language and unashamed imagery. In point of fact, in certain sectors of our newspaper culture we have already encountered a persistent sense of old-fashioned propriety which wants to hold fast to a certain civilized discretion: looking askance at words which should not be printed, pictures which should not be published. Some of this can be put down to an old lingering puritanism; but some also to the new onset of "political correctness" which harbors the hope that self-censorship can be a way of healing society and improving humankind.

I have already referred to some of my friends who attained high places in Anglo-American journalism and made valiant efforts against semantic forms of racism by banning ethnic expletives (e.g., "nigger, kike, dago, chink," etc., etc.). By and large the taboos were (as we have seen) of short duration. The n-word, interdicted in liberal circles for a decade or two (with retroactive penal-

---

In addition, given the fact that "black English" as a linguistic-ethnic fad has been fading fast, this should be taken to mean that (as I have suggested) the word has been defused for in-group usage. In view of the still-existing controversy over dictionary definitions, I quote the rest of this particular entry:

"...in all other contexts it is now generally regarded as virtually taboo because of the legacy of racial hatred that underlies the history of its use among whites, and its continuing use among a minority of speakers as a viciously hostile epithet."

Here *"virtually"* is a soft word which could enrage hard-liners who demand a total taboo in all contexts deemed to be enemy territory.

ties against such older writers as Mark Twain, John Buchan, Margaret Mitchell, et al.), is now freely printed by editors in documentary usage—but who can say that this comeback will not have to be having a knock-down effect and re-enter the derogatory vocabulary of a new generation of hooligans and skin-heads? I had, as I have made abundantly plain, little or no sympathy for even the most well-meaning enterprise of blacklisting words (and ideas) in a mood of political rectitude. Still, I remain clear in my own mind about the dangers of popularizing slurs and sneers, and I inevitably shudder a little when I read front-page stories like the one in my London newspaper this morning—

MP URGES PRINCE OF WALES TO INTERVENE
IN ARMY RACISM ROW

Prince Charles is honorary colonel in chief of the Cheshire Regiment, and it was at a military reception that incidents occurred involving women guests, including "chants to them publicly of 'nigger, nigger, nigger.'"[8] This suggests that on the black, or Negro, front the double taboo—that of the original term of abuse, and then its subsequent newspaper outing—has crumbled for the time being. What of the others?

It would take something like a taboo-meter contraption to measure the ten-sile strength and weakness of the various verbal inhibitions. What will crumble next? Which foulness slouches in the dark corner? One is prepared to be un-pleasantly surprised. But I was mildly amused by a non-incident in an English vaudeville show the other day where a trio of comics, making merry with their own ethnicity and sexual orientation, actually refrained from an obvious gag which would have added to the rhyme and ribaldry. As the *Standard*'s theater critic reported, the evening was "packed with social comment" as the enter-tainers moved to their rousing closing number entitled "Niggers, Dykes and Jews (they are all three)."[9] It could be that "Jew" is sufficiently loaded to suffice for their rude purposes; but I would have thought that in the current debaucheries of our comic spirits the taboo-breaking threesome would have wanted to be known as, say, "Niggers, Dykes and Kikes." Or, again, it could be that a playful and ill-advised touch of anti-Semitism would actually be more upsetting to their sub-urban theatergoers than a simple slur about local lesbians and far-away darkie folks. Two down, one still to go. At any rate, the good news from the Ware-house Theater, Croydon, is that polite civilization as we have known it has not yet completely collapsed.

Given the apparent universality of human antipathies, and their expression in ethnic, racial or other forms of group conflict, there would seem to be no end to the epithets of contempt. Benevolent spirits nowadays label them "in-correct," and in some circles even their accidental or harmless usage is de-plored and interdicted. As a result there is a certain sensitivity and reserve in our Western newspaper culture when words, through their complex etymology, cause offense and call for conscience-stricken apologies. I hesitate, therefore, to go on to explore the whole vocabulary of viciousness lest I be similarly misunderstood. I recall how William Safire was unfortunate enough to be caught out in his use of the word "patsy." He was explaining, in one of his "Language" columns, the meaning of *a pushover* as in "the patsy prosecutor." He reported that he got letters of protest from Irish-Americans who objected that the word is rooted in the traditional Irish name Patrick, and, like "paddy wagon"—presumably a New York or Boston police van, rounding up in its day delinquent Irishmen— is "an ethnic slur." *Caveat scriptor!* [10]

In the speech of the gangster underworld, limited and endlessly repetitive as it is, neither the ethnic slurs nor indeed the profanity retain the force and vitality which they still manage to retain in the straight over-world. Of late even the Mafia has been affected by the liberal spirit of "political correctness," and it is touching to note how one Brooklyn gangster tries to disassociate himself from the racists that he happened to meet as a draftee in the U.S. Army:

> when I had my first real experience with rebels and rednecks and racism and all that bullshit. Now I use words all the time like *nigger, spick, Polack, Jewboy, Mick,* even *greaseball* which is people from Italy [writes the Italo-American Sammy "the Bull" Gravano]. That's just the way you talk on the street. I don't think I am a racist. But these rednecks, they are real hard core. [11]

Semanticists, thus, must get around to explaining the persistent inventiveness of ethnic prejudice as old slurs lose force and new ones are coined or revived. "*Buckwheat*" was a new one on me; I had never heard or seen it in a racial context until the other day. I knew it as an expression for "*greenhorn*" and as an alternative to "*hey, rube!*" (and other disrespectful terms of address for a rustic or novice, mostly with a jocular tone), although some may remember that in the old short film comedies starring the Little Rascals there was one black female child character among the slum kids who was called Buckwheat.

From Chicago the *New York Times* (in March 1997) reported the incident of a black boy who had been beaten into a coma by a gang of whites ("Chicago's Soul at Stake in Hate Crime"). The teenagers were "bragging about keeping blacks out of the neighborhood." This brought about a renewal of "tense times of racial hostility" since it followed on the heels of another ugly incident, during a local Bridgeport basketball game, "dozens of students from a predominantly white, Roman Catholic boys school taunted players from a largely black school with chants of 'Buckwheat.'" [12] "Buckwheat," of course, is a small black grain used for chicken food (and, says one English dictionary, "in America for making cakes"). But Dr. Lighter in his *Historical Dictionary of American Slang* (1994) gives no specifically black-and-white reference. Still, his quotation from an Hispanic scene in *Miami Vice* (NBC-TV, 1987) with Afro-American cops and Cuban refugees—"Hey, buckwheat, lemme in, man!"—puts it into a colored context in which the disrespectful/jocular reference to rustic rubes is re-popularized. An old put-down is getting a new lease on life. After the *Times* usage, syndicated newspaper efforts will do the rest for infectious re-circulation. Can it be that certain semantic vacuums need always to be filled? Obsolescence invites replacement.

The novelist Anthony Burgess—who in his fiction had invented vast amounts of slang and even in one of his novels a whole exotic language —once told me that he had abandoned attempts to devise a new vocabulary of expletives. His futuristic heroes and apocalyptic villains, if they could not resort to old Adam's time-tested dirty realism, couldn't be made to say anything which would outrage or titillate. The dialogue needed too much extra explanation to function properly as profane or obscene. Explicating four-letter clockwork-orange words is as supererogatory as explaining a joke. The shock of the obscene is in the instant recognition, in the time-dishonored taboo.[13]

As so often in these pages, C.S. Lewis offers us wise guidance: for he had considered the spectacle of writers "writhing in the mixed smart and titillation of a fully indulged resentment." He thought it, in its way, "too big a thing to leave us free for any literary considerations" and felt himself "in the presence of tragi-comedy from real life." Comedy? Lewis was at times a light-hearted spirit, and something of an optimist who had seen words do and die, resurrect and reform. Hence he can come to console: "Thus, in criticism as in vocabulary, hatred over-reaches itself. Willingness to wound, too intense and naked, becomes impotent to do the desired mischief."[14]

The prospect of a General Colin Powell candidacy for the White House has in the 1990s come and gone; and with it the vision of "a first Black President in the White House." But its lively discussion in the African-American community, often in the idiom known as "black English" or Ebonics, has been opening up new dimensions for rough phrases, wisps of slang, and indeed miscegeneous profanities which have not hitherto been published in the public prints.

Thus, in the recent ups-and-downs in the career of the black singer, Ms. Whitney Houston, there was an outburst against the (white) media in which Ms. Houston was reported to have said: "they tried to f— with me; white America tried to f— with me."[15] An indignant *Time* reader, upset by the "foulmouthed" quotes, hit back with more of the same, "If white America really wanted to f— with her, she'd feel it in her pocketbook." Loot, not language, is the final litmus-paper test. Americans look to the bottom line and expect the cash value; profanity has become a form of historical materialism. Sex violates; and the violators scramble among themselves for the available money. By these standards Ms. Houston is doing very well, and should have no cause for complaint.

A final surmise.

Would it be far-fetched to suggest that in the world of so-called "gangsta rap"—dominated by certain musically talented underworld types, not a few of whom had serious convictions for mayhem (and even manslaughter)—there is not a dissimilar n-word process at work, taking some of the curse off gangster and its rowdy reputation? Once again the innocent and uplifting final *a* softens the word, gives it a certain leniency, puts it free on parole. The roughnecks of gangsta rap give themselves a hooded name of their own choosing (and spelling), and thus preclude the offensive charges of hostile critics that they were indeed delinquent creatures from a plug-ugly underworld.

Mark Fuhrman's "N-Word"

I return to the usage in so-called "stagy black-talk" of that old Mississippi stand-by, *"nigger,"* which is also overlaid with complex twists and turns.

Newspapers in their daily simple-mindedness tend to ignore the historic, or dialectical, layers of meaning, as we have seen in the n-word crisis of the O.J. Simpson trial. There, in the famous Detective Mark Fuhrman episode, panic and disarray set in when editors had suddenly to decide whether a crucial bit of evidence (or, at least, testimony)—in this case, decisive *for* the cause of the accused black defendant—was indeed fit to print! Shouldn't they have been more confident and appear to be *knowing*: to be hip, with-it, cool? Shouldn't one have been tempted to see it, basically, as a black-and-white issue of "Publish and be damned!"? But we are plagued by uncertainties. Can we trust that the words which we use mean what they say, and not wander off in suggestiveness?

Consider this passage from one of the most popular novels of the day, written by Elmore Leonard, that poet of gangsta rap-talk in the multiracial netherworld of hoodlums and hit-men. In his recent "crime story," *Riding the Rap* (1995), a Negro and a Hispanic have this exchange:

"How come you call each other nigga?"
Louis said... "You say it like you calling you calling him 'my brother'...."
So what happened, Bobby Deo tried him that time in the yard. Looked Louis in the face with a kind of smile and said, "Yeah, nigga, like that." To see how Louis would take it, the man standing there waiting.
Louis said to him, "Yeah, like that. Only it ain't fine to say if it ain't a brother. Understand? Unless you being P.R. [Puerto Rican] has nigga in you"....

And when, in the climax of an escape scene, Louis has to betray a brother by leaving him behind, he says to him in quite a kindly tone, "You ain't going, nigga...."[16]

If *nigga* can be a soft, caring sign of brotherhood, and even *nigger* can be a term of endearment, it is only natural for newspaper editors and the rest of the white world to tread lightly as if walking on eggs. Mark Fuhrman's use of the n-word, played back on Judge Ito's courtroom tape-recorder, was the single most emotive element in the Simpson defense-team's strategy. With it Johnny Cochran, Simpson's main defense counsel, could triumphantly play his "race card." It trumped the main police witness who had found a key piece of evidence (the bloodstained right-hand glove). It terminated the L.A. detective's career: leading to his conviction for "perjury." It made him a pariah, even among the police and the trial prosecutors, one of whom (the D.A., Marcia Clark) went so far as to say in her summation:

> Is he a racist? Yes. Is he the worst LAPD has to offer? Yes. Do we wish the LAPD had never hired him? Yes. In fact, do we wish there was no such person on the planet? Yes....

There was even worse to come. In his personal collection of political cartoons, clipped from the newspapers, there was one about Berlin with a swastika; this plus some other hearsay led to his being called a neo-Nazi and compared to Hitler. In point of fact the man who became an un-person made a belated defense of himself—crucified by Simpson's team of lawyers, vilified by the media, dropped by the L.A. Police Department, and abandoned by the prosecution, he desperately turned to writing a book, a tract in his own defense. He argued, with little or no echo in the press, that the forty-one usages of the n-word on those damnable and regrettable tapes were not used in his direct speech, in his own name, but were "torn out of context." The exculpating context was the outline of movie-story scenarios which he and a co-authoress, Laura Hart McKinney, were intending to sell expensively to Hollywood for epic cops-and-robbers films. Mrs. Laura Hart McKinney, who had an affair with her co-author or "technical advisor" and became a professor of screenwriting at a North Carolina institute of film-making, phrased it more cautiously. Like all storytellers, the man was expressing views "not necessarily his own." But *Time* and the *Los Angeles Times* which had early access to the transcripts of the seven audiocassette tapes and four microcassettes (actually there were twelve in all) reported that so far from being "fictional episodes invented for a screenplay" the "dirty realism" of the tales narrated was "based on verifiable incidents," some in the career of the officer himself.[17]

The whole text—properly transcribed (shorthand secretaries are notoriously erratic) and "in full context"—would confirm or deny the portrait which, for a few, amounted to a caricature, quickly sketched by thousands of newspapers throughout the country. I was curious, and pored over the pages which I could summon up on the Internet and its various web sites and home pages. The presiding judge, Lance Ito, had struck a weak courtroom compromise between the two juridical contentions. The policeman's speech patterns were "irrelevant" for the prosecution—"irrelevant" by and for themselves (for if prejudice prompted the perpetration of evidence-tampering then it was *this*, not simply his bias, that had to be proved); for the defense the tapes were "relevant" (for they revealed a compulsive, and doubtless a compelling viciousness, which could—*must?...did?*—lead to a frame-up). The judge allowed a brief quotation of two passages, and no more. It was enough for the largely black jury, since the papers had already printed—if radio and television refrained from pronouncing—all the choice bits of racist slang. What was played in the tapes in the L.A. courtroom was minimal, but it authenticated the general impression that here was a man whose speech was helplessly contaminated by a lowlife vocabulary.

Reading the full verbatim text of the twelve tapes (1985-1994) one can also sense an effort to put a measure of a would-be writer's distance between the nasty chatter he is spouting and the fictional end-purpose:

> *Hart:* I just transcribe you.
> *Fuhrman:* Verbatim?
> *Hart:* I have to.
> *Fuhrman:* All the "cocksuckers"? Everything?...That's important. That's policeman's talk.
> *Hart:* That's life talk. It's not just "policeman's talk."
> *Fuhrman:* But, we have mastered it. No, the Marine Corps mastered it.

Having been both a Marine and a policeman, he was only talking what comes naturally to masters of undeleted expletives. I came away from reading the transcribed tapes with the impression that only rarely—one or two times on Tape 12—was Detective Fuhrman assuming the persona of a pulp-fiction character when he spat out the *n-word* or any of the other "slam terms" (e.g., "Bubba") that mark common idiomatic speech. Once Fuhrman had a flap with a friend of Professor Hart McKinney who was sitting in on the talks, and he became angry: "You don't even know what it is like [patrolling the violent neighborhoods of L.A.'s black ghettoes]. You're talking shit. You sound like a nigger talking shit..." This is surely not Clint Eastwood or Robert De Niro or a Tarantino movie character shooting his mouth off, but the man himself.[18]

Fuhrman's defense of himself in his book also has its problems—the fulsome apologies and expressions of regret (at the same time claiming that the bigotry was not his but "made up" for the film scenario); the lack of straightforward openness on a number of personal "racist" incidents ("irrelevant and immaterial" as they might have been to the strict case against Simpson for two murders). Still, the Fuhrman book is, in my view, an important contribution. It contains, stewing in the juices of his resentment, the most bitter and trenchant critique—almost worthy of a Sherlock Holmes—of the police's careless work in gathering the bloodstained evidence. This evidence may well be technically "contaminated" (and so, possibly, arguably inadmissible), but in its sickening massiveness, it still convinced most of the nation that the Los Angeles murders were done as charged.

Fuhrman's partisan side of the story also serves in its way as a critique of almost all of the journalism on "the greatest American trial of the century"—casting yet another shadow on the whole journalistic enterprise and its capacity to stick to the facts, report objectively and, above all, fairly. This is especially difficult when the big story, even when it is sensational, must provide a new and different sub-sensation each day.[19]

What, then, of Fuhrman's "racism"? He had served mainly in Los Angeles' black ghettoes, and was considered a no-nonsense street-wise cop. His supporters claimed that among the several hundred arrests that he had made of black felons in his career not one, in jail or out, came forward to accuse him—nor to help support the Simpson defense claim that O.J. Simpson's innocence could only have been impugned by a biased detective whose vile prejudices led him to "plant evidence" and contrive "frame-ups."

I am not concerned here with the merits and demerits of the opposing arguments. But it is noteworthy that one prominent U.S. lawyer and writer, although distancing himself from a complete endorsement of Fuhrman's spirited apologia, braved an overwhelmingly hostile public opinion against an audibly "bad cop." He supported several significant points which neither the long courtroom proceedings nor the vast coverage of the gripping case by the media had made sufficiently clear:

> But if Fuhrman was such a racist that he was willing to frame black people, how come out of the hundreds upon hundreds of black people he arrested throughout the years, how come there wasn't a parade of black people taking the witness stand at the criminal trial to testify that Mark Fuhrman had framed them?...You would do this not just to get even with Fuhrman, which would be your primary motivation, but in doing so you would also be a hero to many in the black community, and could even sell your story. Yet not one single black person took the witness stand.[20]

But back to the n-word—in saying it the cop destroyed his own career and saved the neck of O.J. Simpson. It could be that Mark Fuhrman may only have been reciting the expletives he had put into the foul mouth of his would-be Hollywood screenplay, another "Dirty Harry" in pulp fiction. But the words were in his own voice, and millions had shuddered when he spoke them again and again. Vincent Bugliosi refers to "his unfortunate error or lie on the witness stand (I speak in the disjunctive because it is not clear, at least to me, which it was) that he had not used the 'N' word in the previous ten years...." The possible perjury was small matter; it was the dirty-real injury that caught the conscience of the predominantly black jury. That most eloquent of practicing black lawyers, Johnny Cochran, pulled out all the stops. In his final summation he referred to the white villain in the case who tried to bring down a black hero as "a genocidal racist, a perjuror, America's worst nightmare, the personification of evil." In the beginning there was the word, and the word led to the deed, and both were evil. The wordy detective—who had foolishly perjured himself in saying under oath that he had not used the racist n-word "in the last 10 years"—was found guilty by a judge. The violent suspect—against whom the incriminating evidence for two murders had once appeared to be so overwhelming—was pronounced innocent by a jury. This twist in the plot was unpredictable. As the shocked and humiliated detective put it, "The trial of O.J. Simpson became the trial of Mark Fuhrman."[21] Not since the Dred Scott case of 1857—or perhaps, in more recent memory, *Roe vs. Wade* and the confrontation in Little Rock—had the n-word made such dramatic legal history.

The Color Spectrum of "Race Card"

The reporting of Johnnie Cochran's triumphant eloquence, only heightened by his occasional courtroom histrionics, provides a rich source for the vagaries of the *n-word* in our contemporary discourse. His rhetorical powers in defense of his accused "black brother," once a national football idol, guaranteed headlines. His quasi-Biblical imprecations, in cross-examination, effectively destroyed the reputations of two L.A. detectives (Vanatter and Fuhrman) who had been called as trial witnesses for the prosecution. His tactics discredited as well the evidence they collected at the scene of the crime on the day after the mutilated corpses were found. *Distrust the messenger!* Cochran had thundered (and he made both out to be incompetent liars, and possibly worse). Therefore: *Distrust the message!*...The messengers, namely two white cops, were labelled "twins of deception," and what evil they represented was already foreseen in the Books of *Luke* and *Ezekiel*. (Two copies of the Bible were always at hand in Cochran's defense office.) As one not unfriendly reporter observed,

> Johnnie's style echoes Malcolm X and Louis Farrakhan. The term "twins of deception" was intended to invoke the devil. In the jargon of the Nation of Islam, "devil" meant white. Vanatter and Fuhrman were twin devils of deception, white devils.[22]

Thus was the "race card" played, an ace of spades, the most powerful trump. He had a deck full of them, and their manipulation alienated, among others, another senior counsel (Robert Shapiro) who was a member of Cochran's "dream team"* of legal experts. Shapiro said they were "playing the race card from the bottom of the deck."[23] As if it would not have been equally disrespectful had it been played from any other place in the deck.

A certain ambivalence in the black use of the n-word has already been detected. The ethnic sense of personal identity in a people who have good reason to resent a hostile society is connected to very volatile emotions. It has multiple layers of meaning and insinuation. In the end, who is or is not a racist for thinking-and-talking racism only he could determine. When the Japanese-American judge, Lance Ito, criticized Cochran's behavior in (and out of) the courtroom as bordering on formal "contempt of court," Cochran was told reprovingly by his associate F. Lee Bailey, "Johnnie, you let Ito give you a whipping. Don't let that happen again." Whereupon Cochran smiled and said, "I've been beaten up by a white man today." We are told this in the "uncensored" story of the Simpson defense, and the author (Lawrence Schiller) adds in an even milder reproof that Cochran's "white man" was "referring, not quite accurately, to Judge Ito." There is a whole metaphysics of racism in that little adverb "quite." Under other circumstances he might have said, if anything, that the Judge was obviously...er, well, yellow. A color in a race conflict is a many-complexioned thing.

As I have been suggesting, in the confusions of newspaper reportage, the color of things (and of people) in a racialist context can be a kaleidoscope of varying hues. The naming of the various shades of the primary colors can be subjected to comic overtones or to tragic undertones, and indeed to any mood in between. One instance. In the light of the fact that the body of the female victim in the trial had been one of a famed Hollywood blonde, Nicole Brown Simpson, it was conspicuously gruesome for a writer to record one remark of Johnnie Cochran's. The tense relationship between lawyer and client (between the defender Cochran and the accused ex-husband) had become momentarily worse. O.J. Simpson evidently had turned angry, and "Johnnie's professional mask had slipped": "'He scared me'...Cochran says, 'It's a good thing I didn't have blond hair.'" Tastelessness has rarely been judged to be in contempt of court; but then the insensitivity suddenly gives way to...ultra-sensitivity. One of the Cochran team's star defenders would be responsible for cross-examining Detective Fuhrman about his rumored racism, but Cochran had a problem with F. Lee Bailey's vocabulary:

[He] was amazed to hear Bailey say "nigger" so often....We don't want a white guy throwing this word around on television, Johnnie had said. They'd assumed Bailey would use it sparingly, if at all.[24]

---

*   Detective Mark Fuhrman, or his unnamed ghost-writer, remarked wittily that O.J. Simpson's defense attorneys were quickly dubbed the "Dream Team" by a media that "never met a cliché they didn't like...." (*Murder in Brentwood*, p. 87.)

"So often" here means too often.

Then, again, racism would come into the jocular mode, not grisly but very much playful. In one lighter moment, towards the end of the trial, the lawyers of the "dream team" allowed themselves to think happily of celebrating a famous victory. The talk turned to cheering celebrations, social life...and women. Cochran offered the advice that "when O.J. gets out, the best insurance for him is to get a black date." This time blondes would be ruled out, and not only blondes. The new, suitable companion would be, preferably, "somebody with a big Afro." Another lawyer (Shapiro) also cautioned against "cream color" or "bronze." A female passer-by came into view, and one lawyer cracked, "*There's a girl for O.J.!*" But Johnnie Cochran had said, "'Not dark enough. I want a black woman with black, black hair. Got to be *real* black.' Johnnie can't stop laughing."[25]

If race cards were to be dealt around, Johnnie Cochran would slip himself a few wild cards, jokers. They could be any color at all, and were quite good for a laugh. In the end, the ace of spades would be the winning trump.

But if justice is to be done to the tale it must be recorded that, in the end, Fuhrman the racist proved to be abjectly apologetic, full of contrition; and Cochran the fiery black rhetorician turned out to be ambivalent, to be speaking with a forked tongue. Detective Fuhrman rushes to remorse:

> I don't want to sound as if I'm trying to justify what I said on those tapes. I am ashamed of my words. Taken out of context, they are worse than horrible. And even in context they are ugly. There is no excuse, not even literary license, that can justify or condone the pain I caused people of all colors. I had no idea that the tapes would ever be made public, but I should have thought about how my friends, black and white, would feel if they heard them.[26]

The harsh n-word and its admission as formal evidence in the courtroom created an atmosphere in which an ethnic judge and a colored jury decided what was justice in the case of a black accused of the crime of murdering two whites. But the "n-word of shame" has (as we have seen) its racial complexities.

Such loaded words, words which can be fired and can wound, are often unsteady, unstable, deviant. Fortunately they often (as C.S. Lewis pointed out, hopefully, piously) cannot be relied upon to do the desired mischief. They dissent and defect, and with an embarrassed sense of guilt are put to new purposes. Johnnie Cochran—like Dick Gregory, like James Baldwin—also treasured the *n-word* as a special word among brothers. In his own law firm (according to one attorney) there were few whites, "the white world stayed outside," and there was a special camaraderie—"inside the firm you were family." One of his admirers (Lawrence Schiller) has sketched the office atmosphere: "Words that shocked and offended white society were coin of the realm. 'Nigger' and 'motherfucker' were terms of affection."[27]

It is all too human, as Lewis Carroll famously remarked, to use a word and have it mean just what one chooses it to mean. And if the question is (as Alice asked) whether you can or should make words mean so many different things, the answer is (as Humpty Dumpty replied) "Which is to be master—that's all." More than a century after Lincoln's Emancipation Proclamation the infamous n-word is no longer enslaved to one meaning.

Ebonic Demotic

In American journalism, self-centered as it is, originality or the gold-medaled aspiration for same, is doing what comes naturally.

In British journalism there is, as we have seen, a self-styled neophiliac imperative wherein there is (ever since the Beatles) a self-conscious pride in the breakthrough, a national need to create a note, a tone, a phrase, a vogue before anyone else—especially an American—happens upon it. This kind of success cannot be planned or programed. Whenever the Brits "lose out" in the transatlantic competition they are content slavishly to follow the latest innovative Yankee precedent on the theory that they are at least showing themselves to be quick, up-to-the-minute, fashionable—in a word, "*in*." On the matter of "black jive talk" they take their cues, with strict political correctness, from Harlem, or for that matter anywhere in Manhattan. Thus, when a leading London gossip columnist—Atticus, aka "Taki," in the *Sunday Times*—waxes sentimental over the best modern jazz concerts he's ever attended ("Bop until You Drop," in Gstaad, led the field), he tells a personal anecdote about one of the star performers, the "rock'n'roll icon," Chuck Berry. The conversation between Taki and Chuck was presumably historic enough to warrant recalling and registering in print, thus:

> I found myself next to Chuck. "Haya doin', man?" said the great man. "Veddy, veddy well indeed, old bean", answered Atticus, in my most affected pre-war Etonian accent.
> "Old bean? Old bean? What's this mutherf****r callin' Chuck Berry?"[28]

The reader is then cautioned about a possible misunderstanding because "Chuck Berry always refers to himself in the third person." For the reader in New York this kind of explanation is not quite necessary, since the whole of what can be called the "ebonic demotic" has worked its way up, or across, from the smoky rooms of jive sessions to the back-rooms of American "rainbow" politics and the salons of intellectual discourse.

Consider the remarkable series of articles—perhaps the very best journalistic reportage on black affairs by a black writer in living memory— which Henry Louis Gates, Jr., published in the *New Yorker*. The place of its publication (once the classical home of burnished prose) and the fact that its author was an academic who taught modern literature at Harvard gave it (as he himself would say, putting on the dog) a *frisson* of special postmodernist importance. It marks the journalistic turning-point at which the n-word joins forces with the f-, m-f-, and s-words as the proper and authentic diction for the robust discussion of delicate issues of race relations. A significant irony can be detected in the curious situation that this transpired not in the years of the emergence on the national scene of Martin Luther King and Jesse Jackson, both of whom were ordained Christian preachers and attached to their traditional sources of eloquence—but in the subsequent period when a U.S. Army man, something of a war hero and a four-star general who had come up from the ranks and knew how they "tell it like it is" in the barracks. Colin Powell is a well-spoken officer and a gentleman, but his recent projection into the national political limelight—and he might yet have become a candidate and thus, possibly, the "first black American president"—introduced, as I have suggested, an "ebonic" element into the political vernacular which may have more impact than meets the ear.

In the long article on "Powell and the Black Elite," Henry Louis Gates, Jr., proceeded from the position that the general might well have been the most popular man in America...but what did the nation's black leadership think of his rise, and where did Powell see himself in the politics of race? Here are a few excerpts to document what I suspect to be the historic confluence of two vernacular currents. The *New Yorker*'s current need for singularity in the world of newspaper culture has led to the "outing" of a strain of political profanity which now colors the American scene a shade or two differently:

> [I]f you are Colin Powell, let's agree, you have heard a small voice inside your head repeating, like a mantra, one simple thought: You could be the first black man to be President. What does that do to you? Vernon Jordan— political impresario, Clinton counselor, Powell friend—says bluntly, "It's got to fuck you up."

There's no reason to avoid such bluntness nowadays, unless you think that some other words in the language—such as: *confusing,* or *disorienting,* or *emotionally upsetting,* or *spiritually stupifying*—might express parts of a meaning that the *f-word* doesn't reach. Similarly on the question of whether the man is—as a colored man (the blood-line is, as is common with West Indians, complicated with African, Scottish, Jewish and Arawak-Indian strains), and as a soldier who has spent his life in uniform—whether he is what is called a "regular brother." Does he sing *doo-wop* and Motown tunes?

> When I ask him to do the Camel Walk the General gets up from his chair and does his best to perform James Brown's now classic dance. Jordan says, "The notion that he is not a regular brother is bullshit."

We will be seeing in another place how the b**l-s**t-word emerged in the argumentative culture as the last term in logical proof and refutation, more powerful for some than even the rules of inference and Q.E.D. Still, the impression is that the "light-skinned" hero of a race is an "un-Negro," insulated from his own people by his uniform, with its braid and medals. And it is also seen in his carriage and manner. As for his voice, for those critics who pay attention to the sounds of color, "he has a kind of diction that isn't black American. He's not verbally black." This is all the more reason for the man to come up with the ritualistic lingo of the city streets which would confer the blessing of the racial ghettoes. All of his friends and relatives, bless their souls, rally to help out. As Gates records Powell's business partner (and a cousin of his),

> He talks about America, the great land of opportunity, and how a poor West Indian kid with Jamaican parents and living in the South Bronx can work his way to be Chairman of the Joint Chiefs of Staff.
> "An All American story," I put in.
> "They all love this shit," he says with a characteristic mixture of candor and acumen...."White people love to believe they're fair. One of the things that upsets the living shit out of them is when you confront them with the fact that they are really a bunch of racist, no-good motherfuckers."

The general (bless his soul too) tried on occasion to help his own rehabilitation as a regular brother in the black community by touching on an "ebonic" note. He is talking of what has become known in military theory as "the Powell Doctrine" which cautions against military involvement where political objectives remain murky:

> Powell worries that there are certain essentials that get lost in the ozone of theory. "I believe in the bully's way of going to war," he says. "I'm on the street corner, I got my gun, I got my blade, *I'ma kick yo' ass*....

He confesses that there was a paragraph like this in an early draft of his published book of memoirs. "But it sounded a little too, shall we say, 'ethnic', and a little too Bronx, so I took it out." The b**l-s**t-word is, to be sure, rather different; and he leaves it in. It is multi-ethnic and many-boroughed and the General uses it in his dismissal of critics of the Powell Doctrine, for example, William Safire, with the nicely alliterative putdown, "Bullshit, Bill."[29]

Bill Safire may have been able to make a more effective reply to General Powell, but for the fact that his paper, the *New York Times*, wouldn't allow him to quote the offending word. The B-s-word was out; the profane argument fizzled.

With increasing successes in American cultural life, black celebrities are especially hard put to pay warm and intimate tribute to each other and still maintain, in the white world of mainstream publicity, their special relationship as brothers. More and more in literature and the cinema the artists have risen to the top, not from the urban ghettoes, close to poverty and profanity, but from cultivated middle-class suburbia. Accordingly they have to make a particular effort to sound what passes for authentic not only to their own less fortunate ethnic colleagues, but also to white editors and reporters. Whatever the official status of "black English" or "Ebonics" the demotic usages which happen to be current among the brothers come in very handy, and become compulsory in mainstream white publications that aspire to be politically correct.

Here Harvard's Professor Gates, reporting regularly on these matters for the *New Yorker* magazine, is again a good guide. "Nigger," apart from rare bursts of Gregorian humor, remains vicious: demeaning in effect (on the part of the aggressive whites), bitter in tone (on the part of self-deprecating blacks). "Nigga" is how to vary it with respect; and the proper plural is "niggaz"*—just as gangster became "gangsta" (as in gangsta rap), with the plural being gangstaz. (It looks as if regular rules for conjugation in black slang are being worked out.)

Gates' profile in the *New Yorker* of two young and very successful movie directors, the twenty-one-year-old twins, Allen and Albert Hughes, is headlined "Niggaz with Latitude." In it they explain the rivalries in the black movie community and the emulation of the luminaries that have already made it (viz., Spike Lee, John Singleton): "There's a nigga in New York named Spike. There's a nigga in L.A. named John. Where's the next nigga going to come from?" Well, apparently he is going to come from nice neighborhoods where well-behaved children (like our protagonists, the Hughes twins) grow up "playing camcorders, not semiautomatics." Claremont, "a real white area, smack dab next to Pomona," is a problematical place to come from. It would have been easier, as the Hughes twins concede, if they had been "*niggaz*...raw, hardcore, smelling of asphalt." And then they made it—with a prize-winning film entitled "*Menace II Society*"—if to somewhat grudging praise from black brothers like Spike and John: "And then we pop up and it's like 'Oh, shit, I got to kick those motherfuckers down.'" Professor Gates transcribes it like it was spoke. He doesn't persist with the question—against their explosive objections—of what happened to the Claremont language and the Pomona diction on the way to Hollywood fame. They may have worn white collars and ties to graduation day—but they soon shaved their heads "in that Michael Jordan

---

*   The notion that there is an *okay* (i.e. politically correct) plural to the still taboo singular is an exportable attraction. I note in an English review of a U.S. TV film called *"Fear of a Black Hat"* (all about "a controversial rap band") that it is rated *"NWH."* This stands for "Niggaz With Hats": no clue to its quality but vaguely suggestive of its style. (*Sunday Times*, TV Supplement, 9 October 1997, p. 21.)

back-to-your-roots style." They could look like a Sidney Poitier in a dinner jacket when accepting their awards—but when they opened their mouths they needed to sound like Bigger Thomas, Richard Wright's *Native Son*, full of murderous fury.

Claremont, with its suburban accents and pretentious schooled speech, has been put behind them. Shooting what is reported to be the toughest gangster movie ever made resolved the question "whether the Hugheses were real enough, hard enough, *black* enough—whether the brothers were, well, *brothers.*" You see, the "interracial" matter of it was that their mother happened to be Armenian; but nobody now cares, or can remember, how *her* brothers spoke. The Hughes twins exceeded all hopes for the new representations of what they call "ultraviolence." The lesson that was learned (and Henry Louis Gates, Jr., points it up): "It's not where you're *from,* it's where you're *at.*" But this is, of course, only slangy question-begging. To be "where you're at" covers not only an awareness of your present (i.e., what you are, and what you want to do) but also your inescapable past (i.e. why you came to be that way, or *how* you got to be where you're *at*). Allen Hughes is quoted as saying, "It's like, can we have our own identity, please?" Albert is quoted as groaning, "Every fucking interview, 'Where did you guys grow up?'" And he explodes, "You don't ask Spielberg that shit." Sad to say, Hollywood, in its celluloid enlightenment, still continues to discriminate among box-office hitters. It lionizes white luminaries (e.g. Steven Spielberg, Quentin Tarantino) as geniuses, but only embraces two blacks (although "interracial kids") from Claremont "as their little pets, like they always do niggers...."

Thus does the n-word in several guises perform a whole variety of functions for the changing careers of young men of talent in the black community. As the hero-character in the *"Menace II Society"* film puts it (as quoted by Professor Gates), with the blessing of the house style liberalized in London fashion by the then (English-born) *New Yorker* editor in chief : "He was the craziest nigga alive. America's nightmare. Young, black, and didn't give a fuck."[30]

The special issue of the *New Yorker* ("Black in America," in the spring of 1996) contributed decisively to the "outing" in the white world of the standard profanities which have highlighted African-American loquacity. Now even "the little old lady from Dubuque"—Harold Ross' notoriously typical reader— has been exposed to a new diction.

To be sure, the n-word has not thereby been completely assimilated. Professor Gates notes in a small *New Yorker* anthology devoted to "the n-word" that "it's not what you say, it's how you say it," and, consequently, inflection and intention can also play a role here in the disarming of expletives. He knows that the days when the use of the word "nigger" was an occasion for unpleasantness are not yet over—but nowadays it "ain't, necessarily, your father's slur." Various cultural upheavals have taken place and now, as we have seen: "some people are now using the less toxic 'nigga' to connote affection."

A young black actress named N'bushe Wright has apparently been caught up in this historic "new spin." She would prefer a distaff word of her own, still,

> I don't feel like it's a feminine word, but my friend Stephanie will see you and be like, *"Hey, nigg-ah!"* with all the love in the world and a big smile and come hugging you and kissing you 'cause she hasn't seen you in forever. And that's the same exact way that I hear it in the barbershop or walking down the street hearing boyz talking to boyz.

The n-word has in effect been naturalized in the whole gamut of ethnic emotions. At one end it continues to be a war cry, for "being called 'nigger' had the threat of death behind it." At the other it has the heartfelt affection of *"the luvvies."*

Somewhere in between are the liberal utopian optimists who are convinced that one fine day racial antipathies—and the nasty words devised to convey them—will disappear with the coming of equality and fraternity (and the compassionate welfare economics that should, at long last, be their accompaniment). A young black photographer named Barron Claiborne sounds the classic note of democratic hope: "If everyone had a decent job and the same rights as everybody else, people call you 'nigger' all the way to your nice home and your nice car, and you wouldn't care." Usually, as in the intellectual projections of such fundamental or revolutionary change (see Jean-Paul Sartre, Noam Chomsky et al), there is a bright future for a fresh new language. Here, at least, in such shining renovation the nasty words of the old one are condemned to the dustbin of history:

> If we eliminated racism, we could have Nigger University and Honkytown and Yellow Fever College, and my Chinese friend and my white friend and I could go to Sambo Burger and have some Whitey french fries and nobody would care, because everybody would have equal opportunity and the word would have no power.

This utopianism, simple and sweet as all such visions tend to be, would look a mite more flawed and improbable if the n-word godfathers had reflected on the historic lessons offered by the J-word and the thousands of years in which the anti-Semitic expletives had not yet lost their power. Only a half-century ago, until the *Kristallnacht* of the Nazi *Reich*, a German minority had enjoyed equal opportunities and went back to nice homes and nice cars and *still* found themselves on the eve of a holocaust.

Alas, neither powerful words nor hateful cultures allow themselves to be detoxified so easily.[31]

The transformations of the n-word have gone so far and so fast that the new mutant form of "nigga" has, in more and more inter- and intraracial contexts, displaced the old expletive.* Once again, a best-selling novel and its graphic translation into film with a booming sound-track dialogue is leading the way. Another of Elmore Leonard's tales of the shabby underworld has been adapted by Hollywood: *Rum Punch* (1992), directed by Quentin Tarantino (of *Reservoir Dogs* and *Pulp Fiction* notoriety). One foreign newspaper, makes the offer to enlighten its non-American readers as to what the "verbally dextrous hood"— "Ordell, a gun smuggler and small-time psycho," played by the black actor Samuel L. Jackson—is actually talking about. He explains that his

> chief medium of expression is language, specifically the n-word (nigga) which he uses as five of his eight parts of speech, always with a poetic flourish that stings like the tip of a whip.

Thus, the n-word has now taken on the revised orthography, and is accordingly the heir to all the black man's burdens. The *Guardian* (31 December 1997), borrowing its information from the *Washington Post* a few days earlier, registers a note of liberal concern by reporting that the black film director Spike Lee, of *Malcolm X* fame, has already complained about Tarantino's script which was for him "too black," especially from a white writer. (Does it help extenuate crossing-the-color-line by adding that "the f-word is also used a lot"? Expletives love company.)[32]

"A lot" is a timid estimate. My calculations suggest that if the n-word and the F- (and m-f) words were to be cut from the Tarantino scripts the films would no longer be feature-length...and the poor tongue-tied man would have to go back on location for a couple weeks to shoot an extra hour of fillers. In an excerpt from the shooting script of *Jackie Brown*, the London paper quotes this passage:

> *Ordell:* Look, I hate to be the kinda nigga does a nigga a favor—then BAM —hits a nigga up for a favor in return. But I'm afraid I gotta be that kind of nigga.

Tarantino's work is a language-immersion course in the new fantasy phonetics. Each sentence is a concentrated lesson in the latest lore about whatever happened to the "natural speech of common man." With a brainwashing intensity this trend is moving towards the profanization of our media culture. Nobody's gonna be talking no clean or straight talk no more. Except in the BBC's eighteenth-century Jane Austen world (and even there the TV scripts are being updated).

---

* The 1997 edition of the *Oxford Dictionary of New Words* (p. 216) recognizes the vernacular respelling, and already registers it formally as "a black man," explaining that "it represents a conscious, politically motivated reclamation by blacks of the term *nigger*...a form of self-assertion, with the aim of reducing the term's derogation." It also notes a similar development – transmuting the pejorative – in the adoption of the word *queer* by the gay community (as in "Queer Nation").

Defusing the Enemy's Vocabulary

There are, of course, polemical uses of the n-word by white proponents of the black cause who take sly advantage of its pejorative burden of prejudice. Naturally they think it is clever and therefore an effective propaganda device. (Whether it is, or not, remains a moot question.) The intention, however, was to turn the point of the expletive the other way, and thus strike a blow for the good common cause. John Lennon, for example, in the radical hey-day of the Beatles, once composed a series of radical songs for the '68ers which were recorded and released in 1969. Among them were "Give Peace a Chance" for the pacifist friends; "Happy Christmas (War Is Over)" for the Vietnik comrades; and "Power to the People" for fellow-revolutionaries everywhere. One number, dedicated to his (and Yoko Ono's) feminist front-liners struggling to liberate oppressed womanhood, was entitled: "Woman is the Nigger of the World."*

There was something of the same dialectical twist in the young Norman Mailer's effort to define the radical literary personality—presumably himself: the crusader, the champ, the enlightened friend of Afro-Americans (including his rival, James Baldwin). He coined the new label, "White Negro."** But since Mailer's views and his self-awareness change with the regularity of his publishing a new book, the n-word synonym for marginalized outsiders, for beatniks and hipsters, disappeared before it could be damned as chromatically incorrect. Today it would not even pass over his lips, not to mention through his mind.

Thus, within this form of semantic apartheid, the separate life among the brothers, a sense of an oppressed existence becomes an active value in its own right. It is no longer defensively reactive against a hostile white world, which becomes, in turn, all the more real. "Whitey"—"the dude," "the Man"—becomes, in his turn, all the more sinister in the spotlight, when his words are turned the other way, neatly exploited for other purposes by dulling or defusing the enemy's vocabulary.

The disarming wit of Dick Gregory even changed a deficit into a profit. He had dedicated his books *Nigger* (1964), a best-selling indictment of "an oppressive social system," to his mother: "Dear Momma—Where ever you are, if you ever hear the word 'nigger' again, remember they are advertising my book." But these were only the first lines of a revolutionary manifesto: something light, a joke to begin with, even whistling in the dark. His last lines are in deep tones, in a peroration, in a *basso profundo* which is the soul of gravity:

---

*   Ian Macdonald, *Revolution in the Head: the Beatles' Records & the Sixties* (1995), p. 287.

**   Norman Mailer, "White Negro," first published in *Dissent* (1957) and reprinted in *Advertisements for Myself* (1959).

And now we're ready to change a system, a system where a white man can destroy a black man with a single word. Nigger.
When we're through, Momma, there won't be any niggers any more.[33]

This was written in the 1960s, in those semi-Marxianized militant days when zealous men of ideals were always venting their anger at "the System." Today the bitterness would be against "the Culture," and the triumphant counterculture would bring total emancipation.

Has, then, the n-word anything in common with the J-word? Beyond, that is, the obvious and often lethal violation of the pious precepts of our universal enlightenment. To answer is to return to the semantic maze of what happens to expletives of racial hostility and ethnic exclusion when they cannot be conveniently deleted. Just as one reforms, patching up here and there, when one cannot revolutionize, so are the injured and oppressed tempted to try tiny and tricky verbal devices to better their abject condition.

This kind of detoxification of the pejorative phrases that sat like a plague on black life in urban ghettoes was done with admirable high spirits; and if it betrayed a bit of desperation in the "'hood" it also suggested verbal black dexterity. Christopher Darden, the ill-starred U.S. district attorney who (with Marcia Clark) prosecuted in vain in the O.J. Simpson murder trial, grew up in an all-black neighborhood near San Francisco. He ran with boyish gangs in petty raids on local shopkeepers, and might have (as he confesses) grown up to be a gangster beyond the law. It is almost as if, as in Hawthorne's tell-tale A-mark, there was a G-mark on all the ghetto kids. (While Darden went on to become a prominent lawyer, his brother died young of dirty-needle AIDS after a brief career as a thief and drug dealer.) Who would call him a gangster? All were brothers, and G served as a kindly, even tender abbreviation. Addressing some of his friends and colleagues on the Los Angeles Police Force, Chris Darden would call them "G." And in one especially moving moment in the O.J. Simpson trial (1995-6), this exchange was reported between the two co-prosecutors. Darden was having one of his temper tantrums in open court—he insists he was not being "immature and petty" but making "an important stand" (or so he still believes)—and Marcia Clark was sweetly trying to calm him down. Referring to the judge, she pleaded with her partner "He's got you cold....It ain't worth it G." And Darden explains: "I'd been teaching Marcia some common phrases from the 'hood like G, shorthand for gangster." The term of endearment helped to end the fit. Darden calmed down and apologized to the court like, he admits, an unruly "third-grader." Marcia hadn't called him "darling" or "baby" (as on other occasions). G was tender, G was sweet. Defused words have a special anodyne power.[34]

No one could possibly quantify the amount of affection with which G-for-gangster was invested as whites and blacks declare on occasion their personal solidarity. Who wears the badge of sufferance with more pride? In the relationship between the two unfortunate prosecutors, slated for failure in the O.J. Simpson trial, Marcia Clark, white, forty-three, thought of herself as a rootless waif as compared to Chris Darden, black, thirty-seven, who seemed to her to be so strongly rooted in the local African-America ghetto's "[neighbor] 'hood." In her own book of memoirs about the historic trial she notes that at one sensitive point when the two Los Angeles prosecutors had begun their "euphoric" relationship, "Chris had started calling me G. for 'gangster,' an expression of friendship and respect in his old neighborhood." She felt this term of endearment to be deeply—if, to an outsider, inexplicably—reassuring. Perhaps because as a first-generation daughter of recent immigrants she had been restlessly moving around the States with her ex-Israeli parents, as if they were fated to be wanderers in an Egyptian desert. Accordingly, she had never had a 'hood of her own.[35]

The disarmament of taunts and expletives in the ethnic or racial context can be pacific or militant, gentle or angry, calculating or unintentional. For example, the systematic omission of the n-word in the well-intentioned liberal American journalism of the 1950s-1960s did little to relieve its sting when it suddenly broke out into the open. One wonders whether the smoked glasses of the would-be colorblind was not a pose that was readily seen through. There is an illogicality to the argument, but it may well be true, as the Rev. Jesse Jackson argues: "To ignore race and gender is racist and sexist."

At the other extreme, what are the unintended consequences of the outraged insistence of breaking, for one reason or another, the polite benevolence of the n-word taboo? I suspect that derision by repetition also has a surprising dialectic: repeating it, as in a child's litany of "much-much-much" (which turns it into mush), can render it meaningless, or harmless, or too familiar to register. Or, as I tend to think, it compounds the bile and other emotional ingredients into an incantation which is anything but anodyne. Thus, a columnist for the *New York Times* named Bob Herbert became so incensed at the Republican and generally conservative backlash against liberal legislation in favor of blacks (affirmative action, civil rights, equal opportunity, and the like) that he exploded in print against "the execrable Bob Grant," a right-wing broadcaster of notorious repute:

> a sewer-swimming, garbage-spewing individual whose life is so utterly devoid of meaning he has staked his all on a shtick that calls for him to go on the radio every afternoon and babble the equivalent of nigger-nigger-nigger-nigger-nigger.[36]

Not only is this a far cry from the paper which the Managing Editor A.R. ("Abe") Rosenthal tried to keep colorblind in the 1960s (i.e., unsoiled by any usage of the n-word), it establishes a *Times* record for repetition in a single full-length newspaper column (30 inches long, 13-ems wide). By my count it came to a total of 15 (although they were always grouped in a hyphenated quorum of 5, which presumably sang out in chorus each time the execrable Mr. Grant was quoted with his "vile and spiritually empty" sentiments). The columnist thought he was striking a blow against bigotry, against "the ugly and the dangerous." But it was, as many dismayed *Times* readers skeptically thought, only fighting fire with fire. Arsonists were at work on all sides, and their incantatory rhythms in the end were only fanning the embers.

Still, there are chromatic differences. A BBC correspondent, traveling in the Deep South in the mid-1990s, was much struck by a hymn-like blues song which he heard in an old Negro church concert taking place in a little town called Jonesville.* Indeed he sounded overwhelmed by the obsessive-compulsiveness of the one line, repeated "differently" a hundred times—"You Don't Know How Black You Are"—as if the color deepened each time in the litany of the endless troubles they've all seen. The white man's angry defense of the harassed people is militant, insistent, aggressive. The colored counterpart, in an equally meaningful monotone, is gentler, subtler, long-suffering.[37]

A not dissimilar pattern emerges in the Caribbean, for example in Cuba, where the African slaves were duly referred to as *"Negron...the black ones"* (with the usual slave-holders' sentiments). But when a plangent folk music developed—now, after centuries, called "traditional music"—the song style was affectionately referred to as *"Nengon"* and, as such, enjoys wide multiracial popularity.[38]

The illusion of an easy way to such verbal disarmament is fostered by the curious changes in certain expletives which emerge transformed, as in Nietzsche's celebrated "transvaluation of values." They are, in our context, mostly superficial or uncomplicated terms, relatively free from the complexities of old hatred and nasty prejudice, or of sexual and ethnic imputations. Slang words can be easily turned around, can become ambivalent or, in certain unusual cases, slip into their own antonyms. *Bimbo*, in its original Italian, has no demeaning suggestion, but in English has a rude note of sleazy looseness about it. Polite salesgirls in good Roman children's shops in the Via Condotti will sell you small-sized jeans for your *bimbo* (or *bimbi*, as the case may be). In a conventionally macho vocabulary any nubile female, young or old, can be called deprecatingly a gold-digger or a call-girl or some related form of mistress. Presidential candidates, even presidents these days, have been known to play around with "bimbos." In recent years there have even been "bimbo eruptions."

"Nerd" which used to be a purely pejorative term of utter contempt is now, as I write, on the brink of a turn-around. It is moving from a colloquial American put-down to an Anglo-European term of grudging respect. The nerd was once a social outcast, peculiar and dislikeable in his individual qualities, something between an eccentric jerk and a hopeless nut-case. In a time of spreading

---

*   BBC broadcast, Michael Goldfarb, "Going South," World Service, 20 May 1996.

computer enthusiasm, even the stereotypical image of an obsessive fan as a nerd is fading among young people. One center for so-called "Media Studies" has pronounced that

> While there is still the label of being a nerd, for young people it has become a term of praise or a label for somebody who is an expert.
>
> In the last two years, the nerd has become trendy and quite chic in the fashion world and the expression is now less pejorative than ever before.[39]

In his "Language" column, William Safire aptly replied to a question from the editor (Alan Levy) of the *Prague Post*, "Is there a lexicographical term for words that become antonyms of themselves through distortion, if not misuse?"

> The word is *contranym* or *antilogy,* but the popular phrase for it is *Janus* word....One sense of *Janus*-faced is "deceitful, two-faced" and another is "sensitive to dualities and polarities."

In the above we have been adding to the sense of dualism disarmed, or of polar opposites resolved, by citing cutting words that face in two directions; and they can go into reverse. What lexicographers are mostly concerned with are comic linguistic curiosities such as: to *best* or to *worst,* to *table a motion* (Anglo-American antonyms meaning quashing a proposal in Washington, but actively proposing a measure in London). More recently, the slang flippage of "showstopper" from positive (a spectacular number which commands applause) to negative (a disruptive, even insurmountable obstacle). Two of the most profound examples in political history are "utopia" and "revolution"; and in my book on that subject (University of Chicago Press, 1976) I described how "utopia" veered from a speculative imaginary no-place to a realistic this-worldly ideal—and how "revolution" developed from a circular return or restoration (England's Glorious Revolution of 1688) to a forward-marching linear-progressive innovation (the French Revolution of 1789). Words have lives of their own; they are things in their own right.[40]

The adoption of a term as a badge of pride...and its being whittled away to an insult...is an unusual phenomenon. Hopes have occasionally run high for a similar transformation, a semantic disarmament and psychic reevaluation, to overtake the n- or J-words and other racial epithets of pejorative current discourse. But in their twisted traditionalism there is not discernible any sure sign of a magical change for the better. No one as yet has tried to wear for long the badge of pride which featured the label of *nigger* or *kike* or *wop* or *mick* or *chink* or *dago*....

In point of fact the movement appears to be other way. It seems almost to be a lexic law trying to formulate itself. One can try to put it this way: the ethnic outrage of semantic sensitivities expands to fill the blank quiet spaces vacated by the tidy self-censorship of political correctness. That is to say:

once an Augean stable has been cleaned up, every speck of dirt or lingering odor seems to amount to the old foulness. In certain gentrified areas of civilized societies old and hoary anti-Semitic slurs fade away or disappear; but, as we have seen, the simple appellation of the J-word can intrude to enrage delicate feelings. The n-word, too close to Negro for comfort, appeared to be becoming rather rare, at least in the enlightened half-century since Jackie Robinson's starring career broke the color barrier in major league baseball in the American sporting world. And yet a recent incident, with no expletive to be heard or seen, aroused as much anger and protest around the head of a "racist" athlete and his "victim" (a new black champion) as in the taunting days of explicitly bad language. The grotesque details are notable.

The two men in question were Fuzzy Zoeller—an intelligent, likeable and rather do-gooding middle-aged golfer who had been born into a wealthy New Orleans oil family—and who had won many a professional championship in the last twenty years; and Tiger Woods, a young so-called African-American who had just broken all world golfing records to win the coveted U.S. Masters trophy in Augusta, Georgia (1996).

The trouble began with a TV interview in which Zoeller referred to Woods as "a little boy." In addition to which Fuzzy advised Tiger "not to serve fried chicken next year...or collard greens or whatever...." That was about it. "Boy" was a genial diminutive for the slightly built twenty-one-year-old, albeit with an echo of an old-style ante-bellum cotton-pickin' usage *("Boy!"* shouted the master). Choosing the menu for the Augusta Club ceremonial meal is the new champion's annual prerogative; but neither of Zoeller's ironic culinary suggestions were particularly "black dishes" these days. Colonel Sanders's Kentucky fried chicken is now a standard multicuisine dish throughout all ethnic communities from coast to coast. As for those special kind of greens, very few gourmets in the country could readily tell the difference between "collard greens" (from the Germanic *Kohl*, I suspect; but this unnecessarily complicates the matter) and Tobacco Road turnips, favored by "white trash."

And yet....The *Washington Post* exploded: "This is a vicious racist remark. How will Woods feel when he sees it? Will it scar him?" The *Post*'s sports columnist (Thomas Boswell) lashed out with a proposed penalty: "Knock Zoeller flat with a public reprimand, a big fine and a long suspension." The *New York Times* sports writer, Richard Sandomir, referring to "the inflammatory ethnic remarks," warned that "Public figures make blatantly offensive remarks at their occupational peril." And the perilous prospect was underlined by Roy Innis, head of the Congress of Racial Equality, who urged sternly that Zoeller's apology be rejected, and that the golfer be "condemned" by all Americans and "shunned" by fellow professionals.

It is as if the derogation had been patently vicious and insulting, and the "ethical enormity" had amounted to a plea for the nullification of Abraham

Lincoln's Emancipation Proclamation and the Thirteenth Amendment. Although, as his friends have attested, "he doesn't have a bigoted bone on his body," Fuzzy Zoeller's regret was abject. He had not intended to be "racially derogatory"; the remarks were "misconstrued." He had, unfortunately, been trying to be "humorous." Nevertheless, one big business sponsor of marketing contracts, K-Mart Corporation, began cancelling prosperous deals.

As for the new champion himself, he had been unreachable for a while, having turned down President Clinton's invitation to attend "Jackie Robinson Day" commemorating the breaking of baseball's color line. (Tiger was busy fulfilling his own sponsor's lucrative contracts.) And then, just to confound matters, he made a remark in his turn which surprised, shocked, and left the apostles of political correctness high and dry. Evidently Earl Woods was a proud father and thought of himself as "a black" and his son as a "black" or "African-American" golfer. But the perfect ethnic success story was not to be. His son, Ethridge Tiger Woods, born of a Thai mother (and not purely Asian at that), clarified his racial make-up by cryptically calling himself on nation-wide television "Cablinasian." He explained that the neologism "Cablinasian" (by which he thought of himself and had personally invented, as a middle-class big-city boy) was a compound blend of "Caucasian, black, American Indian and Asian." Which was what he was or said he was. His identity, take it or not.

A new pundit was brought in by the *Washington Post* to deal with Tiger Woods. The melting pot had been stirred. The golfer had "broken the mold." He had even gone so far as to evade the conventional definition of Negro or colored which was if anyone had "even one drop of black blood...." Yet another commentator (Michael A. Fletcher) hastened to broach basic issues by

> bringing into sharp focus the wrenching debate over how the increasing number of mixed race Americans are seen and categorized....Are the racial categories Americans use to define themselves becoming outdated by a dramatically changing demographic portrait?

Such antiquated nineteenth-century classifications as "mulatto... quadroon...octoroon" have long ago ceased to provide "exacting measures of someone's black heritage" (or, less anachronistically, a chattel slave's inherited burden).[41]

"I'm not black," says Tiger. He broke ranks by refusing "to deny his mother" through whom he can be labeled "a quarter Chinese" and even "an eighth white." Tiger was distressed that everyone was "claiming ownership" and "wanted a piece of the action."

Whatever the next phase of racial nomenclature may bring, the categorical imperatives of ethnic biography and chromatic identity may not be as likely to be as simple-minded and all-embracing, indeed as easily manipulable (for good or bad vibes) as they once were when "colored man" or "Negro" was

summarily abolished and "black" was pronounced "beautiful." Old epithets
will be abandoned, new labels can be reevaluated, and will, in turn, be in-
flected to suggest different innuendoes. Labels for identities will be multifarious—especially if the utopian cry which one paper quoted Eartha Kitt intoning as a human right: "Shouldn't we be allowed to be what we please?" is heard
and followed throughout the land. It's a cry of absolute libertarianism, but no
present-day theory of colors will allow the large antinomian latitude to be "anyone one pleases." Each choice has, alas, still to be graded for its correctness.

Reporters for *Time* and *Newsweek* who in the insurgent sixties maintained a
high liberal self-confidence on racial matters have given way in the subsequent decades to a new generation of observers who were troubled by the
chromatic uncertainties that were complicating the black-and-white scene.
Small matter that the fashionable enthusiasms were new and a little strange
(that's the function of pop *chic* on the multicultural front). But then the very
perception of realities appear to have changed:

> In the increasing global youth culture, the notion of identity itself is up for grabs.
> When you can go to a Korean hip-hop club in Los Angeles and dance to the all-
> black Wu-Tang Clan rapping about being Shaolin fighters, in a crowd sporting
> Tommy Hilfiger WASP-wear, who's to say where racial boundaries lie?

The scene has become a no-man's land, and where there are no clear or
fixed boundaries, nothing can be out of bounds. Who calls you friend, who
enemy? What's the pass-word? The reporters on the newspapers seem to be
bewildered; the journalists on the newsmagazines venture to speak of a new
ethnic terrain; they report a cultural tumult which has made America "a more
colorful place" with "a hyphen-happy generation for whom old racial and
ethnic categories—black, white, Asian, Hispanic—no longer work...." Dailies
like to use the old words—weeklies prefer to go in for something fancier like
the altered lines of "racial phenotypes." These are said to induce an optimism
about "a racial cognizance their elders never had," all of which leads one to
suspect "changing parameters":

> James Williams, a sophomore at Wesleyan College, shakes his head over the chang-
> ing parameters. James' mother is white, German. His father is black, with a mix-
> ture of Cherokee and Choctaw. The other day, he says, "this white kid came up to
> me and said, 'what up, nigga?'" This was, he says with a laugh, the kid's idea of a
> friendly greeting.[42]

The contrast here with the slow-moving simplicities of the London press
could not be sharper. The British atmosphere, reflecting the racial stabilities
of its Hindu, Muslim, and Caribbean communities, doesn't quite know "what's
up." It hasn't been hit yet by the "changing parameters" and is still struggling

with the phenotype problems of the old terrain. The newspaper house-style dilemmas which I have pin-pointed in Abe Rosenthal's *New York Times* of the 1960s echoes today in London when, some thirty years later, the *Sunday Times* is still wrestling with the "political correctness which prevents us facing facts that could help fight street crime."

A mugged white newspaperwoman who was reviled as "honkey bitch" (and "white meat"), criticizes London's Metropolitan Police for "color blindness that shields the mugger." Fearful of a wave of racial hatred in the aftermath of a plague of street muggings, the authorities are "now so sensitive that they will not release the ethnic identity of either the muggers or the victims."

What will happen when a Tiger Woods comes along and they all have to deal with bewildering name-tags which read "Cablinasian"?[43]

The imputation of a "culture lag" or being "out of touch" (or not "with it") is only justified if American developments are the measuring rod to be used. Is it "only in America" can the Europeans glimpse the shape of things to come? If the resemblances don't yet fit, "it will, it will!..." (as Picasso is said to have reassured Gertrude Stein, standing skeptically before her unrecognizable portrait). The postwar Germans persisted during their whole period of imported foreign labor (mostly, from Turkey) in ignoring the checkered history of U.S. immigrant "acculturation," of the transatlantic "Melting Pot" experience, and are only now catching up with the lessons of Ellis Island. The Gaullist French were confident that in absorbing and integrating their post-colonial North African population they would master their own emancipation-proclamation problem; and, in fact, they have been haunted by Lincolnesque fears of living in a half-way house, divided against itself. As for the British, the vaunted "Commonwealth spirit" has not mediated the "colored ghettoes" which feature little harmony and less tolerance, in all the old urban centers. So long as the dynamics of social mobility don't change, English disharmonics will have a jarring note of their own and not necessarily sound like a Harlem or Watts race riot. And still, some migrants move, and when they migrate the transatlantic similarities and differences break through, as in this report of an "English student" transplanted to New England:

> Sean Brecker's father is white, Jewish. His mother identifies herself as African-Indian; Sean was born in Pakistan, raised in Tanzania and London. He has piercing blue eyes, and says he has to go out of his way to tell people he is "not, contrary to popular belief, the token white." When he got to Wesleyan, he says, he was first recruited by the African-American students organization, then the Latino, Asian, and interracial groups. "I came to Wesleyan and realized I was out of touch," he says. "I got to thinking about what I was."

He was out of touch? It could be that *they* were out of touch. If he could be all things to all men, it could be that he was asking himself the wrong question—

not what he was, but *who* he was? But, perhaps, there was no easy way of getting *right on!*, in the expostulatory hope of yesteryear. One of his school-mates thinks of herself as "Korgentinian," and some of her friends (with no Korean or Argentinian connections) identify themselves as "China-Latino" or "Blackanese." As for her own group, "Her group is called Hapa, from a Hawaiian word for 'half'— once derogatory—now, in parts of Asia and America, hip." In time there will be an alphabet-soup of combinations taking easy advantage of the *jus solis* and the *jus consanguinis*, determinants of the line of one's heritage without, for the moment, factoring in the element of shade and color (not to mention a soupçon of improbable patriotism). Young James Williams—of *"What up, nigga?"* notoriety (above)—flies a German flag in his room and has a Korean girlfriend. His last confession is of the ultimate colored man's burden: variously said to be losing one's soul, or shadow, or *macho*, or (in one bad blow) losing one's whole culture:

> At times I think "I don't want to have kids lighter than me." I have Native American in me, but I don't recognize that, because it's not pushed on me. If my kids were lighter and had the chance to "pass," maybe they would do that with my black half, [and] lose the culture.

That way, some may think, lies madness or, at the very least, manic mathematics. As I write, calculators are at work and one has come up with the identity-fit of somebody like Tiger Woods. It is said to be, "in strictly mathematical terms,"

> one quarter Chinese, one-quarter white, an eighth Native American and an eighth black. But by the confluence of marketing and ideology, he became golf's great black hope.

The "color of the soul," as Shakespeare sensed, is more important than the correctness of the genetic calculation. Especially if white turns out to be a form of brown (and of black too). Why should our Wesleyan student want to pass muster—and where?—with his "black half"? Who in our media culture is failing to push properly if the "Native American" in him—perhaps Cherokee, perhaps Choctaw—doesn't come to get recognized? What, in the last analysis, does determine "phenotype cognizance"?

We may well be nearing the heart of the darkness, what one U.S. journalist has called "the nation's racial irrationality":

> Most constructions of race in America revolve around a peculiar institution known as the one-drop rule; anyone who acknowledges a single black ancestor is considered black. The rule is a warped legacy of slavery, devised to ensure that the offspring of slaves would remain enslaved.[44]

Evidently it holds its sway even today. Give a peculiar name to a contentious thing and it will surround it like a cage. Misnomers have enslaved spirits.

The Shock Threshold

The Fuhrman tapes of August 1995 may well have altered the balance of justice as perceived by the 12 jurors in the O.J. Simpson trial; but it certainly upset the frame of mind with which American journalism had conventionally approached the race question, unbalanced its sense of judgment, and left all previous rules and guidelines in a riotous disarray. One New York paper put it graphically by quoting a Los Angeles lawyer: "Would a Jewish jury convict a Jewish defendant on the testimony of an S.S. officer?'"—noting nine blacks on the Simpson panel.[45] Some editors, holding fast to their traditional liberal good will, thought that the public playing of the transcribed "vulgarities" in court—and then reproducing them, in whole or in part, in their news-columns—would only aggravate racial and ethnic tensions. One enlightened white Los Angeles police officer was quoted as saying, presumably with utter sincerity, "I was shocked to hear these words said by anybody, regardless of whether they came from a police officer or not."

Others had a lesser shock threshold. The racial epithets, said a NAACP spokeswoman, "There was nothing new about them." All the responses were ringing false in the general dismay and bewilderment.

A police league spokesman dismissed "the whole thing as a bunch of garbage" (arguing that it was only a smokescreen to cloud the original reason—a double murder—why O.J. Simpson was on trial). Other colleagues stretched the thin language of analogies even more with vague and bizarre metaphors about being "way off base here" or "barking up the wrong tree."

Yet the practical editorial question was to be, or not to be, ruthless in the rigor to tell it "like it was." Mark Fuhrman's vulgarity-laced conversations had been recorded in a private chat with an aspiring Hollywood screenwriter Laura Hart McKinny, who evidently led him on to get color for her script. Detective Fuhrman thought of them as a contribution to the "dirty realism" of a Hollywood scenario which would feature shocking language. Whatever the dialogues represented they presented even the TV documentary editors at CNN with a moral problem. Famed for "recording history on-the-spot as it happens," CNN confessed that standards were revised for the Simpson trial and that it did indeed "edit out language.... which we felt was most offensive to widespread standards of custom and decency."[46] But some tapes were used "unexpurgated"—which, according to the *New York Times* (31 August 1995), was not the case with the three major U.S. over-the-air networks. CBS reported on the tapes, "but neither the vulgarities nor the racial slurs were heard." They were also "non-audible" in NBC's coverage, "although 'nigger' appeared on a graphic." As for the ABC's broadcasts, "the purely vulgar language was not audible but the word 'nigger' was."

In the event the CNN compromise saved the day for the media, for as the *Times* reporter wrote with fraternal sympathy,

> while CNN's regular newscasts omitted the worst of Mr. Fuhrman's vulgarities, the word "nigger" was shown (although not heard) because CNN journalists thought it was crucial to understanding the issue.

Is, then, the price of "understanding" an "ultimate exacerbation" of general public opinion? Good question, as sensitive as it is insoluble.

Meanwhile, down at the popular competition, among the Manhattan tabloids like the *New York Post*, there was a veritable field day of copious excerpts and finger-wagging moralizing. It was a rare occasion that the "purely vulgar" comes one's way in the public interest. Still, the old Hamlet-like indecisiveness obtained in the newsrooms, and the *Post* did the n-word in full orthography in its actual stories but, on the screaming front-page make-up, three key quotations from "the Voice of Hate" used asterisks as in "n****r," as if the abbreviated form indicated an extra measure of cautious and dignified disapproval. Here are only a few paragraphs which adorned a full page of the *New York Post* (30 August 1995, pp. 1, 5):

> People there [Washington] don't want niggers in their town. People there don't want Mexicans in their town. And any way you can do to get them out of there, that's fine with them. We have no niggers where I grew up.
>
> If you put a bruise on a nigger it's pretty tough to see....I used to go to work and practice [martial arts]. Niggers, they're easy to practice my kicks.
>
> You know, policemen also use *bubba* lot, 'cause it's a slam term [to use] niggers, and niggers, you know, call each other *bubba*. Sometimes you go—so you go, Hey, *Bubba*, what's happening, you know. And stuff like that. So there is a lot of that conversation.... "Don't you ever fight or f— around with a policeman. You'll do what you're told. You understand nigger? Run, run, run...."
>
> Take one in the basement and beat the ... out of him without even asking him a question....That's how you get information. What is this pattycake, pattycake shit psychology?.....How do you intellectualize when you punch the hell out of a nigger?

There were more than twelve hours of playing time on the incriminating tapes—for Detective Fuhrman had sworn on oath that he had never used racist terms such as "nigger" in his police career and certainly not "in the last 10 years"—but all listeners appeared to be too agitated to do a reliable word count. The *Times* referred to "more than three dozen times," the *Post* to "more than 40 times." One imaginative journalist speculated on "the pungent sound of epithets" which she speculated was the response of the Los Angeles prosecuting attorneies who, sensing the trial's turning point, were "watching their once iron-clad case cascade right down the toilet." She printed one pungency: "Oh, # % $ %Q@#$!" Such hieroglyphics were the fine old time-honored way the American press, especially in the ubiquitous comic strips, used to print a breakthrough to obscenity, or a burst of profanity—a regrettable Dick Tracy cuss-word or Dagwood's occasional slip into bad language. The cryptic expletives were drawn nicely and legibly by the cartoonists in the cartoon-strip's usual conversational balloons. Or, as others claim, they were the invention of the linotype printer, improvising on his Mergenthaler keyboard (and he came up, famously, with that greatest of all newspaper by-lines, *Etaoin Shrdlu*"). In any case it had journalistic tradition, for the papers were always trying to say something of the sort. I was reminded of this continuity when Detective Mark Fuhrman's fateful amanuensis was asked in the Simpson trial, after the playing of the d*@# %ed tapes, whether she had felt "any discomfortment" in prompting the original cascade of expletives in her Hollywoodesque interviews; and Miss McKinny replied, "Yes, very uncomfortable," she said in a near whisper. "But I was in a journalistic mode."[47] So, alas, for better or worse, are we all.

There followed, in the wake of the Fuhrman breakthrough, general concern—and perhaps justifiably so—that the new reportorial routines would be striking deep roots in the newspaper culture; and that racial expletives will become a daily feature of journalistic realism, issuing in (as the optimists feel) a benign indifference or (as the pessimists suspect) in an even more widespread infectiousness in the nastier corners of public opinion.

Thus, the case of the owner of the Cincinnati Reds baseball team came to a climax in June 1996, although Marge Schott had been suspended by the commissioners of major-league clubs three years earlier. She had been charged with repeatedly making disparaging ethnic and racial remarks, "justifying the Nazis" (she had said that Adolf Hitler was "good at the beginning"), and generally being a "pernicious influence." Critics of Ms. Schott argued that "Nazi sympathizers, blatant racists, foul-mouthed public figures and pinch-penny owners have no business being in Major League Baseball." The short-lived original suspension had, in fact, stated that she "commonly used coarse language that is racially and ethnically insensitive."

That was pre-Fuhrman. Now the *New York Times* found that reportorial detail which was once felt to be illicit could now be taken to be explicit; and it reported on the final agreement between the baseball council and the Reds' owner whereby she agreed to step down:

The council said it found "convincing evidence" that Schott frequently used the terms "nigger, lazy nigger, damn nigger and dumb, lazy nigger" and called people of the Jewish faith "Jew bastards and dirty Jews."[48]

The old-fashioned reference to "people of the Jewish faith"—although obviously the victims may well have been agnostics or even faithless atheists (as liberal "non-practicing" Jews often are)—recalled the arch sensitivities of yesteryear to using the J-word. Some readers will recall the daring *Beyond the Fringe* joke of the 1960s when a young cabarettist protested that he was "not a Jew"...but "Jewish." In German, too, as we will have occasion to point out, standard ethnic correctness calls for the adverb *(jüdisch)* rather than the noun *(Jude)*, although the notorious "J"-labels of Auschwitz viciousness did double duty.

Speaking with a Forked Tongue

The time-honored ploy in the side-stepping of anti-Semitism, an evasive move which is common to many Jewish communities (viz. in the U.S. and Britain)—and also in the official *pro*-Semitism of post-Hitler Germany from Adenauer to Kohl—is the avoidance of the noun and the substitution of the adjective. The noun was associated with shouts and insults, hurtful labels and other badges of degrading discrimination—"*Jew!*" The adjective and adverb seemed to be somewhat lighter, with a qualifying touch of civility about them. I have already mentioned the scene in the political cabaret (it became a London and an international hit) where Dr. Jonathan Miller, then a young comedian and star of *Beyond the Fringe* (1960), tried to explain himself, confessing: "I am not a Jew...I am *Jewish.*" The distinction is important, indeed it is taken to be profound—presumably by-passing, as I have hinted, the anti-Semitic insult. To be called "*a Jew*" appears to be menacing, one step towards the ghetto and the concentration-camp; whereas slipping sibilantly into an alternative denomination of one's own—say, "Jewishness"—could be considerably less fateful, certainly less fearful.

The slight phonetic advantage accrues only to assuage in liberal and/or mildly anti-Semitic societies where the sounds of racial appellations can play a small role in modifying the attitude of hostility and discrimination. But in extreme situations very little can help. An incident in the year 1945, in the first months of the U.S. Occupation of post-Nazi Germany, illuminates this distinction.

Two American officers of the U.S. Army's 42nd Division came to arrest Ernst von Salomon and detain him for questioning. (Out of which came only a few years of prison detention and a thick manuscript of *Der Fragebogen*, a best-selling book of the 1950s spelling out at great and colorful length all of von Salomon's answers to the official questions put to him in interrogation.) Von Salomon, who had a brilliant literary reputation in the Weimar Republic, was "not really a Nazi," only a stubborn right-wing intellectual who began his extremist career by helping to assassinate the Weimar Foreign Minister, "the Jew Walter Rathenau," in 1922. (He was tried and imprisoned; behind bars he was always creative, for in jail he completed his first best-selling book, rationalizing the foul deed of murder). Back in circulation, during the whole period of the Nazi *Reich* he busied himself by writing unimportant film scripts, and living happily with a Jewish girl named Ille. Two American officers named Sullivan and Murphy had orders to pick him up in the summer of '45 as "a big Nazi." When he packed his things he instructed Ille, then thirty-two, not to say anything about her non-Aryan origins, for fear of somehow complicating things unduly. Which it promptly did. After she identified herself she was told to pack her own clothes and come along as well for questioning and detention. She had tried, in her fluent English, to help her common-law husband as a common-law wife should; but in the lawless chaos of the postwar ruins no mitigating circumstances could help very much. She told Messrs. Murphy and Sullivan (as von Salomon has recorded it in his book): "Sir, I am Jewish" *(Ich bin jüdisch).* *

This served indeed to complicate the affair. "This makes it all the worse!" one of the Americans said, for what kind of a nice Jewish girl, a Jewess or a *Jüdin*, could be mixing it up with this bunch of Nazis? In other circumstances Ille's confession might have earned her a little more sympathy.

In the Anglo-American West, things were rather different. I recall in my prewar college days in New York that nobody asked in our student sessions (looking for friends and comrades or for ethnic heroes or other roots) whether a previously unknown literary genius (Marcel Proust, Franz Kafka, Hugo von Hofmannsthal) were "Jews," only "whether they were Jewish."

The noun is burdened with the hateful imprecations of the past. The postwar Germans shudder at the usage. The Jews, on their way to the gas chambers of Auschwitz and Treblinka, wore *Davidstern* badges identifying each one of them as a "*Jude.*" Jewish shops during the so-called *Kristallnacht* of 9 November 1938 had "*Jude*" (and the Star-of-David—or, even worse, *Juda verrecke!*) smeared on what remained of their storefront windows. Even in these prewar years the Swiss, eager in their neutralist weakness to appease Hitler's *Reich*, made the suggestion (in 1938) that the letter "J" be stamped in German Jewish passports and all other identification papers to facilitate recognition by the Swiss border police. (And, as we know now, for proper tagging by Zurich bank-tellers when Jewish refugees were trying to open secret Swiss bank accounts.)[49]

The contemporary Germans, cleaving to the postwar line of anti-Nazi orthodoxy, have developed their own version of a "political correctness": German writers who happened to be Jews are called "*jüdische Schriftsteller.*" Even the more modest, less conspicuous lower-case *j* in the language's required spelling cuts down the uneasy sense of guilt; the umlauted *ü* softens the plosive effect into a milder, quasi-diminutive; and the hushed suf-

---

*   Ernst von Salomon, *Der Fragebogen* (1951); *The Answers* (tr. Constantine Fitzgibbon, 1954), p. 433.

fix, as in English, quietens the whole tone. Heine and Marx were of "*jüdische Abstammung*" (of Jewish descent). The famous literary sons of Thomas Mann, Klaus and Golo, should never be called "half-Jews" (as had once been infamously prescribed by Hitler's "Nuremberg Laws") but half-Jewish; for their mother Katja Pringsheim Mann was not "a Jewess" *(Jüdin)* but...Jewish.

And yet. I suspect that there is something of a double standard among what happens in these recommended usages to be in or out. Ambivalently enough, in writing their own history, chroniclers and journalists and even playwrights swallow hard and record the direct noun usage for the sake of ugly truth or shocking dramatic accuracy. I note in the New York theatrical weekly, *Variety* (Oct. 23/29 1995) a review of a play which was being put on at the Theater Artaud by a group called the "Traveling Jewish Theater." The subject is Trotsky and Frida Kahlo, and their "odd-couple" relationship in the years of his Mexican exile. In one scene, as the *Variety* reporter notes, there is a sudden flashforward to Gorbachov's *glasnost*-Russia wherein a racist punk is on stage screaming the staccato three-letter word which wounds so deeply: "Russian people vas never Commie! Commie is all Jew! Jew! Jew!" The audience flinches. Try to have the same chilling effect by calling attention to Marxist-Leninists who happen to be of Jewish extraction.[50]

In Germany where, as I say, the post-Nazi newspapers have been on their best behavior for more than half-a-century now, there are occasional lapses, with the resultant shock, dismay, alarm. Optimists think of them as editorial inadvertencies and of no import; pessimists see ideological turning points and a sinister sign of a recrudescent racialism. One highly dramatic incident involved the controversy over a "Hollywood Manifesto" where some thirty leading American entertainers and film stars defended the so-called Church of Scientology from the attacks on its "dangerous totalitarianism" by the Bonn government. The protest compared the legal and bureaucratic difficulties which the Scientologists had been experiencing in the *Bundesrepublik* to the Holocaust of the Jews in Hitler's Third Reich. Among the American signers of the "Open Letter to Helmut Kohl" (published in the *International Herald-Tribune* in January 1997) were: Tom Cruise, Dustin Hoffman, Larry King, Oliver Stone, Gore Vidal, Goldie Hawn. The misguided petition was poorly written, inadequately argued. Its political charge was patently absurd, and it aroused the ire of Chancellor Kohl, who led a loud chorus of public outrage against the invidious comparison. The German measures against the Scientologists (and they have been refused recognition as a religion or a church...for tax purposes) are of the utmost legalistic mildness—the Germany of today cannot be compared to the Germany of yesterday (i.e., the murderous Nazi régime).

The newspaper reporting of the stormy affair was generally straightforward, except for one Munich publication which felt it significant that "Jewish

Hollywood stars were recruited for a dirty campaign against Germany." The otherwise unexceptionally liberal newsweekly called *Focus* went on, in a flash of suspect journalistic inspiration, to single out the stars in question. *Focus* published little colored photographs of them, as if they were wanted men and identified each—Dustin Hoffman, *Jude;* Larry King, *Jude*.... The dismay, and even distress, among the *Focus* readers was palpable. There had surely been no discreditable "Nazi" intention, perhaps only a thoughtless reversion to styles which remain virulent, at least in the language. How could they excuse themselves? I was told by a most embarrassed Munich editor that headlines are sometimes erratic, that photo captions often get it wrong, that the senior staff just didn't get around to proof-reading pages 186-187 of the 13 January (1997) edition of *Focus* before it went to press. Etc. etc.

Still, a taboo had been broken, a code had been violated; and both had been key pieces in the new postwar German support-system for normalcy: interfaith tolerance, ethnic understanding, multicultural enlightenment, and the like. Would all Jews now have to stand up to be counted, obliged to be identified with little badges of sufferance? The J-word is still at the inflamed center of a national neurosis.

The linguistic correctness of *anti*-anti-Semitism required, as I say, the avoidance of the J-word whenever possible (and especially in Germany where it still can have a fearsome effect when uttered at mass meetings, in the theater or on television). Anglo-American lexicographers have also been pressured to omit from their dictionaries traditional usages which denote the old denigrating myths and echo slurs about greed—namely, the almost obsolete verb for bargaining, "to jew down," and the not unrelated anti-Romany G-verb for cheating, "to gyp." Most editors refuse to play the censor and prefer the evasive strategy of "playing down and, if possible, omitting." A few journalists I know contend that it is best to use and over-use the words until they are exhausted and incapable of any kind of demeaning impact. One dedicated feuilletonist of my acquaintance delicately avoids even the turn to circumlocution and the cowardly euphemism in such references as "Albert Einstein, the scientist of Jewish ancestry" or "Franz Kafka, born into a Jewish family in Prague," and the like. Others go even further with this tactic by attempting to neutralize and render harmless, at long last, what was for centuries, indeed for millennia, an offensive appellation: they insist on writing bluntly, "Heinrich Heine was a Jew" or "As a Jew, Disraeli naturally took a long perspective..." etc.

These are valiant and well-meaning efforts, but I suspect that these highminded stratagems of linguistic subversion will prove to be of questionable value for the cause of tolerance and enlightenment. This particular word has thousands of years of historical encrustation, and it is not easily dusted off. In a brilliant book on "the Jewish question," the Irish writer, Arland Ussher, once pointed out that no small part in the violent history of anti-Semitism in Christendom was played by the fortuitous phonetic closeness of the name of the "traitor" Iscariot who betrayed Jesus, with the name of the people who lived in a land called Judea and were hated and persecuted as "Christ-killers"—*Judas* and *Jew* (in English), *Judas* and *Jude* (in German), etc. This is yet another case of what C.S. Lewis called "infection by phonetic proximity." As he once wrote (in his *Studies in Words*, 1960), "A word needs to be very careful about the phonetic company it keeps."[51]

In this spirit of verbal confusion, one Bonn journalist had a sinister explanation of the popularity in Germany of a Beatles' hit song entitled "*Hey Jude.*" He ascribed it to a resurgent neo-Nazi anti-Semitism among the hippie young, mispronouncing the proper, quasi-Biblical name as if it were a peremptory command to a hapless Jew. For, in this far-fetched mini-knowledgeability, Jude was not as in Hardy's novel *Jude the Obscure* (1895) about "Jude Fawley of Wessex," but "*Jude,*" as in the Hitlerite propaganda badge.

In point of hard fact, "*Hey Jude*" (1968) was, as the historian of the Beatles has documented it, "originally sung as if to Lennon's five-year-old son Julian ("Hey Jules") before McCartney changed it to something a bit more country and western." John Lennon later "described the song as the best his partner ever wrote."*

And yet, and yet... When is "a little knowledge" too little to legitimate a surmise or a theory? It could be that a little more knowledge—an hour or two of extra investigative research, a few more telephone calls, an Internet query—would only reinforce the original outlandish supposition. When I called my Bonn friend's attention to the awkward facts I have just summarized, he did a bit more digging and came up with lurid additional details which only thickened the plot. The Beatles had lived and played for quite a time in Germany, and had learned enough of the language to know what the word for Jew was. They had a penchant for double-entendres (the most famous one being the pun on "Come Together" which was thought of as a "sex-political" title, borrowed from Timothy Leary). The pop cognoscenti of the day always suspected that the "Jude" song was "aimed at Dylan," for Bob Dylan had been a great influence, now a close rival, and his real "Semitic" name was Zimmerman... Q.E.D.**

---

*   Ian Macdonald, *Revolution in the Head: the Beatles' Records* (1994), pp. 242-244.

* * Jude was, according to Matthew 13:55 and Mark 6:3, the brother of James and Jesus. His impassioned epistle is known as the Book of Jude (or Judas) in the New Testament. Judas Iscariot, the Apostle who "betrayed" Jesus, was also called "Jude."
    Various Biblical translations and exegeses have often made an unholy mess of all this. The confounding of names and sounds, the confusion of the godly and the ungodly (who were held to be guilty of the crucifixion of the Messiah) made for sectarian hatreds with recurrent bloody bouts of "theological cleansing"—sometimes known as pogroms, sometimes as inquisitions.

Whole legends can be concocted by tricksters in the black art of mistranslation and misinterpretation, poisoned with a drop or two of sheer misanthropy.

Be that as it may, it is clear that ecumenical progress in what is called "interfaith relations" will not be decisively influenced by countermanding verbal tricks, by strategies of semantic prestidigitation. Playing experimentally with old names that have mortally wounded may be an honorable exercise but, in the end, probably futile. Rabelais once wrote that there were some "bloody" words that were very cutting, "horrific, throat-cutting words." Must we live with them forever? The J-word, for one, can still draw blood, can still cut as sharply as the broken glass of Hitler's infamous *Kristallnacht*.[52]

Ultra-sensitivities in this connection have a notable side-effect in rendering reference books out-of-date (if, for their ultimate rarity and re-sell rates, more valuable). My *Dictionnaire* of synonyms and antonyms, published by *Le Robert* (Paris, 1994), has been subject to controversy, and its current edition has just been withdrawn from sale. This followed protests "over the word 'miser' and 'miserly' being equated with 'Jew' and words that might be translated as 'Yid.'" According to the promise of *Robert*, the offending words would be suppressed in a revised edition.[53]

Grammarians and etymologists often disagree and on occasion fall out violently amongst themselves; but philological revision is one thing, bowdlerization of dictionaries quite another. There are increasingly powerful ethnic-minority groups at work and each has its own posse of word hunters, riding hard on every new edition of popular reference books. Although there is a professional deformation involved—in addition to Samuel Johnson's "Sheer ignorance!" (his reply when asked why he had defined some word incorrectly)—changes nowadays do not come about when there is a sudden recognition that lexicographers who are daily poring over hundreds of thousands of words can grow blind to bias and deaf to inflection in what has been called "a slur blur."

The most recent example of polemical pressure is the case of the word "Nigger" as defined by Merriam-Webster in the current edition of the *Collegiate Dictionary*. A mail protest (amounting to thousands of letters) combined with a threat of a "national boycott" seems to have won this particular dispute. It is revealing that not the editors but the director of marketing at Merriam-Webster should announce the prospect of sensitive revisions: "We are definitely looking at it very closely. It is very, very likely that there will be a change in the definitions of all offensive words." It appears that a very, very new philological principle will be involved. To counteract a "slur blur" it is no longer sufficient to label an unfortunate or distasteful expletive as "offensive" when that very labeling also causes ethnic offense. Here is the disputed entry on "Nigger" in its entirety as published in the current Merriam-Webster:

1: a black person—usually taken to be offensive. *2:* a member of any dark-skinned race—usually taken to be offensive. *3:* a member of a socially disadvantageous class of persons [it's time for somebody to lead all of America's niggers...all the people who feel left out of the political process —Ron Dellums].

usage Nigger in senses 1 and 2 can be found in the works of such writers in the past as Joseph Conrad, Mark Twain, and Charles Dickens, but it now ranks as perhaps the most offensive and inflammatory racial slur in English. Its use by and among blacks is not always intended or taken as offensive, but, except in sense 3, it is otherwise a word expressive of racial hatred and bigotry.

The newspaper story I first read (as in many others I subsequently saw) failed to mention or otherwise identify who was conducting the "campaign." Nor did it suggest what a proper or likely compromise would emerge from the protesters' general insistence to "strike or re-phrase" the above-quoted definition. Many enlightened liberal readers would have thought the existing paragraphs quite unexceptionable and the fourfold references to the word as *"offensive"* in no way constituting a glossing over, "almost as an afterthought," of a slur.

But, as I say, philology does not follow etymology but the rules of the market-place; and most (if not all) publishers will be found in a capitulating mode when librarians, school-boards, and customer-friendly book-stores react as if they were tainted by a putative insult. The threat of a boycott is an especially powerful weapon (and it is a good thing that the family descendants of old Captain Boycott are not putting their own eponymous sensitivities into the mêlée).[54]

What causes a confusion amounting almost to moral disorientation among alert mainstream editors and journalists is precisely this single-minded dissatisfaction which regularly descends on spokesmen for ethnic disadvantaged minorities. Generally, there is a sense in the established world that, as one headline put it,

> THOUGH RACISM PERSISTS,
> PROGRESS IS UNDENIABLE.

Where once Ku Klux Klansmen and their fiery cross-burnings raged, Mississippi now leads the nation in black elected officials. This strikes the black columnist of the *Washington Post*, William Raspberry, as an effective argument against those bitter and impatient spokesmen of his black community who insist that "Nothing has changed!" Raspberry would agree that the road taken, i.e. democratic reform politics, is in point of fact what I have referred to as "viable," and he contends that on a wide front—from education and enfranchisement (where, in the deep South, millions were voteless) to a prospering dominance in various national sports (viz., basketball)—progress has indeed been "undeniable." Why, then, has it been denied? Whence the conviction that racism has remained the same? "How to explain it? Glass-half-empty myopia? Political gamesmanship? Whining as a substitute for analysis?" Doubtless, serious injustices remain, and Raspberry offers the practical (and, alas, rather boring) liberal advice to the radical voices in his own community, that it might be useful to keep those injustices in perspective:

> to separate the major from the minor, the urgent from the merely annoying—in order to put the most effort where it is likely to do the most good. It is hard to get an intelligent sense of priorities about what to do next when you are convinced that the net effect of all you have done to date is that: Nothing's changed.[55]

Is, then, the problem merely one of strategy or tactics in the further struggle for ameliorations, or solely one of maintaining morale in the camp of the reformers? Hardly.

In Britain, where both the scale of the racism and the countervailing progress have different dimensions, there are also voices in public opinion which smolder in similar denial. One explanation offered is the variant of Professor Parkinson's law by which no matter whether an evil is abolished or ameliorated, the vigor of the general protest and sense of outrage remains the same or, if anything, is intensified. This, as Peter Simple has argued in his column in the *Daily Telegraph* for many postwar decades, is due to the vested interest in outrage and its virulence as sustained by the so-called "race relations industry" and its special service known as "Rent-a-Crowd." How can things ever be perceived to get better? Whatever the real situation may be, what Raspberry refers to as "the same dismal assessment" applies to all the lives and livelihoods of one's underprivileged constituency. Nothing's changed, even if most everything is different.

Another account of the deeper factors at work has been circulating in the American press, stimulated by the theory of U.S. Senator Daniel Patrick Moynihan who draws on his Harvard-trained knowledge of the French sociologist Emile Durkheim. William Raspberry, distressed by the "nothing's-changed phenomenon"—and, possibly, disturbed by the amount of energy devoted to hair-splitting with harmless dictionary-makers—offers a version of his own. The Durkheim/Moynihan insight suggested that the amount of deviancy in a community is always roughly equal to that community's capacity for handling deviancy (viz., the number of policemen, courts, prison-cells). Should the amount of deviancy change, then we "Define Deviancy Down" (or "Up," as the case may be). Just as we use our existing capacity to punish deviant behavior that used to be considered tolerable (or vice versa: i.e., to tolerate what used to be punishable), movements for ethnic justice and equality maintain their piercing war cries to rally the troops—simply because we have agreeable formulas at hand and, indeed, a finite capacity for dealing with such problems:

And maybe that capacity will tend always to be fully engaged, no matter the actual amount of racial injustice. Thus, the mechanisms that once were used to deal with the most blatant forms of discrimination are not retired when Jim Crow ends; we merely redefine racist behavior up and proceed as though nothing's changed.

This remark does, I submit, illuminate. In other words: Moving between bouts of irritation and outrage, indignation intensifies to fill all the time and space allowed for it. This pattern of protest—always ardent and constant, never appeased or allayed—might well be memorialized in the sociology books as "Raspberry's Law." A little knowledge, often so wayward, can sometimes do a newspaper a power of good.[56]

Revisions and suppressions are a crude kind of solution, and doubtless of limited effect. In the newspaper culture the question of whether to print—or not to print—remains supremely challenging. Under what circumstances can offensive words be used, even at the risk of giving offense, in order to indicate the enormity of the rough expletive? President Richard Nixon often lost his cool in his quarrel with the Democratic Party and its constitutional opposition to his political career. As we now know, he took every challenge personally, even racially. Enemies were always trying "to kick him around." On occasion it called forth an unprecedented anti-Semitism within the walls of the White House which one observer (or, rather, auditor) deemed "sickening and incomprehensible" in its proportions.

Nixon was quite upset when he had heard, in preparation for the 1972 electoral campaign, that "big Jewish contributors" had been rallied to the support of such Democratic candidates as Vice President Hubert Humphrey, Senator George McGovern and Senator Edmund Muskie. Who were those (expletive deleted) Jews? "We have all this power and we're not using it. Now what the Christ is the matter?" He wanted their names. He wanted them "investigated." He made scathing references to them, which the press still bowdlerized, still withheld from the sensitive ears of the American citizenry who, presumably, might be offended by the language (as well they might!). Even one of his own campaign contributors he called "a cheap kike" (which, if it were quoted in the press, would emerge cryptically as "k—e").

A new set of scandalizing tapes emerged first in a report in the *San Francisco Examiner* in late 1996, and I was mildly surprised to see that the paper's correspondent (its Washington bureau chief, Christopher Matthews) was allowed so far as to quote this paragraph:

Bob, please get me the names of the Jews....You know, the big Jewish contributors to the Democrats. Could we please investigate some of the c—s—ers?*[57]

---

*   The actual words are, of course, clear on the tapes, and are duly transcribed in full in the National Archives documents, being made public. See: Stanley Kutler, *Abuse of Power: the New Nixon Tapes*, published by the Free Press in 1997, pp. 31, 451.

The *Washington Post* (and its *International Herald-Tribune* for readers abroad) edited the story a day later to read,

> "Please get me the names of the Jews," Mr. Nixon told his chief of staff, H.R. Haldemann, in an Oval Office meeting on Sept. 13, 1971. "You know, the big Jewish contributors to the Democrats," he continued. "Could you please investigate some of the [expletives]?....Go after them like a son of a bitch."[58]

No one has ever spelled out how an s.o.b. goes after people—for starters, perhaps, by ordering a sharp-eyed examination by the I.R.S. tax authorities— but the gross antipathy expressed in the highest Washington quarters would cover a multitude of disagreeable reprisals. For, as Richard Nixon was convinced, "The Jews, you know, are stealing in every direction...." "Stealing," here, is ambivalent. It could be the stealth of enemies who are coveting every opportunity to harm him; or, alternatively, it could be (as is notoriously well known) the greed of a people far beyond the dreams of avarice. In any case, one would have to wait for the published transcripts of these new "200 hours of Nixon tapes," made public recently by the U.S. National Archives, to find out how nasty or dirty or rude Richard M. Nixon could be. But as Russell Baker, the witty syndicated *N.Y. Times* columnist, caustically remarked, "printing Nixonic language will bring charges that you are corrupting children by writing such stuff in a family newspaper."[59]

Newspapers, whether devoted to familial niceties or not, have given a necessarily limited picture of Nixon reviling his sinister enemies; even the historical record is incomplete. When, in 1974, Congress mandated the release of Watergate-related tapes "at the earliest possible time," three years elapsed before the National Archives began processing the material; and when, in 1987, the transcriptions were ready, "the Archives chose to cooperate with Richard Nixon's continual efforts to prevent their release," as Professor Stanley Kutler charges. (Kutler was involved in the successful litigation which obtained disclosure.) In all there were approximately 3,700 hours of Nixon tapes, including several hundred more hours of conversations regarding the Watergate affair. Kutler has published only a first volume of some 600 pages, diligently edited, and he promises more. On the matter of the J-word which is our special subject here, he observes,

> Nixon's jarring language about Jews recurs throughout the tapes.... An anti-Semite? Perhaps.... Probably, what was at work here was that corrosive cynicism that pervaded Nixon's remarks.[60]

This is respectably tentative for an editor who has yet to publish all the evidence. Still, newspapers have already come to conclusions about the role of rage and racialism, of bias and self-pity, in the President's campaign against "the cannibals" who were surrounding him, and to what ex-

tent "liberals," "communists," "Jews," and "moneyed men" were leading the pack howling for his head. In Kutler's index there are eighteen
references to "*Jews, Nixon's comments on.*" Taken all together, they point
not only to a "cynical" attempt to hit back rudely at one ethnic element in
the anti-Nixon camp, but to the whole panoply of kinky little *idées fixes*
which has characterized manic anti-Semitic prejudice ever since the century-old dissemination of the *Protocols of the Elders of Zion* (later promulgated in the early 1920s by Henry Ford in his *Dearborn Independent*). Jews in America were rich and dishonest as the day is long;
when they are caught stealing, they have to be exposed and named in
full; and more than that:

> PRESIDENT NIXON: Scare the shit out of them. Scare the shit out of them. Now there
> are some Jews with the Mafia that are involved in all this, too.[61]

Indeed they are everywhere: running the Democratic Party, controlling Wall
Street, infiltrating Washington, and no wonder Nixon confesses abjectly at
one point (23 March 1973) that "we've been trying to run this town by
avoiding the Jews in the government...." The specifically "Christian" elements in his xenophobia are minor, although it is relatively unusual in a
Quaker to be taking so often the name of Jesus in vain—from delays in the
counter-campaign ("Christ, what's the matter?") to the exact religious af-
filiation of some suspected Government source who is leaking stories to
the press:

> PRESIDENT NIXON: Is he a Catholic?
> HALDEMANN: (unintelligible) Jewish.
> PRESIDENT NIXON: Christ, put a Jew in there?
> HALDEMANN: Well, that could explain it, too.[62]

Explain what? It is all too murky. Even the trusted Dr. Henry Kissinger comes
under a shadow when the *New York Times* – like the *Washington Post*, "Jewish-
owned"—manages to obtain fresh and inside information:

> PRESIDENT NIXON: There is another possibility, that he called Frankel [Max Frankel,
> a *Times* editor]....But Henry is compulsive on Frankel. He's Jewish.
>
> COLSON: Frankel, he's the Sunday editor. This was the Sunday edition, so he could
> well have—
>
> PRESIDENT NIXON: The *Times* works that way....They pass it around. You should
> check the Frankel calls....Henry—the *New York Times*, see if he talked to
> Frankel.[63]

In the evaluation of all this, it is the historians, not the journalists, who will be having the last word; and they are not likely to agree with the archivist (Susan Naulty) at "the Richard Nixon Library & Birthplace" in California who tried, unconvincingly, to argue that Nixon's enemies are only continuing "their work trying to perpetuate the false caricature that he is villainy incarnate." Was he not a Quaker (and Quakers are famously unprejudiced)? Didn't he earn the plaudits of Zionists in Jerusalem with his pro-Israeli foreign policy?

Still, alternating a certain diffidence with vague inexplicit denial, Ms. Susan Naulty argues that "there are no saints in the world." Hence Nixon was no devil. She also seeks a grammarian's refuge by suggesting that the slurring anti-Semitic reference to the American Jews who opposed him was "one of a series of proper nouns in an indistinct clause," as if that qualified in any way its odious impropriety. She seems to be saying that "it was a matter-of-fact use of a word, in an inaudible context," as if that cast any acoustical doubt as to the transcription of the malicious expletives in question. She contends that we are all caught up in "a crisis of murkiness," but nowhere in her long apologia in the *Washington Times* (28 February 1997) does she offer a direct and unambiguous refutation. She mentions "misunderstandings promoted by half-truths" (which can be held against us all, at most any time); she posits "the viciousness of double standards" (but surely other people's vices do not negate Nixon's own); she protests "the imbalance of Justice's scales to the advantage of rhetoric over deeds" (and it is indubitably true that some anti-Semites only stoop to mere calumny but others reach out for sticks and stones).[64]

The eminent conservative commentator, William Buckley, Jr., also thought it morally significant, and even decisive, for the assessment of guilt and/or obloquy, to distinguish between "anti-Semitic banter" and its translation into "anti-Semitic activity." President Nixon did, after all, hire as his close collaborators men like Henry Kissinger, William Safire, Herb Stein. Thus, some of his best friends (or, at least, White House colleagues) were Jews...despite the man's "loose bigotry."

In effect Bill Buckley, in his syndicated *New York Post* column, went a bit further, able Catholic casuist that he was. He tried to explain— perhaps even explain away—Nixon's views by insisting that the "paranoid" remarks were indeed rooted in the man's real paranoia:

He was a paranoid who consoled himself by excoriating real and fancied enemies. His anti-Semitism, we are by now entitled to conclude, was...a psychological buzz activated when he felt threatened or victimized or simply querulous.

Can, then, an ill speaker be blamed for speaking ill?

Nixon, as a human being, was a sad mess, with his suspicions, his fears and his loose bigotry.

In the end it was the paranoia that did it—blame the song, not the singer, the bigotry not the bigot. Indeed, in the final reckoning, not even the message was to blame but the message-machine:

> The tapes were a dismal mistake, perpetuating ideological and psychotic doggerel that fascinate the minds of those who are intrigued by scandal.

To be sure, it is also of some fascination to minds involved in moral issues; still, we are forced back to the scandalizing doggerel, to what we know from what the papers have been disclosing albeit with their dashes and asterisks and [deletions]. (Even Buckley, in his quotes, resorted to [expletive].)[65]

The newspapers, for the various and complicated reasons we have mentioned, are still reluctant to tell the full story. It is a wonder that even the offensive J-word was not deleted and put in safe square brackets. For long periods in their millennial history the Jews were a people that dared not speak their name. Even in its abbreviation the J-word appears to have its dangers. It cannot escape its tragic etymology, nor can it ever be uttered in phonetic innocence (as we shall see in what follows).

In the whole record of modern journalism there was one important story— and the efforts of scholarship did not round out the picture—that was rarely news and never effectively registered in the contemporary consciousness. Publicists have for a century now paid one-sided attention to the racism and bigotry of the Radical Right and its totalitarian ideology, with Fascism and Nazism as exemplars of hatred for Jews and Negroes. Ever since Emile Zola gave polemical passion to the *Dreyfusard* cause, the liberal and radical Left appeared to be wholly suffused with the Enlightenment values of tolerance and civic fraternity. Readers the world over were, as a consequence, ill-prepared for the news that the crusading Left harbored an illiberal temper, that Communism could also embrace anti-Semitism, that Marxist-Leninist parties instigated purges of "Jews and Zionists," that Soviet universities (in Moscow in the name of Lumumba of the Congo!) established an apartheid for their African students....

Yet the unimpeachable documents were there for all to read—and report on and make reference to (which was rarely done). A subtle mechanism of bias in the Western ideology blurred whole generations of publicists from registering sensitively another fateful source in our common tradition which predisposed social systems to genocide; they failed to spot the n-word and the J-word in whatever context they may occur. I conclude with a striking phrase from Karl Marx, who did not speak with "a forked tongue" when he was venting, privately, his full feelings. Here are the lines from his writings which, surprisingly if characteristically enough, disclose the elective affinities of the N- and J-words. Marx is writing to Engels (in July 1862) about a hated rival in the intellectual and political leadership of the socialist movement, Ferdinand Lassalle:

It is now completely clear to me that he is, as is proved by his cranial formation and [curly] hair - descends from the Negroes who had joined Moses' exodus from Egypt (assuming his mother or grandmother on the paternal side had not interbred with a *nigger* [in English]). Now this union of Judaism and Germanism with a basic Negro substance must produce a peculiar product. The obtrusiveness of the fellow is also *Nigger*-like [in English].... One of the great discoveries of our Nigger [in English]—which he only confides to his "most trusted friends"—is that the Pelasgians are descendents of the Semites.

So much for "the Jewish Nigger Lassalle...the grimy Breslau Jew with all kinds of pomade and make-up—all this was always repugnant."[66]

It is, regrettably, the inescapable conceit of intellectually playful wordsmiths, chronically unable to resist the temptation to believe what first occurs to them. They give credence to every new impression or inspiration and are instantly persuaded by a simple paradox or unexpected verbal association. They hold fast to what they can readily verbalize, what they can easily spell and punctuate and prettily paraphrase. For yet another example, here is Ken Tynan, a wordmaster of his day, writing in 1963: "Excerpt from Lenny Bruce's autobiography very funny: he says all Negroes and all dwellers in large industrial cities are Jews..." Tynan – unlike Marx (of the "Jewish Nigger"), unlike Mailer (of the "White Negro")—was utterly without larger pretensions to political theory and so found only humor in what others were persuaded to think of as a dazzling sociological insight...a sign of n-word and J-word solidarity. The permutations are not, to be sure, endless; but the combinations are considerable, each toying portentously with symbols of race, religion, or color. I even found a seventeenth-century usage in which James Howell, the future historiographer royal under King Charles II, warned against sinister political advisors who "infuse pernicious principles." He referred to the blackguards as "white Jews."[67]

The Case of "the Jew Rifkind" and Howard's End

Old-style press communications used to end with the editorial injunction: *"Copy Editors Please Note."* But there are days when experienced copy editors have time off, or their off-days. One incident on such a day (20 February 1997) followed on closely to the *Focus* misdemeanor which, regrettably, caused little newspaper comment and even less protest. A significant reaction to the first contretemps might, conceivably, have prevented the second; but, then, sensitivities on the subject in the second half-century after Hitler are discernibly on the wane.

A recent Anglo-German altercation over the J-word—following on from a German journalist's ill-starred reference to the British foreign secretary as *"der Jude Rifkind"*—was unusual. British public opinion has often been so inflamed, indeed has had ever since 1945 its regular outbursts of being "beastly to the Huns." As I say, that's what comes from the chronic habit of refighting World War II every other weekend on the TV screen (and winning every time). There is no comparable *Schadenfreude* on the German side. They only refight the Russians; all's quiet on the Western front. For whatever the Germans may have felt about their Anglo-Saxon enemies in the run-up to 1914, and the aborted cross-Channel invasion of 1940, there has for a half-century now been a deep longing to be European friends with their "English cousins." In that time-span I have sensed almost no important current of anti-British feeling (except, possibly, yesterday in front of the store windows of my local Berlin butcher-shop when I heard some grumbles about this alarming last winter of "mad-cow" discontent).

Still, political tensions were running pretty high—over the European boy-cott of British beef and the British aloofness towards prospective European integration—when Malcolm Rifkind arrived in Bonn to confer with Chancel-lor Kohl and also to make a public speech. The so-called "Euro-scepticism" of many leading Tories in Westminster led to much concern in the orthodox pro-European circles of the Kohl administration and in German public opinion generally. Accordingly, Malcolm Rifkind's remarks on the subject could hardly serve the battered cause of Anglo-German relations. His speech turned out to be diplomatic but not particularly conciliatory—in fact he went even further than the "neutral" Prime Minister John Major in declaring his own "hostility" to the *euro* single currency. The mounting British intransigence was duly re-ported in fairly non-committal dispatches to the European papers but only one was highbrow enough to be amused by the fact that the man, like Luther, stood his ground and could do no other.

The *FAZ*'s account was fairly brief and was printed on page two but it con-tained a single unfortunate phrase which triggered an international scandal. The paper's Bonn correspondent (only identified by initials, *mic*) had com-posed a dutiful summary but went in her last paragraph a mite further and tried to turn an ironic phrase—possibly it was a sort of a mild joke—and she concluded with an indelicacy which caused what I have called the J-word inflammation to flare up yet again.

In this light there was surely no deeper political significance in the whole Anglo-German case of the misplaced slur. The *Frankfurter Allgemeine Zeitung* meant no harm, the British foreign secretary took no offense. It could be that Malcolm Rifkind might have inadvertently started the whole tragi-comedy of errors by thinking that he could get a rise out of his Bonn audience by quoting a German quote in Germany: it was only, as they say there, carrying owls to Athens. More than that, he was ending a crisp speech with a crashing cliché (*Here I stand, I can do no other*) that every schoolboy is taught to avoid. And was he aware of the special spin involved in citing a subversive Protestant in the heartland of Rhenish Catholicism? The chairman of the Konrad-Adenauer Society's meeting (a former German ambassador to Britain, Dr. Jürgen Rufus) knew no better than to pick up the hackneyed phrase. And then the young *FAZ* reporter unthinkingly repeated it and made it her own—expressing surprise, in a whippersnapper of a remark, that "the Jew Rifkind" should be referring to Martin Luther.* She was blithely ignorant of the fact that not only have innumerable Jews been quoting Luther for a long time— indeed ever since his notorious anti-Semitic pamphlet of 1542—and have over the centuries even made their significant scholarly contributions to Protestant Reformation studies. How did the cool and calm Malcolm Rifkind, from the Scotland of John Knox, get into this god-awful historic-theologico-linguistico mess? But, I am afraid, that is the whole unfortunate story of the J-word ever since Pontius Pilate insisted on its being nailed to the cross on which yet another local protester and reformer (and Jew) had been condemned.

The British press had an excited week of "Teuton bashing," and the London tabloids made a meal of it, really went to town. The *Daily Mirror* made the silly, superficial, and in any case casual sentence into a deliberate act of aggression:

STORM OVER 'RIFKIND THE JEW' ATTACK
German paper in racist slur

The *Daily Mail* added fury to the storm with

OUTRAGE AS GERMAN PAPER USES 'NAZI' LANGUAGE ON RIFKIND

The bellicose headline writers of the *Star* went a step further and declared the matter to be something of a *casus belli*:

WAR ON HUNS
OVER JEW JIBE[68]

The quality broad-sheets were a decibel quieter in their presentation of the story but not conspicuously better informed. The *Observer* told us that the phrase in German "is as offensive as its English translation," which is palpably untrue (it is more so, in most circumstances, but not in this one). The *Guardian* on the same day told us the opposite, contrasting it with a nicer alternative,

---

*   The full sentence read: "Als habe ihn seine Rede nicht ganz überzeugt, schloss der Jude Rifkind—ironisch apologetisch—mit dem deutsch hervorgebrachten Lutherwort: 'Hier stehe ich, ich kann nicht anders.'"

In the *Times*' literal translation: ".As if he was not completely convinced by his own words, the Jew Rifkind concluded—ironically, apologetically—with a quote from Luther, delivered in German: 'Here I stand, I cannot do otherwise.'" *The Times* (London), 22 February 1997, p. 1.

"the Jewish Rifkind" (which is grammatically absurd, because this would be a
contrast with the Catholic Rifkind or an Anglican of the same name). The *Times*
correspondent offered a bit of erratic expertise of his own, asserting that "the use
of the expression 'the Jew' is not as jarring in German as in English..."; and even
an English scholar of Judaism averred "it doesn't sound as harsh in German as in
English...." (Chaim Bermant). The statements of the political parties were not more
helpful, a Labour M.P. expostulating "disgusting...appalling...," and a Conservative opining that "it stirs up our worst forebodings about closer political union
with Germany." A Sunday paper proceeded to muddy the waters by asking the
rhetorical question in a headline across four columns: "WHAT IS WRONG WITH
CALLING A JEW A JEW?," but answer there was none. A few days later a *Spectator* columnist ventured to suggest that "nervous genteelisms" like referring
to someone as "of Jewish ancestry" were to be avoided; and on the authority
of Marcel Reich-Ranicki, the veteran literary editor of the *Frankfurter
Allgemeine*, a Jew should be called just that.* (I have on occasion disputed this
point with Reich-Ranicki; but as a survivor of the Warsaw Ghetto in Nazi-
occupied Poland, he is entitled to have the last word.)

What of the reaction of the British newspaper readership to this potpourri
of reportage? To judge by the letters to the editor which a number of London
newspapers published in their correspondence columns, the readers out there
were evidently more informed and distinctly more sensible than the editors in
the hub. Several interesting differences emerge when one contrasts the newspaper culture (which always assumes it knows best what its public wants) and
the readership culture (which sometimes objects to what it is mindlessly fed).

*1. Eagle-eyed editors, so eager to spot foreign motes, had better pay atten-
tion to their own beams.* Fair-minded readers of the liberal-left *Guardian* reminded the editor that "Mr. Rifkind is not the only Jew to be described in
terms which recall the past...." Only the day before the *Guardian* had referred
to "ugly Jewish guys like Dustin Hoffman." As the constant (but self-critical)
reader concluded, "The spirit of Shylock seems to be alive at the *Guardian*
too."

*2. An informed conclusion by an experienced reporter can, despite its self-
confident air, amount to the very opposite of the truth.* A number of knowledgeable and sensitive readers pointed out to the Editor of the center-right
Times that there is no "moral equivalence" of the J-word as used in English
and in German, although anti-Semitism is immoral and deplorable everywhere.

---

*   I checked this quotation with the author, and in a reply Marcel Reich-Ranicki
     qualifies the remark by stating that half-a-century after the end of the Third Reich
     there is the "stubborn consequence" that the word "Jew *(Jude)*" is still a form of
     insult and abuse. Nevertheless, he himself doesn't feel put out when some scoun-
     drel or hooligan is identified as such "so long as the same tag is applied to Einstein
     and Freud when their names come up...." (Personal letter, 3 July 1997.)

The differences are as night and day. In England the anti-Semitism harasses a small Jewish community daily with annoying social and political restrictions. In Germany it darkly resounds to the murder of millions.

3. *A little knowledge, confined merely to the very recent past, can be a poor guide to a deeper understanding of complicated current events.* A letter from a history-minded Oxford don to the Tory *Daily Telegraph* recalled for its editors, who had rationalized anti-Jewish sentiments of the past as a regrettable part of bygone times, that even by the given standards of past times the diatribe of Luther *Against the Jews and Their Lies* (1542), had been deemed shocking and offensive. Erasmus had been notably alienated by the roughness of Luther's views and the rudeness of his tone. And within Germany itself, the Rabbi Jossel of Rosheim made plain his objections to "a man who had bowed in fear and humility before the infinite majesty of God" and yet could contend that "we Jews should be treated with violence and tyranny...because we decline to believe what Luther believes." In that spirit—and the references underlined the historic presence of "the other Germany"—a violent plunderer of the *Judengasse* in Frankfurt was executed in 1616; Hamburg refused in 1648 to extradite a Portuguese Jew to the Catholic authorities (who claimed him as a renegade from baptism); and in 1671 Jews exiled from Vienna were welcomed to Berlin. "The people whom Our Lord once dearly loved, from whom our Messiah was sprung," as Frederick I of Brandenburg decreed (in 1703), should be treated with compassion. The history lesson was not intended to "relativize Auschwitz" or moderate the general sense of German guilt, but it threw light on the ignorant and indeed cynical over-simplifications with which contemporary J-word incidents are reported in the papers.

One other item of history, contributed by a writer in a weekly which, happily enough, has several extra days to put a news-item in perspective. The argument she put, underlining her warning to *Mind Your Language*, was that "any English use of *Jew* from past centuries tends to seem now deliberately offensive, innocently offensive or offensive only to the ignorant." Coleridge is cited from his *Table Talk* (1830): "Jacob is a regular Jew, and practices all sorts of tricks and wiles...." This she calls *offensive*. As for a character in an Iris Murdoch novel (1956) saying, "I'm as rich as a Jew," this was deemed *innocently offensive*. The matter, alas, can get even more complex:

> And in the mid-17th century translation by Horn and Robotham of the *Janua linguarum reservata* we find: "Saltpeter, brimstone, Jew's slime, petrol, bolearmoniak...are called mineral juyces." Here *Jew's slime* is a mere reference to Genesis xi 3, where the builders of the Tower of Babel put their bricks on a layer of pitch (as later translators than King James' committee render it). This usage was never meant to be offensive, and only sounds so to ignorant ears.

The conclusion is not so dialectical or complicated as it might be—

There is a street in the City of London called Jewry. I doubt if its name will be changed; nor should it be.

There is also a restored *Judengasse* in Frankfurt and even an intact *Judenplatz* in Vienna. May they long evoke memories which keep a vital life-line to the truth as it actually was.[69]

As for the conclusion to the "Rifkind scandal" itself, the British Foreign Secretary, true to the unflappable diplomatic tradition, put the incident quickly behind him. He wanted no, and expected no, apology. The young Michaela Wiegel (28, *mic*) kept sedulously silent after having, in a few further bursts of innocence, tried to defend her genuine surprise that a Jew might—could, would, and did—quote a German Protestant; and left the field to one of her paper's Frankfurt publishers, Günther Nonnenmacher. He had similarly blundered with defensive explanations—"We were only trying to be funny"—adding injury to insult by claiming that the phrase as published by his paper and picked up angrily by every British paper in the land was utterly harmless. German jokes, as the *FAZ* publishers were gingerly reminded, have a reputation for going astray (and not only Mark Twain found them often too grim for a smile). In any case there had to be a measure of damage-control since the British press reaction was running amok, even to this wild parody of the German response which actually had been brief and almost taciturn:

> How dare they impugn our honorable motives! We are as magnanimous as Siegfried, as pure as Brunnhilde! And what impudence that this Rifkind, this Britisher, this Jew, should quote our beloved Luther, our German Luther, in our own innocent faces! It is an outrage. We demand satisfaction. Our patience is exhausted.

Dr. Nonnenmacher was finally persuaded to offer an apology for whatever misunderstandings and offense a sentence published in his newspaper might have caused in foreign eyes. He also committed himself to a "guarantee" that his newspaper would never use the offensive phrase in the future. Does this presage the end of the J-word in Germany?

A backward glance and an historical aside, following on from my reference to Pontius Pilate. The J-word had its earliest origins, if a little historical imagination be allowed, as a fateful Roman acronym, the alphabetical abbreviation of *Iesus Nazarenus Rex Iudeorum*. It signaled the contemptuous Latin tag at Jesus' crucifixion: "King of the Jews," inscribed traditionally over the cross as *I N R I.* * This particular "scarlet letter" of victimization,

---

* According to Luke, 23:38 (tr. King James), the mocking "superscription also was written over him in letters of Greek, Latin, and Hebrew...." This was, to be sure, the main point of the Roman indictment: namely, that Jesus had set himself up as "King of the Jews" or as "Christ the King of Israel" (Mark 15:2). In Martin Luther's German translation it is rendered as "der Juden König" (*Lukas* 23:38), *Lutherbibel erklärt* (ed. 1974, N.T., p. 167).

also rendered pictorially over centuries in classical Christological art, goes back a shamefully long way. It is not likely to disappear by simple editorial command.[70]

The J-word case of Michael Howard, a senior minister in Prime Minister John Major's cabinet who was in the running for the Tory Party's leadership after the Conservative defeat and Major's resignation (in May 1997), followed hard on the heels of the Anglo-German altercation over Malcolm Rifkind (which I have described above). The essential life-and-death difference between the two scandalizing incidents was that, in the one, a man was called "Jew" by foreigners who had half-a-century ago murdered many millions of his co-religionists but today, in a profoundly altered Europe, could not harm a hair on his head. In the other, his own anti-Semitic countrymen could do in Michael Howard, at least liquidate his political ambitions. A London paper reported that his wife, during the heated campaigning among the various Conservative candidates, was

> clearly irritated that her husband's unpopularity is, in some way, connected to his Romanian-Jewish origins: "The country has moved on from that. I don't think such things are relevant."

This was audibly whistling in the dark as, in the next days, the factor of Jewishness skulked more and more into the controversy. It came up in the very newspapers which had preached enlightened reticence (to the Germans) in the Rifkind affair but were making a meal of it when the J-word (in English) broke into their own national politics:

> "In many ways," said the experienced MP chomping lightly grilled steak opposite me, "Michael Howard would be a good leader, but there's no chance of it happening." "Why not?" I asked. "The man's a Jew," he replied, evidently piqued by my inability to see what to him was glaringly obvious.

The newspaperman should not have been so surprised. Alan Clark, another senior Tory politician, records in his published diaries that many of his colleagues (and he agreed with them) were contending that Nigel Lawson, later chancellor of the exchequer under Margaret Thatcher, could not "as a Jew" be a contender for foreign secretary. It was felt, as the *Sunday Telegraph* candidly reported, "that Jewish parentage was disqualification enough."

The qualities of mercy were very much strained by the press. The *Daily Mail* wrote that Howard's problems with his party "stem from his origins... his father Bernard Hecht was a Romanian-Jewish refugee" who "changed his name to blend in." Howard comes from an "insecure 'outsider' background."

The unfortunate turn in the anti-Howard campaign began with a critique of Howard's administration as a strict and powerful home minister (in charge of law, the courts, the prisons, immigration, etc.) by one of his former deputies.

But she was robust, if a tad tasteless, in rejecting talk of her being anti-Semitic: "I can *kibosh* that...".* She had, she revealed, been for many years a member of the Conservative Friends of Israel; and, presumably, some of her best friends in the Middle East were Jews. But her telling phrase about Howard—she hinted darkly that there was in his character *"something of the night"*—sounded sinister enough to be taken up again and again. Her critics retaliated by calling her "Doris Karloff." Monsters be here, and the argument began to draw blood. Although there was nothing sharp about the phrase, neither witty nor aphoristic, it was quoted several hundred times in the innumerable articles about the shadowy character of the man—as if Dracula (also of "Romanian origins") or Fagin (of Dickensian shadows) were loose in the land. Even Howard himself (in defensive denial of course) spoke of "the diabolic darkness of my inner soul." Indeed in his energetic campaign he nowhere mentioned the "anti-Semitism" factor in the mounting opposition to his aspirations.

There is, I am afraid, a ubiquitous embarrassment on the part of Jews in such circumstances, soul-trying moments when accusatory fingers are being pointed and one is not quite sure what to confirm or deny. Recall the dramatic American case of Secretary of State Madeleine Albright, who learned so late in life that she was not born as a Roman Catholic in her native Czechoslovakia but as a Jew; her parents, alarmed by Hitlerism, had the child converted and sent abroad for safe refuge. There ensued a not dissimilar congeries of unclear emotions. As Martin Peretz asked in the *New Republic*, "Why does she seem so embarrassed?...Why could she not simply have said, when asked, 'Yes, although I am not a Jew myself, I descend from Jews.'"[71] I suspect that Peretz knows as well as Mrs. Albright that there has never been anything "simple" about it. The German writer Kurt Tucholsky also, like Heinrich Heine, "left Judaism" and confessed, shortly before his suicide, to "not realizing that this simply cannot be done."

Or, cannot be done simply. The theological formulations are difficult, the ethical sentiments complex; and even at the last moment the proper and possibly correct words are liable to fail one. The J-word, prickly with thorns, is in many contexts just too sharp to bring easily over the lips.[72]

In the case of Michael Howard, to what extent did anti-Semitism explain the public unpopularity of Michael Howard or the party-political reservations of his colleagues? A perceptive British commentator, Bruce Anderson, addressed himself to the embarrassing question. Unlike some others he saw no evidence that it did. He conceded that the Tory party could not normally be

---

*   *Kibosh* was used here because it is widely taken to be a Yiddishism (and Mrs. Widdicombe surmised that one who uses Jewish phrases can't be all bad). Mencken refers to it in his *American Language* (pp. 307, 704) as a 19th-century Anglo-American usage. The *Oxford Dictionary* (p. 118) is uncertain about *kybosh* and cites a paper in Glasgow in 1834.

considered philo-Semitic, but there have been in the last two decades two Jewish home secretaries, one chancellor, and one foreign secretary; and at one time in the Thatcher era there were five Jews serving in the Cabinet. He insisted, and it seems to be true, that there is no bar to Jews rising on merit in the Tory party, and that there was no reason why there should not be a successor to Benjamin Disraeli...except, possibly, for the *anti*-philo-Semitism that was now seen lurking under the surface. Everybody recognized the Star-of-David when they saw it (especially when they took the trouble to draw a six-pointed star), and everybody seemed to be tallying up the score of contenders and keeping a little list of ethnic origins.[73]

Columnists hurried to dredge up old and hoary anecdotes about famous Jews in Britain and their friends among the Tory grandees (for whom anti-Semitism is said to be simply an extension of profound, if polite, snobbery):

> "Since you are known to hate Jews", Victor Rothschild said to one of the most prominent Tory Cabinet ministers of the 1980s who had agreed to be his guest, "why are you coming to lunch with me?" "Oh, you're different"....a characteristic variant on "I decide who's Jewish", Goering's famous answer when accused of having Jewish friends.

Wounds which were thought to have healed long ago were re-opened with earnest discussions about whether the Jews were "rootless cosmopolitans." Could they truly "belong" to any nation? Were they likely ever to be fully integrated? Lord Denning ("the greatest Law Lord" of the time, comparable to a U.S. Supreme Court Chief Justice) was quoted as referring to the widely respected Sir Leon Brittan, the British commissioner to the European Union, as "a German Jew telling us what to do with our English law." The *Mail*'s city editor, Andrew Alexander, who felt that the prospect of Howard's leadership was "appalling," explained that "Lord Denning was in fact trying to make a perfectly sensible point about Leon Brittan." A hundred and fifty years ago they were making such perfectly sensible points about Disraeli and his ancestry. Old antipathies can only thrive again when they are recycled into circulation. Repetition of slurs, as has long since been sadly recognized, tends to add to their renewed dissemination.

Perhaps it was of some help to enlightened attitudes when the British press, unlike the equally serious and perhaps more sensitive counterparts in Western Europe and the U.S. "let it all hang out," as one troubled observer remarked, trying to salvage some little grace from a disgraceful episode over an agitated week in democratic politics. At least issues, long slumbering, were brought out into the open. New code words of prejudice were identified and outed. As Alasdair Palmer wrote in the *Sunday Telegraph*:

> "Insecure outsider background" is exactly the code you hear from people who want to remind you that Howard's origins render him unsuitable for leadership.

"You can't change Michael," I have heard it said. 'It's in his blood.' He hasn't got the manner which blends in. He just doesn't understand the conventions of English behavior....

Perhaps if Howard wasn't so combative, being Jewish would not be a problem. All the pejorative adjectives that were used about him were used about Mrs. Thatcher. But given that he is Jewish, those characteristics become a convenient code for why he is genetically unsuited to become leader. The obstacle, as they say, is "in his blood".

What begins in the semantics of a J-word ends up in blood and tears, with genes playing more of a role than genitives, and whole vocabularies are conscripted to do service in dubious battle. Our newspaper culture, like the hospital surgeon dealing with his patients and their grim diseases, can be clinical or be circumlocutory, holistic or economical, that is, can tell the whole hurtful truth or be genteel, humane and evasive with little white lies. Either way, as Brecht-Weill used to sing, the circumstances remain just what they are. Our well-meaning short-sighted editorial stratagems—on behalf of truth-telling or of doing good, two valiant causes which are often mutually exclusive—get hung up on recalcitrant realities.[74]

On the Most Powerful Words

I venture the argument that the most powerful words appear to be Janus-faced. When spoken in the extremes of anger, of hope and passion, they often echo as if pronounced with a forked tongue, sometimes twisting and turning antonyms into an ambivalent whole, as if besting (or worsting) the language represented the subtlest of profane victories. This, I suggest, may be part of the answer to the question which Anthony Burgess has raised about the human paradox involved in taboos, euphemisms, circumlocutions, and other vagaries of our language.

In another place—in my book on *Utopia and Revolution* (1977)—I paid attention to the political words in ten centuries of Western idealism whose historic power came from the various and conflicting layers of meaning. The ruling élites need watchwords, and the wordy intelligentsia feel themselves called upon to formulate agreeable populistic variations. At their high points, connected to electrifying events, they had both direct and alternate currents of suggestibility. My thesis was that "Revolution" was just such a word, and the concept had just such energies as it moved around, in one phase, in Copernican circles—and, in another, straight-on in linear progress to a Robespierrean "republic of virtue" or a Marxist-Leninist "realm of freedom." Its associated metaphors also have this positive and negative energy, a circuit of plus and minus, which give their imagery its special galvanism. Revolutionary events resound with the metaphorical joy of, at long last, the *"earthquake...storm...flood...volcanic eruption...spark* and *fire* and *conflagration,"* as if it were perfectly natural to welcome such catastrophes as beneficent turning-points for mankind!

But I digress. My only point in this context was to call attention to the complexities in two of my basic themes of newspaper culture: *"a question of style"* and *"the quest for meaning."* They are often overlooked in modern journalism as it struggles with "political correctness" which tries to re-edit style and censor meanings. Our newspaper culture lives in the tension between loyalties to liberal decencies and the necessities of truth-telling. It often compromises itself between democratic commitments and professional straightforwardness. This is, as we have been seeing, especially troublesome in what the papers say (and how they say it) about two subjects of special journalistic concern—namely, about races, in societies where enlightenment wrestles with bigotry; and about obscenities, in languages where liberal permissiveness strains to be absolute.

Diluting the Deadly Epithets

Clichés, true to their technical origins, get mechanically reproduced and end the way all stereotypes do, in the scrap heap: broken, useless, and sometimes even unrecognizable. But in the beginning, if a first coinage can be recorded, it was all fresh and different, newly-minted and attractive to behold. Every reader knows the sensation: you see an unfamiliar word or a phrase once, and then again, and thereafter simply everywhere. Sooner or later, if one reads and listens attentively enough, one begins to react to the buzzwords in the environment as to a small electric shock. I have been paying attention to some of the most highly charged clichés in our daily vocabulary, and have been suggesting that in certain flamboyant periods they can attain a certain special wantonness. We know of debauched words—ranging in origin from the erogenous to the ideological—that are still actively around; and we have pinpointed some corrupt phrases and verbal practices that exhibit themselves daily in our newspaper world.

One caution must be added. This literary routine of repetition, marked ultimately by verbal over-work and semantic exhaustion, can in a curious way produce a certain immunity to its own worst effects. Earnestness can give way to coyness, and ingenuity to playfulness; both serve as a kind of reader's protection against more serious damages. When the style of referring alphabetically to the verbiage of obscenity became widespread enough—and Random House has published a whole book under the title, *The F-Word* (1995)—it proliferated into other contexts. This functioned to give a *soupçon* of pseudo-obscene implication to other P-words and s-words that needed a bit of enlivenment; and in so doing, I am afraid, the four-letter tradition of scabrous signs demeaned itself for all serious lovers of low language and profanity-fanciers. Thus, in newspapers of ideological passion, whether Liberal or Conservative, there has been much editorializing about the "L-word" or the "C-word," and in between the lines one can catch the saucy imputation of illicit expletives. This represented the ideologization of an originally blue or off-color alphabet. In the presidential campaign of 1996, when practically no one wanted to be identified as a *liberal,* President Clinton was seen to be "running away from the *L*-word," and such abandonment of liberal values was alphabetically classified in such a way as to give a rough touch of the power and danger of dirty words. Illiberal opportunism was indeed held to be *obscene* (and Senator Eugene McCarthy, the valiant old standard-bearer of liberalism, said as much in his press conferences). The bright-eyed trend-spotters for the *Economist* newspaper quickly caught the echoing pattern of the "resonating rhetoric" and simply concluded: "The *L*-word is back."[75]

Similarly, the Republican candidate, Senator Bob Dole, in his efforts to move to the middle where the electoral majorities are supposed to live, was accused by the right-wing faithful of fearing to use the "C-word." In the American context where "conservative" is taken to be a synonym for a hide-bound reactionary, the senator was caught trying to avoid a word which some millions of "unconservative" voters might consider rude, coarse, and alienating. As for some of his neo-conservative intellectual followers they were also charged with the concise vice of "overlooking the *G*-word," G- standing here for greed as in "the unacceptable face of capitalism" (and in the financial scandals associated with shifty characters in Wall Street). In an editorial entitled "Democracy and The *P*-Word," the editors of the *Washington Post* observed in that treacherous summer of 1996 when this kind of quasi-acronymic habit spread like the plague: "In a notable departure from the overriding message sent out by the Democratic convention, Jesse Jackson dropped a four-letter word: *poor.*" How shocking can you get? But in a time when all four-letter words are, or should be, "outed" and are to be used resoundingly when necessary (and even when not), this is in the mode of straight-talking and telling-it-like-it-is. Alas, the Clinton strategy was disappointing the *Post* and driving it to write about the *poor* and their *poverty* although this was a rude issue in the eyes of "swing-voters." The paper remonstrated, "Thus the Democratic platform avoided the p-word....Once it had seen itself as the advocate of the poor as well as for the working class." Suddenly Clinton had betrayed the cause. For some he was an Iscariot turned informer; for others it was as much of a culture-shock as if Lenny Bruce had just cleaned up his act. What liberal hope remained for "an administration and apparently now a party so deathly afraid to use the *p*-word"?[76]

In the end the politicization of the profane innuendo, this stratagem of sharing the shock, serves to add to the diluting of the power of the slang, the *in*-lingo, which has come to mark the contemporary journalistic demotic style.

Realpolitik is being seduced by "dirty realism." None of it comes out very happily, but the family of rude expressions has grown extensively.

In this extended family of shady words (or the abbreviations thereof), there is not only a weakening of meaning and suggestibility but also an essential domestication of tones and tropes that were once considered outrageous. Ice-cream companies, advertising their new delicious flavors, boast of the "F-"-of-the-month; fat-free diets play with the f-word to give their recommended nutrition extra sex appeal. A Chelsea haberdashery on the King's Road in London—it was called saucily, for no obvious reason at all, "The French Con-nection" (or *FC*)—once covered its show windows with the good news of its English connection, i.e. its commercial incorporation in the United Kingdom. The acronym was also plastered all over its other shops—*FCUK*. Someone—an alert passer-by? A quizzical critic of "advertising standards"?—suspected it was a devious typically Gallic double-entendre, in fact an anagram of the f-word, aimed vulgarly at the funny-bone, with a nudge and a wink, from the *French Connection* world. Could it possibly help sell their special line in men's blue jeans or ladies' skirts? Might it not upset, offend, or otherwise alienate customers? It did. The Council on Advertising Standards issued a high-minded reprimand (in October 1998). The company's directors then announced, pre-sumably covering for their pale blue joke, that the f-word hadn't occurred to them, was (you better believe it) very far from their minds. They had thought of it simply as a catchy logo, and were not in the least implying that their clothes fashion was "sexier." So did *FCUK* have an interrupted career on a Chelsea shop window. All traces of it have been removed. None of the local newspapers which had reported the story even bothered to spell it out. Anagrams of four-letter words have a very limited suggestive range. There is, then, an extra dividend to the f-word popularity in coarse general usage, producing a kind of illicit black-market titillation, a sort of salacity by the side-door. One gets something of the rude force of the expletive in a context which has nothing to do with dirty realism. Thus, in the stormy discussions on the European scene as to how much centralization the vari-ous nation-states will willingly cede—how far all real power is to be del-egated to the EU Commission—there is constant reference, smilingly and slyly phrased, to "the dirty *f-word*," which stands for federalism. But in every European political culture the concept of what is "federal" is differ-ent, ranging from a strong unitary super-state to a visibly weak balance between the central power (in Brussels, in Strasbourg) and the old powerful local parliaments in Britain, France, Germany, etc. Consequently, the talk about *"the dirty f-word"* amounts to an "effing euphemism"; and its emptiness as-sumes almost Australian proportions, full of s—d and f—y, signifying noth-ing. I note in the *Frankfurter Allgemeine Zeitung* that *"dirty f-word"* is used by German journalists as a risqué Anglicism, adding an exotic bit of foreign-language eroticism to its high-minded political reportage.

The dissembling deployment of foreign words and phrases has, of course, been a favored strategy of evasion and euphemism. Only language-wise insiders get the sly point; and even they, with the years, often forget the original traces of an embarrassing etymology. Accordingly, we have to be rudely reminded by a Washington expert on "Philadelphia lawyers" that the derogatory vernacular name for them, namely: *shysters*, had its scatological origins in the German (i.e., *Scheisse*). It is still a bit tangy, but has been nicely cleaned up as a nearly acceptable, if still *vulg.*, sub-category of the legal profession. Shrewd underworld defendants, angling to get off lightly, often hire "a shyster of a lawyer" to handle their cases. He can be counted on to be clever and endowed with all the courtroom trickery to deal with tough judges or impressionable juries. But, as Safire notes, the nature of *"the so-called Philadelphia lawyer"* has itself undergone a transformation. Once—so far from being a *Scheisskerl*—the name denoted the perspicacity of "an especially learned advocate," preferably "from Philly." What a fall was there! (Blame it on the Germans and their penchant for domesticating the crudities.)[77]

An extra thought on this blue aspect of the jabberwocky which may soon obtain in the "global villages" of the West when fashions in language, as in all else, turn multicultural.

The gross difference in the German usage of faecal references in contrast with Anglo-American practices in English surprises, and even shocks, many foreign visitors. The latest on this front is the *Gegendarstellung*—a compulsory statement-of-correction under the Federal Republic's Press Laws—which was obtained by no less an injured party than *Bundeskanzler* Helmut Kohl.

Stern magazine, a liberal-left picture weekly with the largest national circulation (almost two million on good Thursdays), reported that the chancellor at a Christian-Democratic party meeting had called one of his critics a *"Klugscheisser"* (a rude pejorative which, pithily, refers to "the witty-shitty arrogance...of a clever shit-ass," or something like that). Dr. Kohl denied it, and he demanded that *Stern* publish his own version of what had been said; which *Stern* duly did, and all the country's newspapers reported the "retraction." The headline in the *Süddeutsche Zeitung* (Munich, 26 June 1997) read:

KEINE "KLUGSCHEISSER"

The official transcript of the CDU meeting was cited and, sure enough, the K-word was not to be found therein, at least not as a noun. It did make an appearance as an adjective, and Dr. Kohl quoted his irony verbatim: "I've been reading many *klugscheissende* newspapers that just know everything...." And in another place, as the standard eight-letter word, quoting a critical voice in his Pfalz homeland: "What kind of *Scheisse* are you up to in Bonn?"

The German gradations of rudeness and the differences in social acceptance of the several variables are, I find, altogether under-appreciated. In fact the film technicians who are responsible for dubbing Hollywood films for Germany's movie houses (and for the television screens where, again, somewhat different standards apply) have their work cut out for them. In many cases—the Quentin Tarantino films, namely, *Pulp Fiction*—they have to rewrite chunky bits of screenplay dialogue and even to invent whole expletives of equivalent profanity!

Mutatis mutandis, this applies also to the translations of novels from the English and, as the Germans insist on saying when it comes to overseas fiction, "*from the American.*" One classic and prize-winning translation of James Joyce's *Ulysses* (by George Goyert) was recently denigrated and withdrawn from circulation, and replaced by another edition in which another translator tried again to grapple with obscenities and the puns thereon which are, in the last analysis, untranslatable.

This "culture gap" between the various f-words (and other four- and eight-letter words) gives a writer like Elmore Leonard a distinctly different "atmosphere" in each foreign country—although his popularity in every language apparently remains steady no matter what his raunchy characters happen to be saying. Nowadays any kind of dirty word can get clean away with everything.

Strong words do not live well with disabilities. Beyond the natural wastage, there is also the unnatural phenomenon of over-loading certain casual bits of language with quasi-profane or pseudo-obscene implications.

It used to be conventional in pacifist circles to proclaim, at the height of impassioned peace-loving rhetoric, that "War is an *Obscenity!*" Years of semantic dispute were to no avail. War is *not* "obscene." It is hell, a crime, a holocaust, whatever you will; to call it obscene is not only inaccurate and incorrect but basically too good, too benevolent, and is even flattering to the phenomenon of mass murder on the battle-field.

It was not simply philological finickiness that drove Kingsley Amis in his small book on *The King's English* (1997) to repeated protests against the use of *obscene* and *obscenity* to refer to things that may be undesirable but are not "grossly indecent, or lewd." But when the *Oxford English Dictionary* numbered a reference to Vietnam among its citations from the ideological usages of the militant 1960s Amis had an additional political motivation, angrily challenging its quotation to the effect that "Vietnam was the most obscene episode of the century." He usually hesitated to quarrel, even on a small scale, with the authority of the *OED*, but "to my mind, it goes wrong here":

> What we have seen, I would maintain, is...the impious and impudent hijacking or bagging of a word for sensationalist purposes. The kind of person who calls the events in Vietnam *obscene* is being irresponsible under the guise of moral shame. Dreadful things happen in the world all the time, and they are not made more

objectionable by being misdescribed. These are not grossly indecent or lewd; in a word they are not what we have nowadays come to understand by *obscene*, however disgusting and depraved they may be.[78]

Any kind of distinction along these lines gets lost or becomes meaningless in the agitated and demagogic discussions of whether pornography as well as politics enjoys the absolute protection of the U.S. Constitution's First Amendment. A lively recent debate was occasioned by Milos Forman's film entitled *The People vs. Larry Flynt* (1996), Flynt being the owner of America's largest and most profitable "porn empire." Forman's film has been called a "raucous hymn to the First Amendment"; and since pornographers have also been included as rightfully expressing their constitutional "freedom of speech," what the "redneck vulgarity" of this movie amounts to is a portrait of "an unabashed smut peddler as its patron saint." It is also a raunchy mélange of porn wrapped up in a stars-and-striped patriotism.

In one scene Larry Flynt asks, "What is more obscene, sex or war?"—as scenes of gentle porn are intercut with grisly episodes from My Lai and Hiroshima.

What I have referred to as the demagogy comprises the insincerity of a happy and dedicated pornographer who asks self-serving rhetorical questions about "immoral equivalents" and answers them to his advantage. Obviously, if wars can be called "obscene," then even the hardest of porn is less so. A soldier is, then, more sinister than a smut salesman. In the final contrast, according to the porn credo, murder and death are set against love and *joie de vivre*.[79]

By now this verbal pacifistic misdemeanor has almost completely disappeared, since real obscenities—gross expressions of lewdness— have become *de rigueur* in many enlightened and avant-garde circles of our new culture. If obscenities are "in," what shocking expletives remain to serve our revulsion in the denunciation of war? "In-lingos" do not survive outing.

As a consequence, other words—and some harmlessly lightweight in appearance and movement—have turned out to do the heavy duty in an excitable time of semantic sensitivity. One such was the subject of a front-page story in the *Times* of London. It recalled to mind the tempest-in-a-teapot altercations that once, centuries ago, accompanied immodest and insulting name-calling in Parliament or, abroad, the use of the *mot de Cambronne* and the *Götz-von-Berlichingen* aspersion. The *Times'* headline:

LUVVIE IS A TERM OF ABUSE,
SAY THE STAGE FOLK

Here is a case when a new and young and very raw recruit is conscripted into the front lines of fire where the battle over words is part of a war to the death. Not to be confused with the traditional Cockney term of salutation and endearment ("Good morning, *luv*"), the word luvvie was apparently coined in 1991 by the editor—then Ian Hislop— of *Private Eye*, a satirical London weekly which already had popularized other terms of abuse (i.e., "hack" and "hackette" for all journalists, good or bad—and Randolph Churchill had obtained a writ of libel against being called one).

"Luvvie" caught on very quickly as a descriptive noun for actors (and, especially, actresses) of every sort, from quiet and polite matinée idols to darling divas, gushing and all-embracing. After five years or so of wounded vanities, the theatrical profession hit back: "One of Britain's leading directors, Trevor Nunn, has declared war on the word *'luvvie'*. It is, he said, 'as appalling and abhorrent as any racist word.'" Since in our tender epoch of ultra-sensitivities there is no culture or sub-culture worthy of the name that has no *cause célèbre* built into its outraged sense of dignity and honor, groups and grouplets must find enemies that hate them. They search out epithets that offend pride, parenthood, and profession, and then proceed to thunder against special names that denigrate and have to be expurgated from the language.

Ours is an age of new universal imperatives: driven by the promise of aspiration and fulfillment, of entitlement and empowerment. Let a hundred cultures flower; let a thousand utopian dreams flourish. Each people and every race has it and does it. So do the genders and each of the sexually-challenged split-offs...not to mention the long and the short and the tall who, not unlike Boston beans, also do it. As an irreverent old cabaret song cracked, Where lesbians can flaunt, can thespians be far behind? One actor (Nigel Hawthorne) said, "Actors loathe the word *luvvie*. It's the same as *queer* or *gay* applied to homosexuals. People don't like being categorized."

Worse than that, according to Trevor Nunn,

> It's a word that's had a deadly impact. I think it's a word as disgusting as the word "yid" or "nigger". It categorises everyone of a particular grouping as the same; and not only categories them, but patronies them and puts them down. It's a word that says you are hysterical, trivial, under-educated, self-indulgent, absolutely regardless of your background, education, lifestyle or manner.

It is a philistine word, evidently invented by "the Philistines," and a glance back at Josephus' history of the wars of antiquity will tell you why that tribe was unloved by Samson, Saul, and David. And if the Philistines were not Semites, and so rendering a reference to "holocaust" racially incorrect, the theatrical profession has been warned. *Love* (the word, the feeling) is, as is well-known, very close to hate. Accordingly, the "L-word" is taken to be deadly, and all l**vies have been cast to live in fear and trembling.[80]

The Bard, as so often, hit just the right tone:

> As in a theater, the eyes of men
> After a well-grac'd actor leaves the stage,
> Are idly bent on him that enters next,
> Thinking his prattle to be tedious;
> Even so, or with more contempt, men's eyes
> Did scowl on Richard.

> *(Richard II*, ii, 23.)

I suspect that in times past the popular usages of the pejoratives represented not merely the prejudices of the age but the semantic availability of easy locutions, a recourse to strong and simple words that came trippingly off the tongue. The expressions were short and pithy, often fashionable; and one was mindlessly (and without too much emotional or moral commitment) carried along with the identifiable sentiments.

This is surely true of such English-language tags like *wog* ("the wogs begin in Calais"), like *yid* ("the yiddle with the fiddle"), like *wop* and *coon* and many others. Sometimes one or the other word dramatically loses its vogue, not infrequently under moral pressures—and one wonders incredulously how the writers and the politicians of only yesterday could have been so blithely indifferent to ethnic or religious sensitivities.

Sheer verbal exhaustion plays a role. But the so-called conversation of mankind undergoes regular and, on occasion, fundamental changes of vocabulary; and the moving and shaking force is, of course, the *Zeitgeist* with all its own determinants in the life of society. Obviously *"Industrial Personnel"* are no longer the lowly grubby *mechanicals* of a century or two ago; and although the universal presence of a trade union movement has contributed to cleaning up and humanizing our language, I am afraid that workers can still be maltreated, snubbed, exploited, excluded. No amelioration is total or global, and if our speech has in some ways been laundered—"ethnically cleansed," so to say—the hard improvement in social relations and perhaps even in basic personal/ethical sentiments is not necessarily equivalent and corresponding. After all, one doesn't need the n-words and the J-words to be a bigot. One doesn't have to be saying *"Sir!"* all the time in order to be respectful or polite. Love and hate, bigotry and civility would find their way in life without such verbal coaching on the side.

Still, I like to think that the linguistic laundering of our time, for all the absurd excesses of the commissars of correctness, has helped a bit toward an enlightenment. I can recall a classic put-down in a liberal newspaper of a generation ago which one laughed at, admired, quoted repeatedly; and yet I, for one, am pleased that it belongs to a *buzz* that can never come again. The occasion was the attempt at a film version of *Othello* by that titanic figure in the history of the cinema, Orson Welles—whose masterpiece was *Citizen Kane* (1941), but he never approached its force and originality again. Ken Tynan, famed for his ruthless wit, mixed praise and criticism in his *Observer* review, and—throwing his liberal-left ideology to the winds—couldn't resist cracking: "Welles' Othello is the lordly and mannered performance we saw in *Citizen Kane*, we have adapted to read 'Citizen Coon'."[81] Unworthy, even at the time (1952)? Maybe—but worth looking back at in tranquillity. No English or American editor would publish this pun today; even more, no reader would find it funny. At least this C-word* rests in peace.

Mysterious are the ways in the art of the insult, especially in an era when slurs may or may not be deemed to be politically incorrect and even take on a special character if they are pronounced to be officially one thing or another by a court of law. Does name-calling get less vicious if a judge declines to find guilty a certain popular expression which features nastily in streets, saloons, and stadia? Do the victims wince less, or do the hooligans seek whingeing alternatives, if offensive remarks are held to be... inoffensive?

Complaints in Australia provide a case in point. Recent complainants, mostly British expatriates, have taken a Brisbane newspaper, the *Courier Mail*, to court for repeating that hurtful cry of their grand-stand enemies—"*lousy Pommy bastards!*" (here the matters of lice and legitimacy are of no importance but the central pejorative is). It was the Human Rights and Equal Opportunities Commission, no less, which sat in judgment. Sir Ronald Wilson, its president, said the term Pom was unlikely to offend, insult, humiliate or intimidate: the criteria which would merit a ban.

Well, hundreds and even thousands of the annoyed who do claim to feel the smart of contempt and hostility still keep on "whingeing"; but Australia's Anti-Discrimination Board also joined in the general understanding that a fair degree of journalistic license and oratorical excess is essential in a democracy. And this particular expletive does not bear the ear-marks of impermissible malice or scurrility. London etymologists have long assumed that the origin of Pom was an acronym for "Prisoner of Mother England" which is now only a mild out-of-date reference to penal exile; and even the *Australian National*

---

*   Why was this, historically, ever abbreviated from raccoon?

   Bartlett, in the 1841 edition of his *Dictionary of Americanisms* (p. 91), gives only "a nickname applied to those who belong to the [American] Whig Party"—"coonery" being a political abomination and "Rout the 'coons!" an electoral cry of the Boston Democrats.

   In point of fact, its slangy derogatory ante-bellum usage for the "Negro slaves" has been recorded earlier, i.e. in minstrel tunes of the 1830s about "dandy niggers." In *Uncle Tom's Cabin* (1852), Harriet Beecher Stowe has them referred to, with more affection than hard feelings, as "coons" who were escaped slaves. Later on they were loafers, banjo-players, black bastards, etc. See: *Random House Historical Dictionary of American Slang* (ed. Lighter), vol. 1, p. 477.

   As late as 1992, CBS Morning News was broadcasting it in connection with racist police actions: "It was a classic 'coon hunt'...."

Dictionary says it is a shortening of pomegranate which somehow was related to a corruption of "immigrant."

Does this smack of the loyalism of an establishment-minded academe? Australian loyalists to England, beholden to the monarchy and other features of the old country, tend to accept relatively harmless derivations. Trivialization helps to pacify hotheads. On the other hand, rabid republicans and nativists, for whom the English will always remain the hateful eighteenth- and nineteenth-century prison wardens who transported convicts across the seas to the penal colony down under, are naturally tempted to come up with ruder versions. I will refrain from citing other, more salacious ascriptions. The fictionally enhanced etymology is interesting but not credible. Playing anagrams with the P- and M-words, detectable in *lousy Pommy bastard*, reveals only the hostility held to be inherent in the history of a humiliating colonialism and its hapless victims.

In the end it all imposes on the fragile word of disparagement a heavier burden of antipathy than it can credibly carry. It becomes weighted down with extra apocryphal elements so as to accommodate the ultimate rudeness. This is a rather unusual and rare semantic phenomenon. Where the expletive is not strong or verbally resourceful enough to support an expanding public emotion (hatred or defiance, disrespect and disdain, resentment and rivalry) it is reinforced by random apocrypha about the obscenity of the origins.[82]

All languages with a pretense to literary discrimination are known to go to extreme lengths in devising aggressive expressions that can wound and even destroy or, at the very least, do dirt upon their enemies. Herodotus, the so-called "father of history" (*circa* 850 B.C.), records one of the earliest ethnic slurs by which an ancient Greek conqueror, in "a spirit of contempt," changed the "heroic" names of his subject tribes, once glorified in Homer's poems. His own tribe was to be known as the *Archelai*: "rulers of the people." As for his victims, the changes were, as Herodotus notes, "highly invidious...full of bitter mockery":

> for the names he chose were derived from the words "donkey" and "pig" with only the endings changed....*Hyatas*, "pig-men," *Oneatae*, "donkey-men," and *Choereatae*, "swine-men." (*Book. V, 68*)

Over the milennia the intractable spirit of conquest embodied itself in more indirect and even subtler ways, resorting to slight inflections, minimal mispronunciations, and other phonetic devices to register a similar contempt and sense of superiority. Sometimes, when the occasion called for more invidious originality, the words coined were of a cruel and vicious ingenuity. But often they came up with damp squibs. It is a wise victim—and a sensitive editor and keen-witted reader—who knows the difference.[83]

17

The Art of Punditry

Slanguage

I have already touched upon the splendours and miseries of slang in journalism; but the balance in this context—the search for significance in the reported events, the quest of meaning by the so-called pundits—this balance-sheet is almost totally negative.

I did not always agree with Walter Lippmann's columns—except in my very early teen-age years when I first discovered how good English sentences (in this three-pieces-a-week column in the old *New York Herald Tribune*) could, in each brief contribution, no longer than a thousand words, make a thoughtful point, clear and incisive, and worth further thinking about. I imagine he didn't ever give a moment's consideration about whether he was being "entertaining," or amusing or catching the reader's attention. He was not an entertainer but an educator, a publicist trying to shed light on the public and national interest. His prose was fashioned accordingly. Not even in his conversation—and I lunched with him a dozen times, in London, Berlin, and Washington—did he allow a slangy word—"demotic" he called it—to divert him from his effort to formulate precisely. And this was, as he was persuaded (and so am I), only possible if the language of discourse is conventionally concise.

What about "color"? Was it all to be good, slow grey pontificating? In Lippmann's case, the color was in the clarity, and the pace was in the movement of his reflective mind.

There are dozens of other examples, famous and forgotten figures, about whom much the same could be said. In my short list: Raymond Aron's columns on world affairs in the Paris *Figaro*; the commentaries of Richard Löwenthal and Sebastian Haffner in the *Observer* of London; the short essays on the *"terza pagina"* of the *Corriere della Sera* (Milan) and later his own paper *Il Giornale* (Rome) of Indro Montanelli. I would also add the star over many decades in the *Times* (London), when he was not off writing about Wagner's *Ring,* Bernard Levin: florid rather than compact, persuading more through his eloquence than his logical argument. But a master, nonetheless, of clear, forceful prose in the style of great traditions (and, as I fancy, Samuel Johnson and John Stuart Mill would have approved). A case should also be made for Max Lerner in his later, memorable *New York Post* days, pronouncing lucidly on the state of the world till his death at eighty-seven (in 1989), and with a journalistic flair that didn't subvert his paragraph-by-paragraph qualities of learning and sage judgment.

On the other hand, "slanguage" is a means of being amusing, colourful, attention-grabbing, if, at times, making a nice point for all that. But the addiction to slang, to in-language, to jargon, and street-smart lingo in contemporary journalism has tended to make a mockery of thoughtful communication. When professional commentators turn to writing like sports reporters, rock-and-roll chroniclers, and sob-sisters, we all begin to sound like the Rolling Stones, gathering no moss nor meaning. If foreign policy of great (and small) powers is still a serious matter, involving life-and-death issues, then it should still be written in a manner in which Messrs. Jefferson, Montesquieu, Tocqueville, Bagehot, and their ilk, would have recognized. Would they have recognized this? "Sending the U.S. Army into Haiti is more like sending the police to break up a game of a three-card monte on an urban street-corner."[1] This is from a senior *Washington Post* commentator, Jim Hoagland (usually a straightforward and intelligent writer); and even if he would explain to all and sundry what kind of game "monte" is, the analogy could not be saved or defended. He could have used "blackjack" (possibly more familiar), or changed the game to rolling-the-dice (with "snake-eyes" coming up more often than it should); and it still would be a tacky, puerile way of making a point. But, then, who wants to be taken to be a long-hair using long words? Even pundits like to be one of the boys. It is, I am afraid, the tell-tale mark of the smart-aleck.

Another estimable member of the *Washington Post* "Writers Group," syndicated to millions of readers throughout the U.S., is a commentator called Edwin M. Yoder, Jr.; and he is addressing himself to the consequences of the Republican landslide over President Clinton's Democrats in the November 1994 elections. He tries to make the level (which was low) credible to his readers by referring to the hit movie of the day which was a piece of violence and vulgarity entitled *Pulp Fiction.* Thus, politics is just like the movies: full of "moronic verbal violence," of "low-life cheapness" which ends up becoming "hilariously self-satirizing."

Expertise, Then and Now

Whatever connotations the "punditry" of "the Pundits" may have—and they range among the columnists from impassioned polemics to a pretense at profundity—that which we get served up in our newspapers is a mixed bag of commentaries that try to make out the meanings of war, and editorial paragraphs that mark out fine-principled attitudes. Profundities are not to be expected. As Oliver Wendell Holmes famously remarked, original thoughts need to be stated obscurely before they can be put clearly. But the newspaper is enjoined to clarities and indeed to simplicities, and over-simplification can be the scourge of journalistic style in our newspaper culture.

The *New York Times* has never been a vehicle of subtleties. Its coverage of foreign as well as home affairs falls far short of any touch of complexity, and until fairly recently it did not require of most of its writers more than elementary expertise on the subject, even when reporting from abroad in far-away countries about which nobody knew very much. In the 1930s Herbert L. Matthews's dispatches during the Spanish Civil War were naive to the point of venality; and in later years he practically admitted as much (and confessing as well to related mental lapses in his guileless coverage of Castro in Cuba). The *Times*'s mediocre reports over long years from Hitler's Berlin and Mussolini's Rome by Otto Tolischus and Arnaldo Cortesi, respectively, were (apart from the fact that the reporters spoke the local language) less superficial than insensitive and stolid in the light of the tragedies which overtook Nazi Germany and Fascist Italy, and indeed all of Europe. As a youthful reader in New York I myself turned away impatiently from the *Times* to follow the incisive dispatches of Edgar Ansel Mowrer in the Scripps-Howard newspapers and even to the high-pitched cries of warning from Dorothy Thompson. No further word should be lost here on the case of the unworthy Walter Duranty, accepted as a reliable and brilliant correspondent in the Soviet Union during his extensive stay as the *Times* representative, but long since exposed—first by his colleagues Malcolm Muggeridge and Eugene Lyons, who both served in Moscow at the same time—as a cynical liar, a fraud, and even worse (i.e., a "Gaypayoo" agent). Such apologists, all wily, experts in whitewash, are well known in history; and the historian Lord Acton remarked (in what was called an "immortal adage"), "Every villain is followed by a sophist with a sponge."

The editorial-page column of foreign-affairs analysis was conducted in the *Times* of those days by good, grey Anne O'Hare McCormick; and I defy any researcher to go back to thousands of her columns and come up with even a brief, useful quote of any prescience. Still, the prose was at least stately; sentences and paragraphs were traditional in form and vocabulary, circling trimly in-and-around any diplomatic subject as in some slow waltz they danced in the Congress of Vienna. Her successor was the estimable C.L. (Cy) Sulzberger of the *Times* publisher's family—a patrician of a journalist; and I encountered him in a dozen European capitals, breezing in and out, writing as he roamed. He was short on interpretive insight but long on travel, and he conducted quick interviews indefatigably. The anthologies of his *Times* pieces still make for evocative reading; and, here and there, one runs across historically revealing remarks which he diligently recorded from the mouths of the high and mighty on the world's diplomatic stage over the period of his decades with the *Times*. (I still recall, with a quiver, a quote from Maxim Litvinov in wartime Moscow which, had it been paid attention to in time, might have prevented half-a-century of Cold War between East and West....)* [2]

The *Times* column on foreign affairs, which could doubtless be the most influential commentary in the formation of Western public opinion, is written currently by Thomas L. Friedman, who started out as the correspondent in the Middle East and is a press veteran of the wars in Lebanon. For in the beginning was his end. As one acidulous critic who has followed the first year of Friedman's travels to illuminate the world for the world's greatest newspaper (and I reckon it is that, even if by default), has sharply written,

> As an observer of foreign affairs, Friedman's primal and paradigmatic scene was Lebanon. That country has become his metaphor for all wars and all truces. Wherever Friedman goes, he sees Lebanon. Ireland is like Lebanon, Bosnia is like Lebanon, Oklahoma is (sort of) like Lebanon. [3]

Shameful thing to have to say, but the *Times* columnist needs to be reminded that neither Ireland nor Bosnia are "like Lebanon"; and that Chechnya, Rwanda, Colombia, Kashmir, and Somalia are also not like Lebanon. "Lebanon is like Lebanon."

> That is why there are foreign correspondents to distinguish between the wars of the world, rather than conflate them all in a single image of war and peace. And what makes Lebanon the measure of all things? Only the columnist's experience. Friedman seems almost completely incapable of considering his subject without referring to himself. It is always "I think" or "I have a feeling" or "my guess" or "I can be the first columnist to write...," as if writing a foreign affairs column is a form of autobiography.

Notable is the new folksiness in the land; in the old days in the *Times* it was exceptionally represented by a touch of populism in the one-paragraph "Columns" contributed by the wit and folklorist, Will Rogers. Now it echoes reedily through the whole paper (and not only there), with Friedman opining,

---

*   On C.L. Sulzberger, see: *The Big Thaw* (1956) and *A Long Row of Candles: Memories and Diaries* 1934-1954 (1969).

> I don't know much about Bosnia. But I have a feeling that I've been to this play
> before. It was an almost identical conflict between Muslims and Christians, and it
> was called Lebanon.

The homely confession of ignorance in a foreign-affairs expert is the least of
it; in his next column a few days later (on 7 June 1995) he gives vent to the
pseudo-emotion of an outraged unconcern: "I don't give two cents about Bosnia,
not two cents. The people there have brought on their own troubles." Noble
sentiments indeed, and in an elevated language which would do justice to the
penny press of the yellow period of our popular journalism. (In a mix of callousness and demagogy the editorialists of the day used to insist that the poor
have only brought it on themselves; that the Jews were to blame for anti-
Semitism; that victimized foreigners or raped women or other unfortunates
deserved what they got; etc.)

Neither the ethical nor the intellectual content improves when the man moves
closer to home and contemplates the foreign policy of the current Washington
administration. He is not uncritical of President Clinton, but in his judgement
"he has good instincts on foreign policy." Will it be instincts that will conduct
us safely through the perils of world conflict? Our Manhattan Clausewitz has
come up with the ruling dictum: "Foreign policy is just politics with a bigger
map." Which leads directly to the sage advice he gives to a man whom he calls
"Chris," namely, the then Secretary of State Warren Christopher: "Unless you
are willing to out-Serb the Serbs and out-thug the thugs, stay at home." If this
means what it can be read to mean, that the *Times* could be advocating policies
of "ethnic cleansing" to beat the Serbs at their own war games (which include
in the mid-1990s thuggish massacres of men, women and children), then the
editors together with the foreign-policy expert of their own choosing might
wind up before the International War Crimes Tribunal in the Hague. But they're
only joking, fellas....

Are our British cousins any better? For several generations now they have
been sitting through the same Hollywood A- and B-pictures (now made for
TV) as their American cousins, munching the same kind of popcorn in the
dark and coming away with the same flickering impressions, give or take a
black-and-white fade-out or two. We all know in our bones that the John Waynes
in the end will manage to save the big ranch, the decent homesteaders, and the
hard-pressed town folk from the depredations of the villains. The heroic imagery is transatlantic, the shared impressions on the juvenile imagination in-
delible.

And so here is a British correspondent in the Balkans recently, stepping
dangerously into a mine-field of loaded clichés:

> A simple way of looking at the UN role in eastern Bosnia is to see it as a sort of
> cowboy movie—but a movie in which the bad guys always win. A small town is

threatened by a brutal and rapacious band. A group of righteous gunslingers step in to help, to the relief of the citizens. When the show-down occurs however, the good guys bottle out. Instead it is the drunken, unshaven aggressors who carry the day.

If this is, "more or less," what has been happening in Srebrenica and in the other beleaguered safe-havens in the Yugoslavian civil war, then one can retire whole academic faculties of Balkan scholars whose expertise has been leading one to think that things were rather more complicated than that. The reporter—Patrick Bishop, in the *Daily Telegraph* (12 July 1995)—persists with his Western scenario: "Inevitably the question is being asked again: What is the point of having good guys if they don't do any good?" If one accepts for the moment (as addicted newspaper readers are condemned to do) the populistic conceit which can distort every world conflict into a showdown of the good guys versus the bad guys, then a half-column later the patient reader can emerge, in this particular case with several valuable insights, and they do serve in extenuation. Such a dispatch can be saved from trivialization by the sheer experience of an open-eyed correspondent in the field—three years on all the ex-Yugoslavian fronts, in Bishop's case—and a spot of earnest, if clever, writing:

> Humiliation is a way of life for the UN in Bosnia, in which new depths of abasement are continually plumbed. Daily they are insulted, ignored, cheated, robbed and shot at. The shaming experience of the Dutch UN troops in Srebrenica counts among the worst of the indignities the Blue Helmets have had to suffer, and resuscitates the old debate: should we stay or should we go?

And, in the end, on to a clear and important conclusion, well put and quite far from the opening Wild West vulgarities (although the Biblical invocation of the military apocalypse is a bit of a muddle itself):

> The attitudes of the UN and the countries leading the UN effort are formed by a mixture of *realpolitik*, concern for prestige, and genuine humanitarian sentiment. It does not make for a very coherent policy. Professional seers gazing into Bosnia's future tend to predict either Armageddon, or a process of muddling through. There is a third, particularly Bosnian alternative—that of muddling through Armageddon.

As I say, triviality and vulgarity lurk perilously, and sometimes even the most thoughtful of columnists slip badly. Here is the estimable Andrew Alexander of the *Daily Mail* going on about the "surprising" victory of Prime Minister John Major in a recent Tory re-election contest in which many conservative papers (the *Times* and the *Telegraph* among them, sensing the unpopularity of a lost cause) shifted allegiance. Did the Tory press "get it wrong"? No, they didn't, as Alexander valiantly argues. They were accurate: but they were, after all, "dealing with a remarkably slippery electorate," hence bluffing and double-bluffing in order "to confuse the various camps and the lobby journalists." So far, so good—these are the conventional lame excuses of false prophets ever since the *Literary Digest* got it notoriously wrong with its Gallup-Poll in the U.S. elections of 1936. But Alexander goes on to write,

> Ah—say the Majorites—but the Tory press got it wrong and got egg on its face because it advised MPs to ditch Major and they declined to follow that advice. This, you must surely agree, provides a whole new slant on human affairs.

Well, what was this "whole new slant on human affairs" that was suddenly breaking in on our old perceptions?

> By this logic, Jesus Christ got it wrong because his advice has been largely rejected by mankind. What a lot of egg on His face! Ho ho, how embarrassed He must be, eh? Using the same logic, Adolf Hitler "got it right" because he gave the Germans a lot of advice which, alas, they were only too happy to take.[4]

After so much fuzzy logic, one is driven to ask how much nonsense a columnist is obliged to write before his columnar space is amply filled? The long perspective of decades and centuries is being invoked in order to try and win a little argument over boring old yesterday in Parliament. Neither Christ nor the *Führer* have been making the news headlines for a long time now.

18

In the Pseuds' Corner

Neuro-Linguistic Shadows

It is cheering to be able to register the fact that within the business community itself, plagued with hucksters whoring after vocabularies wearing heavy make-up, there is a self-critical note that provides at least a minority dissent. Probably there is a bottom-line profit in it, or a special consultant's fee for managerial advisors who offer some new dish, some simple fare which begins, like all good morning cereals should, with a *snap-crackle-pop!* A writer in *Business Life* observes, "Now that we've been outward bound, inwardly motivated, moved sideways and vertically challenged, is there anywhere for management training to go?"[1] The answer is: almost nowhere, for we have had

> team-building, bonding, energizing, empowering, de-stressing, and all the other buzz-words that boldly verb their nouns....Where does all this go? It creates an office environment of people who've recycled their giants, got empowered and downsized their globalization. Re-calibrated, re-engineered, and ethically cleansed, they good-step around the canteen yelling "sell, sell, sell."

The onset of psychology in the world of managerial culture has introduced a new style in programing which is referred to as "neuro-linguistics"; and it is popular enough to be seen to be replacing previous techniques called "psychometric testing" and "mind-mapping" in the education of capitalism's cadres.

But, in the end, we appear to be left with a linguistic residue, with increased "noun-verbing." The executive classes, whether trained in Tokyo or Topeka, Kansas, continue to get their pithy, if woolly, instructions, as in *"If you always do what you've always done, you always get what you've always got"* or *"Life must be lived forwards, but can only be understood backwards."* The new courses have an elemental earthiness about them—*"Tame that phone!"*...*"What Do You Say After Hello?."* But the neuro-linguistic improvement is more apparent than real, for how improved can prose style become when the emphasis is increasingly on non-verbal communication? At the moment there is less about *re-engineering* (replacing people with machines) and *effective non-verbal communication* (which "means kicking ass"); *outplacement* ("meaning kicking ass over the hill"); *time management* (i.e., "making sure it seems like you're always the last out of the building"); *ethical cleansing* (sacking anyone who disagrees); and *going through the personal visioning processes* ("calling dial-a-horoscope").

There is more about *shadowing*. It is supposed to be "a good catch-phrase, nicked from a dead philosopher"; but, in this case, no intellectual derivation is obvious to me except possibly German-language men of letters who wrote in and about the shadowy subject (Strauss/von Hofmannsthal, *Die Frau ohne Schatten"*? von Chamisso's *Peter Schlemihl?*). Alas, there is also a technique of verbal shadowing, and the example is

> [A] growled "teach the postroom boys a lesson" becomes...a suggestion that the postroom needs the correct instructional objectives with sequenced learning materials to produce a facilitated visionary session.

In any event, what a "new generation of satellite-empowered psychologists" have come up with is

> The effective shadow should study what could be described as the chairman's non-verbal communications: the width of his pin-stripe, his preferred lunch venues, and tell-tale logos such as b**** Lloyd's on his socks.

Whatever the logo actually told when deciphered, *noun-verbing* may be coming in *via* the back-door. Certainly the stereotyped asterisks have long since qualified as tired old buzz-words in the business life.

A complex reply, with some difficult words, is sometimes reported straightforwardly—in order to give the reporter a chance to explain arcane concepts. (He could have asked another question, and then included the simple explanation; but he didn't, a little complexity being better than a surfeit of simplicity.) And so we get a European Union story about a possible new leader, "They're not looking for a very visionary European....They're looking for a down-to-earth, pedestrian sort of president who would emphasize subsidiarity."[2] The reporter then adds, with a slight touch of acerbity, "'Subsidiarity' is EU talk for limiting the role of the Brussels bureaucracy." This kind of obscure vocabulary coagulates in clots in even the prose efforts of popular writers who aim at a large readership, although they are not beyond the temptation of appearing to be professionally technical masters of an "in-lingo." The book reviewer for the *New York Times*, a knowledgeable man in many fields, objects to the "incoherencies" which annoyed him in a new account of the bankruptcy of Macy's department store in New York, especially the jargon in the chapters on its financial follies:

> We are all economists now [writes Christopher Lehmann-Haupt]. But we are not all sophisticated that we can follow, without a little coaching,...rapid-fire references to "senior subordinated debentures," "non-recourse senior real estate debt," "clean-down requirements," "debtor-in-possession financing" and "the cash flow ratio coverage covenant relative to debt."

It not only rained on Macy's parade (which can happen in New York's inclement weather) but also on the parade of infelicitous abstractions which makes financial journalism so wet and clammy.[3]

The standard joke about the parents having to wait for their children to come home from camp in order to press the video buttons to time-record a favorite TV program also tells us something about DIY prose. Neither Sony nor anybody else has apparently been able to explain the procedure in any manual of English-language instructions which has the merits of simplicity and confidence-building persuasion. The general literary difficulties with such manuals which have proved such a bane to consumer happiness persist. Obscurantism rules, and it has been a Sisyphus labor for decades now to improve the practical clarity of the prose in instructional guides so that you can in fact, without doing the contraption an injury, do-it-yourself. What, then, are the hopes for a semantic change in the style of "Jargontua" which plagues the consumer society, buyer and seller alike?

A thousand critiques in our newspapers and magazines seem to have been composed in vain, and the corporate efforts to employ "professional writers" and experts from "the communications world" have not appreciably ameliorated the general impenetrability. Journalism, in its helplessness, has been reduced to making futile little jokes about how badly everyone else is writing nowadays. Here is one, from a columnist on the *Financial Times* who is musing (in the summer of 1996) that "in the world of cyber-babble perhaps the concept of word rationing may be useful." His quasi-Orwellian panacea is simple:

> Every employee is given their ration of over-used, abused or meaningless words per month. Thus you may have four 'empowerments', five 'paradigms', three 're-engineerings' and six 'diversitys'. You may use them where you like: a memo, a seminar, an official report, even a casual conversation. But once they have been used up, that's it until your next ration.[4]

What of the black-marketeers who will spring up to deal illicitly? Well, all we can do is "resist" them and inflict stiff fines for "ration abuse."

This is, I am afraid, the Swiftian fallacy: making fun or making light of the misdemeanors will get you no further than a wan smile. It could be that the Augean stables will just not ever be cleaned. There may be something in the language that doesn't like a plain word or a clear sentence, or tends to make of either before long a cliché or stereotype. It could be, perhaps, that in the speaking and the writing of it there is a form of obscurantist imperative at work, something that is addicted to muddle, joined inseparably to jabberwocky.

Given, as I say, the cultural and commercial imperatives, the print-media will be seizing upon every opportunity to compete with the soundtrack of TV- and-film media for which "salty language" is an ineluctable ingredient ("smut" is optional). It would seem that—as one prudish newspaper reader put it in an anguished letter-to-the-editor—almost any excuse to "write dirty" will serve. The low art of *haute cuisine* will need that extra pinch of salt, and the high art of *avant-garde* sculpture stirs the pungent mix of profanity and pomp. Thus, the restaurant critic of a London paper, the reputable (and otherwise tasteful) Fay Maschler of the *Evening Standard*, can write,

> There are many routes to the making of a great meal. Whatever the adherents of the chuck-it-in, biff-it-about, slosh in some plonk and if you haven't got any chicken stock, don't worry, just piss-in-the-pot school of cooking claim, taking infinite care is invariably involved.[5]

But the confines of the kitchen, and its normal style of hygiene, limits this kind of thing. Not so with the W.C. (or the loo, or the bathroom) which, ever since Robert Rauschenberg's urinals and water-closets, has come into a new artistic dignity. If a painter like Jackson Pollock could use the drip technique in his classic action painting style, then a sculptress like Helen Chadwick is not far behind. On the occasion (in London, July '94) of an exhibition of her work which consisted of something she called "piss flowers" (not to be con- founded with "p— flour" which belongs to the cookery, above), The *Independent*'s arts reporter quoted her in an interview explaining the creative source of her inspiration:

> The sense of urgency out of the sharpening up of desire formed the concept of "piss flowers"....We heaped up piles of snow (in Canada) and first I would piss into it and then he [a lover named David] would piss around my mark. I made casts of the indentations which were eventually exhibited as bronze sculptures.

So impressive were the results that the art critic of the *Guardian* was inspired to write,

> Chadwick aimed a single jet into the middle of the templates, and this created tall encrusted forms that are like a cross between stamens and stalagmites. In this re-

spect she is Goliath, and David is David. He slung his urine modestly and diffusely around the edges. Yet his efflorescences are as fluffy and dazzling as any cloud-study by Constable.

This passage promptly won a prize of place in *Private Eye*'s collection "Pseuds Corner" (£10 paid for each entry). James Hall's *Guardian* review, hitting the planetary mark with jet-like dazzle, was itself so albumin-rich that it earned additional prizes for these memorable passages:

Chadwick describes Piss Flowers as a unique form of love-making, "metaphysical conceit for the union of two people expressing themselves bodily". Her logic may seem perverse, but the results are strangely moving. On Planet Piss, one of the most ephemeral and private activities is apotheosised. Urine is sent skywards, and given a quasi-geological certainty and solidity.

And

at the same time, though, we get an acute sense of sterility and impotence. These flowers could be the world's first monuments to incontinence. They are icy memorials to clapped-out couples whose leaky bodies can no longer get it together.[6]

Whether at its most fashionable in the business world—busying itself inordinately with a vocabulary which manages to disguise its element of sheer greed, or at its most faddish in the art world, always alert to slogans and catchphrases which would make a fortune for its ingenious innovators—language becomes totally agglutinative. Words and phrases stick together and, as if embedded in some masticated chewing gum, cannot easily shake themselves loose.

Here is an example from an interview in Greenwich Village with Julius Schnabel, painter and poet whose celebrity was recently accentuated by his film about the short creative life of Basquiat, the so-called "graffiti artist" who died aged twenty-seven of a heroin overdose. No matter that the highly profitable sale of Schnabel's paintings was called by one critic (Robert Hughes of *Time*) "the biggest hype since the South Sea bubble"; and Hughes also described Schnabel's film as "the worst living American painter making a movie about the worst dead one." Schnabel impresses interviewers in his three-story studio on West 11th Street. The man from the *Observer* came armed with his notebooks and wrote down every word he heard:

Schnabel's conversation bears comparison with his paintings. He drawls in broad verbal brushstrokes, dredging for fresh images and breeding similes....Any sentence that starts out in an art gallery in Manhattan will most likely fetch up, mutliple clauses later, in a Cuban shanty town, or in a reminiscence of a long night in a Mexican beach bar.

If the words stick together, the ideas ooze forward and run off the page, as on some luridly technicolor canvas, "like blood, like some body fluid, some very vast physical thing."

The *Observer* interviewer preserves for us the basic Schnabel credo: *"If you declare something so, it is."* Well, the film on Basquiat is declared to be a masterpiece, or something like that, the difficulty being in the connection between the *something* and the *so*. What are the associations, the sticking parts of the agglutinative process? In the reply to a question about how Schnabel fared as a film director we see the process at work:

> Schnabel booms across the studio, "Michael [Wincott, a friend who plays the role of Basquiat's dealer in the film], tell him how I got you, how I got each actor to focus on a certain object like a painting."
>
> How did that help?
>
> "Oh, in lots of different ways, I guess." Michael looks down into the glass of Coke he is holding. "You know, well, as a focus, Rene [the dealer] was in many ways a sad character but it was the painting that gave the guy a focus. And that is why I borrowed that focus, to be more, more...."
>
> Focused?
>
> "Yeah, I guess. Focused. That's right...."[7]

For the rest the *Observer* interviewer focused on his dead friend, Jean-Michel Basquiat; also on the star who was his dear friend, David Bowie, who played the role of his old friend, Andy Warhol. This was, all focused together, rather important news: for the forty-five-year-old Schnabel has had a major exhibition at the Whitney Museum in New York and thereafter, as the first young American to have a solo there, at the Tate Gallery in London. That should put the picture in real focus.

Self-consciousness, not to mention a note of critical self-awareness, is very rare in the world of the pseud's prose. The writer usually appears to be possessed at once by an uncontrollable vanity and the arrogance which accompanies the discoveries of insights almost too deep for words. One welcomes, therefore, those infrequent moments when a critic or a scholar admits—if only in a fleeting piece of journalism—that pseudery is rampant. The distinguished biologist, Stephen Jay Gould, whose scientific works owe their popularity, in part, to a certain lofty stylishness, has written recently in a newspaper article about "the cardinal pitfall" which calls for "a minor carping":

> Nature really is gorgeous and sublime in the most Burkean sense. But only poets can capture all this in words; when most of us try, we lapse into parodic writing suited only to travel magazines....Most of us should keep the true romance of field work silently in our souls.

But it surely is the essence of romanticism not to keep its silence, and this burst into a peroration embarrasses Professor Gould:

> The starlight is so strong, it can even make shadows....In the bush, night insects buzz incessantly in the trees. From time to time a dingo yelps strangely in the far distance.[8]

When pseudery is not obscure and pretentious, it is unabashedly banal.

The American contributions to this genre, as in so many other Anglo-American contrasts, are heavier, stodgier, more substantial in an exculpatory kind of way. Brilliant nonsense in London or Oxbridge writing has no excuse for itself other than excessive facility with words and phrases, at its most allusive deriving from precocious schoolboy perusals of Shakespeare and childhood echoes of the King James Bible. In the U.S. highbrow jabberwocky has to work harder, and becomes inevitably connected to the larger, simpler American mythology, in which the modern sense of the avant-garde gets mixed up with new frontiers and manifest destiny. The outsourced inspiration of a promised land of unlimited possibilities appears to lend a larger cultural purposefulness to what otherwise would be recognized as rather prosaic pretentiousness. How much gibberish in prose and the pictorial arts gets conscripted to the cause of a Walt Whitmanesque "sense of the infinite"? How many of our contemporary creative artists have paraded their talents to the forward march of limitless newness and novelty? Here is an American critic paying tribute to the "grandiosity" of Jackson Pollock's canvases and the whole achievement of the New York school of Action Painting:

> It is an idea of losing one's own tiresome, ordinary self in the unbounded promise of the New World; liberated from history, one is reborn with primordial stength and integrity.[9]

This is an all-purpose idea which could have launched a thousand different drips and squiggles, and it did. The vaulting ambition was recognized; the novel products on canvas were hailed before they were quite dry. The chorus of art critics agreed that Whitman and his *Leaves of Grass* served as "a useful prism" for aesthetic considerations which needed to import a transcending vision of immanent national greatness to welcome, at long last, the emergence of American masters. Some became rough desperadoes; others dreamers of distant horizons; all thought their avant-gardism kept them well ahead of the times. Whitman boasted he was, like America, "large," and even Jackson Pollock grandly declared, "I am nature." Presumably his *oeuvre* constitutes—as in Ratcliff's book on Pollock, *The Fate of a Gesture* (1996) quoted above – a liberation of his natural self, some kind of primordial rebirth, and when Sol LeWitt stacked groups of cubes in different combinations, an appreciative critic in the *New York Times* thought it was "a process that in itself implied a sense of the infinite." The stacking could indeed go on and on, not unlike the pushing back of the Wild West frontier, just like the American space rockets overtaking Mars, passing it on the left and heading for Jupiter straight on....

It all goes into the making of a special American "gesture," a kind of "high five" which seemed to promise that you could "hold infinity in the palm of your hand," and the grip would help to turn out long-awaited masterpieces. This credo is our special Yankee sort of pseudery, encountered everywhere where the ineffable is pursuing the inexplicable.

Is It Cricket?

The pursuit has left its trail across all the efforts of our newspaper culture to keep up with the contemporary scene, its avant-garde artists as well as its pop stars. Here is an art critic relentlessly sniffing down the prey of precious meaning in an item of surrealistic collage which we thought had gone out of fashion with Max Ernst and Kurt Schwitters, assembling their bits of Weimar detritus:

> Dean Hughes is showing this ticket, among other works, at the Laure Genillard gallery. Some relate to the two years he spent secretly resewing the upholstery on the buses with carefully chosen threads of the same color as the pattern: a virtually invisible ritual invented, it seems to me, to hold the world together and re-enforce the commonplace by delicate intrusion—but with a sensible futility which carries a kindness to the shared world.
>
> So this ticket signed by the driver—a celebration of a completed journey of one man. The Cubists used tickets as bits of life that could be stuck down into compositions of artistic merit. This one is left floating, uncertain of its value but allowing us to reconsider those daily rituals that bring us closer to each other and keep art and life going.

Another ritual that keeps art and life going in some kind of togetherness is the indefatigable effort to find deeper truths in the rock-and-roll culture, here in the music of a pop group called Oasis who, for a moment, are enjoying their season (1996-7) of fame and notoriety. The *Independent* newspaper, with a slight *faiblesse* for the work of Jean Baudrillard, thought it worth its newsprint to publish this classic example of pseudery from one of its contributors:

> It is right to say that Oasis can gain our attention without absolute justification, but this does not mean that their status is entirely false. This is because they occupy what Baudrillard calls the *hyperreal*. This is not the unreal any more than it is the absolute real. Rather, it is a dimension of indistinction between (particularly media) representations and what they purport to represent. The real status of

hyperrealities is undecidable, because the media image is real (for example, effective, even if not truthful) just as real things are always minimally mediated (for
example, televisually).[10]

There are, to be sure, more significant lessons to be learned from an unfortunate passage of pseudery prose than to be warned against mere obscurantist or
euphuistic excess. Sometimes the absurdity touches on the surreal, and the
unfashionable becomes more quaint than anarchronistic. On occasion, we are
brought up by a sharpened sense of the passing of time, of how evanescent or
mutable in history the cadences of style and its appropriate vocabularies can
be. The week of 14 August 1997 in England provided one such useful historic
reminder. Cricket was no longer what it used to be.

I was watching the exciting contest between Glamorgan and Essex, and
I must have blinked for I didn't quite catch the unprecedented moment
until it was repeated on the evening news in slow motion. A batter had
protested; the bowler turned angrily on him; both glared and shoved each
other ever so lightly on their white, somewhat sweaty shirts; and the captain of one side or the other was reported to have addressed the third man
in the altercation by "vouchsafing such sentiments as 'You are a *******
awful umpire.'" Taken together, it wasn't cricket. The TV commentators,
and the sports correspondents the morning after, thundered such epithets
as "disgraceful...shameful...unforgiveable." What would have been in other
games a minor and quickly forgettable incident was recognized throughout the nation as an historic turning point. The attempt to sustain the myth
of "gentlemanly cricket" was now seen to be futile. The *Times* headline
asked: CAN WE AFFORD TO PLAY THE GAME ANY LONGER? The
anguished conclusion was to the effect—

> You cannot turn the clock back. Nor can you sustain that level of competitive ani-
> mosity on the field without the occasional outburst of crude and even violent be-
> havior. Of course it has to be controlled. One doubts if even the most avid of fans
> wants to see matters deteriorate to the point where an outraged bowler takes a Mike
> Tyson-style bite out of the umpire's ear simply because he has turned down an *lbw*
> [leg-before-wicket foul] appeal.

Well, things were bad enough. Cricket was no longer what it used to be, and
what it used to be could no longer be evoked without the wonderment, puzzlement, and sheer disbelief that those Etonian playing-fields had once featured
such a triumphalism of the human spirit. Or was the nostalgia itself drenched
in pure pseudery? The *Times*, for its own melancholy part, risked quoting something that one noble cricketer, a Lord Harris, had said only a generation ago
when cricket was more than just a game, when it was a way of life, the epitome
of civilized behavior:

It is more free from anything sordid, anything dishonorable, than any game in the world. To play it keenly, honorably, generously, self-sacrificingly, is a moral lesson in itself, and the classroom is God's'air and sunshine.

Here was a fleeting moment when pseudery—and the noble Lord was a proper toff and an immortal pseud—flashed its hidden qualities of sincerity and authenticity. *Sic transit gloria mundi.*[11]

Of a High Dumb-Down Tolerance

Everything, to be sure, can be parodied, and every readily identifiable literary style, in prose or poetry, can be useful as a broad or blunt parodic instrument. In the newspaper culture such exercises in high-spirited writing are rarely called for, but I raise the matter of journalistic sources since the vast amount of "pseudery" which gets published annually as undeliberate, unwitting pastiche can be classified into two grand Anglo-American categories, with minor intellectual exceptions (mostly among academic and ad-copy writers).

One is rough-hewn, the other is burnished; one usually harks back to the severe school of Hemingway, the other to the ornate "euphuistic" tradition of John Lyly. One almost always gets away with it, for it happens that in the U.S. the suspect passage is deceptively close to the way people really talk. Fat chance in England, even among the dons in an elegant Oxford college, to catch anyone at head table speaking sentences six inches long, replete with abstractions pretending to be meaningful. I have been particularly attracted in recent years to the genre in pseud's corner which combined two pieces of transatlantic pomp—on the film pages, for example, when London reviewers take their turn at criticizing (and sometimes praising) the big American movie. And I cannot escape the conclusion that an enthused Englishman is rather better at gush than we are. I suspect that a well-educated London *cineaste* can out-gush any star-struck Hollywood sob sister, even if she was trained in the all-embracing school of Louella O. Parsons and Hedda Hopper when those fluffy lady-columnists were in the celebratory mood. Here is a young London film critic, Quentin Curtis of the *Daily Telegraph*, son of a distinguished literary critic, doing his best to acclaim Alfred Hitchcock's *Vertigo* (1958/1997), now released in a new version which was both re-edited and re-colorized. What he saw was a masterpiece re-discovered, "obsessive, thwarted, necrophiliac," "a tortuous blend of yearning and repulsion"—for it is "the master's most personal film." In addition it featured nothing less than "immortal performances" by James Stewart and Kim Novak. Is the picture that good? Sure must be.

the hushed intensity in his voice, the note of pleading, yearning, is heartbreaking. Stewart's perfect mixture of softness and strength, the hint of suspicion in his appraising gaze, suggests vulnerability, while showing a man still aching for truth and rightness. Without this dimension the movie's conclusion would be meaningless. No actor in the history of film has better conveyed the moral being.

(Surely, that is, if one omits the early history of German film in which such actors as Conrad Veidt, Emil Jannings, and Peter Lorre were conveying their version of "the immoral being.")[12]

> In *Vertigo*, ideas of dream and desire, power and freedom recur (the last two words are spoken together three times, as has been noted by the French director Chris Marker, who is obsessed with the film). But, above all, the film is a meditation on time and death. That spiral at the beginning mimics the manipulations of mortality. Scottie's desire—like all lusts and loves—is a futile struggle against oblivion. His attempt to re-create Madeleine stands for all of our loss of the past. It is one of the cruel jokes of film—which Hitchcock, more than anyone, understood—that while something as vibrant as a human being must die, a strip of celluloid survives, preserving a teasing simulacrum of life.

Well, before the thought could occur to one that a cruel fate might also overtake even the most vibrant of life's simulacra, it flashed upon him, in full meditative flight:

> Film, in fact, fades too. The colors soften and the sound deteriorates. The stupendous achievement of the restoration work on this 70mm. print of *Vertigo* is that it restores the movie to pristine newness....The colours are as striking as figments from a dream. Bernard Herrmann's score with its references to Wagner screams at you like an uneasy conscience....

Etc., etc. The trouble with bad writing in pseud's corner is that it is always wrestling with an uneasy conscience, and always winning.

What facilitates the steady dissemination of such pseudery prose in our newspaper culture is a certain tradition of editorial generosity. Harrassed editors of serious papers give nowadays much space and even prominence to dubious or unworthy themes and execrable enterprises out of an unhappy mixture of motives. A misconceived respect for a spurious avant-garde compels openness to whatever announces itself as way-out, forward-looking, progressive, or taboo-breaking. More than that, there is out there a loyal audience for every innovative folly, and new recruitable readers have to be tempted and appeased. The language may hurtle towards jabberwocky, and the life of the mind can become a parody of a sick joke. Still, we must maintain our standards of cultural correctitude even if enlightenment ushers in an impenetrable darkness—or, better still, a frabjous day. One critic on a mainstream newspaper, weary at finding all the jokes "wearing thin," confessed after a performance of the Reduced Shakespeare Company of their version of the Bible *(The Complete Word of God, Abridged)* that what kept him going through all the silly, scornful mockery was "a high dumb-down tolerance." It is, I think, an accurate and useful phrase. Pity the forebearance of the patient *Times* critic when the prophet Abraham, fitted out in top hat and a Lincoln beard, unable to believe his ears when God asks for his foreskin. A thought is spared for "strictly observant Jews" (but observance has nothing to do with it) as for believing Christians who were not exactly "splitting their sides at the sight of a pregnant Virgin lifting up her legs in order to catapult a Holy Infant across the stage...." The *Times* man confessed that he did not split his sides at that one either. Between absurdity and the tediously unfunny he has to endure a musical version of Armageddon, dwarfed by a triptych of Michelangelo's God creating Adam.

In this beginning there appears to be his end: one of our modern critics is teetering on the verge of defection:

> The jokes? Well, banal play on words: e.g., raising the dead means floating them in the air. Cheeky irreverence: a Last Supper painting with holes for heads, seaside photo style. Some gags could fit in all categories, e.g. 'There was a computer in the Garden of Eden because Eve had an apple.'

If our contemporary critics, diligently reporting on all the hijinks of the low world of pop culture, manage to lose their capacity for "high dumb-down tolerance," there is one refuge left: the abject recognition that *excellence* has nothing to do with such artistic success, its notoriety or its prosperity. The last viable credo is that nothing succeeds like excess. This is indeed the aesthetic which has been sustaining the *Documenta* exhibitions in Cologne, especially under the directorship of Mlle. Catherine David; and we will be returning to additional defections in the ranks of critics when we take up the newspaper controversies a recent *Documenta* has aroused.

19

Pop Kulcher

A Drag on Death and Love

I call attention to the illiteracy factor in Pop Kulchur more in sorrow than in anger. Beyond the pleasurable fury in polemicizing against errors in grammar and orthography, against solecisms and other semantic corruptions, there must be (and is) an element of sympathy for so many gifted young men. They make a fortune out of mass communication but are poor wretches struggling disastrously with language and words when they are called upon to cope with some personal crisis. An appalling example from the career of the Beatles will have to stand for many.

It was well known that the professional rivalry and "personality conflicts" between Paul McCartney and John Lennon led to the disruption and disbandment of the classic pop group of our time. In time, years and decades after the murder of John Lennon in New York, Paul McCartney learned to talk of complexes and insecurities, of childhood protective devices and other modish bits of psychology, to account for the estrangement of the two Beatle stars. But then he also conceded that he was a young man who kept his own true feelings "bottled up," and also put on a "suit of armor" to hide emotions for which he had no words. Or no words that were appropriate, commensurate, or honest. ("I was trying to come up with the most meaningful thing.") And so it came to that ugly remark on the occasion of the news of Lennon's death which was so widely taken to reflect not merely the snideness of a shallow young man (who had nevertheless written moving sentimental songs like *Yesterday*) but the callousness of a whole youth culture, devoid of humane feelings and/or of the vocabulary, the verbal decencies, with which to express them:

I'm very funny when people die [Paul told his recent biographer]. I don't show grief very well. It actually leads some people to think I don't care, and I do. I'm not good at it like some people....

Was he better at being unfunny, at being very bad at it? The dismal fact remains that he gave a measure of world-wide offense that still gives him trouble today.

The incident involved a reporter sticking a microphone in front of him and asking, "What do you think about John Lennon's death?" And he replied, "It's a drag." It was a one-liner that went into the book of records for *gaucherie*. For one would like to believe him when he now tells his biographer, "Of course when I got home that night I wept like a baby. If my true feelings would have come out in the press, I would have looked better...." He looked worse because whatever his "true feelings" were or were not, there was not a vocabulary, perfunctory or heart-felt, available to him to deal with the real-life calamity except in the gagged-up cliché way that he did. If he hadn't said it the quip would have to be invented. Death was a drag, and love was lucy-in-the-sky-with-diamonds (LSD). That was all you needed, or needed to know.[1]

For my foreign readers I should add that "drag" was here intended to mean "tedious, tiring, colorless, dull, unexciting." In jazz-musical circles one knew that even sunny Louis Armstrong could sometimes find his wonderful life "such a drag," and when Billy Holiday's career collapsed in drugs—"she was crying and everything..."—her friends said: "It was a real drag."

The phrase, even without special broad intonations to suggest cool distance, invokes vague echoes of the dozen other meanings (from *dragging* on a cigarette, having *drag* with the waiter, being on the main *drag* of town, cross-dressing in *drag*, going to a festive end-of-term *drag*, to sitting through a play that *drags*, etc.) that are recorded and are still in usage.*

A word more on "drag" as a pop signal for grief. I should add the surmise that in the McCartney-Lennon case it was not even original or properly spontaneous but already a stereotype for sorrow among the swingers. Writing about

---

*   See the *Dictionary of American Slang* (ed. Wentworth & Flexner, rev. ed. 1975), pp. 160-1, 694. The entries in H.L. Mencken's several volumes on *The American Language* are eccentric, to say the least, listing only "a train...a slow freight...the rear end of a moving flock..." and the like. Mencken's deficiencies are amply made up for by Eric Partridge's material in his *Dictionary of Slang and Unconventional English* (1991, 8th ed.), albeit mostly British in reference (and, after all, both the Beatle stars were Liverpudlian by birth).

In any case, "drag" is rich and suggestive in its traditional and topical associations. Had Paul McCartney said, "It blows my mind" or "Wow!" not to mention "I'm devastated" or "It's the pits," his rejoinder would surely not have merited further notice.

the American jazzmen of Europe, Mike Zwerin records (in the *International Herald-Tribune*, 28 July 1995) the association of Chet Baker, the "patron saint" in Italy, with the pianist Romano (son of Benito) Mussolini. Baker learned to speak Italian, caught up on a bit of Italian politics, and his line to Mussolini Junior about his father's death, hung up by the heels after his capture by anti-fascist partisans in 1944, was memorable and oft repeated: "Gee, man, it's a drag about your old man." The line is said to have "entered the folklore"—presumably because it was (a) incongruous, (b) tasteless, (c) cool, or (d) politically incorrect. Not a mean demotic achievement for a simple four-letter word.

Pliable Platitudes

The ingenuity of pop culture, its management and manipulation, is that as fast as it devises new terminology for its various performances it nimbly varies the names and slogans before they harden into heavy clichés. The platitudes are pliable; the styles of pop stars are pigeonholed for a season or two and then become yesterday's sentimentalism. In the rare event that nostalgia is freshened up with comeback successes or new popularity in related careers (singers become actors, songwriters become talk show favorites, actresses become best-selling novelists, tired comedians become show-masters and impresarios), the biography or psycho-portrait reads like a recapitulation of contemporary crazes, fads, fashions and passing cultural caprice.

And so when a celebrity named Cher (a songstress turned actress turned film director) became fifty she was suitably celebrated for her "survival skills." The longevity of her stardom was attributed to "a mixture of self-discipline and street-smarts." (The fact that she spent a sum estimated to be a million dollars on plastic surgery and top-to-toe cosmetic replacements was, gallantly, not mentioned except for a polite reference to "adjustments.") The stages of her life's way were summed up vividly by one newspaper reporter who obviously knew his stereotypes:

> Lithe and statuesque in a black jump suit, she paused to wash down a pill from a fistful of capsules....The room was pungent with burning incense.
> With a face as smooth and translucent as white marble framed by plumes of jet-black hair that set off her jutting cheekbones, Cher exuded the aura of an image-conscious teen-age rebel whose personality is an eclectic accumulation of styles: basic beatnik black, hippie nonchalance and fashion-model hauteur toughened with biker-chick bravado. Her casual use of profanity suggested the defiant misfit who continually ran away from home as a child.[2]

Put this way the star, "regaining her foothold in the Hollywood firmament," takes on the authenticity of virtual reality. It is one way in which prose, polished to a glitter, can compete with the dazzle of the electronic media. And every pop star, if he or she survives long enough, will be available for such instant analysis. Most of the vignettes, recapitulating the same eclectic styles, will prove to be interchangeable, and can be recycled to fit the misfit.[3]

There is a little something to be said for the widely criticized inclusion of "Pop Kulchur" courses and even seminars on the Western university level, especially in our schools of journalism; for otherwise there is no hope whatsoever for an intelligent and even literate journalist coming forth to assist us with comment and criticism of the flowering world of mass youth entertainment. Newspapers of quality tended until recently to ignore the rock, pop, and grunge scene. The competition forced one or another editor to pay attention. There were tens of thousands, possibly hundreds of thousands, of readers out there, and even the hyped publicity about their favorite groups would attract them.

The writers on the scene were mostly post-graduates and drop-outs from the scene itself, and despite occasional revelations of special literary aptitudes and streaks of professional critical insight, they were in no position to offer a solution to our unenlightenment. They were essentially part of the problem of cultural illiteracy. Ideas were scarce, vocabulary meager, and the temptations to half-baked pretentiousness—and "Pseuds' Corner" is crowded with pop pomp—very seductive. Here is the former manager of a punk band called "The Pack," Paul Tickell—who has made a documentary film for the BBC entitled *"Punk & the Pistols"*—writing in the *Evening Standard* from the historical perspective of the last twenty punk years:

> Punk yelled and the rest of the country listened. Punk, although it delighted in fragmentation and destruction, was an address to the nation as a whole. Like some bizarre Churchillian parody it was perhaps the last such address, coming at a time that marked the end of the political consensus and the beginnings of Thatcherism and the era we live.[4]

If we take this farrago of nonsense seriously for a moment, we will recall the Churchillian call to the U.S. to "give us the tools and we will do the job." And so it came to pass: the famous Anglo-American victory over Hitler's Western front and the end of Nazism.

The "bizarre" version would have the Brit punk militants taking over from their Yankee helpers the "trappings" and *they* would finish the movement and even victoriously re-export it back to the U.S. (and around the world). London took over from New York such tools as the ripped clothes, the spiky hair, and a life-style of conspicuous excess. It all had the "feel of outrage for art's sake," as Tickell claims, commemorating the occasion when "it all started," the glorious summer of 1975 when Johnny Rotten "foamed and flapped next to the juke-box in *'Sex'* (Vivienne Westwood's shop on the King's Road) as he sang along to Alice Cooper's *Eighteen*...."

Cultural historians, if they can give credit to such primary sources with their anecdotal evidence, might well take note of the various historic turning-points which in a few decades twisted Rock into Rave: "Out of this audition was born the 'Sex Pistols', brand new pop icons whose mission was to smash all the old ones." But, as so often in history, the revolutionary smashers were fated to absorb and incorporate and plagiarize the past—in this case they took over teddy-boys footwear which became essential to punk armor, Hippy drain-pipe trousers, the Rocker's black-leather jackets, the Mods' Italian-tailored suits, etc., etc.

> It was a case of cutting up the old order to fashion the new....The shop *'Sex'* had to take on rubber and leather gear which owed much to an older provincial crowd who were into bondage.

Alas, the parameters of innovation and creativity are, in these throwaway cultures of ephemeral popular fashion, drawn narrowly and very restrictively. As in the perennial problem of the "latest" style in Paris *haute couture*, the celebrated figures are necessarily trapped in a short list of alternatives as they ponder what they will be doing with this season's fashion in skirts. It can only be a full flowing length to the ankles; or a *mini*, clinging suggestively to the thighs; or something in between, hanging just above or just below the knees. Not even pure genius could expand those material possibilities; no other pemutations or combinations of the cloth will serve, even in the thimbled hands of the most dexterous seamstresses.

So it is, with similar frustration, among the desperately energetic pop groups: all seeking a personal tone and a touch of class, a symbol, an icon, a gesture which will give them distinction. They wear clodhopping boots and unlaced trainers—or elegant and shiny little slippers—or they frolic about on the boards, big-toed barefoot. Some wear rags, a few take to velvet or leather or silk, others sporting tight-fitting custom-made iridescent jackets with flashing trousers. Newspapermen—there were few women (until the success of the Spice Girls*)* in this macho world where the men croon and the girls swoon—perpetuate the myth that once upon a time one or the other hit-or-miss choice of three possibilities was "truly original." Journalism, largely fed by a self-educated cognoscenti, reinforces the publicity bumph that the inspiration to rock or to twist, to jump or to break, to dance or to prance, was so innovative as to create "a culture" (of course: less than that it could not be) all of its own. And then, as tomorrow displaces yesterday, come the shameless copy-cats. One young pop authority, named Caspar Llewellyn Smith, writes as if he had seen it all before:

> No youth cult is safe from revival these days...20 years since the 'Sex Pistols' played their first gig, a painfully hip style magazine [publishes] a feature called 'Punk's Not Dead!'....

Meanwhile, the mod renaissance continues apace. groups such as this season's darlings, 'Menswear', have copied Sixties acts like the 'Small Faces' right down to the tailored suits, never mind the music....The break-dancing culture, the precursor to hip-hop is suddenly popular again.

This curiously cyclical phenomenon, or what one old philosopher thought to be an "eternal recurrence," provokes our Mr. Smith to some larger considerations:

There's no darkness, no danger, everyone has seen their kind before. Deciding to be a punk or a hip-hop B-boy or a mod or a hippie means catching some of the excitement the phenomenon had the first time round, but without the uncertainty of throwing in your lot with something that is truly original.[5]

The good old days in the underground were heroic. But the grand cultural revolution did not turn out to be permanent. "The real hippies and punks," it has to be conceded, "were never very many. Coexisting with them were other cultures."

Why should this be surprising? Fashions in *haute couture* are only a sensation for a season, and the fashionable successes of pop stars and their individual styles are equally evanescent. It is only the egomaniacal element in the first flush of fame which leads to the self-deception that being top-of-the-charts could be a permanent arrangement. The onset of nostalgia is programed for the aftermath of the next concert, the next scheduled ten-city-tour, or the big album after that. Rock longs for the days when it was on an easy roll; soul loses itself in the disco; punk slows down into a new wave. There is, as one pop historian regrets, always "a little death." George Melly, the self-styled jazz supremo, has put it another way, and I have heard him define the Cycle of Pop:

[E]very few years a new generation of pretty young things roars out of the clubs, claiming moral purity and artistic originality, popularizes a hair length or trouser width, offends a few parents, makes money, largely for the record company, and disintegrates bloodily or dissolves into golf-club land....

And the fans?...Somewhere tonight they will be queuing up to see another unknown bunch of pretty things in the hope it will be love at first note. The need for cheaply potent pop is always with us.[6]

Those of us who rarely take our places in that queue can follow the cycles of pop in word and picture in all of our media—a little belatedly, perhaps, for the wheels spin so speedily, but with enough detail to recognize in each succeeding generation the hordes of free-floating fans looking for a new enthusiasm: a frenzy, a palpitation, a throb, or whatever it is that is so exciting, gives such fulfillment, and allows so much spending money to exchange hands.

Obviously, not only hip journalists and right-on critics will have to be given a higher academic training to make something coherent and cogent out of all this. We will also need our new, sensitized historians who can pick their way in the over- and under-ground through the provinces of bondage and co-existence, alert to every stylistic change in "S&M accoutrements," and cool to every generational claim that it was innovating or smashing or creating something utterly new. The highbrow canon of originality, which Sir Herbert Read once analyzed so acutely in the context of classic and modern art, has become a fetish of the streets. An old trick, a new talent, a visible talisman, and you're on the golden road to fame and fortune. Who remembers the spasmodic gigs of yesterday? Each generation of youthful fans is experiencing everything for the very first time; all the sound and fury appears fresh and liberating; but in a few years they become an unoriginal throng of sentimental revivalists, waiting for some aging group to oblige by playing their song. As the *Pack* manager, Paul Tickell, retreating in some confusion, admits, "Punk was in many ways a return to the pre-hippie 1960s, to the violent three-minute pop of the likes of the Kinks." As the *New Yorker*'s Harold Ross might have scribbled in the margin, "Who they?"

Help!

Pop Critics' Folklore

It is, to be sure, no accident that in the world of "pop culture" more and more demands are being put on anthropology, especially the loose words which it has left lying around and can be freely picked up for possible tagging. What is "trance" music? what are the "primordial sounds of a 4,000-year-old rock 'n' roll band"?

Trying to help, the Pop correspondent of the *Times* thinks it important for us to know one neglected aspect of the Rolling Stones' legacy. This occurred in the years just before the guitarist Brian Jones committed suicide, and was rooted in the ceremony of Bou Jeloud in the Morroccan mountain village of Jajouka. Unfortunately for bohemian tourists, the goat-god Bou creates his "havoc" at one specific time of the year only: the new moon that marks the end of Ramadan.

"I don't know if I possess the stamina to endure the incredible strain of the festival," the tragic Brian Jones wrote, inevitably putting the blame on his white man's burden. "Such psychic weaklings has Western civilisation made of so many of us."

The Jajouka story has, I am afraid, too many facets to be explained fully here: the villagers singing a song "with a memorable refrain" of *"Brahim Jones, Jajouka, very stoned"*; the role of an expatriate named Brion Gysin who (according to the *Times*' quote from Ted Morgan's biography of William

Burroughs) was "a cheap shit guy"; the foresight of Brian Jones who sensed "the relevance that these ancient powerful trance rhythms would hold for future generations."

Sufficient unto the day is for the *Times** to be giving us an appetite for "this swirling trance music" and an insight into the way it was ultimately put together for a Rolling Stones Records release. Apparently Jones "went to the source":

> recording the flute, drums and double-reed *rhaitas* and then manipulating the tapes with the most common studio devices of the psychedelic era: phasing, echo and tape reversal. The end result was an immersing, intoxicating noise....

One pop participant who wrote an "epic" on the whole Jajouka affair (for *Rolling Stone* magazine, and it has since been reprinted) has confessed, "I don't think we ever figured out whether we were playing the tape backward or forward, but we had a lot of fun trying." The "purists," as the *Times* tells us, were "offended by the added pschedelia."

As for the rest of us, authentic weaklings of Western civilization, we are still trying to figure it out. Neither anthropology nor Pop expertise seems to be helping very much.

The report on the "charismatic" activities of a young Church of England preacher in Sheffield, speaking of anthropological Pop Kulchur mis-usages, is instructive. It seemed that he attempted to attract a "lost generation" of worshippers and "drew heavily on nightclub culture, using loud music, synthesizers, video projections and imaginative lighting." Since there were reports of bikini tops, short skirts, and much sexual misconduct it was also referred to as the Sheffield group's "embracing of the 'rave culture....'"[7]

*   David Troop, "Stoned on the best Moroccan," in *The Times*, 22 July 1995.

20

The Art of Explanation

The Chronic Abuse of a Little Knowledge

There is an unforgettable incident in the history of nineteenth-century socialist intellectuals which involves an arrogant and angry Karl Marx and his victim of the moment, an autodidactic young worker named Wilhelm Weitling. It was at an international meeting in Brussels, the year was 1846; and, whatever the argument was about, Marx knew he was right, Weitling wrong, and pounding the table he leaped up with a shout, "Ignorance has never helped anybody yet!"

But the habitual, self-indulgent abuse of a little knowledge has led whole movements into historic dead-end failures. Marx read the Paris newspapers avidly, and did a number of brilliant and influential pamphlets (*The 18th Brumaire*, etc.) on the basis of the "first-hand reports" he read therein. No Marx scholar I have ever known has gone back to that body of reportage and evaluated its accuracy critically as a reliable primary source. Newspapers in Paris, even Marx's favorite ones, often got things wrong; and I have no doubt that alternative explanations of the events of 1848 or 1871 (say, Victor Hugo's equally brilliant version on "Napoleon the Little") had an arguably better claim to ultimate historical veracity.

A little ignorance not infrequently helps, especially when foreign correspondents are desperate to round out their dispatches with explanations that represent some semblance of authentic clarity. The reader is panting to know: What caused the horrendous sinking in the Baltic of the ferry *Estonia* with its 990 passengers? How dangerous is the combined outbreak of pneumonic and bubonic plague in India?

I suppose it is good and useful to know, amid the sudden loss of so many lives in the icy sea off the Finnish port of Turku, that (according to a Swedish expert):

the chances of identifying bodies trapped in the ship were relatively good since the water temperature at the sea floor is 4 degrees centigrade (39° Fahrenheit), the same temperature as a morgue.[1]

This smacks of instant oceanography; and even if true, a transparent effort to whistle in the dark. But it may be a consolation of sorts, and I can be easily persuaded that the press in all its truthless immediacy should not always be the cruel and heartless bearers of bad news. If a bit of contrived meteorology can help, let it.

Scientists who take time out from their laboratories to scan a daily newspaper often express knowledgeable outrage at the misdemeanors in the reporting of the news emerging from their own fields of specialization. Experts are even unhappy when a trained "science correspondent" simplifies the result of some medical discovery or suggests the social implications of some new biological data. A few newspapers accept this skepticism and make it into a self-criticism of their own. The science writer of the *Los Angeles Times* (Robert Lee Holtz) concedes that recent findings in, say, bio-chemistry and genetics are ("understandably") "viewed through the prism of our vulnerabilities...." How to be cool and objective when there is a temptation to be the first to write about experimental half-truths and to fulfill "our greed for self-knowledge"? Then, too, the truths of even simple relationships are notoriously elusive. The readers of at least one popular newspaper have been warned. The cautionary warning makes the apparent links between violence and maleness:

> Is the aggression of boys, as some new research data hints, merely a matter of a biochemical imbalance between trace levels of copper and zinc? Or is it associated with the extra copy of the male chromosome that sometimes occurs as a reproductive error during conception? Or is excessive testosterone, the hormone found in such high levels among men, at fault?

We should be watching this space in the *Los Angeles Times* diligently, even if a little knowledge misleads and a little more can nullify new certainties:

> Men's testosterone levels, however, drop dramatically when they are in happy marriages, so much so that some researchers speculate that women instinctively use monogamy to control male behavior. Other new research shows that many women in high-pressure professions show a rise in the level of testosterone. Does this mean they also have become more aggressive? More male? Or just more stressed?[2]

This is impressive, admirable journalism; but will hypotheses make for scoops, and can question marks ever be relied upon to sell papers?

None of which is to be mistaken for an outsider's critique of journalism gone astray, for many of the best journalists of the day, proud and despairing by turns of the splendors and miseries of their profession, often pronounce candidly in the same spirit. Nowadays it is occasioned mostly by media rivalry, and sometimes by the bitterness which accompanies the uneasy co-habitation within the newspaper culture of the highbrow broadsheets and the lowbrow tabloids. Here is one example of the former, wherein Christopher Booker is taking several of the leading Radio and TV-program-makers to task:

> it is that supreme example of that pernicious disease now rampant all through our journalism—the disease of cleverdickery, the self-important urge to pose as a fearless journalist, making sneery little points, without any idea of what is really going on in the world.
>
> The overwhelming characteristic of the cleverdick tendency is to want to appear knowing, without actually knowing anything at all....

This is somewhat hyperbolic, but the shared thesis is that a little knowledge can lead to great pretensions.[3]

When total ignorance is very often the rule of the day in the television studios of the world, then a bit of pretentiousness and a dash of bluff seem almost to be intellectual virtues. They are the tribute paid by know-nothingism to a little knowledge. Here is a gleeful newspaper report, pious as well as knowing, about the television experiences of a German bishop of the Protestant Church. Dr. Horst Mirschler is citing a taped telephone conversation with an interviewer from *RTL*, a new, commercial, and highly successful TV station on the crowded German band of some 26 available channels:

> "Well, yes, I am a Bishop."
>
> "Terrific....A real Bishop. We're sending a camera team to do a recording, but first I have a question. Tell me, there is in the Catholic Church, isn't there, something like commandments. Do you know them?"
>
> "Yes, I do, but they are actually the same as in my own Evangelical Church."
>
> "*Ach,* what's in them, can you tell me? Are there many?"
>
> "Yes, there are ten of them, known in German as *Gebote.*"
>
> "Ten of them?"
>
> "Yes, and there are a lot of reasonable things summed up in them. The fifth commandment, for example, saying you shall not kill. Or the seventh: you should not steal. And the sixth you can remember because it has to do with sex: you shall not commit adultery...."
>
> "*Ach,* that's all very interesting."
>
> "And what's more, one can look up Martin Luther's commentaries on all of them."
>
> "Terrific. Rules and regulations, and with instructions on how to do-it-yourself. Tell me, can I ask you to take the trouble and fax them through to us?"

The bishop obliged and, proud evangelist that he was, duly reported to the other Church elders that was how Martin Luther's little catechism got on to the German television screen.[4]

Such interviewers are rarely put out by their mindless performances since they are seldom intelligent enough to be self-critical. At the other end of the IQ spectrum, nothing is so embarrassing as a specialist who is caught out on his own subject. Not only scholars slip up, practical men of action lapse from their tried and true vocabulary, and then the pedants descend like wolves on the fold or (to remain in the metaphor) sea-gulls on to the incoming cruiser. The good ship *Achille Lauro* sank off the coast of Africa after a fire, and in his commentary on the rescue operation, the U.S. Navy spokesman, Commander T. McCready, referred to the "backend of the ship." His face was as red as the ill-fated liner's glowing hull, when he was reminded that the proper word is *"stern."* Even former naval persons or landlubbers knew as much.[5]

In December 1995 a half-dozen of the leading political intellectuals of *Time* magazine, led by editor Walter Isaacson and writer Lance Morrow, made an attempt to deal thoughtfully with the new radical factors in U.S. politics as represented in the sudden emergence of Congressman Newt Gingrich into national prominence. Should they manage to make more than a tired inventory of old attitudes, exhausted phrases, clichés that have long been past serviceability? Hardly.

Gingrich's vision? "A utopia...a renewed civilization...Norman Rockwell in the 21st century, a wholesome Utopia...." Which utopia was to be preceded, of course, by a revolution. Indeed it was even to be a special form of "permanent revolution" (and *Time* dragged the old Trotsky-Parvus phrase of 1905 into play again). But the "dialectic" had also come into play, and now the utopian revolutionary is suddenly seen as "the greatest liability to the revolution he launched." Will he betray the revolution? Or reform it? This may be a shade too political for the visionary politician, for he is quoted as expressing his unpolitical dedication: "The core problem is culture." On this occasion there were no glosses on the intricate subject of *"cultural* culture" or *"countercultural* culture" (although some bright *Time* researcher dug out the embarrassing fact that a leading Republican ally was the owner of a framed photograph of the homosexual artist Robert Mapplethorpe—but it turned out to be only a harmless seascape).

The core problem was becoming, increasingly, one of language—not language as an instrument of reflection but of power-politics, of cut-and-thrust. It has become known, *Time* says, as "serrated language" (viz., "Democrats were to be described as traitors and with such adjectives as *sick, corrupt,* and *bizarre...*"). This may be a coinage, I suspect, known only to the wordsmiths who originate these kind of phrases; but *Time* remains its bright little self by doing a notable double portrait of President Clinton and his challenger House-Speaker Newt Gingrich, two Southern boys who made it big in American politics:

Born three years apart, each was the eldest child of a lively and worshipful mother; each tangled with a gruff stepfather. Both can produce elementary school-teachers willing to testify that they each landed exactly where they always intended. Both are natural teachers, verbally promiscuous and deeply pragmatic. Both sacrificed everything for their public lives, but indulged themselves in their private lives: both are overeaters who tried marijuana and chased women. Neither served in Vietnam. And both own '67 Mustangs.

This is *Time* writing in its characteristic effulgence, with fascinating and mostly irrelevant detail in an ornate wrapping. By the way, the significance of the last climactic item above will be lost on all those (especially *Time* readers of the various International editions abroad) who don't follow the fads and fantasies of old-car vintage drivers in the U.S.—the '67 Mustang, made by Ford, being the current "in" model of worshipful hot-rodders. A very "little knowledge" is sometimes sufficient, but too often taken for granted.[6]

This is dated 1996. Unrecorded is the daring surmise that one would slip from power and headlines within a year or two (and Gingrich did)—and the other might in another year or two be slipping away in disgrace (a fate for the other Southern boy that appears likely). One can't know these things. Is there place in our newspaper culture for wild guesses?

There were spontaneous and unusual public reactions at the formal occasion of Diana's funeral (1997): for example, unashamed shedding of copious tears rather than the vaunted British keeping-a-stiff-upper-lip. Every paper (and photographer) recorded the tens of thousands of bouquets deposited in many places in London (and also in the Great Park in Windsor), all still wrapped in their florist's cellophane, as if no prickly rose should scratch the memory. Each story, and the whole world press was covering it, made a point of registering the slightest departure from the historic royal protocol or even traditional behavior on state occasions. Who ever saw city crowds applauding as the coffin on the gun-carriage rolled by? And when the gigantic TV screens brought the sight and sound of Elton John's gig to the outside millions, applause for the pop star swelled into the Abbey and, perhaps for the first time in a thousand years, the ancient church heard hands clapping at the sound of music in the nave. A few of the press and TV commentators reacted sniffily, but such gestures had their own standard conventionality, even if they were better known in crowded TV-studios when the stars came out at night.

On certain occasions, when the news is hugely controversial or universally tragic, there is a thoroughgoing immersion in opinionated expertise; and whenever it is monotone in its repetition of a cliché it turns out to be barking up the wrong tree. The innumerable analyses of the "deeper meaning" of Princess Diana's public life, and its conflict with or disapproval by the stuffy royal establishment, underlined unswervingly one thesis. This had been a young woman of the modern spirit, who wanted to go places and see things for herself. It reflected, so it was said, a contemporary generation of dissenting young people who, for example, would have liked to have seen the flag flying at half-mast when Diana had passed away—even though it never flies at half-mast at Buckingham Palace, where it serves as the unbroken emblem of sovereignty, never to be lowered not even on the passing of Queen Elizabeth II's father, grandfather, and great grandmother (respectively, George VI, George V, and Queen Victoria). But the expressive sentiment of simple respect from a million mourners for the "People's Princess" triumphed against stiff-necked historical protocol: and the standard was indeed lowered to half-mast for the very first time in recorded history. The end-result was a world-wide impression of a victory of the modernistic vs. the traditional all along the line. Was this really the case?

I, for my own part, sensed that a little knowledge had, again, done duty for more wide-ranging thoughtfulness; and when an attentive scholar came up with an alternative explanation the whole impressionistic tissue of newspaper punditry seemed to crumple. One editor—who quoted what Simon Schama, a well-known and incisive British historian who teaches at Harvard, said on the subject—was moved to confess, "I wonder if Diana's true legacy to the monarchy is not that it should become more modern, but that it should return to something altogether more ancient and mystical." Some polls have indicated the increasing unpopularity of the Royal Family, and indeed that only 15 percent of the survey sample agreed that "the monarchy and the royal family should stay as they are now." The pathos of the Princess' death led many to believe that her approach ("more modern...be with it!") should be adopted. She visited hospitals in war-torn Africa and leper colonies in India, embraced AIDS victims and fondled crippled children, etc. But, as Schama has written,

> When Diana laid hands on the sick, especially on the victims of AIDS, she was tapping one of the most ancient rituals of royal magic: thaumaturgy or touching the king's evil. Medieval kings, at their coronation and on each subsequent anniversary, would extend their hands to those suffering from the disfiguring disease of scrofula. It was believed that through their divine appointment they were able to absorb the evil of the disease in their own bodies and exorcise it. This was the emblematic miracle of monarchy, distantly related to the Gospel of Jesus washing the feet of the poor.

Still: the contemporary pressure for change will not be denied; Buckingham Palace will be, more or less, "re-styled." But whether a reformed monarchy will move into a modernizing future (with royals using mobile phones on bicycles in urban traffic, en route to hard-rock cafés by way of the local cancer clinic) or forward into another phase of the thaumaturgical past, we can safely leave to the small band of high-tech royalty-watchers. The paparazzi may get the picture, but still won't catch the real meaning.

Of Rats and Men

In one Indian tragedy we have had to do with instant anthropology, for when and where modern medicine appears to fail, there is always recourse to the customs and mores of what Ruth Benedict called (fatefully, I think) "patterns of culture." Whether pneumonic or bubonic the plague has to do with the rodent called *rattus rattus,* and it is well-known that poor sanitary conditions breed huge rat populations. But not a reader in a million—as I roughly calculate the élite versed in comparative religion or the sociology of theology—suspected (I quote from the dispatch by the *Washington Post's* John Ward Anderson in Surat, India) that "there has never been a program to combat the scourge because the animal is often worshipped as the companion of Ganesh, the popular Hindu elephant-headed god."[7]

If true—and there is reason to doubt it as sound or pertinent Hindu iconography: as if the rat shared in the protected sanctity of the holy cow, wandering in India's streets—then the bubonic plague would have obliterated the Hindu homelands in the Indian sub-continent long since. And if there was an element of pious neglect in doing something about the contagion-spreaders, then the rodents had good company in the animal kingdom with the local donkeys, cats, pigs and goats, the rotting carcasses of which lay about in thousands. In point of fact, in the next days, Ganesh or no, the Indian government (with, presumably, no risk of heresy or excommunication) mobilized vast reserves of rat-poison and -gas with which, in addition to emergency supplies of antibiotics, it attempted to control the spread of the plague. As Amit Roy reported from Surat ("a ghost town ravaged by fear"),

> this is not a good time to be an Indian rat, which last week became the target of a nation-wide extermination campaign (especially in Bombay, where there are an estimated 50 million rats—five for each resident).[8]

And is each and every quintet traditionally protected—"the holy companions of the elephant-headed God Ganesh," as *Der Spiegel* suggested (3 October 1994)—as part of a personal pantheon of deities? Hardly likely. As a matter of fact, another school of Indian bacteriology believes that dead rodents may be more harmful, that (to quote the Health Minister in Delhi) "killing rats may have the opposite effect ... since if all the rats were killed, rat fleas, more likely to spread plague, would have nowhere to go." Why, just for the appearance of sounding anthropologically "meaningful," drag Vishnu and Shiva and their furry friends into it?

No, Marx was wrong, yet again. Instant social science is as erratic as takeaway ideology. On occasions a little bit of ignorance helps. But then it is probable that it isn't ignorance that I'm after—but (as Mark Twain pointed out) "knowing so much that ain't so...."

The Troubles of the Queen of Green

Our newspapers, being themselves regular victims of "a little knowledge," are the valuable source for information (occasionally sauced up with a note of knowing superiority) of the gaps in other people's mental make-up. How could it be that they—erring professors, half-educated politicians, blank-faced tycoons—know so precious little?

Here is our favorite business enterprise: the fabulously successful cosmetics empire The Body Shop, founded by Anita Roddick, that tireless ecological crusader who, in addition to knowing how to make money, is an expert on the rain-forests, the arid deserts, and affiliated Green concerns. The company suddenly stumbled into financial crisis. The expansion from Britain into the U.S. with several hundred additional shops incurred severe losses. How to get back into profit again? Surely by "upwardly revising" that meager fund of knowledge which the Roddicks had brought to their discovery of the new world.

Now they sure knew better. Gordon Roddick announced something unprecedented, a campaign of advertising commercials, in an attempt to boost its flagging transatlantic sales. Advertising, according to grey theory of the Green movement, is so capitalistic, is such a low manipulative technique, that they never went into it before. As he confessed to newspaper interviewers, *1. "A recognition that the American culture and psyche is completely different."*

Shouldn't a measure of difference have occurred to them before? More could have been gained by reading a book or two by Sir Denis Brogan, the eminent Cambridge historian, or even consulting a simple U.S. history textbook by, say, Nevins and Commager. But still, in the end, America's psyche will not have proved to be so *completely* different! And, poor man, he will just have to think yet again. He and his good wife, they admit, "need time for reflection and re-invention."

2. "America is so huge that perhaps we need to give awareness levels a bit of a kick." It is indeed so huge that there may well be room in its gigantic advertising industry for "kicking awareness levels." And perhaps even for something so pseudo-Madison-Avenue-ese as the snappy jingling slogan the Roddicks are offering for consideration—*"There's more than one ingredient in this product...."* If the extra ingredient, as in the ill-fated *Edsel*, is failure, then the *Body Shop* is in for yet another round of self-examination and soul-searching.

3. "America is a society that expects advertising." Americans also expect businessmen, especially foreign ones, to know their stuff. Who is not hep to the power of the Madison Avenue copy-writer? After such little knowledge, what forgiveness? Not on the part of the financial editors of the English newspapers who on this grey Thursday morning in London are having their bit of fun at the expense of The Body Shop. They themselves have often enough gotten their America wrong.

For the harsh fact of the matter is that anybody who wants to compete can come up with the knack of fabricating vitamin-packed moisturizers and "all-natural" cosmetics which contain nothing but environmentally-friendly ingredients (and not-a-one cruelly tested on live animals!). Anita Roddick's unique touch for The Body Shop, in its prospering empire-building stage, was that she was an attractive, loquacious ideologue, in fact the "Queen of Green." Her general eloquence has led to a certain popularity as a spokeswoman for eco-tycoonery or as an anthropo-intellectual in her own right. The *Guardian* once published the following from her pen,

> The Inca maiden is my heroine, defrosted by a melting glacier half a millennium after her sacrifice to the volcano Ampato. In the universal scheme of things, she's been gone for a moment, but to me she is so many worlds away that she suggests an eternity.[9]

Ms. Roddick, unhappily enough, is able to talk in just the same stylish manner that she writes, and accordingly is a favorite highbrow conversationalist on television chat shows. This particular species of jabberwocky appears to be taken by producers and audiences as either crypto-comical or serio-profound so long as the sound-bites are kept brief enough.

Now the colorful laurels have faded. In her latest interviews she is heard railing against finance capitalism that "ignores the human spirit." The bankers and the speculators are in it only for the money, whereas she stands on her "squeaky-clean ethical record." She dismisses the nasty aspersions cast by mean-minded researchers that some of The Body Shop's ingredients were "unnatural" and that a few of the oils and skin-creams were not quite so innocent of the beastly sins of laboratory malevolence. She is busy now with the desperate initiation of Body Shop house-parties to sweep the country "in an off-beat attempt to boost the performance of the company." She is also undertaking a "massive social audit" in order "to define and cement the unique culture of the company."[10]

But what doth it profit a woman "to upwardly revise" by kicking awareness or boosting peformances and thereby lose her soul, even worse her company's unique culture? (I refer, if I may, to the passing evidence of Biblical wisdom [*in re*: ignoring the human spirit] which is to be found in *Matthew* 16:26, or thereabouts.) "Or what can we give in exchange for our souls?"

An article in the *Daily Mail* (24 August 1994) started a whole new wave of bad counter-cultural publicity which hit "the performance of the company." It had started out—with a small £4,000-loan from a neighborhood bank—to do good and serve the light; and it came into the clutches, by its very success, of old conventional capitalistic standards, for patents and especially copyright legalities. Was the idea, and indeed the very name, original? Evidently "Body Shop" was not borrowed from a funny California garage (where Anita's car had been repaired and the anecdote became folklore), but rather from a serious alternative establishment in Berkeley. And years later, after legal wrangles, the Roddicks paid millions to the two little old Berkeley ladies, owners of the original Body Shop, in cosmic compensation for biodegradable damages (or whatever this kind of a rip-off is called in alternative California circles).

The *Mail* correspondent rubbed it in with an on-the-spot interview in Berkeley with Peggy Short and her sister-in-law Jane Saunders. And the *Mail*'s unfriendly editors added nasty headlines to acid effect:

> WE STARTED THE BODY SHOP AT CJ'S GARAGE.*
>
> *The patchouli masked the smell of pot.*
>
> *Exclusive:* American Woman recalled the Heady Days of Her Hippy Perfume Store...and a £2.3 Deal with the Roddicks.

The whole story is one of ideals lost, of utopian disappointment or betrayal: yet again a tale of the pot that failed. A little knowledge gained from Timothy Leary did not make up for what they did not know either about the hippy world (and the temptations of greed) or about America with its business culture—and, as they have since learned, its advertising outreach to consumers and its "formal structures and controls in place at the operational level."

An attentive reader of the newspaper's financial pages comes to realize very early on that success stories often feature know-nothings, and indeed that knowing nothing does not necessarily preclude making good.[11]

Mistranslation and Misunderstanding

The black pejorative carries such a fullness of bile that polemicists are tempted to borrow such loaded words in arguments far away from Ol' Man River. Thus, in a recent book on the *Bundesrepublik* in which the *Washington Post* correspondent, Marc Fischer, is eager to prove that the postwar Germans haven't really made a sharp break with the ugly past. He reports that the appearance of "normalcy" is only a "veneer," and the term *nigger* is hijacked to add to the indictment (which the *Economist*, defending the record of postwar Germany, thought added up to "slander"). In his *After the Fall* (1995) Fischer deals sternly with still-virulent German racism—and he translates the German word *Neger* as "nigger."* He thinks it makes his point; but the traditional term only means (strictly and exclusively) "Negro"; and you might as well cite bad

---

* Marc Fischer, *After the Fall: Germany, the Germans, and the Burdens of History* (1995). "Germany Slandered," in *The Economist* (London), 12 August 1995, pp. 80-81.

Third World relations with a country darkly called Nigeria as even more proof of racial prejudice.

It could be that Mr. Fischer whose dispatches I have followed closely is "one of the best American journalists to cover Germany recently"; but in his book he is, mostly, jumping at shadows. In its exaggerations, misunderstandings, and sheer astigmatism, he has gotten "the big story" wrong. In his rushing around in a two-year stint to interview a neo-Nazi here, an aggressive Autobahn driver there, and "old ghouls" everywhere, it is yet another example of how misleading for a deadline-harried daily newspaperman "a little knowledge" can be. As in the mistranslation of "Neger" as *nigger*, he can be (as one critic puts it) "downright silly."

German usage for propaganda purposes in Hitler's Third Reich did, in point of fact, target American Negroes; and Dr. Goebbels was memorably embarrassed by the victories of the black sprinter, Jesse Owens, "the fastest man in the world," at the 1936 Olympics in Berlin.** The Nazi ideology propounded the thesis that through the "hot music" of jazz (which was prohibited in Nazi Germany) and miscegenation, among other factors, there had been a *Verniggerung* of American culture which boded mortal danger to civilization-as-they-knew-it....Nowadays it turns up, regrettably, in German football matches as a racial slur of irate fans against some allegedly incompetent dark-skinned player; again, in some neo-Nazi conclaves of delinquent youths. It is also to be found in some liberal-left polemics against right-wing writers who are charged with being xenophobic "racists" and with harboring old prejudices about *"die Verniggerung der Kultur"* (a quote from the *Frankfurter Allgemeine Zeitung*, 4 December 1995, p. 32).

Moliere's *bourgeois gentilhomme* spoke prose for "more than forty years without knowing it...." I imagine that many young German readers of *"unser Shakespeare"* have been surprised that the Bard's characters did not speak Schlegel-Tieck German but some foreign language. Television has some virtues and serves as a corrective. One hears, although the translator's voice soon comes up-and-under, that foreign statesmen speak *'furrin*. But the press necessarily translates and, very often, misinterprets and renders falsely. And even when accurate it cannot help giving a false impression, for almost every effort at translating is a traducing.

I can remember in the old New York days when I could only read Thomas Mann in English, wondering why Mynheer Peeperkorn or Professor Settembrini were always saying, "Stuff and nonsense!" like Dickensian fuddy-duddies. I was relieved to find that the word in *Der Zauberberg* was simply *"Quatsch!"* That's more like it.

** Jesse Owens (Alabama-born, 1913-1980), author of a semi-autobiographical book entitled: *Black Think: My Life as Black Man and White Man* (1970).

Some time ago, in the reports from America on the German defeat in the World Cup, the *Herald-Tribune*'s soccer reporter thought that the one-word headline in *Bild* "said almost everything: 'OUT.'" Of course, what the *Bild* said about Germany's exit from the Cup play, if you want to be literal (and I want to be) nothing of the kind—it said "*AUS!*" Translatese is often confounded with the real thing, often distorting seriously; Hitler never said "*Bosh!*" to the British in Munich, and Dr. Adenauer never "*okayed*" the Marshall Plan. It would help if one began with such little things, tiny differences, perhaps mini-peculiarities that one could get used to. Foreigners speak in foreign tongues; a few strange words should remind us.

I am not for the mish-mash of all languages which global-villages are going in for these days—I heard on German TV the reporter saying "*Hier kommt der Team der deutschen Mannschaft!*" (here comes the team of the German team). But what I call the Bi-National Blur is beginning to reach myopic proportions. You begin with "outing" *Bild*, and then you record that "Berti Vogts [the ill-fated German manager] is not without guilt" (when his *Schuld* is only in not being "entirely blameless"). And then you go on to cite a comment from something called the "*Süddeutsche* newspaper" because you are too lazy to spell out *Zeitung* and proof-read it. (*Daily Telegraph*, 12 July 1995.) In this case the fault was not in the foreign correspondent. Robin Gedye, then the *Telegraph*'s Bonn correspondent, was fluent in German (and is the knowledgeable son of the legendary Central European newspaperman, G.E.R. Gedye, whom I met in Vienna in 1946, a sage old fellow!).

It was doubtless the Sub-Editor's fault (or "guilt," if one wants to press charges against him). But it is quite the same all over. Each morning I listen to the press review on the BBC's "for Europe" program and remain astonished how the chap in London ascribes this-or-that newspaper excerpt to this or that "*zheetung.*"

After all, DeGaulle, that nabob of negativism, will be quoted as saying *Non*, and Yeltsin (when things begin to get get worse) *Nyet*. Isn't it worth the trouble to make every effort to get the language, one's own and theirs, reasonably right?

The Dying Woodlands: First the Bad News (then the Good)

The press has been the main echo of our communications system for maintaining an informed public opinion. Books, especially best-sellers, often play a role; but book-readers in the large are eclectic, and the range of literary interest is random, wide, and variegated. The other media, particularly television, have in their original broadcast impact far more force but they are rarely insistent, taking up subjects and dropping them as quickly in kaleidoscopic variety. Our newspapers—and, to be sure, the news-magazines included—

alone have the multiplier effect which put themes on the political agenda, set fashions in attitude and speech, give currency to slogans and catchwords, solidify reputations of the famous and other celebrated public personalities, stir the circulation of grievances and gossip, and altogether play a major role in shaping the way we talk, think, and generally make do in civil society.

Its demerits are well-known, yet even the sharpest of critics are necessarily driven to use the press in order to criticize the press. They have (with the rarest exceptions) no secret sources for facts about what is happening in the world nor any kind of special illumination from on high. The legendary "Constant Reader" can protest and dissent and counter-attack only on the basis of public information derived from...constant reading. In my own youthful experience in New York we used to refer to our knowledge-hungry newspaper-reading habits as costing "eight cents"—a nickel for *PM* (a stylish, opinionated, highbrow paper which offered radical-chic attitudes on all the issues of the day) and three cents for the *New York Times* (the indispensable "newspaper of record" which gave us the facts to corroborate our radical-liberal predispositions). This was, we learned very early on, the open-ended virtue of growing up in a changeable imperfect society but various enough to offer the tools for mental self-development and intellectual independence. Each new adult generation needs to be in some measure grateful to society for its maturity; and if there is no irreversible linear progress, the wherewithal to make up one's own mind has been sufficient unto the day thereof, and the major serious daily newspapers have made significant contributions to this educational democratic progress.

Yet, as I have argued in assessing the information imparted by our well-informed press, a little knowledge can be a danegrous thing; and anything more than a handful of facts, wrapped in some notional analysis and elemental attitudinizing, has never been the journalistic assignment for even the best of our broadsheet press. In its need to simplify, producing a vast corps of columnists (aka *"les simplificateurs terribles"*), small insights regularly prove themselves to be insufficient. In its drive for popularity among the hundreds of thousands, its reader-friendly short-hand often shows itself to be woefully inadequate. But if errors only mislead—and they can be corrected and apologized for in the next morning's paper—there are, I am afraid, more substantial implications to the moral consequences of the conventional wisdom that is being peddled. I, for one, have an easily vulnerable conscience, and it doesn't take very much to plague it with a discomfiting feeling of mild guilt. One personal illustration, and a lesson in how newspapers (and not only they) can get things wrong or, at the least, straddle ambiguities.

The quarter-of-a-century, beginning in the mid-1960s, was characterized by a plethora of crusades, a few of which have been furtively abandoned but not a few have succeeded more than liberal and conservative skeptics found credible at the time. It was a time of heightened awareness of the mortal dangers to peace, to the environment, to health, to nutrition, to animals, to minority peoples, to the weather, etc. etc. For my own part I stopped smoking; disposed cleanly of my litter; treated my largely female staff with conspicuous equalitarian politeness; cut down on my calories; bled for several blood banks. I also viewed with alarm the asphalt jungles of the urban ghettoes, the seasonal extremes of hot and cold, the melanoma lurking in the holiday sunshine, and (last but not least) the apparent blight of our woodlands. This last was especially troublesome. Since I was, in general and at bottom, an eco-skeptic I was fairly lukewarm on the burning issues of "acid rain" and "sick trees," "global warming" and related disasters. I put off doom-saying articles on the subject for *Encounter* magazine, and indulged in ironic dialectical arguments about the contradiction in fighting for animals' rights and trying to save trees at the same time (what was mystic-green for one was natural forage for the other).

I came to regret it. My contributors sent me long screeds which marshalled the counter-arguments; my relations (especially my children and my nieces) sent me lurid newspaper cuttings on the sad state of Latin American rain forests, Southeast Asian and Canadian woodlands, and, closer to home, the Black Forest. Belatedly, I went along with the bandwagon. I still feel phantom pangs of a guilty conscience for not having earlier raised my voice in the chorus.

The newspaper is not usually the place for intellectual reconsideration. But after several decades of apocalyptic headlines announcing imminent calamity, we might well ask how come God is still making so many trees? Were the endless reports on the lethal assaults by pollutants and climatic changes misleading or exaggerated? The ecologists have been having second thoughts; and, especially in Germany where the national cultural temperament has been conditioned for centuries by a romantic mysticism in word and song (and paint) about the forest primeval, the old shock and the new relief have been of historic proportions. A *Washington Post* correspondent, writing from Freiburg in southwestern Germany (in July 1996) rightly considered it big news, and so left us all with a sense of disenchantment:

FAST-GROWING BLACK FOREST DEFIES THE DOOMSAYERS

Evidently the "evergreen cemetery" was not to be. The forest was not "on its deathbed," and all the trees were not dying. As the *Post*'s Rick Atkinson reported,

[R]umors of the forest's death were premature. Not only is the Black Forest still marvelously verdant, but recent studies show that—like forests across most of Europe—it is growing faster than ever.

The scientists themselves were perplexed, even embarrassed, for nobody in the 1970s and 1980s would have believed it—since the measuring began a century or so ago, there has never been a higher volume of wood per acre than there is now. They concede that the earlier, pessimistic prognosis of a rapid, widespread dying of our forests has not occurred; for the forests from Finland to Greece have survived prophecies of their death "largely unscathed." One authority remarked, "Forest death is the classic example of a media phenomenon."

What the press has done, the press can undo: but not always, and not everywhere. The Germans especially are having serious trouble with the story. An important full-page article in one of the *Bundesrepublik*'s best newspapers, the *Süddeutsche Zeitung* (Munich), concedes that only when the "good news" came in from abroad—from the U.S., with the *Washington Post*'s dispatch; and from Switzerland, in the reports of the *Neue Zürcher Zeitung* (which, in its venerable untroubled conservatism, never went in for the gloom-and-doom scenario)—were German newspaper-readers allowed to ponder the spectacle of *das grosse Waldsterben* as a non-event. This was particularly dismaying since the Summer 1996 conference which produced the surprising twelve-nation study of "Growth Trends in European Forests" had actually taken place in Germany, and it was the Freiburg-based *Institut für Waldsterben* which had played host to the scientists who had come together "to expose a myth."

To the extent that the press paid attention to the results there was skepticism and disbelief. The weekly *Die Woche* sniffed a sinister "conspiracy" linking biologists and journalists to the automobile industry; the *Stuttgarter Zeitung* called the whole story a cheap trick with statistics and a futile effort to get around a most serious threat to all mankind; the *dpa* news-agency also went in for a bit of editorializing and dismissed the Europe-wide scientific report as "superficial and fundamentally wrong." Others thought the plot against the ecology of true believers could be traced to lobbyists of the Finnish log industry.

So it was that Professor Heinrich Spiecker (of the Freiburg University's Institute for Forestry) had difficulties getting his message through. The apocalyptic thesis—"We have sinned against Nature, and now Nature is taking its revenge"—he held to be theology, not science. "We Germans have always been susceptible to ideologies which preached decline-and-fall, due to the malaise of a decadent civilization (a mix of *Untergangsromantik, Zivilisationsfeindschaft, und Hysterie*)." A young scholar named Rudi Holzberger added his suitable name to the support of the scientist's dissent, describing "the journalistic madness" as an "extraordinary orgy of morbid German *Gesinnungs-kitsch*," reinforced by post-'68 "mood, motives, metaphors, method"—all alienated from technology, urbanism, and any kind of "exploitation" (of men, women, and other natural resources). What the French had learned to call *le waldsterben* was now proclaimed to be *"passé."* Individual trees may die, substantial inroads on forests may be thoughtlessly executed, bad spells of weather may have deleterious effects; but there is no discernible "global danger," and the forests in Europe are, by and large, undeniably flourishing.

Still, the old "paroxysm" lingered on. Even a Freiburg mayor was outraged, and ordered his parks commissioner to write an immediate and comprehensive reply. Even *Fachzeitschriften* (the professional specialists' journals) refused to print articles which cast doubt on the indubitable ecological conviction that the trees were all dying and the forests would soon all be gone. And indeed the Munich daily, the *Süddeutsche Zeitung*, in printing its full-page account by Burkhard Müller-Ulrich and upsetting the debunking campaign against the report of the Freiburg scientists, promised to publish another article next week, giving the other side of the story (in the tasteless pun of the day, "the horror in the woodpile"). As the mass-circulation picture-weekly *Stern* had argued: What point is there to be protected by American cruise missiles and hydrogen bombs when what we are protecting is rapidly turning into arid acreage, fields of death, a dioxyde steppe?[12]

Thus, sad to relate, another crusade bites the dust. Here is an example of a simple news-story which functions to stand a whole ideology on its head. At least one of our grim environmental concern of only yesterday, so fashionable, so persuasive, was just "misplaced hysteria." Was there, then, no ozone depletion, as we suspected? and wasn't the sulphur in the acid rain rapacious in its unnatural effects? We had seen with our own eyes, hadn't we, the unsightly woods in a desperate yellowing state; shedding needles to minimize transpiration or leaf vaporization, littering hills and valleys with branches and spindly tree trunks. But at the end of the day, lo and behold, the firs are still there, and the conifers have grown, and the spruce trees have flourished. If this ecological recovery and surprising spurt has "mystified" the experts, at least they have shown themselves to be chastened by their earlier false alarms. The Black Forest, for one, has had a startling growth, showing 20-to-30 percent more volume than a few decades ago. Damaged areas have been "stabilized" and restored. As one leading forester was quoted, "Honest people will admit that they don't understand what's happening....It's just that everything's a bit more complicated." I leave the cautionary tale there, with the feeling that this chastened sense of complication is alone worth the annual subscription price for your morning newspaper which dares, every now and then, to print good news and subvert its own fondest discontents.[13]

By and large, it is ideology with its corps of simple-minded enthusiasts—brandishing burning lists of intolerable grievances which can be eliminated at a stroke—which provides most of the meaningful errors characteristic of our newspaper culture. How many stories have we not read in recent decades about the most dire threat to our Mother Planet—this time, not the death of the forest primeval but the growing threat of aridity from the lifeless desert? It is the well-known melodrama of

> giant clouds of dust blown off the arid drought-prone lands round the Sahara desert, grabbed by passing winds and propelled to Berkshire or Barbados or sometimes right around the globe.[14]

It is a matter of well-known seriousness; and even the most mathematical meteorologists make the news headlines when they estimate that up to a billion tons of dust a year blows off the parched African plains and takes the trade winds to the Caribbean. The figure has more than doubled in the past thirty years. And it has been routine to argue that North African farmers have since time immemorial been turning their dry fields to dust. Western environmentalists have used innumerable columns of newsprint to argue that incompetent African farmers and animal herders have been creating irreversible "desertification" of their continent by misusing their soils and allowing them to blow away. One surely had to help the Third World in enlightened aid-programs for the modernization of agriculture.

Yet something curious happened in the summer of 1996. The figure which had been steadily rising—as the needs of the Third World were neglected by the First World—suddenly slumped. The dust output from Africa was the lowest for more than two decades. Had all those aid programs—and indeed these most ambitious and practical projects of the Ford Foundation (new devices for irrigation, plowing, harvesting, etc.)—induced a sudden turn for the ecological good?

Nothing of the sort. The Western scientists looked into the problem, and came up with a different story, first broken in the staid columns of a professional journal (*Nature*, June 1997). What is actually happening, for good or bad, in the fields of Africa has little to do with the extent of the density of the annual African dust clouds. The decisive factor (according to Cyril Moulin of the "Climate Modeling Laboratory" in Gif-sur-Yvette, France, and his colleagues), emerges after a careful examination of the data of thirty years showing how much dust Africa exports on the winds and where it goes. The explanation is rather intricate, having to do with something called the "oscillation" factor, including the difference in air pressure between the two semi-permanent features of the atmosphere, the "Azores high" off Portugal amd the "Icelandic low." Put bluntly, when the Azores high and the Icelandic low are both intense, and the air-pressure difference high, North Africa and the Mediterranean region become very dry. And when the pressure differences diminish, these two regions become wet:

> The "oscillation" between these two extremes drives much of the region's weather year by year, creating droughts and storms across North Africa and western Europe

from Timbuktu to Tipperary. What Moulin has discovered is that the oscillation also dramatically influences the intensity of each year's Saharan dust cloud.

Is this yet another of our newspaper-fed myths biting the dust? When the story gets around will it have a deleterious effect on the noble efforts of the rich to help the poor? We know that the greatest inspiration for philanthropy is the hidden clause which persuades us that compassion is also in our own material interest. Should the funds in the Aid budget be diverted Westward where the real source of the fall-out problem lies? One reporter raises related questions: "Did Africa's farmers suddenly learn the error of their ways? Or should their critics be offering apologies?"[15] The same queries can be directed to the storytellers and the doom-sayers in our newspaper culture. But learning the error of one's ways, and making even the most humble of apologies, will not dispel the residual problem. A continent's failure to feed its own people remains. The need for a new plow is written in the old stars. But will the press be able to discover another collateral self-interest which can ease our light-headed instincts for doing good?

21

Keeping Up with the Avant-Garde

Rewriting the Classics, Modern-Wise

For years now I have not been able to walk into any theater or opera house without fear and trembling. What outrageous feat of transubstantiation would be perpetrated tonight? Characters get transmogrified, centuries (and even millennia) get displaced, gentle romantic melodies become militant war chants, ancient gods become bourgeois bosses, scenes of classical dramaturgy get inter-cut like the broken montage in a television mini-series. And the cultural critics, in New York and London, in Paris and Berlin, proceed to welcome— almost without exception—something original, something new, in tune with (if not far ahead of) the times.

The other day one talented German theater director put on a new opera production of *Macbeth*. It was happening in, of all places, Vietnam. Saigon, of course, lost; but Shakespeare and Verdi even more. Actors ran around in camouflaged boiler-suits, corpses in the chorus were air-lifted from the battlefield by whirling, roaring helicopters; the stage was strewn with empty Coca-Cola cans and crushed Lucky Strike cigarette packets. Macbeth faces his fate, looking out through glinting dark glasses; and he and Macduff play Russian roulette, squeezing triggers, instead of "laying on" until one cries "Hold, enough!"

The first-night audience, as a newspaper critic wrote the next day, was converted into a "bawling, brawling mob" by the provocations of a *Regisseur* called Günter Krämer, until the conductor mounted the stage and begged for "respect for the singers." And a heckler cried, "But they can't even sing!"

> And be these juggling fiends no more believ'd
> That palter with us in a double sense;
> That keep the word of promise to our ear,
> And break it to our hope. (*Macbeth*, V.vii.48)

313

In London, as I recall, this kind of fiendish thing is more politely received. In the Coliseum, at the English National Opera's production of Rossini's *Moses* a few years ago, I seemed to be the only one in the audience groaning and moaning audibly at the proceedings. The arias were sung against the background of blown-up photographs (Johannesburg demos, Belfast riots) and poster-size "relevant" quotations (Menachem Begin, Nelson Mandela). The Mosaic liberation of the promised land was converted into some kind of guerrilla warfare, with the children of Israel taking their Kalashnikovs (from under their ragged biblical robes) to shoot it out with the Egyptians (in smoked spectacles and grey double-breasted suits).

The Germans order these things better; that is to say, with less simple-minded political naivety and more absurd metaphysical complications. A new Viennese version of *The Merchant of Venice* is Peter Zadek's third neo-German attempt to do justice to Shakespeare's anti-Semitism. Himself a Jew (and a returned émigré from England), he seems to be obsessed with the idea that it is wrong for the Germans not to be willing to play Shylock for the unmitigated villain he is. (Indeed Zadek defended Rainer Werner Fassbinder's scandalizing German play about the character—a Jew, of course—who was responsible for most of the current evil on Frankfurt's city-streets.) I once saw in Berlin that fine actor Ernst Deutsch portray Shylock in the first postwar performance of *The Merchant*; he played as if he were a cross between Nathan the Wise and Moses Maimonides; but Zadek won't have any of this nobility, this hypocrisy, at all.

But perhaps Shakespeare's Elizabethanism has been getting in the way of the clear contemporary message that evidently cries out to be conveyed. So Peter Zadek transforms the story into the Merchant of Wall Street. It all takes place in a skyscraper like Manhattan's Trump Tower. A youthful Shylock reads the *Wall Street Journal*, does his money calculations on a mini-computer, wears fashionable Dior shirts, carries his commercial documents in an attaché case, and takes calls on his cordless telephone. If he impressed one German reviewer as being the "coolest" character in all the Bard's work, he is nevertheless leading—ever universal, always relevant—the stormy wave of current resentment against "the Yuppies." Into the bonfire of vanities with them all! In the new translation which Peter Zadek commissioned, the jokes are "in," the puns are "right on," not all of them redeemed by snappy delivery on the part of clever actors in pin-striped suits, revealing in shirt-sleeved moments the broad yellow suspenders that mark brokerage-*chic*. (I thought: is there anything so baleful as ingenuity when its genius takes a wrong turn?)

By the time I got to *The Ring of the Nibelungen* at the Deutsche Oper (although Götz Friedrich's famous production has toured most of the world's great opera houses) I was prepared for anything; but Götz Friedrich's *Siegfried*, to listen to it, is almost conventional Wagner. True, there are no longer any spears and helmets, and the Fafner monster which our hero strikes dead looks (from where I sat) more like a Mark VI-*Panzer* left over in the surrealistic ruins of the next World War. Still, Mime forges the magic sword in a credible smithy's fire, and Siegfried follows the song of the Woodbird like the melodic country boy he is said to be. Wotan the Wanderer wanders through the painted scenery believably.

Could it have been as old-fashioned as it seemed and sounded? Was there no secret message between the chords of the recurrent motifs? How could the furies of modernism—or, rather, modernization—have stopped short of this stage? They didn't. I soon discovered the hidden meanings as disclosed in the official "Diary Notes" of the production which had been going around the world; and I append here a few extracts for the benefit of ultimate clarification and for those, apart from Bernard Levin, who are interested in the authentic de-structural explication of the text.

In Wagner's first act, in the scene between Wotan and Mime, we have to understand that the latter is like *"Ein kaisertreuer Sozialdemokrat im Marschtempo"* (which is supposed to suggest, if you can bear it, old social democrats in loyal goose-step for their Kaiser). As the plot thickens the woodland woodwinds are to hint at "an androgynous bird-form as in Chagall" and Mime becomes, before the curtain, a kind of "modern psychopath." As the producer tellingly remarks: "Isolated intellectuals become childish...." Even worse, it is in such moments (as Götz Friedrich himself instructs us) that "these kind of people invent the H-Bomb"!

Siegfried presents similar problems that we knew not of. "Don't discredit him as a anti-Nazi, he is no blond beast!"—although he does have a bit of "a Super-Man touch." But then he is intended to be, in the last analysis (after entrancing Wagnerian hours), *also* a bit of an "anti-Hero." Altogether there must be an element of *Heimat*-drama to it all, an echo of "émigrés" and exile. In the second act the plot should constrict to a point "where it is worse than Ibsen...." Evidently worse also than in Marx, because it must add up to the thesis that the "classical class struggle is outlived."

As for the monster scene with Fafner, I was right after all, catching on with my first guess. The production diary reveals that the evil "worm" is actually "a Panzer with a crazy colonel who has survived World War III."

If you were puzzled afterwards by bits in the second half of the second act, you will be reassured to know that "the whole scene is the quintessence of Absurd Theatre—a hundred years before Ionesco and Dürrenmatt...." More than that, Siegfried, in killing Mime by sheer accident, shows himself to be at heart something of "a Pacifist." Nevertheless, when Siegfried approaches the cliffs of the *Walkyrie* he has to move like the US Navy's "Astronauts who first landed on the moon."

And if you find this psychologically chaotic, it goes back to the fact that Wagner was writing "a model psychoanalytical drama." Sexy Brunnhilde remembers what happened to "the Olympian Call-Girls." Siegfried, recalling his mother, has taken "an embryonic position" (I missed this one completely in the semi-darkness). But then, as in his battle with the mad colonel of World War III, he is quite capable of scoring a hit "at the very center of *Angst.*"

Much Nordic nonsense spooked around in the recesses of Richard Wagner's fertile brain, but nothing compared to the strange brew in which musical drama is cooked these days. *Götterdämmerung*, the next afternoon, would seem to present no additional problems, except to keep the soap opera flakes stirring in the pot. And so we have in the *Vorspiel*, where Siegfried takes his farewell of Brunnhilde, joy and sadness mixed but something more too: "as if the next Coca-Cola could contain poison." That sense of sinister pollution carries even into Act III, Scene 1, when the Rhine Maidens swimmingly return: but almost lifelessly, with difficult movements, as if they were sick, polluted fish in the North Sea.

But I am getting ahead of myself. In the great Gibichung castle Siegfried must arrive "like Tarzan breaking into the big city." Then, of course, Gunther —who is, after all, at home—can "behave himself as an English Lord, intolerably aristocratic." So it follows that Gutrune would be "playing Lady Di."

If you think that this is rather a complicated family situation even for Wagnerian gods, we have to realize that the whole atmosphere is suffused with "a hatefulness rather like in *Dallas* or in *Dynasty*" (known to the German TV millions as the Denver Clan). In the second scene of Act III, when Siegfried gets into some trouble, the atmosphere worsens to "that of the Ku Klux Klan," and this might be in some way connected to the atmosphere a few scenes earlier in which Siegfried feels displaced as "a woodsman in Wall Street" or "Dustin Hoffman as 'Midnight Cowboy.'" At any rate the tension is altogether supposed to be that of Alfred Hitchcock's "psycho-thrillers" and when emotion touches horror it shifts rapidly to "Jack Nicholson flying over the cuckoo's nest."

If we have got it all correctly, and down to the last subtle innuendo, we might as well have gone to the movies.

Wagner, I seem to recall, once said that he wanted to emigrate to America, to the Wild West, possibly to California; and who knows whether, in our era of modernizing sensibility, it might legitimate this kind of Hollywoodization of the *Ring*. One scene between Siegfried and Brunnhilde (Gwynneth Jones: magnificent in this role, but clad in tight punk leather) is, as Götz Friedrich guides us, supposed to be "like a Hollywood director's," and the business of dragons and dwarfs is supposed to be something out of "Disneyland."

Still, Berlin is, in the end, where it's all at; and the realities around us—a post-Communist confusion and disarray—can't simply be ignored. I was almost relieved to note on the last page of the Berlin Opera House's "production diary" that those two arch-villains Alberich and his son Hagen, slouching around the stage and noisily plotting their conspiracy and revenge, were compared to nobody less than "a Trotsky in exile." No matter that this is more the "reality" among the remnants of the old Kremlin orthodoxy (where Stalin is still a worthy and Trotsky still a wrecker) than of West Berlin (where Gorbachov's and Yeltsin's truth-telling, even about Trotsky, circulates freely). After all, we're fast friends now; memories of concrete walls and iron curtains have almost made us good neighbors.

Towards a Negative Cultural Tax

Far be it for me to propose moving the clocks back to the days when Hamlet had more to do with Hecuba than with Hitchcock, and the Nibelungen more to do with the Norsemen than the nattering nabobs of neo-modernism. But if the reader can bear with a modest proposal it might look like this.

"A Fund for Contemporaneity," dedicated to the defense of time and place and atmosphere, might be administered by a Trans-Atlantic Arts Council (British delegates: Lord Annan, Lord Quinton, Lord Beloff; American delegates: Hilton Kramer, Tina Brown, Oliver Stone), and it would use for appropriate cultural charity all monies which the cash penalties hereunder specified cause to flow into its coffers.

I remember having dinner in London with Sir Georg Solti, and although he was "a modernist" as befits a friend of Béla Bartók he agreed to sit in hostile judgment in order (in his own energetic phrase) to "stop the rot." (But he died, in 1997, before we would finalize our strategy.)* He consented to act on the jury and, possibly, dissent—as he often did in his career at the Royal Opera House—in favor of a few efforts which go beyond making some vapid statement about Cleopatra taking dope and how Caesar would have died of AIDS whether conspirators cut him down or not.

Meanwhile, the cultural St. Vitus dance continues, and in the operatic world (as our newspapers report incessantly) with compulsive and very predictable twists of plot and character. Clever directors are not facile or mobile enough to walk around their modernizing ideas and pronounce, with much-needed self-criticism, that one or another inspiration (or gimmick) of theirs was bad and, consequently, not being worth putting on the stage. My young friend, Luc Bondy, could not resist the "twitch" to put in his Berlin production of Shakespeare's *A Winter's Tale*, just before the famous "exit of Bear," a snatch of "relevant" or "alienating" music which came from an old-fashioned Wurlitzer juke-box in the corner of the stage. (If Bohemia has, as the Bard thought, "a seashore," why not a discotheque? Fantasy is free.)

In the season I am writing, the operas of Rossini seem to be more of a target than Shakespeare. One would have thought that his main operatic characters including Moses the law-giver and the Algiers Sultan were exotic and multicultural enough to interest late twentieth-century music listeners. But no, in an old London production (as I have mentioned) Moses and his band of Hebrew

---

* And so have several other admirable counselors who died too soon.

exiles carry Kalashnikovs under their ancient Biblical robes. And in a performance of Rossini's opera about the lovely Italian girl in Algiers in the brilliantly ornate Semper Oper in Dresden (glitteringly restored), Mustafá the Arab
potentate turns up in the obligatory general's vanilla uniform (Pinochet, yet
again?), sporting the usual smoked glasses. Where there's smoke there's fire,
and somewhere in the middle of the opera's complications a Tourist Cruiser
burns and sinks in the harbor. This, surely, offers more action than the conventional hijinks in traditional Italian opera.

Even in Washington, D.C., so respectful of the past in political circumstances, inspired directors take operatic liberties, this time in the opening night
of *Pagliacci* (November 1997 with Placido Domingo in the title-role). We
are treated in a Franco Zeffirelli production, as one newspaper reviewer
reported, to "drug-dealers and transvestites, roaming children and their
worried mothers, rollerblading teenagers that looped across the stage, set
as a grimy Italian ghetto." Placido Domingo, as the tragic clown, has his
work cut out for him, asserting himself against a noisy stage-crowd of
hundreds. Small wonder that his classic aria, *Vesti di giubba,* is so full of tears
and heartbreak.[1]

If Jonathan Miller wants (and he wanted, so badly) to stage *The Merchant
of Venice* in nineteenth-century Manchester—with Shylock pacing the Mid-
lands *Bourse* in a long coat and shiny top hat—he can certainly get on with it.
But for the copyright permission to circumvent, or indeed violate, the classic
text so extravagantly, two fines would have to be paid.

First, 1 percent of theater takings, or a flat royalty (whichever is the greater),
for the *geographical* misdemeanor, calculated on the number of miles or kilometers between the original and the displacement (in this case, between Venice
and Manchester, roughly 1,800 miles as the crow flies).

Secondly, for the *chronological* offense which is based on the number of
years involved in the distortion of the contemporary integrity (in Miller's case,
roughly, 375 years—"holding a candle to his shames" for recklessly moving
the Renaissance to the Industrial Revolution). Tricksters like Bert Brecht who
try in sharp practice to shift the Hitler story to the South Side of Chicago
gangsterdom (the *Führer* comes to power in 1933, but Al Capone shoots his
way to the top in 1929) would be caught by my "Negative Cultural Tax"; and
minus three-or-four years would be punished doubly for the obvious and premeditated interference with chonological justice.

It was surely inconceivable in the classic era of operatic achievement—the
century of Verdi and Puccini, Rossini and Wagner and others of their format—
that in a later period it would be only stage business, a young director's touch
or a clever producer's modernistic inspiration that would reputedly save such
masterpieces for changing tastes and new audience appetites. Who would have
thought that even the well-made plays of Shakespearean libretti would be

felt one day to be lacking in adequate dramatic appeal? that they could not hold together, or grip the imagination, without recourse to the optical fads of our underworld gangster types (hooded behind dark spectacles), or the leather-jacketed fashion of the sinister Gestapo and SS (jack-booted, heel-clicking)?

An observant correspondent in post-Soviet Moscow reassures us that the heritage of Stalinism is also proving helpful. A *Washington Post* notice of a new *Aida* production at the Helikon Theater in Moscow does its bit to make ancient Egypt more believable – it has the scenic marching columns wearing scarves "reminiscent of Communist youth groups." But never fear, the standard stratagems of modernization are still deployed to give the plot its usual touches of totalitarian topicality. Our reporter duly spotted that the costumes in *Aida* (director, Dmitri Bertman, 1997) "grafted pharaonic garb onto Nazi-style uniforms" (rather than the other way around, which adds a flash-back element of time-warp). He also recorded that the inevitable Verdi chorus "resembled a Communist-era parade in Red Square more than anything familiar to King Tut...."[2]

Whatever cultural tax may be imposed on the Muscovites for their enterprising, if not very original heresies, they will be relieved to know that they can pay in fairly worthless rubles. Paying the fine in black-market dollars or new *euros* could bankrupt them and might make them long for old-time orthodoxies, even Stalin's rigid formalism.

Atmospheres are a thornier problem to deal with, but my "Cultural Clean Air Act" for the new millennium would deal with the more obvious pollutants —Moses as Yasser Arafat, Creon as Castro, Julius Caesar as J.R., Shylock as Yuppie, Kean as Sartre, Siegfried as Jack Nicholson, Macbeth as Murdoch or Maxwell, Othello as Nelson Mandela, Faust as Albert Einstein or J. Robert Oppenheimer, Freud and Sherlock Holmes as men with golden arms....

But how to deal with new, imaginative projects which are in the hopper?* Eugene O'Neill's *The Iceman Cometh*, set in an igloo somewhere near the

---

*   According to a current item of theatrical news from Bremen (where great phantasts like Peter Stein and Peter Zadek have directed), there will be yet another new production of *The Merchant of Venice*, seen now to be a tragedy of "a figure who far from his homeland becomes a stranger unto himself...." Thus, Shylock will be played as Othello.

My proposal for the U.N., in its future culture-keeping activities, is to hit back, apply sanctions, quarantine the aggressor. My program, in a supplementary protocol for this kind of high-brow vandalism ("transposed heads"), calls for: (1) a one-day strike in Stratford-on-Avon; (2) the breaking-off of relations with Bremen and all its "twinned cities" in Europe; (3) the Schlegel brothers and Ludwig Tieck, the Bard's original translators, to turn noisily in their graves; (4) an infliction on the part of Bremen of a violent Shakespearean tempest followed by a liberating invasion by Fortinbras' forces; and (5) a freezing and requisitioning of all official bank accounts which subsidize the city's *Schauspielhaus*.

North Pole; Terence Rattigan's *The Deep Blue Sea*, played as a submerged drama of underwater divers. Do we need extra punitive categories to capture such and similar metaphorical outrages, involving thermal or nautical displacements? And what should the noble English lords (Beloff, Annan, and Quinton) and the American delegates (Kramer, Brown, Stone) of our Euro-American Arts Council be doing with all the millions?

I welcome any suggestions and advice from jurists, dramaturgists, and philanthropoids. Payment for contributions on the normal royalty scale will, of course, be adjusted by calculating similar differences in time, space, and climate, as well as the mix of mixed metaphors.

A Forward and Backward Glance

Just as in the patter of a stand-up comic, where there is no consistent theme running through except the frenetic attempt to get you to laugh, just so one wants to ask whether individual artists, in this inspired jumble of gags and "art one-liners" (in the phrase of a critic), maintain a line of general intention, perhaps even an aesthetic purposefulness. Most of the time we are in intellectual silence, with the artists insisting that their works must speak for themselves; subsequently, the critics and the curators must supply the rationale and explicate the statements. I have been recently interested in the work of a young English woman, Rachel Whiteread, who has won first prizes in Vienna, Venice, and many points in between. Writing about her meteoric career, the *Sunday Times* art reviewer makes, as always, a valiant attempt to be as near as fulsome in his praise of avant-garde meaningfulness as he can credibly get without tipping over into pseudery:

> What gives her work such splendid and unmissable presence is the contrast between the austerity of the shapes she ends up with in her casts and the richness of the memories they evoke. The irrevocable passage of time is her favourite theme, and her instant memorials are a doomed attempt to arrest the process. All this is sad and nostalgic, but never grim.[3]

The *Times* man was not referring to her sculpture but an installation which was awarded the best artist's prize in the forty-seventh Venice Biennale—she had presented an imaginative piece of toiletry which was hailed as "a monument to every rusty bath that has ever been yanked out of an old house to make way for a new one." Her first and substantial claim to fame was the first prize that she was given in Vienna, for a proposed Holocaust memorial in the open square of the *Judenplatz*. She had wanted (as a critic interprets her inspiration) "to erect a monument to lost knowledge, a kind of library in reverse, in which only the imprints of the tomes that once filled the shelves remain." The prize-winning model has been shown in several European cities, but it has yet to be built. When I saw them on exhibit I found the sketches and the model which she had submitted to be cold and insignificant and a very far cry indeed from the evocation of "rich memories." In a discussion with representatives of the Jewish communities in both Vienna and Berlin I sensed that they, unlike the jury of avant-garde experts, had also been left unresponsive and indifferent. The young woman had captured nothing of the tragedy, had created nothing that could move a Holocaust survivor, not to speak of a visiting tourist. It was perfectly appropriate for her to go on in her career to rusty bath tubs. One felt intuitively that her shelves of untitled books, of "missing volumes"—presented in her style of sentimental minimalism which contrasts unfavorably with, say, Anselm Kiefer's formidable preoccupation with ruined libraries—evoked a feeling of general illiteracy rather than the bookish melancholy of Dr. Goebbels' infamous literary bonfire of 1933, not to mention the torching of the sacred scrolls of the Torah in the *Kristallnacht* of 1938.

One American art critic, reporting to his newspaper on the same Venetian Biennale, underlined the suggestion that is mostly suppressed (or repressed) in the milieu, namely, that we may be at "the end of a cycle," that we were about to see a "reincarnation" of other, older artistic motivations, which would resolve the differences between "so-called post-modernist art and real art." He quoted one painter (a Russian artist, as it happens) to the effect that the disregard of true individuality and "rendering art anonymous" has been, in his view, "the greatest crime against art." In many quarters this journalistic note in the reporting of the artistic scene is taken to be the tone of heavy old philistinism, of mindless know-nothingism, of familiar splutterings against the contemporary achievements of the avant-garde. Some say it takes courage to swim against the tide, no matter in which direction the main currents are flowing. (Maverick critics like Robert Hughes, Brian Sewell, Fritz Raddatz, Hilton Kramer, among others, are far from sharing a common ideology or aesthetic.) It is certainly unusual for a major contemporary exhibition to be looked at askance, with cool:

> Many exhibitors have done pieces specially for the show, and among them are "found" works, such as a brand-new, exceedingly expensive-looking mechanical digger thereafter festooned with tinsel and Christmas decorations, a giant sphere coated with dead beetles, a pile of rubble intertwined with copper funnels and tubes, photos, videos, beer bottles, distressed furniture.

Can a reader detect a new, if slight, note of disenchantment in this dreary inventory of witless objects which otherwise would have been presented in the expensive catalogues as an array of major artistic achievements, if not masterpieces? The six-column headline in the *Herald-Tribune*—A PARTING OF THE WAYS IN VENICE—might have been a shade too melodramatic, for there was nothing (nor could there as yet be) in Robert Conway Morris's long dispatch which hinted at "the other way." Except for our Russian friend, Maxim

Kantor, who was offering "echoes of the painters he admires, from Goya to van Gogh...." (So what else is new.)[4]

From what our papers have been saying, only a handful have deviated from the prevailing present trends. How does this bode for the future? Is it conceivable that whole regiments (nay, armies) of the avant-garde forces can be persuaded to take a backward glance, to look over their shoulders, perhaps to consider making an about-turn, to mix and mingle with the exhausted combat-fatigued rear-guard? Might there be substantial defections from (in Harold Rosenberg's famous phrase) "the herd of independent minds" which has, in modernist times, always run predictably with the bulls? In our newspaper culture the news has all been for half-a-century now about "the revolution of the new." The grumbles of the scattered counter-revolutionaries—famous conservatives and notorious reactionaries like Bernard Berenson (in Florence), Hans Sedlmayer (in Munich), Herbert Read (in London), Hans Sahl (in New York) —have long since been put aside or forgotten. What has been notably happening is that our mainstream press, seduced by—or intimidated by—the avant garde, is giving signs of enough self-confident non-conformism to pay attention to "the revolution of the old" when and if it should begin. It might, after all, even provide a good human-interest tale, a fast-breaking fifteen-minute story under the banner headline, "The Day that Andy Warhol Ceased to Be Famous," sad news but still fit to print.

Meanwhile, there are mounting indications of "deviance" as reported by newspapers previously allied to the money and power which have come in our century to the trend which is fashionable and *chic*. In a series of scintillating interviews with Madame Catherine David, the brilliant and self-possessed high priestess of the Documenta in Kassel, the grilling is almost unprecedented. As in all revolutions an old guard feels that a young guard has just been going too far, that a new zealotry of enthusiastic latecomers is distorting or corrupting the early revolutionary promise. There are many examples of European, and even American, intellectuals who have fought the good fight over the last three decades on behalf of any and every "radical breakthrough" in literature and the arts putting their angry and embittered questions. One can only hope that when the next trend preoccupies tomorrow's newspaper culture that the pendulum will not be swinging too sharply in a new direction.

Bert Brecht's Three Dots

The avant-garde, as in the sense of disorientation as early as George Sand,[*] tends always to be losing its way, by the very virtue of its being so far up front.

---

[*]   See Curtis Cate's long and useful biography, recording her constant struggle to be loyal to the traditional credo of France's *avant-garde*, including the pure ideal of "revolution" *à la* 1789 (or 1793). Curtis Cate, *George Sand: A Biography* (1975).

It commits itself to being first, even a lonely point in an advancing column, pioneers wanting to be ahead at all risks. Let me conclude with the case of a little phrase—an off-color line in a play by Bert Brecht—and how, in the light of what has been happening to "night words" in our liberated language, it suffers a kind of sad post-coital fate.

The camouflage of the F-words on the printed page, as was our mid-twentieth-century custom, presents a certain special phonetic difficulty if a salty text, peppered with one or more four-letter words, is supposed to be, on one occasion or another, "read out loud." How do you pronounce three asterisks, four dots, five hyphens? The challenge comes up rather rarely, one admits, even though the pursing of the lips in the phenomenon of what I have called "participatory obscenity" needs to be pornographically correct. One calculates the omitted letters quickly, and lets the blandishment fit the rhyme. Most readers of the press, if they are not altogether cut off from the ways of the world, make the match in a slightly embarrassed and discomfiting instant, and go on.

The profanity in the texts of film scenarios—the F-word occurs several dozens times per hour in the snappy Hollywood filming of Elmore Leonard's novel *Get Shorty* (1996)—needs no spelling tricks or orthographic disguises, and is spoken as written. Novels too—in the enlightened era after Hubert Selby's *Brooklyn* liberation—are unproblematical: all spaces are now properly filled. Still, there is a dimension beyond space that I want to mention briefly: the dimension of sound when calculatedly discreet prose needs to be spoken audibly.

One example. In Bert Brecht's famous play of 1948, *Herr Puntila und sein Knecht Matti*, currently enrichened with the dramatic atmosphere of some orgiastic, bacchanalian scenes, the sexy question is put (and this is how the playwright put it): *"Kannst du anständig f...?"* How does an actor pronounce the three dots of the F-word? He doesn't—he says the whole word, which in German cultural contexts (especially in the serious avant-garde postwar theater) causes rather less upset than on the stages of New York and London. Surprisingly enough, German reviewers of the latest Berlin production of the play (in the Schiffbauerdamm Theater which still houses Brecht's Berliner Ensemble) have taken serious exception. If an artist goes in for a bit of self-censorship, let no man uncensor him. Too many liberties are being taken with the texts of the Master, and B.B. did in fact write *"f..."* He had no time for the *risqué*. (Raunchy he may have been in his private life but his real and rude message was revolution.)

This criticism (and an outraged review appeared in *Tip* magazine) was rather on the absurd side. Was the objection some sort of burst of neo-puritanism? How else could you give voice to such f..r-l....r words? Omit them? Mouth them in a whisper? Mime them with coarse gestures? Stutter along with a couple of f's and swallow the rest? The issue is entertaining, if not universal. I imagine that even the BBC, when it gets around to adding spice to its routine Press Review broadcasts, will have no trouble pronouncing, quoting, and expleting the standard salacities as they are suggestively printed in the London daily papers. The latest stumbling block is the latest Royal Court theater hit, a play listed in lights (and the small ads) as *Shopping and F———*. One wonders whether Norman Mailer, in one of his readings from his early work at, say, Manhattan's 92ⁿᵈ Street Y, will stick to his *friggin'* evasions in, say, *The Naked and the Dead* (1948), or freely rephrase the self-censored language in his later rougher mode.

Brecht in present-day Berlin is more complicated. "Revolution"—and the famous Brechtian "alienation" from bourgeois society—has gone out of fashion. The Master's dramas are still being performed everywhere but in sensationalized unorthodox productions where the *Regisseur* is driven to up-date, modernize, or otherwise transform the sacred texts in order to interest audiences who no longer can take the old message of exploitation and class struggle. In the current Berlin production (by a director named Einar Schleef), in addition to the staging of two "brutal" orgies and a "lusty" nude rape scene, Puntila's servant Matti is converted into ten roles with as many utterly naked actors (and, with this band of brothers, presumably, poor isolated B.B. finally gets a mass movement). The cultural critic in *Tip*, normally sympathetic to any wild experimentation, found it all too *grob* (vulgar) and *unerträglich* (intolerable).

What matters, then, a small liberty taken with an F-word in restoring it to its full phonetic power? But cultural correctness argues: What even the greatest of writers themselves "bowdlerized" in their own work must be "outed." From such little proof-reading tactics, I surmise, can grow large-scale aesthetic methodologies (like deconstructionism or structuralism). One could perhaps be justified in suspecting that forbidden sentiments and indeed unpublishable expletives lie almost detectably visible between the lines of all the masterpieces. What could the masters not have said and written, not have achieved, if they had been freer—as, presumably, we are—of their own epoch's inhibitions and repressions?

Should our negative cultural tax for such misdemeanors and editorial malpractices ever get on the books, it may be in time to discourage the re-writing in this spirit of the oeuvre of, among other possible victims, Jane Austen, Charles Dickens, Henry James, Oscar Wilde, and even the Bard.[5]

22

Hard Words and Generation Gaps

All changes in our language—the styles of usage, and even the ways we think about them—come largely from a combination of two eternally recurring factors.

One is the natural effort of an older generation to adjust to inevitable changes while maintaining (with what firmness the social crises allow them to be held fast to) the old familiarities and the traditional names of things. The second is the periodic insurgence of a new generation which takes up whatever it fancies to be new, attractive, and seductive, and seeks to give self-indulgent scope to its own individuality, its fresh energies and youthful vanities.

In such evolution and revolution, meanings evolve and revolve. Language, thus, preserves a sense of old safeties and a taste for congenial notions and creates—often simultaneously, in hurly-burly years of radical conflict—new labels, identities, watchwords.

In another place* I have recorded at length this semantic history at the very beginning of the modern world, in seventeenth-century Europe, when there was a great debate about a linguistic peculiarity which the savants of the time referred to as "old-new." It was an era of outlandish discoveries that had to be fitted into ancient maps; of original ideas that had to be reconciled to received values; of strange words whose clarity and significance seemed to be obscure. Indeed there were several useful hand-books published, a *Dictionary of "Hard Words"* (1613/74), glossaries of the "unusual" and "unheard-of" (i.e., buzz-words of the day). Such compendia were all intended to make the acceptance of *"A New Worlde of Words"* (to use the title of Florio's earlier and similar work [1598/1611]), which Shakespeare knew) with its difficult items just a bit easier, a bit less hard. Among the hard, new-world words which John Florio (who is identified as

---

* Melvin J. Lasky, *Utopia and Revolution* (Chicago/London, 1976), Chapters 5 & 6, "The Birth of a Metaphor."

Holofernes in *Love's Labour Lost*) is taken to have made readily available to
Shakespeare are:

> affectionate, bellyful, catastrophe, contentious, curiosity, depraved, disaster, eva-
> sion, frustrate, impetuous, incestuous, intelligent, jovial, monopoly, mutation, plan-
> etary, rebellion, reciprocal, revolt, revolution, ripeness, sophisticated, sterility,
> waywardness....**

Historians through the ages and, on occasion, old poets and modern novelists have been able to catch such dramatic moments between slow evolution
and hectic revolution, moments when harmony breaks out and discord rules.
John Donne's much-quoted lines in *An Anatomy of the World* (1611) are a
famous source:

> And new philosophy calls all in doubt,
> The fire is quite put out;
> The sun is lost, and th'earth, and no man's wit
> Can well direct him where to look for it.
> And freely men confess that this world's spent....
> 'Tis all in pieces, all coherence gone,
> All just supply, and all relation....
> This is the world's condition now....

Spent words signalized the incoherence, as men of the old philosophy had
always warned. This is Francis Bacon, discoursing on the "Idols of the Marketplace" in his *Novum Organum* (1620), arguing that "words plainly force
and over-rule the understanding, and throw all into confusion, and lead men
away into numberless controversies and idle fancies...." But since Bacon's day
the decay had only deepened. Still and all, as even John Donne hoped when he
found "the world's whole frame/Quite out of joint," there might be some promise for a renewed coherence, a prospect for men finding "a new compass for
their way." Might this presage a successor generation with other words to reinforce a different understanding of the world's condition?

Thomas Sprat, that indefatigable propagandist of the new European movement of experimental science (and the historian of the pioneering Royal Society), was only a boy when the British Isles—and many other lands on the
Continent—were wracked with civil war and rebellion; and he could later
look back with post-Cromwellian acuity on the correlation of old language,
old-new words, and a new generation. As he writes, it was

---

* G.C. Taylor, *Shakespeare's Debt to Montaigne* (1925); Shakespeare had read
  Florio's majestic translation of Michel de Montaigne. F.E. Halliday, *A Shakespeare
  Companion* (1964). Frances A. Yates, *John Florio: the Life of an Italian in
  Shakespeare's England* (1934).

a time wherein all Language used, if ever, to increase by extraordinary degrees; for in such busie and active times, there arise more new thoughts of men which must be signified, and varied by new expressions. Then, I say, it (our own language) received many fantastical terms which were introduced by our religious sects, and many outlandish phrases which several writers and translators, in that great hurry, brought in and made free as they pleased. Withal, it was enlarged by many sounds and necessary forms and idioms, which it before wanted. (1667)

As I have contended, "Revolution" was such a varied expression, a difficult word being refashioned (from *rivolutioni*, an Italian coinage in 1648) in busy, active warring times, to signify that men were beginning to consider a wanting new thought.

The pathos of such great historical dramas, tragic, ruinous, or absurd as they may be, has been graphically caught a thousand times, as I suggest, between the chronicles of ancient historians and the imaginative realism of modern novelists, concerned with fathers and sons and other forms of the generation gap. It would, I am afraid, take us too far afield to go on charting more than a few milestones in this historic rhythm of stabilities and destabilization which we have been surveying in our contemporary newspaper culture. Two striking passages will have to suffice.

One is Polybius's account of the *Rise of the Roman Empire*, written over two thousand years ago:

After these defeats there was for a time quiet and peace.... But as time went on, and those who had actually witnessed these terrible conflicts passed away, they were replaced by a younger generation, men who were filled with an unreflecting desire for struggle and who were completely without experience of suffering or of national peril; and their impulse, not surprisingly, was to destroy the equilibrium.[1]

And the other is from the twentieth-century novel written midway between World War I and World War II, *All Quiet on the Western Front* (1929) by Erich Maria Remarque:

and the generation that has grown up after us will be strange to us and push us aside. We will be superfluous even to ourselves, we will grow older, a few will adapt themselves, some others will simply submit, and most will be bewildered;—and the years will pass by and in the end we shall fall into ruin.[2]

Remarque's Germany and practically the whole of the European continent did indeed fall into ruin; entire generations of the old as well as the young were wiped out; and the conventional language of traditional cultures was (just as Francis Bacon and Thomas Sprat had surmised, centuries before) forced and over-ruled, thrown into confusion, disrupted by the many "fantastical" and "outlandish" phrases which signified the strength of the ideologies of Messrs. Mussolini and Hitler.

I return, in this roundabout and discursive way, to our present preoccupation with the problem of language and cultural change, of an enlarged vocabulary by a voluble generation of American (and Western European) youth, who transformed the speech, and hence the prose, of their contemporaries. I refer to the heritage of the '68ers: to the rebels and radicals of the turbulent decade of the 1960s, to the youngsters on both sides of the Atlantic who broke the peace and quiet of the immediate postwar years, who were filled with a desire to struggle, and who (yet again!) "destroyed an equilibrium" and pushed oldsters aside, rudely and crudely.

Part 4

The F-word and Other Obscenities

"No, no; remember that Bad Customs, like Consumption, admit of Remedies in the beginning but grow still more incurable by delay; and Vices, like young Trees, the longer they are let grow, the greater difficulty there is in felling of them; each single sin being not bad only for the evil of the act, but the propensity it gives to repetition,"—Robert Boyle (1695)

"Why the most pleasurable activity known to mankind, and the organs by which it is procured, should be debased through the use of the basic, or quadriliteral, terms as expressions of opprobrium has never been adequately explained....There is perhaps a fundamental puritanism in such usages, a denial of the holiness of sexual pleasure, which, of course, explains the taboo....

"As for the euphemism (from Greek eu—well, good, pleasant—and pheme - speech), it is a device for hiding the harsh or offensive through circumlocution or gentle falsification, and it is used to operate in those areas—sex and excrement—where taboos were most rigidly enforced...." —Anthony Burgess, A Mouthful of Air: Language and Languages, Especially English *(1992)*

"Our softest consonant (fluff), followed by one word of thrust (uh!), or blankmindedness (uh...), followed by our hardest consonant (clack); and that's it. Enough to perpetuate the race.

It's one of the best things we can do with someone, one of the worst to someone....

It's our worst word, at least of one syllable, and maybe our strongest. Shakespeare, Dickens, Mark Twain never used it, at least in print. Norman Mailer in The Naked and the Dead *(1948) had to render it as fug. Now the F-word is 'heard in the best-regulated living rooms.' In American gangsta rap and British working-class novels it appears with more regularity, probably than the. Still, if my parents were alive I would not be writing this....*

Do you think English-speakers in general will ever get over getting a charge, positive or negative or both, out of the F-word? I don't....

And the next thing you know, fuck will start popping up in Republican Congressman's novels, and then in Presidential debates, and then in supermarket ads, and people will start referring to the third Sunday in June as Mofo's Day....

No! There are limits!...the trend henceforth may be to euphemism. Effing will come back, and other eff-words...." —Roy Blount, Jr., "The F-Word" (1995)[1]

23

Skirmishes in the Sex War

Evidently the most painful challenge to journalism today, when porno-permissiveness is running rampant, is that viewing is more seductive than reading, that pictures and spoken words have the colour and sound that makes the pulse beat faster as against truncated acronyms on the printed page decorated with dashes and asterisks.

But, on occasion, the newspapers can take revenge. Sometimes with brightly written parodies—or, in a graver mood, with a stern broadside from the high moral ground against prurient pictorial sensationalism—but, every now and then, with what newspapers can do best: investigative reporting, muckraking, criticizing the performance of even the most professional erotic demonstrations on screen. The Gutenberg galaxy strikes back, O.K.?

The high-point in the sexual war between television and the press came, as I keep the score, in the affair of a famous British anthropologist's BBC series on *The Human Animal*, the third installment of which featured the "Biology of Love" and what was boasted as the first interior view of the male and female sexual orgasm in action. (The consenting couple did indeed have mini-cameras in all the proper, or improper, places.) One London newspaper critic was almost beside herself with wild sarcasm:

> Some readers may wonder what we can possibly learn from observing the uterus greet the sperm during orgasm. Having seen a preview, I can tell you that what we learn is that it looks like a pink hippopotamus kneeling down for a drink of vanilla milkshake. Should make a marvellous post-coital talking point; if any of us can ever face doing It again, that is. And don't go raising your eyebrows, madam; this is science and not to be confused with pornography which is disgusting and would not be allowed on prime-time television.[2]

In the highbrow *Independent*, the reviewer (even if it happened to be the same word-drunk young lady, and it was) was not to be outdone by her alter ego in the low-brow tabloid:

A heat-sensitive camera turned the copulating couple into a molten Warhol: Tony's sperm got famous for 15 seconds, arching through the Jello labyrinth formerly known as Wendy's private parts.

Another TV-reviewer in a middle-brow British newspaper went in for a put-down a shade more sedate than analogies with soft drinks in a zoo and avant-garde pudding:

'How was it for you?' I hear you ask. I hate to disappoint anyone who expected the ultimate in shock-TV, but those few moments were not very different to the casual eye from a film taken somewhere deep in the throat of a person gargling—unpleasant, disgusting even, but emphatically not a turn-on in any way....It succeeded in making copulation look just like one of those maps from outer space showing the earth's oil deposits, or the amount of rice growing in Asia, with Morris explaining: 'Lower down the body it is possible to see the genital region of the female becoming intensely heated as sexual arousal progresses....' Red and blue splodges danced before your eyes.[3]

Another male critic, John Naughton of the *Observer*, registered his mild surprise that it all went on "without a peep from the Mary Whitehouse brigade" (that is, the pro-censorship pressure-group for cleaning-up broadcasting). No censor, he, but Mr. Naughton could have gone without "the first internal footage ever filmed of a female orgasm in all its spasmodic glory":

It was so bad that by the time the climax arrived my spectacles were completely steamed up by Mr Morris's commentary and I missed the shot of Wendy's cervix dancing like the creatures in the Kia Ora ads and had to rewind the tape.[4]

The man, alas, missed the whole point of the exercise.

Is, then, the female of the species more deadly than the male? In an era of weakened masculinity (or of macho self-confidence), the pornography industry, in word and in picture, has spent much enterprise in featuring the image of the strong, predatory woman. And the newspaper industry, for its part, has been increasingly assigning leading editorial positions to young, stylish, female writers, not least for their fresh outspokenness on the issues of sex and gender. My impression, at least from reading the London press, is that the new generation of woman journalists have taken the lead in the F-word steeplechase, whipping swiftly forward as if they were trying to catch up on a century of sexual discrimination by jumping all the hurdles, by taking all the liberties they can. Their pieces stand out in the various papers. They are colorful, witty, saucy, fast with a turn of phrase, quick off the mark with the F-words (or a suggestive play thereon).*

---

* 　I add a personal incident. Last night at a dinner of the Foreign Press Association in Berlin, Sally M.-S., a talented young British journalist (*Oxon.*, etc.), who had just published a rather sensational article on local lesbian prostitution, argued at my table that she couldn't "for the life of me understand why the language taboos

The Galaxy Strikes Back

But rough reviewing is not quite enough. One clever woman reporter—and the English are pioneering the starring roles of female writers on every front, from Bosnia to the boudoir—was enterprising enough to interview Dr. Desmond Morris's lovemaking couple; and the self-criticism they offered was decisive.

We know that late-night porno films are all staged affairs, and all the positioning and grunting are simulated. Can vaunted BBC documentaries on the science-of-love be equally faked? Evidently Mr. and Mrs. Tony and Wendy Duffield were outraged by the element of "hoax" in the virtual reality of copulation on screen. Ms. Anne Barrowclough of the *Daily Mail* quoted them as revealing the fakery involved. The "scientific script" called for them to exhibit certain physiological actions—for example, that women's breasts enlarge by 25 percent during arousal—but this simply didn't turn up on the first takes. Wendy confessed that she had to do special exercises and then be filmed from the side to make the point. The *Mail* reporter writes that Wendy said this "angrily" (but who knows? professional performers can simulate anything...): "We agreed to do the program because we thought it would be breaking new ground, and we're still proud of the orgasm scenes, but the rest of it was irresponsible." Tony gave Wendy, as always, the needed male support, confessing for his part:

> When certain things didn't happen as quickly as the producers hoped, they took short cuts to get the same effect. I had to get on an exercise bike for 25 minutes to work up a sweat because the script said that men sweat during love-making....

Pictures may be more powerful than mere words, but one can't believe what you see. The camera is exposed as an imposter, offering spurious evidence in an elaborate duplicitous exercise....Rarely did the press win such a famous victory over the imagistic media. Readers may be for a time turning more eagerly to their newspapers—even if the F-words remain modestly abbreviated, even if you move your lips while spelling them out. What the lady

---

could not be broken," all of them; and (in her words) "why the f— those F-words could not be spoken freely and without any shame, even in the presence of the children!..."

This young lady will go far as soon as she learns to use her uninhibited verbal instincts, evidently now shaping the language natural to women, with a prudent sprinkling of hyphens and asterisks (especially in her pieces for self-styled family newspapers which might conceivably be read by the very young). She is a Sally Bowles mutant for our times. If it didn't smack too much of an Isherwood remake, she would soon be writing the follow-up story of what happened to the gay Berlin underworld since the heyday of Weimar transvestites.

With (if she can help it) no holds barred, absolutely no taboos.

from the *Standard* called "a marvellous post-coital talking point" may well be that virtual reality is touched up. As I say, the Gutenberg galaxy can strike back.

The female commentators on "The Biology of Love" evidently had an element of gender difficulty. They detected a note of arrogance on the part of a male "expert" announcing the very first internal view of a female orgasm, as if it were a challenge to the long-fought-for and now victorious sovereignty over their own bodies. One snapped: What about internal views of *male* orgasms? Well, that would be another film; for now it would be sufficient unto the day, and to the evening's prime time, to put the man down, "a man so intent on watching everybody else that he can't see how ridiculous he looks himself...." Ms. Julia Grant in the *Independent* went on to relent a bit after letting off some of that suspicious and controversial "steam":

> The Morris version was a bit like an airbag going off inside a crimson pup-tent, something of a white-out after the first few microseconds, but I have to confess that the female orgasm was a startling thing to watch, the cervix clenching and expanding like a pupa doing an impression.[5]

For Ms. Libby Purves, the star columnist of the *Times*, Dr. Morris's clinical-biological curiosity almost amounted to rape on live camera, "one very small, very weatherproof camera, riding shotgun on the male volunteer, the female cervix dipping disdainfully into the preferred lake of fertility." She sneered at the very notion that women were "the only orgasmic female animals." She protested with every measurable inch of her body and soul against

> the indecorous nature of Dr. Morris' safari through human lovemaking: up the nostrils, down the arteries, chasing drops of sweat, measuring nipples, lingering inexplicably on long red fingernails, and pointing out the steam rising from the woman's mouth (but how cold was the bedroom?).

She threw everything at him except possibly the kitchen sink and the bathroom bidet. At the risk of exhibiting "age-ism" she even dared to show her years by matronly remarking that "from the moment the male and female apes stood up, thereby revealing their sexual organs, the emphasis was on youth and beauty." Surely these would be passé in a new era "in which children are conceived by egg-donation and test-tubes." But, in the end, her assignment for the élitist *Times*—now seeking mass circulation and thus also troubled by the competition of a sex-obsessed small screen in the people's living rooms—was not the old Thurberesque struggle between male and female; it was the new media rivalry between colourful pictures and critical prose. The task was to defend civilization's investment in the written word. The final verdict from Ms. Libby Purves was a sniffy, a lofty warning *not* to "rely on prime-time television and a pop biologist to illuminate the central mysteries of human love."

A last word on the scandalous affairs of the human animal. I give it to a young critic, Matthew Norman, on a popular middlebrow tabloid, who has been straining to get a masculine word in edgewise. He says he is grave and serious, "for this is no time for smutty wordplay....It is too sticky a controversy to be treated with flippancy." He insists he was—unusual quest!—looking for "a valuable academic point." No surprise that he didn't find it. Academic points are too valuable to be left to biologists; armchair anthropologists can do better:

> What that point was I have not the vaguest idea; but it must have been there, because otherwise this would have been the crudest, crassest, most gratuitous, pseudo-scientific-sub-pornographic nastiness ever broadcast. If you managed to miss it I congratulate you, for it was enough to put anyone off sex for life.[6]

This amounts to the ultimate, cosmic advertisement for the press and our newspaper culture—turn off TV, read your favorite daily, and you can save your sex life (and maybe even get the illumination of the central mystery of human love).

Young Mr. Norman, professional TV-critic and sentenced to viewing the small-screen crudities, immunizes himself by not believing a sound or an image of what he sees and hears. Here is a passage of muckraking in the great and crass tradition:

> A thermal-imaging camera (converting body heat into bright red) showed how [Wendy's] lips swelled and reddened as she became aroused (or rather ... after she sucked an ice lolly); their pupils dilated and their eyes glistened (bright lights had been shone directly at them); her breasts enlarged (she was clenching her chest muscles); her nipples became elevated (she'd rubbed them with an ice cube); and they breathed faster (they'd just come off exercise bikes) and became drenched with sweat (they'd been sprayed with water).

Some, if not all, of this is factually true; but the protagonist of the word cannot resist word-play, and he gets himself stuck in the "sticky controversy" he feigned to disdain. My last quotations have all the irrepressible English schoolboy enthusiasm for metaphorics which has become the hallmark of British journalism's struggle to survive in the media awash with moving pictures:

> So then, here was something unique—coitus in which almost everything was faked *except* the female orgasm. But there was no disputing the veracity of his erection, which the heat-sensitive camera turned a comic electric pink, nor of its emission of what looked like washing-up water which brought it to a timely end....

He wants to end there: more would be too pictorial:

A graphic description of what this and her own orgasmic muscle contraction (politely put, it looked like a quivering piece of dead whale flesh) resembled is the stuff of pub talk at closing time, but it does not belong here. They were truly repellent and nauseating sights that had nothing useful or interesting to communicate that could not have been communicated by words alone.

This is the classic message of the print media—words alone will save you (and protect your sex life, and unravel the mysteries of human love), and in addition give vitality to grass-roots democracy. For, as the *Standard* reported, "viewers went to the telephones to jam the switchboards of national newspapers in disgust"; and the *Mail*'s headline about Wendy and Tony's "on-screen frustrations" was:

"WE KNEW IT WAS IRRESPONSIBLE
BUT THE BBC TOLD US
WE HAD NO RIGHT TO COMPLAIN..."*

Tabloid scoops keep intact (in Robert Hughes's phrase) the culture of complaint. The free press is the last resort—as Thomas Jefferson in Virginia, so long ago and far away, hoped it would be—for hard-pressed liberty, for freedom from onsetting social evils. Dissidence is all.

And the guideline for such dissidents in our newspaper culture amounts to this. Praise the innovations of miniaturized technology, but let the mini-camera be kept in its proper place. Revel in the chromatics (and acrobatics) of late-night television, but hold the black-on-white brickbats in readiness for the morning-after's editorial assault. Beware of the perils of Ying and Yang: for example, of females flaunting a feminist chip on their shoulder (or wherever); and of young male hacks troubled by their macho identity crises. Above all, try and keep men and women off the subject of coitus.

English invective is at its literary best when, in this fashion, it thunders in a high moral rage against low attempts to venture into the libidinous netherworld of a certain sexual indiscretion. The uproar changes only a very little over the centuries. At a recent London auction I was strongly tempted to buy "a Superb Statue in Wax," being (according to the old catalogue) an early nineteenth-century wax model

---

*   It would take us too far afield to consider the international impact of this whole affair. For the BBC has been busy trying to sell the Desmond Morris film to any foreign TV station that would be shrewd (or enlightened) enough to show it.

Switzerland, of all odd places, was the first. The front-page headline of a Zurich tabloid asked whether it was *"Mutig oder schamlos,"* courageous or shameless, for the Swiss TV to be showing the *"Orgasmus-Film,"* and at prime time too. (*Blick*, 23 May 1995, p. 1.)

offering at once the double advantage of a most highly finished Statue, and an accurate exposition of the anatomy of the human body. The above has also this advantage over other anatomical exhibitions, that while they are in general calculated to inspire unpleasant sensations, this esteemed piece of mechanism is entirely free from anything of the kind, or from the least indelicacy to either sex.

Despite this assurance in the broadside advertisement of 1825, the *Literary Gazette* of the day saw the exhibition in another light:

Under the pretence of imparting anatomical knowledge, this filthy French figure, the property of one Monsieur Esnaut, is exhibited. It is a large disgusting Doll, the alvus of which is being taken off like a pot-lid, shows the internal parts...as remotely from anatomical precision or utility as any of the sixpenny wooden dolls which you may buy at Bartholomew Fair....The thing is a silly imposture, and as indecent as it is wretched.

The latter charge—*"as indecent as it is wretched"*—rings out resoundingly over the years whenever science and sex come ambiguously close to touching each other. One can hear the echo of the storm over the French Doll of M. Esnaut in the controversy over the English pair of lovers in Desmond Morris's BBC efforts at "anatomical exhibition." My intended purchase remained unconsummated, since I had no chance to get a good look at the "Superb Statue in Wax" to confirm or deny the "filth," or the extent to which it might inspire unpleasant sensations or even disgust. But, in the famous porno-polemics, sight unseen has never been a hindrance to such indelicate excitements. Even with the wide-eyed viewing of several millions in front of their TV-sets, vision fixed on the anatomy of the human body in living color and transports, there have been difficulties in recording what anybody really saw. It could be that something indescribable happens to sex when it goes public.[7]

Of Circumlocutions and Pleonasms

What would appear to be a lingering conservatism about the propriety of improper language, or a "lewdness lag," can be deceptive. In some cases it is indeed an old-fashioned reluctance to employ words and phrases traditionally deemed to be rude or vulgar; in others it is a sly continuation of the titillation imperative by other means. The reluctance leads to a familiar variety of circumlocutions, conventional and even genteel; also to cockney back-rhymes and even an up-to-date "Pig-Latin." The round-about salacity is often devoted to puns, double-entendres, and echoes of old blue jokes.

Several illustrations, the first being from the German which uses S-words so freely and ubiquitously that a paper like *Der Spiegel* is hard put to find synonyms and pleonasms in order to give a bit of verbal variety to the weekly stories.

In an account of the rock singer Nina Hagen's rage against a popular tabloid which had been irritating her with criticism of her philosophy of drug use, *Der Spiegel* (9 January 1995) quotes her as expostulating, *"Euer Blatt ist und bleibt totale Scheisse!"* (your paper is and remains total shit). On the same page there is also an item in which two SPD politicians are berating each other on NATO military policy, and one accused the other of a kind of fear of weaponry: *"Du würdest Dir doch in die Hosen machen!"* (you'll be making it in your pants). Political argument still maintains a certain reserve in what the Germans refer to as the "E-world," the earnest context of serious matters; but in the "U-world" of *Unterhaltung* or entertainment, anything goes.

Anything, and as near to it as you can get. Thus, a music critic in the *Daily Telegraph*, reviewing some new pop recordings, looks vaguely away from the F-word, and instead of the harshest expletive only comes up with a put-down to the effect that somebody called Kristin Hersh (star of the hit album, *Hips and Makers*) has only offered her fans "a collection of funked-up folksy guitar songs."[8] Does it help to know that a related album, *Funky Little Demons*, also didn't (alas) "live up to the promise of *Queer*"? Evidently it was a bad week for "electro, indie, grunge, ambient or 'nineties electronic music." All of the groups were accused of merely "doing their best to resurrect their 'angst'-ridden punk past." To the outsider of this In-language scene it might have seemed to be, in the grunge phrase of the 1940s, *Snafu*, or situation-normal-all-funked-up.

In the discussion of serious literary matters the semantics are a shade more complex. In its review of an edition of the letters of the Australian Nobel Prize winning novelist, Patrick White, the *Times* (London, 12 January 1995) agrees with its editor that the correspondence is "earthy, camp, savage, very funny and free," and adds: "It is all these things, and more besides." A word to the knowing is sufficient, and the critique refrains from offering any earthy quotations or camp samplers. We only learn from White himself that "If I am anything of a writer, it is through my homosexuality which has given me additional insights, and through a very strong vein of vulgarity...." It seems to be a vein "which marbles his correspondence." The only glimpse we get of the incisive vulgarity is White's description of the writer Robin Maugham of having a "face like a wizened cow's twat." The *Times* concedes that these characterizations "are sometimes over-agricultural," which may in turn be a circumlocution for barnyard language. Sir Sidney Nolan, the famous "Ned Kelly" painter, was often the target of White's pen. Which may account for the fact that in one of Nolan's works Patrick White is consigned to the circle in Dante's *Purgatory* reserved for sodomites.

All of which can be read as having precious little to do with literature, just fun and games, despicable or foolish as the *argumentum ad hominem* may be.

In fact the word *twat* is given a second meaning in the dictionary of slang* (the first being, of course, "the female genitals, 1656")—namely, "a despicable or foolish person." The *T*-word can have its special use, especially in the hands of an experienced writer.

An editorial aside for copy editors. To the usual literary warning of *rep.*, scrawled disapprovingly in the margin, one extra reminder can be added here: namely, that the urge to repetitiveness, as in the sexual urge itself, tends to a self-satisfied sameness. After a decent interval (a year or so will do), here is the guardian of the blue ration at it again, same quote, same raunchy remark (if expanded a bit to include one significant other). The *Sunday Times* reviewer actually goes out of his way to cite another reviewer of a book on *Somerset Maugham and the Maugham Dynasty* (1997) to the same effect:

> What a horrid pair they were, Robin [Maugham] and his uncle [Somerset]; there were few people in this world who deserve to be described, as Robin was by Patrick White, as resembling "a wizened cow's twat", but here, I am afraid, are two of them.[9]

If, as I say, properly spaced out, the T-word may well prove to be a hardy perennial.

Is nothing sacred? Well, up till now, the efforts of modernizing churchmen to retranslate the Bible—in order to make it more appealing to the contemporary reader who has been estranged by the arcane and archaic language of the traditional versions—have been relatively clean.

The temptations must be very great. Introducing a vocabulary of slang has clearly served the various Christian denominations to get a bit closer to the modern youth culture; and if jazzed-up editions of the Old and New Testament manage to capture the cool attention of with-it generations who may now respond to the call of religion and its promise of "good news," how far away are we from divine messages which multi-mix the sacred and the profane? Every schoolboy used to hear of certain good bits of eroticism somewhere in the books of the Bible (viz., Onan's sin: "spilling of seed on the ground"), and they can surely be rendered even more stimulating to the teenage ear. One can easily conceive of a song of Solomon for the fans who sing the hits on the hit-parade charts. Whether the ecclesiastical committees who feel the call to devise an updated Gospel can muster the courage—or the verbal ingenuity—to take on the street-wise eloquence of current language is another matter.

There may well be insuperable semantic limits. What do we really know of ancient argot, or what constituted profanity in Aramaic among the historic Hebrews, or how the old-time Judaeo-Christians gave verbal vent to their lusts

---

*   *Oxford Dictionary of Slang* (1992), p. 272.

and impious anger? What might Pontius Pilate have said, in an incautious moment, about his perfidious Jewish subjects? Will sensitive research come up, at long last, with all the improper words? One surmises that, given (in the millennial past) the more vivid sense of the sacred, there might also have been an earthier, even barnyard, feel for the profane. If we can only recapture what Socrates muttered when stubbing his toe on loose stones in the *agora*, or Plato's expletives in his annoyance at excessively stupid questions during his morning dialogue with his students. Surely this would open up new possibilities for rendering the Septuagint into a Vulgate for our own times!—enrichened with the Alpha- and Omega-words of our heart's desires....

Scholars will be demanding authentic and valid transliteration, that is, the low language actually used by the Caesars (with luck the lewd epithets of the Roman henchmen heard perhaps in the Jerusalem of Herod and Pontius Pilate). But rewrite men may be tempted to compromise old texts with latter-day idioms, thus producing anachronistic oddities (viz., the Jewish historian Flavius Josephus reporting that all the military heroes in the wars of "antiquity" had the habit, or so it stands in one modernizing English translation of the classic work, of "ratting" on each other). Thus, between the Scylla of authenticity and the Charybdis of anomaly, Biblical modernizers may well be advised to cut their risks and simply bluff their way through by resorting to vague and diffuse abbreviations, touched up by asterisks and hyphens and the euphemistic usage of other acceptable markings (#, @, &, and !).

Meanwhile, enlightened churchmen in our days have to make do with poor substitutes. In the case of the notorious revisionists in Westminster Abbey it has come to be known as the "Happy Clappy" approach; but even its periphrastic attempts at "dirty realism" have been running into trouble. Traditionalists, as always, think of them as being "blasphemous." Many walked out on a recent Good Friday passion play when an actor described Jesus on the Cross as "a sorry-looking bastard." London newspapers were well-informed enough, even over this long Easter week-end, to report that Cardinal Basil Hume, Archbishop of Westminster, left half-way through the "Evangelical Arts" production. He said he had hoped for something more meditational. He suggested a silent procession for the cross-carriers.

But in the beginning, as the cardinal knows, there is always the word; and if the semantic reformation is ever to bless us with a revival of faith it will just have to turn to the street-smart demotic, or at least to come up with language closer to the common speech before it gets to be dressed up in its Sunday best. The suggestive report on the Westminster Abbey drama in one English newspaper may well be indicating the shape of things to come:

> In another scene, Jesus' clothing was described as "a pair of frigging overalls' and one actor told another as they carried the Cross into the Abbey: 'If you drop it, I'll cut your balls off".[10]

Although civil law forbids a newspaper's repetition of a libel, the reporting of blasphemies uttered in Church precincts comes under no ecclesiastical prohibition, at least one that nowadays is legally enforceable. For centuries now free speech has always risked charges of sacrilege, and freedom of the press has just been one damned irreverence after another. One looks forward to the onset of Testament texts for the Man Who Reads Joyce and Lawrence (and watches late-nite television). The reviewer's quotations on the literary pages from the first edition of a so-called *"Barnyard Bible...*designed to be read as realistic up-to-date literature"* will prove to be rich etymological fare; and, under the ecologically correct circumstances, it may well be dispensing with the protective subterfuges of dashes and asterisks. Our press can be unafraid. No one can censor the good book. Even with bad language it will be bringing its good news.

24

World War II, Fifty Years After

The memorial celebrations were over, in London, Paris, and Berlin, and the newspapers as ever were scraping for bits of features that would rival the color and the immediacy of the apparently overwhelming pictorial coverage by the television stations. Matthew Norman who has transferred his scabrous expertise from the *Standard* in London (see his soft-porn critique of the BBC's "skirmish with the sex war," above) to the *Guardian*, equally hard up for relevant tid-bits. He just discovered "the most obscene record for years [that] has just been released" and, playing the irony for all its worth, he reported that it could be bought by mail-order "from, of all fabled disseminators of filth, the British Legion." The record, *Come On Lads,* a collection of wartime songs, as well as the *Guardian*'s report on it were, of course, both in the proper spirit of documenting the great War "like it was": "It is potent stuff, and many old soldiers may not approve of the Legion's involvement."

Still, Denis Healey (World War II officer, Labour minister of defence, and father of the owner of the record company) found it "magnificent" as a V-day record of authentic songs. *"Anzio and Sangro were a farce/We did fuck all and sat on our arse...."* No bars of music with the melodic line are, alas, reproduced; but we are given a liberal sprinkling of verses, including a reference— "Is that why we fought the war? or this?"—to a controversial line about an act of bestiality with a pig..., the *Guardian* gives us a last verse which we may find singable, for it is the British Fifteen(th) Army's Group parody of *Onward Christian Soldiers:*

> Ike and Monty left us
> Jumbo's gone away
> Gone to reign in glory
> In the USA
> Even Alexander's
> Left the sinking barque
> AA-1 is lee-eee-eft with
> General fucking Clark.

343

Norman, for balance, quotes an incensed decency campaigner (Mrs. Mary Whitehouse) to this effect: "Good grief....Soldiers may have sung them in the trenches, but, believe me, they wouldn't sing them in the home." Thanks to the *Guardian*'s journalistic enterprise all of us can softly hum along anywhere.[1]

I turn now to Vietnam, twenty years after. Here, several decades after the Americans left "the sinking barque" in the Mekong, visiting Yanks in Saigon are either being welcomed or insulted, depending on which edition of the *Telegraph* in London you read. Richard West, a serious and experienced reporter, quotes a friend in Saigon:

> Yes, I know we used to prefer the French and despised the Americans. But now the Americans have gone, we realize how much we liked them. That's why I say the Americans really won the war. They won because we all want them back.

On recent visits, the *Daily Telegraph* correspondent (and author of a new book on *War and Peace in Vietnam* [1995]) goes on to report,

> people were so pro-American their faces fell when I had to admit I was merely an Englishman. Former Vietcong were the most outspoken; one told me she now regretted that the Americans had not fought harder.[2]

In the Sunday edition of the same newspaper, another correspondent, Paul Mansfield, finds himself in "a lovely little town on the banks of the Thu Bon river near Danang" when a Vietnamese teenager met a young American backpacker sitting in an outside café. It's quite another scene:

> "I no like Americans. You fight my father! His leg is...." (Here he made a chopping gesture below the knee.) "You go home." His face was full of black hate, and he was close to tears...."No say goodbye to you! F—k you, American."[3]

There may be another view of the truth, possibly more objective and less emotionally colored. But we will have to wait for another round of quotations from witnesses in Vietnam who don't happen to be so familiar with a foreign language and its plosive four-letter words.

25

A Trio of As*ter*isk*s

Lexicographers, and grammarians too, often have sex as well as gender on their minds, sometimes getting the thing wrong on their index cards, occasionally conceding and correcting an embarrassing error. The great Henry Fowler of the *Oxford Dictionary* assumed, as he said, "a cheerful attitude of infallibility"; but when he missed out on the sexuality of "Adultery" the faulty definition was amended. Fowler had defined it thus: "Voluntary sexual intercourse of married person with one of opposite sex." Colleagues pointed out with a certain amount of glee (such is the nature of male jealousy) that he did not appear to be excluding from "adultery" the sexual intercourse of married couples, husband and wife.* Sex is much too important to be left to men who make only dictionaries.

But, as I have been arguing, the language of sex becomes even more erratic when left to the journalists.

Reporters often come away with a notebook full of quotable quotes, and what is the compelling osmosis that takes the casual, redundant F-word from the scribble to the printed page? They, and/or their editors, have a secret agenda. It is, on one level, the breaking of all linguistic taboos—and thereby attaining liberation, self-fulfillment, and (so the credo goes) non-repressive anti-authoritarian naturalness. On another level, it may also serve to increase newspaper circulation in the media wars.

In a time of affirmative action and equal opportunity it is the upwardly mobile female journalist who volunteers, or is conscripted, to take the rude lead. Newspapers are pioneering the offensive strategy of pushing women forward to the front—the no-man's-land where F-words be. For example, when the features editor of the *Telegraph* in London wants to assign a story about the British variant of what in the U.S. is called "road rage"—anger, violence,

---

* Robert Burchfield, *Unlocking the English Language* (1989), ch. 4, "The Fowlers: Their Achievements in Lexicography and Grammar," p. 146.

even murder as a result of frayed tempers in appalling traffic conditions—he is certain to overlook all the available male reporters and choose somebody like Ms. Tessa Boase and send that attractive young person into the fume-filled firing line of London traffic jams. She is driving a Mercedes 250. It stalls. A BMW drives up beside her (this story has nothing to do with Teutonics which I treat on another page). The driver, well dressed in a suit, explodes with rage. As Ms. Boase transcribes it in the *Sunday Telegraph* (1 January 1995), "For Christ's sake, f***ing f*** off the road!" She is duly challenged but records her own counter-blast a shade more modestly:

> I get the message and find myself swearing back and gesticulating wildly. He drops back and mouths some more. A van-driver behind me, enjoying the scene, drives past making lewd gestures.

If this (on page 4) is not quite satisfactory—what *were* the wild gesticulations and lewd gestures?—and do only *males* get fingered, in a form of verbal sexual harrassment, for mouthing the F-words in direct newspaper quotation? —then the dear reader can turn to page 12 of the Foreign News section where some reparations are made in the story from New York by Ms. Emma Gilbey on "Smoker's Rage." Here the apoplectic point at issue is the new metropolitan ban on smoking tobacco in all Manhattan restaurants seating thirty-five people or more. That includes Elaine's: "'F*** 'em,' declares Elaine Kaufman, owner of the hard-drinking, smoke-filled *Elaine's,* when asked about the new ban. 'The next thing you know the Alcoholics Anonymous will get us to stop drinking—f*** them too.'" What Tessa won't put into the mouth of a woman, Emma obliges us with simple professional éclat. You don't have to send reporters on to the street to fill the F-word ration for the day (by my rough count, once or twice an issue, at least on the *Telegraph*)—be patient, the street will come to you. Rushing out on assignments to touch up drab columns of the paper with "copulative verbs" is not really necessary. There are enough straight-talking men and women around to give one an effing piece of their mind for free.

Are my suspicions outrageous? I've no doubt that my argument will—and it has, when I tried it out in Anglo-American round-table discussions—give offense to newspaper editors of declared high and moral purpose. Ulterior motives are being imputed, editorial strategies made suspect...it's all a theoretician's twaddle.

But seasoned journalists are more candid, more realistic; and the thesis of systematic sexual simulation (if that's what it is) is greeted with a knowing smile. We have to do with a culture without restraint, with no fig-leaves to cover its free organs of mass communication—a Hollywood without the Hays Office; a late-night TV empire without the law; a porno underground protected by constitutional ambiguities; a universe of discourse that is post-

Lawrence, post-Joyce, post-Hubert-Selby, Jr., flashing fitfully before the last exit to Brooklyn.

Thus, that eminently conservative pundit of the *New York Times* (and a hundred other syndicated newspapers in the U.S.), William Safire, begins his new book with this:

> The subject is copulation.
> That is known in the trade as a grabber of a lead, attracting on false pretenses those browsing through a family newspaper and looking vainly for sexual arousal.*

This was only a periphrastic way of broaching one of Safire's favorite grammarian subjects: "copulative words." He goes on to "predicate nominatives," and, finally, to his love affair with Norma Loquendi which, being Latin for common speech or "the everyday voice of the native speaker," has little enough erotic about it. We should thank our lucky little stars that there isn't a trio of asterisks in sight.**

Some of the periphrastic euphemisms for referring to the *"F-words"* have long since become anachronistic. Who, amidst the torrent of explicit language flowing through our cinemas, inundating our city streets, sweeping everything before it (except for newscasts and children's programs) on our television screens, would ever refer to the old circumlocution of "barn-yard epithets"? This almost obsolete synonym smacks of an agrarian pre-industrial world. Modern times make do with few barns, fewer yards, and almost no farmers who still expostulate in an earthy fashion all their own. Barn-yard as a locus for profane language should, perhaps, give way to schoolyard.

A London newspaper quotes a bewildered and angry parent in Derby as saying: "You teach your children not to swear and then you find they have been told to do it at school." This is not quite what happened at Derby's "Nightingale Junior School," for the dissonant birdsong was not exactly on the class-

---

*   William Safire, *In Love with Norma Loquendi* (1994), introduction, p. xi.

**   The playful, eccentric, or compulsive omission of letters is not, of course, confined to sexual texts, nor to the shy or tactical avoidance of profane explicitness. Writers have often fiddled with gaps in the alphabet—not to mention the theological prudence to be found in sacred Biblical texts where the Almighty, Providence, G— is not to be directly named.

     I am told that in E.V. Wright's *"Gadsby"* (1939), a story of more than 50,000 words was written in English without its most frequent letter, "E." And it is also said of the German poet Gottlob Burmann (1737-1805) that he composed 130 poems for a total of 20,000 words without the letter "R" (actually suppressing that letter from his daily speech for the last 17 years of his life). William R. Bennett Jr., in the *N.Y. Times Book Review* (2 April 1995, p. 27).

room curriculum. It appears that a Nightingale teacher found the F-word scrawled (probably in its imperative injunctional form) on the bulletin board. No pupil, of course, would confess to the expletive, and nobody would snitch (or, as they probably would say in Derby, inform). Whereupon the school-teacher, a Mrs. Ann Pool who is also a governor of the school, adopted a drastic class-room strategy for getting to the bottom of the matter. According to the front-page report in the *Daily Telegraph* (a family newspaper avid to spot a threat to family values):

> A teacher ordered 30 pupils to write an obscene word to find out who had scrawled it on the notice-board.
> The pupils at Nightingale Junior School, Derby, were told to write the F-word five times in capitals and five times in normal script.
> But the strategy failed when blame fell on an innocent pupil and the culprit was never found.[1]

One surmises that the spelling was correct in each of the 300 scribblings which were sedulously compared. But, presumably, the handwritings in question were so uniformly sub-standard that the incriminating script could not be quite made out. Bad language can hide behind even good orthography if only the penmanship is poor enough.

On some occasions it would seem that journalists and editors are rather pleased when they are not forced—that is, by their own high ethical commitment to low language (and the faithful transcription thereof)— to publish the expletive, or delete it, or dress it up in the emperor's new clothes. Counting the hyphens and/or the asterisks can be a boring, tiresome business. I sensed widespread elation when an angry Democratic strategist in Washington, explained an unexpected turn in the electoral debate: "This would never have happened to the Republicans in this campaign if they hadn't started futzing around."[2] The phrase "to futz around," according to H.L. Mencken (*The American Language*, ed. 1993, p. 262), has "in the original a scatological or obscene significance"; but such loan words (from the German, from the Yiddish) have long since been "naturalized." Still, as Mencken suggests, "higher society [has] no need to resort to foreign phrases or expressions." Higher society has fallen a little lower since then.

26

Gender in the Combat Zone

The grunge-like repetitiveness of the phrase "the Peace Process" has become almost numbing and meaningless. The so-called "process" covers everything ongoing from a sudden and very temporary cease-fire to long drawn-
out negotiations for a lasting truce. It is probably an intentional pleonasm or a
so-called "weasel word" to cover up the true state of the political conflict or
the armed struggle between the warring parties. Misleading as it is, it attracts
additional befogging phrases like "decommissioning arms"—which does not,
of course, mean putting the IRA's guns out of commission but serves to disguise what is really being asked for: the handing-over of the terrorists' weapons (which had never been "commissioned" in the first place), the surrender
of an entire armory which has been waging war for decades in Ulster. It is
hard, therefore, to discern whether there has been "progress" in allaying the
Irish troubles; and I turn for hope to the literary front. But there, too, there are
semantic complications.

It seems, I learn, that Miss Edna O'Brien is angry. Her most recent novel,
House of Splendid Isolation (1994), was not being taken as seriously as she
thought it deserved. After all, she based the character of "McGreevy," the IRA
terrorist, on a real underground militant, none other than Dominic "Mad Dog"
McGlinchy whom she had interviewed at length in jail. (He claimed to have
murdered thirty people, and was himself recently shot dead by a rival band of
would-be Gaelic liberators.)

It was not so much that Ms. O'Brien, "deeply impressed by this very grave
and reflective man," tried so hard to show the human face of the terrorist that
her novel could be taken for an apologia. Even more grievous than that was
the charge by the literary critics that she was not "entitled" to take up this
theme, that she no longer had the "language" to tell an accurate and convincing story. True, she was Irish and had grown up in County Clare, with her
father being a violent alcoholic and her mother sternly opposed to all "sinful"

books (except the Bible). After a Catholic girlhood "steeped in guilt and dread and religious passion," she abandoned Ireland for England, made a successful career writing book after sinful book, and became a darling of the London press. Her latest interviewer leafed through his researcher's sheaf of recent clippings and found only sweet talk: "beguiling...flame-haired...blithe-tongued, wistful seductress...her London home (red walls, deep sofas) reminds you of sex." And the sophistications of her conversation, all full of Yeats, Camus, and Gogol, and "Samuel Beckett used to say...." After all this, what credibility to deal with a mad dog of a terrorist?

As I note in the latest feature about Ms. O'Brien, entitled "The Sweet One Gets Angry" (*Daily Telegraph*, 17 April 1995), the f-word exploded into the conversation.... About time, too. Writers can't live quietly by sex alone.

> "There was one [English critic], I remember, saying I wasn't entitled to have the verbal fluency to write such a book, that I didn't deserve it. Well, f***ing hell...y'know." The anger flushes her face.
>
> "And I work like a beaver to get those words. And it's such a condescending thing to say...."

That disposed of, they went back to "the richly simmering language that is her hallmark" and the idea of love as a form of power and energy. "I like men who have a certain force. I love energy. Energy's everything." At which point certain other expletives (perhaps the b**l-s**t-word) might have exploded into the conversation.

After all, she's not the only one who is working like a beaver to get "those words." Newspapers also have their problems with asserting their entitlements, and journalists too, not least in how to transcribe conversational explosions into acceptable house style within the limits of the daily allotment.

I was pleased to see, on the feminist front, a momentary return of an old-fashioned element of male gallantry, of a kind of collegial honor; for one columnist should not be allowed—at least in the *Guardian*—to insult another. The quarrel involved to "wimmin's page writers," and if they had all the masculine rights they would be duelling at dawn with drawn pistols. As it happened Germaine Greer's column was refused publication by the *Guardian* editors (otherwise, stalwarts in the defense of "the free press"), and she promptly resigned from the paper. Her intended victim was a fellow-feminist (if that is not a censurable contradiction in terms) named Suzanne Moore who is a founder member of a worthy outfit called "Women in Journalism" and campaigns, according to the *Mail* (17 May 1995), for the rights of "wimmin in the meejar [i.e., media]." In fact the *Mail* made a meal of it, finding "nothing so bloody—or entertaining—as a good feminist spat." It also made a point of reporting, tossing hypocrisy to the winds, that Ms. Moore is "also keen on four-letter words and scatological references, in private and, alas, in print."

Well, Ms. Greer is herself no shy slouch in these turns of phrase, and had wanted to go into print—but, alas, the *Guardian* would have none of it (although it was reprinted soon enough in every other paper in the land)—with a number of choice references. Ms. Moore was a "lip-stick feminist," and "so much lipstick must rot the brain." In addition to which she shows, "three fat inches of cleavage and wears f*** me shoes." This gave the ration-minders of Fleet Street an easy day; and when the controversy (what it was actually about no reader could fathom) ran on for several days, our newspaper culture had over-fulfilled its statutory obligations to the slow but regular dissemination of the f-word.

Frank Johnson in the *Daily Telegraph*, although it surely had no need for such frugality, had been saving up for a rainy day and he splurged it all in a single paragraph in which his curiosity about the Greer/Moore footwear became curiouser and curiouser.

> What *are* f*** me shoes?...Are all men shoe-fetishists? Are the objects of the lust the shoes or the women?...Would it be sexist to ask whether men too could wear f*** me shoes? I envisage the males in one of those grand men's shoe-shops in Jermyn Street. "I'd like a good pair of f*** me shoes, my man...."

Frank Johnson is a wit capable of going on like this to keep his paper ahead of all effing competition in the foreseeable future. He wins our hearts by finding his own workaday, Isle of Dogs pair of shoes "positively obscene." And persuasive columnist as he is, he has succeeded in proving that Germaine Greer's monotone from Down Under, modulated in the profane Australian rhythms that pommies know so well, are as repetitively catchy as, say, the refrains of "Waltzing Mathilda."

An amateur Fleet Street etymologist settled the matter. Who did first use the phrase? In the photo-finish of his researches, California managed to edge out Australia by a shoe-string: "I gather that they are properly referred to as 'Joan Crawford f*** me shoes'. The Hollywood actress Bette Davis used the phrase about another Hollywood actress, Joan Crawford." All that remained was the question as to what the shoes in dispute actually looked like. There was a consensus for "high-heeled," "ankle-strapped," and "with a small platform." One English editor volunteered the information that they make one's legs look "fabulous"—but he hastened to add: "if, that is, one is female."[1]

So does profanity—in traffic jam stories, and elsewhere—exhaust itself. Sensitive newspaper editors, looking for alternatives, periodically turn to crowded super-markets where the managers of great chain stores throughout Western consumer societies increasingly complain of "hell on wheels." It is called "trolley rage"; and it ranges from smashing (for some unknown reason or another) a last bottle of sale wine over a rival customer's head (for which a woman was jailed in London after the assault in an otherwise genteel Marks &

Spencer branch shop) to mayhem in the crowded queues at the check-out counters, usually accompanied with ramming, pushing, shoving, and noisy locked-wheel collisions. The rude language of anger and outrage is, however, disappointing: that is, up till now. One reporter, a Mr. Charles Jennings, was assigned to the trail of supermarket punch-ups and found only small pickings for the feature in his paper:

> There was none of the grinding of teeth and bitter cursing you get at the more crushed [incidents of "Car Rage"]....
>
> "I actually found myself calling someone an *'old cow'*," one perfectly genteel lady shopper recently confessed....[2]

Perhaps the genteel note was hit only in the presence of a gentleman of the press or male mediaperson. Female feature writers, as is well-known, are more perceptive and quicker of hearing;* and in Frankfurt-am-Main they have recorded "trolley rage" which begins with the scatological *"Scheisse!"* and goes on from there. But the German press, unlike the quasi-puritanical Anglo-American broadsheets, has no editorial problem with publishing the whole range of expletives which may come up in the course of the daily news.

Something of a journalistic letdown, too, are the inquiries into the lubricious advertising which is rumored to accompany the sexy holiday tour business. Reporters rush to investigate the tour operators, especially when *Club* 18-30 had a successful year featuring slogans such as *"I saw, I conquered, I came."*** But if sex sells holidays, aimed at young singles, it also threatens to taint or stigmatize the less aggressive, and (concedes one tourist director) "This sex, sex, sex image puts people off, especially young women." Well, if they want a vacationer's round of local museums and scenic routes, they can go elsewhere. The club for singles who want to see and conquer are not alienated from the prospect and official promise of the sexy sales-pitch. The text in the brochures (not explicit enough, I suspect, to

---

* The assertion of equal women's rights to such literary expletives was first put forward aggressively by Aphra Behn (1640-1689). Her various London plays and novels had to contend with charges of "lewdness" – attracted, in her view, by her sex (or, as we would say now, gender), and countered in her turn by an open defense of "indecencies written by women." As late as 1905 her work was described as "lurid and depraved." See the *Oxford Companion to English Literature* (ed. Margaret Drabble, 5th ed., 1985), pp. 81-82.

  But Virginia Woolf in her *Room of One's Own* (1928) considered Aphra Behn's work as having "the plebeian virtues of humor, vitality, and courage." Since then the plebeian virtues of having *F*-words of one's own has proliferated exponentially. One man's macho realism is another woman's brave bawdry.

** Also see in the second volume, for the history of the double-entendre with Benetton and the Beatles, "Swearing by the Ad-man's Prose."

be quoted in even the most vivid stories I have seen) "is not meant to be raunchy—it's the language of that type of client. This age range understands these sort of terms." Still, not an f-word in sight.

It is so much more productive to move away from cynical businessmen who are interested only in what they call, with a wink, "the bottom line" and rejoin the cultural world wherein raunchy language flows more copiously, if less explicitly and action-oriented. On this same day when the *Daily Telegraph* had meager pickings in the supermarkets and at the tourist agencies they came up with a winner in the person, just arrived for a come-back concert in London, of James Jewell Osterborn, the Detroit-born aging pop star *aka* "Iggy Pop." No gentility here, although at almost fifty, he is decades away from that "outlandish freak" who drummed for a group called the Iguanas and for whom a local junkie named Jim Popp catered (hence "Iggy Pop"). In a rousing interview he tells the "grunge expert," also improbably named Caspar Llewellyn Smith:

"There's always going to be a side of me that wants to break a glass and put it into your – – ing throat!" he laughs with a hyena's grin. "When I hear a song I like, I just go, 'Yeahh!' There are other sorts of music, with a wider emotional range. But I keep coming back to, Let's *smash* something!"[3]

That's more like it—although the typo-form of two long dashes make the adverb somewhat obscure and sexually incorrect. Small matter. After he had adopted a "low profile" in the 1980s and early 90s the transatlantic reunion with Iggy Pop was smashing in every way. As I am reliably informed, his influence was still evident in the emergence of grunge, "still the most vital development in American rock this decade...." But what is a decade among icons? After having put the obligatory f-word behind him, Mr. Smith goes on in his merry, meretricious way to tell us—

He is physical, he is sexually provocative, he gives the audience a palpable thrill. The girls are half his age, but that is all that has changed in almost 30 years....

Naughty Little Doggie...features his familiar repertoire of squealing guitar licks, anguished yelps and lascivious growls, but he attacks the material with unabashed glee. There is no flab on the record, everything is pared down to the essential bone....

We accept with, possibly, less than glee the conclusion that this latest album adds to "the portrait of a life spent stumbling through a chemically-fashioned haze."

English lady correspondants may feign shock in New York when they run into the profanity of "car rage" in the gridlocked traffic jams of Manhattan streets, but their American counterparts are more blasé and manage to keep their equanimity in even more outrageous incidents of brutal thievery. A *New York Post* newspaperperson named Ann Bollinger covered the story in a Manhattan courtroom where rap star Queen Latifah (real name: Dana Owens) told how she had been affected by the shooting of her bodyguard in a harrowing carjacking. The vehicle in question was a $73,000 green BMW, and the Queen had been sitting in the car with friends, waiting for other friends, near the Apollo Theater. As Miss Bollinger reported, filtering the court testimony of Ms. Latifah with the usual calculated discretion and still preserving (as all good newspaperwomen should) the sense of menace and insult:

> "We sat there for a couple of minutes", Latifah said, "We were laughing and joking. I can't remember being that happy. Then a black kid walks up to the car and says, 'Get the f— out of the car! Get the f— out of the car.'...[As] she was getting out of the car, she heard a gunshot...."

Since there is a carjack in Manhattan almost every day of the year, our New York press is simply doing its duty by the hapless citizen and his endangered automobile in informing him of the current vocabulary of highway robbery: Get out quickly at the sound of the first F-word, its repetition might well be bloody.[4]

It is in some circles an occasion for regret that male newspaper-persons can no longer compete with this sort of thing, namely, the lean and hungry look in distaff journalism which maximizes the appetite for expletives. A man is reduced to this kind of account: a story in the *Miami Herald* of a local traffic accident wherein a woman driver sped through a stop sign and injured a pedestrian trying to cross the road. As Dave Barry explains,

> In Miami it is not customary to stop for a stop sign. If you stop for a stop sign, the other motorists will assume that you are a tourist and therefore unarmed, and they will help themselves to your money and medically valuable organs.

The traffic lights are also subject to peculiar local interpretation, according to which green means *"proceed,"* yellow, *"proceed much faster,"* and red, *"proceed while gesturing."* The Miami incident was aggravated by the decision of the injured pedestrian to remain calm and only to punch the fender of the aggressive automobile. As Barry confessed, it was he who struck the first blow in the "road rage."

> I punched the car and I pointed to the stop sign and I yelled, "THERE'S A STOP SIGN!" The woman then rolled down her window and expressed her deep remorse as follows: "DON'T HIT MY [UNLADYLIKE WORD] CAR, YOU [VERY UNLADYLIKE WORD]!"*

---

* As Dave Barry would say, I am NOT making any of this up nor blue-pencilling anything—these are verbatim quotes....

Writing in his newspaper as an afterthought, he "should have yelled a snappy comeback." But before he could think of anything (so slow have the steeds become in the profanity sweepstakes) "she was roaring away, no doubt hoping to get through the next intersection while the light was still red...."

As I say, males are increasingly hard put in an era of militant feminism to indulge in what could be misconstrued as macho prejudice or gender bias or, for the older folk, what used to be thought of as very ungentlemanly behavior.[5]

In the so-called Clinton sex scandals of the years 1997-1998 men and women played, to be sure, their usual gender roles; but at one notable point it was, again, a female reporter who took (or, some would say, was allowed to take) a step over certain conventional fenced-off limits of language. For the *New York Times* it was Maureen Dowd—touted by an acerbic editor of the *Los Angeles Times* to be "reckless and supercilious...nasty, sparky, but invariably funny"— who would take her place in the paper's book of records. Mrs. Paula Jones was still pressing her charges of "sexual harrassment" in a Little Rock hotel room. And Mrs. Dowd speculated in print about "those rumors about that bald eagle tattoo" on the President's penis. What Paula could allegedly report, Maureen could pass on to readers who might (like me) have only heard tell of some "intimate biological peculiarity" which was supposed to have been revealed in the hotel room confrontation between Ms. Jones and the Arkansas governor in 1991. Genital evidence, whether attested to or solemnly denied, was now fit to print.[6]

The flirtation with this kind of flash vocabulary on the part of female journalists has many prickly aspects, not the least of which is the irony of feministic professionals accommodating themselves to the rude expressiveness of generations of macho hacks straining to get a bawdy bit or two into print. It is as if equal opportunity implied equal obscenity (and a bit more)—anything he can do, she can say better....And yet, in the face of the mounting rudeness from the distaff side, one suspects another victory in the age-old pubertarian plot on the part of the boys to get the girls to "talk dirty" (as in, below, Hollywood's loutish f-word therapy for the young, nubile Elizabeth Taylor). In talking "like a man" they were only being manipulated; in adapting themselves to writing "like it is" they were turning their high heels on the ladylike traditions of Jane Austen and her ilk.

I note in today's newspaper in London the column of a young critic named Maureen Paton, discussing a TV documentary of the night before. It exposed the macho bravado in the local police precincts near various football stadia, plagued by yobbo hooliganism; and she prefaces her remarks with a manly thrust of her own, to wit: "The trouble with soccer is that they don't always kick the correct balls; I know which ones I would aim at, given half the chance...."[7] Her half-a-literary-chance she takes with feet flying as she quotes a pompous policeman talking back to one of the unruly yobs: "'If you ever swear at a policeman again...do not call me a f****** d***head,' said one, his moustache quivering."

As for the male hacks, seeking their tit-for-tat against this kind of farmyard competition from female poachers, they are seen to be covering their portions by making every effort to record women of all sorts (not merely bawdy babes in big-business or in incidents of road rage) indulging in obscene expostulation or moving roughly in the indelicate vicinity of four-or-more-letter words. Thus, in an American account of the career of Arianna Stassinopoulos Huffington (Greek beauty; Oxford scholar; best-selling Picasso- and Callas-biographer; Washington columnist and political hostess), a campaign manager named Ed Rollins tells of his difficulties with the ambitious millionairess and, finally, of his angry turn to her spouse at the time:

> I threatened to quit, telling her husband: "If I stay I don't want to have a f****** thing to do with your wife for the rest of this campaign. Nobody calls me a liar."
>   "Please don't swear at my wife," he [Michael Huffington] said as he hurried her out of the hotel room and into an elevator....[8]

Having put the lady in her place, the *Sunday Times'* informant goes on his uninhibited way to put some of his fellow Americans into similarly immodest context. After all, Ed Rollins spent years in the White House on Ronald Reagan's staff and he knows all the expletives before they were ever deleted. How "f****** modest" was the president when, in his presidential limousine cruising through midtown Manhattan to the reverberating cheers of countless enthusiasts, he had every reason to believe that he was being approved of by History? The crowds were almost worshipful, but the man had humility:

> "Mr. President," I said, "don't you find this outpouring overwhelming?" He looked at me with that infectious Reagan grin. "Just wait about half a block," he said. "Some guy will be flipping me the finger and yelling, 'F*** you, Ron, you prick.' That's the guy who always puts it in perspective for me."

Since this treasurable bit of historical information is not likely to be considered fit to print in the American press, one ought to be publicly grateful to London editors for their journalistic grossness which allows heroes on straight-talking occasions to use expletives as part of their naked natural-born style. "The Brits" have in recent years had an altogether hard time of it in American hands and they are desperate to get some of their own back, even if only by irony. Commenting on yet another Hollywood catastrophe film (*Independence Day*, 1996) which confounds American adversities with dangers for the whole of the planet, Alexander Walker writes with full-frontal directness in his London newspaper, "The rest of the world outside America doesn't get much of a look-in. I'm afraid we Brits are represented as patronising pricks who welcome Uncle Sam's initiative."[9] Thus the f- and p-words, it remains to record, have already taken over some sectors of the high discourse between the classic English-speaking peoples. Some think they have already become indispensable and unavoidable in order to convey a real sense of the transatlantic relationship.

When the backlash comes, with a neo-puritan vindictiveness against major sinners in the corruption of discourse, the blame will be put by hypocritical Anglo-Saxon guardians of our speech on foul-mouthed Americans—and by double-talking macho males against hapless females who were only trying to do their modest fair share on behalf of "dirty realism."

The argument that the domain of profanity and obscenity has been since time immemorial—and therefore will (and should) always be—a natural and exclusive privilege of men is already being heard in the land. Men are identified by one newspaper columnist, risking the wrath of the politically correct lobby, as being "ambitious, aggressive, assertive, dangerous, penile—the p-sex." Being "foul and abusive" must be in the genes. If so, then the wheel of language fashions will turn again; and, in the spin, old readings will be given new intonations. It is no simple pendulum swing or cyclical reversion, because no one can hold fast to what is writ in dirty waters. The following passage suggests what is old (male pride) and what is new (self-criticism) in the resurgence of the insolent masculine principle:

> It is members of the p-sex who dominate art and industry, war and politics, engineering and exploration....Testosterone, not profit, drives members of the p-sex, from the preposterous vanities of Ozymandias, the homicidal impulses of Drazen Erdemovic, the Serb mass murderer, or the acquisitive urges of Kirk Kerkorian, the 78-year-old who has just bought MGM. The p-sex fills our cabinets and our jails, mugs strangers, flies fastest, dives deepest, builds cities, massacres prisoners, creates companies and trades on the floor [of the Futures Exchange]....

The last reference was to an incident on the floor of the International Financial Futures Exchange wherein a young trader was heavily fined for his "foul and abusive behavior" while making a transaction. His gutsy defense was "This is a high testosterone business." Which led to our columnist's conclusion: "The world is a macho world, made that way by the maddest hormone of them all."[10]

Whether or not the seminal factor in sexual language is hormonal we can leave to those others amongst us who have a little knowledge of endocrinology. It could be that the phenomenon of women swearing along with the best of us is yet another "two-cultures-clash" between, say, testosterone and estrogen. All the more reason that the so-called p-sex will not be lightly forgiving the "c-sex." ("Men are not merely the p-sex; they are the everything-sex, except in one regard; it is women who are the c-sex.")

The first witness to attest to the prosecution's case against the new role of women in our newspaper culture is my old friend, the battle-scarred veteran of gangland warfare over linguistic taboos, Sir Peregrine Worsthorne, whom I have called one of the godfathers of the f-word in contemporary English-language discourse. After his triumphalist high-point in the 1970s and then the onset of abject compunctions in the 1980s, he has now been outraged by the shocking recrudescence of the "foul and abusive," flying under the flag of feminism. He had been, he confesses, under the illusion that the "empowerment" of women could possibly make for a less crude and course environment, even a gentler, kinder society. Even in literature, it is doing (or so he finds) exactly the opposite. He reads books written by women novelists containing passages that would have brought a blush to the cheeks of D.H. Lawrence, and indeed brought on, in his own case, the signal for a counter-offensive I have been grimly awaiting for years. He singles out Pat Barker's 1995 Booker Prize-winning novel *The Ghost Road* about the First World War:

> Her officer hero, while resting behind the lines before the final offensive (in which he is killed), has a chance fleeting sexual encounter with a French farm boy, which is described in such disgusting detail as to be unprintable in this newspaper and made all the worse for me by the knowledge that it is a woman's imagination coming up with such crudities....I doubt whether any male writer would have either wanted or dared to go that far. Only a woman would get away with it.

I am not sure how well or widely read Perry Worsthorne is in the hard, or even soft, semi-professional literature of sexual encounters to know with such assurance how far men have been getting away with similar sorts of things; but that is beside the main point. After decades of winning friends and influencing people, the feminist movement may, at least in the world of the public prints, be in for a few beatings. To be sure, one snap of the old Nietzschean whip does not quite make a whole backlash, especially in the case of a tried-and-true circus-performer like Worsthorne of the *Telegraph*:

> At a party last week I heard a journalist say "I don't give a f—whom Polly Toynbee is shagging." It was a female journalist speaking, of course. It is out of the mouths of women nowadays that the real filth springs.[11]

Hedging my bets I venture to suggest that this may be only a transitional phase in journalistic salacity wherein the male journalist could be heard saying the converse, that he "didn't give a shag whom the lady in question was f—ing." The variations are not infinite. Circumlocutions like "shag" will go out of fashion. The f-words will pall and bore, and may fall into desuetude. It will turn out to be, possibly, a big story in the new century.

The Politics of the F-Word

This kind of dissembling usage of a pseudo-blue word has also appeared in the political argumentation of the British press. Although the sexual-verbal wordplay is rather different on both sides of the Atlantic—reflecting, I hasten to say, less real customs than surreal complexes—journalists like the easy way to an apparently bright turn of phrase and the suggestion that something daring is being reported. Was the issue of "Europe"—its increasing federal unity, and especially its imminent single currency (the *euro*, with or without the pound sterling)—central to the 1997 election campaigns of Tory John Major and New Labour Tony Blair? Commentators who thought it was found it "one of the more surreal aspects" that others, including the BBC, were pronouncing it "not an issue." Why so discreet? Why so "stiflingly unreal"? When had the explosive question become an unmentionable? A fortnight before polling day Christopher Booker waxed indignant at its repression since "the E-word had already been erupting over the front pages for 24 hours."[12] Are many readers amused, or even titillated, by the suggestive abbreviation? There was an ever so tiny bawdy touch in the implication that the gentlemen of the press, and all of the rest of prim and proper toffs on the political scene, were reluctant to mention the dirty word for fear of bringing a blush to the face of the electorate. Unashamed and unafraid, veteran anti-European campaigners like Booker had been spelling out the expletive, without sneaky benefit of a single asterisk or dash, for many years now. Booker had been a stentorian tribune of the "Little Englander" camp for a long time now.

But the reluctance to "out" the e-word at the time was, in point of fact, a cold matter of strategy and tactics—neither major party calculated there were any votes in it, either way—and not any kind of political prudery. The language on the hustings is in the Queen's English and is, if anything, clean as a whistle.

The "l"-word, at least in British political campaigns, is rather a more likely candidate for the American category of bad language. A few weeks into a heated campaign (as in mid-April 1997) and tempers get frayed, with loose talk inching to the edge of the tolerable or permissible. Someone may even have stooped so low as to call a rival a "prevaricator" who is being "economical with the truth." Dr. Bryan Macwhinney, the Prime Minister's forlorn campaign manager in a landslide defeat for the Tories, had difficulty pulling out all the verbal stops; and the *Sunday Times* reported,

Alerted by Macwhinney on his flight from Coventry to Newcastle, Major agreed to use "the L-word" himself, the ultimate abuse in British politics. "Liar" he specifically barred in parliamentary exchanges.

Previous elections have had their flashpoints but incumbent prime ministers normally choose to remain aloof from street in-fighting. For Major, however, Blair's tactics warranted the strongest counter-measures. "Blair really has lied. If he is elected he will become a British Richard Nixon."

Now that is a real dirty word, if only the reporters could get it on tape.[13]

This uptightness in the use of political language pertains, to be sure, only to the public dimension of the debate. What may get actually recorded on the tape-recording machines is rather different. Some are overt, under the illusion that they will come in handy some day in the writing of history; some are covert, to be leaked any day now for love or money. The excerpts that get "outed" can be safely said to reflect the conventional standard of rude words that now obtains in pubs, bars, and throughout the land. How soon will the newspaper culture catch up with this hidden demotic dimension of the democratic debate? And what revised house styles will prevail when a newspaper of some quality finally has an opportunity, if one should present itself, to publish the historic expletive (or as near to it as they can dare) with which one desperate candidate finally expostulated to the world his true estimate of the character, probity, parentage, and secret life-style of his altogether unworthy opponent? When might we reach the point—whether it is desirable or not is another question—at which what the papers say approximates how the people actually talk, with no holds barred? So far it's not yet got. Still, progress can be registered in the de-bowdlerization of the hidden political drama. The unexpurgated Starr Report, featuring the notorious Lewinsky-Tripp tapes, was an American milestone (and we will be returning to it).

When journalists actually participate in the political process—a TV correspondent deciding to run for office (Martin Bell of the BBC in Tatton), a *Daily Telegraph* reporter trying, in vain, to hold a parliamentary seat for the Conservatives in Wales (Boris Johnson)—it is obviously easier to get hold of "the real thing" and catch the conflict of political passions in the raw, possibly unbowdlerized, by eavesdropping on the insiders. But Johnson's electoral diary was a mite disappointing; newspapermen have the chronic habit of hesitating a moment for thought or for a small joke before putting anything on paper, and his day-by-day paragraphs had much of a journalistic sameness about them:

> *Monday, April* 21. We're getting closer. Someone has stuffed an old sock through my letterbox in Llangollen. Presumably psychological warfare, by the same person who writes "You Tory w*****" on the battlebus. This enables me to say in speeches how much I look forward to receiving the other sock—not necessarily on the jaw, ha ha.

No suggestion of a break-through here. The *Sunday Times* proved to be more venturesome: not planting a sleeper among the candidates but putting one of the insiders on their own payroll and commissioning the lowdown from a straight-talking professional in the midst of things.

The new Labour cabinet was still being formed by Prime Minister Tony Blair, and the Queen was still going through the "kissing hands" procedure of swearing in the new ministers when one of the old ministers, routed from service at the Treasury under Kenneth Clarke, but alert enough to have kept "a revealing and far from respectful journal," rushed into print with revelations. On the eve of the campaign the Rt. Hon. Philip Oppenheim is dining with another M.P., the Olympic gold-medallist Sebastian Coe, when

> *Tuesday, Febraury 25.*—...On cue, Alan Duncan comes to join us. Duncan's an ambitious s*** but a good class of ambitious s*** because he's so overt it's almost tongue in cheek....

This bit of earthy realism about a colleague, also soon to be bereft of all hope (and ambition), leads on to another entry which appears to be more classified in its secrecy if only the editor had given us a clue as to how to decode it: *"Wednesday, April* 16.—Someone has opened the box and the f***wits have popped out." Which box, what wits? Who knows, and no wonder an "uneasy boredom" is setting in which the candidate is finding "hard to handle." He recalls good old days of ministers' meetings when one could lean over and ask, even "loudly"—"What the f*** is he going on about?" (19 April) Towards the end of his "Diary of an Underdog" Oppenheim senses that his lot have lost their bark and bite—"I know I'll lose, but I won't disgrace myself" (30 April). He tells us that he "was feeling free, almost light" and went home to sleep, "for the first time in months, like a baby." (1 May) The pabulum he's ditched to his newspaper readers. The *Sunday Times* encouraged us to think that we were only a scoop away from a scabrous turning-point. We're only left with a couple of casual expletives, and a funeral. Meanwhile, down at the ranch where triumphalism runs high, we await another opportunity to listen in to the cacophonic sounds of power. It sounds promising. We will be having "unique access" through the novelist Robert Harris (*Fatherland*; *Enigma*) who has been traveling as a member of Tony Blair's private staff, with special contact to the next Chancellor of the Exchequeur, Gordon Brown. What will this bunch of "ambitious s***s" be going on about? A literary man's eye and ear is always an enrichment for our newspaper culture. Harris does not disappoint:

> *Wednesday, April* 16.—...on a gloriously sunny afternoon two weeks before polling, I get my first proper glimpse of Tony Blair the candidate. He is climbing out of the back of a Jaguar....

Thursday, April 17—...The only evidence of tension I encounter is the name given to Brown's suite of offices. These are known apparently as "Planet F***." ('Because every time you're called inside, you know they're about to f*** something up.')...

Well, they didn't. They won, by a landslide, ambitious little sods that they are, eluding the spell of the f-word. One is, in the end, very much relieved that no one ever found a better, ruder way of putting it. This planet may thrive.[14]

Still, the larger cultural forces gather darkly, and the shadows of "dirty realism" in politics and the press are ubiquitous. In the first days of the new Parliament a Blair administration, busy weighing its words for an innovative Queen's Speech, was greeted with an official report as to what the state of the English language is, so far as a representative sample (25,000) of primary school children are concerned:

Pupils are excelling at a new language—of four-letter words....While children have always mimicked adult language, a study of 100 primary schools suggests that they are now more fully aware of the meanings of swear words and are using them in an increasingly hostile and aggressive way....The schools said the bad language and sexual innuendo covered the whole range of adult swear-words.[15]

The usual suspects are being rounded up. Teachers, despairing at the Sisyphean labors of cleaning up the language, blamed television. The Prince of Wales accused the whole nation of swearing too much and relying on clichés which could only encourage "a mean, trite, and ordinary view of the world we inhabit." Football stars were blamed by school-principals. Even the multi-cultural scene was, at the risk of political incorrectness, not excluded from responsibility: "When children who cannot speak English come to school, the first thing they learn is 'pass' and the second thing they learn is 'f***ing pass'...." Older charac'.ers around the schools could remember when children used to call each other such innocuous names as *"piggy"* or *"smelly"*; now they pepper their abuse with profanities "as well as sexually suggestive and racist comments." One hopeless observer offered his cynical vision of tomorrow's proud parents, beaming at their precocious child who had—at such a tender age!— "just said his [or her] very first expletive."

Couldn't a professional psychologist, well versed in the twists and turns of the learning curve, see a shimmer of hope? He could. Dr. Michael Boulton of Keele University ventured the thought, "It is becoming so normal for children to use swearwords that the shock value has gone for children themselves." This is a glimmer of optimism which, as we shall see, will sustain many readers, writers, and editors in the newspaper culture as they reel from the coming tremors and shock waves of an old under-language crawling up into the light of day.

Repeating the Error, or Compounding the Offense

In libel affairs an editorial apology, usually not voluntary but conceded under pressure of legal action and the costly shadow of indisputable evidence to the contrary, never repeats the error—for this would constitute compounding the felony. In matters which involve a mistaken cussword, possibly misheard or misattributed, the studied repetition of the error, with humble and contrite words from the repentant editor, is another way of fulfilling the nominal ration of obscenities for that particular edition of the paper. A gross f- or c-word (or both) get a special rebate. It saves scouring the news-stories and the interview features for the salt with which the salt can be salted. Unless, of course, the error is the wild and improbable attribution of a salacious remark to, say, Mother Theresa. Lesser mortals may well take a quiet manly pride in the rough talk and still go on to obtain the editorial atonement for the scabrous quotation which, in one manner or another, is deemed to be embarrassing.

Thus, in the unending campaign against Rupert Murdoch, hated rival of the media in the Anglo-American world (not to mention his native Australia), the *Observer* published a story under the headline "PUT MURDOCH IN THE DOCK, SAYS FOOT." The objection came not from Mr. Rupert Murdoch and/or Mr. Michael Foot, whatever the vendetta they may have been conducting, but from a Mr. Alastair Brett who happened to be the lawyer for the (Murdoch-owned) *Sunday Times*. The *Observer* had a report about the former Labour leader "wining and dining" a former KGB agent. The paper now confessed that "we now understand that he [Michael Foot] did not." Why this, apart from its nonfactuality, should have a moral or emotional dimension is neither here-nor-there. After all, the *Guardian* which owns the *Observer* had a foreign and features editor who was wined and dined by (and took money from) real and functioning KGB agents, and it defended him to the last.* Ideology may be, as Sartre put it, the soiled province of *les mains sales*, but nothing is dirtier than dirty words. So, drawing on its wonted dignity, the *Observer*, that traditional organ of liberalism ("Independent Journalism since 1791"), published the following additional "CORRECTION": "We also reported that Mr. Brett called Michael Foot's lawyer 'a fucking cunt' after the reading of a statement in open court which apologized to Mr. Foot." The paper went on to accept a rather prim and flimsy defense, but slyly contrived to "compound the libel" or the label (although these kind of statements are usually subject to word-for-word agreement by the legal parties involved): "Mr. Brett has pointed out that he does not, and did not, use the word 'cunt', and that he was misheard in the mêlée outside the court."[16] Did this mean that the f-word came away with flying colors, clearly heard

---

*   See my pages on the case of Richard Gott, pp. 43ff.

in the mêlée and presumably also deeply felt? Only speculation. Mr. Brett had his apology "for any embarrassment this may have caused him." Even if the Murdoch-owned *Sunday Times*' lawyer had been cleared of using embarrassing language, Michael Foot had also been exonerated for breaking bread with secret agents of a foreign power.

It could be that only the KGB came away from the affair with any honor. But then who knows what the appropriate dirty words are in the Russian language? As former KGB Major Oleg Gordievsky has disclosed, the use of obscenities in the espionage directorate of the old Moscow headquarters was always *nyetkulturny*.[17]

Tyrannies have it easier, and their *ukases* on behalf of puritan censorship is peremptory and effective. Democracies have it more difficult, and liberality tends to encourage the publication of "corrections" and, at the very least, dissenting letters to the editor. Provided the mailbag is full and various enough, here is another cheap and easy way to fulfill the minimum ration of a paper's need for the daily dose of vulgar nutrients. On one Sunday the *Observer* apologizes for its sins; on another it gives an indignant reader a bit of space to vent his rage against (as the caption had it) an "F-WORD TOO FAR." An angry subscriber from Heathfield, East Sussex, writes as a representative of the younger, under-thirty generation—no old fogey, he (and no young fogey either, for he is explicit enough about the explicit language he deplores):

> I was disgusted to have to read the uncalled-for language...last week. I liked the style in which the article was written and found it informative and amusing, but was there really any need for the inclusion of 'fucking', 'fuck' and 'tits' (although 'tits' was not quite so offensive)? I did not mind 'condom', as it was a great description....I am not some old fuddy-duddy.[18]

This was all on a pleasant, very private Sunday morning; and if financial compensation were to be paid for the press's intrusive obscenities, clearly there would have to be an alphabetical scale, with the c-words and t-words not being nearly so costly as the f-word on the charge sheet of alleged damages. If salacity, needless and gratuitous, turns out to be an offense of editorial malpractice in the newspaper culture of the future, self-censorship by the purse may change all this. Or (it could be) economy-size and low-budget profanity may prove to be the safe and prudent way out. Some cheap words, although they are "not quite so offensive," simply cost less.

From Jefferson to Ochs to Murdoch

There is a noteworthy Anglo-American discrepancy here that must be registered and taken account of, for it will have surely occurred to the reader before this. Generally speaking, the Americans say the word more and publish it less; with the British it is the other way around. The preponderance of our examples of free-for-all usage, so far as serious journalism in our newspaper culture is concerned, is from London newspapers.

Why is the *New York Times*, in the rules and regulations of its style book, subjecting itself to more "puritanical" rigor than the *Times* of England? The latter is owned by Rupert Murdoch who comes from Australia, not conspicuous for its compunctions about profanity; but he also owns the *New York Post* which, despite its wild penchant for the demotic in slangy headlines and for colloquial idioms in stories and features, also (like the *New York Times*) keeps sedulously clear of the scabrous.

All the more reason for the English to seize upon every opportunity which presents itself to involve their transatlantic cousins in the common aberrations of a shared language. For example, nothing is taken more seriously for the *Guardian*—one great tradition which it carries over from its noble predecessor, the *Manchester Guardian*—than the issue of freedom of the press. It regularly musters earnest arguments from morality, political science, sociology, and even philosophical metaphysics, to persuade its readership of the liberal centrality of clashing opinions. But, as in its recent report from the U.S. on the emergence of "one-newspaper towns" as competition dies and dailies go under, it jumps at the chance of getting a dose of street-wise straight-talking into its act. Nobody less than the salty-tongued Pete Hamill—once a '68 militant, clawing at the establishment, now a guru of liberty and a defender of the status quo which "at least" offers a measure of variety—is interviewed to sum up the Jeffersonian lesson; and the *Guardian* (24 July 1995) quotes him to this unveiled effect: "If you're the only one in town you've lost the independence you would have if you just say fuck these guys."

In good part this represents something of the immemorial wonder that proper English literacy has always had for the free ways of American speech and writing; and famous British travelers from Trollope to Dickens have filled their notebooks with jottings of unusual expression among the post-colonial Yanks. The American newspaper culture has remained, more or less, faithful to its nineteenth-century formative years: crisp and colorful, innovative and easygoing. But in Britain the quality press has opportunistically adapted itself in the struggle against television and "one-media towns" where almost all the people get their news (and most other knowledge of the external world) from the living-room TV screen.

In America the institutional conservatism of the press has proved itself so strong that it won't "talk dirty" even at the price of survival. The New York *Newsday* has recently suspended publication (summer 1995), and it remained to the end an intelligent paper replete with classically good journalistic prose (first and foremost, the columns of Murray Kempton). If the founder of the *New York Times*, Adolph Ochs, could return to read today's edition of his newspaper, he would be surprised by very little and shocked at nothing. If Geoffrey Dawson, the great force in the *Times* of London for so many decades, could return, he would perish again at what happened to his prim and staid, if occasionally still "thundering," newspaper. For him, the barbarians would have evidently taken over. For Ochs the good old pride of Manhattan's Times Square was still publishing only (in its original slogan) "the news fit to print."*

Papers like the *Guardian*, then, have few easy pickings in what is actually published by its transatlantic counterparts, and so it is noteworthy that its "Jackdaw" department, which specializes in chromatically off-color items (all of them, mind you, of sociological significance), managed to locate an adequately juicy item, anomalously reported in full-frontal prose, printed in of all places, Texas. The story in the *Dallas Morning Star* was something to crow about, for it not only caught an outraged American protester in linguistic liberation but, at the same time, took on one of its favorite mass-cultural enemies, the Walt Disney Corporation. For a decent American parent had taken his son to "Disney World" in Florida, and the following untoward incident occurred (as published in the Dallas paper and in the *Guardian*, 24 July 1995). After a pleasant and invigorating morning in Orlando, a parade began which featured a marching band and many of the famous Disney characters. Everything was fine, writes the indignant American, until "Mickey Mouse" came marching by, and then his son—"who is a bit hyperkinetic (probably from all the junk food we feed him)"—broke loose from the parental grasp and ran up to Mickey, "anticipating no doubt a cartoon adventure":

> I followed my son out of the crowd, but before I could reach him, he had wrapped himself around Mickey's left leg for dear life. As I walked up, "Mickey" began screaming at both my son and myself. I paraphrase his words: "Get the fuck OFF ME, you little pile of RAT SHIT! I gotta put up with you little FUCKERS every goddamn day and I'm so sick of it I swear to God I'll bury my paw up your goddamn little butt hole if you don't LET GO!!!"

The artful irony of the word "paraphrase" indicates the quality of parental protest which ensued. After the first burst of commotion—Mickey was screaming and kicking his legs, trying to dislodge the lad, other Disney World fans

---

*   "All the News That's Fit to Print." The *New York Times'* slogan first appeared on its editorial page on October 25, 1896. But it did move to the upper left-hand corner of the front page of the newspaper on February 10, 1897, where it has remained.

were taking photos of the action—a "mortified" Dad stepped in to save the situation.

> *Nobody* treats my son like that. I suppose I lost my composure, and it pains me to say it, but I'm afraid I acted precipitously. I began to beat the shit out of Mickey. I understand he is a Disney employee, but I felt justified on the grounds that he was mistreating a member of the paying public, who happened to be my only child. Would you have done differently?[19]

There the "Jackdaw" document ended, with a well-phrased rhetorical question. The reply from the Disney Corporation, in the name of its senior vice president of public relations, is presumably of no other public—or linguistic—interest, offering as it apparently did only a few routine words of apology and a small discount voucher for other Disney entertainments.

All in all, journalistically speaking, the day was a success, beginning in New York with an f-word on behalf of the free press and ending up in Florida with a scabrous but perfectly understandable protest against the violation of a little boy's human rights—and hence utterly fit to print, even in its explosive rudeness. Profanity, in the *Guardian*'s style-book, is only a continuation of politics—indeed of liberalism—by other means. What noble, if nasty, battles will it be fighting on our behalf and in common cause in the tangy columns of tomorrow's paper?

Lady Di's In-Laws

There are special f-word usages which, in an act of unusual orthographic deference, the opening letter is discreetly omitted. But then extra care must be taken to get the number of vowels and consonants exactly right.

What's the coarse style among kings and queens? How does one cuss in Court, and has any royal reporter recorded it faithfully? Did even the Bard catch all the lewd lingo of his Elizabethan day? In our times, has our investigative journalism, peeping into the young lives of princes and princesses, eventually established how they pick up the off-color vernacular? (Do their commoner playmates spread it around? or is it a deviant little ducal cousin who knows all the blushing words? Is there off-color graffiti on their school's toilet walls?) If our thoroughly modern media-men are—even in these thaumaturgical precincts—desirous of telling-it-like-it-is, what loyal and royal limits are set (if any) not to run the risk of *lèse-majesté?*

The scandalizing loucheness of the affairs of Crown Prince Charles and the late Princess Diana which had been unsettling Britain's House of Windsor provides a crowning example of how one of London's most posh Sunday newspapers deals with such a delicate matter. (In certain centuries earlier one false step, or even a misheard word, might have landed a Rupert

Murdoch, like Walter Raleigh and Thomas More before him, in a cell in the Tower.*)[20]

Our editors are almost at their wit's end. Either they move ahead to what I have called full-frontal candor—Hollywood is already there, so are diverse ladies' and gentlemen's magazines (and even presidents don't get their expletives deleted any more). Or, falling short of naked truthfulness, they remain at the razor's edge, risking close shaves, and cutting and running whenever an embarrassing situation calls for a tactical retreat.

More than this is not needed to comprehend the cunning of the *Sunday Times* faced with the task of coming up in print with something to upstage the BBC which on the following Monday would be televising *live*, and on *prime time*, its exclusive interview with Princess Diana discussing *intimate* details of her private life. All the issues are being laid bare:

> Is Diana's decision to speak out on [the BBC's] *Panorama* tomorrow night the act of a desperate woman or a world-class manipulator?...[We] investigate how the Princess of Wales trumped the palace. How the public became Diana's hand mirror. From ingenue to old ham, [we] explain why the Princess is so keen for a TV confessional.

All this is well and good—but the BBC-TV can go it one better, for it has its cameras and studio lights and zoom-lenses for even more intimate close-ups. And the *Times* knows it is on a losing wicket here since it recognizes that "her facial expressions are amazing"—like Garbo's, like Norma Desmond's—and

---

*   This punishment—as the press, in its constant reminders, would have it – is, theoretically, still possible. As *The Sun* reported (22 November '95) with a touch of sadistic glee, "Princess Di and ex-lover (Captain) James Hewitt could be hanged for treason under centuries-old laws which have never been repealed. Princess Diana broke an Act of 1705 by suggesting that Prince William could become King instead of Prince Charles. And Hewitt broke a 1351 law banning anyone having sex with the wife of the heir to the throne...." With the usual cheekiness of blunt tabloid style, *The Sun* (also owned by Rupert Murdoch) gave it the headline:

HANG 'EM BOTH

Which violent threat is, one suspects, punishable as well under some convenient ancient ordinance.

A Tory M.P. also suggested the invocation of the Treason Act of 1351, "for which the penalty on conviction remains death by hanging"; but, presumably, he is protected by some Parliamentary immunity dating back to the time of Cromwell's Protectorate. Even then, "extenuating circumstances" could be pleaded in the light of Captain Hewitt's would-be martyrdom when he gallantly confessed that "I would have died for her." (*Sunday Times*, 26 November 1995, p. 15.) The moral of the story: what's news today can be centuries old. Historians can always come up with clues to manslaughter, or threats thereof.

"in one minute convey everything from misery to heroism to flirtation, everything a camera could ever want...."

And yet the news media has a trump card, for what the papers can say is not for the BBC sound-track to emit, not even in the post-godfather era of the Kenneth Tynans and Peregrine Worsthornes. Black-and-white has got it all over living color and digital sound. The *Sunday Times* tells us exactly (or thereabouts) what the princess said, ten-point type, printed left-to-right and black-on-white, about the Royal House of Windsor and her relatives in the richest and most illustrious monarchy in the world: "'After all I've done for that ******* family,' she cursed...."[21] Remember, when the audience-ratings are all done and the Sony is shut off, you first read it here. Indeed you first heard it here, for readers—and we have eavesdropped on such occasions before—have been caught murmuring and moving their lips. If there must be participatory obscenity, at least we are in good regal company.

Jacqueline Du Pré, or Tragedy in the Family Circle

What we could be edging toward is an honorable usage of the f-word. It would not amount to a grave breakdown of social communication, but there are in serious newspaper accounts of persons and events whose shape and significance would not be altogether clear if one persisted with style-book euphemisms. In the light of all the hijinks we have been recording, from the buffoonery of bright reporters to the cynical hypocrisy of copy editors and their superiors, it is often difficult to credit such virtuous motives. For the shock effects of the obscenities, and indeed the whole of the phenomenon of creeping profanity, appear to be an indistinguishable mess of farce and trickery. Still, as in the old days when *le mot de Cambronne* and *das Götz-von-Berlichingen-Wort* defined, or at least indelibly characterized, a battlefield emotion or a power-political crisis, there are times when a word can "make free," can encapsulate a truth, or (if you will) tell it like it is. Consider one last expostulation.

The readers of the *Times*, put upon so often in recent years by salacious frivolities, were hardly prepared to be shocked into authenticity on this occasion. For what we were being offered, one week long, was a mournful memoir of a young and famous musician who was cut off in her prime by a dreadful paralyzing disease and whose untimely death in 1987 at the age of 32 still causes distress in the widest circles. She had been married to the Israeli conductor Daniel Barenboim, and their recordings (she on the cello, he on the piano) were prized worldwide. The first few installments of the *Times*' serialization of a new book remembering Jacqueline Du Pré by her devoted sister (and an equally devoted, as we shall see, brother-in-law) added only the odd sentimental detail and anecdote. By the Wednesday, or "Day 3," sensitive souls began to fear some kind of an editorial countdown. In the story up till now, family tensions were becoming exacerbated; the symptoms of Jacqueline's medical condition were aggravated; the music was beginning to suffer; sister Hilary and her husband Kiffer Finzi became increasingly concerned. Then the *Times* feature tossed out the teasing question on "Day 4":

> What sort of man would sleep with his wife's sister, with his wife's knowledge, while she shared their home? That is what Kiffer Finzi did for 16 months...while his sister-in-law was on the brink....

The *Times* insisted (in a full-page banner headline), *It couldn't have NOT happened*. All the obvious rationalizations of an erotic outing were at hand. It was essential to the girl's stability. It was a human interest story. It even had the necessity and finality of a Greek tragedy. The sister believed, "Sexuality is important for everybody...." The brother-in-law looked into Freud and Jung, and was convinced by the pamphlets of Dr. R.D. Laing. ("Later on," he confessed, this bookish baggage made him "more of a hindrance than a help.") I knew an American rabbi, resident in London, who looked after her and tried valiantly to talk her out of a bitter complex that (or so her family felt) she was suffering a divine punishment for having married a Jew and converted to Judaism.

The first few installments were replete with circumlocutory cues for the *denouément* to come—going to bed, sleeping, bed-hopping, a little bit of fun on the side. "Day 5" with the final extract of the series "Genius & Betrayal" couldn't have *not* begun with a shocker.

> As Jackie became more incapacitated she took an even greater delight in shocking people. Many a male visitor would be alarmed by the greeting "**** me." Some turned it into a joke, others were frightened away. Maybe it was Jackie's way of saying she had not lost her sexuality.

Maybe it was only the *Times'* way of saying that it had not yet lost grip on the f-word and, despite the star-studded camouflage, its puritanical shock of recognition. I suspect the startled readership (and my private poll was only a small sample) was half-persuaded, half upset.

Soon the MS disease had taken its enfeebling toll, and one of the most vivacious musical soloists of the time was "unable to talk, swallow, speak or see." She had never spoken to Kiffer again after he had, at some point in the relationship, turned down her immediate demand to be "made love to." But we—whether we had a need to know or not; whether we were sympathetic or prurient witnesses, as the case might be, to a heart-rending tragedy—we had been told a hard fact of life and love by one of the great newspapers of the world. It was its big story of the week. It had never been told "full frontally" before. A real scoop.[22]

The credo of our newspaper culture is that nothing can or should be sacred, for in every deep crisis of human anguish—in love and hate, guilt and remorse, greed and failure—there is a strangled cry struggling to come out, with a high tone or a low word. I will, in a moment, be coming to an Amis and an Osborne, in the grips of their youthful anger; a Crosland, possessed by a political passion; a Chaplin, taking his revenge *sotto voce* for past humiliations; and many others. I don't know when some poet or a philosopher will commit to paper the ultimate blasphemy, expressing in a horrific cuss-word (expletive deleted) his tortured metaphysical angst in a god-forsaken universe. But when he or she does get around to defying Providence, in utterly free speech, insulting the Almighty to His face, telling the Lord God where to go or what to do with Himself, we can be sure that one or another of the great newspapers of our world will find the space (and the proper orthography) to record the primal cry, to be telling it like it is. It may not be news fit to print but we will, by then, have an insatiable, irresistible, and ineradicable need to know. Everything.

Expletives in Public Life

A word about the f-word in politics. It is difficult to conceive of parliamentarians like Winston Churchill or Anthony Eden departing from their usual prose style and peppering some speech in the House of Commons or some angry reply during Question Time. But since they both had vigorous opponents, in and out of Westminster, the expletives could have roared around them without, however, being recorded in *Hansard*. *Hansard* is notoriously subject to editing and indeed self-censorship; and, after delicate rewriting, abuse on the House floor (*"Liar!" "Bastard!" "Rat!"*) emerges as mildly insulting disagreements when acceptable synonyms are officially substituted.

What of the spectators in the balcony? Does the democratic record register the interpolations of the *vox populi* when it breaks out on occasion into the rude demotic? One recent incident suggests that if the Parliamentary reporter of the *Times* is within hearing distance, then historical truth has a chance of being served.

Matthew Paris, one of the best of the English "sketch-writers" bringing politics close to home for bored unpolitical readers, was in any case in high dudgeon on the Wednesday afternoon in question (the *Times*, 9 November 1995):

> The Commons just risen had developed the air of a long-stay, low-security mental asylum. Here, someone would be shouting at a tree; there, another would be weeping quietly alone on a bench; a third would be stumbling through the marigolds mumbling to herself; while a handful more would be jabbing fingers at each other in inane dispute....

Time to break away from the purple prose. The *Times'* man was slumping in his seat above the chamber, half-listening to a ministerial statement, when "a man's voice was suddenly raised in a string of shouted obscenities...." Of the string we are given only one pearl: "You f—— hypocrites, you're all..." Was this indeed all? We surely would need to know more about the dots and dashes to determine whether this chap in the balcony would be qualifying, along with those other godfathers of the f-word, for an entry into the *Guinness Book of Records*. It just cannot be that this was the *first* time the expletive had been resounding in the sacred halls of the Parliament. How can we find out? Whom should we consult? It might take a whole team of investigative journalists to dig out the dirt on this one. Meanwhile, the *Times* feigns indifference: "Routine stuff," I thought, "but they're warming up." He wonders whether the chair was within earshot, for the house speaker is very sensitive about such indelicacies. At least someone else up there in the balcony heard. A "terrific struggle" ensued as the "mad interrupter was dragged by attendants from his seat. Down in the chamber MPs stared up in shock." Farther down in Printing House Square (or wherever Rupert Murdoch's newspaper flagship is being printed these days), the *Times'* editors hardly looked up from the routine stuff; but it was early hours yet, and the paper would be warming up.

The American style of f-word transcription may be arch in its stiff, euphemistical formality—rarely "outed" in our mainstream newspapers, almost always protected in its [brackets]. But it has its special advantages by diverting a certain attention from the scurrility to the subject of what is held to be the real up-to-date misdemeanor—increasingly, race and religion rather than sex or obscenity. The *Washington Post* sports pages reported the following decision of the National Basketball Association during the '97 season:

> *Chicago.*—The NBA has fined Dennis Rodman of the Chicago Bulls a record $50,000 for a series of expletive-laced comments about Mormons that he made while the team was in Salt Lake City for the finals. Rodman apologized for the remarks....

The Bulls had been in Utah and had not been playing very well, whereupon Rodman had offered the excuse to reporters in a press conference: "It's difficult to get in sync because of all the [expletive] Mormons out here." The derogatory remarks (all "expletive-laced") caused a storm of protest, with the Anti-Defamation League outraged at their defamatory character and, with others, at their ethnic or religious insensitivity. Rodman's infraction of the rules, said the NBA Commissioner sternly, came under the unacceptability of offensive comments "involving race or other classifications." A well-known religious denomination was clearly classified in the protected area—although foul language, by and for itself, might have been tolerated or even excused. Still, the Chicago coach, Phil Jackson, tried to cast doubt on the real character of the derogatives which had proved so scandalizing and so costly. He suggested that "Mormon" in the black slang of an athlete like Dennis Rodman might have just been a nickname for people from Utah, and he might not have even known that "it's a religious cult or sect or whatever it is...."[23]

Such expletives may still have a touch of vulgarity about them but they can be, if semantic or other vested interests dictate it, more associated with grammatical error or a phonetic slip-of-the-tongue rather than to expressions of derogatory viciousness. Not the f-word but the M-word was the clue to the outrage. We (and our newspapers) don't even care to know what exactly the explicit expletive was: it makes no real difference. The slur was already built into the attitude, lurking in the nasty scapegoating impulse of blaming another "classification"—the Mormons, in addition to the Jews, the wasps, the blacks, the furriners, et al.—for all our misfortunes, especially those which happened to lay us low in the game last night.

What presidents can say—and indeed have said, as the Nixon tapes resoundingly document, in the privacy of the Oval Room—comes to involve a new generation of official aides who have to wrestle with the Washington press corps over ticklish stories that call for all manner of resourceful techniques of news management. Formal press spokesmen give way to "spin doctors," and reporters for serious U.S. journals vie with tabloid scoopsters for every little scrap of leaked information.

The antics, or "feeding frenzies," have become so outlandish that by the time of the second Clinton administration an editor of the *Los Angeles Times* wrote gravely (as if his own paper was a thing apart), "The corruption of the Fourth Estate is clearly a major story that needs to be told." For the moment the story could be summarized in a rare outburst of dog-eat-dog rivalry: "The quest for sales and ratings on the part of owners and top managers has reduced once distinguished news organizations to the level of Rupert Murdoch's *New York Post....*" Which led to the bare-boned conclusion that "there is no apparent difference in the behavior of the White House reporters for the *New York Post* and the *New York Times....*"

These are rare tones coming from one of the establishment centers of mainstream American newspaper culture, not only bemoaning "the integrity of journalistic art" and its élite representatives but, while they are at it, viewing with alarm "the general decline of civility in American life in recent decades." Two stories are apposite, both involving—names can be named: nothing is personal, nothing is private – Michael Frisby, White House correspondent for the *Wall Street Journal*, a daily newspaper generally taken to be accurate and well-informed as well as admirably serious. The *Los Angeles Times* writer quotes the media correspondent of the *Washington Post*, Howard Kurtz, who had just published a new book, an "inside story" of "the Clinton Propaganda Machine" (*Spin Cycle*, Free Press, 1998):

"Frisby was renowned inside the White House for tossing poison darts at uncooperative aides in the *Journal*'s gossipy, anonymously sourced 'Washington Wire' column, which ran on the front page every Friday. No one wanted to be the next target." True to form, Frisby seems to love playing the schoolyard bully, threatening to expose one Clinton aide for chatting with ABC executives in the hallway with the charge that he was soliciting a job with the network. "We're desperate for 'Washington Wire' items," he said. "Give me something else or I'm going to have to use this about you."

This is a spectacular American instance of what used to be known in old prewar Europe as *"Revolver-Journalismus,"* practiced at its most ruthless length in Vienna and Budapest. The formula implied was: blackmail...gun-to-your-head, page-of-galley-proofs under your nose(with an imminent deadline)...or else.*

But back to Frisby's soft landing. As the *L.A. Times* has it, "Michael Frisby of the *Wall Street Journal* stands out as particularly vengeful when his ambitions are by-passed. 'I'm going to f— you' he screams at White House aide Rahm Emanuel after being passed over on the leak of some story. Emanuel knew exactly what Frisby meant...."[24] The f-word resounding through the halls of the White House was inevitable, but it was the least of the misdemeanors of the occasion.

The Point of the Anecdote

How, then, can sportswriters transcribe colorful—and revealing—anecdotes about incidents on the playing field and attitudes of coaches and trainers? Australians who are winners in so many games are salty characters who do not hold up to discreet censorship. Scotsmen who are chronic losers need to have their boisterous burrs in trying to explain their tribal pride in unrelenting defeat (except on an especially windy day of golf at the St. Andrews Masters).

---

*   Such editorial exploits in those two capitals by Josef Bekessy are still notorious. I can remember in the years after World War II how U.S. Army Captain Hans Habe (*H.B.*, the son of old Bekessy) personally suffered—and his own brilliant reputation as a writer and newspaperman as well—from the lingering notoriety of his father's sleazy practices. It was no less a thunderer than Karl Kraus who mounted a campaign to "banish the villain" from Vienna.

Habe was the author of a best-selling memoir, *If Thousands Fall* (*Ob Tausend fallen*) in 1943; he published in the post-War Occupation period the official American-sponsored newspaper, *Die Neue Zeitung* (an excellent paper in every way); and then resumed his journalistic and literary career, writing a column for *Die Welt* and many novels. But the dastardly blackmailing feats of his father, the *Revolver-Journalist*, are still unforgotten. Both Kraus and Habe would have been astonished at the news that the sleazy practice has found a new playing field in Washington. Prospective victims still pale at the page-proofs, tremble at the deadline, concede on demand. Who dares say: Publish and be damned!

One soccer story. The fate of Scottish teams in international competition and in the World Cup is made particularly difficult by the lingering tribal loyalties which their Kings and their Edinburgh *philosophes* enjoyed. The Scotland squad can only be made up from the teams that are playing in the Scottish League. Research has to be done to validate the genealogical pedigree of each player. To play for Scotland you must have been born there, or have a Scottish parent or grandparent. Thus, "Scotland" is not exactly putting its best foot forward, and the poor pure-blooded weeded-out remnants get regularly humiliated. But the vaunted land with its philosophical traditions in the eighteenth-century Scottish Renaissance has a quick way with dialectics. As the current Scotland football coach, Craig Brown, explained to one mystified foreign interviewer who could not quite grasp the criticism of one player who was "damned for not playing when the other team's got the ball":

> One of Scotland's strengths, I believe, is that we are very good when the other team has the ball. Pity is that we're hopeless when we've got the ball. No, don't laugh, that's a fact.
>
> I think we're one of the best teams in Europe without the ball, but one of the worst when we're in possession because we haven't got the assurance and the composure to keep it.

Being Scotsmen, their fans are steadfast and never discouraged; and even when losing in Bulgaria, there were the men in Scottish kilts marching as if to famous victory. How perverse, then, is this penchant for not coming out on top? What could possibly account for indifference to the normal addiction to triumphalism and its robust emotions? "The Scots love people with a wee flaw in them, don't we?" The wee flaws amount on occasion to a wilful, dogged preference for defeat: for in its odd way it stimulates patriotic fervor. When two of their skaters were once performing brilliantly and were on their way to Olympic Gold Medals (and a small fortune as professionals), half the Scottish nation were up half the night to cheer them on. But the story that is remembered—the illuminating line, the classic adage of national character—was Jimmy's "Whit were ye up tae anyway?...Seeing that pair? I wish they'd fall on their f****** a****." And the moral of the story? "No, we don't like perfection in Scotland. Which is just as well anyway."[25] Which is the point of the anecdote. Without the f-word, no key and surprise insight into national character. Needless to say, the newspaper copy editors made absolutely certain they got it right, counting the right number of asterisks twice over. A typo-error here would be disastrous. Finicky proofreading guarantees that they are saying what you think they mean to be saying. I have just checked again. It does come out all right.

Motiveless Malignity

I have confined myself in most of the above to tropes of titillation. Still, there are grave situations in which the f-word appears to be, at least for the time being, an essential ingredient in a testimony which, without it, a report of a serious social commitment would be significantly incomplete, perhaps even inconceivable. This was the case in the O.J. Simpson trial which featured (and perhaps was determined by) the taped testimony of Detective Mark Fuhrman in which he used the n-word some forty-odd times (see above). An additional example.

In the trial of four youths in the Old Bailey, accused of murdering in an act of "motiveless malignity" a black youngster who had been waiting for a bus in south London, the white youths were acquitted for lack of overwhelming evidence. Still, the tape-recordings which were made available to the press (but not to the jurors as "admissible evidence") were indeed overwhelming in their "racism." One of the accused was heard saying (according to, among others, the *Independent*):"I reckon that every nigger should be chopped up, mate, and they should be left with nothing but fucking stumps."[26] The story in the *Times*, in fact, omitted the expletive in the last remark; but it offered an additional "chilling insight into the lives and thoughts of a gang of racist thugs" with this quote on an international football match between a Cameroon and a European team. The British television commentary had been irritating, and the youths talked back angrily to the man in the box:

Oh yeah we want Cameroon to win this—why should he want niggers to win it when they're playing something like Italy or something like a European ****team?...You rubber-lipped ****! I reckon that every nigger should be chopped up....Bollocks you nigger! A macaroon better not win it, mate.[27]

In another sequence another of the accused was recorded confessing,

If I was going to kill myself do you know what I'd do? I'd go and kill every black c***, every Paki, every copper, every mug that I know. I would go down to Catford...with two sub-machine guns, and I'd take one of them, skin him alive, torture him, and set him alight. I'd blow their two legs and arms off and say 'Go on, you can swim home now.'

There were many hours of this sort of thing, recorded secretly in their apartment. But while accepting that the videos showed unpalatable racist attitudes, the defense attorneys argued successfully that extreme racist views were neither a motive for nor evidence of a murder (and witnesses to the fatal incident had been vague in their identification at the bus-stop). The court did not allow the tapes—"to show the videos would so prejudice a jury there would be no chance of a fair trial." Justice not only had to be blind but deaf as well.

As for the press, once the prosecution withdrew its case, all metropolitan newspapers rallied to the cause of full and complete public documentation. Its details caused shock, dismay, and anger. For in its loathesome fullness the text revealed something more than the sly and sniggering prejudice which is common to many sectors of society, and more than even the blatant racism to be heard in the football terraces. The court (Mr. Justice Curtis, presiding) ruled it legally inadmissible; still, the newspapers found it relevant and eminently printable. Whether all readers would find the vituperation equally appalling— whether indeed (and this is the eternal risk of a free press) a few might read the racy quotations from the "video nasty" with secret sympathies and even open assent—is another question. Here the f-word did its duty: a vile signal for an emphatic sadism abroad in the land.

27

Remembering the Founding Fathers

The Heritage of the '68ers

Over-simplification is furthest from my mind. There is no intention to reduce the variegated strands of the recent sixties turbulence to a single generational factor. Nor is there any implication to the effect that the corps of young rebels conspired to foist the f-word and its related obscenities on a prim and proper world, which achievement merited the highest accolade (*"super...cool...wow!...wild...right on!"*). They did not succeed in making a revolution and forcing us to live different lives; but they forced us to speak (and write) differently. After all, they did not have the enthused support of radical masses, nor a grand and viable strategy for seizing power through the barrel of a gun. They did not—except for isolated gangs, here and there—carry firearms, employ firepower. The weapon they all could flourish with deadly effect was language; and here they were all—every single boy and girl of them—armed to the teeth with explosive words. When the tumult and the shouting were over, we were left with all our institutions intact, only a bit frayed by wear-and-tear (and, in places, sometimes slightly refurbished). But our vocabularies emerged unrecognizable.

In the beginning, when Mario Savio and his friends with their f-word placards began jumping up and down, the search for an explanatory theory was relatively a simple affair. Having only to deal with the Californian eruption on the Berkeley campus, one could have thought at first this was another aspect of American "exceptionalism"—*only in America*....For here was a uniquely advanced society, affluent as no other, marked by a social mobility to the point of absolute rootlessness, shaped by a liberal permissiveness which was leading its young to the edge of personal anarchy. The question, then, was: Why should it surprise when "Spock-marked" academic adolescents, with money

379

in their pockets and a scramble of every idea that ever appeared in paperback in their heads, rise up and, like young Prometheans, attack old gods and long for fiery new beginnings? Yet it did not turn out to be a singularly American phenomenon; and Europeans, who were moving more slowly, duly went out and did likewise.

Theories had to be revised when explosions were registered from Stockholm to Tokyo. Of course, many of the constituent elements were shared: mass culture, mindless prosperity, and so on. Yet the Swedes had a social order of much justice and equality, with none of the outraging miseries of America's "Negro ghettos." And how could an extensively close-knit Asiatic family-pattern produce exactly the same proto-Western dissidence and alienation? Then, when the young Germans began to be wildly agitated, theories began to go out of the window in utter intellectual defenestration. No other land was so grotesquely divided, with an iron curtain splitting the nation and a concrete Berlin wall dividing the streets of its capital city. The clue, surely, was that there was a "nationalism-deficit," a postwar absence of a patriotic ideal in the Bonn Republic which could give emotional coherence to vague dissatisfactions. As for Germany's universities, what was wrong with them was that they were old fashioned, élitist, and medieval, not (as in Berkeley) mechanical, massive, and modern. As for the "sordid bourgeois family," what was revolting about the German *Vater*, at least in the eyes of his disaffected son, was not that he was a nice, ineffectual, permissive Big Daddy but that he was still a narrow, authoritarian, stuffy little Nazi.... No, it was all too complicated, and has indeed remained so thirty years on. In the ultimate explanation of the international turbulence we have been floundering in an *embarras de différences*. Yet, in the Anglo-American world, the language was revolutionized, even if English proved not to be the serviceable language of revolution.

The Cromwellians—who beheaded a king (as they rationalized: *"Killing, No Murder"*) and established England's seventeenth-century commonwealth – may well once have been "revolutionaries," a new breed of men, dedicated to "root-and-branch" radical change. But they had in their century the resources of another tongue; they had the grand metaphors of Christian theology and the resources of a powerful Old Testament text. Since then the language has been of no service at all to English-speaking men or women of ideology. Except for brief Wordsworthian and Byronic outbursts (and not even then), the words are just not there; the rhythms falter, the echoes are missing. English has become too magnificently humdrum. Marx, in translation, loses half of his power; Hitler became obscure and almost meaningless; Saint-Simon and Fourier and Auguste Blanqui sounded like jejune fantasizers.

How much easier it was for a young Frenchman or a young German, when he heard the call to the extreme life, to sound authentic! A *groupuscule* agitator at the Sorbonne in May 1968 needed only to echo a phrase of Saint-Just

(*"La question du bonheur est posée en Europe"*) and he was securely locked into a magniloquent tradition. I heard at the time a young Berlin *Revoluzzer* hurl the word *"Umfunktioneren!"* at a despised liberal professor; and the heckler's imprecation seemed not only to be blessed by Kant and Hegel but also had within it a certain brutal power which no English academic word could ever convey without resorting to underworld slang (e.g., "Let's get him...fix him...bump him off...whack him out...take him for a little ride").

The American rebels were, at least in this respect, something of a special case. Aware of the profound handicaps of a language in which neither vague metaphysics nor rolling rhetoric could easily flourish, they ingeniously invented a vocabulary of political obscenity. Now suddenly the language could function for them in order to shock and to hurt, and to break out into what appeared to be a brand-new dialogue with their utopian future. The dirty word would help cleanse society.

But what is there left to do when—it was already happening at the time—the outrageous verbalism begins to become familiar and wear off, when the barnyard epithets and the street-corner expletives get taken up by playwrights and script-writers...by racy columnists and night-club clowns...by gutsy novelists and straight, well-dressed businessmen...by athletes and other celebrities...even by diplomats and high public officials? No matter, a famous victory had been won over the repressive restrictiveness of plain and decent English prose.

So the so-called "flight from language" which was imputed to the generation of the 1960s represented, in the end, its singular semantic achievement, its only real triumph over the old order. The oldsters looked askance. I myself grumbled that, apparently, no word longer than four letters seemed to be capable of carrying the delicacy of expressive meaning they wanted so much to communicate. But the genius of the basic f-word vocabulary, which could be mastered in a very few minutes, would be to qualify any four-letter man or woman on campus for greater things. This followed on mellifluously from the experience of the G.I. generation of World War II, when millions of veterans returned home after an immersion course in extensive profanity behind them, wherein barracks speech was just that: free, easy, and almost natural. Now the time had finally come for the outing of the f-word and all the stacked-up rudeness held uptight in reserve.

Here are some of the entries I made at the time; even if some have become somewhat *passé*, most are living happily in open sin ever after.

1. *Wild*. It was never used in a sentence or without an exclamation point. It served as a kind of *right-on* denotation of approval for the progressive excesses of the noble savage. When Ms. Bernardine Dohrn, a student leader at Columbia University and later the impassioned ideologue of the Weathermen gang, heard of the barbarous murders committed by Charles Manson and his

"Family," she said, "Dig it! First they killed those pigs, then they ate dinner in the same room with them, then they even shoved a fork into a victim's stomach. Wild!"

2. *Kill.* This is not to be confused, at least in black usage, with *murder* (or, in IRA usage, with "execution"). It was preferred by white university graduates to older forms deemed to be "square." These included *purge*, as in FDR's efforts in the New Deal thirties to "purge the Supreme Court"; *liquidation*, as in Stalin's terror of 1936-8; *épuration*, as in the French Resistance's summary court-martials in 1944-5; *erledigen* and *Endlösung* ("final solution"), Hitler's policy of extermination in the Nazi Reich (1933-1945); *umfunktioneren* (Rudi Dutschke, 1968), a vague if sinister battle-cry of student militance. One American rebel named Bill Ayers was asked what the *Weathermen* program was:

> "Kill all the rich people," he answered. "Break up their cars and apartments."
> "But aren't your parents rich?" he was asked. (Ayers' father was a Chicago corporation president and a university trustee.)
> "Yeah," Ayers said. "Bring the revolution home, kill your parents, that's where it's really at."

It would take a long in-depth study in psychiatry to explore whether the threat *"to kill"* represented a real intention to murder, to inflict death upon, etc., or perhaps it signified merely a rhetorical effort to simulate extremism, to suggest strongly the perfect hateful act of opposition and hostility. W.H. Auden's notorious defense in a poem of "the necessary murder" was explained away in the latter sense as "only words." Students of the language know that when real blood is to flow—in a political revolution or in a gangland war—men usually reach for a metaphorical equivalent. The enemies of Lenin and Stalin were, famously, "purged" or "liquidated." Rivals in the New York underworld, if we are to believe Mario Puzo's *The Godfather*, were made an offer that they couldn't refuse and then dispatched "to sleep with the fishes." In latter-day usage, as in the Sammy Gravano testimony in the New York Godfather trial of John Gotti, they thought about "whacking" their victims, about "taking them out." As one word-sensitive newspaper columnist has written, pondering the course of such euphemisms in the American context (from the days when the deceased was said to be "a-mouldering in his grave," like John Brown's body, to the time when "he was pushing up daisies"):

> Murderers probably don't say "bumped off" these days. Like most of us, murderers probably hate to seem out of touch with the new trends, and "bumped off" sounds as antique as a black-and-white movie starring Edward G. Robinson.
> In Robinson's day, murderers didn't confine themselves to the "bump-off." Often they took their victims for "a little ride."[1]

There is, Russell Baker detects, "a certain squeamishness about saying 'murder'" even if we can also detect in political history a resort to synonyms which differ by only a hair from the mark of Cain. In the bloodthirsty years of the seventeenth-century English Civil War a regicide's defense of the beheading of the king was, as I have mentioned, the insistent argument "Killing No Murder." In the debate with conscientious pacifists who deny the moral legitimacy of anyone fighting a Just War, defenders of European armies on a thousand battlefields often went to the extent of revising the Biblical translation of the sixth Commandment to read, not *Thou shalt not kill,* but thou shalt not *murder.* Killing enemies to protect God and Country, to defend Freedom or safeguard the Revolution, is not to be confounded with the foul deed of murder. The German Supreme Court recently (1996) came to a landmark decision which rejected the legal suit of the German Army's military command that the quotation of Kurt Tucholsky's famous remark—*"Soldaten sind Mörder"* (Soldiers are murderers)—should be forbidden as a calumny, a dishonoring libel on a patriotic duty. The Minister of Defense had argued: Soldiers are trained to kill, but they do not—at least not in a liberty-loving democracy—commit murder.

Russell Baker is less interested in the morality of the problem than in its semantic ironies:

> "Hit-man" sounds like an honest craftsman who might live next door. Politically motivated killers who murder whole groups of people for publicity purposes are dignified as claimants. After a massacre, the press usually reports that this or that [group] has "claimed responsibility" for the deed.

There are other "comically grisly expressions." In Argentina the victims were done away with and officially became "the disappeared." During the Vietnam war, the CIA's way with inconvenient characters was "to terminate with extreme prejudice." A generation earlier the American GIs were "greased" or "bought the farm" or just "bought it." But with the firepower of their superior weapons they, in turn, just "wasted" the enemy.

War may or may not be, in the standard anti-war campaigner's phrase, an "obscenity" but the words men have always used for killing—and, on the wrong side, for murder—need to be looked at with at least the semantic rigor now given to swear words, dirty talk, and filthy language. Etymology may serve us better than theology. The dictionary may prove to be of more use than the Biblical texts so innocently ambivalent in telling the bloody story of sinful humanity.

3. *Kick.* This was originally of harmless denotation, as in "alive and kicking" and "kick-off time" (every Saturday afternoon in U.S. football stadia). It was re-invigorated as in *Weathermen* instructions for "kick-ass street battles with the police." It packs more political punch when not used as a qualifying adjective but as an active verb as in an SDS resolution in July 1969: "We're not going to Chicago to get our ass kicked, we're going to kick ass."

4. *Bull*. As a fairly polite term for nonsense (classier than, say, *"crap"*) it has become obsolete, since it is mostly used in combination, hyphenated or not, with "-shit." It is taken to be an equivalent of Q.E.D. in the concluding stage of a serious argument, as in Mark Rudd's famous peroration at Columbia University: "Intellectual bullshit!" My suspicion at the time has been strengthened over the years that it is exclusively used by urban middle-class types who have no notion of its agronomic value on a well-run farm—and also by male chauvinists who persistently overlook the defecatory powers of the female of the species. ("Cow-flop!" went nowhere.) The b-s-word has since become popular and quite casual, but among the '68ers it was felt to be the most convincing final term in disputation since the discovery of the syllogism.*

5. *Ball*. This is obviously obsolete in its old pleasurable connotations, as in "having a ball." Also fallen into disuse is its note of nostalgia for aristocratic hedonism (Verdi, *Ballo in Maschera*). It has been nullified by the modernistic style in which no avant-garde opera director of our day will produce it without cladding the conspirators in menacing fascist leather-jackets on the stage, and allowing the lovers in the moonlight to go just a bit too far. Now unmasked, it is to be used only in the plural and with emphasis: "Balls!" (or "Bollocks!"). It serves either as a mild alternative tactic for "b**l-s**t" (see above), or as the guerilla target of the militant's day, viz. as one American Marxist rebel instructed another, "We are tired of toeing up to society and asking for reform. We're ready to kick it in the balls."

6. *Fuck*. Its political usage has almost (but not quite) rendered it *obs.* as a vulgarism for intercourse. It is indispensable in its "Australian" repetitious manner, being a steady *adj*. Qualifier, giving each sentence added rhythm and length. The classic example being an old Down-Under joke in which the Aussie sergeant tells of his great weekend when he finally scored: "I had this effing pass for an effing weekend in this effing town where I went to this effing bar where I picked up this effing broad and had a couple of effing drinks, and we got effing along so effing well that we went to this effing hotel and...and had,

---

*   The ubiquitous expletive in the US Army throughout World War II was *"chicken shit,"* but its surly dissidence was in no way incompatible with conventional army discipline. It was, possibly, associated with the general *sotto voce* downgrading of all strange military values in a new civilian draft army, as in calling the regimental commander a "a chicken-colonel" which downsized the eagles he wore as shoulder insignia.

So far as I am aware this war-time principle of what I call "derogation by dimunition" did not obtain in the obscenities of the '68 generation. A chicken posing as an eagle was a small absurdity, quite sufficient to let off GI steam. The subversive hostility of the '68 generation was larger, more massive, taking on the ultimate macho target, the big bull (and ignoring even the equal rights of the female of the species).

er, sexual intercourse." In recent ideological conflicts it served as the ultimate rhetorical weapon: "Up against the wall, Mother-fuckers!" which, mistakenly, gave some demonstrations in the 1960s an air of Greek tragedy. But "M——f——" is not to be confounded with incestuous Oedipal implications. However, in black or Afro-American usage, it did betimes appear to be a schizoid term of revilement against one's own white father, grandfather, or slave-holding great grandfather. (See the genealogical tables of such colored leaders as Angela Davis, Malcolm X, Michael X, Stokley Carmichael and, recently, Thomas Jefferson.) In white academic usage it is, alas, a consequence of literary amnesia following on from the almost complete disappearance of classical studies in American education. Who remembers the incest of Jocasta and Oedipus? Who's afraid of Sophocles? Among the feminists and single-parent mothers of the Women's Liberation movement, I have not found, curiously enough, evidence that it was interdicted by the "correct" lexicographers. But I did hear Germaine Greer (in her debate with Norman Mailer, in New York City's Town Hall in May 1971) offer alternative transitive conjugations of the verb which would not leave the female so passive, so apparently inactive and nonparticipatory on the receiving end of the manly verb to f—. There were readers of Kate Millett's pioneering book, *Sexual Politics* (1970), who wanted to go on to do research into Amazon literature and graffiti. The quest was to find the liberating expletive of "Father-f—er," the much-needed equalizer.

This changeable variety of incidental use of "Black English" (as it was once known) is usually restricted to brief colorful quotes in a newspaper or magazine feature.

There are other possible variants, and two or three subsequent generations who have not had the historic opportunity to enjoy the excitement of the tumult and the shouting of the '68ers, confined themselves to the exploration of new verbal radicalism. A graduate student at Yale University who has published poetry and devoted himself to the study of the current cultural usages of "Four-Letter Words" calls our attention to notable changes. As young Stephen Burt reports in a well-informed article in the *Boston Review*, "Two years ago, every college radio rock DJ in America was familiar with Superchunk's 'Slack Motherfucker', not only because it's a great song (and it is), but because you couldn't play it on the air before midnight." Evidently the outing of this tune into the early evening and even the open daylight of the afternoon was a famous victory: "conjuring into existence, a social context of youth and confrontation in which calling somebody a 'slack motherfucker' was standard, even laudable. In this context, swearing became...'signs of forbidden identity, sources of value.'"[2] Its valuable quality lasts in this case only a brief season in the hit charts, when apparently new identities emerge, move into crisis, and mutate slackness for firmness or tightness—and then we're into a whole new ball game.

A more serious or systematic representation of such accents or demotic vocabulary comes under what one novelist has referred to a *"ban of silence."* According to the best-selling Chicago author, Scott Turow, such a taboo on "ethnic incorrectness" has prevented white writers from treating black characters and African-American life in contemporary fiction. Breaking that ban, Turow in his recent novel *The Law of the Fathers* (1996) makes an ambitious and extensive use of ghetto street dialect; and one cautious reviewer in the *Washington Post*, the perceptive Jonathan Yardley, registered it as "presumably accurate." The *Post* has been burned its fingers enough on this issue; and Yardley hedges his bets with an additional proviso that "sooner or later Turow is going to catch hell for his presumption in writing about these people and using their language, or his own version thereof. It will be a pity if it comes to pass."[3]

One can understand a black intellectual's "difficulties" with a white novelist's attempt to fill hundreds of pages with a whole variety of "gangsta rap." But it is absurd to think of it as "racist." If none of his blacks talk mainstream English, the white dudes in Turow's book, mostly ex-militant Americans of the '68 generation, don't speak standard English so good either.

More of this anon. Here I have been only trying to register, with rough accuracy, the public emergence of the indelicate and the immodest, of the scabrous and the salacious; or, if you will, the "outing" of closet obscenity. In this act of verbal bravura—the quasi-legitimation of obscene words, normally suppressed and for so long repressed in official society and its flat over-ground culture—the antiwar '68ers excelled even the "G.I." and the "Nam" generations who had come home from the battlefields.

Here, again, there are tonal differences; but, for the most part, the G.I. generation kept the f-words neatly submerged in their old foot-lockers, stuffed deep down in their B-bags. In crasser contrast, there was the Vietnam generation of outcast plebeians and tragic losers who, unsung and unfêted, pinned their f-words on to a tattered bloody flag, if not exactly on their t-shirts. (Which had been the fashion among some Vietnik protest-circles, following on from the injunction of Mario Savio's famous Berkeley campus placard on behalf of "Free Speech!") Thus, there was a confluence of wartime and peacetime exasperations.

A mix of two cursing cultures determined what I have referred to as the outing of a nether-world vocabulary, the emergence of the f-word from its previously natural habitat—foot-lockers and B-bags; locker rooms and smoky macho bull sessions; rowdy club get-togethers in hard-drinkers' hotel rooms; furtive graffiti on schoolyard walls and in students' toilets; high-spirited conventions of "the boys" over a long weekend with rambunctious horseplay; etc., etc. It had now come into the open space of public discourse.[4]

The Godfather of the F-Word (I): Kenneth Tynan

The Outing

Words and phrases have their parentage, and sometimes they can be clearly and accurately ascribed by philologists, etymologists, and their like. Mostly they have relations and well-wishers who offer help and friendship and, on occasion, a godfatherly gesture of power and authority, rich in assertiveness. Godfathers are to be cultivated if a weak and neglected word, of lowly origin, its growth stunted and its very life threatened by taboos, is to flourish and come into its rightful inheritance. The f-word in literature and in journalism has had the good fortune to grow up under the protection of many such godfathers, and none—at least in our media world of newspapers and magazines, film and television—deserves more recognition than Kenneth Peacock Tynan. He was a celebrated drama reviewer in London and New York (and it won him the intellectual reputation of being "the George Bernard Shaw of theater criticism"); he was also the notorious stage producer of *Oh! Calcutta!* (which earned him scandalizing fame as "the P.T. Barnum of pornography"). I do not know why he is not to be found in the *Guinness Book of Records*, for on 13 November 1965 Tynan was the first man "in the entire, known world" to have broadcast (on BBC Television) the f-word. We saw the man, heard the word.

It caused widespread offense because it was crude; it started a scandal because it was coarse; it titillated the intelligentsia and advanced the *Zeitgeist* one parameter; it made literary history because it broke a long-term taboo which had maintained an official ban on language and pictures associated with pornography and related obscenities.

Tynan's widow, Kathleen Halton Tynan, in her formidable two-volume edition of his life and letters, records the night to be remembered:

> On 13 November 1965, on a late-night programme called BBC-3, Ken said "fuck". It was the first time the word had been used on television. The subject of the discussion, with the writer Mary McCarthy, was censorship, which they both wished to abolish. The moderator asked Ken whether, were censorship in the theater abolished, he would allow a play to be done at the National in which sexual intercourse took place. He answered, "Oh I think so, certainly. I doubt if there are very many rational people in this world to whom the word 'fuck' is particularly diabolical or revolting or totally forbidden."

He had switched his answer, from the act to the word; and it was for Mrs. Tynan "slightly out of context, rather suggesting that he had planned to use it." Or, possibly, not. For nothing is harder for a man of the theater to plan than spontaneity. In subsequent incidents of pornspeak bravura, whether impulsive or premeditated, the tactics appeared clumsy and obvious. Some four years later (1969) a poet named Julian Mitchell gave BBC Third Programme listeners ten seconds in which they could switch off before he pronounced the same naughty monosyllable. Novelists like James Kelman, the Booker Prize winner, as well as acclaimed Hollywood film directors, no longer bother to give an "early warning signal" before they unleash natural-born, swear-word utterances on to the public.

In the perspective of permissive time it appears to be a matter of historical indifference whether the televised turning-point was willed, in a calculated act of militance, or inevitable one way or another since the culture was moving towards four-letterization. Still, for many years after the Tynan incident I myself was mildly obsessed with the phenomenon. For one thing my whole generation had found itself committed to absolute cultural liberties and a war to the death against censors and censorship. In 1947 in East Berlin on a rather dramatic occasion I welcomed the end of Dr. Goebbels' infamous cultural controls and went on to warn against the onset of a not dissimilar Soviet-Communist apparatus of totalitarian *Gleichschaltung*. (Incidentally I held up as exemplary the American struggle on behalf of Joyce's *Ulysses* and of James T. Farrell's *Studs Lonigan* and spoke against the prudery which blushed at sex and its vernacular.) Then again in 1960, I—along with Stephen Spender and Frank Kermode as editors of *Encounter*—was involved in giving testimony in the landmark *Lady Chatterley's Lover* case in which the Penguin edition of the D.H. Lawrence novel (unexpurgated, at last) faced prosecution by the Crown.

Was I, for once, on Ken Tynan's side? The Fleet Street press, for the most part, behaved like hyenas. Headlines read: INSULT TO WOMANHOOD and SACK 4-LETTER TYNAN! Thousands of cuttings streamed into K.T.'s press service. In the House of Commons four motions were set down attacking Tynan and the BBC for a lewd conspiracy against established values. In the end, the BBC did issue an "expression of regret" but not an apology, for it insisted that "the Word" had been used in a serious discussion.

Mary McCarthy and Ken Tynan (and all the rest of us) were of one opinion as to its seriousness, but only Ken had risen to the occasion. Only he had said it. Mary had only nodded, but echo came there none. When I subsequently asked her, she regretted that she had not followed suit; but the grand old cause of the avant-garde literary intelligentsia didn't really need her echoing support. A single outing—and for the first time—was sufficient unto the day. Mary would have opportunities enough to catch up with the outed phrase of what a wag at the time called "liberal libertinism."

The wag, I might add, was Hugh Wheldon, a high BBC official in the 1960s, talking to me; I was his occasional consultant on matters of "sex and the literati" (and also of ideological violence, especially the Baader-Meinhof terrorism of the day). Officially Wheldon had dissented from the BBC's "regret"; he was stalwart and unironical in defense of Tynan's f-word. He was appalled that people were appalled—the matter had been handled "responsibly, intelligently, and reasonably." And so, for a season, said we all. Even those middle-class intellectuals, traditional keepers of good taste and high style, who never before that time had brought the f-word over their lips. I was among them, but I had a special problem: I had been living in Ken Tynan's London flat, and the erotical atmosphere had proved haunting. Thereby hangs a tale.

When Kenneth Tynan moved to New York to accept William Shawn's offer to succeed the late Wolcott Gibbs as regular theater critic for the *New Yorker*, I was moving from Berlin where I had been editing *Der Monat* to succeed Irving Kristol as co-editor (with Stephen Spender) of *Encounter* magazine. It was a nice item of cultural coincidence (an American in London, an Englishman in New York). When Ken Tynan offered me his famous Mayfair flat (at 120 Mount Street, just across from the distinguished Connaught Hotel) I accepted it. It was rather small for us (wife, two children) but there were, after a year or so, other reasons for moving out. The Tynanesque atmosphere was all his own. Walls were decorated with floor-to-ceiling enlargements of Bosch's *Garden of Delights*. (They were the same reproductions that had inspired his adolescent talents earlier on, in his rooms at Magdalene College, Oxford.) Midnight telephone calls awoke me regularly with offers of—something rare at the time (the phrase, I mean, not the deed)—"oral sex" and other personal favors. Photographs tumbled out of books on the library shelf, often interleaved with private letters which an embarrassed glance sufficed to suggest love and passion, hate and lust, along with other preoccupations. I grew weary answering my children's question about what was going on behind the door (a futile cover-up) where a panel of Hieronymous Bosch's fantasy was especially fruity or orgiastic in the *Garten der Lüste* (the kids were bilingual and there was no fooling them).

In the end we turned our backs on the books and the bawdry, and never (except for one thing) looked back. Or, perhaps, Tynan thought us not such good tenants. In the collection of his letters there is this passage which his widow thought interesting enough to publish:

> I went into the flat on the pretext of borrowing a book. Melvin Lasky was in Berlin but his wife was there...full of horrid condescension about the Berliner Ensemble.

Didn't like her at all. The place is clean and well, apart from my study which Melvin has tossed into a morass of manuscript. The bull pictures have been taken down and replaced by rather chichi Chinese prints. My whole feeling is of unreality.* (26 June 1959)[5]

For a long time after that historic 13th in November 1965 I myself was trapped in a recurrent fantasy. In the obsessive scene I was back in Ken Tynan's flat, looking at myself in the bathroom mirror, trimming a bit on my beard, and rehearsing—the way I imagined he was theatrical enough to play act—the emission of the obscenity. I pursed my lips with due deliberate speed, clasped my upper teeth over my lower lip, and spat the word out. Each effort was a trial, and I simulated the difficulties and fearful tension. Would it work? Would the word get stuck? Could I—he—bring it off? Mirror, mirror on the wall...it seemed easy enough, with some luck. For Ken Tynan had a fitful stammer, and since he was never sure whether he could deliver a punch line on exact cue; it made him nervous and his listeners restive.**

How did he, with his almost uncontrollable stuttering diction, ever manage to pronounce the f-word at the right time and place?[6] He once confessed that he was "obsessed with word games" and "anything to do with words is sure to make me prick up my mind...." He was elated to discover that *"Hm* is the only English word in the pronunciation of which air is expelled through the nose...." Possibly, in some way or another, this arcane phonetic information helped him with his problems. After all, he had enjoyed a youthful acting career and he was known for his lively conversation in talk-shows.

---

*   Just to set the record straight: I had asked him, before I moved into the flat, whether I could get some wall space by removing some of the bull-fight posters. He agreed amiably. He told me that readers of his 1955 book on Spain had been sending him posters, presumably as souvenirs of solidarity; and he had more than enough to paper anyone's flat, even "enough to paper Versailles."
     As for those "rather chichi Chinese prints," they were in fact not Chinese but Japanese – items that I had bought in Kyoto and Nara several years before (some were 17th-century lithographs, two were classics by Hiroshige).

* * It is no accident that I published at the time a landmark study on the subject: Philip French's remarkable essay on "The Stammerer as Hero: 'O Word, Word that I Lack'" (*Encounter*, November 1966, pp. 67-75). It illuminated the trials and tribulations of the men (why no women?) who were famously afflicted with the speech impediment, among others: Somerset Maugham, Aneuran "Nye" Bevan, King George VI, Melville's Billy Budd and Arnold Schoenberg's Moses (who sings, haltingly, in the opera the aria "O Word, Word that I Lack" which gave Philip French his sub-title).
     Philip French, distinguished film critic, was a colleague of Kenneth Tynan on the staff of *The Observer* newspaper in London, and is still (as he wrote me) a fellow-sufferer of "the stumbling tongue." He refers to Tynan (p. 75, note) as "a genuine stammerer of the time."

I was never sure where Ken's stammer came from, basically. Some said, in a somewhat easy turn at psychoanalysis, that it was rooted in the traumatic discovery, rather late in the day (in fact on the afternoon that a certain Sir Peter Peacock died), that he was illegitimate. His father, known in Birmingham as "Mr. Tynan," was only Rose Tynan's part-time local partner, whose true identity the son never knew (and whose funeral he now boycotted). It was Sir Peter Peacock, a wealthy merchant and powerful local politician in a distant shire, who had sired him. Shakespearean that young Tynan was, it could have been useful in Oxford for "a man who would be king" to have a secret claim to bastardy. Still, such autobiographical complications are known to create some neural difficulties; yet, on that November occasion in the BBC studios, everything came clear. On the night Ken's bronchial difficulties with the plosive—that handicapping tongue-tied f-f-f-f-f- which so endangered the clear, audible and complete outing of the f-word to the outside world—were mastered. Somehow Ken Tynan had gotten the matter off his chest where it was, I suspected, a physiological as well as a psychic urgency. For he was also afflicted with faulty lungs, aggravated by chain-smoking of cigarettes, and was to die of emphysema aged fifty-three in 1980. He was, accordingly, especially sensitive to breath and breathlessness and the rhythms of inhalation and exhalation, on and off the stage. The f-word was air expelled from his soul. That alone should have made it into the *Guinness Book of Records*. In one of his love letters, full of longing and infatuation (as so often), he makes play with Indian music, muses over the dying art of finger plucking, which leads him to write tenderly of his overwhelming desire "to pluck and finger you...." He was slowly, surely, getting there. One more heave and he would be over the hump.

Once over and out, he was sure that a real blow had been struck for freedom, for that liberalizing reform (if not the Good Revolution) which was a'coming. He told Lord (Noël) Annan that he felt "the climate is riper for radical change than you can imagine...."

And so it was. He was right, at last; and prophetic. The f-word four-letterization of the Anglo-American world was to march through the institutions.

As for me, I look back on my paltry walk-on rôle, my one-word psycho-drama in Tynan's Mount Street flat, trying out the liberation of the language in front of the bathroom mirror. If K.T. was the godfather, I felt myself to be a kind of godson, somehow related, if illegitimately.[7]

The Goode Olde Cause

To give him his due, Ken Tynan was a major figure in the long struggle in Britain against the century-old powers of the Lord Chamberlain (and his officious staff of censors). In the 1960s, before his authority officially to license theatrical performances was abrogated, the running conflicts between the National Theater and the Establishment's watchdog left the "Literary Manager" Tynan battered, beaten (more often than not), and secretly building up a head of hissing steam. It would, one day soon, burst.

In the winter of 1964-5 there was a long tug-of-war over a long-forgotten play called *Dingo* (set in the North African desert before El Alamein in World War II). Tynan negotiated with a Colonel Johnson of the Lord Chamberlain's office which refused to grant a license for *Dingo* "in its present form." The changes required were innumerable, and finally the production was dropped by Olivier and Tynan. Bowdler had won the day. There had to be deletion or substitution of all the obvious four-letter words; this also included some indirect imagery (e.g., a sexual image about grease in the breech-block). Needlessly horrific wartime scenes had to be softened (screaming shouldn't be continuous); charred corpses shouldn't be *so* realistic; stage blood doesn't have to seem to be spurting from open wounds. The frequent use of "Jesus" was objectionably blasphemous. Nor should the medal, pinned to a blonde's knickers in Act II, be *readily* identifiable as the *DSO* (Distinguished Service Cross). Finally, impersonation of living persons on the stage would allow some sort of composite general, but not a look-alike Field Marshal Lord Montgomery.

As for Brecht's *Mother Courage* which became a bone of contention a few months later (in April 1965), the Lord Chamberlain himself (then Lord Cobbold) had recommended deletions, among them being "balls." In his translation W.H. Auden was seeking to follow the music note for note, and (as Tynan quoted him) "he finds it difficult to suggest an alternative monosyllable which conveys the same sense of carefree bawdiness." Reluctantly they agreed to delete "bugger"; change "shitting in your pants" to "wetting"; drop other coarse idioms such as "taking a crap"; and tone down cynical remarks about religion in the seventeenth-century context of the Thirty Years War.

Tynan felt "mutilated." Only a few months later (in November 1965) was the f-word uttered in a televised BBC conversation with Mary McCarthy. Damn the censorship, bugger the censors! Give me all your four-letter words, yearning to be free....[8]

In New York he had quite other obstacles which challenged his managerial talents and his devotion to hard porno-liberation principles. While in London he reassured the editor of the *Times* that the phrase "tasteful pornography" could never be ascribed to him (for he had "a horror of the word 'tasteful'").[9]

The defenders of taste in Manhattan, even among the show-business cast of *Oh! Calcutta!* were a different kind of animal. Some he had to tame (for "the queer Mafia" was always going too far); some he had to re-educate, for they found one or another line or gesture too "offensive and disgusting" to bear. Like some beleaguered warrior he appeared to be fighting on several fronts at once, and valiantly. As he wrote in a private letter to his fellow-Calcuttans about the first try-out performances in London of his greatest long-running New York success:

> I believe we are in exceptionally bad shape....As you may or may not know, the cast is split up into cut-throat cliques....Jonathan plays the whole number with his cock hanging out and looked as if he was going to hit me when I suggested he might refrain. At the end he and Tony mime the act of buggery: this is perhaps the lowest point of the whole evening. Brenda has put in a line about being fucked by the Count Basie Band. Could she please go back to the Mormon Tabernacle Choir?[10]

Was this because it was tasteless for Brenda to impute "gang-rape" to Basie's group of fine black musicians? or because it was more impressive, or even politically incorrect, for Brenda to offer greater pleasure for the greatest number by enlisting the massive crowd of Utah choristers? In any case the f-word was no longer the avant-garde signal to arise and conquer, nor even a prompter's call for ongoing titillation. It had become a routine cue in stage management, spoken softly, flatly, without passion or a hint of testosterone.

Yet it was another unconventional milestone of his career, the f-word turning up regularly at every curve or road-crossing. Whether young or old, as journalist or impresario or ideologue, Tynan's f-word could be sighted usefully marking how far he had come as the master wordsmith of the *Zeitgeist*. It was like the recurrent motif of a grand opera, scoring a triumphal high note on even the lowest of occasions. Nothing in his life, if he could help it, would ever be "wordless."

Not too long before he tactically retreated to the silence of mime, where "wordlessly" was the keynote, he diligently collected ideas for his revue's sketches. What was "the idea of yours," he reminded John Lennon, still among the Beatles in 1968, "for my erotic revue—the masturbation contest?" Lennon replied, "you know the idea, four fellows wanking—giving each other images —descriptions—it should be ad-libbed anyway—they should even really wank which would be great."[11] Whether Ken who was well into surrealism and symbolism, and the like, could be persuaded to go back to social or sexual realism (as John Lennon suggested) is doubtful. Was really "great art" ever literally about the real thing? Actors shed tears but do not actually weep; actresses go into hysterics, fly into madness, but remain calm and quiet in themselves. Why should wankers do it for real?

Even if art, like ripeness, was all, politics evidently played a serious role in shaping the course of Tynan's life. But his politics were embarrassingly simple, reiterated over the years with a sameness that indicated that not a minute had been lost in thinking or re-thinking about the issues; but only that some trouble had been taken to convert leaden ideological precepts into bright readable prose. It always came out archly self-confident: for his ironic manner bordered on impatience with all the poor rest of us, so mentally retarded. As he explained in a letter to the editor of the *Times* (in 1971), he was a man of the

Left: "I mean, of course, genuine socialism, and not the sort of coalition-care-taker capitalism which your editorials have been holding out as bait for hesitant leftists." He was, thus, opposed to all the Cold War institutions in the West (from NATO up, or down):

> The EEC is a capitalist power block dedicated to the perpetuation of the postwar schism of Europe....The Market is essentially the economic arm of NATO, and it deplores any backsliding towards neutralism, let alone socialism and its dread concomitants, the public ownership of land and the means of production.[12]

I had given up arguing with him years before. He thought I was merely being "provocative" by asking what difficulties he might expect, comes the Revolution, from the commissars who administered for the proletariat the "public ownership" of the newspapers and magazines he would be still likely to be writing for. He had been having difficulties galore with editors in a capitalist society (William Shawn of the *New Yorker*, Hugh Hefner and A.C. Spectorsky of *Playboy*). Here his otherwise lively imagination failed him—did the blue-pencilling inflicted on his manuscripts by wilful editors in New York and Chicago, marked by different tastes and attitudes, constitute the worst literary fate imaginable? Chinese writers had their spectacles broken and their fingers fractured during the "Cultural Revolution," Russian poets were executed by order of Stalin, and whole manuscripts of important writers were routinely burned by the KGB under the regimes of Khrushchev and Brezhnev. Even in the "good revolution" of Fidel Castro there were poets and novelists sitting in jail for "literary crimes." Why were these not also outrages that would concern him? His conscience was otherwise engaged. The main enemy, in the 1950s and 60s, had been "at home"; the monster was the Lord Chamberlain in 1970, and his censor's office had been happily defeated. The next target was the repressed minds (and bodies) of the Anglo-American middle-classes, ripe for liberation. I find it remarkable how patient he was with the meddling misdemeanors of newspapers and magazines who published him regularly, giving him large fees and international notoriety, and holding his loyalty.

Publicly he went on about the "freedom to choose the socialist path" (letter to the *Times*).[13] Privately he seemed to be driven by quite other ideals and ambitions. He once had an older book project, a Grove Press anthology called *For Myself Alone*. It was to be "a collection of masturbatory fantasies by famous writers"—and now he wanted to take it up "as soon as possible." He seemed to be moving backward, returning to pubertarian sources of inspiration, trying to disregard the mounting disappointments of growing up and getting older. Apparently a vast number of writers had turned Tynan down for the anthology: Vladimir Nabokov said that he had "no interest whatever in pornography"; Graham Greene didn't feel like joining "this children's game"; and Auden felt pornography should be written, if at all, "to amuse one's intimate friends." Ken Tynan was, after all, forty-four years old at the time, no longer the boy wonder of Oxford in a purple velvet suit. In a newsy letter to Penelope Gilliat, the red-haired and otherwise colorful writer on the *Observer* and later on the *New Yorker*, he still exhibited his schoolboy surliness: "Oh and I am a father again, as maybe you knew, a boy called Matthew...: ever fearful of the competing prick, I had hoped for another girl...." Still, he was outraged when friends were "disgusted" with his "money-grubbing sensationalism" and the "odious" turn his career had taken (the harsh words were his own). He was dismayed by all the references to "Tynan, the well-known *Playboy* editor"; but the obvious consequence was not to "quit playing around" but to ask primly that his name be removed "*now*" from the *Playboy* masthead. He confessed to Laurence Olivier a "deep sense of urgency and distress," and it seemed not to be only over the failures at the National Theater. His spirits picked up a bit when Shawn said yes to the *New Yorker* project of a long piece on Wilhelm Reich, inspired by "mysteries of the organism" (which may have been a pun or even a typographical error for orgasm or onanism or something in between). Whatever the trouble—and I am not competent to offer a psychograph in depth-analysis—he himself wrote to his American friend and publisher, Mike Bessie, "I am going through a crunch period of my life...."[14] He had made his choices, and whatever he freely chose appeared to be closing out his other options, which were sadly hinted at in his bit of doggerel—

> Ever a chooser,
> And never a beggar
> (Quoting Marcuse
> And even Heidegger)...
> Be an empiricist
> In socialism and sex!
> Read Wilhelm Reich
> And remember the Czechs![15]

This was high-spirited and cheerful; but his wife Kathleen was "chillingly" preoccupied, figuring out "why our beautiful life was in jeopardy." She had received his half-apologetic letter trying to explain why he had kept an adulterous assignation with some actress he had met at a party: "Then I took her home and fucked her." Some would say that the outing of the f-word in the private correspondence of a marriage was intimately linked to the historic public outing which was fast becoming his greatest, most substantial, if only, claim to fame. Nor that he was insensitive or oblivious to other, more beneficent four-letter words. To Kathleen from his Tunisian hotel of convalescence, he wrote , "*please*, on receiving this, send me a cable employing the word 'love'."[16] He could write the word but, apparently, not say it. "Lack of conversational practice has brought on a fantastic and impenetrable stammer." Alas, he would now be unable even to repeat his historic triumph on the BBC. He also had a low energy level—"*all within?*" he asked his wife, in a letter, "energy stored up for who knows what?...." The crucial question, once associated with the complex secret sources of art and philosophy, was now reduced to: "Does one lose it by fucking, or does fucking release it for other uses?"[17] To be sure, he was still intense about his association with high art and radical world politics. He found a new play, now altogether forgotten, by Trevor Griffifths (a left-wing pamphleteer, not without talent) "*superb*"—even if it "doesn't bother to explain what to Socialists is self-evident but may not be to the whole audience," namely, "why there is a need for revolutionary change."

Between the f-word of his erotomania and the r-word of his juvenile politics, fell the shadow. It may not have been clearly discernible in 1972, but his judgements, whether about sex or politics, were obscenely irrelevant to anything, to everything, except the passing *Zeitgeist*—or, in the most advantageous moments, an innovative local fashion whose time had come.

The f-word remained a fixture of his life and career: inescapable, like Coleridge's albatross around the mariner's neck. It went with him day and night, into his private affairs, into his professional rehearsals. He had not only outed it, he had converted it into a central piece of equipment, a working tool of his everyday life. When he suspected that Peter Schaffer's play, *Equus*, needed a little extra work—to eliminate "the Protestant guilt pang" and accentuate the Dionysiac ritual of "the sexual ecstasy"—he formulated the problem in his National Theater "production notes" by insisting that "the passage from the abortive fuck to the murders needs restructuring."[18] He needed to use it clinically, the biological act itself; and he liked to have it around as all-purpose slang, as in his warning to a young and erratic actress that if she persisted "the audience will neither understand or identify and you will be fucked up." To another he promised her that the end-product would be "an erotic film that looks beautiful and outrageous at the same time." He told her not to fear "scenes and lines that will alarm you—do not be alarmed"; the results would not, repeat not, be "squalid."

I wonder if he was at all times in verbal charge, in semantic control. Funny that he should be pressing the heir to the Getty oil fortune, John Paul Getty, Jr. —who was supposed to be persuaded that Tynan would be coming up again with "a unique work of pornographic art and huge financial success"—to fork over his promised investment money with the off-color Tynan quip: "So the ball is in your court—or, rather, my balls are in your court." Sometimes the lewd lingo came naturally in the circles in which he was mixing. He wanted to win over Gore Vidal for the successor show to *Calcutta* (called then, imaginatively, *After Calcutta*); it would broaden the range of "serious exploration of eroticism." Tynan reassured Vidal he could use nudity, could remain anonymous, could please (and excite) himself. Vidal replied positively from Rome, promising to "put cock to page in your interest." ("Kennie" must himself have been pleased that Vidal had avoided the pedantry of a pee-alliteration of putting-penis-to-page; erotomanes understand each other's subtleties.)[19]

An American Inspiration: Lenny Bruce

It may not directly belong to the cultural history of journalism, but the record of the contemporary break-through of spoken and printed obscenities would be incomplete without a mention of Lenny Bruce, the once-celebrated American satirist (1925-1966). Tynan's achievement was not rooted in English insularity and singularity, but shaped by a "special relationship," an Anglo-American partnership with a traditional ring of Allied liberation about it. The transatlantic influence on Tynan, like on all anti-American figures in the European Left, was necessary (if not sufficient) to inspire a radical movement. The U.S. may be opposed, despised, even hated; but it was Americans who led the way in drastic dissent and, thus, represented strong redemptive characters. So it was that Bruce's American street-smart brashness and daring inspired the Englishman. He, in turn, elevated the large ideal purposes of a stand-up comic who might have turned out to be just another entertainer who "talked dirty" and whose "act" consisted of "routines" or "gigs."

In one of the many U.S. trials for obscenity which Lenny Bruce happened to win—the court was impressed at the recondite Tynanesque comparisons of Bruce's work with Aristophanes, Rabelais, and Jonathan Swift—he recited one of his pieces of nightclub verse (to the accompaniment of drum and cymbal), and it can claim credit for the legitimization of *coming* as an ejaculation or coital word. *"To is a preposition..../Come is a verb, the verb intransitive/ ...To come, to come. It's like a big drum solo...,"* etc. Later the nightly risqué ambiguity became fashionable (although not in mainstream journalism), and lost a measure of its ideal rationalization which it purported to have when Lenny Bruce "outed" it: "Now, if anyone in this room or the world finds those two words 'to come' decadent, obscene, immoral, amoral, asexual, then you're of no use, because that's the purpose of life, to re-create it."[20]

I heard him recite this one evening at the crowded "Establishment" nightclub in London. I wondered at the time whether, earnest social satirist that he was, he was truly persuaded of this. Were the censors and the London police not to allow him to sail in on the flagship of procreativity, proclaiming the purposes of life, would then fertility "in this room" and sex "in the world" fall into desuetude? Found naked on the floor of his flat, dead at the age of forty of a heroin overdose (3 August 1966), possibly Lenny Bruce couldn't have cared less about the unborn generations to come. Still, he became a cult figure and, arguably, something of an historic force shaping the vernacular in the next generation (Mort Sahl, Terry Southern, Philip Roth, et al.). The *Observer* in

London praised him; Kenneth Tynan said he was "a pearl miscast before swine" and welcomed his "public use of harmless, frutiful syllables like 'come' (in the sense of orgasm) and 'fuck'...."

It could be that on one of those evenings in Soho in the early 60s or, possibly, in that cellar room under the Duane Hotel in New York where Bruce held forth when he was not being "busted by the cops," that Tynan was inspired to plan the historic f-word outing of his own. What evidently made a deep impression on Ken Tynan's mind—the man was, after all, an Anglo-American culture-hero, in his way, for half-a-generation—were Bruce's daring and argumentative one-liners, contributing to the radical chic ideology of the day: namely, that the smoking of marijuana should be encouraged (because, after all, it does not induce lung cancer); that children ought to watch pornographic movies (it's sure healthier than learning about sex from Hollywood); and sundry other theses, especially the one about "capitalism"— from which so many of his targets derived—not necessarily being a permanent and unchangeable fact of human existence. Arch ironies, bearable if not harmless.

The write-ups, as they were called then before the pretensions of "critiquing" shows came in, controlled their hostility, trying to match the comedian's jokes with a small gag of their own. *Time* called Lenny Bruce "a sicknik." Arthur Gelb, in one unflappable review in the *New York Times*, referred flippantly to the concern for safeguarding "the dubious innocence of underage New Yorkers, which runs to four-letter words, of which the most printable is Y.M.C.A." If this was a mite too blasé, Gelb reassured his *Times* readers that "a good many adults" would indeed find him "offensive." And if that, in turn, was a tad too stuffy he balanced his judgment with notable liberal compassion: there was "such a patent air of morality beneath the brashness that his lapses in taste are often forgiveable...."[21]

For Tynan, trying to forge not only a lateral united front coalition between subversive vernacularists on both sides of the Atlantic but also a vertical popular front of the upper and lower classes, Lenny Bruce was an ideal ally. He was a product of the poor Jewish ghetto (though, for Tynan's Oxonian tastes, Bruce lapsed into too many Yiddishisms). He was quick and clever but far removed from being an intellectual (and in fact Tynan wished, on second thought, that Bruce "had broadened his viewpoint by a little selective reading of Marx as well as Freud...").[22]

Still and all, he accepted Bruce for what he was: "a night-club Cassandra" or, at best, "a prophet of the new morality." He was "a true iconoclast." Warming to the subject, Tynan thought that Bruce was breaking through "the barrier of laughter" (Lenny's jokes were no mere gags!) to "the horizon beyond where the truth has its sanctuary." Translated into something less heady, and this side of the blue horizon, it meant simply that Bruce was taking potshots at what

Tynan professed to hate most: a capitalistic and obsessive society, thriving on greed and profit, chained to neurotic repression and anal eroticism. (Even that was a cocktail well mixed, shaken but not stirred, with tiny jiggers of "Marx" and "Freud.") He was convinced that when Lenny Bruce was shocking he shocked us by "the right things"—not by four-letter words which violate only convention but by crying out against society: against want and deprivation, poverty and exploitation.

Tynan welcomed Lenny Bruce to London, and when at the Establishment, a Soho nightclub devoted to satire (and run by the late Peter Cook of *Beyond the Fringe* fame), Bruce "roamed out on the stage in his usual mood of tormented derision," Tynan acclaimed him as "the most original, free-speaking, wild-thinking gymnast of language our inhibited island had ever hired to beguile its citizens...."[23]

In the new edition (1992) of *How to Talk Dirty and Influence People*, an introduction by Eric Bogosian—Tynan had written the "foreword"—claimed that "the book was part of a secret collection of sacred texts that unlocked the doors of hipness and rebellion." Even more than that, it was one of "the bridges between postwar African-American culture and the 'counterculture' of the 1960s and '70s." Among those whom Eric Bogosian called "the Saints of the New Attitude" were John Lennon, Jim Morrison, Abbie Hoffman, and...Lenny Bruce. Central to the philosophy of the New Attitude was the painful conviction that they were all being "suppressed and repressed." They were demanding of Society, the System, the Established Ruling Class not only "more" but "better freedom." For an ascetic moment—until the worldwide royalties began to stream in—they held their credo to be: "Money is out. Lifestyle was in." When money became "in" again, and the vows of poverty fell into neglect, the lifestyle (as we have seen) became fashionably chic and hugely expensive.

Tynan could not easily follow this movement—in which he was an acknowledged star—on this journey, or "trip." One of his books was entitled *Commitment* and he devoted his life to dedication. This involved a shared delight in "blowing your mind" but means should not be confounded with ends. The admirers of Lenny Bruce were playing on quite another track, and as one of them confessed, in middle age, "these bohemians had a real commitment to noncommitment; they had a mania for irresponsibility." This explained and excused "rip-offs and hustles, white lies and put-ons, goof-ups and escapades, promiscuity and intoxicated bouts." Tynan, on the other hand, had to keep time, to be on time, to adhere to deadlines, to make an evening premiere or a midnight curtain-call or a *corrida* at 3 P.M. *sharp*. In the end, there had to be a parting of the ways. But it was not only the additives and substances which fell short of inducing a social nirvana.[24]

A tragically serious man can only take so much life-enhancing frivolity. Tynan was very earnest about obscenity; and pornography was no laughing matter. His f-word was on a sacred mission. Lenny Bruce used it in gig after gig as another of those "*b**l-s**t* words," particularly when it was before too long taken over by "the high-brow intellectuals" (e.g., Norman Mailer penning his post-frigging love-prose after pure D.H. Lawrence was permitted). For the shocking vocabulary of four-letter profanity has different functions when it comes in a context of highbrow meaningful expostulation in contrast with a stream of expletives which masks streetwise illiteracy. Its syntax is different, and indeed the whole grammar of obscenity has diverging rules for parsing. In the ghetto it can serve as adjective, adverb, split infinitive, punctuation. On the middle-class writing table and in metropolitan impolite society it signals a rather different message. One leads to the coarse soundtrack of the films of Quentin Tarantino where the f-word cascades off the screen in the thousands, and all the crude bits of dialogue are interchangeable. The other leads to the dialogues in the novels of, say, Philip Roth wherein the profanity is parseable and the phonemes belong precisely to a character's individual voice and vernacular. With Tarantino half of the crudities can be omitted without making the slightest difference to the intended communication or plot (mostly mayhem, featuring violent murder). Even among the cast of characters in an Elmore Leonard novel, swearing serves to differentiate and individuate among the half-educated louts; the novel avoids monotony by varying (and even, I suspect, rationing) the epithets and expletives. There is a point where they meet, e.g., the Tarantino film version of a Leonard novel—*Jackie Brown* (1998, 2 hours, 20 minutes) out of *Rum Punch* (1992, 297 pp.). Tarantino is seen (with the novelist listed as the film's "executive producer" and, presumably, approving) rewriting wholesale, by adding several hundred f-words to the shooting script and soundtrack. Nary a sentence can be read or heard that escapes the T-touch.*

On that evening of 13 November 1965 when Ken Tynan was still, in the phrase of one critic, Joseph Epstein, an "unshy pornographer," he didn't quite realize (although his wife noted the fudge that he made out of noun and verb) what a burden of life's difficulties he had taken on with one singular word. Lenny Bruce had it easier. When one avant-garde institution or another decided to bestow a spurious honorary Ll.D. degree on him, Lenny Bruce quipped with the academic graduation cap on his head, accepting the Doctor of Letters: "To the man who won fame using four of them at a time."[25]

---

*   The distinguished old London firm of Faber & Faber published the Tarantino scenario in 1998. T.S. Eliot, when he was a Faber editor in the 1920s, used to write their dust jackets. On the cover jacket of *Jackie Brown*, the publisher's pap refers to "Tarantino's genius for stimulating the senses with his dialogue." Just like in *The Wasteland*, sort of.

Boomerang

The "bleeding F-word" stabbed like a *muleta* at all of Tynan's life's commitments and engagements. Occasionally it seemed to scratch on the surface, but then it was omnipresent and rattling, like some resonating gong of destiny.

Take the falling out with Hemingway in that Spanish summer of 1959 when the American *aficionado* was fêted in Pamplona and every other place that had an arena which could accommodate Luis Miguel Dominguin and Antonio Ordoñez, those two great matadors then locked in rivalry. At dinner one night, as A.E. Hotchner (who was there) has told us, Tynan had given a blow-by-blow account of a particular kill he had seen that day, and Hemingway had challenged him.

> *Hemingway:* "You know, just because you wrote one skinny book doesn't make you an authority. On what authority do you make those statements?"
> *Tynan:* "On the authority of my eyes."
> *Hemingway:* "Fuck your eyes. You need glasses."

Tynan rose to his full height (a gangly man, but not as tall as Hemingway); announced that there was no point to staying at the table any longer; and left— promising (after Hemingway called attention to the unpaid check) to make later arrangements to take care of the bill. He was "disturbed," as a friend noted, who saw him storm out. He was hurt. The f-word could boomerang.[26]

It was still boomeranging—with Tynan again on the taking, not giving side —when in an altercation about the rehearsals in the National Theater of a Samuel Beckett play named *Play* the vituperation got out of hand and Laurence Olivier became involved. Tynan objected to Beckett's influence at rehearsals, made a "snide" remark about him, was called by the play's director (George Devine) "impertinent and ignorant," and tempers simmered at a boiling point. Olivier was paternal and stern with his assistant:

> This is a detonation with an alarming sound-off, but if we just wait till our ears stop tingling, I think we may not see much wreckage about. I don't know whether you were conscious of the first *V*'s arriving in London. I remember shooting up in my bed thinking the whole of London has had it; what happened was that it hit a gasometer, and that's really what has happened in this case....

Could a slight, nostalgic anecdote about a World War before Tynan's time be strong enough for an admonition to one of the postwar plain speakers? Profanity had since become a passport to liberty and real meaning. Olivier would have to hit a bit harder, straighter, and added: "I like you. I like having you with me, apart from it rather tickling me to have you with me, but you can be too fucking tactless for words." Again, the old f-word had veered off course and had wounded its young master. Like the heroine in Hawthorne's *Scarlet Letter*, the man was almost wearing a black-and-blue F-letter on his forehead. He was a marked man.

He sensed it himself. When his marriage to Kathleen Halton Tynan was in jeopardy (betimes she grew weary of his philandering adultery) he tried to parse the verb and give it a range of meanings which might call for his being forgiven. It *was* an actress, and he *had* met her at a party, and they *did* arrange to meet, and she was *very* ambitious, and there just *might* be a good acting role for her somewhere. Then Tynan wrote to his wife in an intimate, decisive letter (24 October 1974), which I have already mentioned, using the f-word in his confession: "Then I took her home and fucked her." But *no*, not at all, this was *not* what had transpired. The word had no reality. He said it, he wrote it, but it didn't really happen. Several tortured sentences further he abandoned his four-letter word strategy and simply waxed lyrical: "I began to whistle to myself and to think of simple congenial everyday irreplaceable things like caviare and Diamant Bleu champagne and the New Oxford Book of English Verse and you." She believed him, at least they went on together with her trying "to figure out why our beautiful life was in jeopardy"; and when, with a widow's loyalty, she went through his papers for her two volumes about his life and letters, she may have learned the truth, real or virtual. The f-word on the lips of its godfather has some cunning ways.[27]

In point of fact the f-word in Ken Tynan's life and letters and achievement was less a spontaneous expletive, expressing anger or lust or a low folksiness, than an instrument of reflection. He loved the idea of it, its obscenity, and indeed the sound of it. It also had a clean political thrust, for it could be used as a kind of verbal battering-ram on behalf of the revolution which would dismay the enemy, put the old society in disarray, herald a new era of pleasure and purpose, all the while marking the progress of true art which had to stoop to conquer. These matters raised thorny issues and he gave them his best thought. There was an argument on at the time (and *Encounter* joined in it occasionally), featuring Maurice Cranston (a philosopher) and Wayland Young (a journalist and political writer, also a member of the House of Lords as Lord Kennet) as to whether the sublimation of sexual energy was the mother of most art and progress. Since Kenneth Tynan was devoting considerable portions of his own time and energy to sexual activity, he surely did not want to be excluded from high achievement or include himself out of the loftier regions of humanism. Will you, he argued in a handy analogy, if you hoard enough milk, will you produce better wine? Or, put another, more characteristic way (in a letter to his wife): "Does one lose it by fucking, or does fucking release it for other uses?"[28] His thoughts on saving or expending sacred fluids took on urgency. He needed very much to disbelieve "the fantastic theory that art and progress are contingent on continence." Alas, he could not invoke the creative muses in this debate; many of his admirers thought him to be a genius but, in the end, not talented enough to produce works of art. This might prove an insuperable obstacle; he had to find another way. Perhaps he could weave 'em together, marry art and sex, link the high points of both achievements. He pondered the possibilities of "wordlessly" achieving erotic stimulation by stagecraft, and became obsessed with fine authors (among them Harold Pinter, Gore Vidal, Edna O'Brien) providing him with sketches to which he would attach music and other sound-effects that would approach ecstatic climaxes never before experienced in the theater. Putting it into words still faced obstacles, whether in New York (where he devised the notorious popular success, *Oh! Calcutta!*) or in London where even the *Observer* did not choose to go along with him in all his adventurous "extension of the parameters." Tynan had written, "Language can be employed in many and delicate ways to enliven the penis." As the publisher David Astor explained to him, fearing readership reaction, "It will be said that this phrase is published so as to shock, rather than to advance the argument." Tynan modified the sentence, was convinced he was being treated "shabbily," and threatened to defect to the paper's great Fleet Street rival, the *Sunday Times*.

The effort to advance the argument was also beset with difficulties back in Manhattan. Having burned his fingers even with the p-word he turned to appeasing editors, who published and paid well for his articles, by guaranteeing that "naturally, no four-letter words would be involved." One piece tried to argue the case "In Defense of Hard-Core Pornography," in (of all places) the *Saturday Evening Post* which rejected it, and it was ultimately published in *Esquire*.[29]

As for nudity—until he perfected the total striptease for *Oh! Calcutta!*—he was rather thin-skinned about that; for when a famous Happening arranged for a nude young woman to streak through the Edinburgh Festival (in August 1963) he had condemned it and called it "totalitarian and apocalyptic." Which it wasn't; for if it were, he might have had sneaking sympathies for a radical gesture of dramatic holism, stripping realities to the essential.[30]

I should mention here, for whatever interest this recondite bit of etymology might still have, that the famous title was, of course, another of Tynan's ingenious puns, in this case a blue bi-lingual one. The Grove Press' edition (1969) of *Oh! Calcutta!* was formally sub-titled "*An Entertainment with music devised by Kenneth Tynan.*" The obscurity of the title is explained by the Grove Press editors—who, on more forthcoming days, shied away from no explicitness—on the back cover. Grove distributed the hugely popular film, "*I Am Curious (Yellow),*" which broke the path for soft-porn cinema, but here is its discreet, not quite satisfactory explanation:

The title of this revue, which is taken from the title of a painting by the French surrealist painter Clovis Trouille, contains a phonetic French pun: 'Oh! Quelle— t'as!' Or, freely translated: 'Oh! What a lovely—you have!'"

Barney Rosset's Grove Press, American pioneers in so-called "dirty realism" and brave booksellers of Henry Miller as well as of Jean Genet's works, had never been so prissy in its publishing history.

As for Tynan it represented a triumph of wordplay over principle; for beyond all the full-frontal nudity and erotic simulation of his show he wanted viewers "to prick up their ears." The wag in him trusted an Anglo-French *double-entendre* to help do the trick.

At that time, he had not yet found himself, the true inner self. When another collection of his pieces was published, *Tynan Left & Right* (1967), he confessed that his critics were divided: one said *Snob!* And the other said *Charlatan!* But, deep down, in his self-recognition the snobbery was really only fastidious devotion to values and the charlatanry was merely a means to a noble end. For the moment he had been whirling at the center (so his wife Kathleen claimed) of the celebrated "Swinging London." And I recall another minor altercation between us at another of Lord (George) Weidenfeld's *soirées*. Tynan was, as always, full of gossip, if a bit slow in getting it all out, and he was saying that Michelangelo Antonioni, planning his great "swinging" film *Blow-Up* during an evening in Mount Street, had created the tag. I dissented flippantly, mostly to annoy him rather than to take out a serious copyright claim, asserting that *I* had invented the phrase, and that Horace Judson had popularized it with a cover story for *Time*. It did not go down well. Words that changed the world were his department; the revolution would be made only by his approved comrades.[31]

Of Sex and Revolution

Sometimes, in moments of soul-searching, Tynan sought to give a total coherence to his life and all its flamboyant impulses, from acting and producing plays and films (and "sex shows") to theater criticism of all the stages in the West (from Brecht's East Berlin to New York's off-Broadway) and then on to writing books and seducing every eligible woman or girl in sight, like Don Giovanni totting up his score in Spain. He always believed (at least, until the very end) that he was standing up for the spirit of integrity and stalwart conscience. No, he wouldn't go out of his Havana hotel room, despite his sympathies for Castro's "good revolution," to witness officially (as did Tennessee Williams) firing squad executions of Fidel's class enemies. Nor would he praise Truman Capote's masterly *In Cold Blood* (1966), for the author had preferred a sensational scoop to the chance of saving the two protagonists' lives by submitting his evidence to the court. A red thread of radical political opinions also ran through his literary activity, from time to time signing a petition for reform or social protest and consistently, over thirty or forty years, firing off an eloquent letter-to-the-editor stating the short case to be made on behalf of his current ideological passions. Why socialism would replace capitalism—why Soviet planning is better than Western unemployment and inflation—why some writers should or should not be reprimanded for their anti-Semitism (viz., Evelyn Waugh)—why the West was responsible for the Cold War (and hence, its nasty nuclear weapons had to be abolished immediately). One such letter was published in *Encounter* (in 1958, the year I came to live in London). "But why," Tynan asked, "should anyone be horrified at being called Jewish? The suggestion is not, by any stretch of the imagination, slanderous."[32]

This naivete, or failure of the imagination, or unfamiliarity with the ways of the real-existing world, was characteristic of the man. His liberal intentions overshadowed his political realism. In an anti-Semitic society to call a man "a Jew" (and even "a foreigner") was, to be at the very least, pointing a mildly accusing finger. He was a tribune of the Left who saw nothing untoward in accepting a fascist friend's invitation for him to take tea with Sir Oswald Mosley, the old prewar leader of the British fascist movement. In June 1959, he wrote (to his first wife, Elaine Dundy Tynan), "I spent most of [East] Berlin with the Ensemble and nearly defected." His so-called near-defection consisted merely of an offer to take a job with Brecht's East Berlin troupe as a *Dramaturg* (a play reader and advisor), a post he was later to fill in Sir Laurence Olivier's National Theater in London. But he was always conceiving his life on the outer edges of melodrama: nearly getting married once or twice a year (offering gold or diamond rings to the smitten girls); nearly going off to fight in a revolution or class struggle; nearly buying a Spanish ranch to raise brave bulls (and even to fight some of them himself as a matador); nearly transplanting himself across the Iron Curtain, from West to East where the Soviets were busy fulfilling his socialist ideals. When Tynan first saw Brecht's play, *Mutter Courage*, in Paris in 1955, he declared: "I have seen 'Mother Courage' and I am a Marxist." Nearly.[33]

Between, as I say, the outer edges of theatricality and the inner rim of conviction he figured for some decades at the center of transatlantic cultural attention. We never met in New York where the verve of his prose (not to mention his strongly held views of what theater should be) immediately ensconced him as a fearsome dean of Broadway critics. Oxford and Mount Street seemed far away. But he did return, and even his passing visits were fraught with a certain tension. Our paths crossed once in Stratford on Avon where we were both in the audience at the performance of *Coriolanus* with Laurence Olivier (and Peter Hall directing). For him it was a "surprise visit" since his New York accountant had advised him to stay out of the U.K. for another half-year or so. But the Stratford masterpiece, he cracked, "was worth being double-taxed for." We made an appointment to meet at the flat, to borrow a book (one of his, or mine). I used the occasion to talk up my friend Martin Esslin's work on Brecht (which he had neglected because of its anti-Stalinism), but when he had read it he was forced to revise his piece for the *New Yorker* on the "Berliner Ensemble." As he wrote to the editor (Shawn), apologizing candidly for the delay, "So much that was new to me that I decided to revise the article in the light of what I'd learned."[34]

He was, if anything, at once openminded and hardheaded. At times he held fast to a schoolboy prejudice as if it were a lifetime's wisdom; at others he shed a life-style enthusiasm as he changed his flashy white alpaca jackets or his purple corduroys. I once asked him about what time he had left over, after his total commitments to theater and revolution, for bull fighting: for he had, in his youth, written (as I told him) one of the three best books I knew on the subject (the others being Hemingway and V.S. Pritchett).

"I don't care," he said, poising himself for the old phonetic difficulty, "f-f-frankly I don't care if I never see a f-f-f***ing bull again!" I now note that in the edition of his published letters Tynan's favorite expletive became "a bleeding bull" (which version was surely not a playful punning euphemism, for he had turned against blood sports). Since he had previously mentioned to me that his "ultimate ambition" was to buy a half-interest in a bull ranch in Spain (and even to retire there), I assumed that he had once again changed his long-term perspective on life and his own human commitment.

Perhaps he lost his way because he was always being caught up in storms and driven off course. He was constantly being frustrated by editorial blue pencils, especially in his own friendly camp; and it more than evened out the score which took into account the personal liberties he himself took. *Playboy* published his interview with the actor Richard Burton; Tynan received his copy (August 1963) and was *"HORRIFIED"*—"They have rewritten all my questions in their own idiotic jargon, attributing to me opinions I don't hold, so that hardly a word remains of what I wrote."[35]

He was back in Mount Street, and when once I called on him there to pick up a set of corrected proofs, he was still—months had gone by—furious at the magazine's drastic editing. I teased him with a remark to the effect that "this was not the way he was treated in the good old *Encounter* office." He used to contribute pieces, and we never touched a word, although we disagreed on most things. Ah, but his comrades in the sexual revolution at *Playboy*—"they have chopped up and re-shuffled everything…creating totally misleading answers to their own dreamed-up questions." He estimated that about 80 percent of the words attributed to him were words he never uttered, and in a prose that was vulgar and coy. More than that, it also wounded him that Richard Burton's exposition of his "socialist ideals" (glowingly shared by his interviewer) was omitted entirely. A few anachronisms were included: references to the film premiere of *Cleopatra* and to the announcement of Burton's intention to marry the star (Elizabeth Taylor), neither of which had happened when the interview took place. Tynan's letter of protest to the *Playboy* editors in Chicago was never published. He hurled four-letter imprecations at them, but the playboys were not listening. They had, as Tynan had preached, other hard-core preoccupations.[36]

Had things been easier in Manhattan? The forty-one New York previews which *Oh! Calcutta!* had in the spring of 1969 (at the Eden Theater on 2nd Avenue and 12th St.) elicited from Tynan a series of "production notes," re-examining every detail with a diligence and an ingenuity which would have done any veteran Broadway play doctor proud. (I once knew such a professional, the masterful Abe Burrows, whose stagecraft often had the stamp of ebullient last-minute improvisation. This could be, perhaps, the clue to popular entertainment.)

Tynan thought laughs were being lost because of timing and inflections. He felt some songs to be a little dirge-like and overlong, and one number could end with a white light on "a frieze of frozen nudes." Above all, there should be no premature publicity and he made a furious effort to keep any snooping journalists, critics or gossipers, out of the theater. ("Could the box office be instructed to check on ticket buyers with English accents by asking them if they are press?")

The cast was easier to deal with than obstreperous prudes in the audience. Tynan had apparently converted them, and as Kathleen Tynan has recorded, "The cast, liberated beyond recall, told stories of the dramatic change in their private lives."[37] Was it his stagecraft? Or his *Weltanschauung*? Or a bit of both, joined magically on cue? If the sexual liberation were to work, every comma in the emancipation proclamation had to be in place. Here are a few excerpts from the sage's last-minute instructions before the premiere on 17 June 1969 when the winter palace of the establishment's prudery was to be stormed:

The way Jack pulls the ruler out of Jill is too rough: couldn't he extract it more gently and leave the rough stuff until the fuck....And doesn't she shriek too much during the fuck?...

Margo must either wear just the flower in her cunt or we should cut the Can-can altogether....

The gusset: Fred should be advised that the gusset must fit snugly into the crotch. Nancy's dangles about four or five inches from her cunt. This isn't sexy....

Please bear in mind the harem syndrome—men like girls on stage with no male competition, and girls also like to see girls making love to each other because it removes their fear of men....

And couldn't we consider freezing the masturbation fantasies whenever anybody comes up with one that's authentically personal and really bizarre?...

Also I feel we're missing a laugh when Leon notices Margo's tits. I don't think it's clear from "See somethin' you like" that she means her tits. Could Bill say "Some set of boobs, huh?" Also: "I don't mean folks where you just come in and lay your pecker on the table"—surely the stress should be on "table" rather than "pecker"....

I thought Nancy was a little too reticent last night in the rectal spread department—a touch more disclosure would be appropriate....

Tynan's inexhaustible expertise could have made a lusty edition of *Gray's Anatomy*. He didn't shriek too much and knew every syndrome. He knew when a man was too rough and a woman too quiet. All in all, the message with all the minutiae was getting across. He was certain that a reference to "one of the two best sexual experiences I've had in my entire life" should involve "not only a manual gesture but a fantastic squirm of the whole pelvic area." (And he laughed because he knew it was also hip.)[38]

When it all added up—the flowers and the gussets and the squirms—it appeared to fulfill his wildest ambitions, a climax to his dreams far beyond the hopes of orgasm. He was moved by the praise from Jerome Robbins (of *West Side Story* and *Fiddler on the Roof* fame) who used Tynan's phrase about "High Definition Performance" originally defined as

> supreme professional polish, hard-edged technical skill, the effortless precision without which no artistic enterprise— however strongly we may sympathize with its aims or ideas—can inscribe itself on our memory.....the hypnotic saving grace of high and low art alike, the common denominator that unites tragedy, ballroom dancing, conversation and cricket.[39]

Nor was this all. What of the "aims and ideas"? Would the winter palace fall, would the cold warfare chill out the establishment? To those who maliciously wrote that they found the show boring, he countered that this was what the early critics had said about *Lady Chatterley*, Henry Miller, and Joyce's *Ulysses*. But the critic of *Newsweek* magazine (Jack Kroll) had gotten it right, for he "saw the point of what we were trying to do and said that I had brought the sexual revolution to the middle classes for the first time!" Thus, it was also a triumph for the r-word. He had, for an off-Broadway season or two, put out more flags on the barricades than anyone else had ever dared.[40]

Crusade's End

If it wouldn't be literally misunderstood one might say that *Oh! Calcutta!* represented the interrupted climax of his career. One London reviewer (Frank Marcus in the *Sunday Telegraph*) got under Tynan's skin whereupon he fired off another letter-to-the-editor restating what it, and he, and the message were all about. Refuting the charge that he had been "reduced to propagating titillation by nudity and chemically induced ecstasy," he said he "thoroughly approved *titillation*" (dictionary definition: *tickle, excite pleasantly*) but insisted that he never advocated or recommended "chemically induced ecstasy." He and Marcus were quibbling about the name of the drug; Marcus replied that he had not meant XTC, but marijuana. So sounded all the quibbles in the 1970s. What was important was that Tynan had joined the herd of independent titillating minds, each seriously convinced that he was making his contribution to the erotic regeneration of the race.

One of his skits would, like travel, broaden the mind (it was called "See Nipples & Die"). Whatever the shock administered to willing or unsuspecting audiences, each of his sketches had to be politically correct. He was against racist slurs. Accordingly, he instructed one of his flippant actresses to refrain from that line about "being fucked by the Count Basie Band." One had to break taboos correctly. After all, he was bringing to *Calcutta* the enviable expertise of half a lifetime. Tynan had the writer's and director's touch for every scene.

Nothing escaped his attention except possibly the suspicion that, at this rate, his other reputation—as a critical intellectual, rich in language and ideas, fêted in all the cultural capitals from Berlin, London to Paris and off-Broadway—would be mutating to something else. Perhaps he had gone too far, one or two f-words too far. He still considered the critical hostility he was encountering to be conventional, simpleminded, and reactionary. It was more difficult to cope with Germaine Greer who was on the faster track to sexual liberation, and was overtaking him on the left. He was having trouble with her about the piece she had written for the National Theater program for Shaw's *Mrs. Warren's Profession*. In a memo to Laurence Olivier (4 December 1970) he confessed,

> I've already cut 200 words of her piece, including two other uses of the word "fuck," the word "cunt," a reference to the anal practices of prostitutes and to the amount of semen in a prostitute's vagina.
>
> I've blackmailed her into doing this by saying that the printers refused to print the offending passages. At first she saw no reason to agree to any cuts, saying that it would be ludicrous and contemptible for someone like myself, who had always fought against censorship, to insist on censoring others.
>
> I finally wore her down...but she insisted on retaining one four-letter word because she loathes the pedantry of words like "copulation."
>
> If we bring any further pressure on her she will either despise me, tell the story to the papers or both. Please bear in mind that she is a highly respected authoress and a university teacher.[41]

Sir Laurence (as he then was) called Ms. Greer and "got her to change 'fucking' to 'sexual intercourse.'" Olivier modestly confessed to "Kennie," "I blamed myself, Kennie. I told her that you had shouted at me. I said it was my fault." The f-word was fast threatening to prove Tynan's unmaking. He was making a spectacle of himself; and once he got into the act his penchant for cleverness reduced him to writing quips for improvised Shakespearean mobs being filmed in Roman Polanski's famed production of *Macbeth* (London, 1971). He made suggestions to Polanski as to what the crowds should shout:

"Hail the son of Duncan!

"Hail the King of Scotland Hereafter!"

"Death to the Tyrant!"

"WHERE THE FUCK IS DONALBAIN?"[42]

Thus, he struck a phonetic blow for the good old cause of tyrannicide and at the same time assuaged, a little, Germaine Greer who didn't "tell the story to the papers" and needed reassuring that Tynan, the man who would be the Great Utterer, was not a despicable f-word backslider. He also reassured himself as well as his other four-letter friends that he was still in heated pursuit of that "hypnotic saving grace."

Was grace slipping away? Or hypnotic art, or the whole "good revolution" which would save us all by embracing sex and socialism? It was a dispirited and troubled man who confided to his journal, "I disbelieve in art because I no longer believe that there is a secret something inside me which, when properly expressed, will take on a high reality and deserve the name of 'art.'"* [43] This deep loss of faith, of engagement, of the commitment he preached, was a secret—as his wife tells us—he confided to no one, only to his diary. For the rest, he was a man of the f-word to the last; it followed him like nemesis. Kathleen Tynan writes that he wants to make good for his compromises and other shortcomings, he "wanted to make amends...and to that end he spent much of the next decade devising other projects with sex as the theme, designed to deliver what *Oh! Calcutta!* failed to achieve." In his journal he confided to other heresies and failings (e.g., noting that he had never liked, or practiced, "group sex"). He contemplated a film in an "atmosphere of secrecy and slightly decadent sensuality"; nothing came of it. He enthused about the life and work of Wilhelm Reich after chancing upon a copy of Reich's *The Sexual Revolution* (1936/1945), and he thought of writing Reich's biography to probe the secrets of "orgasmic potency." It remained unwritten.

Something had gone deeply wrong. It was as if he had subjected himself to false gods, "obscene" perhaps in the original sense of the word (according to the *O.E.D.*) which was of an ill-omened augury. By embracing the cause of life's obscenities, breaking taboos on the immodest and the indelicate, defending what the uptight hypocrites of the past had pronounced to be "impure,

---

*   In a perceptive newspaper article entitled "Pagliacci," Richard Eder also quotes this "secret" passage and observes "a melancholy curve of decline." But he only ascribes this to the conventional loss of the "visionary fire" of Tynan's early enthusiasm. Whoever keeps to the youthful utopias of 19?

Tynan had written of Olivier (in obvious contrast to himself) that "he makes no attempts to insist, and invites no moral response, simply the thing he is shall make him live." Now Eder writes of Tynan that "at some point he lost the thing he was, beneath the preening and the peacockery. That fierce knowing of the theater, that will to become it, had dwindled. Nothing else would entirely make him live."

But this had not "dwindled"; it was willfully down-sized, lustfully depleted.[44]

indecent, lewd," he was choosing what Shakespeare (in *Richard II*) and his contemporaries thought of as a "black" path of "ribald scurrilitie." A singular *O.E.D.* entry under "Obscenity" tells of one victim of a "Juggernaut": "A well-made young man who danced a while before the idol…then rushing suddenly to the wheels he shed his blood under the tower of obscenity." Here are allegories galore, warnings in abundance, metaphors rich enough to stop a poet in his tracks! And then, too, there was the stern lesson that Milton taught as Talmudic wisdom, "All words which are writ obscenely must be changed to more civil words." He who would leave them, cultivate and praise them, was only condemning himself to inauspicious adversity.[45]

A last letter he received before he died in California in May 1980 was cheering, and it would have written a happy end to the careers of most men who enjoyed by-lines in newspaper columns. It came from Harold Hobson in London, the old and retired critic of the *Sunday Times*, recalling "the great days when you and I did weekly battle over the plays—generally, indeed almost always, ending in your victory." He opined that "they now seem a part of some legendary Homeric past." Kenneth Tynan hadn't made it with the classics of art and sex (say, Joyce's *Ulysses*); but then a friend was good enough to remember Homer, a related titan to be spoken of in the same breath. These are the niceties of a classical Oxonian education. He wanted to be remembered for love and art and wit, a triad of taboo-breaking ideals, whereby masterpieces and ecstasy and high style would be created. But the one greatness he achieved—or was born to…or had thrust upon him—turned out to be the godfather of the f-word. It was "a figure in the carpet," and had proved as ominous and ineluctable as in Henry James' tale.

A last backward glance. Should the man have spent so much of his last years pursuing sexual liberation, like some lewd Lochinvar or a porno-Parsifal in a crusading quest for a holy grail? He pursued the cosmic and earthly drama of orgasmic sex as if the crusade for the grail was on the verge of imminent fulfillment, and he was always getting reports of its last sightings, full of tempting details of its color and brilliance, its size and shape, its capacity.

Alas, the man who invents a *Zeitgeist* is, in the end, overwhelmed by it: its hectic changeableness, its belated and unforeseen costs and consequences. Tynan was confident that he had a nose for the real thing: the dialectic of history, the high climax of art. In the fifties he turned up as a Brechtian in Berlin, in the sixties a Castroite in Cuba, in the seventies an erotomane in Manhattan, as if the *Zeitgeist* had regularly been making him offers he could not refuse. After all, he had repossessed a sacred word, and once it had been outed it was really out there, hanging in the wind for all to see and hear, the great f-word itself in full sight and volume in front of millions of incredulous lip-reading television fans, yes the four-letter word with all the letters in place. An historic moment!…He—and we—would not look on its like again. But like the proverbial warrior who lived by the sword and died by the sword, the f-word was his making and his undoing.

The Godfather of the F-Word (II): Peregrine Worsthorne

The f-word appears at first blush to be a willful personal aberration, or a regrettable and tasteless editorial lapse, or a boorish gesture of social aggression. But it has also taken on in our time a key function in an *ideology*, in a coherent set of beliefs and attitudes which holds that rude change is on the agenda of the day and that a utopia beckons with the promise of unabashed and liberated love. Those enlightened spirits, D.H. Lawrence and James Joyce, masters of an English prose which had shaken loose of old fetters, had pioneered the way. Sex was far too important to be left to the censors; words would make us free; circumlocutions were shackles. Freud, in his way, helped to open up the dark continent with its erotic secrets and erogenous zones (although, in fact, his psycho-conservatism affirmed forms of repression as essential to a stable civilized balance).

As we have seen, certain pioneers of the f-word in public discourse—Kenneth Tynan, for example—had an impassioned faith in the ideological force of an obscene expostulation or a lewd gesture (*Oh! Calcutta!*). It could indeed be the onset of a revolution, comparable in its radical semantic (or semiotic) way to the attack on the Bastille or the storming of the Winter Palace. The vocabulary of forbidden and profane words would provide an arsenal of explosive slogans; for the word that could, at long last, dare to speak its name would signal a natural breakthrough to a new felicity in human intercourse.

I have already touched upon this streak of utopian optimism in the hyperactive generation of the "'68ers," but more than thirty years on we observe the age-old disillusionment of a youthful romanticism, the ruins of a utopian faith when ideology (as it must, as it always has) disintegrates, when we are left only with "the God that Failed." As one veteran of "the swinging '60s" who had reluctantly abandoned the whole psychedelic dream, with its politico-sexual disenchantment, rudely put it, "It was the orgasm that failed." Self-satisfied old men have nodded wisely in assent. I even heard the mutterings of those battle-scarred veterans of ideological disappointment, Arthur Koestler and Ignazio Silone (in the presence of Richard Crossman who had published their historic recantations) as the *idèologues* of '68— from Herbert Marcuse to Timothy Leary, from Jean-Paul Sartre to Tariq Ali and Richard ("Oz") Neville—faded out into the sunset. "The gods are failing, yet again..."

But it is one thing to try and make a revolution—and dream of achieving "that terrible beauty...changing things utterly" (in Yeats' phrase)—and quite another to influence, even if the movement's grand cause failed, the *Zeitgeist* and thus have a lasting influence on the temper of the times. We are all children of the *Zeitgeist*, and none of us have been immune to the informal lifestyles that dominate our social conventions ("Come as you are!") and indeed to the cruder speech habits that have intruded into the conversation of mankind. One example from the recent history of the media will, I am sure, be sufficient to illustrate the point that even conservatives give out with the same sounds of penitent survival. I refer to the case of Sir Peregrine Worsthorne, that dean of Tory intellectual commentators, a former editor-in-chief of the right-wing *Sunday Telegraph*, and still an elegant and patrician figure on the London scene.

Let him tell his instructive story in his own words:

> A great many years ago I used the four-letter f-word on television. It was only the second time it had been broadcast, the first being some time earlier by the radical-chic drama critic Kenneth Tynan. Because bad language was more expected from him than from the *Sunday Telegraph* deputy editor, as I then was, it caused rather more of a shock, and if I am to be remembered for anything—most unlikely—it will be for this egregious piece of taboo-breaking.

This all happened in the year 1973, when the BBC had invited him to a "nationwide" discussion-program on the current scandal of British parliamentary life, the resignation from his ministerial position by Lord Lambton (whose daughter, as it transpired, Worsthorne was later to marry). The noble Lord had been found in bed with two prostitutes, one black and one white. The TV program was live, and when Worsthorne was asked how he thought the great British public would react to yet another sex-sensation involving the Conservative government, he replied (as he records his fateful reply),*

> Probably they won't give a... there's only one word for it... won't give a f***.

It was a quip, a calculated double-entendre, and the wordplay got no laughs.

I once asked him about the incident, and he told me that the joke had been thought up in a taxi on the evening in question by him and a fellow-journalist, the music critic (sophisticated, and with a rather more dry wit) Philip Hope-Wallace. At other times the off-color plot was said to have been hatched at Fleet Street's El Vino's bar; but, flamboyant and imaginative chap that he is, officially in his autobiography he denies that he had "planned to use the word" and attributed the affair to "spontaneous bravado." More than that, far from offering apologies as he was pressed to do, he affirmed that "it was exactly the *mot juste*."

---

* Quoted from Peregrine Worsthorne, in his autobiography, *Tricks of Memory* (1993), p. 223; it was also published, with a slight omission, in his article "Why We Should Watch What We Say," *Daily Telegraph*, 12 July 1995, p. 19.

In any case the *mot* in one scandal caused another, the word rivalling the thing, and *le mot de Peregrine* kept pace with the call-girl confessions that studded the press coverage of the Lambton case. The owner of the *Telegraph*, Lord Hartwell, and especially his formidable wife, Lady Pamela, were outraged; and Worsthorne was suspended from the newspaper. The BBC put him on a blacklist for years. A host of irate *Telegraph* readers wrote in to cancel their subscriptions. From the whole furore the patrician journalist drew the not surprising conclusion that "clearly a very large section of the public still found sexual swear words unacceptable." Yet in his rueful memoir of the notorious incident he imparts his impression that nowadays he would have clean gotten away with it.

But perhaps that had not been the point of the exercise; the shock was the thing that would catch the conscience of the king. At the time the battlelines were sharply drawn:

> My promising career on the box came to a virtual end. The BBC at once cancelled a major political series in which I was to be the anchorman.... I was not invited on even the most marginal programmes. No such punishment is meted out to today's producers, who put on documentaries, plays and sitcoms where the foulest of language is the rule.

Perry's quip had been playful. It could be that he had not even really meant to shock, only to pretend to for a passing moment. He was no *idéologue* (like Tynan), only a fellow traveler of fashion, surfing on a new wave of radical chic rap. He was no crusader, only a stylist who liked to try on words: in Shakespeare's phrase, "dressing old words new/spending again what is already spent." He had, in what turned out to be something of an historic occasion—which turned him, memorably, into the "Godfather of the F-word (II)" —indulged himself in an eccentric folly, meaning no harm, intending no good. He was never a reformer nor a radical in the camp of the sex-liberators. In the tradition of schoolboy pranksters he wanted, I suspect, to be caught, wanting merely to embarrass and be embarrassed. Products of a sentimental education, such sentimentalists may be permitted to believe that in the old days a dirty word had a certain rare innocence.

But our wordsmith today is owning up to rather profound regrets. He has pondered the lesson from experience, and the moral of the story: he wishes now he had not set such a bad example. Overcome by the importance of being earnest he has given us a re-consideration which comes from having second thoughts on the f-word and its discontents. The poacher turned gamekeeper? The schoolboy turned headmaster:

> Bad language on the telly does shock. It shocks enough in public places, on public transport, in pubs and most of all in school playgrounds, from where it rises nowadays like a bad smell. But there is no escape from it in public places, which is

precisely why the public should not also have it thrust down their ears in the privacy of their own homes. Even now for the great majority of the population foul language is still abnormal and aberrant—a form of verbal pollution from which they wish to protect their homes and their families, and it is inexcusable for the broadcasting authorities to disregard these wishes.

One hears the resounding words of remorse: "Such was the hell of a lesson I learnt all those years ago that I have never attempted to offend again."

And yet, and yet... one is not entirely persuaded. Like so many penitents, he wants in his contrition to take his turn at dispensing punishment, "to mete out the same condign chastisement to my all too numerous successors." But will he be hitting out at "the others" or at his own mates? Let's face it: his successors on his own two great newspapers have been inexcusably involved in institutionalizing the f-word, apportioning it in daily doses (and twice over the week-end), sweetened slightly by (see above) asterisks and hyphens but which, according to the rule of "participatory obscenity," has me saying *le mot de Worsthorne (et Tynan)* every weekday once or twice and over again on Sunday. I, and a million other captivated readers, say it to myself, quietly, pursingly, but if you read my lips—to use Sir Peregrine's phrase so long ago when he became the second man ever to be so bold—"there's only one word for it, isn't there?"

What chastisement is condign enough for us silent offenders? Probably another year's cut-rate subscription to the paper coming discreetly through the mailbox. It will never fail to disappoint, for there is an *omerta* to every Godfather and they all remain, above all, loyal and steadfast. We have not seen the last of the *mot juste*.[46]

In Perry Worsthorne's case it could not be long postponed. His penchant for the occasional street-corner expletive and farmyard epithet to give a certain cross-class accent or aroma to his elegant paragraphs has grown undiminished over the years. In a more recent feature in the *Daily Telegraph* (November 1998) about his noble wife and their altercations, in private and in public—"*My Wife Threw a Chair at My Head*"—he confesses that Lady Lambton, as she is still known, is "like all intelligent women very difficult." This he ascribes to the fact that women are better than men at judging human character (including his own). He recounts how she would break into loud outbursts in the decorous Garrick Club, and how she would often "bristle with disapproval and contempt" at certain friends of his whom he brought home. Decorum and domesticity may be upset; but women have their uncanny talents: "my wife can spot a charlatan, a poseur, a creep or a s— miles off." No matter the distance, the pungency is (as I say) still there in the well-fertilized prose.[47]

Osborne's Effing Anger

The wind bloweth where it listeth. I would not have thought that the passing of John Osborne (aged sixty-five, on Christmas Eve 1994) would have provided any kind of special occasion for the vocabulary we are documenting. But his own liberties with language, embracing (as the obituaries recorded) "bawdry ... invective ... sleaze ... vitriol ... sedition ... misogyny..." as well as a brimming mouthful of ordinary cuss words, was evidently infectious beyond the grave.

In the *Times*, obit writers (and readers) rushed into print to suggest that the revolution in British dramatic writing, which Osborne's memorable play, *Look Back in Anger* (1956) came to symbolize, could still stimulate the adrenalin and nearby glands. Writing effusively about his life and death, the memorialists aped the master and indicated that the anger could still burn or boil over, and the coarseness still tingled in the nostrils. For, after all, this was the man who, breaking radically with the theatrical traditions of silly, snobbish unrealities, brought "the smell of the kitchen-sink on to the English stage." It was mixed in his stormy life with the aromas of love and hate.

Of Osborne's many wives, as Bernard Levin recalled, the one Osborne disliked the most was the actress Jill Bennett whose autocratic ways earned her his term of endearment (she was, famously, called "Adolph"). And when she committed suicide her former husband's response to the news was, "She was the most evil woman I have ever come across—she was a bitch." He was not being nasty, as he tried to explain; it was only his "style." Levin dissented: "he pisses in his once-beloved's grave, and he is really astonished when people find him unpleasant."[48]

The unpleasantries that discolor the two volumes of his memoirs are legion, the most distasteful being embedded in the hundred unhappy pages he devoted to his mother (always referred to as Nellie Beatrice) whom he reviled; consequently he took a special scabrous delight when, during the war, an enemy bomb fell on their squalid little suburban house and "she was blown off the lavatory."

The day's papers went on from the kitchen sink to the toilet bowl, moving gingerly from the p-words to the f- and s-words. The *Times'* drama critic, Benedict Nightingale, remembered Osborne's splenetic hatred of all unfriendly reviewers, especially "the shit Nightingale." He also recorded a long list of the playwright's indiscriminate attacks—with the Osbornian verve of his wild and notorious manifesto from St. Tropez, *"Damn You England!"*—on Australians, gays, trendy Bishops, American academics, vegetarians, people called Debbie and Kevin, and, last but not least, the Brussels bureaucrats (including the Strasbourg parliamentarians, the so-called MEPs, whom, we are told, he referred to as "Ministers for European Pricks").[49]

Another theater critic[50] deemed it important to tell us that the acting cast in Osborne's later plays referred to them, succinctly, as *"Whatshit"*: which is of course our old friend the s-word slightly covered up. An *Independent* columnist, Wallace Arnold, a humorist of sorts, went on to make fun of himself as a would-be interviewer who tried in vain to get the famous man to agree to speak with him. As he records, the first time he got only "Piss off you fat prat." "Prat" may be taken to be (as the *Longman Dictionary* gives it) a "worthless, stupid" person; but it is usually a synonym for the a-word: for "back-side, buttocks," to wit, ass, arse, *Arsch*... In either case, it represents no great and colorful enrichment of the language to be treasured over the years, especially when it happened repeatedly to the hapless Mr. Arnold: "Don't mess with me again, you pompous stinkarse, or I'll slit your bloody throat in two." Unbloodied, unbowed, he came back for more, this last time in the otherwise congenial rooms of the Garrick Club in London, where he was peremptorily dismissed as a "fat-arsed toad."

Grateful readers were indebted for all the tangy journalism, so evocative— as only Fleet Street on the scent can be—of the dank spirit of kitchen sink leftovers. Thankful, especially, to the *Times* and the *Independent* for all the bits of scatological evidence which helped to round out the portrait of the aging Angry Young Man with, as one reader pungently put it, "farts and all."

Osborne's dramatic achievement was for me, at least, less solid than that sound-and-fury signifying diffuse discontent; but the British press paid him handsome tribute in tens of thousands high- and low-falutin words, obviously using the occasion to pull out all the stops in between. I found few enough hyphens-and-asterisks, and there was very little shocking that was left out, not even his praise for the Teutons (for in a world full of hateful abominations Osborne was grateful for some un-English spirits: "Thank God for the Krauts and the Wogs!"). We are assured by the *Times* that he remained an "AYM"— an angry young man—to the end, threatening any so-and-so who called him a "senior citizen" that they "would get one last almighty smack in their mealy effing mouths." The *Times'* conclusion: "The right valedictory, surely, from the feisty father of modern English drama, John Osborne." Funky and flaky too, he was.

His reputation had been first made by the *Observer's* Kenneth Tynan after the première of *Look Back in Anger* at the Royal Court Theater on the day, 8 May 1956, which "made history." Tynan went on from hailing the Poet of the Kitchen Sink to realistic achievements of his own—being the first (on the BBC in 1973) to broadcast the f-word and he was also the first, in *Oh! Calcutta!*, to present the full frontal f-deed on the London stage.

I knew them both men personally, and I look back with satisfaction that they enjoyed living and dying "in the best of times, in the worst of times." For if it was a liberating age of light and wisdom, it was also (to complete the

Dickens quote) the age of foolishness and incredulity and despair. If you'll pardon the expression, Osborne's "effing anger" has just sort of become part of the culture. And as that wry philosopher of twentieth-century civilization, Auberon Waugh, insists on putting such a grave question, can we really, as a culture, afford this sort of thing for another century? More and more liberation, and endless self-fulfillment?

It was a rough passage, but in two aspects the familiar aspects of Osbornianism prevailed. First, at the memorial services in St. Giles-in-the-Fields, just off Charing Cross Road—in the little London church at which he arranged for his friends and admirers to assemble—there was a sign which he had wanted to put up on the door. The names thereon guaranteed more headlines, looking back in anger at fellow-playwright Arnold Wesker; theater critic Nicholas de Jongh; "Fu Manchu" (i.e., Sir Peter Hall), and "the Bard of Hay-on-Wye" (i.e., the actor Albert Finney), all of whom he hated. He forbade them entrance to St. Giles in the event that they should turn up.

Then, again, there was the vaunted coyness in some of the newspaper accounts which would have led to more histrionic outbursts. The *Daily Express* columnist, Paul Callan, reported that "There was many a joke, particularly about Osborne's ability—rare in the world of the Luvvies—to extract the, er, you-know-what out of himself."[51] Readers are invited to spend a creative moment or two and try to puzzle out exactly what it was—adrenalin and anger? hate and more cuss-words?—that was being "extracted."

Amis *Père et Fils*

Kingsley was nothing if not paradoxical in his choice of language and squeamish reasons for so doing. The last book of his to be published—a small posthumous "guide to modern usage" entitled *The King's English* (1997)—oscillated between the characteristics he called "Berks and Wankers." Left to the berks, the English language would die of impurity (for they are "careless, coarse, crass, gross"); left to the wankers, it would die of purity (for they are "prissy, fussy, priggish, prim"). One Oxford professor of language and communciation (Jean Aitchinson) did not think much of Amis as a genuine "linguachondriac"—someone with real, if excessive, fears for the health of the language: He was merely a mild "linguaphobic," a person who shudders at certain usages, particularly certain words. These were less likely to be scabrous stereotypes (to which he was hopelessly addicted) than harmlessly mispronounced clichés. He disliked the words *belly* and *kids*; he found "parameters," badly spoken to rhyme mistakenly with "kilometers," quite repulsive. And what of our f-word for which we have appointed him as an honorary godfather? As the linguist in the *Sunday Times* has written,

His squeamishness over *belly* contrasts oddly with his tolerant attitude toward *f****:
"I have forgotten when I first said or made a character say f*** [*i.e.* the *Times'*
asterisks] in print, but no one seemed to care."

Least of all Kingsley Amis. He quietly accepted the drama out of the demotic
break-through. He casualized the f-word; and accommodated the s-, p-, and c-
words to routine literary conversation, whether in his novels or when standing
at the Garrick bar. And yet he was among the most caring of writers in the
English language, as I knew from his various manuscripts, at least a dozen of
which I published—elegant essays ("Farewell to Cambridge"), splendid polemics ("More Means Worse"), fastidious poetry.[52]

Amis *père* died in October 1995, widely mourned as "England's foremost
man of letters" who had as an Angry Young Man* given another tone to the
language. Who will now continue the tradition of the fathers when the sons
look away?

But no fears for the heritage. If novelists now go whoring after the "clean
bits," then the "dirty bits" will have to be in the good natty hands of our journalists. Only a few days after Kingsley Amis' death—he had not yet been
buried—a newspaperwoman named Elizabeth Grice seized her opportunity
during the London launching of a new book by Elizabeth Jane Howard. Ms.
Howard was the second Mrs. Amis who had aroused the first Mrs. Amis into
an "effing fit of jealousy" on a Spanish holiday beach. Ms. Grice showed
scarce interest in the new Howard novel and pressed forward on the burning
literary issue of the day: Why was the widow not turning up for the funeral?
Elizabeth Jane Howard spoke sadly of the passionate love that once had been
—until his alcoholism had driven them apart. She had "bolted," and they never
saw each other or spoke again.

But Ms. Grice of the *Daily Telegraph* knew a bit more, and her quotation
from the private letter from Kingsley Amis to the poet Philip Larkin indicated
that the heritage was going to be well preserved. At least we would be getting
two sides of the story, for he described the profound sense of relief at his
second wife's departure which, he said, was partly "because she realized I
didn't like her much" and "partly to punish me for stopping wanting to f...
her." If the three discreet dots were Kingsley's, then the correspondence is
showing new facets of his character; if it was inserted by the copy editors on
the *Telegraph* desk, it suggests yet another variant of the f-word. There can be

---

* Who first used the phrase? The coinage is much in dispute. Claims have been
made for various figures in what one obituarist called "a tatterdemalion group"
(including Amis, Kenneth Tynan, John Wain and, of course, John Osborne). Informed experts in the Sloane Square milieu attribute it to a quick-witted press-
relations man (George Fearon) at London's Royal Court Theater of the day. But
several years earlier a London writer, Leslie Paul, had published a volume of
memoirs entitled *Angry Young Man* (1951).

life and love after the era of asterisks and hyphens, of circumlocutions and periphrasis. *Dots!*[53]

Kingsley Amis was a more gentle and circumspect adumbrator of character; but in narrating the story of his life and works, the *Daily Mail* went to great lengths to pinpoint an intimately related Amis theme. In a stormy episode in Kingsley's first marriage, he had run away to have an affair with "another woman" (the novelist Elizabeth Jane Howard) and then rejoined the family for a holiday in Majorca. One afternoon he had fallen asleep on the beach. The *Daily Mail*, and its serviceable biographer Eric Jacobs, picks up the story from there (in the first installment of "Words, Whisky, and Words," 15 May 1995):

> Overwhelmed with misery at the latest evidence of his infidelity, Hilly [Kingsley's first wife, and mother of Martin] seized the lipstick from her bag and she wrote on his bare back *"1 Fat Englishman"* (the title of the book he was working on). Underneath she wrote *"I F*** Anything"*....

The word, evidently, is no passing expletive: it has family traditions, and the Fleet Street press can be relied upon to respect them.

In the memorial service for the first anniversary of Kingsley Amis' death (October 1996), held in St. Martin-in-the-Fields and presided over by Martin Amis, there was full coverage in the newspapers involving their gossip columnists, their literary critics, and their theology editors. The critical evaluation of the "old devil's" work came somewhat short but the church was still crowded by the London literati, and the *Times* noted that it was "a memorial as eccentric as any chapter in the old devil's life": "There was no service paper, no vicar, no blessing, no prayers, no hymns and, but for a burst of jazz to play out the congregation, no music." Only the *Independent* was heavy enough to seize the religious issue by the horns:

GOD MEETS THE OLD DEVIL
A memorial service for an atheist?

Why indeed commemorate with a church service, however bare-boned, a man who boasts in his memoirs of his life-long atheism and, more than that, was proud of his "hatred for God"? With some empathy a good case could be made out, based on a subtle interpretation of many of the fictional characters he had created in his twenty-odd novels; for if they were "drunken, lecherous, God-fearing" protagonists for whom, no matter how terrible an eternity with Him may be, it was surely preferable to an eternity of being merely themselves. Thus, "drunken, lecherous, God-loathing Kingsley Amis" made sin and redemption far more real and natural than they appear in the works of most professedly Christian novelists. How proper-and-generous it was for the church "to lend its high windows to his memory."

As for the gossipy angle, it cried out for—and it was duly republished in several papers, including the *Sunday Times*—that "lecherous" bit about the lipstick scrawled on the beach in the summer sunshine. It was retold yet again, and on the second telling it was repeated with both hyphens and asterisks but in lower-case letters. The deadly sin was still clear and current, and at least the old devil was being given his due.[54]

Old literary friends, and Amis' authorized biographer has evidently consulted them and had access to letters and diaries—none of this "invasion of privacy" stuff with our "foremost man of letters"!—help in the burden-sharing. On next-to-the-last day of the *Mail*'s series we came to the climax of a gaggle of dreary extramarital affairs with one that got away. A disappointed but still enterprising amorist writes to his friend (Robert Conquest, the historian) for help with an extra measure of deviousness that would protect the next assignation:

> Now listen...can you fix me up with a bed for tomorrow week (Dec. 19)? From say 11:30 onwards. Reply if you will to the above address, not Glanmor Road, because a fault in my security system has led Hilly to connect a Conquest letter with an impending Amis screw.... So please, chum, no leaks to anyone on this, & christ, as you'll readily understand, what bugged me was having to serve my sentence without having had a chance to commit the f***ing crime, so to speak.[55]

The asterisks, one takes it, were not present in the original; otherwise all the documentation in this not unfriendly, if cheerless, biographical effort is in point of fact faithful to the infidelities in word and deed. And, to be sure, the *Mail* in such cases of *coitus interruptus*, finds the "crime" not in the intercourse but in the interference.

On Friday, when the *Mail*'s week-long excursions into the deep background of sexual life in our time usually conclude, there is still time to maintain par with one more stroke, one-putting on the greens of literature. A writer ages, alas; and all passion spent he thinks now only of his unfinished page in his typewriter (an *Adler* office manual), the malt whiskey (*Macallan*) on his desk, and the echoing lines of his Oxford mate (the poet Philip Larkin) who once set the ideal for an ambitious postwar generation:

> The s*** in the shuttered chateau
> Who does his five hundred words
> Then parts out the rest of the day
> Between bathing and booze and birds.

The latest is that the hoopla in New York and the kerfuffle in London have quieted down in the Martin Amis scandal. The story up to here involved the astonishing risk taken in Manhattan by an adventurous American publisher who was persuaded by a fast-talking hotshot literary agent to offer the English novelist a million dollars, give or take a few percent, for his new book.* Back home in England his colleagues and competitors (plus his old agent) were flabbergasted, incensed, envious.

Now the novel, *The Information*, has without undue delay been published in the U.S. and throughout Europe. Is it good? Will it make back its enormous advance? One American newspaper reviewer says yes; and yes, the novel is "wonderful" and "should also be a big popular hit." Its story of the nasty rivalry between two ambitious writers who used to be friends—set in "Martin Amis's world of angst, drugs, sex and literary revenge"—is written in "wonderfully edgy, street-smart prose." I think I'll order a copy (Harmony Books, $24).

Another reviewer makes me hesitate. The Manichaean struggle between "Richard Tull and Gwyn Barry" amounts only to "a bad book." Obviously one street-smart aleck deserves another. In the latest Manhattan mugging the *Newsweek* critic, Jeff Giles, writes,

> Amis has loosened his belt, and his slangy scattershot prose veers towards self-parody. Sentences are either impossibly short or impossibly long. Commas, colons, parentheses and dashes crawl all over the page like flesh-eating microbes.

A small sampler of Amis' "edgy" prose, attempting to define the great personal conflict:

> Then and there it crystallized: the task. A literary endeavor, a quest, an exaltation—one to which he could sternly commit all his passion and his power. He was going to f—k Gwyn up.

No, thanks, cancel that copy; I can get my f-words cheaper.

Distinctions have to be made. It is far from my intention to lump together the whole host of novelists and newspapermen who seem to have enlisted themselves among the cursing classes in our societies. There are almost as many gradations among them as there are categories of swear words, and in

---

*   According to the *New York Times*, Martin Amis and his high-powered New York literary agent, Andrew Wylie, "fought diligently to prevent the story's publication and were caught unaware when it happened...." The *New York Times* also, in its profile of Wylie in its Magazine (11 August 1996, pp. 26-29), registers "his gallant defense of Martin Amis' honor." This is not necessarily accurate or meaningful since the *N.Y. Times* erratically reports that it was *The Times* of London which had run the excerpts from Eric Jacobs' biography (it claimed to be "authorized")—it was, actually, as in our footnotes, the *Daily Mail*. The Magazine's writer even went on to praise something beyond "gallantry" in literary character, namely, *"nonpareil chutzpah."* Which only indicates that literary gossip has some difficulties in crossing the Atlantic intact.

this wide spectrum Kingsley Amis could hardly be taken as a protagonist of excess. From the early, stormy, and very litigious days (of Joyce and Lawrence before the U.S. courts in the 1920s) to more recent climactic turning-points (the *Chatterley* case in London, followed by the prosecution of Hubert Selby, Jr.'s *Last Exit to Brooklyn*, and throw in the likes of James Jones, Norman Mailer et al. in the permissive sixties), there emerged only a rough general awareness of writers who did and writers who didn't. Writers who did belonged to the enlightened avant-garde of what was yet to be called "dirty realism." They distanced themselves from the stuffy traditionalists who were charged as only wanting "to write like Jane Austen."

But, as in other human contexts, there were doves and hawks, compulsive extremists, mild liberals and, ineluctably, Colonel Blimps. Amis has often wrestled with the dilemmas he faced in writing his first novel, *Lucky Jim* (1954) and trying to make the "womanizing" of his hero, Jim Dixon, intelligible within the language prescriptions of the day. He often told one anecdote which was memorable. Some character is saying of someone else, "I feel sorry for the poor bugger." His English publisher at that time was the ebullient Victor Gollancz (of Left Book Club fame), and he quickly warned that if Amis insisted on that six-letter word he might lose thousands of copies which would otherwise be taken by the popular lending-libraries. Amis considered briefly:

> "What about 'bloody fool'?"
> "Perfectly acceptable," said Gollancz.

Still, Amis always used to add that he had never felt entirely easy about the change, because "bugger" in such a context did not count for him as swearing. It was not comparable, say, to Hemingway's loss of "three little words" (see below, "A Thought on the Hall of Ill Fame") in his *A Farewell to Arms* (1929):

> What a long time ago it all seems [writes Amis in his last book, 1995]....I have forgotten when I first said or made a character say *fuck* in print, but no one seemed to notice or care, any more than they did when my son Martin used the word several dozen times in one page in a novel published in 1978.[56]

Only a man who didn't pay very close attention to newspapers, films, and television—the time saved he employed to continue writing excellent verse—could state that, in the last year of his life (1995), "Four-letter words are probably less in use conversationally than they were and, with the exception of one denoting the female parts, of less impact." In his mid-century experience, cursing and swearing and bad language were associated only with "a boyish desire to show off," acts of small revolt which simultaneously revealed oneself as "a diminutive dissident." It was all about "recognition signals." Sending whole pages of scurrility to each other was a way of signaling a deep literary friendship between Amis and the distinguished poet, Philip Larkin. It was also, in his manner, a way of being entertaining; and, even to the last, Amis was only playful with profanity, and not deadly serious about the idea of liberating mankind from its verbal shackles: "The power of making one male character say to another, 'She's a fucky *nuck* case' is not to be lightly surrendered." With humor like that what need to read Freud or Jung to describe such cases with unfunny psycho-jargon? Tell it like it is, ducky; and Bowdler is still the main enemy at home.

All in all, Amis' status as one of the English godfathers of the f-word is properly diminished by his modesty, by his moderation in the cause of excess. He thought "present-day writers make more fuss about physical sex than I care to do, or describe it in more detail than I find comfortable." Mailer would have argued in reply that the truth—about war and peace, about love in ancient Egypt and Jesus' Biblical times—resides in these very details; and they live on very comfortably indeed in his books.

As for the guardians of our newspaper culture, chronically dependent on literary role models, they are pleased for a while to share the dilemmas of the hesitant modern school which predispose journalism to (what someone has referred to in a bastardized Latin) a kind of *lingua interruptus*. When worse comes to worse, and things get better, they can always fall back to full-frontal fanaticism, to unexpurgated obscenities no longer hiding behind green "fig-leaves of reticence," to the utopians of the sexual revolution whose liberated language promises the ultimate in felicity and freedom.

In contrast to the erotic peccadillos in the newspaper culture, the best of contemporary literature, it must be said, exhibits a far greater range and richness of vocabulary—think of Céline and Jean Genet, Joyce and Lawrence, Updike and Philip Roth—in dealing with matters of fornication and scatology, and the like. But for an ordinary week, catching up with the Anglo-American press, we have had enough to be getting on with.

The last word must be given to Amis *fils*. For, like all f-wordsmiths who have extended the frontiers of "dirty realism," he fancies himself to be the only realist the realists who reflect the realities of speech as she is really spoken—it is *the others* who write dirty, even to outrageous porno excess. Thus, Martin Amis has been having an uncomfortable time of it when he reads his competition: say, Philip Roth. Writing about one of Roth's latest novels, *Sabbath's Theater* (1995), Amis protests that "Philip Roth has gone too far this time." In words strikingly similar to the ones that hostile critics applied to his own lusty prose, Amis notes, "Yes, this is what morbid erotomania must really feel like. It's an itch in the brain—a cerebral nettle rash."[57] Unfortunately, he is condemned to silence in the face of all this "schlock and pornography...lusting and rutting"—for, as he confesses, flashing a prim unwonted literary discipline, "I am writing in a family newspaper...." The most he will give us is a warning that Philip Roth's novel is "unbelievably dirty." Believable dirt must be quite another thing, and requires rather different talents than are exhibited in this "450-page spasm of hysteria...about the hysteria of an hysterical man [which] leaves you feeling— hysterical."

Still, I like to think the hysteria is presaging a new sobriety, in which even Bacchus sobers up and Priapus has his regrets in the morning. There are some signs that the heroes of the flesh (and all the ribaldry and bawdry that it is heir to) are getting weary. The confession of Martin Amis may signalize that here too the gods are failing. A disenchanted penitence may be setting in: "After awhile it provokes in the reader only one desire: the desire to skip. You toil on, looking for the clean bits."

Martin Amis' latest novel (*Night Train*, 1997) continues the expected, customary provocation, and the journalistic tradition of being hoist with his own petard; or, rather, of being hit by those effing boomerangs he hurls about with such abandon. This time it is John Updike who serves the f-word back at him in a hateful, dismissive front-page quotation (in the book section of the Sunday *New York Times*). Amis and the paper are battle-scarred veterans of the expletive, but it surely must be a first in journalism for Updike: in his decades of writing for the old *New Yorker*, he surely never had a chance of getting past William Shawn's formidable lot of prose-minders and word-checkers who used to launder every page.

> Amis, beneath his banter, is a scowling atrocity-minded author who demands we look directly at things we rather would overlook....In *Night Train* he makes us closely watch an autopsy and spotlights the void...in which criminals "f*** a baby and throw it over the wall" and "chop up eight-year-olds for laughs."[57]

One feels that the critic is less upset with the author's atrocities than with his faux-demotic mannerisms which evince the simple stylistic faith that "repeating something magically deepens it."

> "I'm sorry. I'm sorry. I'm sorry...."

> "She'd always leave you with something. Jennifer would always leave you with something."

> "But I cannot get the good guys. I just cannot get the good guys."

> "But the seeing—the seeing, the seeing—was no good at all."

Next it will be the turn of the babies, the babies, the babies, if not for laughs then just to fill out the page. What for Amis are boring expletives in the work of a Philip Roth are, in his own work, a kind of protected privileged profanity, a necessary and proper demotic to deal with the gravity of his themes—the Holocaust, a Nuclear Disaster, our Moral Void—all calling for any horrific locution he can think of. In the end it always comes down to the f-word, that "old reliable" so fully deserving of literary loyalty for it has given some writers a lifetime's good service.

Jeeves in Sardinia

It could be argued that what George Steiner once called (in a controversial *Encounter* article dissecting pornography) "the night words" occupy such a small space in the vast newspaper output that one needs to be pruriently searching for the "f-words" to find them so ubiquitously there. I have not, I confess, done a "content-analysis" with the usual sociological apparatus of counting and tabulating. At the risk of being impressionistic I have contended that a proliferation of profanity is proceeding apace. It is true that I wade through thousands of column-inches before I find the examples with which I have studded these pages. But found them I have. And when in an indolent moment I reach out for yet another journal in which to browse in a desultory fashion, I am almost always forced to sit up and take note—yet another example *in situ*.

Just a few moments before I was driven to write these paragraphs, I dipped into a long, pleasant, innocuous account by a bright-eyed traveller who thought he had found an expatriate's haven on the island of Sardinia. It was mildly amusing as such tales go—his Cardiff accent mangled his Italian conversation; he had difficulties submitting a Welsh birth certificate to get a residency permit; he fell in love and married a local girl from Tempio Pausania in the island's far north. It was all bland and easy-going, and occasionally instructive: as when he learned that his neighbour was to "*assist*" in the soccer match against Juventus but he did *not* mean he was playing in the team. ("*Assistere*," you see, means to watch....) Yet, a few paragraphs later, I had my illustrative specimen. How come?

Profanity, of course, has its parallelisms, and all the obscenities also have their diffusion. But the pattern of proliferation has an additional element. I think of it as a part of the curve of the familiar market-economy recurrence, a supply-demand cycle which overheats into inflation. Editors more and more need, or want, what puritanical spirits dub the daily installment of smut: to satisfy (as I have said before) their drive to keep up with the competitive realities pressing them; and also to appease their own sense of being "in" or "with it" or whatever the fashionable conformities are. In addition to which there may well be cynics and immoralists among them. I remember in my school days in New York watching the antics of the most populistic editor of the day, an ebullient tabloid editor named Emil Gauvreau, whose paper, the *Daily Graphic*, I followed avidly. He specialized in "sensational scoops"; and he prided himself, when on having to announce the tabloid's demise (it had sensationalized itself into a shameful bankruptcy), he had the last scoop. His Manhattan motto in the 1920s had been: "One dirty story a day, no more, no less." Is there nowadays a similar, slightly accelerated schedule for salaciousness?

Back to my Welshman, a Mr. Peter Gregory-Jones, and his Sardinian expatriation. (The department in the *Daily Telegraph*'s special foreign edition, published weekly, is called "Expat World") It was indeed a strange world where a Briton, and a provincial one at that, necessarily seemed to appear as a character in a P.G. Wodehouse novel. He even took to wearing an old grey trilby at a properly rakish angle and, of course, an old school-tie. I will spare my readers, as he did not, the additional details of the "jolly tweed suit" and the "lapelled waistcoat twinkingly adorned by a grandpaternal watch-chain." And then he reported—"Then it happened."*

As I say, the inflationary cycle amounts to editors wanting it, soliciting and paying for it, that small voluptuous thrill with which any paper and any story can be twinkingly adorned. Old editors look for it; young writers give it to them. Life and language will never be the same again in "Wooserish Wodehousian dreams." In the inevitable *denouément*, the Welshman met his local Sardinian match: "Yuck! I mean, God, who the bloody hell do you f*****g well think you are, a bleeding Inglese?" The Welshman protested, "But I *am* English...," gingerly smiling. It worked. The enemy had become a friend; and they both went out for a drink to Mario's, after which the Sardinian confessed that he detested those local "apes" who pretended to be what they weren't and "never sh****g could be."

After this who could wish for a p—ch line? But in this faded expat world of would-be Woosters this had to be: "I had met my Jeeves." In telling the story Wodehouse might have added an asterisk or two; or, probably, he would have even deleted the expletives altogether.

A Thought on the Hall of Ill Fame

Cultures, if they are not inert or monolithic, tend at times to yearn for the new and its renewal, at others offering only cold conservative resistance to change and innovation. In the recurring cycles of utopian disenchantment, one comes to learn that there are no literary ideals, no lofty ambitions for a purer or truer or more liberating language, without disagreeable social complications. Of our twentieth-century writers I have taken Hemingway, among many other modernists, as representative of all the restless spirits pressing forward to some breakthrough to vaunted authenticity. They all entertained

---

*   *The Weekly Telegraph*, Nr. 176, 23-29 November 1994.

their literary objectives as precious theory, but actual practice was laden with dangers and pitfalls. The enthusiasm for a new culture often favors dogma and a new (or old) orthodoxy. Cultural fundamentalism on the part of a powerful establishment is all too easily drawn to a favored weapon, the censor's blue pencil. But things did not always have to go so far. Writers and publishers proved, more often than not, to be amenable to small compromises and large defeats; and huge battles have been fought in our time over tiny words. A prudent or pragmatic self-censorship often prevented things from heading regularly towards do-or-die confrontation. In the long perspective we can make out the emergence of a usable profanity for a profane society. But the stages along the way are irksome, quarrelsome, tedious.

In my own editorial experience, mostly in Europe,* I was caught up a number of times in the cut-and-thrust of censorship duels. In the United States the difficulties of my older contemporaries were with the post office which had the power to withdraw a class of mailing privileges and thus effectively block circulation (i.e., fulfillment of subscriptions, or wholesale distribution) of troublesome literary materials. In Britain the very thought of a large newsagent, like W.H. Smith and its hundreds of shops throughout the country, turning down a newly published book or, even more disastrously (at least in my own personal case), the next monthly issue of a magazine, was enough to discourage any adventurous plan to come out with some unusual piece of imaginative writing or piece of reportage. In the notorious case of Wayland Young's documentary on London prostitutes, called saucily *Sitting on a Fortune* (and replete with four-letter words), I managed to convince the directors of W.H. Smith that there was no real risk of "consequences" (from the law, or the police, or the Lord Chamberlain's office). I was supported by a persuasive red-ribboned advisory paper in defense of the suspended issue of *Encounter* (September 1959) from the pen of a

---

*   In New York in the 1950s I edited *The Anchor Review,* published by Doubleday (who were then doing Jason Epstein's pioneering *Anchor* paperbooks). In the second number we risked excerpting *Lolita,* plotting with Vladimir Nabokov to avoid or evade the "shadow of censorship" which caused the novel's boycott or simple rejection by every Anglo-American publisher. The "daring novel" had only been printed in Paris in Maurice Girodias' questionable off-color "Olympia Press" list.

We had it critically presented by Columbia professor Fred Dupee, and Nabokov himself gave us a witty postscript ("...I have not re-read *Lolita* since I went through the proofs in the winter of 1954 but I find it to be a delightful presence now that it quietly hangs around the house like a summer day which one knows to he bright behind the haze."). *Anchor Review* was the first to break through the haze. Epstein and I were rather surprised that neither the *Anchor Review* nor the publishers "suffered consequences" of any kind. Or so I thought. No subsequent numbers of the *Anchor Review* were ever published by Doubleday.

prominent Queen's Counsel of the day—in fact it was Gerald Gardiner, Q.C., later the solicitor-general in the Harold Wilson Labour cabinet, who happened to turn the trick. It was a close-run thing, especially when the agitated young author was at first reluctant to use safe synonyms for unsafe sex. We compromised. We did trade-offs in obscenities, and met each other half way.

Ernest Hemingway himself was battle-scarred, and his letters to his editor at Scribner's on the eve of the publication of *A Farewell to Arms* (1929) were recently published by the revamped *New Yorker* with the teasing front-cover caption (and it lured me into buying the copy from the newsstand): "Three Dirty Words." The pre-publication problem with the page-proofs of what was to prove Hemingway's masterpiece was that they were to be excerpted and serialized in *Scribner's Magazine*, and there was the concern of the book's editor (Maxwell Perkins) and the publisher (Mr. Charles Scribner himself) that the U.S. Post Office would "stop delivery if the language or the scene were judged to be too graphic...." (In point of fact the June 1929 issue of *Scribner's* was banned in Boston.) As Hemingway wrote to Perkins from Key West, Florida (in February 1929),

> About omissions. They can only be discussed in the concrete examples. I told you I would not be unreasonable—don't mind leaving out a word if a blank is left or if the omission is unavoidable and as for passages—almost every part of the book depends on almost every other part. You know that....

What was also known was that the writer needed money; the novel would be earning a small fortune (and his advance on royalties was already substantial). Hemingway's exchanges with Perkins show him to be tough, rough, and a little cynical. He notes that "the operation of emasculation is a tiny one," and it "is very simple and easy to perform on men, animals, and books." He adds that "the Price is fine" (sixteen thousand dollars was the magazine's fee) and that "the bull fighter is worth whatever he gets paid."

Maxwell Perkins has a deservedly great reputation as a sensitive editor and his advice to the novelist was touching in its tentativeness: "if you could reduce somewhat the implications of physical aspects in the relationship I doubt that harm would be done. But here I may be influenced by the dangers of censorship." Many months later Hemingway was still trying to work out his own bottom-line "attitude on the publishable or unpublishable word business":

> You know what I want—all we can possibly get. It's a fight with me for the return to the full use of the language and what we accomplish in that direction may be of more value in the end than anything I write. I never use a word if I can avoid it, but if I must have it I know it.

What if the decision was to "emasculate" just a tiny bit?

> Then if you decide it is unpublishable really unpublishable I suppose I must leave it blank. But I want the blanks to indicate what the word is.

Thus was the art of blank indicatives born, and we have seen how far the see-through camouflage with asterisks and hyphens can be perfected.

In the end the emasculation seemed really to be only a tiny operation, and Perkins informed Hemingway,

> the three words we have talked so much about could not be printed, or plainly indicated...except that I do not see how anybody could fail to get the sense.... Everything else in the book goes, of course, as you have put it, exactly.

By July 1929 Hemingway was in Spain, and he wrote from Valencia about the "three words," one of which he stiffly referred to as "the word b——," the other as "c—s——" (and he concedes that he "never expected" they could ever print that one). Then he goes on to the subject of money matters—"You have been swell (what a lousy word to mean so much)"— but not before adding a postscript to his letter which was more Roget than ribald: "What about kicked in the *scrotum*....Remember the last time balls was changed to Horns— isn't that O.K.?" As for the English edition which was being prepared by Jonathan Cape, his publisher in London, he was "disgusted" with their cowardly cutting which he referred to as "yellow deletions."

All in all it was a time that was trying a novelist's soul. Affecting his usual manner young Hemingway put it a little more modestly: "I'm a Professional Writer now—than which there isn't anything lower...." But the other news (now from "Paris, France") was good and bad: "It's been raining all day....Haven't had a drink for a week."

By the way, the "Three Dirty Words" that the *New Yorker* had promised us turned up fresh and unadorned only in the Editor's preface to the article. There she coolly explained, "The three words 'fucking,' 'cocksucker,' and 'balls' caused considerable concern."[59]

When we contemplate the busts in our contemporary hall of f-word fame, the gallery is impressive: from John Osborne and Norman Mailer to Edna O'Brien and Germaine Greer. At the outset the battleground was on the printed page of novels and plays in the grand liberating tradition of D.H. Lawrence, and subsequently of Hubert Selby and in Terry Southern's green-covered Olympia novels in Maurice Girodias' Paris press. These famous victories having been won, the triumphal aftermath was celebrated in literary journalism, especially in feature interviews where the conversation is quoted "like it was spoke," free and unfettered in its spiciness.

It appeared to be, as I think, a case of the prurient in pursuit of the profane; or, perhaps, the other way round. Who takes the erotic inititative is unimportant among consenting adults. In any case we have to do with, again (as always) a complicitous arrangement—not between the reader and the reporter, an understanding which I have referred to as "participatory obscenity"—but between the writer and the journalist, between the voluble interviewee and the avid note-taker. The final salacious touch as to orthography and frequency is in the hands of the newspaperman, or his sub-editor; but the literary personality (and here handsome female authors are most desirable) provides the salt wherewith the story can be salted.

The peppery playwright John Osborne never failed to spice up the public prints. Even beyond the grave (as we have seen) the voice can be heard cursing and hurling rich and quotable imprecations. At the recent funeral of another English dramatist, Robert Bolt, who otherwise phrased his thoughts in abstractly elegant prose, there was the familiar "explosion" which has become the commonplace badge of honor for writers of candor and integrity.

The memorial meeting for Robert Bolt, as reported in the *Guardian* (6 June 1995), was held at St. James' Church, Piccadilly, and the London congregation of mourners and fans heard excerpts from his well-known works (*A Man for All Seasons*, about Sir Thomas More; and the film scripts of *Lawrence of Arabia* and *Dr. Zhivago*). Among the speakers was his wife, Sarah Miles, who was the star of other celebrated films based on Bolt scripts, *Ryan's Daughter* and another on the love life of Lady Caroline Lamb. The *Guardian* man knew a good quote when he heard one, and he wrote in his opening lead: "The actress Sarah Miles stood near the altar of St. James', Piccadilly, yesterday and said explosively: 'Fucking hell'!" It may not have exactly been an historic breakthrough in recorded London speech; still, as we were instructed, "It may well have been a modest first for the English church but the rector, the Rev. Donald Reeves, didn't turn a hair. The congregation laughed affectionately." Did Sarah Miles need an excuse? Under the unusual circumstances of sacred soil and memorial remembrance, evidently she did. We were re-assured that "Ms. Miles had the most flawless of a widow's alibis for her language." She was quoting the first words spoken by her husband a year after being partially paralyzed by a stroke. Fantasizing, as was his dramatic wont, about the history of convalescence, he was drawn to the first phrase every recovering stroke victim uttered—for it was (as in his own case) "a good phrase to get your tongue around. So much so that he used it whenever he found himself—unfamiliarly—wrestling with words until he died in February [1995], aged 70."[60] It could indeed be considered a modest first, for this time—and it is rare in the vulgar history of expletives—the f-word came armed with a medical certificate.

Otherwise any piece of paper will do, shorthand scribbles in a reporter's notebook or, better still, a crackling tape recording. In any case the newspaper of record has the last word on what has or has not been said, and how (and how often) it should be spelled out.

I once conducted an interview with Henry Miller in the days before the printing of profanity in our newspaper culture became seemly and stylish. I am afraid I winced at the time at the profusion of f- (and other)-words. But, I imagined, I heard through the still sad music of obscenity a thoughtful man offering incisive reflections on our "air-conditioned nightmare" as seen through his "cosmological eye." And if they were somewhat paraphrased (which I dutifully did) they might, on publication, provide some important testimony on the state of life and letters in our time.

Today the feature story would take a rather different turn. I would be obliged —by an editor, or his addictive house-style, or even more by the *Zeitgeist*, the spirit-of-the-age—to give a saucy sampling of the remarks that actually punctuated the conversation. In the end I would have wound up, in free preference, with a couple of dozen asterisks rather than as many po-faced hyphens. It would have constituted an arbitrary editorial selection, and an uncertain and cowardly rationing of the speech natural to macho men—for which neither I nor Henry Miller (at least for this) would have made it into our gallery in the hall of ill fame.

One Newspaper Comes Out of the Closet

There are, inevitably, a limited number of opportunities to engage in an illicit traffic in such suggestive abbreviations. Twenty-some letters of the alphabet, and you are done with—the c-word which is still lusty and attractive (meaning only a resurgence of Communism behind the ex-Iron Curtain); the s-word which is still foul and to be avoided (but the *s* stands merely for Statism and evidently F.A. Hayek and Milton Friedman got it right). One can also record coy references to the forbidden or dangerous or unfashionable use of the l-word (for Liberalism), the p-word (for the poor or Poverty), and the like. In the end, after such fun and games the newspaper headline-writer (in cahoots with, preferably, a taboo-breaking female journalist) goes for broke. Above a long feature by Valerie Grove, illustrated by a photo-panel of other distinguished women (Florence Nightingale, Germaine Greer, etc.) one sub-editor devised a six-column *Times* headline:

THE F-WORD—AND WHY WOMEN SHOULD NOT BE ASHAMED TO USE IT

Was this the ultimate breakthrough? Were all the Lady Chatterleys in the land being given august advice from the old Thunderer of the Establishment to speak loud and clear and to pull no prudish punches, to stammer no stuttering f-f-f's? Not at all. This was the last coyness—a blockbuster of f-word suggestiveness, with names and faces to match—but the actual subject of the story was...*feminism.* The word recently has been falling into political disuse, even disrepute. Many of the feminist demands have come to full fruition in the last decades, and women with more civil rights and recognition than ever before in history are increasingly reluctant to use the old slogan. Have they no pride? A gender revolution has almost been won: still there is a growing antipathy to fly the movement's flag. Ms. Valerie Grove presses the point in a number of *Times* interviews, and she recommends to "SAY IT LOUD," viz. *"We are feminists. Without it* [presumably, the word, the movement, the great cause] *we would not be here* [that is, high in politics, way up there in the media, near the top in the business board-rooms] *and aren't we looking good."*

After such disingenuous duplicitous punning, what room for verbal maneuver remains? The taboo has finally to be faced front on, and so it has come to pass.[61]

It is always easier in such transitions to have celebrities involved in a scandalizing turning point. An ordinary actor may get censured for "indecent language"—or a run-of-the-mill footballer sent off the field for "insulting" the referee—and nowadays a newspaper sub-editor doesn't even bother to raise the newsworthy question about what was actually said (and why, and when). But a glittering Hollywood star, a powerful Washington politico, and in England a Royal (preferably in the first ten in the succession line to the Queen) will do very nicely indeed. Two recent Royal incidents changed quantity into quality in the upsurge of a four-letterized culture we have been examining.

The first involved the Duchess of York in a global television show, in which she was only a passive player in the drama (and, in any case, she was really only a commoner and a divorcée at that). The prestigious MTV pop-culture awards were being given in Milan before a live-TV audience of hundreds of millions with the duchess presiding. She gave one Best-Video prize to a group known as *Massive Attack* and, true to form, the band's leader, a youngish man called Del Naja and known as "3-D," exploded. One newspaper account reported (in November 1998): "She offered her hand but the gesture was rejected and Del Naja announced: 'Someone's having a ******* laugh, **** you very much.'"[61] Ms. "Fergie" Ferguson, as she once was, was visibly appalled at the language, but she attempted to laugh it off; and later she approached the band backstage and simply asked,

"What's all this about?" Del Naja, 32, retorted: "**** off!..."
  Asked later about his behaviour, the singer said: "What the **** has she got to do with music for a start?...It's just ******* ridiculous."

It was evidently a misguided blow struck for political purity, or at least the class integrity, of the "youth culture." The *Telegraph* reported that the next day the Duchess was "very good natured" about the swearing incident which had been recorded with such manic editorial attention to indecorous detail.

But the nature of the beast or the beastliness was aroused; and when Prince Charles, a few days later, was involved in another incident in which he actually had a speaking part (if only a word or two), we found ourselves moving towards something of a grand denouément in the drama of how an immemorial taboo is broken, nay shattered, in our very own time. The Prince of Wales, the middle-aged Royal who would still be King, had said "bloody."

In a response to a heckler at some opening at which he was officiating, Prince Charles shouted back: "Why don't you come and open the bloody thing yourself?" Not even the *Times* could give credence to the expressions of polite shock and conventional horror at what was once taken to be a blasphemous swear word ("By our lady!").* Newspaper editors used the occasion to ruminate about the straits of the language. Photographers dug out old stills of Audrey Hepburn playing Liza Doolittle in the film version of *My Fair Lady* —which resonated G.B. Shaw's most famous "bloody" in his play *Pygmalion* (1913). The *Times* itself, once so reluctant to publish any kind of photograph where an elegant paragraph of English prose would do, now filled half a newspaper page with snapshots of William Shakespeare (the onlie begetter of so many obscenities); the foul-mouthed pop star, the late Sid Vicious; and Kenneth Tynan (who had dented the BBC taboo on the f-

---

* Of *bloody* it has been said that it is barely acceptable in Britain, is the essence (albeit embarrassingly so) of the national vocabulary in Australia; and of virtually no importance whatsoever in America. As an intensifier, its use is universal, meaning: *exceedingly*, *abominably*, or *desperately*. However, it is good to be reminded, in a time of increasingly one-tone vocabularies, of other impressive and graphic intensifiers that once appealed to the imagination of the so-called "rough classes," saving them from the standard repetitive obscenities. Green suggests: "jolly, awfully, terribly, devilish, deuced, damned, ripping, rattling, thumping, stunning, thundering, etc."

As for the Australian usage, a 19th-century English writer (Alexander Marjoribanks, *Travels in New South Wales*, 1847) noted that he heard a bullock driver use it 27 times in 15 minutes. At that rate of speech he calculated that over a 50-year period some 18,200,000 repetitions of "the disgusting word" would have been produced. (See Jonathon Green, *Slang Down the Ages*, pp. 143-4.)

The use of the *F*-word in the sound-track of Quentin Tarantino's Holywood films is necessarily rather more concentrated and hence speedier; I have calculated, in some scenes, "27 times in 5 minutes"; and if this style of *gangsta rap* persists for a half-century, the Australian mark of some 18 million would long since have been overtaken.

word). This was conspicuously opportunistic but still within the realm of what we have been outlining as the current conventions of English-language newspaper culture. Even the headline of its descriptive-interpretive-etymologico-feature piece which warned EXPLETIVES NOT DELETED was marked by the characteristic mixture of coyness and cowardice which keeps titillation available for occasional journalistic pleasure:

> From gosh to damn to *!*!*!: how we have come used to swearing

The glyph was double-edged, for it reappeared rather more daringly elsewhere on the page in a cartoon wherein a figure looking like Queen Elizabeth II is christening (as she often does) a new ship, and saying with Royal sourness, "I name this ship F@!!%!" Like son, like mother. In fact this was a good moment to resurrect the oldie about the last, dying words of King George VI, expiring in the Royal bed at the unhappy English Channel resort called Bognor Regis—"Bugger Bognor!" Still, the recent incident turned out to be more than that, indeed a fairly serious occasion.

For the *Times* the instructive lesson of the morning remained the acknowledgement of the power of taboo words to shock even in a relatively uninhibited society. True, many of our famous works of library reference still carry no entry between "*fuchsite*" and "*fucoid*." But it added, disingenuously (the significant note of the day),

> And most publications, including *The Times*, print the 'four-letter' words rarely and reluctantly and with asterisks for the last three letters. This subterfuge cannot deceive any readers. But the naked words still upset many.

This was, of course, as far as *Times* practice is conceived, patently untrue, for its editorial record has been embarrassingly inconsistent about hiding its taboos under circumlocution and euphemism.

Whatever the house style may or may not permit or enjoin, the maintenance of double standards has persisted. Actually in the official *Times Style Book*, it instructs journalists with respect to "four-letter words"—a euphemism dating from 1934 – that they should be avoided because they upset many readers; but that "in direct quotes and where they are essential to the story" obscenities should be styled thus: "f***," "c***," etc. In point of fact the *Times* (Robin Young) author of the long, historic, half-page account of "Expletives" suggests gingerly for us to "count the asterisks in the remainder of the piece and you will be able to see how we are doing...." "Not very f——g well," commented one reader, but then he was grateful for the concession that using asterisks (and even little dashes) to disguise four-letter words "only heightens their illicit status."

In the last analysis, could it be that hell hath no fury left, at least no ready lingo with which to express it? The *Times* proceeds to take stock, in an inventory which moves from old religious blasphemy to metaphors derived from Anglo-Saxon bodily functions and anatomical parts to (in Geoffrey Gorer's phrase) a new "pornography of death." In the future, speculates the *Times*' leading article on "BLANKETY BLANK," trying hard to identify unmentionable topics which are still available to a rude vocabulary, the most shocking curse may be, "*You, putrefying old corpse*'." Surely the *Times*' editors can think up more pungent, less necrophobic scurrilities, but they do at least coolly confirm the staple elements which are still available and still enjoy "unfamiliar notoriety":

> The short words definitely with us since Anglo-Saxon times are "shit", "turd", and "arse". "Fart" is an unproven probable. "Piss" arrived with Norman French. "Fuck" (first recorded 1503) and 'cunt' are of uncertain origin...[63]

I detect a slight hesitation in the *Times*' man to instruct his readers "all the way"; and Robin Young admitted that (in his own self-defeating phrase) "there are people, of course, people who frankly do not give a f***" about any of this. Still, there is a little bit more that we need to know, and the *Times* obliges us:

> Overemployment of the participle "fucking"—now often used to precede every noun—has already led to its being described as the British Unit of Excess but "fuck" is in fact only the third worst word in the Broadcasting Standards Commission's current league table. It is worsted by "cunt" (already a source of lubricious enjoyment when Shakespeare had Hamlet slyly referring to "country matters") and the inelegant Americanism "motherfucker" (first recorded 1956)...

As always in these exercises of lexicographical derring-do, as if a delicate line between virginity and defloration were being transgressed, the brave transmitter of such argot words regrets, or repines, or becomes otherwise sweetly conscience-stricken and begs forgiveness for, possibly, having offended. On the historic, decisive day when it came out, or let it all hang out, or told it like it was, or whatever the current euphemism for candor may at the moment be, the *Times* takes refuge in a classic literary anecdote. Dr. Samuel Johnson was being congratulated by two English ladies on leaving all the dirty words out of his famous eighteenth-century dictionary. The lexicographer countered, "What! my dears! Then you have been looking for them!"[64] One day soon nobody will have to waste a precious moment looking for them; they will be everywhere.

From the narrow but long-established bases in the language's sexual and obscene areas, the f-word (and related expletives) has been colonizing other vocabularies. These include literature, politics, cinema, journalism, and even, in straight-talking circles, polite conversation. It is on the verge of moving on to become an indispensable part of public discourse, ubiquitously and almost universally deemed appropriate. We shall see in the next volume the causes and consequences of this oceanic change in the tides of style and meanings, and how the unshackled language of journalism is faring with its new-found liberty and license.

Notes

Preface

1. Professor Benjamin Nelson, who died in 1977, was the teacher who first opened the world of scholarship to many young (and very provincial) students at City College. He wrote a major work on *The Idea of Usury* (1969) which he modestly referred to as "only a long footnote" to the ideas of Max Weber on the Protestant ethos and the rise of capitalism. He was also author of a book on Freud and a collection of essays. I will be subsequently referring to him in the analysis of how our papers cover the story of an Islamic ethos and the rise of capitalist societies in the Middle East.
2. H.L. Mencken (1880-1956): his most enduring work is his three volumes on *The American Language* (1919/1936). His memoirs of his "newspaper days," as well as the anthologies of his articles from his monthly journal, *The American Mercury*, are replete with stimulating remarks on "newspaper culture."
3. The text-book by Cohen and Nagel which we treasured, studying philosophy in our student days, was entitled *An Introduction to Logic and the Scientific Method* (1934).

    Of the two "old-timers" at *The New Yorker* one, the versatile humorist, Frank Sullivan (1892-1976), is largely forgotten. A.J. Liebling (1904-1963) is still remembered, not only for his witty studies of "The Wayward Press" but also for other pieces of reportage (on sporting events, on restaurants serving grand food, and especially on World War II, *e.g. Normandy Revisited* (1958) and *The Road Back to Paris* (1944)). The anthologies of their "best writings" are still worth looking into, especially Sullivan's pieces on "Mr. Arbuthnot" and his adventures among clichés. They both figure prominently in the histories of *The New Yorker* by Dale Kramer (1951) and Brendan Gill (1975).
4. Dwight Macdonald (1906-1982) left the Henry Luce establishment in the 1930s and emerged as a revolutionary Marxist (of the Trotskyist persuasion). Because of his achievement and talents in journalism, as an editor of *Fortune* Magazine, he brought an unprecedented freshness and vigor to the tired rehashing of old dogmas which passed for prose on the Left. There is a biography by Michael Wreszin (1994), many studies of his

career—by Gregory D. Sumner (1996), Stephen Whitfield (1984), etc.—and a number of readable anthologies of old articles: *Against the American Grain* (1962), *Discriminations* (1974), *Memoirs of a Revolutionist* (1957; reissued as *Politics Past*, 1970), among others. His film criticism, especially that written for *Esquire* Magazine from 1960 to 1966, had a large, devoted following, and was collected in a paperback, *Dwight Macdonald on Movies* (1969).

Jacques Barzun (1907-), well-known as an historian of ideas—I heard him lecture when I attended Columbia University. Among his widely-read books: *Darwin, Marx, Wagner* (1958), *The Use and Abuse of Art* (1974), *Teacher in America* (1945), and *Berlioz and the Romantic Century* (1950). Of special importance to this book is his introductory essay to the volume on *New York Times'* newspaper style by Theodore Bernstein (who wrote the *Times'* style book of the day, *Watch Your Language: A lively, informal guide to better writing, emanating from the News Room of The New York Times* (1958)).

On Sidney Hook (1902-1989) and the "culture of controversy," see his calm and sovereign autobiography, recounting a thousand stormy arguments of a long, polemical life: *Out of Step* (1987).

5. There is a brief history of *Der Monat* which was published in Germany: Marko Martin, *Orwell, Koestler und all die anderen: M.J. Lasky und "Der Monat"* (Mut Verlag, 1998). There are many histories of *Encounter* "in progress" but none has yet been published. There is also a representative (and massive) anthology of memorable articles published in *Der Monat* (1948-1985), put together by Marko Martin for Beltz-Athenäum (Weinheim, 2000) under the title *Ein Fenster zur Welt* ("A Window to the World").

6. Andrew Sullivan, "You Cannot Be Serious: Why do the British chatter so wittily but say nothing of any substance?," *Sunday Times*, 26 November 1995, News Review, p. 5. Michael Kinsley, *Prospect*, October 1995 (London), p. 4.)

I have often written on the "transatlantic factor," and the reader may find a useful and, I suspect, revealing history of American attitudes towards Europe (on Jefferson, Hawthorne, Henry Adams, Henry James, *et al.*) in an essay published in Arthur Schlesinger, Jr., and Morton White's anthology of *Paths in American Thought* (1963). It originally appeared in *Encounter*: "America and Europe: Transatlantic Images" (January 1962, pp. 66-78).

7. Jean-Jacques Rousseau, *Essai sur l'origine des langues: où il est traité de la mélodie et de l'imitation musicale*, available in a paperback edition, published in 1993 (Flammarion, Paris); and the remarks by R.A. Wilson, in his *Miraculous Birth of Language* (1937), chapter III: "Rousseau (1712-1778): The Old and the New.")

Part 1: Question of Style
Epigraphs

1. Epictetus, *Discourses* [Loeb ed., tr. Oldfarther, 1925], vol. I, p. 285.
2. Canto III, 1xxxvii. *Works*, p.684.

1. Words Win, Language Loses

1. *International Herald-Tribune* (hereafter abbreviated as *IHT*), "Seventy-Five Years Ago," 14 November 1994.
2. *IHT*, 29-30 October 1994.
3. *New York Post*, 25 April 1996.
4. *IHT*, "Amex," 19 September 1996, pp. 13, 15. *Agence France-Presse/IHT*, 19 September 1996, p. 7. Samantha Power, "The Reporter of the Crime," *Washington Post/IHT*, ? 1995, ed. page.
5. *IHT*, 5 January 1995, p. 1. *AP/IHT*, 12 April 1995, p. 3. *Washington Post/IHT*, "Nato," 19 September 1995, p. 6.
6. Alessandra Stanley, "Russian Wrangle," *New York Times* (hereafter abbreviated as *NYT/IHT*, 9 May 1995, p. 2.
7. *IHT*, 19 September 1994, p. 11.
8. Dave Barry, "Official Olympic Grammar," *Miami Herald/IHT*, 22-23 June 1996, p. 24.
9. "Usage and Abusage," Fritz Spiegl's weekly column in the *Daily Telegraph*, 24 August 1996.
10. Minette Marrin, "It is obvious that abortion is bad for you," *Sunday Telegraph*, 20 October 1996, p. 39. Ms. Marrin's point is not heavily polemical, going on to say merely that "Even the best regulated of abortions carry the risk of infection and sterility" (among other greater risks); and that the research on this subject is given, for obvious reasons, disproportionately little attention in the Western press.
11. Robert Burchfield, *The New Fowler's Modern English Usage* (1996, 3rd ed.), p. 738. Burchfield, *The Spoken Word* (1981). Kingsley Amis, *The King's English* (1997), pp. 217-219.
12. *Times*, 18 May 1992, quoted in Burchfield/Fowler, ibid., p. 737.
13. Letters, *Times*, 14 August 1998, p. 14.
14. Frederic Raphael, "Equaller, Hopefully," *Times Literary Supplement*, 16 October 1998, pp. 7-8.
15. Keith Waterhouse, column in the *Daily Mail*, 17 August 1998.
16. Frank Johnson, "Notebook," *Daily Telegraph*, 15 August 1998, p. 18.
17. Andrew Roberts, "Triumph of the plastic language," *Sunday Times*, 16 August 1998 (News Review), p. 5.
18. Simon Jenkins, "To split or not to split," *Times*, 15 August 1998 p. 18.
19. Tom Utley, "New Dictionary to boldly give approval for split infinitives," *Daily Telegraph*, 13 August 1998, p. 6, and also his "Sorry, Ms. Pearsall, but up with this I will not put," 14 August, p. 20. "Dictionaries redefine

the word 'marketing'," *Times*, 14 August 1998; *Daily Mail*, 13 August 1998, p. 21. "Why today's writers are split over a quest of infinitives," *Evening Standard*, 13 August 1998, p. 7. Frank Johnson, "Perhaps Shakespeare was only dreaming," *Daily Telegraph*, 15 August 1998, p. 18. Simon Jenkins, "To split or not to split," *Times*, 15 August 1998, p. 18. Andrew Roberts, "Triumph of the plastic language," *Sunday Times*, 16 August 1998, p. 5 (News Review).

20. Henry Louis Gates, Jr., "Thirteen Ways of Looking at a Black Man," *New Yorker*, 23 October 1995, p. 56.

2. The Equality of Sentences

1. Nicholas Bagnall, "To Who It May Concern," *Sunday Telegraph*, 27 October 1996, p. 36. *New Fowler's Modern English Usage* (ed. Robert Burchfield, 1996), published by the Oxford University Press.
2. *New Fowler's Modern English* (ed. Burchfield, 1996), p. 457.
3. Christopher Lehmann-Haupt, review of Fowler, *NYT/IHT*, 6 January 1997, p. 9.

3. The Slang of an In-Lingo

1. *Daily Telegraph*, 11 October 1994.
2. Dr. Steve Jones, in *Daily Telegraph*, 12 October 1994.
3. John Morrish in the *Daily Telegraph Magazine*, 1 October 1994.
4. Review of "Pal Joey," in *Daily Telegraph*, 12 October 1994.
5. Edward Stourton, in *Sunday Telegraph*, 9 October 1994.
6. Barry James, in the *IHT*, 20 April 1995.
7. Mike Zwerin, in *IHT*, 23 June 1994.
8. *Sunday Times*, 26 June 1994, p. 6.
9. *Washington Post/IHT*, "'Cool/Cooling' Stones, 3 July 1996, pp. 1, 12. For the once "in" style in New York avant-garde art, see the exhibition catalogue entitled *The Birth of the Cool* (Cantz, Zurich, 1997).
10. David Denby, "Buried Alive: Annals of Popular Culture," *New Yorker*, 15 July 1996, p. 50, 52.
11. *Horace* (tr. Wickham, 1903), pp. 343-44.
12. "A Few Words from the Victors," *Financial Times*, 24 November 1997, p. 10.
13. Andrew Gowers, "Prize-winners in the business of jargon," *Financial Times*, 24 November 1997, p. 10.
14. *IHT*, "Business: Market Intelligence," 21 November 1997, p. 13.
15. *IHT*, 29 September 1995.
16. AP report, in *IHT*, 10 April 1996, p. 3.
17. *New York Times/IHT*, 16 April 1996, "Christopher Reeve: The Will of Superman."
18. *Washington Post/IHT*, 5 April 1996.

19. "Behind Albright's Canceled Visit: Irked Cambodians," *Washington Post/ IHT*, 28-29 June 1997, p. 5.
20. KR (Kurt Reumann) in the *Frankfurter Allgemeine Zeitung*, 17 October 1995, p. 3.
21. George Vecsey, *NYT/IHT*, 9 November 1995.
22. *IHT*, 7 June 1995.
23. *N.Y. Times/IHT*, 27 February 1995.
24. *NYT/IHT*, 26 September 1994, p. 22.
25. Christopher Fildes, in *The Spectator*, 2 March 1997. *Daily Telegraph*, 1 March 1997, p. 7.
26. *New York Times*, 27 September 1994.
27. *Times*, 17 November 1995, p. 47.

4. Sort of Suspicious, Kind of Guilty

1. Quentin Tarantino, *Natural Born Killers* (Faber, 1995). *Natural Born Killers: The Strange, Wild Ride of Mickey and Mallory Knox* (Penguin ed., 1994). The Signet paperback's credits are given thus: "A Novel by John August and James Hamsher. Based on a story by Quentin Tarantino. And a Screenplay by David Veloz & Richard Rutowski & Oliver Stone. With an Introduction by Oliver Stone." Kind of enough authors to be getting on with...

5. Of Plastic Prose, in Bits and Pieces

1. *NYT/IHT*, 20 September 1996, p.3, Russell Baker, "A Press Monument," *NYT/IHT*, 25 September 1996, p. 22.
2. *New York Times/IHT*, "Who Will Win the House?," 14 October 1996, p. 3.
3. R.W. Apple, Jr., "Campaign," *New York Times/IHT*, 8 October 1996, p. 1, 10.
4. Nelson Warfield, Dole's chief spokesman, *New York Times/IHT*, 23 October 1996, p. 3.
5. "Real 'Character' Issues," *Washington Post/IHT*, 19-20 October 1996, p. 6.
6. "A Decorous Debate," *New York Times/IHT*, 8 October 1996, p.8.
7. *Washington Post/IHT*, "Dole Gambit Fails," 25 October 1996, pp. 1, 3.
8. Howard Kurtz, "The Dole Affair: A Campaign Story That Wasn't," *Washington Post/IHT*, 14 November 1996, p. 3.
9. Maureen Dowd, *NYT/IHT*, "Limboing with Clinton," 11 October 1996, p. 9.
10. Maureen Dowd, "Inside the Oval Office," *NYT/IHT*, 14 January 1997, p. 8.
11. Maureen Dowd, "All This Talk About Sex...," *New York Times/IHT*, 12 June 1997, p. 9.
12. Maureen Dowd, "Columnist Tells All, For a Bargain Price," *New York Times/IHT*, 19 March 1997, p. 9. Karl Meyer (ed.), *Pundits, Poets & Wits: an Omnibus of American Newspaper Columns* (1990).

13. Maureen Dowd, "Papa as Product: It Is Not Good," *NYT/IHT*, 14 April 1997, p. 8.

14. Dowd, "Counting the Days," *NYT/IHT*, 28 April 1997, p. 8.

15. Neil Strauss, "Oh, All Those Wacky Celebrities!," *New York Times*, 14 November 1996, p. 15.

16. Joe Murray, "Proud to Live in America," *IHT*, 6 November 1996, p. 11.

17. Thomas Friedman, "Saudi Arabia's Strange Moves and Some Possible Explanations," *New York Times/IHT*, 8 November 1996, p. 8.

18. *New York Times*, Sunday ed., 16 June 1996, p. E 7.

19. Frank Rich, *New York Times/IHT*, 7 November 1996, p. 11.

20. Frank Rich, "Scientology, Hollywood and the Power of Money," *NYT/IHT*, 28 January 1997, p. 9.

21. Thomas L. Friedman, "To Counter the Iraqi Dictator? Attack His Ample Cash Flow," *New York Times/IHT*, 14 October 1996, p. 8.

22. Thomas L. Friedman, "Clinton Had a Honeymoon," *New York Times/IHT*, 24 October 1996, p. 10; "Bibi's Moment of Truth," *New York Times*, September 29,1996, Section 4, p. 15.

23. "Presidential Campaign Bucks and Stutters Into Slow Motion," *Washington Post/IHT*, 4 October 1996, p. 3.

24. Friedman, "For Russians, Iraq and Iran Aren't the Problem," *New York Times/IHT*, 2 December 1997, p. 8.

25. Thomas L. Friedman, "The Only Option May Be Bombs and More Bombs," *NYT/IHT*, 2 February 1998, p. 8.

26. Thomas Friedman, "Get Real on Russia," *New York Times*, 19 June 1996, p. A23; "Turkey Wings It," 26 June 1996, p. A23.

27. Thomas L. Friedman, "Wise up and Help China Adopt the Rules of Law," *NYT/IHT*, 27 May 1997, p. 8.

28. Tim Weiner, "Clinton's Education on Defense," *NYT/IHT*, 29 October 1996, p. 9.

29. Thomas L. Friedman, "The Arab Burden," *NYT*, 20 November 1996, p. A25.

30. Thomas L. Friedman, "Hong Kong," *NYT/IHT*, 16 December 1996, p. 10.

31. Thomas Friedman, *NYT/IHT*, "Unrest in Morocco," 24 February 1997, p. 6.

32. Thomas L. Friedman, "Grand Bargain," *NYT/IHT*, 28 October 1996, p. 8.

33. Friedman, "Watch and Help as China Acquires a Free Press," *NYT/IHT*, 13 January 1997, p. 8.

34. Friedman, "A Fateful Moment," *NYT/IHT*, 6 January 1997, p. 8.

35. Thomas Friedman, "Egypt Set to Join the Global Economy" and "Europe Has 18 More Months to Get Its Bosnia Act Together," *NYT/IHT*, 14 November 1996, p. 10; 25 November 1996, p. 8.

36. Friedman, "Italian Vices Turn to Virtues," *NYT/IHT*, 13 February 1997, p. 8.

37. *NYT/IHT*, 11 January 1999, p. 8.

38. *New York Times/IHT*, 25 March 1997, p.8. *New York Times/IHT*, 4 April 1997, p. 8.

39. Jim Hoagland, "What About This Campaign, You Ask?," *Washington Post/ IHT*, 14 October 1996, p. 8.
40. "Chancellor's Flirting," *Daily Telegraph*, 27 November 1996, p. 2.
41. Matthew Parris, *Times*, 14 October 1996, p. 22.
42. Adam Nicolson, "Perpetual emotion...uses cold calculation to get the tears flowing," *Sunday Telegraph*, 6 October 1996, p. 32.
43. Joel Achenbach, "Help for the Campaign-Impaired," *Washington Post/ IHT*,17 October 1996, p. 11.
44. William Safire, "Are Soccer Moms the Key to the Election?," *New York Times/IHT*, 28 October 1996, p. 9.
45. Mark Steyn, in the *Sunday Telegraph*, "Fight an election...," 20 October 1996, p. 31.
46. Ian Thomsen, "Soccer? Too Much Like Real Life for American Tastes," *International Herald Tribune*, 19-20 October 1996, p. 26.
47. John Carlin, "Soccer...a golden goal to relish," *The Independent*, 22 October 1996, p. 24.
48. *NYT/IHT*, "For Football Fans, It's Freaky and Fun," 7 January 1997, p. 1, 18.
49. David J. Morrow, "What's My Line? Try an Easier Question," *NYT/IHT*, 14 October 1996, p. 16.
50. Patricia Volk, "Plastic Is Us," *NYT/IHT*, 16 October 1996, p. 11.

6. Life-Style Crosses the Ocean, and Returns

1. "Paradigm Lost: U.N. Takes Heat as Cambodia Slides Toward Civil War," *Wall Street Journal*, 7 July 1997, p. 1.
2. Minette Marrin, "The rich are different: they always want more," in the *Sunday Telegraph*, 29 October 1995.
3. *Los Angeles Times/IHT*, "Charles T. Powers, 53, L.A. Times Reporter," 4 October 1996, p. 6.
4. Douglas Martin, "Deathstyles of the Rich and Famous," *New York Times*, 12 January 1997, "News of the Week," section 4, Sunday, page 2.
5. Re: "famous economist," see Eli Ginzberg, "Choice of the Term 'Life Style' by One Research Group," *Journal of Individual Psychology*, vol. 23 (1967), p. 213.
6. From A. Van Kamm, in *Existential Foundations of Psychology* (1966), p. 239.
7. Ulf Poschardt, *DJ-Culture* (Hamburg, 1996). *Frankfurter Allgemeine Zeitung*, "Kratzer auf der Platte," 3 July 1996, p. 32.
8. Maureen Dowd, "Behind and Inside the Oval Office," *New York Times/ IHT*, 14 January 1997, p. 8.
9. Mike Zwerin, "Bob Brozman," *IHT*, 3 November 1995.
10. John Bryant, in *Times*, "Taking the game of life into extra time," 23 Nov. 1995, p. 46.
11. Full text of the BBC interview with the Princess of Wales, in *Sun*, 22 Nov. 1995, p. 6.

12. Laura Colby, in the *IHT*, 8 Nov. 1995.
13. "Of Walls and Wanting: Martha and Ralph just don't sell paints—it's a major lifestyle fetish!," *Newsweek*, 6 January 1996, pp. 50-51.
14. Linda Hales, "Forget Chintz, This Year It's Provence," *Washington Post/ IHT*, 12 August 1997, p. 7.
15. Mike Zwerin, on "Chris Blackwell," *IHT*, 18 September 1997, p. 26.

7. Teutonics, or Refighting World War II

1. *Evening Standard*, 14 July 1995.
2. Benedict Nightingale in *Times* (London), 14 March 1996.
3. Petronella Wyatt, in the *Sunday Telegraph*, 25 September 1994.
4. *Times*, 26 April 1996, "Touch of Leather: A 30-Years War for football's Holy Grail."
5. *Daily Telegraph*, "An off-the-ball incident as press seeks World Cup goal," 27 April 1996.
6. *Daily Telegraph*, "How Casement the 'Martyr' was Exposed," 19 October 1995, p. 9.
7. *The Standard*, 12 July 1995.
8. Waldemar Janusczak, "Brave new worlds," *Sunday Times*, 22 June 1997 (Culture), p. 11/7.

Part 2: The Art of Quotation

Epigraphs

1. Ralph Waldo Emerson, "History", in *The Portable Emerson* (eds. Bode/ Cowley, 1981), pp. 115-137. C.S. Lewis, *Studies in Words* (1960), p. 313. Charles Lamb, *Last Essays of Elia*, Penguin ed., p. 229.

8. The Little Goose Feet

1. *The Lynching of Language: Gender, Politics, & Power in the Hill-Thomas Hearings* (ed. Ragan/Bystrom/Kaid/Beck, 1996), pp. 28, 32-33, 139, 261-2.
2. Clines, *IHT*, 3 October 1994.
3. *Wall Street Journal*, 27 February 1995.
4. "Teen-Age Sweethearts," *New York Times*, 18 November 1996, pp. B1, B5. "Teens Face Death," *New York Post*, 19 November 1996, p. 4.

9. TV and Press "War"

1. *Times* (London), 27 December 1994.
2. "Trash TV," *Independent*, 18 July 1995.
3. A.A. Gill, "Lights, Camera, Faction," in the Culture section, *Sunday Times*, 2 March 1997, p. 2.
4. *IHT*, 1 March 1995.

5. *New York Times* dispatches by Louis Uchitelle and Michael Specter, *IHT*, 19 August 1996.
6. *Washington Post/IHT*, "Needing a Transplant, Japanese Must Leave," 23 July 1996, p. 1, 8. *IHT*, "Bumpy Road for Europe," pp. 1, 8.
7. *New York Times/IHT*, "Microsoft Shifts to the Net," 23 July 1996, p. 11.
8. Chris Hedges, "Bitter Kosovo," *NYT/IHT*, 18 February 1997, pp. 1, 5.
9. Christine Spolar, "The Polish Question: Am I a Jew?," *Washington Post/ IHT*, 4 March 1997, pp. 1, 10.
10. Victor Lewis-Smith, in the *London Evening Standard*, 31 July 1995.
11. Rupert Widdicombe, "The Bare-faced Cheek of It," *Sunday Times* (Culture), 31 August 1997, pp. 2-3.
12. Tom Shone, "Thong and Dance," *Sunday Times* (Culture), 31 August 1997, p. 4.
13. Elisabeth Leigh, "Are TV People Oversexed?," in the *Evening Standard* (London, 3 April 1996), p. 52. "When Kissing Had to Stop": The title is, of course, a famous line from Robert Browning's poem "A Toccata of Galuppi's":"What of soul was left, I wonder, when the kissing had to stop?" It was given additional coinage, and a sharply political one at that, when it was borrowed for the title of a brilliant, if controversial, novel by the late Constantine Fitzgibbon.

The roman à clef was "inspired" by an awkward incident in London at an *Encounter* party when I made an attempt to introduce my friend Fitzgibbon to another guest—Kingsley Martin, the celebrated editor of the left-wing *New Statesman & Nation.* The cocktail party was, as I recall, at the Mount Street flat of Kenneth Tynan (and I had rented it for the year Tynan was away doing his year's stint as the theater critic for *The New Yorker*). *Encounter's* relations with the *New Statesman* had not been, under Irving Kristol's editorship, very friendly; still, in 1958, when I replaced Kristol as Stephen Spender's co-editor, Kingsley Martin turned up, formally speaking, to "welcome" a new colleague on the London scene.

Fitzgibbon, a bitter critic of Martin's left-wing line, was outraged at his presence. Martin, for him, was not merely a soulless pro-Soviet anti-American fellow traveler but a likely figurehead for a tragic occupation of Britain and Europe on that sad day when Stalinist Russia would win the Cold War. Reaching for yet another drink, Constantine vowed he would write a novel about him, "that Pétain...that Quisling," who would be unwilling to face totalitarian realities even "when the kissing had to stop."

A year or so later the novel of that title was written and published; and it was subsequently filmed for television. Kingsley Martin did not sue for libel; the TV actor who played his role had the same shock of silver hair but managed to speak with quite a different accent (Welsh, as I recall, rather than Oxfordshire).
14. "Ooh, ah...," Sport on Television, *Daily Telegraph*, 21 July 1997, p. S9.
15. "Woods takes the fans to task," *Daily Telegraph*, 21 July 1997, p. S3. *NY Times/IHT*, 8 July 1997.
16. "Teed-off Tiger in wee spot of bother," *Daily Mail*, 19 July 1997, p. 77.

11. Citations Sown

1. Frederic Raphael, "French Without Tears," *Sunday Times* (Books), 20 July 1997, p. 3.
2. Charles Bremner, *Times*, 12 October 1994.
3. *International Herald-Tribune*, Ian Thomsen reporting from the Roland Garros stadium in Paris, 8-9 June 1996, p. 20.
4. Michael Parkinson, interviewing David Platt, in the *Daily Telegraph*, 4 November 1995, p. 22.
5. Tom Friend, in the *N.Y. Times/IHT*, 3 November 1995, p. 23.
6. Robin Finn, "Becker Loses His Cool...Upset in Australia," *New York Times/IHT*, 14 January 1997, p. 19.
7. *Independent*, "And Coleman is 70...Quite Remarkable," 26 April 1996, Section 2, pp. 2-3.
8. Michael Calvin, "Motor Racing," *Times*, 10 October 1997, p. 45.
9. Thomas Boswell, "Orioles' Myers Perfects His Non-Image," *Washington Post/IHT*, 4 July 1997, p. 23.
10. *NYT*, 5 November 1994; *IHT*, 5-6 November.

12. Words, Words, Words...

1. *NYT/IHT*, 20 September 1995.
2. *Longman Dictionary of Contemporary English* (London, 1978), p. 651.
3. *NYT/IHT*, 20 April 1995.
4. Jon Pareles, "Patti Smith Comes Back," *NYT/IHT*, 22-23 June 1996, p. 24.
5. *IHT*, 20 April 1995
6. *Times*, 5 May 1995.
7. *Daily Telegraph*, 6 May 1995.

13. The Strategy of Misquotation

1. Carl Sandburg, *The People, Yes* (original ed. 1936, New York, quotation taken from the 1948 ed., ch. 23, p. 43). *Der Sprachdienst* (Wiesbaden, 1983), vol. 27, Heft 7/8, p. 97ff: Rolf Bülow, "Stell dir vor, es gibt einen Spruch...(Just imagine, there's a saying)."
2. Harpo Marx, *Harpo Speaks!* (1961), ch. 22, p. 426.
3. See in *Encounter* (August 1975), J.P. Stern's "Karl Kraus and the Idea of Literature." As Professor Stern has written me: "*Die dritte Walpurgisnacht* was set in the summer of 1933 and should have appeared in *Die Fackel*; Kraus decided against it, being afraid it would unleash an anti-Semitic campaign in Germany. Instead, in July 1934, he published a long piece in *Die Fackel* (Vol. 36, 890-905), 'Warum die Fackel nicht erscheint', on p. 2 of which the sentence occurs. A good many passages in that essay are identical with *Die dritte Walpurgisnacht*, which was finally published in Munich by Kösel in 1952 (ed. Heinrich Fischer)."

4. Matthew Paris, in *Times*, 17 November 1995, p. 2.
5. Simon Hoggart, in *Guardian*, 17 November 1995, p. 2.
6. Mark Steyn, "Where the cowardly lion is king," *Sunday Telegraph*, 27 October 1996, p. 30.
7. *Washington Post* (weekly edition), 10-16 June 1996, pp. 6-8. See, for the novelist's skill with such East-West quotations, the East-European dialogues in Malcolm Bradbury's brilliant pastiche *Doctor Criminale*: (1992).
8. "Crazy Limey," *Times*, 27 May 1997, p. 18.
9. *NYT/IHT*, 23 June 1995.

14. The Interviewer and the Interviewee

1. *Oxford English Dictionary* (1933), Volume V, p. 425.
2. *Memoirs of M. de Blowitz* (New York, 1903). Frank Giles, *A Prince of Journalists: The Life and Times of Blowitz* (London, 1962). p. 149.
3. The so-called interview was first perpetrated in the March 1989 issue of *Encounter*: "The Art of the Interview, or the Difficulties of Asking a Question & Getting an Answer," pp. 61-64. As is well-known, imitation is the sincerest form of flattery.
4. There are a dozen masterful interviews that George Urban published in *Encounter*, and many were never collected in his books. See his interviews there with Milovan Djilas (September-November 1988), Vladimir Bukovsky (November 1987, January 1988), Alain Besançon (May and June 1987), Galina Vishnevskaya (December 1986, January 1987), Max M. Kampelman (February 1985), Alexander Zinoviev (April 1984), Jeane Kirkpatrick (November 1983), Eugene V. Rostow (April 1983), Daniel Bell (February 1983), W. Averell Harriman (November 1981), and Zbigniew Brezinski (May 1981). A previous conversation with Milovan Djilas was in the December 1979 *Encounter*. A book collection of conversations by Urban was published in London, "*Can the Soviet System Survive Reform?*" (1988).

Part 3: The Quest for Meaning
Epigraphs

1. John Updike, *Brazil:a Novel* (1994), p. 1. C.S. Lewis, in *Studies in Words* (1960), p. 327-8. Robert Berwick, a co-director of the Massachusetts Institute of Technology's Center for Biological & Computational Learning, writing about the book by Terrence Green, *The Symbolic Species: The Co-Evolution of Language* (1997) in the *Los Angeles Times* (Books), 7 September 1997, pp. 3-5.

   The Rabbi Rizin quotation was the motto to the following poem written by David Rokeah, translated from the original Hebrew by Ruth and Mathew Mead (in *Encounter*, December 1981, p. 91:

The Truth

He dug with his bare hands
through the floor of mempry,
under the treshold
The truth about the truth
is not found,
a diamond buried deep.

Objects which long for each other
embody the power
of magnets.

15. Race and the Color of Things

1. *NYT*, story by Andy Newman, "Metro" section, 26 December 1997, p. B3.
2. *New York Post*, story, by three reporters and a writer, p. 3. *New York Daily News*, story by two staff writers, p. 4.
3. Wade Henry, *NYT/IHT*, 16 January 1998, p.3.
4. Valerie Grove and Adrian Lee, "Rape Trial," *Times*, 16 January 1998, pp. 1, 3.
5. Nathan Glazer and Daniel Patrick Moynihan, *Beyond the Melting Pot* (1970). See also Nathan Glazer, "The Etnic Factor," *Encounter*, July 1981, pp. 6-15; "The Universalization of Ethnicity," *Encounter*, February 1975, pp. 8ff.
6. *Times*, "Benny Hill Returns," 6 March 1998, p. 2.
7. *Time*, 9 March 1998, p. 100. "Caribbean," *Daily Mail*, 25 December 1985.
8. "When in Rome," *Daily Telegraph*, 30 November 1985.
9. "Haringey," *Daily Mail*, 7 January 1986.
10. J.L. Talmon, *The Origins of Totalitarian Democracy* (1952) and *Romanticism and Revolt: Europe 1815-1848* (1967).
11. BBC-2, 6 January 1986.
12. The "Nazi" reference was used by the editor of the New York *Daily News*, in a leading article (6 December 1985) defending the practice of "racial discrimination" with the conventional (if still perverse) rationalization that the-end-justifies-the-means. It might be "unpleasant" and "distasteful" and—"it is reminiscent of the Nazi Nuremberg racial laws. There's no way around that. But 'reminiscent' is different from 'the same.' Purpose is crucial...."

    Thus, the tragic and self-defeating maxim becomes: Crucial purposes justify unethical practices. Some ethics!
13. For the most perceptive interpretation of what he saw as "the sphinx of affluence" and "the pitfalls of welfare," see the late Ignazio Silone's profound essay (in *Encounter*, March and April 1968), entitled "Re-Thinking Progress."

14. Ellis Close, "Pride and Power," *Newsweek*, 9 March 1998, pp. 42-48. See also Anthony W. Marx, *Making Race and Nation: A Comparison of the United States, South Africa, Brazil* (Cambridge University Press, 1998).)
    Philip Mason, *Race Relations: A Field of Study Comes of Age* (London, 1968), *How Peoples Differ: An Introduction to Race Relations* (London, 1971), *Race Relations* (London, 1970), *An Essay on Racial Tension* (Westport, Conn., 1972), *Patterns of Dominance* (London, 1970).
15. Michael Meyers, in the *New York Post*, 3 March 1998.
16. Keith Richburg, *Out of America* (1997). "Outrage as Black American says 'Thank God for Slavery'," *Daily Telegraph*, 22 March 1997, p. 13.
17. "Gipsy Curse" and "Reggae Row," *Daily Mail*, 12 July 1994.

16. The N-Word and the J-Word

1. Richard Cohen, in *New York Post*, 23 November 1993.
2. "War of Words," *Daily Telegraph*, 31 January 1998, p. A/IV. Martin Duberman, *Paul Robeson* (1989), pp. 604-5, fn. 14.
3. Mark Steyn is an American critic who contributes to the New York monthly, *The New Criterion*, and writes regularly for the *Daily* and *Sunday Telegraph* in London. My quote is from his article, "Hazy shades of rock on Broadway," reprinted in the *Weekly Telegraph*, No. 333, 10-16 December 1997, p. 25. Steyn is the author of a history of "musicals then and now," *Broadway Babies Say Goodnight* (1997), hence his detailed knowledgeability about the ups-and-downs of the n-word taboo on Broadway.
4. Kim Fletcher, in the *Sunday Telegraph*, 11 January 1998, p. 30.
5. Luigi Barzini, *Americans Are Alone in the World* (1953); *The Italians* (1964); *From Caesar to the Mafia* (1971) and *The Europeans* (1983).
6. William Safire's language column in the *New York Times* Magazine, *NYT/IHT*, 16 March 1998, p. 9.
7. *Times*, 8 August 1996; *Evening Standard*, 7 August 1996, on Mal Young, producer of the Brookside series, and "his enthusiasm for finding more taboos."
8. *Independent on Sunday*, 11 August 1996, p. 1.
9. *London Evening Standard*, "A lesson in laughter," 8 August 1996.
10. William Safire, "Language," *NYT/IHT*, 16 December 1996, p. 11.
11. Peter Maas, *Underboss: Sammy the Bull Gravano's Story of Life in the Mafia* (1997), pp. 28-29.
12. "Chicago's Hate Crime," *New York Times/IHT*, 28 March 1997, p. 5.
13. *Longman's Dictionary of Contemporary English*, p. 130. J.E. Lighter, *Random House Dictionary of American Slang* (1994), vol. I, pp. 286-7.
14. C.S. Lewis, *Studies in Words* (1960), p. 330.
15. *Time* Magazine, 4 December 1995, "Letters."
16. Elmore Leonard, *Riding the Rap* (1995), pp. 49, 243.
17. Lawrence Schiller (with James Willwerth), *American Tragedy: the Uncensored Story of the Simpson Defense* (1997), pp. 685, 731.

18. For other Fuhrman quotations on Internet, see: myra@netcom.com, bwitanek@igc.apc.org, alt.fan.oj-simpson.transcripts. See also the *Detroit News*, "Jurors for the first time hear of Fuhrman's use of racist slurs," 6 September 1995; *Time* Magazine, "A Taste of Venom," 28 August 1995.

19. See, among other books in the extensive literature, Dominick Dunne's *Another City Not My Own* (1997). Dunne contributed incisive articles regularly to the monthly *Vanity Fair* but (unfortunately, for our purposes) did not go on to write a straightforward account of his well-researched data and special insight. He chose instead to write "a Novel in the form of a Memoir," thus reducing its value to colorful, atmospheric hearsay. We have far too much fiction already in what purport to be true stories.

20. Vincent Bugliosi, in his foreword to Mark Fuhrman's *Murder in Brentwood* (1997), p. xiii. See, generally, Bugliosi's own book, *Outrage: the Five Reasons Why O.J. Simpson Got Away with Murder* (1996). Bugliosi as a D.A. came to national prominence as the prosecuting attorney in the murder trial of Charles Manson in 1970.

21. Fuhrman, *Murder*, p. 153.

22. Schiller, *American Tragedy*, p. 843.

23. "Race Card," quoted by Johnnie Cochran in his memoir of the trial, *Journey to Justice* (1996), p. 312.

24. Schiller, *American Tragedy*, pp. 780ff., 842, 515.

25. Schiller, *Tragedy*, pp. 780ff., 842, 515, 730.

26. Mark Fuhrman, *Murder in Brentwood* (1997), p. 278.

27. Lawrence Schiller, *American Tragedy*, p. 123.

28. Atticus column by "Taki," in the *Sunday Times*, 16 March 1997, p. 11.

29. Henry Louis Gates, Jr., "Powell and the Black Elite," *New Yorker*, 25 September 1995, pp. 64-80.

30. Henry Louis Gates, Jr., "Niggaz with Latitude," *New Yorker*, 21 March 1994, pp. 143-148.

31. The special issue of *The New Yorker* (April 29 & May 6, 1996) was edited by Hendrik Hertzberg and Henry Louis Gates, Jr. My quotations are from "The N-Word," p. 50.

32. *Guardian*, G-2 Section articles (pp. 2-3, 14) on Tarantino, Leonard, etc. Dick Gregory, *Nigger*, 1964, p. 209.

33. Christopher Darden's memoir of his life and the O.J. Simpson trial, *In Contempt* (1996), pp. 107, 309.

34. Marcia Clark, *Without a Doubt* (1997), p. 258. The "G" usage dots the text of the memoir, viz., "Hey, G, pull up a chair" (p. 258); "Don't let them get you down, G" (p. 295); "'It ain't worth it, G,' I told him" (p. 314); and that most protective and confidence-building of phrases "You know I got your back, G" (i.e., no one could sneak up on her, or him, from behind), pp. 315, 372.

36. *New York Times*, Bob Herbert's "Radio Sick Shtick," 3 May 1996, p. A31.

37. *NYT/IHT*, 8 May 1996, Clint Bolick, "In America, Racial Classification Instead of Color-Blind Law."

38. BBC World Service, "Music in Review," 15 December 1995.
39. Prof. Jean Aitchinson, "There's a word for it...," *Sunday Times* (News Review, p. 6), 27 April 1997. "How the 'nerd' earned respect," *Daily Telegraph*, 25 April 1997, p. 11.
40. William Safire, "Language Column," *NYT/IHT*, 5 May 1997, p. 12. Jeffrey H. McQuain, *Power Language* (1997).
41. "Zoeller's Remark," Zoeller Has Company," "Tiger Woods and the Melting Pot," *Washington Post, NYT/IHT*, 24-25 April 1997, pp. 3, 15, 23. "Tiger Woods' True Colours," *Daily Telegraph*, 26 April 1997, pp. 13, 29. *Newsweek*, "In Living Colors," 5 May 1997 (Int. ed.), pp. 40-41.
42. "In living color," *Newsweek* (Int.ed.), 5 May 1997, pp. 40-41.
43. "Colour blindness that shields the mugger," *Sunday Times* (New Review), 27 April 1997, p. 7.
44. John Leland and and Gregory Beals, "In Living Colors," *Newsweek* (Int.ed.), 5 May 1997, pp. 40-42.
45. *New York Post*, 30 August 1996, p. 14.
46. *New York Times*, 31 August 1995, David Stout, "Some Protest Vulgarities; Networks Back Their Use" (a headline which was belied by the story).
47. *New York Post*, "Fuhrman's Tapes Shock Court," and Andrea Peyser's column on "L.A. Justice," 30 August 1995, p. 4.
48. *NYT/IHT*, "Reds' Owner Agrees to Step Down," 14 June 1996.
49. "Wartime History Haunts the Swiss," *NYT/IHT*, 10 February 1997, pp. 1, 9. On the Kristallnacht, see Lionel Kochan, *Pogrom – November 10, 1938* (1957), and Rita Thalmann and Emmanuel Feinermann, *Crystal Night* (1974). Heinrich Mann's book of 1939, *Der Pogrom*, published in Zurich, is graphic.
50. See Leo Rosten, *The Joys of Yiddish*, (1968); Cecil Roth, *A History of the Jews* (1970); also *From the Fair: the Autobiography of Sholom Aleichem* (1985).
51. C.S. Lewis, *Studies in Words* (1960), p. 141.
52. Arland Ussher, *The Magic People* (1950). The remark by Rabelais (1535) is to be found in *Gargantua and Pantagruel* (tr. Cohen, 1955), p. 569.
53. *Weekly Telegraph*, 15-21 November 1995, p. 17.
54. *Washington Post/IHT*, "A Dictionary Feels Sting of Public Opinion," 2 November 1995, p. 3.
55. William Raspberry, "Though Racism Persists, Progress Is Undeniable," *Washington Post/IHT*, 3 March 1998, p. 9.
56. Michael Wharton, *The World of Peter Simple: Extracts from the "Way of the World" Column in the Daily Telegraph, 1971-1973* (London, 1973) and *More of Peter Simple: Extracts from the "Way of the World" Column in the Daily Telegraph, 1965-1969* (London, 1969). *Merriam-Webster's Collegiate Dictionary*, (10ᵗʰ ed., Springfield, Mass., 1997) p. 784. Daniel Patrick Moynihan, "Defining Deviancy Down," *The American Scholar*, 1993, p. 17-30. Charles Krauthammer, "Defining Deviancy Up," *New Republic*, November 22, 1993, pp. 20-25.
57. *San Franscisco Examiner*, 10 December 1996, p. A-17.

58. "Nixon on Tape," *Washington Post/IHT*, 12 December 1996, p. 3. "Nixon's Anti-Semitism," *San Francisco Examiner*, 10 December 1996, p. A-17.

59. Russell Baker, "Discarded Thoughts," *N.Y.Times/IHT*, 20 January 1997, p. 22.

60. *Abuse of Power: the New Nixon Tapes* (ed. S.I. Kutler, 1997), p. xvii.

61. Kutler, 3 August 1972, p. 115.

62. Kutler, *Abuse of Power*, 19 October 1972, p. 171.

63. Kutler, *Abuse of Power*, 1 January 1973, p. 191.

64. Susan Naulty, "Historical Accuracy and the Nixon Tapes," *Washington Times*, 28 February 1997.

65. William Buckley, Jr., "Nixon and Anti-Semitism," *New York Post*, 8 January 1997, p. 23.

66. Marx to Engels, July 30, 1862. *The Letters of Karl Marx: Selected and Translated with Explanatory Notes and an Introduction* by Saul Padover (1979), pp. 466, 468. This letter is not included in Marx-Engels, *Selected Correspondence*, but is in the complete German edition, Marx-Engels, *Werke* (Berlin 1961), vol. 30, pp. 257, 259. Also Engels to Marx, 7 March 1856, *Marx-Engels Correspondence* (ed. Raddatz, 1981), p. 74.

The Soviet English-language edition of the *Selected Correspondence* published in New York in 1942 (p. vi) states: "With reference to the use of the word 'nigger' which occurs in this book: Marx used the word while living in England, in the last century. The word does not have the same connotation as it has now in the U.S. and should be read as 'Negro' whenever it occurs in the text."

Diane Paul comments that "this explanation does not accord with that of the Oxford English Dictionary or with a great deal of other evidence....If the word 'nigger' was not so jarring in mid-nineteenth century England as it is in England or America today, it nevertheless was a term of abuse....Both Marx and Engels sometimes used the English term 'nigger' to refer to blacks and to others for whom they had contempt...." (*Journal of the History of Ideas*, January-March 1981, pp. 126, 127.)

67. Kenneth Tynan, *Letters* (ed. Kathleen Tynan), 1994, letter to his wife, 4 October 1963, p. 283. Howell quote in Lasky, *Utopia and Revolution*, pp. 301-2.

68. *Daily Mirror*, p. 11. *Daily Mail*, p. 2. *Daily Star*, p. 6, all dated 22 February 1997..

69. *Frankfurter Allgemeine Zeitung*, "Rifkin/Jude," 20/24/25 February 1997, p. 2/p. 2/p.17. Thomas Braun, "Luther," *Daily Telegraph*, p. 15; John Hobson, "Jewish Question," *The Guardian*, p. 8, and *Times*, p. 17, dated 25 February 1997. "'German baiting' over Rifkind row," 26 February 1997, p. 19. Paul Johnson and Dot Wordsworth, columns in the *Spectator*, 1 March 1997, pp. 18-19.

70. See also Paul Winter, *On the Trial of Jesus* (1961); Paul Johnson, *History of Christianity* (1976); Geza Vermes, *Jesus the Jew* (1973).

71. Peretz, *New Republic*, 10 March 1997, p. 29.

72. See, also in the same issue (10 March 1997) of the *New Republic* (pp. 28-29), Walter Laqueur's penetrating article, "Madeleine Albright and Jew-

ish Identity." He quotes Kurt Tucholsky and some others, all in the shadow of "Jewish law" according to which it is technically impossible to leave the faith—"even if he has sinned he remains of Israel...."

Cardinal Lustiger of France has also written subtly about his own problem of "past [Jewish] descent" and "present [Catholic] faith." See the revealing memoir written by his cousin, Arno Lustiger in the *Frankfurter Allgemeine Zeitung* ("Bilder und Zeiten"), 14 September 1996, p. B2, "Ich bin Jude und werde es bleiben: Zum 70. Geburtstags des Kardinal Lustiger."

73. Bruce Anderson, "Politics," *Spectator*, 24 May 1997, p. 8; and in the *Spectator* of the week before (17 May 1997), Michael Howard's reply to Anne Widdicombe, "Maybe I Am Dangerous Stuff," pp. 10-11.

74. Michael Prescott, "Howard's End," *Sunday Times*, 18 May 1997 (Focus) p. 13. Interview with Mrs. Howard, *Sunday Telegraph*, 18 May 1997, p. 3, and in the same issue, Alasdair Palmer, "The genteel art of Tory anti-semitism."

75. *Economist*, "The Roosevelt Legacy," 28 September 1996, p. 72.

76. *Washington Post*, "Democracy and the P-Word," 9-15 1996, weekly ed., p. 24.

77. William Safire, "How Sharp Is a Philadelphia Lawyer?," *New York Times*, 13 October 1996 (Section 6), p. 30.

78. Kingsley Amis, *The King's English: A Guide to Modern Usage* (1997), pp. 139-40.

79. "Flynt as Free Speech Hero?," *NYT/IHT*, 24-25 December 1996, p. 20.

80. "Lebensform Föderalismus," *FrankfurterAllgemeine Zeitung*, 12 December 1996, p. 37. *Times*, "Luvvie is a term of abuse, say the stage folk," 21 September 1996, p. 1.

81. Kathleen Tynan, *The Life of Kenneth Tynan* (1987), p. 98.

82. "Race body turns down whinge about Pom," *Daily Telegraph*, 22 May 1997, p. 3.

83. Herodotus, *The Histories* (Penguin edition, 1954, tr. de Sélincourt), pp. 335-6; (University of Chicago edition, 1987, tr. David Grene), p. 384.

17. The Art of Punditry

1. *IHT*, 10 November 1994.

2. On the history of the *New York Times* and its foreign correspondents, see: Gay Talese, *The Kingdom and the Power* (1969) and David Halberstam, *The Powers That Be* (1979).

On Malcolm Muggeridge's views, see his novel, *Winter in Moscow*, republished in 1987 (wherein Duranty was satirized as "Jefferson"), as well as his volumes of autobiography, *Chronicles of Wasted Time* (1982). Also the recent Muggeridge biography by Richard Ingram which deals with Duranty's GPU connections, "gay blackmail," alcoholism, etc. Eugene Lyons' book, *Assignment in Utopia* (1937), exposed self-critically his own "mendacious" pro-Soviet sympathies as well as the unreconstructed Stalinism of other members of the Western press corps in the Moscow of the 1930s. He quotes from the *New York Times'* dispatches: "There is no actual starvation or deaths from starvation" (and every one there knew how untruthful this was). And, again, "Any report of a famine in Russia is today [1933] an exaggeration of malignant propaganda...."

Nor was his successor, Ralph Parker, much of an improvement; his wartime dispatches from Moscow to the *New York Times* were tendentious and untrustworthy; and his bias was revealed when, after the war (as one historian of the paper records), he "turned up writing for the London and New York editions of the Communist *Daily Worker*...." (Gay Talese, *The Kingdom and the Power* , p. 460, where Ralph Parker is not mentioned by name).

Just to round off this brief chronicle of the troubles they've seen. Maintaining their own correspondent in Moscow the *Times'* editors appointed Harrison Salisbury to the post in 1944, for no better reason, apparently, than that the post was open and Salisbury, applying for the job, had already managed to wangle a Soviet visa which had always been difficult to obtain for any journalist in Stalin's time. (It was correspondingly easier if the American journalist was considered by the Kremlin to be "politically naive.") Salisbury's reporting did not break the tradition of hard luck for the *Times*. He also proved to be "controversial" (especially among American academics and New York intellectuals who were students of Soviet affairs). Indeed, the *Times* had to try and compensate for its reportorial deficiencies by printing additional material and extra analyses from Professor Harry Schwartz, its resident "Kremlinologist." The editors of the *Times* aggravated their difficulties by refusing to publish a caution that all dispatches from Moscow had been "passed by the censor." Obviously they preferred to mislead the reader, by publishing such news as the Bolshevik thought-controllers thought fit to release, and then to attempt to redress the balance as best as Harry Schwartz could.

The remark was copied by E.M. Forster into his *Commonplace Book* after listening [as an undergraduate] to one of Acton's lectures. See George Watson, *Lord Acton's History of Liberty* (1994), p. 4.

The actual remark by Maxim Litvinov was made to Edgar Snow—recorded in his later book of reportage, *Journey to the Beginning* (1959), p. 357—but was repeated to me by C.L. Sulzberger who knew Snow both in China and in the Soviet Union: "Why did you Americans wait until now [April 1945] to begin opposing us in the Balkans and eastern Europe....You should have done this three years ago. Now it's too late..." Litvinov had been the influential foreign minister conducting Soviet policy towards the West in the 1930s. Ten years later, after a period of "disgrace" (how could a Russian Jew serve the Kremlin during the Hitler-Stalin pact?), he was given a vice commissar's post in Moscow.

On "the road not taken" in the history of the Cold War, see the diplomatic writings of George F. Kennan who, at roughly the same time as

Maxim Litvinov, warned that if the USA and its Western Allies did not "resist" or "contain" or otherwise deter the Kremlin from its adventures in expansion beyond its frontier, it would be in mortal danger. Slowly, almost belatedly, the West's policies changed to alarmed alertness (after the 1948 coup in Prague and the "Blockade" in Berlin) and to military preparedness (with the NATO alliance of 1949). But by that time the "Cold War" was raging, and the two ideological camps were locked in a balance of power with the real prospects of "massive retaliation" or "mutual assured destruction."

See also R.C. Raack's well-documented scholarly study, *Stalin's Drive to the West, 1938-1945: the Origins of the Cold War* (1995).

3. On Thomas Friedman's column on foreign affairs in the *New York Times* since January 1995, I am indebted to the withering polemic published in the *New Republic*, "Not Two Cents," by Nader Mousavizadeh (10 July 1995), pp. 12-13. I have already considered the general language used in his work, and touch here only on one aspect of his regrettably narrow intellectual horizon.

4. Andrew Alexander in the *Daily Mail*, 14 July 1995.

18. In Pseuds Corner

1. *Business Life: the Magazine for Europe*, Andrew Eames, "Who's Afraid of Team Games?," April 1996, pp. 58ff.
2. *IHT*, 12 June 1994.
3. Lehmann-Haupt's review of Jeffrey Trachtenberg's *The Rain on Macy's Parade*, *NYT/IHT*, 23-24 November 1996, p. 6.
4. Adrian Furnham, "Merits of Cross-Functional Teams," *Financial Times*, 5 August 1996, p. 8.
5. Fay Maschler, in *Evening Standard*, 2 August 1994.
6. James Hall, in *Guardian/Private Eye*, 12 August 1994.
7. *"The Observer Interview:* Julian Schnabel," Life Magazine/*Observer*,16 February 1997, pp. 6-8.
8. Stephen Jay Gould, in *Times*, 14 August 1997, p. 35. The quoted example is from Richard Fortey's much-praised "one-volume history of life" entitled *Life: An Unauthorized Biography* (1997).)
9. Carter Ratcliff, *The Fate of a Gesture: Jackson Pollock and Postwar American Art* (1996), quoted in a review in *NY Times/IHT*, 1 January 1997, p. 8.
10. Anthony Gormley in *Observer*, and Dr. Martin Murray, in *Independent*; "Pseuds Corner," in *Private Eye*, 24 January 1997, p. 9.
11. Cricket reports in for 13 August 1997, in *Times* (p. 44) and *Daily Telegraph* (p. 40)—and the entire London press with the exception of the soft-porn tabloids on that "black Tuesday." Magnus Linklater, in *Times*, 14 August 1997, p. 18, quoting Lord Harris in 1931.
12. Quentin Curtis, "Dizzying display of Hitchcock," *Daily Telegraph*, 25 April 1997, p. 26.

19. Pop Kulcher

1. See Ray Coleman's biography, *McCartney—Yesterday and Today* (1995) and the *Daily Mail*, 16 August 1995. Also Peter Norman, *Shout!: the True Story of the Beatles* (1981/93) and Hunter Davies, *The Beatles: The Authorized Biography* (1985).
2. Stephen Holden, "Cher at 50: Coming Back for Another Round," *New York Times/IHT*, 2 July 1996, p. 20.
3. See, generally, John Decker, *Post-Modernism and Popular Culture: A cultural history* (1994).
4. Paul Tickell, in *Evening Standard*, 17 August 1995.
5. C.L. Smith, in *Daily Telegraph*, 19 August 1995.
6. I am quoting here from John Harlow, "Is Britpop about to go pop?," in the Culture section, *Sunday Times*, 2 March 1997, pp. 4-5.
7. *Daily Telegraph*, 23 August 1995, p. 7.

20. The Art of Explanation

1. Reuter dispatch, in *Athens News*, 30 September 1994.
2. Robert Lee Holtz, "Mysteries of the Organism," *Los Angeles Times*, 7 September 1997, (Books), p. 6.
3. Christopher Booker was polemicizing against John Humphrys (of the *Today* program) and Jeremy Paxman (of *Newsnight*), in *The Sunday Telegraph*, 21 May 1995.
4. *Welt am Sonntag*, 23 June 1995.
5. *IHT*, 7 December 1994.
6. *Time* Magazine, "Newt Gingrich: Man of the Year," 25 December-1 January 1996, p. 47.
7. *Washington Post*, 26 September 1994.
8. *Sunday Telegraph*, 2 October 1994.
9. *Guardian/*"Pseuds Corner"in *Private Eye*, 24 January 1997, p. 9.
10. *Sunday Times*, 22 October 1995.
11. *Daily Telegraph*, 19 October 1995.
12. Burkhard Müller-Ulrich, "Are the Forests Really Dying," *Süddeutsche Zeitung*, 7-8 September 1996, p. I, and his book entitled *Medien-Märchen: Gesinnungstäter im Journalismus* (Blessing Verlag, 1996). See also: Rudi Holzberger's *Das sogenannte Waldsterben* in which he reversed his earlier position (as an editor of *Geo* magazine) and now calls his eco-crusade "a humbug" (Eppe Verlag, 1995).
13. *Washington Post/IHT*, Rick Atkinson's dispatch from the Black Forest, 15 July 1996, p. 2.
14. "Dust in our Eyes," *Guardian*, 12 July 1997 (Online), p. 7.
15. Fred Pearce, in *Guardian*, 12 July 1997, pp. 44-45, commenting on the recent issue of the science journal *Nature* which included the article "Control of atmospheric export of dust from North Africa by the North Atlantic Oscillation," by Cyril Moulin, Claude E. Lambert, François Dulac, and Uri Dayan, 12 June 1997, pp. 691-694.

21. Keeping Up with the Avant-Garde

1. "Pagliacci," *Financial Times*, 25 November 1997, p. 15; "Rossini," *Die Welt*, 25 November 1997, p. 11.
2. "Moscow's Opera Scene," *Washington Post/IHT*,10 December 1997, p. 24.
3. Waldemar Januszczak, "The 47th Venice Biennale pushes into exciting new territories," *Sunday Times*, 22 June 1997 (Culture), p. 11/8.
4. Robert Conway Morris, "The Parting of the Ways in Venice," *IHT*, 14-15 June 1997, p. 6.
5. On Brecht's *Puntila*, see the review by Rüdiger Schaper in *Tip: Berlin Magazin*, 7 March 1996, pp. 90-91. On Brecht's fading reputation, see the report on an International Theater Conference in Augsburg (Brecht's birthplace: b. 1898-d. 1956) which was dedicated to the "rehabilitation" of the Master who is being unjustly "written off." *Süddeutsche Zeitung*, 13 February 1996, p. 12.

22. Hard Words and Generation Gaps

1. *Rise of the Roman Empire*, "Rome & Gauls" (Book II), p. 132 (Ian Scott-Kilvert's translation slightly adapted).
2. Erich Maria Remarque, *All Quiet on the Western Front* (tr. A.H. Wheen, 1929), p. 298.

Part 4: The F-Word and Other Obscenities

Epigraphs

1. Anthony Burgess, *A Mothful of Air: Languages, Languages...Especially English* (New York: William Morrow, 1992).
2. Roy Blount, Jr., preface to *The F-Word*, edited by Jesse Scheidlower (New Yprk: Random House, (1995).

23. Skirmishes in the Sex War

1. Allison Pearson, in *Evening Standard*, 16 August 1994.
2. Peter Paterson, in *Daily Mail*, 21 August 1994.
3. John Naughton, in *Observer*, 21 August 1994.
4. Julia Grant, in *Independent*, 18 June 1994.
5. Matthew Norman, in *Standard*, 18 June 1994.
6. On the "Wax Model," see the Antiquarian catalogue of Ken Spelman (York, #35), p. 27, where it was again offered for sale for the sum of £35.00.
7. *Daily Telegraph*, 14 January 1995.
8. Philip Hensher in *Spectator*, quoted by the *Sunday Times* in "Books," 10 August 1997, p. 2.
9. *Daily Telegraph*, "Abbey abandons avant-garde," 5 April 1996, p. 12.

24. World War II, Fifty Years After

1. *Guardian*, 5 May 1995.
2. *Daily Telegraph*, 28 April 1995.
3. *Sunday Telegraph*, 30 April 1995.

25. A Trio of As*ter*isk*s

1. *Daily Telegraph*, 14 March 1994.
2. *Washington Post*, 5 November 1994; *IHT*, 5-6 November 1994.

26. Gender in the Combat Zone

1. *Daily Mail*, 17 May 1995; *Daily Telegraph*, 18 May 1995; *Sunday Telegraph*, 21 May 1995.
2. Charles Jennings, "Hell on Wheels: 'Trolley Rage' has been invented after a punch-up in an M&S queue," in *Daily Telegraph*, 2 March 1996, p. 9.
3. "Muscling in on the 90s: In a career spanning 30 years rock icon Iggy Pop has often seemed on the point of self-destruction. Caspar Llewellyn Smith discovers the secret of his survival." *Daily Telegraph*, 2 March 1996, p. 2A.
4. Ann V. Bollinger, in *New York Post*, "Carjack ordeal spurs Latifah's teary testimony," 25 April 1996, p. 22.
5. Dave Barry, "Good Old Miami Courtesy," *Miami Herald/IHT*, 8-9 June 1996, p. 22.
6. *Los Angeles Times*, 29 March 1998 (Sunday Book Review), p. 3.)
7. Maureen Paton, *Daily Express*, 15 August 1996, p. 43.
8. Ed Rollins, "Arianna," *Sunday Times*, 11 August 1996 (News Review), pp. 1-2; also his book, *Bare Knuckles and Back Rooms* (Broadway Books, New York, 1996).
9. Alexander Walker, "Someone Up There Hates Us," *Evening Standard*. 8 August 1996, p. 24.
10. Kevin Myers, "Men who carry excess baggage," *Sunday Telegraph*, 18 August 1996, p. 28.
11. Peregrine Worsthorne, "Out of the Mouths of Women," *Sunday Telegraph*, 18 August 1996, p. 29.
12. Christopher Booker, "How politicians have lost touch with reality," *Sunday Telegraph*, 20 April 1997, p. 14.
13. "In the Gutter," *Sunday Times*, 27 April 1997, p. 11.
14. Boris Johnson, "My Battle," *Daily Telegraph*, 5 May 1997, p. 10. Philip Oppenheim, *Sunday Times*, "Diary," 4 May 1997, p. 15. Robert Harris, "Behind Closed Doors," *Sunday Times* (News Review), p. 1.
15. "Swearing Soars in Primary Schools," *Sunday Times*, 4 May 1997, p. 8.
16. *Observer*, 13 August 1995.

17. *Observer*, 9 July and 13 August 1995. Oleg Gordievsky and Christopher Andrews, *The KGB* (1990), and Gordievsky's autobiography, *Next Step Execution* (1995).
18. *Observer*, 20 August 1995.
19. *Guardian*, 24 July 1995.
20. Neil Hamilton, Conservative M.P., letter to *Times*, 23 November 1995, p. 21.)
21. *Sunday Times*, "Diana's Prime Time," 19 November 1995, pp. 14-15.
22. The book by Hilary and Piers Du Pré, *A Genius in the Family* was published by Chatto & Windus in 1997. The serialization in the *Times* was during the week of Monday-to-Friday, 6-10 October 1997. My lengthy quotations are in: *Times*, 8 October, p. 14, and 10 October, p. 19.
23. "NBA Fines Rodman," *Washington Post/IHT*, 14-15 June 1997, p. 21.
24. Review-article in the *Los Angeles Times* (Books), 29 March 1998, p. 3. The author, Robert Scheer, is "a contributing editor" of the paper. He was criticizing the new book by Howard Kurtz, *Spin Cycle: Inside the Clinton Propaganda Machine* (The Free Press, 1998), as being part of the problem he was presumably diagnosing, namely, "the nauseating ritual of gotcha journalism...."
25. *Daily Telegraph*, 23 October 1995.
26. *Independent*, "Depth of hatred revealed in covert video," 26 April 1996, p. 4.
27. *Times*, "Spy film exposed suspects' hatred of blacks," 26 April 1996, p. 5.

27. Remembering the Founding Fathers

1. Russell Baker, "Pushing Up Daisies," *NYT/IHT*, 18 April 1997, p. 22.
2. Stephen Burt, "High Windows and Four-Letter Words," *Boston Review*, October/November 1996, pp. 18-19.
3. Jonathan Yardley, *Washington Post/IHT*, 26-27 October 1996, reviewing Scott Turow's novel, *The Laws of Our Fathers* (1996).
4. See my articles "Revolutionary Diary: 1968," "Lady on the Barricades," and "The Ideas of '68: Revolt After 20 Years," in *Encounter* (August 1968; July 1972; November 1988); and in *On the Barricades, & Off* (1989), chapters 1 and 2. I have freely borrowed some of my own material (but not without a few self-critical revisions).
5. Lasky reference, Tynan, *Letters*, p. 242. I must be discreet about these letters and not get caught up in other people's quarrels. According to an item in the *New York Times* (24 November 1994) the first Mrs. Tynan (Elaine Dundy) was "fighting mad" at her successor (Kathleen Halton) for publishing her letters without her consent (excerpts had appeared in *The New Yorker* in its October 31 issue). As all careful editors know, the contents of letters belong to the writer or the writer's estate, not to the recipient.
6. *Kenneth Tynan's Letters* (ed. Kathleen Tynan, 1994), pp. 329-330. Kathleen Tynan, *The Life of Kenneth Tynan* (1987), ch. 24, "A Four-Letter Word." I am also grateful to my friend, Herb Greer, journalist and playwright, for

letting me have his account of conversations he recorded with Kenneth Tynan in the 1970s; they were illuminating, even if uncritical (as he readily admits).

Whatever the research peculiarities of the *Guinness Book of Records*, one notes that scandal-trained spirits in our newspaper culture still keep tabs on the peccadilloes of the famous and the notorious in our time: in Kenneth Tynan's case, even some 17 years after his death. A headline in the *Daily Telegraph* (London, 13 October 1997, p. 14), read: IN BED WITH KEN TYNAN. The story featured excerpts from a new volume of Doris Lessing's autobiography, *Walking in the Shade*, namely the paragraphs which recount a strange, one-night affair. Its only conceivable news value for a fairly serious newspaper was not that she was bedded in Tynan's celebrated Mount Street apartment but, as the novelist noted with some shock and wonderment, that "the bedroom walls had been grotesquely transformed, for on them were arranged every sort of whip, as in a whip museum." Ms. Lessing doesn't make clear whether it was on this "bizarre" occasion she encountered "*a sjambok*, always irresistible to sadomasochists."

All I can say is that not any of the whips were there in my time. Doris Lessing, with a novelist's eye, does note that in the morning "a female menial" brought breakfast on two trays "and then she tidied away the whips." I never saw a trace of them.

7. The breathtaking discovery about "*Hm*" is in a letter to an editor of *Esquire* Magazine, *Letters* (February 1963), p. 271. Noël Annan incident in *Letters*, pp. 332-3.
8. Tynan, *Letters*, pp. 320-322.
9. Letter to Lord Salisbury, *Letters*, p. 474.
10. Tynan, *Letters*, pp. 476-77.
11. Tynan, *Letters*, p. 420.
12. Letter to *Times*, in Tynan, *Letters*, p. 497.
13. Letter on socialist path, *Letters*, p. 498.
14. *Letters*, p. 499; *Playboy*, p. 509. Bessie, 4 May 1972, p. 512.
15. *Letters*, p. 513. The lines quoted were from a poem for his daughter Tracy on her 20th birthday.
16. *Letters*, p. 525.
17. *Letters*, p. 530.
18. Tynan, *Letters*, p. 544.
19. *Letters*, to Gore Vidal, March 1975, p. 555.
20. Lenny Bruce's verses are cited in his autobiography, *How to Talk Dirty and Influence People* (1965; 1992), pp. 125-6.
21. Kenneth Tynan, foreword to the first edition of Lenny Bruce's *How to Talk Dirty...* (1992), pp. xi-xv. Gelb, quoted on pp. 113-4; *Time* quoted, p. 99.
22. Tynan, "Lenny Bruce" (1965), in *The Sound of Two Hands Clapping* (1975), pp. 64-69. By the way, "Marx and Freud" were two subjects Tynan had never written on; and there is no evidence that he had ever read widely

and deeply enough in the collected writings of M. and F. to make usefully "select" excerpts for other novices.

23. *Letters*, p. 67.

24. Eric Bogosian in *How to Talk Dirty and Influence People: an Autobiography of Lenny Bruce* (1965, 1992), pp. vii-x.

25. Bruce, *Dirty*, pp. 154-5. Joseph Epstein, "Kenneth Tynan: the Unshy Pornographer," *New Criterion*, January 1996, pp. 10-20. See, generally, Albert Goldman's biography *Ladies and Gentlemen – Lenny Bruce!!"* (1974).

26. Hemingway's articles in *Life* magazine (1960) were later expanded into a book entitled *The Dangerous Summer*. Many years later, when Tynan was desperate for lucrative magazine assignments, he did some additional "taurine" journalism: a portrait of Ordoñez, *Atlantic Monthly*, May 1973. The blow-by-blow account of the Hemingway-Tynan altercation was given by Hotchner to Kathleen Tynan for her edition of Tynan's *Letters*, p. 258.

27. Tynan, *Letters*, pp. 518-19.

28. *Letters*, p. 530.

29. "Saturday Evening Post," Tynan, *Letters*, pp. 380, 417.

30. Tynan, *Letters*, p. 270.

31. On that particular history, see my second volume: Part V, Towards a Theory of Journalistic Malpractice, chapter 3, "The Reporter Re-Arranges the Scene." Also: "Angus McGill saunters through town in search of the swinging sixties spirit: When everyone loved London," *Evening Standard*, Wednesday, 2 July 1980, pp. 22-23. Horace Judson's original *Time* cover story (and my use of the phrase, credited by Angus McGill as a "first") was published in the issue of 15 April 1966, pp. 30-34, "You Can Walk Across It On the Grass."

32. "Jewish," Tynan, *Letters*, p. 217.

33. "Brecht," Tynan, *Letters*, pp. 240, 244.

34. Brecht/Esslin in *Letters*, p. 245.

35. *"Playboy"*/Burton, in *Letters*, p. 278.

36. *"Playboy"*/Burton, Letters, p. 285.

37. Tynan, *Letters*, p. 440.

38. "Rehearsals," *Letters*, pp. 442-445.

39. Tynan quote (Robbins), *The Observer*, "Shouts & Murmurs," 7 April 1968. Tynan, *Letters*, p. 453.

40. *"Newsweek,"* Letters, p. 453.

41. Germaine Greer, *Letters*, pp. 480-81.

42. "Polanski," Tynan, *Letters*, pp. 478-79.

43. *Letters*, p. 460.

44. Eder's review-article appeared in that excellent Book Review supplement of the *Los Angeles Times*, 3 May 1998, p. 5.

45. "Obscenity," *O.E.D.*, vol. VII, O-pp. 26-27.

46. See also by Peregrine Worsthorne, *Peregrinations* (1980) as well as *Tricks of Memory* (1993). There is a chapter on Worsthorne in Alan Watkins' *Brief Lives* (1982), pp. 200-206.

47. Sir Peregrine Worsthorne, "My Wife Threw a Chair at My Head," *Daily Telegraph*, 2 November 1998, p. 12.
48. Bernard Levin, in the *Times*, 27 December 1994.
49. See *Times*, 27 December 1994.
50. Irving Wardle, in *The Independent* (1 January 1995).
51. *Daily Express*, 3 June 1995.
52. Kingsley Amis, *The King's English: a Guide to Modern Usage* (Harper-Collins, 1997). Jean Aitchinson, *The Language Web: the Power & Problem of Words* (Cambridge University Press, 1997), and her review of Amis, "Devil's Advocate for the English Tongue," *Sunday Times* (Books), 16 March 1997, pp. 8-9.
53. "Interview with Elizabeth Jane Howard, with Elizabeth Grice, 'I Couldn't Even Say Goodbye to Him'," in *Daily Telegraph*, 2 Nov. 1995, p. 13. See also the letters of Alan Sillitoe and Eric Shorter, in the *Daily Telegraph*, 30 October and 2 November 1995.
54. *Times*, 22 October 1996, p. 5; *Sunday Times*, "Death of an old devil unites his women," 13 October 1996, p. 3; *The Independent*, 24 October 1996, p. 17.
55. *Daily Mail*, 18 May 1995, p. 53.
56. Kingsley Amis, *The King's English* (1997), "Four-letter words," pp. 72-74.
57. *Sunday Times*, 24 September 1995.
58. John Updike on Martin Amis in the *Sunday Times* (Books), 21 September 1997, pp. 1-2.
59. Letters, Ernest Hemingway and Maxwell Perkins, "Three Words," in *The New Yorker*, June 24/July 1, 1996, pp. 73-77. The letters were previously unpublished and "recently released from private collections." The editor adds that "the punctuation has been modified," but certainly not the d—y w—s in question. What would have been the point in her doing that? Emasculation has gone out of fashion. Nobody, at least in the book and magazine world, pencils in stars or draws blanks any more.
60. John Ezard, in *The Guardian*, 6 June 1995.
61. Valerie Grove, "The F-word – and why women should not be ashamed to use it," *Times*, 21 November 1998, p. 21.
62. *Daily Telegraph*, 14 November 1998, p. 3.
63. The Geoffrey Gorer article on "The Pornography of Death" was published in *Encounter*, October 1955, pp. 49-52. The essay is a characteristic piece of the incisive or, at least, stimulating popular anthropology of the day which made Gorer's writings so quotable. He emphasizes that the immemorial sources of embarrassing and unseemly utterance [anthropo-speak for obscenities] are related to sex and excretion; but this is neither necessary nor universal. And, for want of better proof, he re-quotes Malinowski's old tale about the Trobrianders who surrounded eating with "as much shame as excretion." (In other societies personal names or aspects of ritual come under the same taboos.)

Worth noting, in other connections, is his distinction between pornography and obscenity. The latter appears to be a universal, taking place (producing shock, social embarrassment, and laughter) everywhere and at all times. Pornography, on the other hand, is a rarer phenomenon, probably only arising in literate societies. "We certainly have no records of it for non-literate societies"—although we must not be surprised when some suspiciously suggestive drawings are soon discovered on the walls in prehistoric caves. More than that: "Whereas the enjoyment of obscenity is predominantly social, the enjoyment of pornography is predominantly private."

As for the new preoccupation with different "unmentionables," with death-taboos, Gorer's argument is still pertinent:

"There seems little question that the instinct of those censorious busybodies preoccupied with other people's morals was correct when they linked pornography of death with the pornography of sex....

"Nevertheless, people have come to terms with the basic facts of birth, copulation, and death, and somehow accept their implications; if social prudery prevents this being done in an open and dignified fashion, then it will be done surreptitiously. If we dislike the modern pornography of death, then we must give back to death—natural death—its parade and publicity, re-admit grief and mourning. If we make death unmentionable in polite society—not before children—we almost ensure the continuation of the horror comic. No censorship has ever been really effective."

64. Robin Young, "Explet!ves Not Deleted," *Times*, 21 November 1998, p. 21; leading article, "Blankety Blank," p. 23.

To cover so much forthrightness in the plain and unadorned usage of obscenities, it was a typical nicety of *Times* to choose "blankety-blank," one of the most discreet and harmless circumlocutions of them all. *Webster's* refers to it as "a humorous euphemism"; and it was for a long time very much in usage in children's comic strips with its very "blankness" never giving a clue as to the bad language being euphemized. See *Webster's New World Dictionary of the American Language* (2nd ed., 1970), p. 149.

Index